YUCATAN
HANDBOOK

THIRD EDITION

YUCATAN HANDBOOK

THIRD EDITION

CHICKI MALLAN
PHOTOS BY OZ MALLAN

MOON
PUBLICATIONS INC.

YUCATAN HANDBOOK

Please send all comments,
corrections, additions,
amendments, and critiques to:

CHICKI MALLAN
c/o MOON PUBLICATIONS, INC.
722 WALL STREET
CHICO, CA 95928, USA

Published by
Moon Publications, Inc.
722 Wall Street
Chico, California 95928, USA

Printed by
Colorcraft Ltd.

Printing History
1st edition—November 1986
Reprinted
  May 1987
  April 1988
2nd edition—January 1989
Reprinted
  September 1989
3rd edition—December 1990
Reprinted
  June 1991

Library of Congress Cataloging in Publication Data

Mallan, Chicki, 1933–
  Yucatan Handbook / Chicki Mallan
  —3rd ed.
    p.   cm.
  Rev. ed. of: *Guide to the Yucatán Peninsula. 2nd ed. 1989*
  Includes bibliographical references and index.
  ISBN 0-918373-55-7
  1. Yucatán Peninsula—Description and travel—1981—Guide-books.
  I. Mallan, Chicki, 1933- *Guide to the Yucatan Peninsula.* II. Title.
  F1376.M28   1990
  917.2'604834—dc20   90-41232
                                                                        CIP

Printed in Hong Kong

To the new generation coming along—the "grands":
Stephanie, Kellianne, Misty, Kara, Becky, Peter, Chelsea, Brittany, Tyler,
Serra, Aaron, Stanley, Trevor, plus the two "mystery members" coming
soon. May they all inherit a curiosity about the world!

ACKNOWLEDGEMENTS

And now a third edition. I wish there were a way to thank the entire population of the Yucatan Peninsula, but since that's not possible I would like to mention some of the more outstanding people who have helped bring this book together: Mexicana Airlines for flight arrangements, Javier Rivas and the Ministry of Tourism in Mexico City, Teresa Borge and the State Tourism Office of the state of Yucatan. The Yucatan tourism office in Merida has been an overwhelming help with nuts-and-bolts information about the growing state. Thanks also to Meridano Luis Nevaer, a good friend who kept us posted with the new and exciting events that continue to happen in Yucatan, even when we aren't there.

To all the talented people at Moon, you continue to amaze me with your talents. *Muchas gracias* to everyone involved with bringing this book together from publisher Bill Dalton to editor Christa Jorgensen with the sharp eye and ear, and assistant editor Beth Rhudy. Michelle Bonzey who continues to input and output. And thanks to Dave Hurst, production manager/art director, who continues to make miracles with a few words, a graphic or two, and lots of effort. What a pleasure to work with a craftsman who never loses his cool nor his artistic eye while working with disorganized authors as well. Also, thanks to Anne Hikido for assisting in production and cartography. Thanks to cartographers Bob Race and Brian Bardwell, for taking scratches and scrawls and coming up with beautiful maps.

Asha Johnson, resident computer genius, always has the right solution when the computer (or the author) crashes. One cannot forget the "front office" and Donna Galassi who makes sure the sales continue to spiral, and Virginia Michaels, Moon Publicist, who sees to it the world (CNN, rah rah!) knows about Moon Travel Books and the authors. It's fun to work with all the Moonies: Mark Morris, Rick Johnson, Cindy Fahey, Nancy Kennedy, Lucinda Stram, and Larry Anton.

Last, thanks to my family (all eight children with their never-ending support). I especially thank the other half of this team, Oz Mallan, photographer/husband/pal, who continues to provide dazzling photos—in good humor—even if it means hanging on to the side of a vine-covered pyramid for an hour and 23 minutes waiting for the sun to come out from behind the tropical clouds.

CONTENTS

INTRODUCTION 1
The Land and Sea 1
Fauna...7
Flora...14
History..17
Economy..23
The People...25
Ancient Culture of the
 Yucatan Peninsula............................26
Fiestas and Celebrations 31
Accommodations 37
Food...40
Activities...44
Getting There and Around 48
Car Rental Tips 54
What to Take......................................55
Health Care..57
Cameras and Picture Taking 63
Other Practicalities............................65

THE STATE OF YUCATAN 69
Merida...72
Vicinity of Merida................................98
Progreso..102
Chixulub...107
Dzilam de Bravo and Vicinity 108
Izamal...109
Chichen Itza 111
Vicinity of Chichen Itza.......................119
Valladolid and Vicinity 121
Rio Lagartos 124
Vicinity of Rio Lagartos 127
Uxmal..129
Vicinity of Uxmal 136
Oxkutzcab and Vicinity 139
Ticul 141

THE STATE OF CAMPECHE 143
Campeche City...................................145
Vicinity of Campeche 155
Champoton..159
Isla del Carmen...................................161
Escarcega...163

THE STATE OF CHIAPAS..................165
Tuxtla Gutierrez 170
San Cristobal de las Casas 175
Palenque...186
Santo Domingo....................................190
Vicinity of Palenque 195
Bonampak 197

THE STATE OF TABASCO..................201
Villahermosa..204
Vicinity of Villahermosa.......................216

THE STATE OF QUINTANA ROO 221
Isla de Cozumel...................................223
San Miguel de Cozumel 227
Water Sports..243
Cancun...249
Isla Mujeres 275
Puerto Morelos and Vicinity 289
Punta Bete 294
Playa del Carmen 297
Xcaret 303
Pamul 305
Puerto Aventuras 307
Akumal...309
Chemuyil..314
Xcacel..315
Xelha..316
Tulum Ruins...318
Coba 323
Muyil: Ancient Maya Seaport
 of Sian Ka'an 327
Road to Punta Allen..............................329
Punta Allen 331
Felipe Carrillo Puerto 332
Xcalak Peninsula 334
Chetumal 340
Crossing Into Belize..............................344
Escorted Trips to the
 Yucatan Peninsula..............................345

BOOKLIST 347
GLOSSARY.......................................349
INDEX 355

MAPS

Air Routes to Cancun 50
Bonampak 197
Campeche, City of...149
Campeche, State of 144
Cancun 250
Cancun Hotels..264
Cancun, Downtown...252
Central Caribbean Coast 305
Chankanab Lagoon and Park...............................239
Chetumal..343
Chetumal, Downtown..345
Chiapas, State of..166
Chichen Itza...112
CICOM 208
Coba Archaeological Zone 326
Comalcalco Ruins 217
Comalcalco, Day Trip to 218
Cozumel Hotels..231
Driving Distances 49
Dzilam de Bravo, From Progreso to......................108
Isla Cozumel..224
Isla Mujeres 276
Isla Mujeres, Downtown.......................................282
Kabah 137
La Venta and Tabasco 2000 206
La Venta Park Museum..205
Labna...138
Loltun Caves, Ticul to 140
Merida..75
Merida, Downtown 80
Merida to Celestun 100

Merida to Progreso..102
Northern Caribbean Coast...................................289
Palenque 187
Palenque Village 190
Playa del Carmen...298
Progreso...103
Punta Allen, Tulum to 330
Quintana Roo, State of...222
Rio Lagartos, Tizimin to 123
San Cristobal de las Casas..................................177
San Cristobal de las Casas, Downtown...........179
San Miguel, Downtown 235
San Miguel, Vicinity of 228
Sayil...137
Southern Caribbean Coast 328
States and Capitals 3
Tabasco, State of...202
Tulum...319
Uxmal 133
Uxmal and the Puuc Ruins, From Merida to......130
Valladolid...122
Valladolid, Chichen Itza to 121
Villahermosa..204
Villahermosa City Center 210
Villahermosa to Frontera Day Trip 212
Villahermosa to Palenque....................................214
Xcalak Peninsula...334
Xelha...316
Yucatan Peninsula 2
Yucatan, State of 70

CHARTS, ETC.

Aguadas 2
Airlines Serving the Yucatan Peninsula 51
Amber 171
Anthropological Museum of Mexico 52
Balankanche Caves Hours and Services 119
Bullfighting 33
Cafe de Olla 266
Campeche Accommodations 150
Campeche, Archaeological Zones 145
Campeche, Taxi Stands 154
Cancun Accommodations 261
Cancun, Airlines Serving 274
Cancun, Driving Distances from 251
Cancun, Emergency Telephone Numbers 272
Cancun Marinas 256
Chac, the Maya Rain God 41
Champoton Accommodations 159
Chiapas, Archaeological Zones 165
Chichen Itza, Bus Schedule to 118
Chichen Itza Visitor Center
    Services and Hours 113
Ciudad del Carmen Accommodations 161
Cozumel Accommodations 230
Cozumel, Airlines Serving 236
Cozumel, Bike and Car Rentals 238
Cozumel, By Boat 237
Cozumel Dive Shops 247
Differrences Between Moths and Butterflies 13
Diving Safety References 46
Escarcega Accommodations 163
Fiestas and Celebrations 35
Getting Married in Cancun 271
Giant Turtles and the Indians 306
Hammocks 90
Henequen 73
Hetzmek 167
Important Dates in the History of the Maya 333
Important Maya Archaeological Zones
    in Yucatan 71
Isla Mujeres Accommodations 281
Isla Mujeres, Boats Schedules to and from 287
Isla Mujeres Eateries 283
Isla Mujeres Important Telephone Numbers 285
Isla Mujeres Shopping Hints 285
Loltun Caves Archaeological Zone Hours 140
Longest Reefs in the World 4

Los Topes 48
Luggage Tip 53
Manatee Breeding Program 336
Merida Accommodations 78
Merida Bus Schedules 96
Merida, Car Rentals 97
Merida Restaurants 85
Merida Supermarkets 89
Merida, Taxi Stands 97
Merida Tours 93
Merida, Weekly Schedule of Events 92
Mexican Wine 269
Palenque Accommodations 193
Palenque, Other Sites Near 195
Pre-Columbian? 18
Progreso Bus Schedules 106
Progreso, Driving Distances from 105
Progreso Hotels 104
Progreso Public Services 105
Queen Conch 292
Quintana Roo, Archaeological Zones 225
San Cristobal Accommodations 182
San Miguel Emergency Telephone Numbers 235
Shells You Might Find On the Beach 6
Simple First-Aid Guide 59
Sponges Commonly found
    on the Yucatan Peninsula 4
Tabasco, Archaeological Zones 201
Telephone and Emergency Information 66
Tipping 260
Tortillas 42
Uxmal, Bus Schedules from Merida 135
Uxmal Visitor Center Services and Hours 131
Valladolid Hotels 122
Vehicle Supplies 37
Villahermosa Accommodations 211
Villahermosa Banks 213
Villahermosa, Caves for Explorers 219
Villahermosa Emergency
    Telephone Numbers 215
Villahermosa Nightlife 213
Water Safety 253
What is a Biosphere Reserve? 15
White City 72
Youth Hostels 39

IS THIS BOOK OUT OF DATE?

We strive to keep our book as up to date as possible and would appreciate your help. If you find a hot new resort or attraction, or if we have neglected to include an important bit of information, please let us know. Our mapmakers take extraordinary care to be accurate, but if you find an error, let us know that as well.

We're especially interested in hearing from female travelers, RVers, outdoor enthusiasts, expatriates, and local residents. We're interested in any comments from the Mexican tourist industry, including hotel owners and individuals who specialize in accommodating visitors to their country.

If you have outstanding photos or artwork that you feel could be used in an upcoming edition, send us duplicate slides or drawings. You will be given full credit and a free book if your work is published. Materials will be returned only if you include a self-addressed stamped envelope. Moon Publications will own all rights. Address your letters to:

Chicki Mallan
Moon Publications, Inc.
722 Wall St.
Chico, CA 95928

FROM THE AUTHOR

Most people who enjoy Mexico are aware that many changes are taking place, mostly with the fluctuating *peso*. Even while producing this book, we were aware that prices would be out of date before the book was published. In the past, prices were listed in pesos; in this edition prices will mostly be listed in dollars—which change more slowly. Even dollar prices will change, but not as radically as the peso.

Most travelers want an idea of what to expect in the pocketbook when planning a trip. However, please use the prices in this book as a *general guide only*—we have tried to supply addresses where you can check for the most current prices available.

ABBREVIATIONS

a/c—air conditioned	**km**—kilometer	**R**—right
C—Centigrade	**OW**—one way	**RT**—round trip
d—double occupancy	**pd**—per day	**s**—single occupancy
ha—hectare	**pn**—per night	**t**—triple occupancy
I.—island	**pp**—per person	**tel.**—telephone number

INTRODUCTION
THE LAND AND SEA

The Yucatan Peninsula occupies an area of approximately 113,000 square kilometers, with a shoreline of over 1,600 kilometers. Geographically, the Peninsula includes the Mexican states of Yucatan on the north coast, Campeche on the west along the Gulf of Mexico, Quintana Roo on the east along the Caribbean coast, bordered by the entire country of Belize and a corner of Guatemala to the south.

Geologically this flat shelf of limestone and coral composition is like a stone sponge: rain is absorbed into the ground and delivered to natural stone-lined sinks and underground rivers. The abundant limestone provided the early Maya with sturdy material close at hand to create the mammoth structures that have survived hundreds of years. Limestone was readily cut with hand-hewn stone-cutting implements. This geology creates a problem for the primary necessity of life—water. In the northern region of Quintana Roo there are few rivers and lakes. Only in the extreme south is one sizeable river, the Rio Hondo, which cuts a natural boundary between Belize and Quintana Roo, at the city of Chetumal. Four lakes at Coba are scattered between ancient ruins.

Cenotes (Natural Wells)
Limestone and coral create eerie shorelines, caves, and (fortunately) water holes. When flying over the Peninsula you can see circular ground patterns caused by the hidden movement of underground rivers and lakes. The water level rises and falls with the cycle of rain and drought. The constant ebb and flow erodes the underground limestone and earth around the moving water, creating steep-walled caverns; the surface crust eventually caves in, exposing and allowing access to the water. Around these sources of water Maya villages grew. Some of the wells are shallow, seven meters below the jungle floor; some are treacherously deep, with the surface of the water as much as 70-90 meters below. In times of drought, the Maya carved stairs into slick limestone walls or hung long ladders into abysmal hollows leading to underground lakes to obtain precious water.

THE YUCATAN PENINSULA

John Stephens' book, *Incidents of Travel in The Yucatan,* covers his 1841 expedition with Frederick Catherwood. Catherwood's realistic art reproduces accurately how the Indians survived in the northern part of the Peninsula from year to year with little or no rainfall by burrowing deep into the earth to retrieve water. The two American explorers observed long lines of naked Indian men carrying the precious liquid from deep holes back to the surface in calabash containers.

The Peninsula Coast

The west and north coasts are composed of many lagoons, sandbars, and mangrove swamps. The east coast is edged with coral reefs; several islands lie offshore—Cozumel, Isla Mujeres, and Contoy. The fifth-largest reef in the world, the Belize Reef, extends from the tip of Isla Mujeres 250

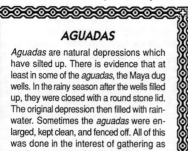

AGUADAS

Aguadas are natural depressions which have silted up. There is evidence that at least in some of the *aguadas*, the Maya dug wells. In the rainy season after the wells filled up, they were closed with a round stone lid. The original depression then filled with rainwater. Sometimes the *aguadas* were enlarged, kept clean, and fenced off. All of this was done in the interest of gathering as much water as possible during the rains.

km south to the Bay of Honduras. Many varieties of coral—including rare black coral found at great depths—grow in the hills and valleys of the often-deep reef that protects the east coast of the Peninsula. In many places along the reef it is illegal to dive for the coral, and where it is permitted it's a dangerous (but money-making) occupation. Since tourists are willing to buy it, the local divers continue to retrieve it from the crags and crevices of underwater canyons. The coral ridges of the reef attract curious divers from all over the world.

AGRICULTURE

The land in the northernmost part of the Yucatan was described by Diego de Landa, an early Spanish priest, as "a country with the least earth ever seen, since all of it is one living rock." Surprisingly, the thin layer of soil supports agriculture. This monotonous landscape is a stony plain dotted with a multitude of sword-shaped plants called henequen. The Spanish settlers on the Peninsula made vast fortunes growing and selling henequen (used for rope-making) at the turn of the century. However, it was the Maya who showed the Spanish its many valuable uses, especially for building their houses. Without nails or tools, the house was "tied together" with henequen fiber twisted by hand into sturdy twine. Wherever *palapa*-style structures are built today by the Indians, the same nail-free method is used.

Food Crops

With careful nurturing of the soil, the early Indians managed to support a large population of people on the land. Though rainfall is spotty and unreliable, the land is surprisingly fertile and each year produces corn and other vegetables on small farms. The northern tip of the Peninsula can be dry and arid on the northwest edge where tradewinds bring more rain, the land is slightly greener. As you travel south, the desert gradually becomes green until you find yourself in a jungle plain at Quintana Roo fringed by the turquoise Caribbean and the Rio Hondo.

Along the coast of Quintana Roo, remnants of large coconut plantations, now broken up into small tracts and humble *ranchitos*, are being developed by farmers with modest government assistance. At one time it was commonplace to see copra lining the roadside drying in the sun. The number of coconut trees afflicted with "yellowing" disease in the Yucatan has greatly decreased the output of copra in the state. As a result of the "yellowing" disease and Hurricane Gilbert, what was once a mixture of thick lush coco trees and rich verdant jungle often looks like a war zone with dead limbs and topless coco trees. Fortunately the jungle rejuvenates quickly and within a few more years nature will cover the dead with new growth. As for the coconut trees, new strains are being planted that are resistant to this dreadful disease. Different parts of the Peninsula produce different crops. In most areas juicy oranges grow which you can find for sale everywhere; in the marketplace and along the road the green peel is often removed, the sweet fruit ready to eat. The early chocolate drink was developed by the Indians in Mexico and presented to the Spanish. Today chocolate is manufactured and shipped all over the world from Mexico. Bananas of many kinds from finger-size to 15-inch red plantains are grown in thick groves close to the Gulf of Mexico coast. Tabasco bananas are recognized worldwide as among the finest.

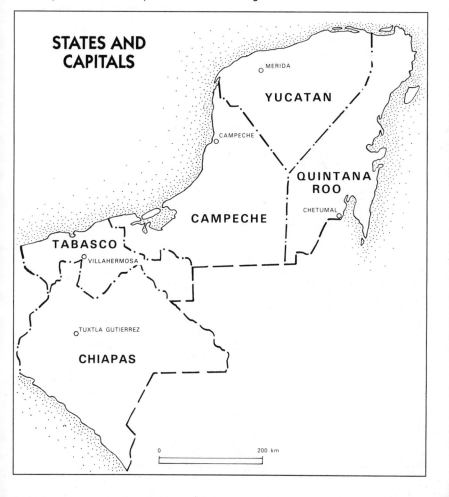

STATES AND CAPITALS

MERIDA

YUCATAN

CAMPECHE

QUINTANA ROO

CHETUMAL

CAMPECHE

TABASCO

VILLAHERMOSA

TUXTLA GUTIERREZ

CHIAPAS

0   200 km

REEFS ALONG THE QUINTANA ROO COAST

The sea is a magical world unto itself. Man is just beginning to learn of the wonders that take place within its depths. Some dreamers predict that a time is coming when oceans of the world will provide man with all the nutrients he needs, and that people will live comfortably side by side with the fish in the sea. For now, men and women are content just to look at what's there.

LONGEST REEFS IN THE WORLD

Great Barrier Reef, Australia	2000 km
New Caledonia, S. Barrier Reef	600 km
New Caledonia, N. Barrier Reef	540 km
S. Louisade Archipelago Reef, PNG	350 km
Belize Reef	250 km

Coral

From tiny polyps grow spectacular coral reefs. Coral is a unique limestone formation that grows in innumerable shapes: delicate lace, trees with reaching branches, pleated mushrooms, stove pipes, petaled flowers, fans, domes, heads of cabbage, and stalks of broccoli. Corals are formed by millions of tiny carnivorous polyps that feed on minute organisms and live in large colonies of flamboyantly colored individual species. These small creatures can be less than a centimeter long or as big as 15 cm in diameter. Related to the jellyfish and sea anemone, polyps need sunlight and clear saltwater no colder than 20 degrees C to survive. Coral polyps have cylinder-shaped bodies. One end is attached to a hard surface (the bottom of the ocean, rim of a submerged volcano, or the reef itself) and the other, mouth end is circled with tiny tentacles that capture its minute prey with a deadly sting.

Coral reefs are formed when polyps attach themselves to each other. Stony coral, for example, makes the connection with a flat sheet of tissue between the middle of both bodies. They develop their limestone skeletons by extracting calcium out of the seawater and depositing calcium carbonate around the lower half of the body. They reproduce from buds or eggs. Occasionally small buds appear on the adult polyp; when mature, they separate from the adult and add to the growth of existing colonies. Eggs, on the other hand, grow into tiny forms that swim away and settle on the ocean floor. When developed the egg begins a new colony.

SPONGES COMMONLY FOUND ON THE YUCATAN PENINSULA

tube	encrusting	basket
vase	rope	barrel

A Reef Grows

As these small creatures continue to reproduce and die, their sturdy skeletons accumulate. Over eons, broken bits of coral, animal waste, and granules of soil all contribute to the strong foundation for a reef, which slowly rises toward the surface. To grow, a reef must have a base no more than 25 meters below the water's surface and in a healthy environment can grow four to five cm a year. One small piece of coral represents millions of polyps and many years of construction.

Reefs are divided into three types: atoll, fringing, and barrier. An atoll can be formed around the crater of a submerged volcano. The polyps begin building their colonies on the round edge of the crater, forming a circular coral island with a lagoon in the center. Thousands of atolls occupy tropical waters of the world. A fringing reef is coral living on a shallow shelf that extends outward from shore into the sea. A barrier reef runs parallel to the coast. Water separates it from the land, and it can be a series of reefs with channels of water in between. This is the case with some of the largest barrier reefs in the Pacific and Indian oceans.

The Yucatan Peninsula has a barrier reef extending from the tip of Isla Mujeres to Sapodilla Caye in the Gulf of Honduras. This reef is known by various names (Belize Reef is the most common), and it's 280 km long, fifth longest in the world. The beauty of the reef attracts divers and snorkelers from distant parts of the world to investigate the unspoiled marinelife.

The Meaning Of Color

Most people interested in a reef already know they're in for a brilliant display of colored fish. In the fish world, color isn't only for exterior decoration. Fish change hues for a number of reasons, including anger, protection, and sexual attraction. This is still a little-known science. For example, because of its many colors, marine biologists are uncertain how many species of groupers there are—different species or different moods? A male damsel fish clearly imparts his aggression—and his desire for love—by turning vivid blue. Some fish have as many as 12 different recognizable color patterns they can change within seconds. These color changes, along with other body signals, combine to make communication simple between species. Scientists have discovered that a layer of color-bearing cells lies just beneath a fish's transparent scales. These cells contain orange, yellow, or red pigments; some contain black, others combine to make yellow or green. A crystalline tissue adds white, silver, or iridescence. Color changes when the pigmented cells are revealed, combined, or masked, creating the final result. Fish communicate in many surprising ways including electrical impulses and flashing bioluminescence (cold light). If fish communication intrigues you, read Robert Burgess's book titled *Secret Languages of the Sea* (Dodd, Mead and Company).

Conservation

The Mexican government has strict laws governing the reef, to which most divers are more than willing to comply in order to preserve this natural phenomenon and its inhabitants. It takes hundreds of years to form large colonies, so please don't break off pieces of coral for souvenirs. After a very short time out of water the polyps lose their color and you have only a piece of chalky white coral—just like the pieces you can pick up while beachcombing. Stiff fines await those who remove anything from the reef. Spear fishing is allowed in some areas along the Yucatan coast, but not on the reef. The spear must be totally unmechanical and used free-hand or with a rubber band only (no spear guns). If you plan on fishing, write to Oficina de Pesca, 1010 2nd Ave., Suite 1605, San Diego, CA 92101, tel. (619) 233-6956, for more details; a fishing license is required.

Hurricane Gilbert

On September 13, 1989, a hurricane of extreme

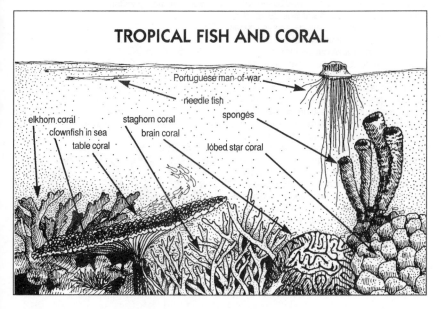

TROPICAL FISH AND CORAL

Portuguese man-of-war

needle fish

sponges

elkhorn coral

clownfish in sea

table coral

staghorn coral

brain coral

lobed star coral

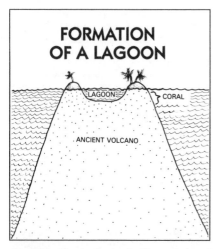

FORMATION OF A LAGOON

LAGOON — CORAL

ANCIENT VOLCANO

force hit the Yucatan Peninsula. Strong winds and high waves washed across the coast, uprooting trees, destroying buildings, and tearing away roadways and coastline. Some locations suffered more damage than others. Cancun probably lost more glass than anything else, and though certain areas of sandy beaches were swallowed by the sea at Cancun, in other areas sand was dumped as though by the truckload creating high sand dunes where not needed. The eye of the hurricane passed between Playa del Carmen and Puerto Morelos. While a few buildings were totally washed away, others were destroyed on the inside (in one case two stories were gutted) with the outside walls left intact. Because so little time has passed, the wounds are fresh and stories abound. One woman in Puerto Morelos tells of taking refuge in a friend's house near the jungle after evacuating her beachfront home. While walking through a dark hall one night (the electricity was off for 15 days along this section of the coast) she was struck by two tropical snakes which were obviously trying to escape their flooded jungle environment. After treatment (in a Merida hospital), she returned to find her house and everything in it gone. However, like most Yucatecans she has built a small bungalow for herself and three others to rent. (See "Puerto Morelos.")

Another man tells of delivering his son at the height of the storm. He, his wife, and their two children had prepared a bag of supplies containing candles, water, matches, canned food, can opener, blankets, and clothes for the expected infant. After his wife announced the birth was imminent, it was obvious the baby would be born in the house while he assisted. The parents carefully boiled a new pair of shoelaces (to tie the umbilical cord), sterilized a kitchen knife (to cut the cord), and began reading directions in the Lamaze training book under emergency deliveries. As the hurricane continued across Cancun, the wind was constantly shifting directions and the small family moved from one room to the next fearing the rattling glass would burst—even though taped. The windows didn't shatter, and the man and his two children assisted his wife in the delivery of a baby boy. No, they didn't name him Gilbert!

The people of the Yucatan Peninsula always felt the reef that protects their coastline from a strong surge would keep hurricane tides away. Now they know the strength of a hurricane as well as their own. Cancun has been rebuilt in record time; it's better than ever. Even the beaches that were destroyed are slowly being rebuilt by the sea. The small villages along the coast have for the most part put their lives and homes back on track. The Caribbean Sea is as beautiful as ever, always welcoming visitors.

SHELLS YOU MIGHT FIND ON THE BEACH

horse conch
cowrie
prickly cockle
queen conch

cut-ribbed ark
West Indian fighting conch
West Indian top
turkey wing

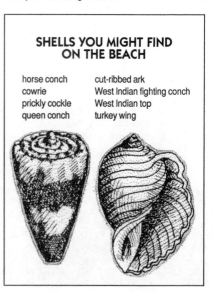

FAUNA

Many exotic animals are found in the thick jungles and flatlands of Quintana Roo, many that aren't found elsewhere in Mexico. With patience it's possible to observe animals not normally seen in the wild. If you're serious about this venture, bring a small folding stool (unless you prefer to sit in a tree), a pair of binoculars, possibly a camera, and plenty of bug repellent! The distribution of animals and plant life is a direct result of the climatic zones, which are in turn affected by their different elevations and proximity to the sea.

REPTILES

Reptiles thrive in Yucatan's warm sunny environment—man is their worst enemy. Though against the laws of most countries today, in the past some species were greatly reduced in number because they were hunted for their unusual skin. Snake and crocodile skin when tanned makes sturdy, attractive, waterproof leather, previously used in luggage, shoes, and ladies' handbags. A few black marketeers still take their toll on the species.

Iguana
This species—American lizards of the family *Iguanidae*—includes various large plant-eaters typically dark in color. Seen frequently in Quintana Roo, they come in many sizes with slight variations in color. The young iguana is bright emerald green. This common lizard grows to one meter long, has a blunt head and long flat tail. Bands of black and gray circle its body, and a serrated column reaches down the middle of its back almost to the tail.

Very large and shy, the lizard's forelimbs hold the front half of its body up off the ground while the two back limbs are kept relaxed and splayed alongside its hindquarters. However, when the iguana is frightened, its hind legs do everything they're supposed to, and the iguana crashes quickly (though clumsily) into the brush searching for its burrow and safety. This reptile is not aggressive, but if cornered it will bite and use its tail in self-defense. The iguana mostly enjoys basking in the bright sunshine along the Caribbean. Though they are herbivores, the young also eat insects and larvae. Certain varieties in some areas of the Peninsula are almost hunted out—for example, the spiny-tailed iguana in the central valley of Chiapas. A moderate number are still found in the rocky foothill slopes and thorn-scrub woodlands. In Quintana Roo it is not unusual to see locals along dirt paths carrying sturdy specimens by the tail to put in the cookpot.

iguana

From centuries past, recorded references attest to the medicinal value of this lizard, which partly explains the active trade of live iguana in the marketplaces of some parts of the Peninsula. Iguana stew is believed to cure or relieve various human ailments such as impotence. Another reason for their popularity at the market is their delicate white flesh which tastes a lot like chicken but is much more expensive.

Other Lizards
You'll see a great variety of lizards, from the skinny two-inch miniature gecko to the chameleon-like black anole that changes colors to match the environment either when danger is imminent or as subterfuge to fool the insects that it preys on. At mating time, the male anole's bright-red throat-fan is puffed out to make sure that all female lizards will see it. Some are brightly striped in various shades of green and yellow; others are earth colors that blend with the gray and beige limestone which dots the landscape. Skinny as wisps of thread running on hind legs or chunky and waddling with armor-like skin, the range is endless—and fascinating!

Coral Snakes
The coral snakes found from the southern part of the Yucatan Peninsula to Panama grow much larger (one-1 1/2 meters) than the ones in the southern U.S. The body is slender, with no pronounced distinction between head and neck. In North and South America are several genera of true coral snakes, which are close relatives of cobras. Many false coral snakes with similar coloring are around though harmless. Nocturnal, coral snakes spend the day in mossy clumps under rocks or logs.

Note: The two North American coral snakes have prominent rings around their bodies in the same sequence of black, yellow or white, and red. They don't look for trouble and seldom strike, will bite if stepped on; their short fangs, however, can be stopped by shoes or clothing. Even though the Mexicans call this the "20-minute snake" (meaning if you are bitten and don't get antivenin within 20 minutes, you die), it's actually more like a 24-hour period. According to Mexico's Instituto Nacional de Higiene, an average of 135 snakebite deaths per year (mostly children) are reported for the country, the number declining as more villages receive antivenin.

Chances of the average tourist being bitten by a coral (or any other) snake are slim. However, if you plan on extensive jungle exploration, check with your doctor before you leave home. Antivenin is available in Mexico, and it's wise to be prepared for an allergic reaction to the antivenin by bringing antihistimine and adrenalin. The most important thing to remember if bitten: *don't panic and don't run*. Physical exertion and panic cause the venom to travel through your body much faster. Lie down and stay calm; have someone carry you to a doctor.

Tropical Rattlesnakes
Called *cascabel* in Mexico and Mesoamerica, this species is the deadliest and most treacherous of all rattlers. It differs slightly from other species by having vividly contrasting neck bands. Contrary to popular myth, this serpent doesn't always rattle a warning of its impending strike. It grows two-2 1/2 meters long and is found mainly in higher, drier areas of the tropics.

Caymans
The cayman is part of the crocodilian order; crocodiles' and alligators' habits and appearance are very similar. The main difference is the underskin. The cayman's skin is reinforced with bony plates on the belly, making them useless for the leather market (lucky them!); alligators and crocodiles, with smooth belly skin and sides, in some parts of the globe have been hunted almost to extinction. There are laws that now protect the crocodilia, though certain governments allow farming the animal for leather production.

Of the five species of cayman, several frequent the brackish inlet waters near the estuaries on the north edge of the Yucatan Peninsula along the Rio Lagartos (loosely translated to mean "River of Lizards"). They are broad-snouted and often look as though they sport a pair of spectacles. A large cayman can be 2 1/2 meters long, very dark gray-green with eyelids that look swollen and wrinkled. Some species have eyelids that look like a pair of blunt horns. They are quicker than alligators and have longer, sharper teeth. Their disposition is vicious and treacherous; don't be fooled by the old myth that on land they're cumbersome and slow-moving. When cornered they move swiftly and are known for not liking people. The best advice one can heed is to give the cayman a wide berth when spotted.

The raccoon has the curious habit of washing its food before eating it. A strictly nocturnal creature, it eats most anything that comes along, and can ruin an Indian milpa (cornfield) in no time. It's related to two other familiar jungle creatures, the coati and kinkajou.

Sea Turtles

At one time many species of giant turtles meandered the coastal regions of Quintana Roo, laying their eggs in the warm Caribbean sands. Though many didn't survive birds, crabs, and sharks, thousands of hatchlings managed to return each year to their birthplace. The Sea Turtle Rescue Organization claims that in 1947, during one day, over 40,000 sea turtles (Kemp's ridley) nested on the one Mexican beach instinct returns them to each year. In 1984 fewer than 500 Kemp's ridleys nested during the entire season.

In spite of concentrated efforts by the Mexican government, the number of turtles is still decreasing. They were a valuable source of food for the Maya Indians for centuries. But only in recent years has the wholesale theft of turtle eggs, coupled with the senseless slaughter of the lovely hawksbill (for its beautiful shell), begun to deplete the species. Refrigeration and freezer holds enable large fishing boats to capture thousands of turtles at one time (male and female) and smuggle meat by the ton into various countries to be canned as soup or frozen for the unwary consumer: processors often claim the turtle meat in their product is from the legal freshwater variety.

Another problem is the belief that turtle eggs cure impotence. Despite huge fines for anyone possessing turtle eggs, every summer nesting grounds along the Yucatan Peninsula are raided. There is *no* hunting season for these threatened creatures, and the meat is illegal on menus throughout the state. Though some restaurants ig-

nore the law and verbally offer turtle meat, it never happens with the eggs! They are forbidden fruit.

Ecological organizations are trying hard to save the dwindling turtle population. Turtle eggs are kept in captivity; when the hatchlings break through their shells, they are brought to a beach and allowed to rush toward the sea, hopefully imprinting a sense of belonging there so that they will later return to their place of "birth." Afterward, the hatchlings are scooped up and placed in tanks, and allowed to grow larger before being released into the open sea to increase their chances of survival. All of these efforts are in the experimental stage; the results will not be known for years.

Pronatura is a grassroots Yucatecan organization valiantly trying to work against the tide looking after certain species that are heading into extinction if guidelines aren't followed. A few current projects: sea turtle protection, a deer reproduction center, coastal and reef management planning, toucan habitat study, jaguar population study, and general conservation funds. For more information and donations write to **Pronatura**, % Joann Andrews, Calle 13 #203-A, Col. Garcia Gineres, Merida, Yucatan, Mexico; tel. 25-10-04. Specify your special interest. Donations made out to "Friends of Pronatura" are U.S. tax deductible.

ENDENTATA FAMILY

Nine-banded Armadillos

This strange creature looks like a miniature prehistoric monster. The size of a small dog, its unusual feature is the tough coat of plate armor which encases it. Even the tail has its own armor! Flexibility comes from nine bands (or external "joints") that circle the midsection. Living on a diet of insects, the armadillo's extremely keen sense of smell can locate grubs 15 cm underground. Its front paws are sharp, enabling it to dig easily into the earth and build underground burrows. After digging the hole, the animal carries up to a bushel of grass down to make its nest. Here it bears and rears its young and sleeps during the day. Unlike some armadillos that roll up into a tight ball when threatened, this species will race for the burrow, stiffly arch its back, and wedge in so that it cannot be pulled out. The tip of the Yucatan Peninsula is a favored habitat due to its scant rainfall and warm temperatures; too much rain floods the burrow and can drown young armadillos.

Giant Anteaters

This extraordinary cousin of the armadillo measures two meters long from the tip of its tubular snout to the end of its bushy tail. Its body is colored shades of brown-gray; the hindquarters become darker in tone, while a contrasting wedge-shaped pattern of black outlined with white decorates the throat and shoulders. This creature walks on the knuckles of its paws, keeping the foreclaws razor sharp. If threatened, anteaters can be deadly; more importantly, they are capable of ripping open the leathery mud walls of termite or white ant nests, the contents of which are a main food source. After opening the nest, the anteater begins flicking its tongue. Ants don't have a chance; the long viscous tongue quickly transfers them to a toothless, elongated mouth.

Tapirs

South American tapirs are found from the southern part of Mexico to southern Brazil. A stout-bodied animal, it has short legs and tail, small eyes, and rounded ears. The nose and upper lip extend into a short but very mobile proboscis. Totally herbivorous, tapirs usually live near streams or rivers in the forest.

They bathe daily and also use the water as an escape when hunted either by man or by its prime predator, the jaguar. Shy and unaggressive, these nocturnal animals have a definite home range, wearing a path between the jungle and their feeding area. If attacked, the tapir lowers its head and blindly crashes off through the forest; they've been known to collide with trees and knock themselves out in their chaotic attempt to flee!

Peccaries

Next to deer, peccaries are the most widely hunted game on the Yucatan. Other names for this pig-like creature are musk hog and javelina. Some compare peccaries to the wild pigs found in Europe, though, in fact, they're part of an entirely different family.

Two species found on the Peninsula are the collared and the white-lipped peccaries. The feisty collared peccary stands 50 cm at the shoulder and can be one meter long, weighing as much as 30 kilograms. It is black and white with a narrow semicircular collar of white hair on the shoulders. In Spanish *javelina* means "spear," descriptive of the two spear-like tusks that protrude from its mouth. This more familiar peccary is found in the desert, woodland, and rainforest forest, and travels in groups of five to 15. Also with tusks, the white-lipped peccary is reddish-brown to black and has an area of white around its mouth. This larger animal, which can grow to 105 cm long, is found deep in tropical rainforests and lives in herds of 100-plus.

CATS

Seven species of cats are found in North America, four tropically distributed. The jaguar is heavy-chested with sturdy, muscled forelegs. It has small rounded ears and its tail is relatively short. Color ranges from tan on top and white on the under-

jaguar

side to pure black. The male can weigh 65-115 kilograms, females 45-85 kilograms. Largest of the cats on the Peninsula, the jaguar is about the same size as a leopard. Other cats found in Quintana Roo are the ocelot and puma. In tropical forests of the past the large cats were the only predators capable of controlling hoofed game such as deer, peccaries, and tapirs. If hunting is poor and times are tough, the jaguar *(el tigre)* will go into the rivers and scoop fish with its large paws. The river is also a favorite spot for the jaguar to hunt the large tapir when it comes to drink.

MANATEE

Probably the most unusual mammal, the manatee is an elephantine creature of immense proportions with gentle manners and the curiosity of a kitten. Though today seldom seen, this enormous animal, often referred to as the sea cow, at one time roamed the shallow inlets, bays, and estuaries of the Caribbean in large numbers. The manatee is said to be the basis of myths and old seamen's references to mermaids. In South America this particular mammal is revered by certain Indian tribes. The manatee image is frequently seen in the art of the ancient Maya, who hunted it for its flesh. In modern times, the population has been reduced by the encroachment of large numbers of people in the manatees' habitats along the riverways and shorelines. Ever-growing numbers of motorboats inflict often-deadly gashes on the nosy creatures.

At birth the manatee weighs 30-35 kilograms, it can grow up to four meters long and weigh over a ton. Gray with a pinkish cast and shaped like an Idaho potato, it has a spatulate tail, two forelimbs with toenails, pebbled coarse skin, tiny sunken eyes, numerous fine-bristled hairs scattered sparsely over its body, and a permanent Mona Lisa smile. The head of the mammal seems small for its gargantuan body, and its preproboscidean lineage includes dugongs (in Australia), hyrax, and elephants. The manatee's truncated snout and prehensile lips help to push food into its mouth. The only aquatic mammal that exists on vegetation, the manatee grazes on bottom-growing grasses and other aquatic plantlife. It ingests as much as 225 kilograms per day, cleaning rivers of oxygen-choking growth. It is unique among mammals in that it constantly grows new teeth—worn teeth fall out and are replaced. Posing no threat to any other living thing, it has been hunted for its oil, skin, and flesh, which is said to be tasty.

The mammal thrives in shallow warm water; in Quintana Roo and coves of Belize the manatee has been reported in shallow bays between Playa del Carmen and Punta Allen but very infrequently anymore. One spring evening recently in a small bay in Belize near the Chetumal border, a curious manatee spent about an hour lazily swimming the cove, lifting its truncated snout out of the water about every four minutes, often its entire head. The few people (this author included) standing on a small dock in the bay were thrilled to be seeing the shy animal.

In neighboring Guatemala, the government is sponsoring a manatee reserve in Lago de Izabal. In the U.S. the mammal is found mostly in the inshore and estuarine areas of Florida. It is protected under the Federal U.S. Marine Mammal Protection Act of 1972, the Endangered Species Act of 1973, and the Florida Manatee Sanctuary Act of 1978. It is estimated that their total population numbers about 2,000.

BIRDS

Since a major part of the Yucatan Peninsula is still undeveloped and covered with trees and brush, it isn't surprising to find exotic, rarely seen birds all across the landscape. The Mexican government is beginning to realize the great value in this (almost) undiscovered treasure-trove of nature (attracting both scientists and laymen) and is making initial efforts to protect nesting grounds. The birds of the Yucatan have until recent years been free of pesticides, smog, and human beings' encroachment. If you're a serious birdwatcher, you know all about Quintana Roo. Undoubtedly, however, change is coming as more people intrude into the rangeland of the birds, exploring these still undeveloped tracts on the Yucatan Peninsula. Hopefully, stringent regulations will take hold before many of these lovely birds are chased away or destroyed.

Quintana Roo is one of the better ornithological sites. Coba, with its marshy-rimmed lakes, nearby cornfields, and relatively tall, humid forest, is worth a couple of days to the ornithologist. One of the

kingfisher

more impressive birds to look for is the keel-billed toucan, often seen perched high on a bare limb in the early hours of the morning. Others include *chachalacas* (held in reverence by the Maya cult), screeching parrots, and occasionally, the ocellated turkey. For an excellent bird book that deals with the Yucatan Peninsula, check out *100 Common Birds of the Yucatan Peninsula* written by Barbara MacKinnon. A well-known birdwatcher, Barbara has lived in the Cancun area for many years, and is donating all of the profits of her book to the Sian Ka'an Reserve. Available for US$30, through Amigos de Sian Ka'an, Apto. Postal 770, Cancun, Quintana Roo, Mexico 77500.

Sooty Terns

In Cancun on a coral island just offshore from the Camino Real Hotel, a breeding colony of sooty terns has been discovered. The sooty tern is not the only seabird which lacks waterproof feathers, but it is the only one that will not land and rest on a passing ship or drifting debris. The bird feeds on tiny fish and squid that swim near the ocean surface, hovering close to the water and snatching the unsuspecting prey.

The sooty tern nests from April till September. The Camino Real Hotel is being urged to warn guests to stay away from the rocky island. Man is the sooty tern's only predator. If frightened the parent birds panic, leaving the eggs exposed to the hot tropical sun, or knocking the young into the sea where they drown immediately.

Flamingos

In the far north of the Peninsula at Rio Lagartos, thousands of long-necked, long-legged flamingos are seen during the nesting season. They begin arriving around the end of May, when the rains begin. This homecoming is a breathtaking sight: a profusion of pink/salmon colors clustered together on the white sand or sailing across a blue sky, long curved necks straight in flight, the flapping movement exposing contrasting black and pink on the undersides of their wings. The estimated flamingo population on the Yucatan Peninsula is 30,000. This wildlife refuge called **El Cuyo** protects the largest colony of nesting American flamingos in the world. Many of these flamingos winter in Celestun, a small fishing village on the northwest coast a few kilometers north of the Campeche-Yucatan state border. Celestun lies between the Gulf of Mexico and a long tidal estuary known as La Cienega. If you're visiting Merida and want to see flamingos during the winter season, it's a closer drive to Celestun (about one hour) than to Rio Lagartos (about three hours). Don't forget your camera and color film!

Estuary Havens

Estuaries play host to hundreds of bird species. A boat ride into one of them will give you an opportunity to see a variety of ducks; this is a wintering spot for many North American flocks. Among others, you'll see the blue-winged teal, northern shoveler, and lesser scaup along with a variety of wading birds feeding in the shallow waters, including numerous types of heron, snowy egret, and (in the summer) white ibis. Seven species of birds are endemic to the Yucatan Peninsula: ocellated turkey, Yucatan whippoorwill, Yucatan flycatcher, orange oriole, black catbird, yellow-lored parrot, and the quetzal.

Quetzals

Though the ancient Maya made abundant use of the dazzling quetzal feathers for ceremonial costume and headdress, they hunted other fowl in much larger quantities for food; nonetheless, the quetzal is the only known bird from the pre-Columbian era that is almost extinct. Close by, the Guatemalan government has established a quetzal sanctuary not too far from the city of Coban. The beautifully designed reserve is open to hikers, with several kilometers of good trails leading up into the cloud forest. For the birder this could be a worthwhile detour to search out the gorgeous quetzal. The tourist office in Coban, INGUAT, hands out an informative leaflet with a map and description of the quetzal sanctuary.

INSECTS

Any tropical locale has literally tens of thousands of insects. Some are annoying (mosquitos and gnats), some are dangerous (black widows, bird spiders, and scorpions), and others can cause pain when they bite (red ants), but many are beautiful (butterflies and moths), and *all* are fascinating studies in evolved socialization and specialization.

Butterflies And Moths
The Yucatan has an abundance of beautiful moths and butterflies. Of the 90,000 types of butterflies in the world, a large percentage are seen in Quintana Roo. You'll see, among others, the magnificent blue morpho, orange-barred sulphur, copperhead, cloudless sulphur, malachite, admiral, calico, ruddy dagger-wing, tropical buckeye, and emperor. The famous monarch is also a visitor during its annual migration from the Florida Peninsula. They usually make a stopover on Quintana Roo's east coast, including Cancun and Cozumel, on their way south to the Central Amer-

DIFFERENCES BETWEEN MOTHS AND BUTTERFLIES

1. Butterflies fly during the day; moths fly at dusk or at night.

2. Butterflies rest with their wings folded straight up over their bodies; most moths rest with their wings spread flat.

3. All butterflies have bare knobs at the end of both antennae (feelers); moths' antennae are either plumy or hairlike and end in a point.

4. Butterflies have slender bodies; moths are plump. Both insects are of the order Lepidoptera. So lepidopterists bring your nets, for you are in butterfly heaven in the jungle areas of the Yucatan Peninsula.

ican mountains and Mexican highlands where they spend the winter. Trying to photograph a butterfly (live) is a testy business. Just when you have it in your cross hairs, the comely critter flutters off to another spot!

FLORA

Flora of the Yucatan Peninsula varies widely from north to south, and even east to west. The Yucatan is subject to tropical storms and occasional hurricanes. Although these tremendous winds seldom reach the interior, they periodically damage vegetation in their paths. They also pick up and disperse seeds from the Caribbean basin (where the storms originate), spreading plants and flowers across political boundaries.

The Forests
Among the plantlife of Quintana Roo are mangroves, bamboo, and swamp cypresses, plus ferns, vines, and flowers creeping from tree to tree and creating a dense growth. On topmost limbs, orchids and air ferns reach for the sun. In the southern part of the Yucatan Peninsula with its classic tropical rainforest are the tall mahoganies, *campeche, sapote,* and kapok, also covered with wild jungle vines.

Palms
A wide variety of palm trees and their relatives grows on the Peninsula—tall, short, fruited, even oil producers. Though similar, various palms have distinct characteristics. Royal palms are tall with smooth trunks. Queen palms are often used for landscaping and bear a sweet fruit. Thatch palms are called *chit* by the Indians; the frond of this tree is used extensively on the Peninsula for roof thatch. Coconut palms serve the Yucatecan well. One of the 10 most useful trees in the world, it produces oil, food, drink, and shelter. The tree matures in six to seven years and then for five to seven years bears coconuts, a nutritious food that is also used for copra and valued as a money crop by the locals. Presently, this source of income has all but disappeared in a good part of the Quintana Roo coast due to the "yellowing" disease that's attacked the Caribbean coast from Florida to Central America. Henequen is a cousin to the palm tree; from the fiber comes twine, rope, matting, and other products. New uses are constantly being sought since this plant is common and abundant.

From Fruit To Flowers
Quintana Roo grows delicious sweet and sour oranges, limes, and grapefruit. Avocado is abundant, and the papaya tree is practically a weed. The mammey tree grows tall (15-20 meters) and full, providing not only welcome shade but also an avocado-shaped fruit, brown on the outside with a vivid salmon-pink flesh that makes a sweet snack (the flavor similar to a sweet yam). Another unusual fruit tree is the *guaya* (part of the litchi nut family). This rangy evergreen thrives on sea air and is commonly seen along the coast and throughout the Yucatan Peninsula. Its small green leathery pods grow in clumps like grapes and contain a sweet, yellowish, jelly-like flesh—tasty! The calabash tree, a friend to the Indian for many years, provides a gourd used for containers.

The tall ceiba is a very special tree to those close to the Maya religious cult. Considered the tree of life, even today it remains undisturbed whether it has sprouted in the middle of a fertile *milpa* (cornfield) or anywhere else. At first glance when visiting in the summer, it would seem that all of the state favors the beautiful *flamboyanes* (royal poinciana). As its name implies, when in bloom it is the most flamboyant tree around, with widespreading branches covered in clusters of brilliant orange-red flowers. These trees line sidewalks and plazas and when clustered together present a dazzling show.

Orchids
In remote areas of Quintana Roo one of the more exotic blooms, the orchid, is often found on the highest limbs of tall trees. Of the 71 species reported on the Yucatan Peninsula, 20% are terrestrial and 80% are epiphytic, attached to a host plant (in this case trees) and deriving its moisture and nutrients from the air and rain. Both types grow in many sizes and shapes: tiny buttons spanning the length of a long branch, largepetaled blossoms with ruffled edges, or intense, tiger-striped miniatures. The lovely flowers come in a wide variety of colors, some subtle, some brilliant.

Nature's Hothouse

In spring, flowering trees are a beautiful sight—and sound—attracting hundreds of singing birds throughout the mating season. While wandering through jungle landscapes, you'll see a gamut of plants thriving in the wild that we so carefully nurture and coax to survive in a pot on a windowsill at home. Here in its natural environment, the croton exhibits wild colors, the pothos grows 30-cm leaves, and the philodendron splits every leaf in gargantuan glory.

White and red ginger are among the more exotic herbs that grow on the Peninsula. Plumeria (in the South Pacific called frangipani) has a wonderful fragrance and is seen in many colors. Hibiscus and bougainvillea bloom in an array of bright hues. A walk through the jungle will introduce you to many delicate strangers in the world of tropical flowers. But you'll find old friends too, such as the common morning glory creeping and climbing for miles over bushes and trees. Viny coils thicken daily. Keeping jungle growth away from the roads, utility poles, and wires is a constant job because warm humid air and ample rainfall encourage a lush green wonderland.

SIAN KA'AN

With the growing number of visitors to Quintana Roo and the continual development of its natural wonders, there's a real danger of decimating the wildlife and destroying the ancient culture of its people. These are *the* two reasons that most travelers come to Quintana Roo—how foolhardy to kill the goose that laid the golden you-know-what. Because of that reality, authorities and scientists first put their heads together in 1981 and the seeds of an idea began to grow.

In 1986 the culmination of this group effort, the **Sian Ka'an Biosphere Reserve,** came to fruition. It takes into account land titles, logging, hunting, agriculture, cattle ranching, and tourist development. The local people feel comfortable with it, and in October of 1986 Sian Ka'an was officially incorporated into UNESCO's World Network of Biosphere Reserves.

Several important issues were addressed. Deforestation is becoming commonplace in Quintana Roo as the growing population clears more land for farms and ranches. Even in traditional fishing

---

WHAT IS A BIOSPHERE RESERVE?

The biosphere is the thin mantle of the earth in which we live. It consists of parts of the lithosphere, hydrosphere, and atmosphere. The biosphere maintains our life and that of all organisms. We need to protect it and keep it liveable.

The program *Man and Biosphere* was created by UNESCO in 1971, and it deals with the interactions of man with his environment. The program contains various projects, among which the concept of biosphere reserve has gained popularity and has become very important worldwide.

The idea of a biosphere reserve is new in conservation. It promotes the protection of different natural ecosystems of the world, and at the same time allows the presence of human activities through the rational use and development of natural resources on an ecological basis.

A biosphere reserve has a nucleus which is for conservation and limited scientific investigation only. A buffer zone would surround this nucleus in which people may live and use the resources on a regulated, ecological basis. Conservation in a biosphere reserve is the challenge of good use rather than prohibiting use. This concept sets it apart from the national parks in which people are only observers. Biosphere reserves are especially appropriate in Mexico where conservation and ecomomic development are equally important.

—from the bulletin of the
Amigos de Sian Ka'an

---

villages growth is affecting the environment. In Punta Allen, to supplement their income fishermen were turning to the ancient method of slash-and-burn agriculture which for centuries had worked fine for the small groups of people that inhabited the Quintana Roo region. But with the continued systematic destruction of the forest to create new growing fields the entire rain forest along the Caribbean could be destroyed in just a few years.

The people need an alternative means to support their families. The Amigos de Sian Ka'an and reserve administrators along with the local population have been working in the field (thanks to support from the World Wildlife Fund U.S.) and have come up with an experimental farm (called "el Ramona") which consists of one acre of land transformed by crop rotation and interplanting of various fruit and vegetables. It is an ecologically sound procedure using biodegradable pesticides and a minimum of fertilizers; this allows for constant production of diverse crops. The fishermen at Punta Allen were able to observe an operating prototype and have seen that this "new" method works. The cost of the farm, including a drip irrigation system, construction of a well plus the purchase of a gas pump and plastic tubing was US$2000, within the means of the Punta Allen fishermen. This compromise provides the fishermen with produce, slows deforestation, and creates a self-supporting farm.

Other problems are being dealt with as well. The palm is an important part of the cultural and practical lifestyle of the indigenous people of Quintana Roo. The Maya have for years used two particular types of palm *(Thrinax radiata* and *Coccothrinax readdi)* as thatch for the roofs of their houses, and in the past 10 years fishermen have been selectively cutting *Thrinax* to construct lobster traps. It is becoming more difficult to find populations of this palm in the reserve today. Amigos de Sian Ka'an, with World Wildlife Funds, are studying the palms' growth patterns and rates, anticipating a management plan that will encourage future growth. Other problems being faced include limiting commercial fishing, relocating an entire fishing village to an area which will better support the families, putting up a red light for tourist development where it will endanger the ecology, and doing a study of the lobster industry and its future. Many more worthwhile projects are waiting in line. Like most ambitious projects, these take a lot of money. If you're interested in helping out, join the booster club. Your donation will really be helping a worthy cause, and you'll get a bulletin/newsletter with fascinating facts about the area and the people as well as updates on current projects. For more detailed information write to: Amigos de Sian Ka'an, Apto. Postal 770, Cancun, Quintana Roo, Mexico 77500.

Ecology Publications

For birders or any visitor intrigued with wildlife and interested in helping the ecological preservation of the Yucatan Peninsula, a fairly new book, *100 Common Birds Of The Yucatan Peninsula,* by Barbara MacKinnon is available through the Amigos de Sian Ka'an. See p. 12 for ordering details.

Another publication, *The Rainforest News,* keeps the world in touch with facts concerning the rainforests of Mesoamerica; a yearly subscription is available with donations of over US$4 per year. For more information, donations, and subscriptions, contact The Rainforest Fund, P.O. Box 140681, Coral Gables, FL 33114. To contact the Mesoamerica Foundation, write to A.P. 1575, Ad. 1, Merida, Yucatan, Mexico.

HISTORY

THE ANCIENTS

Earliest Man

During the Pleistocene Epoch when the level of the sea fell (around 50,000 B.C.), people and animals from Asia crossed the Bering land bridge into the North American continent. For nearly 50,000 years, man continued his epic trek southward. It is believed that the first Indians reached Tierra del Fuego, at the tip of South America, in approximately 1000 B.C.

As early as 10,000 B.C., Ice Age man hunted woolly mammoth and other large animals roaming the cool, moist landscape of central Mexico. Between 7000 and 2000 B.C., society evolved from hunters and gatherers to farmers. Such crops as corn, squash, and beans were independently domesticated in widely separated areas of Mexico after about 6000 B.C. The remains of clay figurines from the Preclassic Period, presumed to be fertility symbols, marked the rise of religion in Mesoamerica, beginning around 2000 B.C.

Around 1000 B.C. the Olmec Indian culture, believed to be the region's earliest, began to spread throughout Mesoamerica. The large-scale ceremonial centers grew along Gulf coast lands and much of Mesoamerica was influenced by these Indians' often sinister religion of worshiping strange jaguar-like gods, as well as the New World's first calendar and a beginning system of writing.

Classic Period

The Classic Period, beginning about A.D. 300, is now hailed as the peak of cultural development among the Maya Indians and other cultures throughout Mexico. Until A.D. 900, phenomenal progress was made in the development of artistic, architectural, and astronomical skills. Impressive buildings were constructed during this period, and codices (folded bark books) were written and filled with hieroglyphic symbols that detailed complicated mathematical calculations of days, months, and years. Only the priests and the privileged held this knowledge, and continued to learn and develop until, for some unexplained reason there was a sudden halt to this growth (see p. 25 for speculation).

Postclassic

After A.D. 900, the Toltec influence took hold, marking the end of the most artistic era and the birth of a new militaristic society built around a blend of ceremonialism, civic and social organization, and conquest.

COLONIAL HISTORY

Hernan Cortes

Following Columbus' arrival in the New World, other adventurers traveling the same seas soon found the Yucatan Peninsula. In 1519, 34-year-old Hernan Cortes sailed from Cuba against the wishes of the authority of the Spanish governor. With 11 ships, 120 sailors, and 550 soldiers he set out to search for slaves, a lucrative business with or without the blessings of the government. His search began on the Yucatan coast and would eventually encompass most of Mexico. However, he hadn't counted on the ferocious resistance and cunning of the Maya Indians. The fighting was destined to continue for many years—a time of bloodshed and death for many of his men. This "war" didn't *really* end on the Peninsula until the Chan Santa Cruz Indians finally signed a peace treaty with the Mexican federal government in 1935, over 400 years later. By the time Cortes died in 1547 (while exiled in Spain), the Spanish military and Franciscan friars were well entrenched in the Yucatan Peninsula.

Diego De Landa

The Franciscan priests were shocked by acts that they believed to be influences of the devil, such as body mutilation and human sacrifice, performed in the name of the Maya religion. The Franciscans felt it their duty to God to eliminate these cere-monies and all other traces of the Maya cult, and gather the Indians into the fold of Christianity. Diego de Landa arrived in Mexico in 1549 as a 25-year-old friar, and was instrumental in the destruction of many thousands of Maya idols. He oversaw the burning of 27 codices filled with characters and symbols that he could not understand, which he believed contained only superstitions and the devil's evil lies. Since then, only three codices have been found and studied, though only parts of them have been completely deciphered. While Landa was directly responsible for destroying the history of these ancient people, he did redeem himself before his death by writing the most complete and detailed account of the life of the Maya in his book *Relaciones de las Cosas de Yucatan.* Landa's book describes daily living in great detail, including the growth and preparation of food, the structure of society, the priesthood, and the sciences. Although he was aware of their sophisticated "count of ages," he didn't understand it. Fortunately, he left a one-line formula which, used as a mathematical and chronological key, opened up the science of Maya calculations and their great knowledge of astronomy.

Landa was called back to Spain in 1563 after colonial civil and religious leaders accused him of "despotic mismanagement." He spent a year in prison, and while his guilt or innocence was being decided, he wrote his book in defense of the charges. During his absence, his replacement, Bishop Toral, acted with great compassion toward the Indians. Landa was ultimately cleared and was allowed to return to the New World in 1573, where he became a bishop and resumed his previous methods of proselytizing. He lived in Yucatan until his death in 1579.

Franciscan Power

Bishop Toral was cut from a different cloth. A humanitarian, he was appalled by the unjust treatment of Indians. Though Toral, after Landa's imprisonment, tried to impose sweeping changes, he was unable to make inroads into the power held by the Franciscans in the Yucatan. Defeated, he retired to Mexico. However, shortly before his death (in 1571) his reforms were implemented with the "Royal Cedula," which prohibited friars from shaving the heads of Indians against their will, flogging them, and keeping prison cells in monasteries. It also called for the immediate release of all Indians held prisoner.

PRE-COLUMBIAN?

The word "pre-Columbian" establishes the time before Columbus discovered the New World. His arrival on the scene was the catalyst that would bring to an end the cultures of the period that were then thriving. Some of the ancient cultures had died out many years before the Spanish arrived, but some of them continued beyond 1492, as in the case of the Aztec culture, which continued until about 1521. The Maya culture endured (though in much smaller numbers) until well toward the end of the 16th century.

Catholicism

Over the years, the majority of Indians were indeed baptized into the Catholic faith. Most priests did their best to educate the people, teach them to read and write, and protect them from the growing number of Spanish settlers who used them as slaves. The Indians, then and now, practice Catholicism in their own manner, combining their ancient cult beliefs handed down through centuries with Christian doctrine. These mystic yet Christian ceremonies are performed in baptism, courtship, marriage, illness, farming, housebuilding, and fiestas.

Further Subjugation

While all of Mexico dealt with the problems of economic colonialism, the Yucatan Peninsula had an additional one: harassment by vicious pirates who made life on the Gulf coast unstable. Around 1600, when silver production began to wane, Spain's economic power faltered. In the following years, haciendas (self-supporting estates or small feudal systems) began to thrive, overrunning communal villages jointly owned by the Maya. But later, between 1700 and 1810 as Mexico endured the backlash of several government upheavals in Europe, Spanish settlers on the Peninsula began exploiting the native Maya in earnest. The passive Indians were ground down, their lands taken away, and their numbers greatly reduced by the white man's epidemics and mistreatment.

Caste War

The Spaniards grabbed the Maya land and planted it with tobacco and sugarcane year after year until the soil was worn out. Added to the other abuses, it was inevitable that the Indians would eventually explode in a furious attack. This bloody uprising in the 1840s was called the Caste War. Though the Maya were farmers, not soldiers, this savage war saw them taking revenge on every white man, woman, and child by means of rape and violent murder. European survivors made their way to the last Spanish strongholds of Merida and Campeche. The governments of the two cities appealed for help to Spain, France, and the United States. No one answered the call, and it was soon apparent that the remaining two cities would be wiped out. But fate would not have it that way; just as the governor of Merida was about to begin evacuating the city, the Maya picked up their primitive weapons and walked away.

Spanish-style ship

Sacred Corn

Attuned to the signals of the land, the Maya knew that the appearance of the flying ant was the first sign of rain. Corn was their sustenance, a gift from the gods without which they would not survive. When the rains came, the corn had to be in the soil otherwise the gods would be insulted. When, on the brink of destroying the enemy, the winged ant made an unusually early appearance, the Indians turned their backs on certain victory and returned to their villages to plant corn.

This was just the breather the Spanish settlers needed. Help came from Cuba, Mexico City, as well as 1,000 U.S. mercenary troops. Vengeance was merciless. Most Maya, regardless of their beliefs, were killed. Some were taken prisoner and sold to Cuba as slaves; others left their villages and hid in the jungles, in some cases for decades. Between 1846-1850 the population of the Yucatan Peninsula was reduced from 500,000 to 300,000. Guerilla warfare ensued, the escaped Maya making sneak attacks upon the whites. Quintana Roo along the Caribbean coast was considered a dangerous no-man's land for almost another hundred years. (In 1936, President Lazaro Cardenas declared Quintana Roo a territory of the Mexican government; in 1974, with the promise of tourism, the territory was admitted to the Federation of States of Mexico.)

Growing Maya Power

Many Maya Indians escaped slaughter during the Caste War by fleeing to the isolated territory known today as Quintana Roo. The Maya revived the cult of the "talking cross," a pre-Columbian oracle representing gods of the four cardinal directions. This was a religious/political marriage. Three determined survivors of the Caste War—a priest, a master spy, and a ventriloquist—all wise leaders, knew their people's desperate need for divine leadership. As a result of the words from the talking cross, shattered Indians came together in large numbers and began to organize. The community guarded the cross's location, and advice from it continued to strengthen the Maya.

They called themselves *Chan Santa Cruz* (meaning people of the little holy cross). As their confidence developed so did the growth and power of their communities. Living very close to the British Honduras border (now Belize) they found they had something their neighbors wanted.

The Chan Santa Cruz Maya began selling timber to the British and were given arms in return. These weapons gave the Maya even more power. From 1855-1857 internal strife weakened the relations between Campeche and Merida. While the Spaniards were dealing with the problem on the Gulf coast, the Maya took advantage of the vulnerability of Fort Bacalar and in 1857 took possession, giving them control of the entire Caribbean coast from Cabo Catouche in the far north to the border of British Honduras in the south. In three years they destroyed all of the Spanish settlements while slaughtering or capturing thousands of whites.

The Indians of the coastal community of Chan Santa Cruz were also known as Cruzobs. For years they had murdered their captives, but starting in 1858 they took lessons from the colonials and began to keep whites for slave labor in the fields and forest; women were put to work doing household chores and some became concubines. For the next 40 years, the Chan Santa Cruz Indians kept the east coast of the Yucatan for themselves; a shaky truce with the Mexican government endured. The Indians were financially independent, self-governing, and with no roads in, totally isolated from technological advancements beginning to take place in other parts of the Peninsula. They were not at war as long as everyone left them alone.

The Last Stand

It was only when President Porfirio Diaz took power in 1877 that the Mexican federal government began to think seriously about the Yucatan Peninsula. Over the years, because of Quintana Roo's isolation and the strength of the Maya in their treacherous jungle, repeated efforts of Mexican soldiers to capture the Indians failed. Long periods of time elapsed between attempts, but it rankled Diaz that a handful of Indians had been able to keep the Mexican federal army at bay for so long. In 1901 under the command of army General Ignacio Bravo the Feds made a new assault on the Indians. The general captured a village, laid railroad tracks, and built a walled fort. Supplies got through the jungle to the fort by way of the railroad, but General Bravo also suffered at the hands of the clever Indians. The garrison was besieged for a year, the Mexicans prisoners within their own fort. Reinforcements arrived from the capital and the upstarts were finally put down. Then began another cycle of brutal Mexican occupation until 1915, but the scattered Indians didn't give up. They persisted with guerilla raids from the rainforest until the Mexicans, defeated once again, pulled out and returned Quintana Roo to the Maya. From 1917 till 1920, hundreds of thousands of Indians died from influenza and smallpox epidemics (introduced by the Spanish). An Indian leader, General May, took stock of his troops, and it was apparent that the old soldiers were fading. They put up a long tough battle to hold onto their land and culture. In 1920, the end of their independent reign in the Quintana Roo jungle began. Foreign gum-makers initiated the chicle boom, bringing *chicleros* to work the trees. It was then that General May demanded (and received) a negotiated settlement. In 1935 the Chan Santa Cruz Indians signed a peace treaty with the Mexican Federals. Now came a time of new beginnings, new growth, and another era of government.

MODERN TIMES

Meanwhile, in the northern part of the Peninsula, prosperity settled upon Merida, capital of the state of Yucatan. In 1875, the henequen boom began. Twine and rope made from the sword-shaped leaves of this variety of agave plant were in demand all over the world. Merida became the jewel of the Peninsula. Spanish haciendas with their Indian slaves cultivated the easily grown plant, and for miles the outlying areas were planted with the henequen, which required little rainfall and thrived in the Peninsula's thin rocky soil. Beautiful mansions were built by entrepreneurs who led the gracious life, sending their children to Europe to be educated, taking their wives by ship to New Orleans, looking for new luxuries and entertainment. Port towns were developed on the Gulf coast, and a two-kilometer-long wharf named Progreso was built to accommodate the large ships that came for sisal (hemp from the henequen plant). The only thing that didn't change was the lifestyle of the *peone.* The Indian peasants' life was still lacking in human rights; they labored long, hard hours to keep henequen production up. Living in constant debt to the company store, where their meager peso wage was spent before it was received, the Indians were caught up in a cycle of bondage that existed for many years in Merida. One legend says it was during this time that the lovely *huipil* (Indian dress) was mandated to be worn by all Indians and mestizos (those of mixed blood) on the Peninsula. There would now be no problem distinguishing Indians from full-blooded Spaniards.

Hacienda Wealth

The outside world was becoming aware of the Peninsula, its newly found economic activity, and its rich *patrones.* In 1908, an American journalist, John Kenneth Turner, stirred things up when he documented how difficult for the Indians and how

Hacienda Yaxcopoil dates back to the turn of the century.

prosperous for the owners life was on a henequen plantation. From this time forward, change was inevitable. In 1915, wealthy hacienda owners were compelled to pay an enormous tax to then President Venustiano Carranza. This tax was extracted under duress and the watchful eye of General Alvarado and 7,000 armed soldiers, who needed the money to put down revolutionists Emiliano Zapata and Pancho Villa in the northern sections of Mexico. Millions of pesos changed hands.

The next thorn in the side of the hacienda owners was upstart Felipe Carrillo Puerto, the first socialist governor of Merida. Under his tutelage the Indians set up a labor union, an educational center, and political clubs—"leagues of resistance." These leagues gave the *peones* the first secular hope ever held out to them. Through the leagues, workers wielded a power that wealthy Yucatecans were forced to acknowledge. Carrillo pushed on, making agrarian reforms at every turn. He decreed that abandoned haciendas were up for appropriation. He was very successful, so much so that his opponents began to worry seriously about the power he was amassing. With the number of his followers growing, conservatives saw only one way to stop him. In 1923, Felipe Carrillo Puerto was assassinated—but not his cause.

The Revolution

The fight against wealthy landowners and the power elite continued after Carrillo's murder. In the south, Emiliano Zapata was demanding land reform; shortly thereafter, the revolution put an end to the uneven control of wealth in the country. The constitution (of 1917) had made some inroads. It was instrumental in dividing the large haciendas, giving the country back to the people (*some* of the people), and making sweeping political changes. The education of all children was decreed and

schools were built to implement the law. Power of the church was curtailed and church land redistributed. In this war of ideals, however, Indian villages (communal groups) were broken up along with the large haciendas, and turmoil continued. Again it was the rich against the poor; a whole new class of rich had been created, those who had the new power. The poor were still the poor. It wasn't until recent years that some of the Indians benefited from this land division, when President Lazaro Cardenas (1934-40) gave half the usable land in Quintana Roo to the poor.

Mexican Unity

Between 1934 and 1940, the Mexican government nationalized most of the foreign companies that were taking more out of the country than they were putting in. Mexico suffered through a series of economic setbacks but gained unity and national self-confidence that enthusiastically heralded the economic strides to come. Like a crawling child trying to walk, the country took many falls. But progress continued; the people of the country saw more jobs, fairer wages, and more products on the market—until the 1970s when inflation began to grow. By 1976 it was totally out of hand. Mexico was pricing itself out of the market, both for tourists and capital investors. Eventually, a change in the monetary policy let the peso float and find its own value against the dollar. This legislation brought back tourists and investors.

The condition of the peso is a boon for visitors, but a burden for the people. The belief is that enough foreigners coming and spending their money will create more jobs so that the economic condition will ultimately remedy itself. Smart Mexican businesspeople began developing the natural beauty of the Caribbean coast, and indeed visitors are coming from all over the world.

ECONOMY

MONEY

Currency Exchange

The peso, the basic medium of exchange in Mexico, has floated on the free market since 1976. The money is issued in paper bills (1000, 5000, 10,000, 20,000, and 50,000 denominations) and peso coins are distributed in 500, 1000, and 5000 pieces. Coins of smaller value are measured in centavos (10, 20, and 50), but no one is really sure what to use them for since nothing sells for centavos.

Usually your best rate of exchange is at the bank, but small shops frequently give a good rate if you're making a purchase. Hotels notoriously give the poorest exchange. Check to see what kind of a fee, if any, is charged. You can learn the current exchange rate daily in all banks and most hotels. Try not to run out of money over the weekend because the new rate often is not posted until noon on Monday; you will get the previous Friday's rate of exchange even if the weekend newspaper may be announcing an overwhelming difference in your favor. The exchange rate in June of 1990 is 2800 pesos for one dollar. Cashing personal checks in Mexico is not easy; however, it is possible to withdraw money against your credit card in some banks. *Wearing a moneybelt is always a good idea while traveling—in any country.*

Mexico is trying valiantly to pull itself out of its status as a developing country and continues to make rapid strides in economic growth. The average yearly wage per person has grown to the equivalent of US$2500, and though inflation is high, it dropped to a much slower pace in 1990. As Mexico controls inflation it will be able to make use of its many natural resources and provide jobs to keep up with the rapid population growth.

World's Largest City

Mexico is suffering from a population explosion. Mexico City, with 20 million people, is the largest city in the world. Each year 800,000 people enter the city's job market; only 400,000 jobs are available. Roughly 65% of the national population resides in cities, partly due to continuing migration from rural areas. In addition, a certain number of young Mexican adults, many accompanied by their families, make their way across the U.S. border, where there's more hope of getting jobs; about six million Mexicans presently live in the U.S. Because of this leave-the-land movement, the country's agriculture has suffered. Mexico imports corn, cereals, and sugar, among other products, and exports coffee, cotton, sisal, honey, bananas, and beef cattle.

Industries

Mexico's chief industries are oil, mining, and tourism. After the oil industry was nationalized in 1938, a time of transition slowed down production. Pemex, the state oil corporation, does not belong to the Organization of Petroleum Exporting Countries (OPEC), but keeps its prices in line with it. Most of the oil produced in Mexico is shipped to

henequen leaves

the U.S. (its number-one customer), Canada, Israel, France, and Japan. Rich in natural gas, the country sends the U.S. 10% of its total output. Two-thirds of Mexico's export revenue comes from fossil fuels.

Mexico is still the world's largest producer of silver and fluorspar. It also processes large quantities of barite, antimony, bismuth, copper, and sulphur. Other minerals mined are gold, tin, manganese, zinc, coal, and iron. Although mining has always been important to Mexico's economy, growth of the industry is slow, about a 2% increase per year. Around 60% of the country's industrial plants are concentrated around Mexico City, though the government is developing petrochemical processing industries along the U.S. border.

The Yucatan

The leading moneymaker on the Peninsula is the oil business. Along the Gulf coast from Campeche south into the state of Tabasco, the oil industry is booming. Yucatan cities are beginning to show signs of good financial health. Yucatecan fisheries are abundant along the Gulf coast. At one time fishing was not much more than a "ma-and-pa" business here, but today fleets of large purse seiners with their adjacent processing plants can be seen on the Gulf of Mexico just south of the city of Campeche and on Isla del Carmen. With the renewed interest in preserving fishing grounds for the future, the industry could continue to thrive for many years.

Maquiladoras

An industry that's growing rapidly all over Mexico, the *maquiladoras* provide jobs for hundreds of Mexicans. Products from the U.S. such as clothing, small equipment, and leather goods are begun in the States, then sent to Mexico to be completed by the cheaper labor force. These *maquiladora* plants are enthusiastically being developed.

Tourism

Tourism is developing into the number-two contributor to the economy. Going with a good thing, the government has set up a national trust to finance a program of developing beautiful areas of the country to attract visitors. Cancun is probably the most successful thus far.

Cancun: Economy

Until the 1970s the economy of the lost territory of Quintana Roo amounted to very little. For a few years the chicle boom brought a flurry of activity up and down the state. Then chicle was shipped from the harbor of Isla Cozumel. Native and hardwood trees have always been in demand; coconuts and fishing were the only other natural resources that added to the economy—but none on a large scale. Today the face of Quintana Roo is changing. With the development of an offshore sandbar—Cancun—into a multimillion-dollar resort, tourism is now its number-one moneymaker. Cancun is one of Mexico's most modern and popular resorts. Construction is continuing south along the coast. Other naturally attractive sites are earmarked for future development and the corridor south of Cancun is already showing signs of growth with several new resorts, a marina, an 18-hole golf course, and rumors of another international airport. New roads give access to until-now unknown beaches and often unseen Maya structures. Extra attention is being given to archaeological zones ignored for hundreds of years: building restrooms, ticket offices, and fences to keep out vandals.

Travel in Mexico gets better every day. For the Mexican people, the deflated peso is a sock in the eye. For the traveler to Mexico, the dollar is worth more than ever and is attracting visitors in large numbers which in turn helps Mexico's economy. There is no time like the present to visit the Yucatan Peninsula.

THE PEOPLE

At one time the Maya, the first settlers of the Yucatan Peninsula, numbered about a million. For hundreds of years, modern scholars of the world have asked, "What happened to the Maya people?" Their magnificent structures, built with such advanced skill, still stand. Many carvings, unique statues, and even a few colored frescoes remain. All of this art depicts a world of intelligent human beings living in a well-organized, complex society. It's apparent their trade and agricultural methods supported the population for many centuries. Scholars agree the Maya was the most advanced of all ancient Mesoamerica cultures. Yet all signs point to an abrupt work stoppage. After around A.D. 900, no buildings were constructed, and no stelae, carefully detailing names and dates to inform future generations of their roots, were erected. So what happened?

Anthropologists and historians do know that thousands, perhaps as many as 500,000, were decimated by such diseases as smallpox after the arrival of the Spaniards. But no one really knows for sure what halted the progress of the Maya culture.

A Society Collapses

Priests and noblemen, the guardians of religion, science, and the arts, conducted their ritual ceremonies and studies in the large stone pyramids and platforms found today in ruins throughout the jungle. More specific questions arise: what happened to the priests and noblemen? Why were the centers abandoned? What happened to the knowledge of the intelligentsia who studied the skies, wrote the books, and designed the pyramids? Theories abound. Some speculate about a revolution of the people or decentralization with the arrival of outside influences. Others suggest the Indians tired of subservience and were no longer willing to farm the land to provide food, clothing, and support for the priests and nobles. Whatever happened, it's clear that the special knowledge concerning astronomy, hieroglyphics, and architecture was not passed on to Maya descendants. Sociologists who have lived with Indians in isolated villages are convinced that this priv-

ileged information is no longer known by today's Maya. Why did the masses disperse, leaving once-sacred stone cities unused and ignored? It's possible that lengthy periods of drought, famine, and epidemic caused the people to leave their once-glorious sacred centers. No longer important in day-to-day life, these structures were ignored for a thousand years and faced the whimsy of nature and its corroding elements.

The Maya question may never be answered with authority. One nonconforming theory suggests that these stone cities were built by people from outer space. Another considers the possibility that today's Maya are no relation to the people who built the structures, made near-perfect astronomical observations, and discovered infinity a thousand years ago—instead a society long gone.

Modern Times

However, there's hope in today's technology. Satellite photographs, for example, have spotted within the thick uninhabited jungle of the Yucatan Peninsula many untouched structures, large treasures of knowledge just waiting to be rediscovered. As new finds are made, the history of the Maya develops new depth and breadth. Archaeologists, ethnologists, art historians, and linguists continue to unravel the ongoing mystery with constant new discoveries of temples and artifacts, each with a story to tell. Native writings such as the *Chalam Balam* follow the history and traditions of the period just before the Spanish came, and a few books written soon after the Spanish conquest provide vivid firsthand accounts of Maya life in its last days of cultural purity, especially Diego de Landa's complete description of Maya life, *Relaciones de las Cosas de Yucatan.*

PHYSICAL CHARACTERISTICS OF THE MAYA

Maya men and women average 1.62 (4' 6") and 1.50 (4' 9") meters tall respectively. Muscular bodied, they have straight black hair, round heads, broad faces with pronounced cheekbones, aquiline noses, almond-shaped dark eyes, and eyelids with the epicanthic or Mongolian fold (a prolongation of a fold of the upper eyelid over the inner angle or both angles of the eye).

Stylized Beauty

Bishop Diego de Landa writes in his *Relaciones* that when the Spanish arrived, the Maya still practiced the ancient method of flattening a newborn's head with a press made of boards. By pressing the infant's forehead, the fronto-nasal portion of the face was pushed forward, as can be seen in carvings and other human depictions from the pre-Columbian period; this was considered a very important sign of beauty. Further, they dangled a bead in front of a baby's eyes to encourage cross-eyedness, another Maya beauty mark. Dental mutilation was practiced by filing the teeth to give them different shapes or by making slight perforations and inlaying pyrite, jade, or turquoise. Tattoo-ing and scarification were accomplished by lightly cutting a design into the skin and purposely infecting it, creating a scar of beauty. Adult noblemen often wore a phony nosepiece to give the illusion of an even longer nose sweeping back into the long flat forehead.

The Maya Bloodline

Isolation of the Indian people kept the Maya bloodline pure. Their resemblance to the people of a thousand years ago is thus understandable, but still amazing!

Today, 75-80% of the entire population of Mexico is estimated to be mestizo (mixed blood, mostly Indian and Spanish), with 10-15% pure Indian. (For comparison, as recently as 1870, pure-blooded Indians made up over 50% of the population.) While no statistics are available, it's believed most of the 15% who are pure Indian live on the Peninsula (including the state of Chiapas).

ANCIENT CULTURE OF THE YUCATAN PENINSULA

RELIGION AND SOCIETY

The Earth

The Maya saw the world as a layered flat square. At the four corners (each representing a cardinal direction) stood four bearded gods called Becabs that held up the skies. In the underworld, four gods called Pahuatuns steadied the earth. The layered skies and underworld were divided with a determined number of steps up and down. The gods and each direction were associated with colors: black for west, white for north, yellow for south, and most important, red for east. In the center of the earth stood the Tree of Life, *la ceiba*. Its powerful roots reached the underworld, and its lofty foliage swept the heavens, connecting the two. The *ceiba* was associated with the color blue-green *(yax)* along with all important things—water, jade, and new corn.

The Indians were terrified of the underworld and what it represented: odious rivers of rotting flesh and blood and evil gods such as Jaguar, god of the night, whose spotty hide was symbolized by the starry sky. Only the priests could communicate with and control the gods. For this reason, the populace was content to pay tribute to and care for all the needs of the priests.

Ceremonies

Ceremony appears to have been a vital part of the daily lives of the Maya. Important rituals took place on specific dates of their accurate calendar; everyone took part. These often bizarre activities were performed in the plazas, on the platforms, and around the broad grounds of the temple-cities. Sweat baths are commonly found at the centers and were incorporated into the religion. Some rituals were secret and only priests took part within the inner sanctums of the temple. Other ceremonies included fasts, abstinences, purification, dancing, prayers, and simple sacrifices of food, animals, or possessions (jewelry, beads, and ceramics) amid clouds of smoky incense.

The later Maya took part in self-mutilation. Frequently, carvings found depict an Indian pulling a string of thorns through a hole in his tongue or penis and the blood that ensued. The most brutal ceremonies were sacrifices including death by a variety of causes, made to gain the approval of the gods. Sacrificial victims were thrown into a sacred well; if they didn't drown within a certain length of time (often overnight), they were rescued and then expected to relate the conversation of the spirits that lived in the bottom of the well. Other methods of sacrifice were spearing, beheading, or removing the heart of the victim with a knife and offering it still beating to the spirits.

Although old myths and stories say young female virgins were most often sacrificed in the sacred *cenotes,* anthropological dredging and diving in the muddy water in various Peninsula ruins has turned up evidence proving most of the victims were young children, both male and female.

Time

The priests of the Classic Period represented time as a parade of gods who were really numbers moving through Maya eternity in careful mathematical order. They were shown carrying heavy loads with tumplines around their heads. The combination of the gods and their burdens reflected the exact number of days gone by since the beginning of the Maya calendar count. Each god has particular characteristics; number nine, an at-

tractive young man with the spots of a serpent on his chin, sits leaning forward, jade necklace dangling on one knee, right hand reaching up to adjust his tumpline. His load is the screech owl of the *baktun* (the 144,000-day period). Together, the two represent nine times 144,000, or 1,296,000 days—the number of days elapsed since the beginning of the Maya day count and the day the glyph was carved, maybe 1,275 years ago. Archaeologists call this a Long Count date. Simpler methods also were used, including combinations of dots and bars (ones and fives, respectively, with special signs for zero). Most Mayanists agree that the date of the beginning of the Long Count was August 10, 3114 B.C.

Status

If the Maya's sophisticated calendar sounds complicated to you, so will the complex, stratified society that made up the Maya civilization. Their society of many classes was headed by the elite, who controlled matters of warfare, religion, government, and commerce. Also in this group were architects who designed the magnificent temples and pyramids. Skilled masons belonged to a class

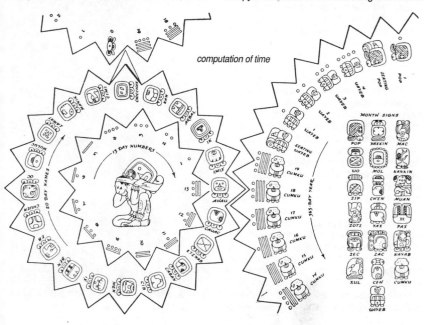

computation of time

that included servants of royalty. Priests directed the people in the many rites and festivals required of a realm governed by a pantheon of gods who demanded constant homage and penance.

Farmers were instrumental in maintaining the social order. They battled a hostile environment, constantly fighting the jungle and frequent droughts. Creativity enabled them to win out most of the time. They slashed fields from rainforest, constructed raised plots in swampy depressions, and built irrigation canals. In some areas farmers terraced the land to conserve soil and water. The results of working by hand and using stone and wood tools were sufficient to feed a growing population. All aspects of Maya life maintained a close relationship to Maya religion.

THE ARTS

Pottery

The Maya were outstanding potters. Some of the earliest Maya pottery art is dated to 36 B.C. and found at Izapan. Evidence of artistic advancement is apparent with the variety of new forms, techniques, and artistic motifs that developed during the Classic Period. Growth has been traced from simple monochrome ceramics of early periods to bichrome and later to rich polychrome; polychrome drawings on pottery work have been found with recognizable color still visible. Three-legged plates with a basal edge and small conical supports, as well as covered and uncovered vessels, were prevalent. A jar with a screw-on lid was found recently in Rio Azul, a Maya site in an isolated corner of Guatemala; an amazing find!

Figurines, especially those found in graves on the island of Jaina, were faithful reproductions of the people and their times. Many decorated pottery vessels used for everyday purposes tell us something about these people who enjoyed a touch of class along with the mundane. Decorative motifs ranged from simple geometric designs to highly stylized natural figures to simple true-to-life reproductions. We have learned much from Maya artists' realistic representations of their bodies (even of those that were pathologically deformed) and garments and adornments that were typical of their time. Through this precise method we get a glimpse into the lives of people of all social classes: common men and women, noble-

men and priests, musicians, craftsmen, merchants, warriors, ballplayers, even animals. Many of these clay figurines were used as flutes, whistles, ocarinas, rattles, or incense holders. Noteworthy are the quantity of female figurines that represent the fertility goddess Ixchell.

Sculpture

The Maya used their great talent for sculpture almost exclusively to decorate temples and sanctuaries. They employed a number of techniques which varied depending on the area and the natural resources available. They excelled in freestanding stone carving, such as the stelae and altars. In areas such as Palenque, where stone wasn't as available, stucco art is outstanding. The Indians added rubber to the plaster-and-water mixture, creating an extremely durable surface that would polish to a fine luster. In Palenque you'll see marvelous examples of stucco bas-reliefs adorning pyramids, pillars, stairways, walls, friezes, masks, and heads. Sculpting was done not only in stone but also in precious materials

Maya art

such as gold and silver. Some of the Mayas' finest wcrk was done in jade, a substance they held in great reverence.

Painting

Paints were of mineral and vegetable origin in hues of red, yellow, brown, blue, green, black, and white. Mural painting reached a high degree of expression by the Maya. Murals found in several ancient sites depict everyday life, ceremonies, and battle scenes in brilliant colors. Bright color was also applied to the carved stone structures, pyramids, and stelae. Today all color has disappeared from the outside of these buildings along with most of the finishing plaster that was used as a smooth coating over large building stones. When Cortes's men first viewed the coast of Tulum, it must have been quite a sight to behold: brilliantly colored buildings in the midst of lush green jungle overlooking a clear turquoise sea.

SCIENCE

Maya inscriptions relate to calculations of time, mathematics, and the gods. Astronomy was also a highly developed science integrated within the cult. The Maya shared their calendar system and concept of zero with other Mesoamerican groups. But they went on to perfect and develop their sophisticated calendar, more exact to a ten-thousandth of a day than the Gregorian calendar in use today.

Hieroglyphics

The hieroglyphics the Maya used in scientific calculations and descriptions are seen everywhere on the Yucatan Peninsula, in carved temple panels, on pyramid steps, and in stelae commonly installed in front of the great structures, carrying pertinent data about the buildings and people of that era. The most important examples of the system are the three codices that were not destroyed with the coming of the conquistadores. In the codices, symbols were put carefully on pounded fig bark with brushes and various dyes developed from plants and trees. As with all fine Maya art, it was the upper class and priests who learned, developed, and became highly skilled in hieroglyphics.

When they suddenly and inexplicably stopped functioning around A.D. 900, long before the Spanish arrived on the Peninsula, science and artwork gradually ceased.

MAYA "BASKETBALL"

Ballparks were prevalent in the ceremonial centers located throughout the Yucatan Peninsula. Though today's Maya are peaceful, at one time bloody games were part of the ancient cult as seen from the remaining artwork (for example the panel in Chichen Itza's Temple of the Bearded Man). The carvings graphically show that the losing (or as a few far-out scientists have suggested the winning) team was awarded a bloody death. The players were heavily padded with leather, and the object of the game was to hit a hard rubber ball into a cement ring attached to a wall eight meters off the ground. Legend says the game went on for hours and the winners (or losers) were ~warded clothes and jewelry from the spectators.

HOUSING

Thanks to remaining stone carvings, we know that the ancient Maya lived in houses almost identical to the *palapa* huts that many people still live in today. These huts were built with tall thin sapling trees placed close together to form the walls, then topped with a *palapa* roof. This type of house provided circulation through the walls, and the thick *palapa* roof allowed the rain to run off easily, keeping the inside snug and dry. In the early years there were no real doors and sparse furnishings. Then as now, families slept in hammocks, the coolest way to sleep. For the rare times that it turned cold, tiny fires were built on the floor below the hammocks to keep the family warm. Most of the cooking was done either outdoors or in another hut. Often a small group of people (extended family) built their huts together on one plot and lived almost a communal lifestyle. If one member of the group brought home a deer, everyone shared in this trophy. Though changing, this is still commonplace throughout the rural areas of the Peninsula.

SPANISH CULTURE

When Cortes arrived, he was greeted by a peasant culture. According to Bishop de Landa, the people still practiced the ancient cult, but the huge stone monoliths were already being overtaken by the jungle. It was inevitable that the Spanish culture would ultimately supplant the Indians'. Maya books were destroyed and the Indians themselves overpowered by the Spanish who believed that Maya ways were evil. Ultimately, the old beliefs and Catholic orthodoxy were mixed in a strange rendition of Christianity. Surprisingly, the Catholic priests accept this marriage of religions, and it can be seen today in many functions and holiday celebrations. In small rural pockets that have had little contact with the modern world, certain customs and ceremonies still take place, but in secret. The Maya learned their lessons the hard way, and some anthropologists believe that they still maintain an underground pipeline of the ancient culture. However, as more tourists and travelers come into the area, this culture is becoming diluted with modern ways.

TODAY'S CULTURAL CHARACTERISTICS

Language
The farther away you go from a city, the less Spanish is spoken—only Maya or a dialect of Maya is heard. The government estimates that of the 10 million Mexican Indians in the country, about 25% speak only an Indian dialect. Of the original 125 native languages, 70 are still spoken, 20 of which are different Maya languages, including Tzeltal, Tzotzil, Chol, and Yucatec Mayan. (Though mandatory education in Mexico was initiated in 1917, like most laws this one didn't reach the Yucatan Peninsula till quite recently.) Despite efforts to integrate the Indian into Mexican society, many remain content with the status quo. Schools throughout the Peninsula use Spanish-language books, even though many of these children speak only some form of Maya. In some of the smaller schools in rural areas (such as in Akumal), bilingual teachers (Spanish and local dialects) are recruited to help children make the transition.

Higher Education
For years, Peninsula students wanting an education had to travel to the university at Merida. The number of students going on to college grows with each generation and universities are slowly being built. The state of Quintana Roo still does not have a university, but college is available in Campeche and Tabasco, and a second one has been built in Merida.

Today's Housing
The major difference in today's rural housing is the growth of the *ranchito*. Only one hut sits on a fam-

teacher and students

ily farm where corn and sometimes a few pigs and turkeys, maybe even a few head of cattle, are raised. The Indians' homes have become slightly more comfortable than their ancestors', with a table and chairs, a lamp, and maybe a metal bathtub as the only furnishings in their homes. In southern Quintana Roo huts are often built of planks with tin roofs. In the north more are constructed with stucco walls. The only modern touch to the house design is the frequently seen electric meter and wires poking through even the sapling walls. Many huts have electric lighting and often radios; some even have refrigerators.

Family
Small children in Mexico are treated with great love and care. Until recently families always had many children. A man validated his masculinity by having a large family, the more children, the more respect. The labor around the family plot was happily doled out to each as they came along. Today's young couples encounter the same problem that plague parents everywhere: the expense of raising children is increasing. Just providing the basics—food, clothing, housing—is creating havoc for the poorer families. Though education is free, many rural parents need their children to help with work on the *ranchito*. That and the cost of books still prevent many Yucatecan children from getting a higher education. Gradually this is changing, and the government is trying to impress upon the people the importance of education by providing school in all areas.

FIESTAS AND CELEBRATIONS

Mexico knows how to give a party! Everyone who visits the Yucatan should take advantage of any holidays falling during the visit. Workers are given a day off on legal holidays. See chart, pp. 35-36, for dates of the biggest fiestas.

As well as the public festivities listed, a birthday, baptism, saint's day, wedding, leaving, returning, good crop, and many more reasons than we'd ever think of are good excuses to celebrate with a fiesta. One of the simplest but most charming celebrations is Mother's Day in Playa del Carmen, Merida, and many other colonial cities. Children both young and old serenade mothers (often with a live band) with beautiful music outside their windows on the evening of the holiday. If invited to a fiesta, join in and have fun. Even the most humble family manages to scrape together money for a great party on these occasions.

Village Festivities
More money means fancier fireworks. Half the fun is watching preparations, which generally take all day and involve everyone. Both big and little kids get goose bumps watching the *especialista* wrapping and tying bamboo poles together with mysterious packets of paper-wrapped explosives. At some point this often-tall *castillo* (structure holding the fireworks) will be tilted up and admired by all. Well after dark, at the height of the celebration, the colorful explosives are set off with a spray of light and sound and appreciative cheers of delight.

Village fiestas are a wonderful time of dancing, music, noise, colorful costumes, good food, and usually lots of drinking. A public fiesta is generally held in the central plaza surrounded by temporary stalls where you can get Mexican fast food: tamales (both sweet and meat), *bunuelos* (sweet rolls), tacos, *refrescos* (soft drinks), *churros* (fried dough dusted with sugar), *carne asada* (barbecued meat), and plenty of beer chilling in any convenient ice-filled container.

Beware "The Egg"
You'll find innocent-looking little old ladies selling the "dreaded eggshell" filled with confetti, ready to be smashed on an unsuspecting head. So be prepared if you're the only gringo around! Your head or any convenient body part will be pummeled with the colorful bombs by anyone tall enough. This is followed by a quick getaway and lots of giggles from onlookers. The more you respond good naturedly, the more you will continue to be the target—and what the heck, whether the headache is from too much beer or too many eggs doesn't matter. (Besides, it might be time for you to plunk out a few pesos for your own bombs!)

A Marriage Of Cultures
Many festivals in Mexico are in honor of religious feast days. You'll see a unique combination of re-

Yucatecan dancers

ligious fervor and ancient cult mixed with plain old good times. In the church plaza, dances that have been passed down from family to family since before Cortes introduced Christianity to the New World continue for hours. Dancers dress in symbolic costumes of bright colors, feathers, and bells, reminding crowds of onlookers about their Maya past. Inside the church is a constant stream of the candle-carrying devout, some traveling long distances to *perigrinate* (make a devout journey), sometimes even traveling several kilometers entirely on their knees to the church, repaying a promise made to a deity months before in thanks for a personal favor, a healing, a job found, or who knows what.

Some villages offer a *corrida* (bullfight) as part of the festivities. Even a small town will have a simple bullring; in the Yucatan these rings are frequently built of bamboo. In Maya fashion, no nails are used—only twine (made from henequen) to hold together a two-tiered bullring! The country *corrida* has a special charm. If celebrating a religious holiday, a procession carrying the image of the honored deity might lead off the proceedings. The bull has it good here; there are no bloodletting ceremonies and the animal is allowed to live and carry on his reproductive activities in the pasture. Only a tight rope around its middle provokes sufficient anger for the fight. Local young men perform in the arena with as much heart and grace as professionals in Mexico City. And the crowd shows its admiration with shouts, cheers, and of course, *musica!*—even if the band is composed only of a drum, a trumpet, and a guitar. Good fun for everyone, even those who don't understand the art of the *corrida*.

Religious Feast Days

Christmas and Easter are wonderful holidays. The *posada* (procession) of Christmas begins nine days before the holiday, when families and friends take part in processions which portray Mary and Joseph and their search for lodging before the birth of Christ. The streets are alive with people, bright lights, and colorful nativity scenes. Families provide swinging piñatas (pottery covered with papier-mâché in the shape of a popular animal or perky character and filled with candy and small surprises); children and adults alike enjoy watching the blindfolded small fry swing away with a heavy board or baseball bat while an adult moves and sways the piñata with a rope, making the fun last, giving everyone a chance. Eventually, someone gets lucky, smashes the piñata with a hard blow (it takes strength to break it), and kids skitter around the floor retrieving the loot. Piñatas are common, not only for Christmas and Easter but also for birthdays and other special occasions in the Mexican home.

The Fiesta And Visitors

A few practical things to remember about fiesta times. Cities will probably be crowded. If you know in advance that you'll be in town, make hotel and car reservations as soon as possible. Easter and Christmas at any of the beach hotels will be crowded, and you may need to make reservations as far as six months in advance. Some of the best fiestas are in more isolated parts of the Yucatan and neighboring states. Respect the privacy of people; the Indians have definite feelings and religious beliefs about having their pictures taken, so ask first and abide by their wishes.

BULLFIGHTING

The bullfight is not for everyone. Many foreigners feel it's inhumane treatment of a helpless animal. There *is* bloodletting. If you can't tolerate this sort of thing, you'd probably be happier not attending a bullfight. Bullfighting is big business in Mexico, Spain, Portugal, and South America. The *corrida de toros* (running of the bulls) is made up of a troupe of (now) well-paid men all playing an important part in the drama. In the country's largest arena (in Mexico City), 50,000 people fill it for each performance on Sundays and holidays. The afternoon starts off (promptly at 1600) with music and a colorful parade of solemn pomp with matadors and *picadores* on horseback and *banderilleros*, plus drag mules and many ring attendants. The matadors ceremoniously circle the crowded arena to the roar of the crowd. The afternoon has begun!

Traditional customs of the ring have not changed in centuries. The matador is the star of the event. This ceremony is a test of man and his courage. He's in the arena for one purpose, to kill the bull—but bravely and with classic moves. First the preliminary *quites* and then a series of graceful *veronicas* heightens the excitement brushing the treacherous horns with each move. The matador wills the animal to come closer with each movement of the *muleta*. He is outstanding if he performs his ballet as close to the bull's horns as possible (oh, how the crowd cheers!). He must elude the huge beast with only a subtle turn of his body (now they love him!). To add to the excitement, he does much of this on his knees. At *the hour of truth,* the crowd gives its permission for the matador to dedicate the bull to a special person in the crowd He throws his *montera* (hat) to the honored person and will now show his stuff.

At just the right moment he slips the *estoque (sword)* into the bull's neck. If he's an artist, he will sever the aorta and the huge animal immediately slumps to the ground and dies instantly. If the matador displays extraordinary grace, skill, and bravery, the crowd awards him the ears and the tail, and their uncontrollable respect.

Bullfighting has long been one of the most popular events in Mexico. Aficionados of this Spanish artform thrill to the excitement of the crowd, the stirring music, the grace and courage of a noble matador, and the bravery of a good bull. A student of Mexican culture will want to take part in the *corrida,* to learn more about this powerful art. *Art* is the key word. A bullfight is not a fight, it is an artistic scene of pageantry and ceremony handed down from the Middle Ages that was celebrated all over Europe.

Records of the first primitive bullfight come to us from the island of Crete, 2,000 years before the time of Christ. At the same time in Spain savage wild bulls roamed the Iberian Peninsula. When faced with killing one of these vicious animals, young men, not to be outdone by the Cretons, would "dance" as closely as possible to the brute to show their bravery before finally killing the animal with an axe.

The Romans began importing Spanish wild bulls for Colosseum spectacles and the Arabs in Spain encourged *tauromachia* (bullfighting). In 1090, El Cid (Rodrigo Diaz de Vivar), the hero of Valencia and subject of romantic legend, is believed to have fought in the first *organized* bull festival. He lanced and killed a wild bull from the back of his horse showing great skill. In this era, only noblemen were allowed to use a lance, and the *corrida* soon became the sport of kings. Even Julius Caesar is said to have gotten in the ring with a

wild bull. Bullfighting quickly became popular, and it was *the* daring event for the rich. Spain's ancient Roman colosseums (such as in Merida) were used. A feast day celebration wasn't complete without a *corrida de toros*. The number of noblemen killed while participating in this wild event began to grow.

To try to stop the *corrida*, Pope Pius V issued a papal ban threatening to excommunicate anyone who was killed while bullfighting. This didn't dull the enthusiasm of the Spanish; the ban was withdrawn, the danger and the fight continued. Queen Isabella and then finally King Philip ordered these encounters halted, and the fight ceased. Whether it was out of respect for their monarch or a new brave twist given the *corrida* by the common man (now facing the bull on foot), will never be known.

Since the lance was forbidden, commoners intrigued with the excitement of the event began fighting the bull on foot, using a cape (*muleta*) to hide the sword (*estoque*) and confuse the bull. This was the beginning of the *corrida* as we know it today.

The *corrida* has changed little in the past 200 years. The beautiful clothes originally designed by the famous artist Goya are still used. Richly embroidered silk capes add a gala touch draped over the railing of the arena. Even in the smallest Yucatecan village *corrida*, the costume design persists. Though made of simple cotton (rather than rich satin and gold-trimmed silk) and delicately embroidered with typical designs of the Yucatan, the *torero* is impressively dressed.

Gone are the wild bulls; the animals are bred on large Mexican ranches (all of Spanish ancestry) just for the bullring. Only the finest: those showing superior strength, cunning, and bravery are sent to the ring. *El toro* is trained for one shining day in the arena.

The season begins in December and lasts for three months. The rest of the year it's the *novilleros* (neophyte matadors) that are seen in the plazas across the country. They must prove themselves in the arena before they are acknowledged as respected (highly paid) matadors. Bullfighting is as dangerous now as when the Pope tried to have it banned in the 16th century. Almost half of the most renowned matadors in the past 250 years have died in the ring.

Outside of special events, bullfights take place on Sunday afternoons and the best seats are on the shady side of the arena (*la sombra*)—and are more costly. Ask at your hotel or local travel agency for ticket information. But remember, the *corrida* is not for everyone.

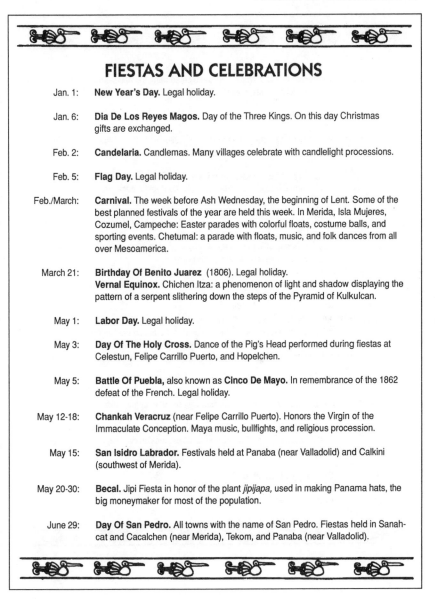

FIESTAS AND CELEBRATIONS

Jan. 1: **New Year's Day.** Legal holiday.

Jan. 6: **Dia De Los Reyes Magos.** Day of the Three Kings. On this day Christmas gifts are exchanged.

Feb. 2: **Candelaria.** Candlemas. Many villages celebrate with candlelight processions.

Feb. 5: **Flag Day.** Legal holiday.

Feb./March: **Carnival.** The week before Ash Wednesday, the beginning of Lent. Some of the best planned festivals of the year are held this week. In Merida, Isla Mujeres, Cozumel, Campeche: Easter parades with colorful floats, costume balls, and sporting events. Chetumal: a parade with floats, music, and folk dances from all over Mesoamerica.

March 21: **Birthday Of Benito Juarez** (1806). Legal holiday.
Vernal Equinox. Chichen Itza: a phenomenon of light and shadow displaying the pattern of a serpent slithering down the steps of the Pyramid of Kulkulcan.

May 1: **Labor Day.** Legal holiday.

May 3: **Day Of The Holy Cross.** Dance of the Pig's Head performed during fiestas at Celestun, Felipe Carrillo Puerto, and Hopelchen.

May 5: **Battle Of Puebla,** also known as **Cinco De Mayo.** In remembrance of the 1862 defeat of the French. Legal holiday.

May 12-18: **Chankah Veracruz** (near Felipe Carrillo Puerto). Honors the Virgin of the Immaculate Conception. Maya music, bullfights, and religious procession.

May 15: **San Isidro Labrador.** Festivals held at Panaba (near Valladolid) and Calkini (southwest of Merida).

May 20-30: **Becal.** Jipi Fiesta in honor of the plant *jipijapa,* used in making Panama hats, the big moneymaker for most of the population.

June 29: **Day Of San Pedro.** All towns with the name of San Pedro. Fiestas held in Sanah-cat and Cacalchen (near Merida), Tekom, and Panaba (near Valladolid).

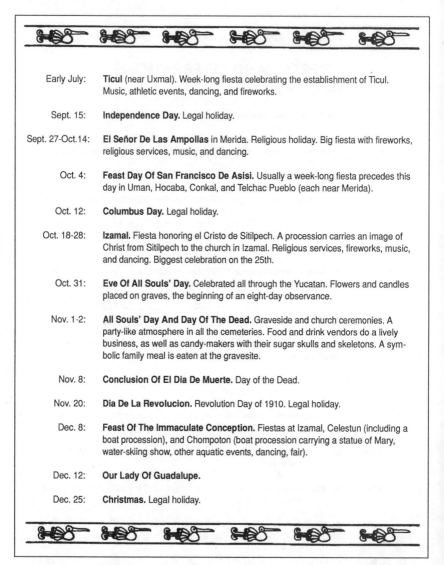

Early July: **Ticul** (near Uxmal). Week-long fiesta celebrating the establishment of Ticul. Music, athletic events, dancing, and fireworks.

Sept. 15: **Independence Day.** Legal holiday.

Sept. 27-Oct.14: **El Señor De Las Ampollas** in Merida. Religious holiday. Big fiesta with fireworks, religious services, music, and dancing.

Oct. 4: **Feast Day Of San Francisco De Asisi.** Usually a week-long fiesta precedes this day in Uman, Hocaba, Conkal, and Telchac Pueblo (each near Merida).

Oct. 12: **Columbus Day.** Legal holiday.

Oct. 18-28: **Izamal.** Fiesta honoring el Cristo de Sitilpech. A procession carries an image of Christ from Sitilpech to the church in Izamal. Religious services, fireworks, music, and dancing. Biggest celebration on the 25th.

Oct. 31: **Eve Of All Souls' Day.** Celebrated all through the Yucatan. Flowers and candles placed on graves, the beginning of an eight-day observance.

Nov. 1-2: **All Souls' Day And Day Of The Dead.** Graveside and church ceremonies. A party-like atmosphere in all the cemeteries. Food and drink vendors do a lively business, as well as candy-makers with their sugar skulls and skeletons. A symbolic family meal is eaten at the gravesite.

Nov. 8: **Conclusion Of El Dia De Muerte.** Day of the Dead.

Nov. 20: **Dia De La Revolucion.** Revolution Day of 1910. Legal holiday.

Dec. 8: **Feast Of The Immaculate Conception.** Fiestas at Izamal, Celestun (including a boat procession), and Chompoton (boat procession carrying a statue of Mary, water-skiing show, other aquatic events, dancing, fair).

Dec. 12: **Our Lady Of Guadalupe.**

Dec. 25: **Christmas.** Legal holiday.

ACCOMMODATIONS

The Yucatan Peninsula offers a wide variety of accommodations. There's a myriad of hotels to choose from in cities, villages, beach resorts, and the offshore islands, in all price ranges. If you like the idea of light housekeeping and preparing your own food, condos are available in many locales. If your lifestyle is suited to outdoor living, beach camping is wonderful along the Caribbean, and the number of small bungalows for tourists is growing rapidly.

CAMPING

If traveling in your own vehicle, a vehicle permit must be obtained when entering the country (see p. 65). Camping with a vehicle allows you to become a "luxury camper," bringing all the equipment you'll need (and more!). A van or small camper truck will fit on almost any road you'll run into. With an RV you can "street camp" in the city. Parking lots of large hotels (check with the manager) or side streets near downtown activities are generally safe and offer easy access to entertainment.

Vehicle Supplies

A few reminders and some common-sense planning make a difference when traveling and camping with a vehicle. Near the Caribbean coast are many swampy areas so check for marshy ground before pulling off the road. When beach camping, park above the high-tide line. Remember that gas stations are not as frequently found on the Peninsula as in most parts of Mexico. If you plan on traveling for any length of time, especially in out-of-the-way places, carry extra gas, and fill up whenever the opportunity arises. Along with your food supply, always carry enough water for both the car and passengers. Be practical and come prepared with a few necessities (see box).

Sleeping Outdoors

Sleeping under a jeweled sky in a warm clime can be either a wonderful or excruciating experience. (Two factors that will make or break it are the heat and the mosquito population in the immediate vicinity.) Some campers sleep in tents to get away from biting critters, which helps but is no guarantee; also, heat hangs heavy inside a closed tent. Sleeping bags cushion the ground but tend to be much too warm. If you have a bag that zips across the bottom, it's cooling to let your feet hang out (well marinated in bug repellent or wearing a pair of socks—a dark color the mosquitos might not notice). An air mattress softens the ground (bring along a patch kit). Mexican campers often just roll up in a lightweight blanket, covering all skin, head to toe to defy possible bug attacks.

The most comfortable option (according to Yucatecans and backpackers) is to sling a hammock between two palm trees, protecting yourself with a swath of mosquito netting and bug repellent. Some put a lightweight blanket between themselves and the hammock strings. For a very small

VEHICLE SUPPLIES

✔ couple of extra fan belts
✔ long towing rope or chain
✔ bottle of Windex
✔ set of spark plugs
✔ points and condenser
✔ emery boards
✔ feeler gauge (to set the points)
✔ oil filter and gas filter
✔ gas can
✔ oil
✔ fuses
✔ extra tire, patch kit
✔ air supply
✔ good-sized machete to hack your
   way through vines and plants
✔ shovel
✔ flares
✔ flashlight
✔ a few basic tools
✔ paper towels

fee, many homey resorts provide *palapa* hammock-huts that usually include water (for washing only); these places are great if you want to meet other backpackers. Though they are fast giving way to bungalow construction, a few hammock-huts are still found along the Caribbean coast.

HOTELS

In many Peninsula cities, modern hotels are springing up faster than any guidebook can keep track of, especially in Cancun. All are trying to outdo themselves with luxury, service, amenities, and beauty. As a result, when construction is completed in 1995, Cancun will probably offer the greatest concentration of world-class hotels than most resorts in the world. Today there are 13,000 rooms available in the hotel zone; by 1995 there will be 25,000.

Reservations
Traveling during the peak season (15 Nov.-15 April) requires a little planning if you wish to stay at the popular hotels. Make reservations in advance. Many hotels can be contacted through an 800 number, travel agency, or auto club. Many well-known American chains are represented in the larger resorts (Cancun, Isla Mujeres, Playa del Carmen, Merida, Villa Hermosa), and their international desks can make reservations for you. Many now have fax numbers, much quicker than regular mail. If not, write to them direct and enclose a deposit check for one night (if you don't know how much, guess). Ask (and allow plenty of time) for a return confirmation. If traveling in May-June or Sept.-Oct., rooms are generally available. Many parts of the coast are quiet in the summer. However, beginning in July Cancun is the destination for many vacationing Mexican families, so reservations are suggested.

Luxury Accommodations
Some of the familiar hotel names found in Quintana Roo are the Presidente Stouffer, Camino Real, Hyatt, Sheraton, Omni, Holiday Inn Crowne Plaza, and Hilton. They offer endless luxuries, including lovely bathrooms—some with hair dryers, marble fixtures, separate showers, and thick fluffy towels—in-room safes, cable television, mini-bars, a/c, good beds, suites, jr. suites, balconies, terraces, gorgeous ocean views, green garden

Some beach huts offer little more than sapling walls, thatch roof, and hammock hooks; this one goes further with hanging beds and mosquito netting.

areas, pools (one is a kilometer long) with swim-up bars, nightclubs and fabulous restaurants, entertainment, travel agents, car rentals, gift shops, and delicatessens; almost all accept credit cards. Refunds are handled on an individual basis.

Condominiums
Cancun has hundreds of condos lining the beach and many under construction. Isla Mujeres, Cozumel, Playa del Carmen, and Akumal have a few condominiums and others are sprouting up along the southern coastal beaches as well. If vacationing with family or a group, condo living can be a real money-saver while still enjoying the fine services of a luxury hotel. Fully equipped kitchens make cooking a snap. In many cases the price includes daily maid service. Some condos (like the Condumel on Isla Cozumel) welcome you with a refrigerator stocked with food basics; you pay only for the foods and beverages that you use each day. Details are given in the appropriate travel sections.

Traveler Beware!

Condomania is putting down roots. One of the biggest complaints from travelers to Cancun and Cozumel in the last couple of years concerns the salespeople who pester visitors to buy condos and timeshare accommodations. Their come-on is an offer for a free breakfast and often a free day's rental of a motorbike, or some other freebies. After the breakfast or lunch, they give a sales presentation, a tour of the facilities, and then each guest gets a hard pitch from a very experienced salesperson. These people have learned American sales methods down to the nitty gritty. If you succumb to the offer of free breakfast and aren't interested in buying, better practice saying *"no."*

Moderate Hotels

In most cities on the Peninsula it's not difficult to find moderate hotels; even in downtown Cancun and a few scattered locations within the hotel zone, moderate hotels are available. They aren't nearly as glitzy, probably don't have telephones, or multiple restaurants and bars, maybe not even a swimming pool, and they are not on the beach. However, the better ones provide transportation or are close to a bus stop. Prices can be one-third the cost of the hotel zone.

Budget Inns

Travelers looking to spend nights cheaply can find a *few* overnight accommodations in Cancun (the downtown area), more in Cozumel, Isla Mujeres, Playa del Carmen, Merida, Villa Hermosa, Campeche, Tuxtla Gutierrez, San Cristobal de las Casas, and many more along the Caribbean and Gulf of Mexico coast. During the peak season in Cancun it takes a little (sometimes a lot of) nosing around (starting out early in the day helps) but inexpensive hostelry is available, and searching for one offers a good way to see the city and meet friendly locals as well.

For the adventurer in small rural villages, ask at the local cantina, cafe, or city hall for a hotel or boardinghouse-type accommodation. These hotels are *usually* clean, and more than likely you'll share a toilet and (maybe) a shower. Sometimes

---

YOUTH HOSTELS ON OR NEAR THE YUCATAN PENINSULA

CREA Cancun
km 3, 200 Boulevard Kukulcan
Zona Hotelera
Cancun, Quintana Roo, Mexico

CREA Campeche
Ave. Agustin Melgar S/N, col. Buenavista
Campeche, Campeche, Mexico

CREA Chetumal
Alvaro Obregon y General Anaya S/N
Chetumal, Quintana Roo, Mexico

CREA Tuxtla Gutierrez
Calz. Angel Albino Corzo No. 1800
Tuxtla Gutierrez, Chiapas, Mexico

For more information write to:
CREA, Agencia Nacional de Juvenil Gloriet
Metro Insurgentes
Local CC-11, col. Juarez
C.P. 06600 Mexico, D.F.
tel. 525-25-48/525-29-74

---

you'll share the room itself, a large area with enough hammock hooks scattered around the walls to handle several travelers. The informed budget traveler carries his hammock (buy it on the Yucatan Peninsula if you don't already have one—they're the best made) when wandering around the Caribbean. When staying in the cheaper hotels in out-of-the-way places, come prepared with toilet paper, a towel, soap, and bug repellent, and expect to buy bottled drinking water. Most of the villages have a small cantina that serves a *comida corrida* (set lunch) or ask your host; credit cards are *not* the norm. However, the price will be right and the family that runs it will offer a cultural experience that you won't forget.

Youth hostels, though few and far between, are good bargains on the Peninsula, especially in Cancun.

FOOD

Many of the crops now produced by American farmers were introduced by the Maya and Aztecs, including corn, sweet potatoes, tomatoes, peppers, squash, pumpkin, and avocados. Many other products favored by Americans are native to the Yucatan Peninsula: papaya, cotton, tobacco, rubber, vanilla, and turkey.

EARLY AGRICULTURE

Enriching The Soil

Scientists believe Maya priests studied celestial movements. A prime function performed in the elaborate temples (built to strict astronomical guidelines) may have been charting the changing seasons and deciding when to begin the planting cycle. Farmers used the slash-and-burn method of agriculture (and still do today). When the time was propitious (before the rains began in the spring), Indians cut the trees on a section of land, leaving stumps about half a meter above ground. Downed trees were spread evenly across the landscape in order to burn uniformly; residual ash was left to nourish the soil. At the proper time, holes were made with a pointed stick, and pre-

cious maize kernels were dropped into the earth, one by one. At each corner (the cardinal points) of the cornfield, offerings of *pozole* (maize stew) were left to encourage the gods to give forth great rains. With abundant moisture, crops were bountiful and rich enough to provide food even into the following year.

The Maya knew the value of allowing the land to lay fallow after two seasons of growth, and each family's *milpa* (cornfield) was moved from place to place around the villages scattered through the jungle. Often, squash and tomatoes were planted in the shade of towering corn stalks to make double use of the land. Today, you see windmills across the countryside (many stamped "Chicago, Inc."); with the coming of electricity to the outlying areas, pumps are being used to bring water from underground rivers and lakes to irrigate crops. Outside of irrigation methods, the Maya follow the same ancient pattern of farming as that of their ancestors.

Maize

Corn was the heart of Maya nutrition, eaten at each meal. From it the Indians made tortillas, stew, and beverages both alcoholic and nonalcoholic. Because growing corn was such a vital part of Maya life, it is represented in drawings and carvings along with other social and religious symbols. Corn tortillas are still a main staple of the Mexican people. Native women in small towns can be seen early in the morning carrying bowls of corn kernels on their heads to the tortilla shop for grinding into tortilla dough. This was done by hand for centuries (and still is in isolated places). With the advent of electricity to the Peninsula it's much quicker to pay a peso or two and zap—tortilla dough! Others pay a few more pesos (price is controlled by the government) and buy their tortillas by the kilo hot off the griddle. It's amazing that the Maya came up with the combination of corn and beans without a dietician telling them it was a complete protein; they did not raise cattle, sheep, or pigs before Spanish times.

GASTRONOMICAL ADVENTURE

Taste as many different dishes as possible! You'll be introduced to spices that add a new dimension to your diet. Naturally, you won't be wild about everything—it takes a while to become accustomed

to squid served in its own black ink, for instance! A hamburger might not taste like one from your favorite fast foodery back home. It should also not come as a shock to find your favorite down-home Tex-Mex enchiladas and tacos are nothing like those you order in Mexican restaurants. Be prepared to come into contact with new and different tastes—you're in *Mexico,* after all!

Seafood

You won't travel far before realizing that one of Yucatan's specialties is fresh fish. All along the Caribbean and Gulf coasts are opportunities to indulge in piscine delicacies: lobster, shrimp, red snapper, sea bass, halibut, barracuda, and lots more. Even the tiniest cafe will prepare sweet fresh fish "à la Veracruz" using ripe tomatoes, green peppers, and onions. Or if you prefer, ask for the fish *con ajo,* sautéed in garlic and butter—scrumptious! Most menus offer an opportunity to order *al gusto* (cooked to your pleasure).

Try the unusual conch (*kaahnk*), which has been a staple in the diet of the Maya along the Caribbean coast for centuries (see p. 292). It's often used in *ceviche.* Some consider this raw fish; actually, it's marinated in a lime dressing with

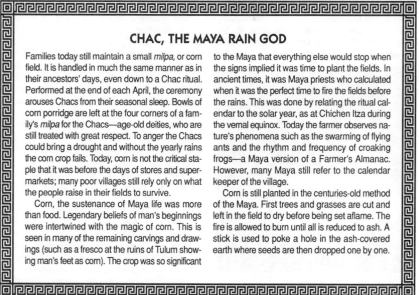

CHAC, THE MAYA RAIN GOD

Families today still maintain a small *milpa,* or corn field. It is handled in much the same manner as in their ancestors' days, even down to a Chac ritual. Performed at the end of each April, the ceremony arouses Chacs from their seasonal sleep. Bowls of corn porridge are left at the four corners of a family's *milpa* for the Chacs—age-old deities, who are still treated with great respect. To anger the Chacs could bring a drought and without the yearly rains the corn crop fails. Today, corn is not the critical staple that it was before the days of stores and supermarkets; many poor villages still rely only on what the people raise in their fields to survive.

Corn, the sustenance of Maya life was more than food. Legendary beliefs of man's beginnings were intertwined with the magic of corn. This is seen in many of the remaining carvings and drawings (such as a fresco at the ruins of Tulum showing man's feet as corn). The crop was so significant

to the Maya that everything else would stop when the signs implied it was time to plant the fields. In ancient times, it was Maya priests who calculated when it was the perfect time to fire the fields before the rains. This was done by relating the ritual calendar to the solar year, as at Chichen Itza during the vernal equinox. Today the farmer observes nature's phenomena such as the swarming of flying ants and the rhythm and frequency of croaking frogs—a Maya version of a Farmer's Almanac. However, many Maya still refer to the calendar keeper of the village.

Corn is still planted in the centuries-old method of the Maya. First trees and grasses are cut and left in the field to dry before being set aflame. The fire is allowed to burn until all is reduced to ash. A stick is used to poke a hole in the ash-covered earth where seeds are then dropped one by one.

onions, peppers, and a host of spices—no longer raw and very tasty! Often conch is pounded, dipped in egg and cracker crumbs, and sautéed quickly (like abalone steak in California), with a squirt of fresh lime. Caution: if it's cooked too long it becomes tough and rubbery.

If you happen to be on a boat trip where the crew prepares a meal of fresh fish on the beach, more than likely you'll be served *tik n' chik* cooked over an open fire. The whole fish (catch of the day) is placed in a wire rack and seasoned with onions, peppers, and *achiote,* a fragrant red spice grown on the Peninsula since the time of the early Maya. Bishop Diego de Landa identified *achiote* in his *Relaciones* written in the 1500s.

Wild Game

The Yucatecans are hunters, and if you explore the countryside very much, you'll commonly see men and boys on bicycles, motorscooters, or horses, with rifles slung over their shoulders and full game bags tied behind them. Game found in the jungle varies. *Pato* (wild duck) is served during certain times of the year and is prepared in several ways that must be tried.

Restaurants

Most small cafes that cater to Mexican families are open all day and late into the night. The Mexican custom is to eat the heavier meal of the day between 1300-1600. In most of these family cafes a generous *comida corrida* (set lunch) is served at

fruit vendor

TORTILLAS

In the public market the fascinating tortilla shop is always the busiest shop. Housewives line up to buy two, four, or six kilograms of tortillas every day. The staple of the Mexican diet, many women still make them by hand at home, but a large percentage buy them for a reasonable price, saving hours of work on the *metate* (grinder) and the *tomal* (griddle). One traveler tells of spending 20 minutes in fascinated concentration observing the whole operation; 50-pound plastic sacks of shucked corn kernels stacked in a corner of the stall, the machinery that grinds it, the pale yellow dough, the unsophisticated conveyor belt that carries it across the live-flame cooking surface, the patrons that patiently line up for the fresh results, and the baker who hands the traveler several tortillas hot off the fire along with a friendly smile that says thanks for being interested.

this time. If you're hungry and want an economical (but filling) meal, that's what to ask for; though you don't know exactly what's coming, you get a table full of many delights. Always expect a large stack of tortillas, and five or six small bowls filled with the familiar and the unfamiliar: it could be black beans, a cold plate of tomatoes and the delicious Yucatan avocado, *pollo pibyl* (chicken in banana leaves), fish, and whatever. Cafes in the larger hotels that cater to tourists don't serve this set meal. Late in the evening a light supper is served from 2100-2300. Hotels with foreign tourists offer dinner earlier to cater to British, Canadian, and American tastes. Some restaurants add a service charge onto the bill. If so, the check will say *incluido propina.* It's still gracious to leave a few coins for the waiter. If the tip isn't added to the bill, leaving 10-15% is customary.

Strolling musicians are common in Mexican cafes. If you enjoy the music, P2000 is a considerate gift.

In certain cities, cafes that cater to Mexicans will commonly serve free snacks in the afternoon with a beer or cocktail. The Cafe Prosperidad (Calle 56 No. 456-A) in downtown Merida is very generous with their *antojitos* (snacks). The place is always packed with locals ordering the *comida corrida,* complete with live entertainment and waitresses

tortilla-makers from Los Almendros in Merida

candy), and barbecued meat. The public markets have foods of every description, usually very cheap. In other words, there's a huge variety to choose from, so have fun.

A ploy used by many seasoned adventurers when they're tired of eating cold food from their backpacks: in a village where there isn't a cafe of any kind, go to the local cantina (or grocery store, church, or city hall) and ask if there's a housewife in town who (for a fee) would be willing to include you at her dinner table. Almost always you'll find someone, usually at a fair price (determine price when you make your deal). With any luck you'll find a woman renowned not only for her *tortillas por manos* but also for the tastiest *poc chuc* this side of Tikal. You gain a lot more than food in this arrangement; the culture swap is priceless.

Food Safety

When preparing your own food in the back country, a few possible sources of bacteria are fresh fruit and vegetables, especially those with a thin skin that don't get peeled, like lettuce or tomatoes. When washing these foods in local water (and they should definitely be washed thoroughly before consuming), add either bleach or iodine (eight to 10 drops per quart) to the water. Soaking vegetables all together in a container or plastic bag for about 20 minutes is easy; carrying along Ziploc bags is essential. If at the beach and short of water, substitute sea water (for everything but drinking). Remember not to rinse the bleached food with contaminated water, just pat dry, and if they have a distasteful lingering flavor, a squirt of lime juice tastes great and is very healthy. Some foods nature has packaged hygienically; a banana has its own protective seal so is considered safe (luckily, since they're so abundant on the Peninsula). Foods that are cooked and eaten immediately are also considered safe.

wearing a long version of the *huipil.* Here you'll get the real essence of the city, and you may be the only gringo present. Remember, we didn't say the cafe is spotless!

Yucatan has its own version of junk food. You'll find hole-in-the-wall stands selling *tortas* (sandwiches), tacos, tamales, or *licuados* (fruit drinks), as well as corner vendors selling mangos on a stick, slices of pineapple, peeled oranges, candies of all kinds (including tall pink fluffs of cotton

ACTIVITIES

DIVING AND SNORKELING

Not everyone who travels to the Yucatan Peninsula is a diver or even a snorkeler—at first! One peek through the "looking glass"—a diving mask—changes that situation. The Caribbean is one of the most notoriously seductive bodies of water in the world. Turquoise-blue and crystal clear with perfect tepid temperature, the protected Yucatan coast (thanks to off-shore reefs) is ideal for a languid float during hot humid days.

Snorkeling

You'll find that the sea is where you'll want to spend a good part of your trip. So even if you never considered underwater sports in the past, you'll be willing—no, eager!—to learn. It's easy for the neophyte to learn how to snorkel. Once you master breathing through a tube, then it's simply a matter of relax and float. Time disappears once you are introduced, through a four-inch glass window, to a world of fish in rainbow colors of garish yellow, electric blue, crimson, and a hundred shades of purple. The longer you look, the more you'll discover: underwater caverns, tall pillars of coral, giant tubular sponges, shy fish hiding on the sandy bottom, and delicate wisps of fine grass.

Diving Wonderland

For the diver, there's even more adventure. Reefs, caves, and rugged coastline harbor the unknown. Ships wrecked hundreds of years ago hide secrets as yet undiscovered. Swimming among the curious and brazen fish puts you literally into another world. This is raw excitement!

Expect to see an astounding variety of fish, crustaceans, and corals. Even close to shore, these amazing little animals create exotic displays of shape and form, dense or delicate depending on species, depth, light, and current. Most need light to survive; in deeper, low-light areas, some species of coral take the form of a large plate, thereby performing the duties of a solar collector. Sponge is another curious underwater creature and it comes in all sizes, shapes, and colors, from common brown to vivid red.

Be Selective

Diving lessons are offered at nearly all the dive shops on the Peninsula. Before you make a commitment, ask about the instructor and check his accident record, then talk to the harbormaster, or if you're in a small village, ask at the local cantina. Most of these divers (many are American) are conscientious, but a few are not, and the locals know whom to trust.

Bringing your own equipment to Mexico might save you a little money, depending on the length of your trip and means of transportation. But if you plan on staying just a couple of weeks and want to join a group onboard a dive boat by the day, it's generally not much more for tank rental, which will save you the hassle of carrying your own.

Choose your boat carefully. Look it over first. Some aren't much more than fishing boats with little to make the diver comfortable. Ask questions; most of the dive masters who take divers on their boats speak English. Does it have a platform to get in and out of the water? How many tanks of air may be used per trip? How many dives? Exactly where are you going? How fast does the boat go and how long will it take to get there? Remember some of the best dive spots might be farther out at sea. A more modern boat (though costing a little more) might get you extra diving time.

Detailed information is available for divers and snorkelers who wish to know about the dive sites they plan to visit. Once on the Yucatan Peninsula, pamphlets and books are available in dive shops. Look for Ric Hajovsky's detailed pamphlet on reefs, depths, and especially currents. Wherever diving is good, you'll almost always find a dive shop. There are a few high-adventure dives where diving with an experienced guide is recommended (see "Diving" in "Cozumel").

DIVING HAZARDS

Underwater

A word here about some of the less-inviting aspects of marine society. Anemones and sea urchins are everywhere. Some can be dangerous if touched or stepped on. The long-spined, black sea urchin can inflict great pain and its poison can cause an uncomfortable infection. Don't think that you're safe in a wetsuit and booties *or even if wearing gloves!* The spines easily slip through the rubber. In certain areas, such as around the island of Cozumel, the urchin is encountered at all depths and is very abundant close to shore where you'll probably be wading in and out of shallow water; keep your eyes open. If diving at night, use your flashlight. If you should run into one of the spines, remove it quickly and carefully, disinfect the wound, and apply antibiotic cream. If you have difficulty removing the spine, or if it breaks, see a doctor—pronto!

First Aid

Cuts from coral, even if just a scratch, will often cause an infection. Antibiotic cream or powder will usually take care of it. If you should get a deep cut, or if minute bits of coral are left in the wound, a serious and long-lived infection can ensue. See a doctor.

If you should get a scrape on red, or fire, coral you'll feel a burning sensation for a few minutes to five days. On some, it causes an allergic reaction and will raise large red welts. Cortisone cream will reduce inflammation and discomfort. While it wouldn't be fair to condemn all red things, you'll notice in the next few paragraphs that the creatures to avoid are all red!

Fire worms (also known as bristle worms) if touched will deposit tiny cactus-like bristles in your skin. They can cause the same reaction as fire coral. *Carefully* scraping the skin with the edge of a sharp knife (as you would to remove a bee stinger) might remove the bristles. Any leftover bristles will ultimately work their way out, but you can be very uncomfortable in the meantime. Cortisone cream helps to relieve this inflammation, too.

Several species of sponges have fine sharp spicules (hard, minute, pointed calcareous or siliceous bodies that support the tissue) that should not be touched with the bare hand. The attractive red fire sponge can cause great pain; a mild solution of vinegar or ammonia (or urine if there's nothing else) will help. The burning lasts a couple of days, and cortisone cream soothes. Don't be fooled by dull-colored sponges. Many have the same sharp spicules, and touching them with a bare hand is risky at best.

Protect Your Hands And Feet

Some divers feel the need to touch the fish they swim with. A few beginners want an underwater picture taken of them feeding the fish—bad news! When you offer fish a tasty morsel from your hand (whether gloved or not), you could start an underwater riot. Fish are always hungry and always ready for a free meal. Some of those denizens of the deep may not be so big, but in the frenzy to be first in line, their very efficient teeth have been known to miss the target. Another way to save your hands from unexpected danger is by keeping them out of cracks and crevices. Moray eels live in just those kinds of places in a reef. A moray will usually leave you alone if you do likewise, but their many needle-sharp teeth can cause a painful wound that's apt to infect.

A few sea-going critters resent being stepped on and they can retaliate with a dangerous wound. The scorpion fish, hardly recognizable with its natural camouflage, lies hidden most of the time on a reef shelf or the bottom of the sea. If you should step on or touch it you can expect a

snorkeling in Xelha Lagoon, Quintana Roo

painful, dangerous sting. If this happens, see a doctor immediately.

Another sinister fellow is the ray. There are several varieties in the Caribbean, including the yellow and southern sting rays. If you leave them alone they're generally peaceful, but if they get stepped on they will zap you with a tail that carries a poisonous sting which can cause anaphylactic shock. Symptoms include respiratory difficulties, fainting, and severe itching. Go quickly to the doctor and tell him what caused the sting. One diver suggests a shuffling, dragging-of-the-feet gait when walking on the bottom of the ocean. If bumped, the ray will quickly escape, but if stepped on it feels trapped and uses its tail for protection. Jellyfish can also inflict a miserable sting. Avoid particularly the long streamers of the Portuguese man-of-war though some of the smaller jellyfish are just as hazardous.

Don't let these what-ifs discourage you from an underwater adventure, though. Thousands of people dive in the Caribbean every day of the year and only a small percentage of accidents occur.

OTHER WATER SPORTS

With so many fine beaches, bays, and coves along the Caribbean, all water sports are available. Because so many beaches are protected by the reef that runs parallel to Quintanta Roo's east coast, calm **swimming beaches** are easy to find and many hotels have pools. **Water-skiing** is good on Nichupte Bay in Cancun, and **parasailing** is popular there also. **Windsurfing** lessons are given, and rental boards are available at most of the resort areas: Cozumel, Cancun, Akumal, and Playa del Carmen.

FISHING AND HUNTING

Fishing

A fishing license is required for all persons 16 years or older, good for three days, one month, or a year, available for a small fee at most fresh- and saltwater fishing areas from the local delegate of the Fishing Secretariat. Ask in the small cafes at the more isolated beaches. Check with the closest Mexican consulate where you can get a permit for

---

SAFETY REFERENCES

Check with your divemaster about emergency procedures before your boat heads out to sea. A safety recompression chamber is located on the Island of Cozumel, tel. 2-01-40. Here are some other useful numbers:

La Costera (Coast Guard)
Radio: channel 16
(canal numero diez y seis)

Divers Alert Network (DAN)
(919) 684-8111
Dial this number for information about Cozumel's recompression chamber or for assistance in locating a chamber in the U.S.

Air–Evac International
(619) 278-3822
located in San Diego, CA.

Life Flight
(713) 797-4011
(800) 231-4357 from the U.S.
(800) 392-4357
air ambulance service located in Houston, TX. Check with your medical insurance company, generally speaking they will pay for these emergency services.

---

your sport-fishing craft; you can also get current information there on fishing seasons and regulations which vary from area to area. Fishing gear may be brought into Mexico without customs tax; however, the customs officials at the border crossing from Brownsville, Texas, into Mexico are notorious for expecting to have their palms greased before allowing the RVer or boater to cross the border. If you find yourself in this position start with $1 bills (have lots of them with you); there are several people that need to be soothed before you can cross. If you choose not to pay the bribe, they can keep you hanging around for hours, even days, before they will allow you to cross. Sadly, it's a no-win situation. For more fishing information write to: General de Pesca, Av. Alvaro Obregon 269, Mexico 7, D.F.

Hunting

A seasonal license for small-game (including birds) must be purchased from the state where the hunting is intended. Any Mexican consulate or tourist office will provide information on obtaining a firearms permit as well as current hunting season dates and regulations, which vary yearly. Big-game hunting is now taboo. Check with the Mexican Department of Wildlife. Start making your preparations well in advance of your hunting date. For more information write: Direccion General de Caza, Serdan 27, Mexico, D.F. After obtaining Mexican information, write to the Dept. of Wildlife in Washington, D.C., or go to the nearest customs office and ask for the booklet, "Pets and Wildlife." This lays out the U.S. government rules and regulations on importing game.

The safest and least confusing way to go hunting is to either travel from the States with an American guide who makes the trek each year (check with your travel agent or hunting club), or to make arrangements in advance with a hunting lodge in Mexico. Another source of hunting lodge information is the back ad sections of *Field And Stream* and *Hunter* magazines. By mail they will walk you through the whole planning procedure, but allow plenty of time!

OTHER ACTIVITIES

Birdwatching is wonderful throughout the Yucatan. From north to south the variety of birds is broad and changes with the geography and the weather. Bring binoculars and wear boots and lightweight trousers if you plan on *watching* in jungle areas. Studying **tropical flora** is also a popular activity. For this you most certainly will be in the back country—don't forget bug repellent and be prepared for an occasional rain shower, even in the dry season. For most orchids and bromeliads look up in the trees. However, Yucatan does have ground orchids to look for. Remember, don't take anything away with you except pictures.

Photography

There's a world of beauty to photograph here, what with the sea, the people, and the natural landscape of the Peninsula. If you plan on **videotaping**, check with your local Mexican Tourist Office for information on what you can bring into the country. Most archaeological zones prohibit tripods. For the photographer who wants to film *everything,* small planes are available for charter in the larger cities and resorts. In Cancun, for instance, you can take pictures from a plane that tours for about 15 minutes over Cancun and the surrounding coast. Per person price is US$30-40. (For further photography info see "Cameras And Picture Taking," p. 63)

OTHER SPORTS

Tennis courts are scattered about Quintana Roo; the large hotels at Cancun, Akumal, Cozumel, and Puerto Aventuras have courts. Bring your own rackets. **Golf courses** are few, but you can plan on playing in Cancun and Puerto Aventuras.

GETTING THERE AND AROUND

For centuries, getting to the Yucatan Peninsula required a major sea voyage to one of the few ports on the Gulf of Mexico followed by harrowing and uncertain land treks limited to mule trains and narrow paths through the tangled jungle. Today the Peninsula is accessible from anywhere in the solar system! Arrive via modern airports, a network of new (good) highways, a reasonably frequent train system (very limited), or an excellent bus service that reaches large cities as well as an incredible number of small villages in remote areas.

BY CAR

An international driver's license is not required to drive or rent a car in Mexico. However, if you feel safer with it, get one from an auto club. At AAA in California you will need two passport pictures and $5 along with a current driver's license from your home state. The international license is another good form of identification if you should have an accident or other driving problem.

When you cross the border from the U.S. into Mexico, your car insurance is no longer valid. You can buy insurance from AAA or an auto club before you leave home. Numerous insurance agencies at most border cities sell Mexican insurance: Sanborn's is one of the largest. Ask Sanborn's for their excellent free road maps of the areas you plan to visit. For more information write: Sanborn's Mexican Insurance Service, P.O. Box 1210, McAllen, TX 78501, tel. (512) 682-3401.

In the last 15 years highway construction has been priority work on the Peninsula. A growing number of well-engineered roads throughout the area provide access to cities and towns. However, before taking your car into the country, consider the manufacturer and the condition of the car. Will parts be available in the event of a breakdown? Volkswagen, Renault, Ford, General Motors, and Chrysler have Mexican branches and parts should be available. If you drive an expensive foreign sports car or a large luxury model, you might be better off making other arrangements. Repairs might be unavailable and you could be stranded in an unlikely place for days waiting for a part. It's always wise to make sure you and the mechanic understand the cost of repairs before he begins —just like at home! **Note:** Selling your car in Mexico is highly illegal.

Highways To Yucatan
In California, main highways cross the Mexican

LOS TOPES

When you see a sign that reads "Tope," slow down! You'll soon learn that it means a traffic bump is imminent. They are often very high, sometimes with spikes sticking up, and if you hit them fast they can cause severe damage to your car, as well as your head! *Tope* signs precede almost every town and school on the Yucatan Peninsula.

border from San Diego to Tijuana and from Calexico to Mexicali. From Arizona go through Tucson to Nogales. From Texas, El Paso leads to Juarez, Eagle Pass to Piedras Negras, Laredo to Nuevo Laredo, and Brownsville to Matamoros. From each of these gateways, good highways bring you to the capital of the country, Mexico City.

From the capital the easiest and most direct route to Merida and other Peninsula cities is on Mex. 190D, a toll road to Puebla. At Puebla there's an interchange with Mex. 150D, another tollway that parallels the older free road (Mex. 150). On 150D you cross the plateau climbing to 2,385 meters at the summit of the Cumbres de Maltrata, after which a 22.5 km curving road drops you down quickly. Though this road is often foggy, it beats the alternative—Mex. 150, which hairpins through the Cumbres de Acultzingo, a narrow, heart-thumping drop of 610 meters in only 11 km.

Mexico 150D eliminates going through Mt. Orizaba; the old road (150) takes it in. In Cordoba 150D ends and the two roads meet; continue on 150 to the humid coastal plain. At Paso del Toro turn southeast onto 180, which leads to Veracruz, then continues through Coatzacoalcos to Villahermosa. From here you can continue on 186 which loops southeast, close to Palenque, and then north through Escarcega where the road meets 261. Stay on 186, travel due east across the Peninsula to Chetumal on the Caribbean coast. At Chetumal, 307 follows the coast northeast to Cancun. From Cancun take 180 southwest to Merida.

Another option from Villahermosa is to take 180 following the Gulf coast. This route includes several ferry boats (that have frequently interrupted schedules due to rough seas) and takes you through Isla del Carmen, Champoton, Campeche, and then on to Merida. With *no* delays, figure the

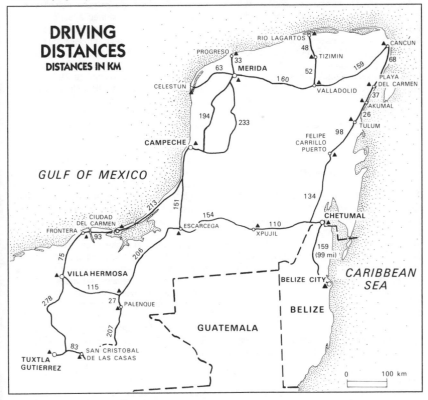

DRIVING DISTANCES
DISTANCES IN KM

trip from Villahermosa and Champoton to take about 8½ hours.

Just past Villahermosa, 186 provides the fastest route to Champoton. Take 186 to Escarcega, turn onto 261 and follow it for 85 km to Champoton. Though longer, this is a much faster and less complicated route and avoids several ferries.

Driving Tips

In Quintana Roo, it's recommended that you don't drive outside the cities at night unless it's a necessity. The highways have no streetlights—it's hard to see a black cow on a black road in the black night. Also, pedestrians have no other place to walk; shoulders are nonexistent on the roads. Public phones are few and far between, and gas stations close when the sun goes down. If you should have a problem while driving during daylight hours on a *main* road, stay with your car. The Green Angels, a government-sponsored tow truck service, cruise the roads several times a day on the lookout for drivers in trouble. They carry gas and small parts, and are prepared to fix tires. Each car is equipped with a CB radio and the driver is trained to give first aid, or will call a doctor. If you foolishly travel an isolated road after dark and break down, your best bet is to lock yourself in and stick it out for the night; go for help in the morning. The Mexican people are friendly, especially when they see someone in trouble; sometimes you have more help than you want.

BY PLANE

Today, planes fly to two international airports in Quintana Roo. The newest and most modern is at Cancun, Yucatan's most sophisticated resort. Jets arrive daily, with connections from most countries in the world. It's also possible to fly internationally to the small island of Cozumel. In Quintana Roo there are several small landing strips for private planes and small commuter airlines.

BY TRAIN

For many years Mexico has had a fairly efficient railway service. Traveling by train is relaxing and

the scenery outstanding. You can make an entire trip from the States to Merida by rail (a 45-minute flight to Cancun). From several stateside cities along the border, buses or trains drop off passengers at Mexican train connections. For example, you can catch a Golden State Bus at the Los Angeles main terminal which crosses the border to Mexicali. Here you board a 1st-class train to Mexico City (48 hours) and for US$100, two people can travel in a private compartment with two beds and a bathroom; the train also offers a dining car, a/c, and daily departures; reservations necessary. In the Los Angeles area call Orozco Travel, (213) 626-2291. In Mexico City you transfer to the daily train to Merida (which is not modern).

It's possible to travel by rail from Merida to most cities in Mexico. The prices are cheap, and for approximately double the price of a 1st-class ticket you can get a sleeping car (a *good* bargain). For 1st-class you need reservations; even if there's not a dining car (ask), you can bring a lunch or depend on the (frequent) stops at stations along the way, where vendors sell everything, including Mexican fast food, tamales, etc. For information on other departure points along the border plus schedules, prices, etc., deal directly with the railway companies; schedules and prices change frequently. Some travel agents have train information, but not all. Government tourist offices can give you schedules and prices for a specific trip. For further information write: Mexican National Railways, 489 Fifth Ave., Suite 2601, New York, NY 10017; tel. (212) 682-1494.

BY BUS

Bus service to Quintana Roo is very efficient. Fares will fit the most meager budget, scheduling is frequent, and even the smallest village is accessible from most cities in northern Mexico. From the U.S. it's smart to make reservations with Greyhound or Trailways to your final destination on the Peninsula. The bus driver will take you to the border and then help you make the transfer (including your luggage) to a Mexican bus line. This service saves you a lot of time and confusion when in a strange bus station. When making return reservations, make them straight through across the border, even if only to the first town on the U.S. side; again you will have an easier time crossing the border and making the connection.

Class Choice

You have a choice of super-deluxe, deluxe, 1st-, 2nd-, and 3rd-class. Third-class passengers can bring their animals (and often do); buses are older models usually, with no toilets or a/c. Third-class bus tickets can be as cheap as a Mexican dinner at Taco Bell in the U.S. First-class and above buses have assigned seats, are more comfortable, and are still very moderately priced. Make reservations in advance. Your ticket will say *asiento* (seat) with a number. Some 1st-class buses sell food and drinks onboard. If you're traveling a long distance, buy 1st-class; the difference in comfort is worth the small added expense. Second- and 3rd-class buses stop for anyone who flags them, and at every small village along the way. First-class operates almost exclusively between terminals. This cuts a lot of time off a long journey.

Luggage

If it fits in the overhead rack, almost anything can be carried on board. Usual allowance is 25 kilograms, but unless you're ridiculously overloaded, no one ever objects to what you bring aboard. If a driver should refuse your load, usually you can come to an amicable (monetary) agreement. Larger luggage is carried in the cargo hold under the bus where breakables have a short lifespan. Purses and cameras are best kept between your feet on the floor, rather than in the overhead rack—just in case. Luggage should always be labeled, inside and out, with your name, address, and telephone number.

Seat Comfort

If you can, choose the shady side of the bus during the day: going south sit on the left side and going north sit on the right. At night sit on the right, which eliminates the glare of oncoming headlights. The middle of the bus is the best place to be. Steer clear of seats near the bathroom, usually the last few rows. They can be smelly and the aisle traffic and constant

AIRLINES SERVING THE YUCATAN PENINSULA

Airline	To	From
American	Cancun, Cozumel	Dallas, Fort Worth
Aeromexico	Cozumel, Mexico, Merida, Chetumal, Monterrey, Cancun	Houston, Los Angeles
Continental	Cancun, Cozumel	Los Angeles, Houston, Denver, San Francisco
Eastern	Cancun	New Orleans
LACSA	Cancun	Guatemala, Costa Rica, New Orleans
Mexicana	Cancun, Cozumel	Miami, Dallas, Philadelphia
United	Cancun	Chicago

THE ANTHROPOLOGICAL MUSEUM OF MEXICO

Passing through Mexico City? Take at least one day to thoroughly explore the Anthropological Museum in Chapultapec Park. The park covers four square kilometers, with a children's playground, a lake with boating activities, water birds including lovely white and black swans, a botanical garden, zoo, Chapultapec Castle, and two important museums: Anthropological and Modern Art. The park is the scene of concerts, theater, children's programs, picnics—and much more. People of the city come to enjoy cultural offerings plus grass, trees, and a feeling of being in the country.

Many flights to the Yucatan Peninsula from the U.S. stop in Mexico City for a change of planes. Though it would take days to really tour the capital city properly, while on your way to Mayaland a highly informative adjunct to your trip would be three days in Chapultapec Park. Devote much of that time to the Anthropological Museum, take in the Museum of Modern Art, and by all means spend half a day at the castle made famous by Maximillian and Carlotta, short-term king and queen from France.

The Anthropological Museum complex was built in 1963-64, beautifully designed by Pedro Ramirez Vasquez. The museum presents a surprisingly harmonious example of contemporary architecture. Incorporated in the roof is an enormous stone umbrella supported on a column 12 meters high with a curtain of water dropping into a basin below.

As you enter the museum, the shop on the left is well stocked with a great selection of catalogs, brochures, and informative books (in several languages) on many subjects including the Indian cultures of ancient Mexico, and an excellent museum guidebook. Some of the finer reproductions of Maya art are available here at reasonable prices. Unfortunately, the store doesn't ship to the States, so you must either lug your purchases around with you on the rest of your trip or take the time to wrap and ship them yourself.

If time is limited, there are well-informed guides who speak English. For a moderate fee you can join a small group that will give you concentrated information either on the entire museum or the salons you're interested in. Each culture is represented in its own well-laid-out salon. Tickets (small fee) to the museum are sold in the vestibule at the main entrance of the two-story building.

In the Salon of the Maya you'll see some of the finest treasures found on the Yucatan Peninsula. The terra cotta figures from the Island of Jaina are remarkable images of people portraying various lifestyles. Reproductions of the colored frescoes found in Bonampak are outstanding, as are the delicate carvings from Chichen Itza.

A theft during the Christmas season of 1985 saw the tragic loss of some spectacular remnants of Maya history. The fabled jade mask of Pacal found in a tomb in the depths of the Temple of the Inscriptions at Palenque was among the valued pieces stolen. It has since been recovered.

After visiting the museum and seeing the artifacts, you will have gained a greater understanding of the people who created the mysterious structures you visit on the Yucatan Peninsula.

If you plan on staying for awhile, the Presidente Hotel in Chapultapec Park is within walking distance of all the park attractions and a colorful Mexican hotel. The Nikko Hotel is next door, a new Japanese-style hostel, very modern, and very large. Mexico City has a plethora of hotels to fit every pocketbook; if you're looking for a luxurious splurge, this is where you'll find sophisticated, beautiful, world-class inns that compete with any in the world.

Budget travelers can find a good selection of hotels all over the large city plus three youth hostels:

SETEJ, Cozumel 57, tel. 286-91-53, four blocks south of Metro Sevilla Station (Line 1), which is on Av. Chapultapec, between Zona Rosa and Chapultapec Park.

CREA Hostel (IYHF), tel. 286-91-53, one block south of Villa Olimpica, on Insurgentes Sur.

International Mexicano Norteamericano de Relaciones Culturales, Hamburgo 115, between Genova and Amberes, in Zona Rosa (no phone).

door activity can keep you awake. Bring a book and ignore the bus driver and his abilities; in other words, just relax.

OTHER TRANSPORTATION

By Ship

Cruise ships stopover at several ports on Mexico's Caribbean coast. Many lines will take you one way and drop you off either at Cancun, Cozumel, or Playa del Carmen. Check with Princess Lines, Chandris, and Carnival Cruises; your travel agent can give you the name of others that stop along the Yucatan coast. New cruise ships are continually adding the Mexican Caribbean to their ports of call. Cruise passengers have the opportunity to make shore excursions from the Caribbean coast ports to Chichen Itza, Tulum, Coba, and Xelha. Shopping and beach time is also included. For less adventurous travelers, this may be your only chance to visit Maya archaeological zones.

Group Travel

Travel agents offer many choices of escorted tours. You pay a little extra, but all arrangements and reservations are made for you to tour by plane, train, ship, or RV caravan. Also, special-interest groups with a guest expert are another attraction. For instance, archaeology buffs can usually find a group through a university that includes a knowledgeable professor to guide them through chosen Maya ruins. Evenings are spent together reviewing the day's investigation and discussing the next day's itinerary. Archaeology laymen will find many opportunities, including trips offered through Earthwatch, Box 403, Watertown, MA 02172; volunteers can physically work on a dig under the supervision of professionals; destinations change regularly. The Intercare Organiza-

---

LUGGAGE TIP

For those who travel *light,* but don't want to carry a backpack, here's a great soft-sided bag that opens flat because of extra long zippers, allowing efficient packing in separate zippered compartments. It has a shoulder strap, fits under the seat on an airplane, and holds clothes and shoes to sustain the careful traveler for three weeks. Dimensions are 20 by 13 by 10 inches, made of durable puncture-resistant ballistic nylon. This is the way to go. Called Bayley's 147 3-zip Carryon, it is available at Easy Going Travel Shop, 1400 Shattuck, Berkeley, CA 94709, tel. (415) 843-3533, and 167 Locust, Walnut Creek, CA 94596, tel. (415) 947-6660. For *super efficiency,* either of these locations offer free packing demonstrations.

---

tion, FACHCA Director, Box 8561, Moscow, Idaho 83843, of interest to nursing home administrators and people in related fields, travels to cities around the globe, visiting nursing homes, comparing and learning about facilities similar to their own, and scheduling lectures and seminars. *Transitions Abroad*, 18 Hulst Rd., Box 344, Amherst, MA 01004, is a magazine that offers information about study and teaching opportunities around the world. Travel agencies, student publications, and professional organizations can give you more information. It's a good way to mix business with pleasure, and in certain instances the trip is tax-deductible.

CAR RENTAL TIPS

Renting a car in Mexico is usually a simple matter but can cost much more than in the U.S.—and is always subject to Murphy's Law. If you know exactly when you want the car and where, it's helpful to make reservations in the States in advance. If you wait until you get to Mexico, you pay the going rate, which can add up to about $60 per day for a small car; most offices give little or no weekly discount. This is not to say that you can't take part in the favorite Mexican pastime, bargaining. You might get lucky. *If* it's just before closing time, and *if* someone has cancelled a reservation, and *if* it's off-season on the Peninsula, it's possible to get a car for a good rate. However, that's a lot of *ifs* to count on when you want and need a car as soon as you arrive. Also, it's often difficult to get a car without reservations; you may have to wait around for one to be returned.

Affordable Mexico
Representatives of Hertz, Avis, and Budget can be found in many parts of Mexico. These are separate franchises. Though not run by the mother companies, U.S. corporate offices will honor a contract price made in the States before your arrival in Mexico. If you should run into a problem and you still want the car, pay the higher price and write a brief protest on the contract right then.

Hertz runs a special deal a good part of the year called "Affordable Mexico." In January 1990, the rate for a VW Bug or a Renault was US$250 per week, including 2,000 km free, 15% Mexican tax and US$ collision insurance. You can only get this rate by making the deal in the U.S. in advance. If you belong to AAA automobile club, many offices will give you another 10-20% discount when returning the car and making the final calculation (have your membership card). This is the cheapest fee for car rentals in Mexico, and unless you plan to use a car for only one or two days, the price is definitely right. Hertz, Avis, and Budget list toll-free phone numbers in the yellow pages of all large U.S. cities. You need a major credit card to make phone reservations.

Insurance
Mexican insurance from the rental car agencies runs about US$6 per day and covers only 80 % of the damages (which many travelers are unaware of). However, it's dangerous to skip insurance; in most cases in Mexico, when there's an accident the police take action first and ask questions later. With an insurance policy, most of the problems are eased over. Rental agencies also offer medical insurance for US$4 per day. Your private medical insurance should cover this (check). If not, many travelers-cheque packages come with some sort of medical insurance for a small extra fee.

Getting The Car
Another advantage to making reservations in advance is the verification receipt you receive. Hang onto it; it's like money in the bank. When you arrive at the airport and show your verification receipt (be sure you get it back), a car will almost always be waiting for you. Once in awhile you'll even get an upgrade for the same fee if your reserved car is not available. On the other side of the coin, be sure that you go over the car *carefully* before you take it far. Drive it around the block and go over the following checklist:

✓ Make sure there's a spare tire and working jack.
✓ All doors should lock and unlock, including trunk.
✓ The seats should move forward, have no sprung backs, etc.
✓ All windows should lock, unlock, roll up and down properly.
✓ Check for proper legal papers for the car, with address and phone numbers of associate car rental agencies in cities you plan to visit in case of an unexpected car problem.
✓ Horn, emergency brake, and foot brakes should work properly.
✓ Check clutch, gear shift, all gears (don't forget reverse).
✓ Get directions to the nearest gas station; the gas tank may be empty. If it's full it's wise to return it full, since you'll be charged top dollar per liter of gas. Ask to have any damage, even a small dent, missing door knob, etc., noted on your contract, if it hasn't been already.

✓ Note the hour you picked up the car and try to return it before that time: a few minutes over will cost you another *full* day's rental fee.

Payoff Time

When you pick up your rental car, the company makes an imprint of your credit card on a blank bill, one copy of which is attached to the papers you give the agent when you return the car. Keep in mind that the car agency has a limit of how much you can charge on one credit card at one time (ask the maximum when you pick up the car). If you go over the limit be prepared to pay the balance in cash or with another credit card. If you

pick up a car in one city and return it to another there's a hefty drop-off fee (per km). Most agents will figure out in advance exactly how much it will be so there aren't any surprises when you return the car.

In 99 cases out of 100, all will go smoothly. However, if you run into a problem or are over-charged, don't panic. You might be at an office that has never heard of Affordable Mexico, even though it is specified on your verification. Go ahead and pay (with plastic money), save all your paperwork, and when you return to the States, make copies of everything, call the company, and chances are very good that you'll get a refund.

WHAT TO TAKE

Whatever time of year you travel to Mexico's Caribbean coast you can expect warm weather, which means you can pack less in your suitcase. Most airlines allow you to check two suitcases, and you can bring another carry-on bag that fits either under your seat or in the overhead rack; this helps if you're planning on a one-destination trip to a self-contained resort hotel and want a change of clothes each day. But if you plan on moving around a lot, keep it light.

Experienced women travelers pack a small foldable purse into their compartmented carry-on which then gives them only one thing to carry while en route. And be sure to include a few overnight necessities in your carry-on in the event your luggage doesn't arrive when you do. Valuables are safest in your carry-on stowed under the seat in front of you rather than in the overhead rack, whether you're on a plane, train, or bus.

Security

It's smart to keep passports, travelers cheques, money, and important papers on your person at all times. (It's always a good idea to keep a separate list of document numbers in your luggage and leave a copy with a friend back home. This expedites replacement in case of loss.) The do-it-your-selfer can sew inside pockets into clothes; buy extra-long pants that can be turned up, and sewn three-fourths of the way around, the last section closed with a piece of Velcro. Separate shoulder-holster pockets, money belts, and pockets around

the neck inside clothing—all made of cotton—are available commercially. If you're going to be back-packing and sloshing in jungle streams etc. put everything in Ziploc plastic bags before placing them in pockets. Waterproof plastic tubes are for sale that will hold a limited number of items around your neck while swimming.

Clothing

A swimsuit is a must, and if you're not staying at one of the larger hotels, bring a beach towel. In today's Mexico, *almost* any clothing is acceptable. If traveling during November, December, or January bring along a light wrap since it can cool off in the evening. The rest of the year you'll probably carry the wrap in your suitcase. For women, a wraparound skirt is a useful item that can quickly cover up shorts when traveling through the villages and some cities (many small-village residents really gawk at women wearing shorts; whatever you do, don't enter a church wearing them). The wraparound skirt also makes a good shawl when it cools off. Cotton underwear is the coolest in the tropics, but nylon is less bulky and dries overnight, cutting down on the number needed. Be sure that you bring broken-in, comfortable walking shoes; blisters can wreck a vacation almost as much as a sunburn.

Necessities

If you wear glasses and are planning an extended trip in Mexico it's a good idea to bring an extra pair or carry the lens prescription; the same goes for medications (make sure the prescription is written in general terms) though many Mexican pharmacies sell prescription drugs over the counter.

Reading Material
Avid readers in any language besides Spanish should bring a supply of books; English-language reading materials are for sale in limited quantities, mostly in big hotel gift shops and only a few bookstores. Both small and large hotels have booktrading shelves. If they aren't obvious, ask at the desk. Most travelers are delighted to trade books.

Backpackers
If you plan on hitchhiking or using public transportation, don't use a large external-frame pack; it won't fit in most small cars or public lockers. Smaller packs with zippered compartments that will accommodate mini-padlocks are most practical. A strong bike cable and lock secures the pack to a YH bed or a bus or train rack. None of the above will deter the real criminal, but might make it difficult enough to discourage everyone else.

Experienced backpackers travel light with a pack, an additional canvas bag, a small water- and mosquito-proof tent, a hammock, and mosquito netting.

Campers
For the purist who vows to cook every meal, here's a list for a handy carried kitchen:
- single-burner stove, 2 fuel cylinders (fuel not allowed on commercial airlines)
- one large sharp machete-type knife; one small, sturdy, sharp knife
- pair of pliers—good hot pot grabber
- plastic pot scrubber
- can opener (with bottle hook)
- hot pad, 2 if there's room
- 2 pots that nest, one Silverstone skillet
- wire holder to barbecue fish or meat over open fire
- small sharpening stone
- soap and laundry detergent
- plate, cup, fork, and spoon, plastic or metal
- 2 large metal cooking spoons
- one long-handled wooden spoon
- one egg spatula
- 3 fast-drying dish towels (not terrycloth)
- plastic Ziploc bags, large trash bags
- paper towels or napkins
- 2 or 3 plastic containers with tight-fitting lids, nested
- coffee drinkers that don't like instant will want a coffee pot
- several short candles and matches
- flashlight (batteries are usually easy to find)

HEALTH CARE

TOURISTA

Some travelers to Mexico worry about getting sick the moment they cross the border. But with a few simple precautions, it's not a foregone conclusion that you'll come down with something in Mexico. The most common illness to strike visitors is *tourista,* Montezuma's Revenge, the trots, or in plain Latin—diarrhea. No fun, it can cause uncomfortable cramping, fever, dehydration, and the need to stay close to a toilet for the duration. It's caused, among other things, by various strains of bacteria managing to find your innards, so it's important to be very careful of what goes into your mouth.

Possible Causes
Statistics show that the majority of tourists get sick on the third day of their visit. Interested doctors note that this traveler's illness is common in every country. They say that in addition to bacteria a change in diet is equally to blame, and suggest that the visitor slip slowly into the eating habits of Mexico. In other words, don't blast your tummy with the *habanera* or *jalapeño* pepper right off the bat. Work into the fried food, drinks, local specialties, and new spices gradually; take your time changing over to foods that you may never eat while at home, including the large quantities of wonderful tropical fruits that you'll want to eat every morning. Blame is also shared by mixing alcohol with longer than usual periods of time in the tropical sun.

It's The Water
Water is probably the worst culprit. Many parts of the Yucatan Peninsula (such as Cancun and the newer developments along the Caribbean coast), have modern sewage systems, but the small villages and more isolated areas still have little or none—all waste is redeposited in the earth and can contaminate the natural water supply. While in these places you should take special precautions.

In the backcountry, carry your own water, boil it, or purify it with chemicals, whether the source is out of the tap or a crystal clear *cenote*. That goes for brushing your teeth as well. If you have nothing else, a bottle of beer will make a safe (though maybe not sane) mouth rinse. If using ice, ask where it was made and if it's pure. Think about the water you're swimming in; some small local pools might be better avoided.

The easiest way to purify the water is with purification tablets; Hidroclonozone and Halazone are two, but many brands are available at drugstores in all countries—in Mexico ask at the *farmacia*. Another common method is to carry a small plastic bottle of liquid bleach (use eight to 10 drops per quart of water) or iodine (called *yodo*, five to seven drops per quart). Whichever you use, let the water stand for 20 minutes to improve the flavor. If you're not prepared with any of the above, boiling the water for 20-30 minutes will purify it. Even though it takes a heck of a lot of fuel that you'll probably be carrying on your back, don't get lazy in this department. One can get very sick drinking contaminated water and you can't tell by looking at it—unless you travel with a microscope!

When camping on the beach where fresh water is scarce, use seawater to wash dishes and even yourself. If you have access to a sporting goods or marine store, ask for Sea Saver soap. Otherwise, Liquid Ivory or Joy detergents both make suds in saltwater. It only takes a small squirt of the detergent to do a good job. (A rub of soap on the backside of pots and pans before setting them over an open fire makes for easy cleaning after cooking.)

In the larger cities purified water is generally provided in bottles in each room, or if the hotel is large enough it maintains its own purification plant on the premises. In Cozumel, for example, the Sol Caribe Hotel has a modern purification plant behind glass walls for all to see, and they're proud to show it off and explain how it works. If the tap water is pure, a sign over the spigot will specify this—except in Cancun which, with its modern infrastructure, brags that they're the only Mexican city in which every tap gives purified water. If you're not sure about the water, ask the desk clerk; he'll let you know the status—they prefer healthy guests that will return.

Other Sources Of Bacteria

Handling money can be a source of germs. Wash your hands frequently, don't put your fingers in your mouth, and carry individual foil packets of disinfectant cleaners, like Wash Up, that are handy and refreshing in the tropic heat. Hepatitis is another bug that can be contracted easily if you're around it.

When in backcountry cafes, remember that fruits and vegetables, especially those with a thin edible skin (like tomatoes), are a possible source of bacteria. If you like to eat food purchased from street vendors (and some should not be missed), use common sense. If you see the food being cooked (killing all the grubby little bacteria) before your eyes, have at it. If it's hanging there already cooked and nibbled on by small flying creatures, pass it by. It may have been there all day, and what was once a nice sterile morsel could easily have gone bad in the heat, or been contaminated by flies. When buying food at the marketplace to cook yourself, use the hints given in "Food."

Treatment

Remember, it's not just the visiting gringo who gets sick because of bacteria. Many Mexicans die each year from the same germs, and the Mexican government is working hard to remedy their sanitation problems. Tremendous improvements have taken place that ultimately will be accomplished all over Mexico, but it's a slow process. In the meantime, many careful visitors come and go each year with nary a touch of *tourista*. If after all your precautions you still come down with traveler's illness, many medications are available for relief. Most can be bought over the counter in Mexico, but in the States you'll need a prescription from your doctor. Lomotil is common, and it certainly turns off the faucet after a few hours of dosing; however, it has the side effect of becoming a plug. It does not cure the problem, only the symptoms; if you quit taking it too soon your symptoms reappear and you're back to square one. In its favor, Lomotil probably works faster than any of the other drugs, and if you're about to embark on a 12-hour train ride across the Yucatan Peninsula you might consider Lomotil a lifesaver. A few other over-the-counter remedies are Kaopectate in the U.S., Immodium and Donamycin in Mexico. If you're concerned, check with your doctor before leaving home. Also ask him about some new formulas called Septra and Bactrim. We count on a combination of Immodium (which stops the symptoms fairly quickly) and Septra or Bactrim (which supposedly kill the bug). Don't forget the common Pepto Bismol—some swear by it; be aware that it can turn the tongue a dark brownish color—nothing to be alarmed about. Septra and Bactrim must be bought in the U.S. with a prescription; check with your doctor.

For those who prefer natural remedies, lime juice and garlic are both considered good when taken as preventatives. They need to be taken in large quantities. Douse everything with the readily available lime juice (it's delicious on salads, fresh fruit, and in drinks). You'll have to figure out your own ways of using garlic (some believers carry garlic capsules, available in most U.S. health-food stores). *Pero te* (dog tea) is used by the Mexicans, as well as fresh coconut juice (don't eat the oily flesh, it makes your problem worse!). Plain boiled white rice soothes the tummy. While letting the ailment run its course stay away from spicy and oily foods and fresh fruits. Don't be surprised if you have chills, nausea, vomiting, stomach cramps, and run a fever. This could go on for about three days. But if the problem persists, see a doctor.

SUNBURN

Sunburn can spoil a vacation quicker than anything else, so approach the sun cautiously. Expose yourself for short periods the first few days; wear a hat and sunglasses. Use a good sunscreen, and apply it to all exposed areas of the body (don't forget your feet, hands, nose, the back of your knees, and your forehead—especially if you have a receding hairline). Remember that after every time you go into the water for a swim, sunscreen lotion must be reapplied. Even after a few days of desensitizing the skin, when spending a day snorkeling, wear a T-shirt in the water to protect your exposed back, and thoroughly douse the back of your neck with sunscreen lotion. PABA (para amino benzoic acid) solutions offer good protection and condition the skin. It's found in many brand names and in different strengths and is much cheaper in the U.S. than in Mexico. The higher the number on sunscreen bottles, the more protection.

If, despite precautions, you still get a painful sunburn, do not return to the sun. Cover up with clothes if it's impossible to find protective deep shade (like in the depths of a dark, thick forest). Keep in mind that even in partial shade (such as under a beach umbrella), the reflection of the sun off the sand or water will burn your skin. Reburning the skin can result in painful blisters that easily become infected. Soothing suntan lotions, coconut oil, vinegar, cool tea, and preparations like Solarcaine will help relieve the pain. Mostly a cure takes just a couple of days out of the sun. Drink plenty of liquids (especially water) and take tepid showers.

HEALING

Most small cities in Quintana Roo have a resident doctor. He may or may not speak English, but will usually make a house call. When staying in a hotel, get a doctor quickly by asking the hotel manager; in the larger resorts, an English-speaking doctor is on call 24 hours a day. If you need to ask someone to get you a doctor, say *necesito doctor, por favor!* Emergency clinics are found in all but the smallest villages, and a taxi driver can be your quickest way to get there when you're a stranger in town. In small rural villages, if you have a serious problem and no doctor is around, you can usually find a *curandero*. These healers deal with the old natural methods (and maybe just a few chants thrown in for good measure), and can be helpful in a desperate situation away from modern technology.

Self Help
The smart traveler carries a first-aid kit of some

kind with him. If backpacking, at least carry the following:

adhesive tape	insect repellent
alcohol	Lomotil
antibiotic ointment	needle
aspirin	pain killer
baking soda	pain pills
Band-Aids	sunscreen
cornstarch	tweezers
gauze	water purification
hydrogen peroxide	tablets
iodine	

Many of these products are available in Mexico, but certain items, like aspirin and Band-Aids, are sold individually in small shops and are much cheaper in your hometown. Even if not out in the wilderness you should carry at least a few Band-Aids, aspirin, and an antibiotic ointment or powder or both. Travelers should be aware that in the tropics, with its heavy humidity, a simple scrape can become infected more easily than in a dry climate. So keep cuts and scratches as clean and dry as possible.

Another great addition to your first-aid kit is David Werner's book, *Where There Is No Doctor*. Also published in Spanish, it can be ordered from the Hesperian Foundation, Box 1692, Palo Alto, CA 94302. David Werner drew on his experience living in Mexico's backcountry when creating this informative book.

Shots
Check on your tetanus shot before you leave home, especially if you're backpacking in isolated regions.

SIMPLE FIRST-AID GUIDE

Acute Allergic Reaction
This, the most serious complication of insect bites, can be fatal. Common symptoms are hives, rash, pallor, nausea, tightness in chest or throat, trouble in speaking or breathing. Be alert for symptoms. If they appear, get prompt medical help. Start CPR if needed and continue until medical help is available.

Animal Bites
Bites, especially on face and neck, need immediate medical attention. If possible, catch and hold animal for observation taking care not to be bitten. Wash wound with soap and water (hold under running water for two to three minutes unless bleeding is heavy). *Do*
continued on next page

not use iodine or other antiseptic. Bandage. This also applies to bites by human beings. In case of human bites the danger of infection is high.

Bee Stings
Apply cold compresses quickly. If possible, remove stinger by gentle scraping with clean fingernail and continue cold applications till pain is gone. Be alert for symptoms of acute allergic reaction or infection requiring medical aid.

Bleeding
For severe bleeding apply direct pressure to the wound with bandage or the heel of the hand. Do not remove cloths when blood-soaked, just add others on top and continue pressure till bleeding stops. Elevate bleeding part above heart level. If bleeding continues, apply pressure bandage to arterial points. *Do not* put on tourniquet unless advised by a physician. *Do not* use iodine or other disinfectant. Get medical aid.

Blister On Heel
It is better not to open a blister if you can rest the foot. If you can't, wash foot with soap and water; make a small hole at the base of the blister with a needle sterilized in 70% alcohol or by holding the needle in the flame of a match; drain fluid and cover with strip bandage or moleskin. If a blister breaks on its own, wash with soap and water, bandage, and be alert for signs of infection (redness, festering) that call for medical attention.

Burns
Minor burns (redness, swelling, pain): apply cold water or immerse burned part in cold water immediately. Use burn medication if necessary. **Deeper burns** (blisters develop): immerse in cold water (not ice water) or apply cold compresses for one to two hours. Blot dry and protect with sterile bandage. *Do not* use antiseptic, ointment, or home remedies. Consult a doctor. **Deep burns** (skin layers destroyed, skin may be charred): cover with sterile cloth; be alert for breathing difficulties and treat for shock if necessary. *Do not* remove clothing stuck to burn. *Do not* apply ice. *Do not* use burn remedies. Get medical help quickly.

Cuts
For small cuts wash with clean water and soap. Hold wound under running water. Bandage. Use hydrogen peroxide or other antiseptic. For large wounds see "Bleeding." If a finger or toe has been cut off, treat severed end to control bleeding. Put severed part in clean cloth for the doctor (it may be possible to reattach it by surgery). Treat for shock if necessary. Get medical help at once.

Diving Accident
There may be injury to the cervical spine (such as a broken neck). Call for medical help. (See "Drowning.")

Drowning
Clear airway and start CPR even before trying to get water out of lungs. Continue CPR till medical help arrives. In case of vomiting, turn victim's head to one side to prevent inhaling vomitus.

Food Poisoning
Symptoms appear a varying number of hours after eating and are generally like those of the flu—headache, diarrhea, vomiting, abdominal cramps, fever, a general sick feeling. See a doctor. A rare form, botulism, has a high fatality rate. Symptoms are double vision, inability to swallow, difficulty in speaking, respiratory paralysis. Get to emergency facility at once.

Fractures
Until medical help arrives, *do not* move the victim unless absolutely necessary. Suspected victims of back, neck, or hip injuries should not be moved. Suspected breaks of arms or legs should be splinted to avoid further damage before victim is moved, if moving is necessary.

Heat Exhaustion

Symptoms are cool moist skin, profuse sweating, headache, fatigue, and drowsiness with essentially normal body temperature. Remove victim to cool surroundings, raise feet and legs, loosen clothing and apply cool cloths. Give sips of salt water—one teaspoon of salt to a glass of water—for rehydration. If victim vomits, stop fluids, take the victim to emergency facility as soon as possible.

Heat Stroke

Rush victim to hospital. Heat stroke can be fatal. Victim may be unconscious or severely confused. Skin feels hot, is red and dry, with no perspiration. Body temperature is high. Pulse is rapid. Remove victim to cool area, sponge with cool water or rubbing alcohol: use fans or a/c and wrap in wet sheets, but do not over chill. Massage arms and legs to increase circulation. *Do not* give large amount of liquids. *Do not* give liquids if victim is unconscious.

Insect Bites

Be alert for acute allergic reaction that requires quick medical aid. Otherwise, apply cold compresses, soothing lotions. If bites are scratched and infection starts (fever, swelling, redness), see a doctor.

Jellyfish Stings

Symptom is acute pain and may include feeling of paralysis. Immerse in ice water from five to 10 minutes or apply aromatic spirits of ammonia to remove venom from skin. Be alert for symptoms of acute allergic reaction and/or shock. If this happens, get victim to hospital as soon as possible.

Mosquito Bites

See "Insect Bites," above.

Motion Sickness

Get a prescription from your doctor if boat traveling is anticipated and this illness is a problem. Many over-the-counter remedies are sold in the U.S.: Bonine and Dramamine are two; if you prefer not to take chemicals or get drowsy, something new, the Sea Band, is a cloth band that you place around the pressure point of the wrists. For more information write:

> Sea Band
> 1645 Palm Beach Lake Blvd.
> Suite 220
> W. Palm Beach, FL 33401

Medication is also available by prescription from your doctor that's administered in adhesive patches behind the ear.

Muscle Cramps

Usually a result of unaccustomed exertion, "working" the muscle or kneading it with the hand relieves cramp. If in water, head for shore (you can swim even with a muscle cramp), or knead muscle with hand. Call for help if needed. *Do not* panic.

Mushroom Poisoning

Even a small ingestion may be serious. Induce vomiting immediately if there is any question of mushroom poisoning. Symptoms—vomiting, diarrhea, difficult breathing—may begin in one to two hours or up to 24 hours. Convulsions and delirium may develop. Go to a doctor or emergency facility at once.

Nosebleed

Press bleeding nostril closed or pinch nostrils together or pack with sterile cotton or gauze. Apply cold cloth or ice to nose and face. Victim should sit up, leaning forward, or lie down with head and shoulders raised. If bleeding does not stop in 10 minutes, get medical help.

Obstructed Airway

Find out if victim can talk by asking "Can you talk?" If he can talk, encourage victim to try to cough obstruction out. If he can't speak, a trained person must apply the Heimlich maneuver. If you are alone and choking, try to forcefully cough object out. Or press your fist into your upper abdomen with a quick upward thrust, or lean forward and quickly press your upper abdomen over any firm object with rounded edge (back of chair, edge of sink, porch railing). Keep trying till the object comes out.

Ivy, Oak, Or Sumac

After contact, wash affected area with alkali-base laundry soap, lathering well. Have a poison-ivy remedy available in case itching and blisters develop.

Plant Poisoning

Many plants are poisonous if eaten or chewed. Induce vomiting immediately. Take victim to emergency facility for treatment. If the leaves of the diffenbachia (common in the Yucatan jungle) are chewed, one of the first symptoms is swelling of the throat.

Puncture Wounds

Usually caused by stepping on a tack or a nail. They often do not bleed, so try to squeeze out some blood. Wash thoroughly with soap and water and apply a sterile bandage. Check with doctor about tetanus. If pain, heat, throbbing, or redness develop, get medical attention at once.

Rabies

Bites from bats, raccoons, rats, or other wild animals are the most common threat of rabies today. Try to capture the animal, avoiding getting bitten, so it can be observed; do not kill the animal unless necessary and try not to injure the head so the brain can be examined. If the animal can't be found, see a doctor who may decide to use antirabies immunization. In any case, flush bite with water and apply a dry dressing; keep victim quiet and see a doctor as soon as possible.

Scrapes

Sponge with soap and water; dry. Apply antibiotic ointment or powder and cover with a non-stick dressing (or tape on a piece of cell-

ophane). When healing starts, stop ointment and use antiseptic powder to help scab form. Ask doctor about tetanus.

Shock

Can be a side effect in any kind of injury. Get immediate medical help. Symptoms may be pallor, clammy feeling to the skin, shallow breathing, fast pulse, weakness, or thirst. Loosen clothing, cover victim with blanket but do not apply other heat, and place him lying on his back with feet raised. If necessary, start CPR. *Do not* give water or other fluids.

Snakebite

If snake is not poisonous, toothmarks usually appear in an even row (an exception, the poisonous gila monster, shows even tooth marks). Wash the bite with soap and water and apply sterile bandage. See a doctor. If snake is poisonous, puncture marks (one to six) can usually be seen. Kill the snake for identification if possible, taking care not to be bitten. Keep the victim quiet, immobilize the bitten arm or leg, keeping it on a lower level than the heart. If possible, phone ahead to be sure antivenin is available and get medical treatment as soon as possible. *Do not* give alcohol in any form. If treatment must be delayed and snakebite kit is available, use as directed.

Spider Bites

The black widow bite may produce only a light reaction at the place of the bite, but severe pain, a general sick feeling, sweating, abdominal cramps, and breathing and speaking difficulty may develop. The more dangerous brown recluse spider's venom produces a severe reaction at the bite, generally in two to eight hours, plus chills, fever, joint pain, nausea, and vomiting. Apply a cold compress to the bite in either case. Get medical aid quickly.

Sprain

Treat as a fracture till injured part has been X-rayed. Raise the sprained ankle or other joint and apply cold compresses or immerse in cold water. If swelling is pronounced, try not to use the injured part till it has been X-rayed. Get prompt medical help.

Sunburn
For skin that is moderately red and slightly swollen, apply wet dressings of gauze dipped in a solution of one tablespoon baking soda and one tablespoon cornstarch to two quarts of cool water. Or take a cool bath with a cup of baking soda to a tub of water. Sunburn remedies are helpful in relieving pain. See a doctor if burn is severe.

Sunstroke
This is a severe emergency. See "Heat Stroke." Skin is hot and dry; body temperature is high. The victim may be delirious or unconscious. Get medical help immediately.

Ticks
Cover ticks with mineral oil or kerosene to exclude air from ticks and they will usually drop off or can be lifted off with tweezers in 30 minutes. To avoid infection, take care to remove whole tick. Wash area with soap and water. Check with doctor or health department to see if deadly ticks are in the area.

Wasp Sting
Apply cold compresses to the sting and watch for acute allergic reaction. If such symptoms develop, get victim to medical facility immediately.

CAMERAS AND PICTURE TAKING

Bring a camera to the Yucatan Peninsula! Nature and Maya combine to provide unforgettable panoramas, well worth taking home with you on film to savor again at your leisure. Many people bring simple cameras such as Instamatics or disc-types which are easy to carry and are uncomplicated. Others prefer 35mm cameras, which offer higher-quality pictures, are easier than ever to use, and are available in any price range. They can come equipped with built-in light meter, automatic exposure, self-focus, and self-advancing —with little more to do than aim and click.

Film
Two reasons to bring film with you: it's cheaper and more readily available in the States. Two reasons *not* to bring lots of film: space may be a problem and heat can affect film quality, both before and after exposure. If you're traveling for more than two weeks in a car or bus a good part of the time, carry film in an insulated case. You can buy a soft-sided insulated bag in most camera shops or order one out of a professional photography magazine. For the average vacation, if your film is kept in your room there should be no problem. Many varieties of Kodak film are found in camera shops and hotel gift shops on the Yucatan Penin-sula. In the smaller towns along the Caribbean coast you may not be able to find slide film.

X-ray Protection
If you carry film with you when traveling by plane remember to take precautions. Each time film is passed through the security X-ray machine, a little damage is done. It's cumulative, and perhaps one time won't make much difference, but most photographers won't take the chance. Request hand inspection. With today's tight security at airports, some guards insist on passing your film and camera through the X-ray machine. If packed in your checked luggage, it's wise to keep film in protective lead-lined bags, available at camera shops in two sizes: the larger size holds up to 22 rolls of 35mm film, the smaller holds eight rolls. If you use fast film, ASA 400 or higher, buy the double lead-lined bag designed to protect more sensitive film. Carry an extra lead-lined bag for your film-loaded camera if you want to drop it into a piece of carry-on luggage. (These bags also protect medications from X-ray damage.)

If you decide to request hand examination (rarely if ever refused at a Mexican airport), make it simple for the security guard. Have the film out of boxes and canisters placed together in one clear plastic bag that you can hand him for quick examination both coming and going. He'll also want to look at the camera; load it with film *after* crossing the border.

Film Processing

For processing film the traveler has several options. Most people take their film home and have it processed at a familiar lab. Again, if the trip is lengthy and you are shooting lots of photos, it's impractical to carry used rolls around for more than a couple of weeks. Larger cities have one-hour photo labs, but they only handle color prints; color slides must be processed at a lab in Mexico City, which usually takes a week or two. If you'll be passing through the same city on another leg of your trip, the lab is a good cool place to store your slides while you travel. Just tell the lab technician when you think you'll be picking them up. Kodak mailers are another option but most photographers won't let their film out of sight until they reach their own favorite lab.

Camera Protection

Take a few precautions with your camera while traveling. At the beach remember that a combination of wind and sand can really gum up the works and scratch the lens. On 35mm cameras keep a clear skylight filter on the lens instead of a lens cap so the camera can hang around your neck or in a fanny pack always at the ready for that spectacular shot that comes when least expected. If something is going to get scratched, better a $15 filter than a $300 lens. It also helps to carry as little equipment as possible. If you want more than candids and you carry a 35mm camera, basic equipment can be simple. Padded camera cases are good and come in all sizes. A canvas bag is lighter and less conspicuous than a heavy photo bag, but doesn't have the extra protection the padding provides. At the nearest army/military surplus store you can find small military bags and webbed belts with eyelet holes to hang canteen pouches and clip holders for extra equipment. It helps to have your hands free while climbing pyramids or on long hikes.

Safety Tips

Keep your camera dry; carrying a couple of big Zip-loc bags affords instant protection. Don't *store* cameras in plastic bags for any length of time because the moisture that builds up in the bag can damage a camera as much as leaving it in the rain.

It's always wise to keep cameras out of sight in a car or when camping out. Put your name and address on the camera. Chances are if it gets left behind or stolen it won't matter whether your name is there or not, and don't expect to see it again; however, miracles do happen. (You *can* put a rider on most homeowner's insurance policies for a nominal sum that will cover the cost if a camera is lost or stolen.) It's a nuisance to carry cameras every second when traveling for a long period. During an evening out, you can leave your cameras and equipment (out of sight) in the hotel room—unless it makes you crazy all evening worrying about it! Some hotel safes are large enough to accommodate your equipment.

Cameras can be a help and a hindrance when trying to get to know the people. Traveling in the backcountry you'll run into folks frightened of having their pictures taken. Keep your camera put away until the right moment. The main thing to remember is to ask permission first and then if someone doesn't want his/her picture taken, accept the refusal with a gracious smile and move on.

OTHER PRACTICALITIES

ENTRY AND DEPARTURE

U.S. and Canadian citizens can obtain a free tourist card with proof of citizenship (birth certificate, passport, voter's registration, or notarized affidavit) good for 180 days. It can be obtained at any Mexican consulate or tourist office, at all border entry points, or from airport ticket offices for those traveling by plane. Hang on to your tourist card for the entire trip. You won't need it after you go through customs until it's time to leave the country. Then you must give it back. If visiting Mexico for 72 hours or less, a tourist card is not needed. Ask at the Mexican consulate about extensions for longer periods. If you're a naturalized citizen, carry your naturalization papers or passport. Citizens of the U.S. or Canada are not required to obtain certificates of vaccination to enter Mexico; other nationals should check with a local Mexican consulate. Those under 18 without a parent or legal guardian must present a notorized letter from the parents or guardian granting permission to travel alone in Mexico. If a single parent is traveling with a minor, he or she should carry a notorized letter from the other parent granting permission. This is important going in both directions.

Bring A Passport

If you have a passport, bring it along even though it's not required (tuck your tourist card inside); it's the simplest ID when cashing travelers cheques, registering at hotels, and going through immigration. If you're visiting an area that has a current health problem and you have a health card with current information, keep that with the passport also. Keep all documents in a waterproof plastic case and in a safe place. Write to the U.S. Secretary of State for the most recent information about isolated areas that might be on the list for immunization. If traveling to such places, you'll need proof of vaccination to get back into the U.S. and perhaps other countries as well.

Driving Procedures

If driving, the tourist card serves as a vehicle permit when completed and validated at the border point of entry. Vehicle title or registration and driver's license are required. If you should happen to reach a remote border crossing at night, you may find it unmanned. *Do not* cross the border with your car until you have obtained the proper papers; if you do, it will cause problems when you exit the country. Mexican vehicle insurance is available at most border towns 24 hours a day.

If traveling with a pet, a veterinarian's certificate verifying good health and a rabies inoculation within the last six months is required. This certificate will be validated by any Mexican consulate for a small fee.

Purchases

When departing by land, air, or sea, you must declare at the point of reentry into your own country all items acquired in Mexico. To facilitate this pro-

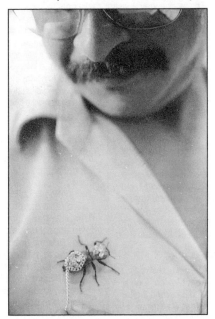

You can buy a live jeweled beetle at the Merida market, but it won't clear U.S. Customs.

cedure, it is wise to register any foreign-made possessions with customs officials before entering Mexico and to retain the receipts for purchases made while there. Limitations on the value of imported, duty-free goods vary from country to country and should be checked before traveling. U.S. citizens are allowed to carry through customs $400 worth of purchases per person duty free and up to $1000 for 10% tax. However, about 2,700 items are exempt from this limit, most of which are handcrafted or manufactured in Mexico. Consular offices or embassies in Mexico City can supply additional information on exempt items. Plants and certain foods are not allowed into the U.S. Authentic archaeological finds, colonial art, and other original artifacts cannot be exported from Mexico. And, of course, trying to bring marijuana or any other narcotic in/out of Mexico or the U.S. is foolhardy. Jail is one place in Mexico a visitor can miss.

Bargaining
This is one way a visitor really gets to know the people. Although the influx of many outsiders who don't appreciate the delicate art of bargaining has deteriorated this traditional verbal exchange, it's still a way of life between Mexicans, and it can still build a bridge between the gringo and the Yucatecan. Some Americans accustomed to shopping with plastic money either find bargaining distasteful or go overboard and insult the merchant by offering far too little. It would not be insulting to begin the bargaining at 50% below the asking price; expect to earn about a 20% discount (and new respect) after a lively, often jovial, repartee between buyer and seller.

Shipping
Mailing and shipping from Mexico is easy within certain limitations. Packages of less than $25 in value can be sent to the U.S. The package must be marked "Un-solicited Gift—Under $25" and addressed to someone other than the traveler. Only one package per day may be sent to the same addressee. Major stores will handle shipping arrangements on larger items and duty must be paid; this is in addition to the $300 carried in person across the border.

COMMUNICATIONS

Telephone
Large cities in Mexico have direct dialing to the U.S., with international operators available to assist whenever necessary. Many cities in the Yucatan still have a less-efficient system, and often a long-distance call can take several hours to place.

Telegraph And Postal
Even the smallest village has a telegraph office. Wires can often be sent direct from the larger hotels. Almost every town in Quintana Roo has a post office. If you can't find it by looking, ask—it may be located in someone's front parlor. Airmail postage is recommended for the best delivery. Post offices will hold travelers' mail for one week if it is marked a/c Lista de Correos ("care of General Delivery"). Hotels will extend the same service for mail marked "tourist mail, hold for arrival."

TELEPHONE AND EMERGENCY INFORMATION	
Information (national)	01
Long-distance operator	02
Time	03
Information (local)	04
Police radio patrol	06
Bilingual emergency information	07
International operator (English)	09
Long-distance direct service:	
station to station (national)	91 plus area code and number
person to person (national)	92 plus area code and number
Long-distance direct services:	
station to station (international)	95 plus area code and number
person to person (international)	96 plus area code and number
Worldwide:	
station to station	98
person to person	99

Radio And Television

AM and FM radio stations, in Spanish, are scattered throughout the Peninsula. Television is becoming more common as well. In the major cities hotel rooms have TV entertainment. The large resort hotels in Cancun, Cozumel, and Merida and surroundings have one or more cable stations from the U.S., on which you can expect to see all the major baseball and football games, news, and latest movies.

MONEY

Currency Exchange

The peso, the basic medium of exchange in Mexico, has floated on the free market since 1976. The money is issued in paper bills (1000, 5000, 10,000, 20,000, and 50,000 denominations) and coins (up to 1000-peso pieces). Coins of smaller value are measured in centavos (10, 20, and 50), but no one is really sure what to use them for since nothing sells for centavos.

Usually your best rate of exchange is at the bank, but small shops frequently give a good rate if you're making a purchase. Hotels notoriously give the poorest exchange. Check to see what kind of a fee, if any, is charged. In today's Mexican economy, it's not unusual to have money-changers approach you in the bank while you're waiting in line and offer you better than the posted rate. There's no harm in this—except, can you tell the difference between counterfeit pesos and the real thing? You can learn the current exchange rate daily in all banks and most hotels. Try not to run out of money over the weekend because the new rate often is not posted until noon on Monday; you will get the previous Friday's rate of exchange even if the weekend newspaper may be announcing an overwhelming difference—in your favor. The exchange rate in June of 1990 is 2800 pesos for one U.S. dollar. Cashing personal checks in Mexico is not easy. However, it is possible to withdraw money against your credit card in some banks.

Credit Cards

Major credit cards are accepted at all of the larger hotels, travel agencies, and many shops throughout the Peninsula. But don't take it for granted, ask. The smaller businesses do not accept them. In some cases you will be asked to pay a fee on top of your charged amount. Gas stations *do not* accept credit cards.

Business Hours

Banks are open 0900-1330, Mon.-Friday. Business offices are open from 0800 or 0900 to 1300 or 1400, then reopen between 1530 and 1600, until 1800. Government offices are usually open 0830-1500. Stores in cities on the Peninsula are generally open from 1000 to1900 or 2000, closing from 1300 to 1600. Government offices, banks, and stores are closed on national holidays.

Tipping

If not already included, 10-20% of the bill is standard. Tips for assistance with bags should be equivalent to US$.50 per bag. Chambermaids should receive about US$1 per day. It is not necessary to tip taxi drivers unless they have performed a special service. Tour guides should receive US$1 for a half-day trip and US$3 per day for longer trips. Gas station attendants are tipped P500 or P1000 for pumping gas, cleaning the windshield, checking the oil and water, and providing other standard services. Often tips are the main part of the provider's income.

MISCELLANEOUS

Time

The states of Yucatan, Quintana Roo, Campeche, Chiapas, and Tabasco are in U.S. Central Time Zone.

Electricity

Electric current has been standardized throughout Mexico, using the same 60-cycle 110-volt AC current common in the U.S. Small travel appliances can be used everywhere; if you have a problem, it will be because there's no electricity at all. In some areas electricity is supplied by small generators and is usually turned off at 2200. The hotels will offer you gas lanterns after the lights go out.

Studying In Mexico

In addition to fulfilling the requirements for a tourist card, students must present documents to a Mexican consulate demonstrating that they have been accepted at an educational institution and that they are financially solvent. A number of courses and workshops are offered throughout Mexico lasting two to eight weeks in addition to full-time study programs. Many adults as well as younger folks are taking part in language programs where the student lives with a family (that speaks only Spanish to them) for a period of two to four weeks and attends language classes daily. This total immersion into the language, even for a short time, is quite successful and popular as a cultural experience.

Write to the National Registration Center for Study Abroad (NRCSA), 823 North Second St., Milwaukee, WI 53203, or call (800) 558-9988. Request their "Directory of Educational Programs," which describes programs in a number of cities in Mexico.

Churches And Clubs

Mexico is predominantly a Catholic country. However, you'll find a few churches of other denominations in the larger cities (if you find a synagogue, let me know!). Local telephone books and hotel clerks have these listings. Many international organizations like the Lions, Rotary, Shriners, and foreign social groups have branches on the Yucatan Peninsula which welcome visitors.

U.S. Embassies And Consulates

If an American citizen finds himself with a problem of any kind, the nearest consul will provide advice or help. Travel advisories with up-to-the-minute information about traveling in remote areas of Mexico are available.

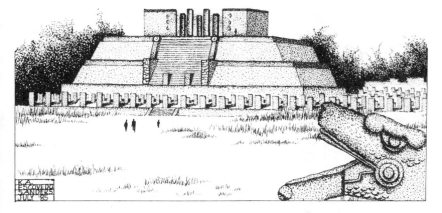

THE STATE OF YUCATAN

Yucatan is a triangle-shaped area bordered by the Gulf of Mexico to the north, the state of Quintana Roo on the east, and the state of Campeche on the west. It occupies 38,508 square km and boasts a population of over 950,000. The climate is hot and humid during the summer months; most of the rain falls between May and October. The average daytime temperature during these months is 37° C (96° F). Fortunately a breeze blows during most of the year and the drier winter months seem much cooler. Daytime temperatures vary only a few degrees between seasons. The state has no lakes or rivers, and for water collection it's dependent upon underground rivers and natural wells called *cenotes* (from the Maya word *dzonot*).

HISTORY

Spaniards arrived to the Yucatan Peninsula in the early 1500s, confiscated the land of the Maya, forced them into slave labor, and established haciendas and cities. It took many years of degradation, but the Indians finally rebelled. In the mid-1800s the state of Yucatan found itself in the midst of a bloody confrontation known as the Caste War. Thousands of lives were lost on both sides. Over the years, through revolutions and the passage of time, Yucatan has seen many changes between

people and government. The state has developed into a small business metropolis and is now a gateway to the Peninsula for both commerce and tourists.

ECONOMY

Yucatan's main industries are the cultivation and processing of henequen into hemp, plus fishing, commerce, and tourism. As strange as it seems, with so many abandoned henequen fields surrounding the large Cordemex plant, it's still necessary for Cordemex to import henequen from other countries. At the turn of the century and into the early 1900s, Cordemex employed thousands of locals who worked the thorny fields caring for and harvesting the sword-shaped spiked fronds with simple machetes. These *campesinos* (peasants) were paid with housing and an inadequate charge account at the company store—a tie that effectively chained a worker who could never find his way out of debt. Other important industries in Yucatan are salt, honey, building materials (including cement, blocks, lime), and the Oxkutzcab area is becoming known for its citrus fruits.

Maquiladoras (finishing factories) are becoming a viable source of employment for more Meridanos. The manufacturing process is begun in the

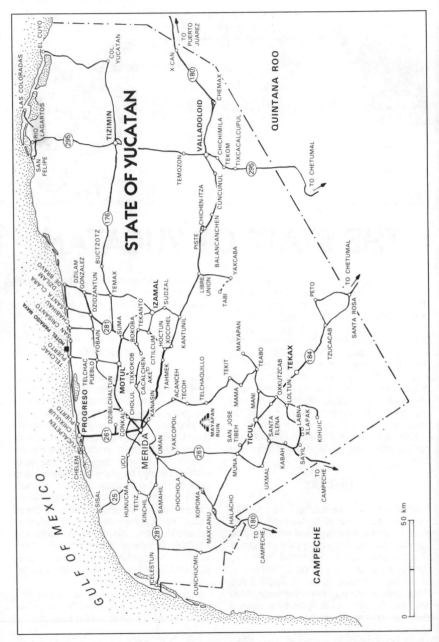

U.S. then the unfinished goods are shipped here to be completed. Clothing, for example has been cut out and shipped from the U.S. to be sewn and finished. This is becoming a popular, money-saving method of manufacture by a number of big companies in the states, and *maquiladoras* are found in increasing locations all over Mexico.

The seat of the government is (and has been for centuries) in Merida, which is also the largest city in the state. Yucatan, along with all of Mexico, is making sweeping changes to lure tourists from all over the world to visit its outstanding archaeological zones—and more. More than ever, travelers are looking for concentrations of wildlife in our fast developing world. Who would've imagined 50 years ago that many of our beautiful birds, animals, and flora would succumb to the ever-encroaching cement which seems gradually to be covering the globe. More and more people are looking for "ecotourism" as a way of celebrating both their vacations and their curiosity about the wildlife of the world. Yucatan offers the possibility of both. And yes, it takes money to continually wage battles with both the elements (such as Hurricane Gilbert which destroyed much of the jungle habitat) and "Big Business," which needs to be educated about the benefits of keeping nature's environment pure. Yucatan has much to offer the world—for instance, did you know that the verdant coastal estuaries of the state are the only ones in the world fed by underwater springs and that they serve as a haven for many exotic resident birds and for thousands of wintering migratory birds? Or, did you know that El Cuyo, the wildlife refuge located at Rio Lagartos, protects the largest colony of nesting American flamingos in the world? Or, did you know that Yucatan is home to

IMPORTANT MAYA ARCHAEOLOGICAL ZONES IN YUCATAN

Acanceh	Labna
Ake	Mayapan
Calcetok	Oxkinton
Chichen Itza	Sayil
Dzibilchaltun	Uxmal
Izamal	Xlapak
Kabah	

one of the continent's most beautiful orchids, the *Rhuncholaelia digbuana?* All of these gifts of nature are being threatened by man's encroachments; you can help protect them as well as many others which give Yucatan so much of its charm and beauty. If anyone wants to donate to this cause (no matter how modest), please send contributions to Pronatura, c/o Joann Andrews, Calle 13 #203-A, Col. Garcia Gineras, Merida, Yucatan, Mexico; tel. 25-10-04. Be sure to include your name and address. Make checks out to *Friends of Pronatura* (a private nonprofit organization); this is a U.S. tax deductible contribution. Specify your special interest: sea turtle protection, deer reproduction center, coastal and reef management and planning, toucan habitat study, jaguar population study, general conservation funds. Money is needed for all areas, including education of the general public, especially visitors to this hidden pocket of the world.

MERIDA

Merida is the largest city on the Yucatan Peninsula, with a population of over 600,000. The colonial capital of the state of Yucatan displays the appeal and grace of old Europe—as it should since much of it was patterned after Paris—with the gentle personality of the descendants of the Maya and Spaniards. The atmosphere is an exotic mix of a bloody past and cosmopolitan present. Merida is a musical city. Heady Latin rhythms and the latest disco steps share billing with Maya and Spanish folkloric songs and dances. Free nightly concerts and other cultural gatherings throughout the week are well attended by local citizens as well as outsiders. Take several days to investigate the many museums, old churches, beautiful government buildings, monuments, and shady, tree-lined plazas everywhere. The longer you stay, the better you'll like this city of contradictions.

"The White City," as Merida has been called for centuries, is very clean. Sewage problems have been eliminated and potable water plants are scattered all around town. However, it is still recommended that you drink bottled water if provided by the hotel. Some of the hotels have purification plants on-site. To be sure, ask hotel personnel—or if there's a bottle of water in your room, you can be certain the water out of the tap is only for washing.

HISTORY

Merida was originally called T'ho or Ichcansiho by the Maya inhabitants (depending on which chronicler you read). The first Spaniards found a large Maya commercial center with ornate stone structures that reminded them of the Roman ruins in Spain's city of Merida—hence the name. Mexico's Merida was founded 6 Jan. 1542, by Francisco de Montejo "El Mozo" (the son), to celebrate his victory over the Indians after 15 years of conflict. The Maya Indians, by then slaves of the Spanish invaders, were forced to dismantle their temples and palaces, and use the materials to build homes, offices, cathedrals, and parks they were not permitted to enjoy. Merida became the capital and trade center of the Peninsula, the seat of civil as well as religious authority. The Spaniards lived in fine houses around the central plaza in downtown Merida, while Indian servants lived on the outer edges of town. It wasn't until the late 1840s that they finally rebelled in the Caste War, one of the bloodiest wars in the history of Mexico. To look at Merida today, one would never know of the enmity of the past. The people are happy and what appears to be an even mix of Indians, Ladinos, and mestizos populates the city.

WHITE CITY

Several legends explaining the reason for the title "White City" hang on. One is simply the white clothes worn by the inhabitants, white *guayaberas, huipils,* and Panama hats. Another is taken from the lime mixture that is used to spread over the rooftops to make them watertight. All of them seem quite accurate, and Merida does linger as a "white" city on the peninsula.

ECONOMY

Merida's economy today is based on commerce and agriculture. Formerly this northern part of the Peninsula was the hub of the henequen industry. Although henequen is no longer the vital moneymaker that it once was, it still employs a very large percentage of people in and around Merida. Fishing has been a way of life for centuries along the Gulf coast; but only in recent years has the activity become mechanized and organized to a point where exporting fish (mostly to the U.S.) is now big business. Tourism is taking its place at the top of the moneymaking list. The state tourism departments are wielding more clout and the government is spending more to provide the traveler with good accommodations, improved highways, emergency road service, and bigger and better attractions; especially noteworthy are the improvements and services at the sites of Maya ruins. Uxmal and Chichen Itza each offer a lovely visitors center with rest rooms, cafeteria, gift shop, book shop, and a mini-museum.

HENEQUEN

Henequen grows easily in the northern section of the Yucatan Peninsula, especially in the area surrounding Merida. At one time hundreds of sprawling haciendas grew the thorny crop in this sparse, rocky soil—precisely what the agave requires along with little rain. Field-factories still dot the countryside. Henequen requires seven years of growth before its first harvest. The men work close to the land using a scythe to cut one selected tough leaf at a time. These are brought into the field-factory in bundles, then shredded and allowed to dry into pale yellow, straw-like sheaves of individual fibers. These sheaves are then processed, dyed, woven, braided, reshaped, and reworked into a multitude of forms by sophisticated machinery. The end product may be wall coverings, twine of many thicknesses and colors, floor mats, interior car cushions, burlap bags, or a simple Yucatan hammock. One of the more recent byproducts is animal food. Adding blood-meal (from nearby packing houses) and protein (from soy beans) to plant residue produces a nourishing (they say) pellet for dogs, chickens, and other animals.

A visit to the grounds of the Cordemex factory (a huge complex covering many acres of large buildings) will take you past the nursery starts of thousands of henequen seedlings. Also interesting to see are mature experimental plants. The result of years of hybridizing are the first thornless leaves —much easier to handle. In one of the field-factories called San Francisco on the road to Chichen Itza, stop and take a look around (if you're lucky you'll miss the tour buses that also stop there). A little old man clad in sparkling white cotton will hand you a small sheaf of bleached heneqen. While you hold one end, he quickly twists and manipulates the threads, finally handing you a neat piece of woven twine. Your souvenir is *Mayan* twine, for the Maya worked henequen entirely by hand!

It's quite obvious to a visitor that OSHA doesn't exist in Merida; workers wear shorts and kerchiefs across their mouths to repel thick dust emanating from the machinery. Some are barefoot or wearing sandals. All have one emotion in common—they're happy to have a job. In many cases the job also includes housing. On the highway to Progreso are several hundred newish small cottages which the Cordemex Co. has built to rent to employees.

SIGHTS

Central Plaza Area

The large green central plaza is an oasis in the middle of this busy town, surrounded by aristocratic colonial buildings. Friends (and strangers) gather here all day and late into the night. This is a city where people stroll the streets after dark and feel very safe and comfortable. In the old custom, sweethearts sit on *confidenciales* (S-curved cement benches) allowing intimate tête-à-tête—oh so close!—but without touching. White-sombreroed men gather early in the morning; visiting mestizas in colorful *huipils* sit in the shade and share lunch with their children excited by the sights of the big city. Sidewalk cafes edge the park, and in the cool of evening locals and tourists enjoy music offered several times a week.

The narrow streets were originally designed for *calesas* (horse-drawn buggies), sometimes called *pulpitos* by locals because they resemble church pulpits. You can still ride the *calesa* through the old residential neighborhoods. From 0800 to 2200 on Sunday a major downtown section surrounding the central plaza is closed off to vehicular traffic. This is the ideal day to tour the city in a *calesa* and see beautiful old mansions built at the turn of the century or earlier. Like taxis, the horse-drawn buggies are not metered, so arrange your fee and route before starting out: average price is around US$8.50 per hour. However, on Sunday a downtown ride through the quiet streets will cost you about US$3 for a half-hour trip. The *calesas* have regular routes for their one-hour tours—the **Paseo Montejo Drive, Old Merida Neighborhoods, Centenario Park,** and **Park of the Americas.**

Merida En Domingo

Sunday is a wonderful day in Merida. Regulars visit a mini-flea market in the **Plaza of Santa Lucia,** followed by typical Yucatecan music performed by a band, often the well-known Merida Police orchestra (Santa Lucia is located on Calle 60). At 1300 at the **Palacio Municipal** the mestiza wedding dance is performed by the City Hall Folklore Ballet. About 1130 a marimba concert begins in Hidalgo Park (also known as Cepeda Peraza located at Calles 60 and 59). The music goes on all day. Everyone in the city (or so it seems) dresses in their Sunday best and comes downtown. The closed-off streets, as well as the plaza, are filled with strolling people.

Sidewalk cafes do a lively business as do the dozens of pushcarts selling drinks, *tortas* (sandwiches), *elote* (corn on the cob), and sweets. In the evening some families take in the cinema, others meet with friends, listen to the music, and chat. But whatever the activity, loud smelly cars are gone for the day and it's a glorious freedom that turns the clock back in time to a more gracious period. The one disheartening aspect about Merida is the traffic in the narrow streets. However, the city is so charming that it's possible to overlook the rush of cars and buses—it's really one of the loveliest old colonial towns on the Peninsula.

A free guided walking tour of the historic structures in the center of town starts at 1000 on Sundays. This program, sponsored by the Dept. of Tourism, is called "Merida en Domingo"; check with your hotel for time schedule and meeting place. This is a good opportunity to see part of Montejo House (one of the oldest homes on the Peninsula) complete with narrative, along with surrounding government buildings. The buildings in Merida are dignified structures—some with magnificent facades created by European craftsmen—each with an intriguing story that contributes to the elegant heritage of this lovely city.

The Cathedral

The most prominent building on the plaza is the Cathedral. Built from 1561 to 1598 with stones taken from Maya structures on-site, it's the largest church on the Peninsula and one of the oldest buildings on the continent. If you search, you'll find an occasional stone with a Maya glyph still visible. The architecture prevalent in Spain at the time is reflected in the Moorish style of the two towers. Surprisingly, the interior is stark in comparison to some of the ornately decorated churches in other parts of Mexico—during the Caste War and the Revolution of 1910, the church was stripped of its

The heart of Merida is the central plaza.

valuable trimmings. Note the impressive painting of the meeting between the nobles of the Maya Xiu clan and the Spanish invaders in 1541. This solemnly portrays the Xiu tribe joining the Spaniards as allies—a trust that was violated, and the beginning of the end of the Maya regime. (There are still a few descendants that carry the Xiu name in the area around Mama outside of Merida.)

On the right side of the church as you enter is a small chapel which houses an honored image of Christ called *El Cristo de las Ampollas* ("Christ of the Blisters") carved from a tree in Ichmul that is said to have been engulfed in flames but remained undamaged. Reportedly the wooden statue then went through another fire in a church, this time developing blisters as living skin would. Though the statue is honored with a fiesta each fall, every Sunday sees the devout crowding around to touch the statue and sigh a brief prayer.

Palace Of The Archbishop

Just south of the Cathedral facing the plaza, this once-elaborate building was the home of the arch-

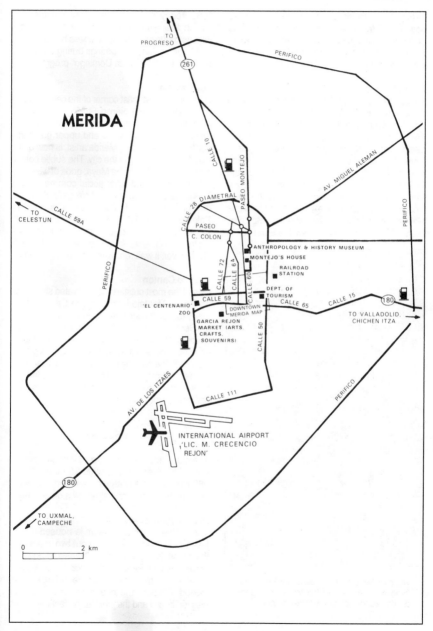

bishop. Since the revolution, when the church's power was restricted, the large structure has housed the local military post. Today, along with the military, an assortment of small shops offers a variety of trinkets from art to clothing.

Casa Montejo
Facing the south edge of the central plaza is the **Banamex Bank** building. This was formerly the home of Francisco de Montejo, constructed in 1549 by his son Francisco de Montejo "El Mozo," using talented Maya craftsmen and recovered stone. The unique carvings of Spaniards standing at attention with their feet planted firmly on the heads of the Maya remain in place today—a blatant reminder of their dominance at the time. These works of art were also rendered by Maya slaves. It's said that 13 generations of Montejos lived in the house until it was sold to Banamex in

This sculpture of Spaniards with their feet planted firmly on the heads of the Maya depicts the dominance the Spanish had over the Maya.

1980. Today the bank takes up the entire structure, including a large second floor. You can see the enormous patio during business hours (0900-1300), or on Sunday mornings during a walking tour with the "Merida en Domingo" program.

Los Palacios
Opposite the northeast corner of the central plaza is the **Palacio de Gobierno.** Striking abstract murals painted by Fernando Castro Pacheco in 1978 decorate the interior walls and upper galleries. Castro, an outstanding Merida artist, is now quite elderly and still living in the city. The subtle colors represent the birth of the Maya, gods of wisdom, sale of slaves, and other social commentaries. This is the seat of government offices for the state of Yucatan; open daily to the public at no charge. **Palacio Municipal** (City Hall), located on the west side of the central plaza, is a gracious building dating from 1543. Architecturally charming with its tall clock tower, it was renovated in the mid-1800s.

Palacio Canton
One of the most outstanding renovated structures on Paseo Montejo is the Palacio Canton. This lovely rococo-facade building was built in 1909-11 for General Francisco Canton Rosado, a former governor of Yucatan. It was designed by the same architect who built the Teatro Peon Contreras on Calle 60. The building served as the official state residence from 1948-1960. Today it is administered under the auspices of the National Institute of Anthropology and History.

MUSEUMS

The museums in Mexico are commonly open to the public Tues. to Sat. 0800-2000, and Sun. 0800-1400. Some charge a small admission, no charge for children, and all are free on Sunday.

Archaeological Museum
The archaeological museum is housed at the lovely old Palacio Canton. About two years ago the old penitentiary on Av. de Itzaes and Calle 59 across from the Park of Peace was to be the new home of the museum. All of the artifacts were moved with care and love, but the new location was too humid and the precious artifacts, some of

Merida Museum

which date back almost a thousand years, were being ruined. So the ancient artifacts were returned to the renovated Palacio Canton. Compared to Mexico City's anthropological museum there are fewer artifacts. However, the Canton building itself is worth the visit let alone such intriguing treasures as an exhibit of the antiquities brought up from the sacred well at Chichen Itza.

City Museum
This is a small museum located in a red building on the corner of Calle 61 and 58 (next to the Cathedral). Here you'll find some unusual antique paintings along with old photos depicting the development of modern Merida over the years; open Tues.-Sun. 0800-2000.

Museum Of Popular Art
This large museum, located behind the Majorada Church on Calle 59 near 50, gives you an introduction to the way of life and style of dress outside the city as well as in the other states of Mexico. A small shop offers a selection of some of the finer crafts of the area.

Pinacoteca Del Estado
This collection of art and sculptures exhibits Yucatecan artists and themes. Many paintings are antique and the collection includes sculptures by Gottdiener, well known in Yucatan. Located on Calle 59 between 58 and 60.

DIVE SITES

Cenote Dives
A surprise to most divers are the unique diving opportunities in and around this inland city. Merida is only nine meters above sea level, and centuries ago the entire Peninsula was under the sea. An organization called the **Club de Espeleobuceo** makes diving expeditions to a half dozen locations around Merida. Some of these are *cenotes,* located on the grounds of old henequen haciendas, an added reason to make the trip. The *cenotes* give the diver a rare view of fossilized sharks' teeth and snails. Diving a *cenote* is a unique geological experience. The waters are pure and crystalline without the currents of the open sea. The diver will witness an ecosystem that includes, among other fascinating creatures, the blind fish—an unusual species of fish that has never seen the sun. Ask about diving on the **Alecrane Reef** off the Gulf of Mexico coast; the water can be cloudy when the sea is ruffled by a passing storm. It's not as breathtaking as the Caribbean, but another reef to conquer.

Certified scuba divers (with a valid card) can join either of two groups. **Dive Mayab** requires two-day advance reservations and provides all dive gear, a qualified divemaster, and lunch. They'll pick you up at your hotel in their VW minibus at 0800 and take you to two different *cenotes,* returning to your hotel by 1700. Price is around

US$56 for two persons. Snorkelers, ask about **Snorkel Mayab;** the price is US$37 for two persons. In Merida make reservations through Molica Tours, located in the lobby of the Hotel Caribe, Calle 59 #500, tel. 24-87-33, telex 753623. **Note:** Always check the credentials of the dive master.

ACCOMMODATIONS

Merida has hotels to fit everyone's expectations—and pocketbook. Large and modern, aged and plain, expensive or cheap, there's something for everyone! You can expect good service, formal dining rooms, casual coffee shops, *tipico* and continental food, swimming pools, discos, indoor and outside bars, purified water, laundry service, TV, room service, tour service—and almost all accept credit cards.

Colonial Hotels
If you have that special longing to return to the past, you'll get a marvelous taste of colonial days

---

MERIDA ACCOMMODATIONS

The state of Yucatan has established a price structure on the star rating. Use the following as a *guideline* for a standard double:

★ = US$15, ★★ = US$21, ★★★ = US$35, ★★★★ = US$68, ★★★★★ = US$?—A five-star hotel can charge whatever they wish. In Merida there is one five-star hotel, the Holiday Inn, which charges for a standard double room about US$81. Remember, a 15% tax is added to these rates.

NAME	ADDRESS	TELEPHONE	FAX
Del Arco ★	Calle 48	23-01-05	—
Posada Central ★	Calle 55 #446	21-61-13	—
Rodriguez ★	Calle 69 #478	23-62-99	—
Latino ★	Calle 66 #505	21-48-31	—
Mucuy ★	Calle 57 #481	21-10-37	—
Del Mayab ★	Calle 50 #536	21-09-09	—
Hotel Del Prado ★	Calle 50	24-94-33	—
Mexico ★★	Calle 60 #525	24-70-22	—
Moody ★★	Av. Itzaes #243	25-21-01	—
Nacional ★★	Calle 61 #474	24-92-55	—
Reforma ★★	Calle 59 #508	24-79-22	—
Del Parque ★★	Calle 60 #497	24-78-44	—
San Luis ★★	Calle 68 #534	24-76-29	—
Peninsular ★★	Calle 58 #519	23-69-02	—
Flamingo ★★	Calle 57 #485	24-77-55	—
Dolores Alba ★★	Calle 63 #464	21-37-45	—
Montejo ★★	Calle 57 #507	28-03-90	—
Londres ★★	Calle 64 #456	21-35-15	—
Caribe ★★	Calle 59 #500	24-90-22	—
Suites Imperial ★★	Calle 17 #191	27-95-77	—
Hotel Trinidad ★★★	Calle 62 #464	23-20-33	—

in a few of the old mansions that have been turned into hotels. A lovely colonial hotel to check out is the **Gran Hotel**. Recently restored, it's moderately priced. A little bit of the good old days lingers on in the high-ceilinged loggias, Corinthian arches, shiny tile floors, and dark woods of this Italianated turn-of-the-century building. Anyone who appreciates old elegance should take a look; check out their clean restaurant, Patio Español, and try the delicious *pulpos en tinto* (octopus in its own ink). Hotel rates are about US$20 s, US$25

d. Credit cards okay. It's located in a small plaza, Cepeda Peraza, also known as Plaza Hidalgo (behind the Cathedral); Calle 60 and 59, tel. 24-76-22/24-77-30, fax (99) 24-76-22.

One of the favorites is the simple turn-of-the-century **Hotel Trinidad.** Don't expect luxury; some people fall in love with it, but not everyone. The pink terra-cotta facade has two globe lights to show you the entrance. Small public rooms are lined with bold, brightly colored paintings of the modern genre. The patios have decorative ce-

MERIDA ACCOMMODATIONS (CONT.)

NAME	ADDRESS	TELEPHONE	FAX
Posada Toledo ★★★	Calle 58 #487	23-22-56	—
Colonial ★★★	Calle 62 #476	23-64-44	—
Colon ★★★	Calle 62 #483	23-43-55	(99) 24-49-19
Cayre ★★★	Calle 70 #533	24-86-55	—
Gran Hotel ★★★	Calle 60 #496 (on Plaza Hidalgo)	24-77-30	(99) 24-76-22
Del Gobernado ★★★	Calle 59 #535	23-71-33	—
Paseo de Montejo ★★★	Paseo de Montejo #482	23-90-33	—
Trinidad ★★★	Calle 62 #464	21-37-45	—
Autel ★★★★	Calle 59 #546	24-21-00	—
Best Western Maria del Carmen ★★★	Paseo de Montejo #482	23-90-33	—
Hacienda Inn ★★★★	Calle 63 #550	23-91-33	—
Merida Mision ★★★★	Calle 60 #491	23-95-00	—
Montejo Palace ★★★★	Paseo de Montejo #483	24-76-44	—
Calinda Panamericana ★★★★	Calle 59 #455	23-91-11	(99) 24-80-90
Conquistador ★★★★	Paseo de Montejo at Calle 56-A #458	26-21-10 and 26-21-10	(99) 26-88-29
D'Champs ★★★★	Calle 70 #543	24-86-55	—
Casa del Balam ★★★	Calle 60 #488	24-88-44	—
Los Aluxes ★★★★	Calle 60 #444	24-21-99	—
El Castelano ★★★★	Calle 57 #513	23-01-00	—
Holiday Inn ★★★★★	Colon and Calle 60	25-68-77	—
Casa Mexilio Guesthouse (Bed and Breakfast)	Calle 68 #495	21-40-32	(99) 23-71-42

DOWNTOWN MERIDA

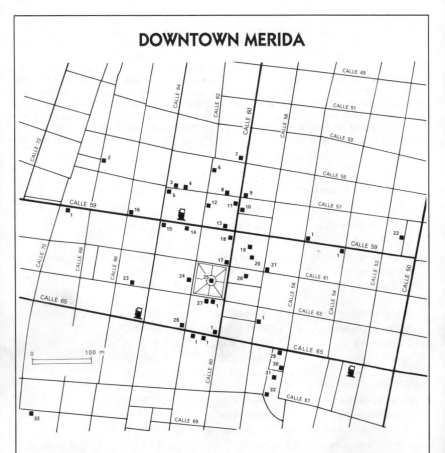

1. bank
2. Hotel Paris
3. Galeria Manola Rivero
4. Hotel Castellano
5. Alberto's Continental Patio
6. Hotel Trinidad
7. Santa Lucia Park
8. Pop's Cafe
9. Hotel Casa del Balam
10. Jose Peon Contreras Theater (information center)
11. University of Yucatan
12. Yucatan Trails Travel Agency
13. Pancho Villa's Follies Restaurant and Disco
14. State Dept. of Tourism
15. Central Telephone Office
16. Hotel del Gobernador
17. Government Palace
18. Cafe Expresso
19. Hotel Caribe
20. Parque Hidalgo (Cepeda Peraza)
21. Mexicana Airlines
22. Los Almendros Restaurant
23. Juan Gamboa Guzman Picture Gallery
24. City Hall
25. Central Plaza (Plaza de la Independencia)
26. Cathedral
27. Montejo Palace
28. Hotel Oviedo
29. post office
30. telegraph office
31. Municipal Market
32. Arts and Crafts Bazaar
33. bus station

ment columns and archways. A small plant-filled courtyard displays old trees that grow up and over the patio walls, providing welcome shade for a good read. Sun worshipers will find lounges and quiet privacy to soak up the rays on the roof.

Some of the rooms have 18-foot ceilings. Where there was space, tile bathrooms were added, so some rooms have private baths while a few share the two community bathrooms (separate for men and women). Antique furniture and old tile floors with an occasional chip here and there give visitors an idea of the elegance that once was. An antique bar in the patio doubles as reception desk and kitchen. It's here that you pick up chilled purified water.

A small breakfast menu is available. Though the hotel has been rated three stars by the inspectors, the price, beginning at US$10 s without private bathroom, up to US$26 d (with bath) brings it into the budget range and it is an excellent value. Guests are invited to use the swimming pool at the **Trinidad Galleria** close by. Hotel Trinidad is located on Calle 62 #464 between 55 and 57; tel. 23-20-33.

The Trinidad's sister hotel, **The Trinidad Galleria** (located on Calle 60 #456) is another old residence that has been transposed into a charming hotel with modern touches, including a swimming pool, green garden, ceiling fans, and a/c. Prices begin at US$10 s with shared bath, and US$26 with a/c; tel. 21-09-35/32-24-63.

Bed And Breakfast

Casa Mexilio Guesthouse is a bit different than most. In another old colonial residence this delightful intimate inn is owned and operated by hosts who speak English, Spanish, and Maya. They are dedicated to providing personal touches in five rooms where guests may enjoy visiting with other travelers, cooling off in a tiny swimming pool, soaking in the jacuzzi, and sitting amid lush plants in a shady patio. Guests are provided a tasty breakfast and a refrigerator where they can store drinks or sandwich fixings. Rates are US$40 s or d, extra person is US$25. Roger and Jorge also arrange tours of Yucatan, Quintana Roo, Belize, and Guatemala. The guesthouse is located four blocks from the main plaza on Calle 68 #495 between 57 and 59, tel. 21-40-32, Merida fax is (99) 23-71-42. For reservations call in the states **Turquoise Reef Group,** (800) 538-6802, fax (303) 674-8735.

Budget

Although there's no youth hostel, numerous small hotels near the plaza offer economical shelter. For the money, **Hotel Mucuy** is an option. Northeast of the plaza, it's in a quiet neighborhood, with a relaxing patio where guests can lounge in the sun and read books from a good selection of English-language paperbacks provided by the management; US$10 d, 10 rooms; Calle 57 #481, tel. 21-10-37. Facing the municipal bus station, **Hotel Rodriguez** is plain—except for its beautiful tile floors and bathrooms. The rooms in the back of the building are the quietest. Handy location, pleasant staff—ask for purified water at the desk. US$7 d, more for a/c; Calle 69 #478, tel. 23-62-99.

Hotel Latino is located between the main square and the bus station. There's a snack bar and TV room with free coffee for guests. Twenty-seven rooms each have a ceiling fan, hot water, a bathroom, and two double beds. Telephone at reception desk. About US$9.50, Calle 66 #505 between 61 and 63.

Hotel Posada del Angel is a very clean and tidy hotel located five blocks southwest of the main square. There's a parking lot, laundry service, 31 rooms, and good *tipico* food served in the small cafe. TVs rent for about US$1.50 per day. A double room with two beds, ceiling fan, bathroom, and hot water costs about US$15; on Calle 67 #535 between 66 and 68, tel. 23-27-54. Another small, modest hotel, the **Hotel Dolores Alba** is for travelers looking for peace and quiet. This is one of Merida's best budget hotels with a pool, laundry service, and rocking chairs in the center hallway to sit and chat or read. Drivers will find a parking lot with a big mango tree to provide shade. The 18 rooms all have bathrooms, hot water, and fans. A good restaurant serves breakfast and dinner; continental breakfast costs about US$2. Double rooms are about US$18; no credit cards, on Calle 63 #464 between 52 and 54, tel. 21-37-45, 28-31-63. You can make reservations for their sister hotel, **Hotel Dolores Alba Chichen Itza,** at the desk. Another sister hotel to check out is **Hotel Janeiro,** more modern in appearance, swimming pool, air-conditioned coffee shop, no credit cards. US$18 d, on Calle 57 #435, tel. 23-36-02, 23-83-73.

Another little gem to check out is **Casa de Huespedes** located near the courtyard on Calle 62 #507. A former home when Merida was the scene of many such mansions, it has high ceilings, spacious rooms, charming courtyard with surrounding balconies—a classy building. However, the gem has a major flaw that may or may not bother you —one small bathroom with toilet and shower to serve all the rooms. Look it over, and ask for current prices. They were very cheap in 1989. This is a popular place with the hip European crowd.

Moderate

If you want a few more amenities and are willing to pay a tad more, the following lodgings offer clean, comfortable rooms with a touch of old Mexico. Certainly not fancy, but clean with a lot of four-star features, three-star **Hotel Caribe** is a good buy. The location is ideal, one block from the plaza and close to everything. It sports a/c, a swimming pool, and a clean restaurant downstairs serving good food at reasonable prices. Rates are US$28 d with a/c, US$25 with fan; beware of laundry rates—expensive. Check out the laundry on Calle 58, between 57 and 59. Located on Calle 59 and 60 #500; tel. 24-90-22.

Hotel Peninsular is standard quality with 49 rooms (some with a/c), small pool, restaurant, bar, cold and warm water, private bath, and a pleasant staff. Rates are about US$14 s and $17 d for a room with a ceiling fan, US$17 s and $21 d for a/c; credit cards okay. Located at Calle 58 #519; tel. 23-69-96, 23-69-02.

Hotel Cayre is located one block from the main bus station and six blocks southwest of the main square. It has 100 rooms, a large shady patio and garden with a variety of big trees that make it cool and quiet; a great escape from the hot and noisy downtown area. All rooms have a/c, telephones, bathrooms, and are clean. A double room is about US$22.50; on Calle 70 #543, near 67, tel. 23-60-24.

Hotel Colonial has no relation to its name except for an old bell on the rooftop. It's a comfortable and pleasant hotel with 73 a/c rooms, a small pool, laundry service, bathrooms, TV, hot water, bar, restaurant, parking lot, travel agency, and places to lounge and be lazy. Rates are about US$29 s, $29 d; on Calle 62 #476 between 57 and 59, tel. 23-64-44, fax (99) 28-39-61, in the U.S. and Canada tel. (800) 428 3088, fax (317) 887-9517; credit cards okay.

Hotel Gobernador is a three-star hotel that is actually quite nice and outshines many of the four-star hotels in the city. With 61 rooms, a/c, telephone, two double beds, bathrooms, hot water, color TV, pool, parking lot, and friendly, polite staff. There's a restaurant and bar with live "trio" music (very romantic type) from 2000 to 2200 on Wed., Fri., and Saturday. A single room is about US$26, $30 d, summer and winter. Located on Calle 59 #535 near 66, tel. 28-13-51, fax (99) 23-27-00, in the U.S., ITI, Laguna Beach, CA, tel. (800) 227-0212, (714) 494-8129.

More Expensive

Merida has a good selection of deluxe hotels. The prices range from about US$35 to US$60 for two.

Hotel Dolores Alba

Hotel Calinda Panamericana

Starting at the low end of the deluxe price range, **Hotel Maria del Carmen** is four blocks west of the plaza. Pleasant carpeted rooms, a/c, swimming pool, coffee shop, restaurant, and garage; US$35 d. Located on Calle 63 #550; tel. 23-91-33. The **Casa del Balam** has been high on the ratings for years. Large, clean rooms have heavy dark-wood colonial-style furniture. All have twin beds except for the honeymoon suite which has a giant *matrimonial* (double bed) in an airy room with windows that open for a rooftop view of the entire city. On the lower floors you may not wish to open windows because of the traffic noises outside. The shady courtyard is planted with lush tropical plants; comfortable chairs placed under wide arches along the tile corridors are perfect for relaxing or reading to the accompaniment of a splashing fountain while enjoying a drink from the new lobby bar. There's a small pool and bar in a back garden; a pleasant restaurant faces the street. Rates start at US$62 s or d, slightly less in the summer; tel. 24-88-44, located on Calle 60

and 57 #488. In the states contact Mayaland Resorts, tel. (800) 235-4079.

Calinda Panamericana has a lovely entrance and large central courtyard that was once part of a gracious mansion built at the turn of the century. Elegant wooden doors, spacious high-ceilinged rooms (now used as offices or banquet rooms), delicate plaster carvings topping Corinthian columns—brought from Europe to enhance the opulent structure years ago—are carefully maintained to add an old-world touch. A multi-storied bedroom wing was added onto the rear of the patio. The hotel offers elevators, rooms furnished in early-1900s simplicity, private baths, a/c, swimming pool, patio bar/coffee shop, dining room, and live entertainment, and credit cards accepted; about US$50 d. Located on Calle 59 between 52 and 54; tel. 23-91-11.

A few blocks' walk from the central plaza, the **Los Aluxes** is a multi-storied hotel providing courtesy valet parking for its guests. The hotel has a friendly staff, the kind that remembers your name as you come and go. Excellent food is served in the lobby dining room, and an intimate bar/lounge provides mellow late-night music. Good swimming in pleasant surroundings, plus a poolside bar, formal dining room, coffee shop, room service, tropical garden complete with fountain, one-day laundry service, travel agency, car rental, and credit cards accepted. Rooms are carpeted and equipped with TV (with satellite dish), and the suites, with individual terraces and tropical plants, are a good buy; especially #317, #417, or #517. Rates: about US$60 d. Located at Calle 60 near 49; tel. 24-21-99. **Hotel Merida Mision** is across the street from Hotel Casa de Balam and the Peon Contreras Theater. In the "old" days, this was Merida's luxury hotel, which entertained many notable celebrities over the years. Still lovely and well equipped, the rooms are comfortable, each has a/c, telephone, TV (satellite dish), and bathroom. There's a gift shop, travel agency, bar and restaurant with live music from 2030 to 2200, a nightclub that offers folkloric music and dancing at 1900 each evening; about US$7 gets you a *tipico* dinner, a show, and one drink. There are plenty of quiet places to relax, including the pool area; the corner rooms offer the best views. This hotel is popular with tour groups. A double room is around US$40; Calle 60 #491 near 57, tel. 23-

95-00. On Merida's lovely broad Paseo de Montejo you'll find **Hotel Conquistador**, one of the city's newer hotels (opened Dec. 1984). This very comfortable hostelry is manned with cheerful personnel and offers a/c, lovely tile bathrooms, indoor pool, solarium, restaurant, bar, telephone, TV, parking lot, car rental, travel agency, plus large and small meeting rooms. Rates are around US$45.50 d; located at Paseo de Montejo #458 near 35, tel. 26-26-90/25-21-00.

Deluxe

The **Holiday Inn** (rated five stars), located a few kilometers north of the downtown area, is the most expensive hotel in town. This well-designed, multistoried, modern hotel has *all* the conveniences. It's often crowded with out-of-town conventions and banquets; US$75 d. Located at Av. Colon between 60 and Paseo del Montejo; tel. 25-68-77.

Trailer Parks

Just north of Merida (a couple hundred feet from Cordemex) on the road to Progreso find the **Rainbow Trailer Park.** RVers will enjoy a swimming pool, hot water (potable), electricity, many tall shade trees, spaces for 100 trailers, and clean showers and restrooms. Rates start at about US$4 per day. For reservations call 24-20-80. Another park, **Maya Trailer Park,** is across the boulevard from the airport entrance. The price is about the same, but its facilities are a bit more rustic.

FOOD AND ENTERTAINMENT

Cafes of every description are found in Merida. Yucatecan as well as Mexican food are included on most menus, and the "hot stuff" is served on the side, so you needn't worry about the infamous habanera chiles making a sneak attack. Be sure to try Yucatecan salsa made from the usual chiles, cilantro, tomatoes, spices, and one addition—a dash of citrus fruit and rind (mostly sour orange). If your palate is ready for a change from Yucatecan gourmet, Merida offers excellent Arabic, Chinese, and European food. For those traveling on a budget, it's a simple matter to find filling economical meals in Merida. As always the park vendors sell good tamales for about US$.50. Or if you prefer, *tortas* (sandwiches on a roll) made from meat, chicken, or cheese combinations are the same price—but at that price the roll is not *loaded* with filling!

Restaurants

In some *cantinas* in Merida when you order a cold beer in the middle of the afternoon, you'll be served tasty snacks (a more than ample lunch!). **La Prosperidad** is a popular spot where Meridanos crowd into the large cafe daily for drinks, snacks, and good live music. Try it either for cold beer or for a large *tipico comida corrida* (typical meal of the day) including a variety of dishes: *pollo pibil, panuchos, pollo escabeche,* tortillas, *rellenos,* cold chicken, and avocado—a big meal for a reasonable price. **El Tucho** (Calle 60 #482) with more of a nightclub atmosphere, also serves good *antojitos* (snacks) when you order a beer.

A spotless health-food store serving good sandwiches and some vegetarian dishes is called **Pronat** on Calle 60 #446—two doors from the Los Aluxes Hotel—and another location on Calle 59 between 60 and 62. Try their excellent frozen yogurt. Another vegetarian restaurant is the **Ananda Maya Gynza Vegetarian Restaurant;** try one of their unusual drinks, either an iced hibiscus tea called "Jamaica," or a creamy green *chaya* drink. They're located on Calle 59 #507 between 60 and 62. For the adventuring gourmand, try *pulpos en tinta* (octopus in its own ink), especially good at the **Patio Español** cafe in the Gran Hotel.

Well worth an evening's visit is **Alberto's Continental**—for excellent Lebanese cooking, plus continental and Yucatecan dishes. Delightful atmosphere, moderate prices. The building alone (dating from 1727) is a must-see; this is old Mexico in your most romantic dreams. Picture five-foot-thick walls weathered to the hue of "ancient" surrounding the patio with plants and vines providing a dappled shade. Here and there are astounding pieces of ancient stonework and antique furniture—at night it's magical with shimmering candles on delicate crystal. Located on Calles 64 and 57.

La Casona has good Italian pasta in a former mansion. Dine in an open patio (in the evening give your exposed skin a good coating of repellent to ward off mosquitos!) overlooking a lush garden or an indoor formal dining room. Great cappuccino, moderate prices; Calle 60 #434, tel. 23-83-48.

For a change of taste **Kon Tiki** serves outstanding Chinese food; Av. Colon and Calle 14. For good French cuisine both **Yanning** (some readers complain the servings are small!), Calle 62 #480, or **Le Gourmet,** Calle 10 #109 Perez Ponce, are well worth the money, although more

MERIDA RESTAURANTS

NAME	ADDRESS	TELEPHONE	SPECIALITY
Alberto's Continental Patio	Calle 64	21-22-98	continental
Ananda Maya Gynza	Calle 59 #507	—	vegetarian
Buffalos	Paseo Montejo #479	27-53-88	—
Cafe Continental	Paseo Montejo #480	27-35-62	Lebanese/cont.
Chateau Valentin	Calle 58-A #499-D	25-56-90	continental
El Marinero	Calle 40 #413	27-38-21	—
El Meson	Calle 59 #500	24-90-22	—
El Parrilon	Calle 22 #388	27-89-78	—
El Tucho	Calle 60 #482	24-23-23	regional
Express	Calle 60 #502	21-27-28	soups, sands, tacos
Hereford	Av. Aleman & Perez Ponce	27-88-43	int'l, Mexican, beef
La Casona	Calle 60 #434	23-83-48	Italian
La Jungla	Calle 62 #500 61 & 59, 2nd floor	28-12-55	Italian
La Prosperidad	Calle 60 #482	—	regional
Le Gourmet	Av. Perez Ponce #109-A	27-19-70	French
Los Almendros	Calle 50-A #482	—	regional
Los Aluxes	Calle 60	24-21-99	continental
Maria del Carmen	Calle 63 #550	23-91-33	int'l, Mexican
Muelle 8	Calle 21 #142	24-49-76	meat & fish
Pancho's	Calle 59	23-09-42	Mexican
Pizza Rock	—	26-75-45	pizza
Pop Cafeterria	Calle 57 #501	21-68-44	American breakfast & lunch
Portico del Peregrino	Calle 57 #501	21-68-44	continental
Romano's	Av. Perez Ponce #443	27-21-68	Italian
Santa Lucia	Calle 60 #55	21-56-70	continental
Siqueff	Calle 59 #553	24-92-87 24-74-65	Lebanese
Soberanis	Calle 60 #503	21-19-71	seafood
Thai Cafe	Paseo Montejo across from museum	—	Thai
Tulipanes	Calle 42 #462-A	27-09-67	regional
Vito Corleone	Calle 59	27-54-54 23-68-46	pizza
Yanning	Av. Perez Ponce	—	French

outdoor cafe, Merida

expensive than average. The lobby dining room of the **Los Aluxes Hotel** serves excellent continental food with the best-trained waiters in Merida.

Cozy and intimate, the **Santa Lucia Restaurant** (located across the street from the Santa Lucia Church on Calle 60 and 55) has a special charm and a delicious pepper steak, in a delightful brandy sauce prepared next to your table—tasty and tender. The **Cafe Continental** is another outstanding Lebanese restaurant on the Paseo de Montejo #480, tel. 27-35-62. Here you have a choice of a spacious outdoor patio or charming formal a/c dining room. For a light appetizing snack, order *labne* (great thick Lebanese yogurt), *garbanzo con tahine* (tasty puree dip served with fried Arab bread), and a mixed green salad covered with a light blend of olive oil, vinegar, a hint of garlic, and a smidgeon of fresh chopped mint leaves. Perfect for a warm tropical evening.

Gourmets, at **Portico del Perigrino,** taste the delicious *berejenas al horno* (stuffed baked chicken and eggplant), a specialty prepared at this low-key, charming cafe next door to Pop's Cafeteria on Calle 57 between 60 and 62. You have a choice of dining on the intimate, vine-covered patio or in a/c dining rooms. The kitchen staff is very cooperative with vegetarians; even though it's not on the menu, the chef will happily fix something that fits into your diet plan.

For the purist whose mouth waters for hand-made tortillas, **Restaurant Los Almendros** is one of the few places where you can still watch them being made. Enjoy *poc chuc,* a zesty marinated meat dish; located on Calle 50 and 59 off the Mejorada Square. **Pancho's** is a touristy restaurant with a bright atmosphere and fairly good Mexican food served by cloned Pancho Villa-type waiters right down to the hat and ammunition belts across the chest. As the evening progresses, the disco music begins—if you like a quiet dinner get there early—by 1900. Other choices for spirited disco nightlife are the **Holiday Inn** disco or Merida's newest and biggest **Bim-Bom-Bao Disco** located 20 minutes north of downtown by car or taxi. The taxi drivers know where it is.

If you're feeling more in the mood for classic Mexican cuisine (sometimes outstanding, and other times just so-so), spend an evening at **Tulipanes** or **La Ciudad Maya;** both serve *tipico* Yucatecan food and put on exotic shows with rather tacky-looking costumes of the ancient Maya—again very touristy. However, Tulipanes has been importing a great Cuban show nightly during high season. If you're craving good (Mexican-style) Italian pizza go to **Vito Corleone's** on Calle 59. And for even more—spaghetti, lasagna, or pizza—go to **La Jungla de Vito Corleone.** Located in one of the city's oldest buildings next to the main plaza, you can watch the comings and goings of the park or enjoy the colorful decor of a jungle atmosphere playfully created with real exotic plants dangling in front of colorfully painted walls of green jungle, and giant ceramic jungle animals and papier-mâché birds guarding it all. Find it on the second floor of Calle 62 #500 between 61 and 59. As you wander up the steps into the old colonial building, check out the art exhibit and several gift shops including **Casa del Alguacil Mayor** where you'll find indigenous handcrafts, silver, papier-mâché, T-shirts, and more.

Breakfast And Sandwiches

Pop's Cafeteria (on Calle 57 between 60 and 62) is still the solid standby for a good economical continental breakfast (fresh orange juice, toast, and coffee; about US$1.25), and this writer, for one, would like to hang a sign in front that says, "Best BREWED Coffee in Merida." (For those who don't know, most of the coffee served in Yucatecan restaurants is made from instant granules.) You can also get a good American-style hamburger (somewhat smaller than in the U.S., but tasty!), with a few (very few) french fries and coleslaw for under US$2, plus other fine sandwiches, cakes, pies, ice cream, and malts. This is a gathering place for both locals and visitors.

Speaking of gathering places, for local color with a splash of tourists thrown in, visit the **Express,** located on Calle 60 near the corner of 59, across from the Plaza Hidalgo. Here you'll see throngs of white-shirted businessmen along with the T-shirt crowd, sightseers, writers, photographers, and travelers, and you'll hear a cacophony of languages that includes Spanish, English, German, French, Italian, and those unrecognizable. The food is plain but good—and reasonably priced. This no-nonsense open-air cafe has dark wooded trims and friendly waiters that have been around for 33 years *mas o menos.* They make terrific soups and always serve a generous basket of fresh French bread as an accompaniment. Great meal for few pesos, about US$1.25. Coffee lovers, this is another Merida restaurant that serves brewed coffee—strong, but good. Hamburger-heaven is an hour spent at **Tommy's;** or as the younger set claims, **Leo's** isn't just a hangout: the tacos are the best.

Drinks And Goodies

The Yucatan Peninsula offers several drinks not commonly found anywhere else: *horchata* (ground rice, raw sugar, cinnamon, water, and—today—ice) and *pozole* (made from ground corn). These two drinks are classic Maya specialties dating back hundreds of years; *pozole* was described by Bishop Diego de Landa in the 16th century as used for offerings to the gods when planting corn.

Easy-to-find nourishing drinks quench your thirst, satisfy your sweet tooth, and are easy on the pocketbook, while providing a taste of everyday Maya life. In all honesty, one must *develop* a taste for them. On the other hand, the more modern Maya produce *licuados* (a liquified fruit crush made from a selection of melons, pineapple, oranges, and any other fruit that happens to be in season) that everyone loves at first sip. *Licuado* stands—filled with rows of brightly colored fruit—are found all over the city. You can also buy fresh fruit platters from these vendors. Another Meridano treat is called *champola,* a sherbet created in many tropical flavors including tamarind, corn (yes!), mamey, lemon, orange, and chocolate. Find it at the *dulceria* under the arches where you see the white wire "ice cream chairs" across from the *zocalo* after a late-night supper. For good local color and tasty sherbet, try **Dulceria Sorberteria Colon,** a local hangout since 1907. Another *dulceria* is on the Paseo de Montejo between 39 and 41. Frozen yogurt is sold by both Pronat vegetarian shops.

SHOPPING

Merida is definitely *the* place to shop on the Peninsula. Prices at the **mercado municipal** are hard to beat and you'll find a selection of quality crafts from all parts of Yucatan. Even if you're not interested in a shopping spree, take a trip through the busy *mercado* for a wonderful social and cultural experience. You'll see many women from the rural villages of Yucatan state wearing *huipils* (ee-PEELS).

At the *mercado municipal* many small *fondas* (food stalls) are on the second floor with a vast selection of fruits, vegetables, tortillas, sweets; these and other prepared foods are also scattered throughout the market. Don't overlook the *super mercado* (supermarket). These are the easiest places to find scotch tape, boxed crackers and cookies, paper goods, canned or boxed sterilized milk, or dried pasteurized milk, dehydrated soup mixes, soap, and a number of other items that are often hard to locate in the public market unless you're a whiz in Spanish. Just as in the States, the supermarket is a cheap place to purchase liquor and beer. Mexican brandies (El Presidente and Don Pedro), or other liquors manufactured in Mexico (Kahlua, Tequila, and Xtabentum), often go on sale. Remember that imported liquors carry a high import tax, making American gin or Canadian whiskey high priced in Mexico. (The same goes for American peanut butter or coffee.) If you haven't already, try the dark beer made in Yucatan, Leon Negro; or if you prefer light, try Montejo and Carta Clara. For a special gift to take home, buy locally made Xtabentum; this liqueur, made from fermented honey and anise, has a spicy licorice flavor.

Mercado Municipal

Along with the euphoric pleasures of color—bundles of brilliant flowers and rainbows of neatly stacked fruit and vegetables—watching the steady stream of people makes a visit to the bustling market a diverse entertainment. Here are foods of all description: cooked tamales, raw meat, live chickens, and pungent odors from mounds of unusual-looking herbs, spices, and

mercado municipal

fruit. The candy man offers delicate sugar flowers, shoes, and skulls (if it's near the Day of the Dead holiday) for just a few pesos. Be sure to stop by the *tortilleria.* Upstairs, a series of tiny fast-food windows serve the cheapest meals in Merida: tacos, tamales, *tortas,* and *licuados.*

Chattering merchants invite you to inspect (and bargain for) their colored woven hammocks, huaraches, and gleaming chunks of clear amber-colored *copal* (incense) in use since the days of the Maya. Narrow little "gold-stalls" have thousands of dollars worth of gold earrings along with charms and bangles of every description stored in their small glass cases. You'll see the common and the uncommon, ordinary and extraordinary. Some things you may not want to see, such as *mecech,* jeweled lapel beetles—the crawly kind outlawed in the U.S. The ordinary seems always in demand: straw baskets of every shape, pottery bowls for every use, Panama hats in the final stages of manufacture, *guayaberas* (wide-lapel, pleated, cotton shirts), and white *huipils* with thickly embroidered flowered borders in every color. Located at Calle 56 and 67.

Contraband Market

Called "Chetumalito" by Meridanos, after the border city of Chetumal between Belize and Mexico which offers excellent tax-free bargains. The contraband market offers good buys in imported goods. It's just behind the municipal market. Don't be alarmed if a couple of burly men approach you at the entrance and ask what you want (they want your dollars first if possible and can get it for you wholesale, whatever *it* is!). Tell them you're just looking and continue on your way. This market's even more crowded than next door (if possible), and louder: tape recorders blast out the latest rock, and vie in decibels with lively Latin rhythms.

SPECIALTY SHOPS

Huipils

The *huipil* is a lovely garment (first used by mestiza women at the insistence of hacienda patrons), edged with bright-colored embroidery around the squared neck and hem, with a lace-finished petticoat peeking out below the dress. Similar, the *terno* is a long dress that is more elaborate than the *huipil* but with the same ornate embroidery; it's used at all the fiestas and other celebrations.

Most Merida women are fashion-conscious and vitally into the clothes of the 1990s. *Huipils* are worn almost exclusively by women who have come to market for the day from small rural communities surrounding Merida. The *huipil* is a unique rememberance to take home and a cool *tipico* garment to wear in warm weather. Unfortunately, machine embroidery on synthetic fabrics is the norm in most shops. All-cotton hand-embroidered garments are available but you must search them out and the cost is much more. The thick embroidered designs (usually brilliantly colored flowers) are often symbolic to the woman who is wearing them. If the price of the hand-embroidered discourages you (US$150 and up), shop around for good-quality machine work (US$45). Try the *mercado,* the small shops that line the streets around the plazas, or hotel gift shops like the boutique at the **Hotel Casa del Balam,** Calle 60 #488, **Agoras Fonapas Crafts Center,** Calle 63 #503, between 64 and 66. Here many are cotton, but seldom hand embroidered.

Guayaberas

Yucatecan men wear the *guayabera* in place of a white shirt with tie and jacket. This shirt is perfectly acceptable for any dress occasion you may encounter in Merida or any other part of Mexico. The most common color is white, but they're also available in pastel tones. They're found in most of the shops, but for a large selection and made-to-order *guayaberas* go to **Jack's** at Calle 59 #505. The **Camiseria Canul** at Calle 59 #496B is another popular place to buy or order the Yucatecan shirt. Prices range from about US$18 up to US$50 for made-to-order. Visitors on tour buses are brought to these shops so they're apt to be crowded, but both have very large selections and a great variety of sizes.

Panama Hats

If you're in the market for a hat, look for a local *jipi* shop and pick up a Panama hat. (By the way, these hats are not made in Panama; the name originated because of their popularity during the building of the Panama Canal.) They're made in several towns in the states of Yucatan and Campeche, and the finest are made of the *jipijapa* fiber; ask for *finos* for the most supple. They can be folded and stuffed in a pocket and then will pop back into shape when needed. But buyer beware, many cheaper "palms" are used as well and these will not take that kind of treatment. Browse around *La Casa de los Jipis* (Calle 56 #526) where you'll see the hat in many qualities. Ask questions, they'll educate you on the subject of Panama hats. Not cheap here, the *finos* may cost US$65, but if you want classic design and the best quality that should last forever, it's worth it. For a simple sun hat, street vendors are seen near every plaza and at the entrance of many hotels—bargain!

Hammocks

Yucatan is noted for producing the best hammocks in Mexico. Street vendors try to induce tourists to buy them, which is okay as long as the buyer knows what to look for. Many shops sell them including **La Casa de los Jipis** (Calle 56

MERIDA SUPERMARKETS

Here are several supermarkets located around the city:

☞ San Francisco De Assisi
(supermarket and dept. store)
Calle 65, between 50 and 52
Paseo de Montejo and Calle 21 (on the way to Progreso)
Calle 59 between 82 and 84 (close to Centenario Zoo)

☞ Blanco
Calle 67 and 52
Calle 72 between 59 and 61 (across from Santiago Square)
Calle 56 between 63 and 65 (close to post office)
Paseo de Montejo and Calle 21

☞ Super Maz
Calle 56 between 63 and 65
Plaza Buenavista (Calle 60 and Circuito Colonias)
Plaza Oriente (Circuito Colonias and Calle 65)

☞ La Italiana
(supermarket and dept. store)
Calle 58 and 63 (one block east of Main Plaza)

#526, near Calle 65). Don't hesitate to ask the vendor to stretch the entire hammock out while you inspect it carefully. To judge whether a hammock will be long enough for you, hold one end of the body of the hammock to the top of your head and let it drop. The other end of the body should be touching the floor for you to be comfortable. Ask what it's made of and don't be afraid to bargain.

Antique Shops

A few antique shops are scattered throughout Merida. The ones that are really "junk shops" are the most intriguing! If you like to get lost in dusty shelves of rare old books (if you can read Spanish, you're in luck), chipped 17th- and 18th-century religious art (a large collection), empty rococo frames, odd pieces of bric-a-brac, delicate glass, all complete with resident cobwebs, you must visit Manolo Rivero's shop called **Ridecor;** Calle 60 #456. Manolo is an artist, and to walk into his shop is like walking into a lovely old painting of your aunt Minnie's attic. When speaking to him about the works that lie gathering dust, you get the feeling that perhaps he really cares little about selling any of his precious "junk," that the shop is just another facet of the love of his life—art. (He has an art gallery practically next door.)

Art Galleries

For the art buff interested in the world of modern art, a visit to **Galeria Manolo Rivero** is well worth the trip (Calle 60 #456). Here you may happen upon a show of the works of such outstanding avant-garde artists as Jose or Alberto Lenero, Roberto Turnbull, the controversial Gustavo Monroy (whose show in Mexico City was closed for several days in 1988 due to the complaints of the traditionalists of the city who disapprove of his artistic religious disrespect). Perhaps you'll arrive during one of the occasional shows of the imaginative Jose Garcia Ocejo. His gently erotic work—done in a combination of subtle to brilliant color to black and white—is shown in galleries all over the world.

Arts And Crafts

On Calle 63 between 66 and 64 is the **Fonart**, center for arts and crafts from all over the state of Yucatan. You'll also find silver, gold, leather, ceramics, onyx, and typical clothing from the 31 states of Mexico. *Occasionally* you'll find good reproductions of Maya images that were made under the supervision of artist Wilbert Gonzalez in Ticul. Gonzalez uses the same techniques to create his pottery as the Maya. His work is so extraordinary and authentic that he was thrown in jail (some years back) by ignorant police who accused him of stealing original art when in fact they were his own creations. He sat in jail for three months while the "expert archaeologists" studied the pieces and agreed they were indeed original Maya art. Only when his friend Victor Manzanilla Schaffer (now governor, then senator of the state of Yucatan) returned from an extended trip to Japan and came to his rescue was he released and the matter clarified. He shrugs the incident off with a wry smile and the comment, "That's my Mexico." He now inserts a hidden code on each piece to protect himself. Today Gonzalez creates his art in the small town of Ticul where he also instructs students in the style of the ancient Maya under the auspices of the government; his workshop and gallery are called **Arte Maya.**

HAMMOCKS

Yucatan hammocks have a reputation for being the best in the world. Many local people sleep in them and love it. *Hamacas* are cool, easy to store, make wonderful cribs that babies cannot fall out of (at least not easily), and come in a variety of sizes.

It's important to know the size you want when shopping. The Yucatecans make a *matrimonial* which is supposed to be big enough for two persons to sleep comfortably; for even more comfort, ask for the *familiar*, weavers say the whole family fits!

A good hammock stretches out to approximately five meters long (one-third of which is the woven section), and the width three to five meters pulled out (gently, don't stretch!). Check the end strings, called *brazos;* there should be at least 100 to 150 triple loops for a *matrimonial.*

A variety of materials is used: synthetics, henequen, cotton, and linen. It's a toss-up whether the best is pure cotton or linen. The finer the weave the more resilient. Experts say it takes eight km of thread for a *matrimonial.*

Each Sunday from 1000 to 1500, a **Bazaar of Arts and Crafts** is held in the Centenario Park and Zoo. See artists and their paintings, sculpture, and crafts, and—to add a little zing—chess instructors go knight to rook with students. On the same day from 1000 to 1400 an **Antique and Crafts Bazaar** is held at Santa Lucia Park. Sellers bring worn books, antique bric-a-brac, old stamps, furniture, typical clothing, and lovely artwork—good browsing! A large handcraft market is located on the corner of Calle 65 and 62 with a good selection of crafts.

Maya Feather And Shell Art

The Maya created lovely art in a variety of forms. Using shells and feathers was considered a lost art for years; but more and more this form is surfacing in bazaars and tourist shops. The ancients used brilliantly colored feathers to weave elegant garments from the richly hued birds of the Yucatan Peninsula, especially the blue-greens of the now seldom-seen quetzal bird. Some fine examples of this art can be seen at the Anthropological Museum in Mexico City.

Books, Magazines, And Newspapers

Visit the **Mesoamerican Bookstore** on Calle 59 #520, between Calle 64 and 66, two blocks west of the main plaza. The shop benefits various ecological organizations on the Yucatan Peninsula. Books in English and postcards displaying nature's subjects are sold as well as appropriate T-shirts urging all to save the rainforests. Free video-show presentations are given explaining the plight of Central American rainforests. Ask for information about **Pronatura**, a local ecological organization dedicated to saving flora and fauna of the Yucatan including the flamingos, orchids, and sea turtles. Nature-tour schedules available. **Note:** Anyone interested in buying an acre of the rainforest can do so for US$50. Simply sign an agreement that specifies there will be no development on your acre. For more information ask at the Mesoamerican Bookstore.

As usual, the large hotel gift shops carry a good supply of English-language books, both fiction and pictorial books about the area. You can also get American magazines and often *The News,* a Mexico City-published English-language newspaper. This paper can also be found at the small newsstand in the arcade on the north edge of the central plaza. **Discolibros Hollywood,** located on the south side of Cepeda Peraza (Plaza Hidalgo)

facing Calle 60, has a great selection of American magazines and English-language paperbacks, plus the *New York Times Weekly Review.* **Burrell's Book Stores** (there are four) carry a good line of English-language guidebooks dealing with the entire Peninsula as well as stationery goods. One store is located on Calle 59 between 60 and 62. **Dante's,** another bookstore chain, has six locations in Merida; one is on Calle 59 near the crossing of 59 and 68, tel. 23-37-91, plus shops at the larger archaeological zones, Chichen Itza and Uxmal. (Dante's sells English-language books at inflated prices; the second edition of this guidebook was marked US$32!)

Photo Supplies

A complete line of photo equipment, film, and one-hour color processing can be found at **Omega,** Calle 60 off 59. Kodak and Fuji are most common here, a little more expensive than in the States; but if you must buy film on the Peninsula, Merida's probably the least expensive place, and offers good processing services. Some travelers find it convenient to buy Kodak mailers at home and drop them off at post offices (or large hotel mail pickups) along the way, with processed results sent directly home. (For more photo information, see "Cameras" p. 63.) **Mericolor** has shops scattered around the Peninsula and offers one-hour color service as well as black-and-white and transparency processing.

CULTURAL EVENTS

Music

Music is heard all over Merida, and Sundays you have your choice of marimba, classical, or folkloric. Informal entertainment is provided for Merida's residents and visitors at parks and plazas throughout the city. Families and friends gather under the stars in the warm tropical night for a variety of music each evening year-round beginning at 2100—free. All day Sunday at a variety of parks, family events take place. For more information about these evening concerts, check at your hotel or any one of the city's tourist offices. This is casual entertainment, so don't hesitate to speak to your benchmate—very often you'll make friends with a great Meridano who will take delight in showing off his city, or at least give you the opportunity to ask questions or practice Spanish.

WEEKLY SCHEDULE OF CULTURAL EVENTS IN MERIDA

SUNDAY

Santa Lucia Square	popular art and antiques bazaar 1100 live band music
Park of the Mother	"Children in Culture" (arts and crafts)
Cepeda Peraza Square **(also known as Hidalgo Sq.)**	1130 live marimba music
Plaza de Independencia	Handcraft bazaar 1100 free tours of city hall 1100 concert at Hall of History in the Governor's Palace, 2nd floor 1300 Mestizo Wedding (folkloric dance)
Centenario Park	1000 Children's Festival. Zoo is open all day

MONDAY

Palacio Municipal	2100 Vaqueria Regional Dance

TUESDAY

Santiago Square	2100 live band music

THURSDAY

Santa Lucia Square	2100 Yucatecan Serenade (folkloric music, dance, bards)

FRIDAY

University of Yucatan **(Central Patio)**	2100 University Serenade

Teatro Peon Contreras

This theater, built in 1908 during Merida's rich period, was patterned after European design. A lovely old building, it continues to offer a variety of concerts and other entertainment, worth visiting just to see the classic interior. During the busiest seasons (winter and spring), colorful folkloric dances are presented every Tuesday night, admission about US$4. Located on Calle 60 and 57, admission varies depending on the event. For a list of attractions at the theater, call 24-92-90/24-93-89. Located in one corner of the theater building is the Tourist Information Center.

For Children

Sunday is family day in Mexico, and Merida is no exception. The tree-shaded parks are popular for picnics, playing ball, buying giant colorful balloons, etc. Children's movies are offered from 1000 throughout the day at **Pinocchio's Movie House** located just across from El Centenario Park. On Sunday, festivals are held at **El Centenario Park Zoo** and **La Ceiba's Park** at 1100, **Mulsay's Park** at 1800. Here children (and parents) are entertained by magicians, clowns, puppets, theater groups. All take part in organized games which even include the smallest child, and offer prizes to winning participants. The Merida zoo is outstanding and a popular stop for both children and adults, across from the museum on Av. Itzaes and Calle 59. Also on Sunday at the **Plaza Maternidad** children take part in drawing classes and play chess.

SERVICES

Remember that many businesses in Merida close between 1300-1600 and are open evenings until 1900. Restaurants and food stores are the exception.

Travel Agencies

Yucatan Trails is a reliable travel agency where English is spoken, and the staff is very helpful, making or changing airline reservations, hotel reservations, or group tours. A daily city tour (pick-up at your hotel) is available for US$7 pp. This is a good way to get the lay of the land when you first arrive in Merida. There are many other tours available, including custom tours. These can all be arranged through Yucatan Trails; ask for manager Denis Lafoy (from Canada) for more complete information and updated schedules. Located in the heart of town on Calle 62 #482, between 57 and 59, tel. 28-25-82/21-53-58. **Molica Tours** is located in the lobby of the Hotel Caribe, Calle 59 and 60, tel. 23-84-33. **Buvisa** is on Paseo de Montejo between 37 and 39, tel. 27-79-33. **American Ex-**

Office of Federal Tourism In Merida
Calle 56 #514
Merida, Yucatan, Mexico

press has recently opened a travel agency on Paseo de Montejo, one block south of the Palacio Canton on the opposite side of the street. Among other things they cash and sell Amex travelers cheques. **VN Travel** is run by a delightful lady, Alicia del Villar, who is friendly, helpful, and speaks perfect English. VN Travel is located on Calle 58 #488, tel. 24-59-96/23-90-61, fax (99) 24-82-19.

Tourist Information Centers

Several tourist information centers are found in Merida. One is at the Teatro Peon Contreras on Calle 60; they speak English and give out lots of good information. Another is located at the Palacio Gobierno (facing the north side of the main plaza). The address of the Office of State Tourism is Calle 86 #499, C.P. Merida, Yucatan 97000,Mexico, tel. 24-57-26, fax (99) 24-97-81, Apto Postal 752. Each of these offices gives information, maps, and other important literature. If you have a problem and need assistance, call SECTUR, the federal tourism office, tel. 24-94-31/24-95-42.

Laundry Service

The laundry on Calle 58 between 57 and 59 does a good job, washes and irons, and is more reasonable than most of the hotels.

Medical Or Emergency

For a medical emergency most hotels can provide the name of an English-speaking doctor (see "Health," pp. 57-63). You can also go to one of the small clinics located around the city. The San Jose clinic on Calle 54 between 55 and 57 has

---

MERIDA TOURS

Mayaland Tours offers escorted tours in air-conditioned buses to most of the sights on the Peninsula. Their headquarters are in Merida at Av. Colon #502, Box 407, Merida, Yucatan State, Mexico.

In the U.S. make reservations and get more information by calling (800) 451-8891, in Florida call (305) 341-9173.

Prices listed below are in U.S. dollars.

Balancanche Caves	from Chichen Itza	from $15
Chichen Itza	from Merida	from $30 lunch
Colonial Tour	from Uxmal	from $54 lunch
Dzibilchaltun	from Merida	from $25
Merida City Tour	from Merida	from $12
Merida City Tour	from Uxmal	from $59
Progreso	from Merida	from $33
Uxmal	from Merida	from $28 lunch
Uxmal Light and Sound Show	from Merida	from $40 dinner
Uxmal & Puuc Region	from Merida	from $120 lunch

three doctors who speak *some* English (two brothers and a sister). A reader recently had occasion to visit the doctor for a throat infection and reported good service and the cost was about US$5; tel. 21-73-61. For extreme emergencies, medical or otherwise, call the **U.S.** or **British Consulates.** If you need medications or a prescription filled, a reliable pharmacy is **Farmacia del Bazar** located on Calle 65 across from the post office. The prices are economical, and manager Carlos Montero can understand a *little* English. **The Dept. of Tourism's** hotline for all of Mexico is (5) 250-0123, 24 hours a day. **Merida Police Station,** tel. 25-25-55; the **Fire Station,** tel. 24-92-42; **Federal Highway Patrol,** tel. 24-79-33; **Red Cross,** tel. 21-24-45.

The Green Angels

This government-sponsored road service cruises the main roads daily; they recommend staying with your car in the event of a breakdown if it's daylight (they don't cruise after 2100) and you're on a paved artery (they don't cruise dirt roads).

Car Parts

If you should have a problem with your car while in Merida and need parts, contact **Lubcke Repuestos Del Golfo Y Caribe.** Ask for Jaime (pronounced HI-mee) Lubcke; he speaks English—a friendly helpful guy! Using his fax machine he can get parts quickly (for Mexico). Located on Calle 58 #471, tel. 24-15-45/23-04-85.

Banks

Banks are everywhere you look in Merida; hours are 0900-1330 Mon. through Friday. Get there early during the busy seasons, there's usually a line. On Calle 65 alone are five banks. Changing travelers cheques at a bank is usually more advantageous than at a hotel. Often shops will give an even better exchange than the bank (with a purchase); usually a sign is posted—if not, ask. If you go to **Banamex** facing the south side of the central plaza, take a look around; until 1980 it was the home of the historic Francisco Montejo family. At this printing only the Banamex and Bancomer were changing Canadian travelers cheques.

When the banks are closed, a good place to change money is **Casa de Cambio Canto** on Calle 61 #468, between 52 and 54, about three blocks east of the main plaza. Rates are competitive (check) and they have longer hours than the bank; open Mon.-Fri. 8-1:30 and 4:30-7:30, Sat. 8-1:30. Travelers in a bind can usually talk the proprietor into sending a fax to the states; tel. 28-04-58, fax (99) 24-77-84.

Post Office

The post office and telegraph office are located on Calle 65 and 56, near the *mercado;* business hours are 0900-1900 Mon. to Friday.

Long-distance Telephone And Telegraph

For *larga-distancia* (long-distance) telephone calls go to **Condesa,** Calle 62 and 59, or to the bus terminal on Calle 69 #554. It's much cheaper than at your hotel where a service charge can be as high as 100%. If you must phone from the hotel, ask about the service charge structure—it may be cheaper if you call collect, but you may still have an added charge. Telegrams can be sent from Calle 56 between 65 and 67; or from the bus terminal on Calle 69 #554.

Churches

Catholic churches are predominant in Merida. On the east side of the central plaza (Calle 60 at 61) the **Cathedral,** built in the late 16th century, is the largest church on the Peninsula. Other churches in Merida include **Santa Ana,** Calle 60 at 45, and **Santa Lucia,** Calle 60 at 55. A Presbyterian church, **El Divino Salvador,** with an English-speaking pastor, is located at Calle 66 #518.

Consulates

In case of lost passports, legal problems, or emergencies, get in touch with your consulate. The **U.S. Consulate** is located at Paseo de Montejo at Av. Colon #453. Office hours are 0830-1730; tel. 25-50-11/25-50-09. For emergencies after working hours call 25-50-39. Former football great Brian Salter is the American Consul and is always ready to help with a problem. There's also a U.S. Consular agency in Cancun open from 1000-1400. The **British Consulate** (which also handles Belize business) is on Calle 58 #450, tel. 21-67-94. The Canadian Consulate is closed temporarily, in the meantime for emergencies call Mexico City, 254-32-88. Calls will be answered between 0900 and 1700. An answering machine accepts after-hours messages and your call will be returned.

GETTING THERE

Since the Spanish first settled the city of Merida, it has been the hub of travel and the easiest city on the Peninsula to get to by a variety of transport.

Airlines Serving Merida

Mexicana Airlines, on Calle 58 #500, tel. 24-50-78/24-66-33 (in the U.S. 800-531-7921), has destinations and connecting flights to Mexico City, Cancun, Oaxaca, Monterrey, Chetumal, Cozumel, Tijuana, Guadalajara, Puerto Vallarta, Houston, New York, Miami, and Los Angeles. Please check with the airlines or a travel agent for prices and schedules. **Aeromexico** (tel. in the U.S. 800-237-6639) offers service to Miami, Cancun, Villahermosa, and Mexico City. **Continental** (tel. in the U.S. 800-525-0280) flies direct to Miami, Newark, and Houston.

By Plane

Planes fly into Merida's airport from most cities in Mexico. The airport service road is off of Av. de Itzaes (Hwy. 180) seven km southwest of town. Cafe, post office, long-distance phone, money changer, car rental counters, and several gift shops are inside. The terminal is (usually) air-conditioned. A taxi charges about US$4 *to* the airport but *from* the airport a collective cab will deliver you to downtown hotels for about US$1; buy your ticket at a counter in front of the air terminal. Hang on to your ticket until all packages, baggage, purses, and carry-ons are accounted for at your destination. The cabbies in Yucatan have a great reputation for honesty, but there's no point in pushing your luck. For bus transportation from the airport to the downtown area, look for bus #79. It runs between the air terminal and a downtown bus stop on the corners of Calles 67 and 60; the fare is less than a U.S. dime. **Note:** For General Merida airport information call 24-85-54.

By Train

Merida's train station is located on Calle 55 between Calles 48 and 50, eight blocks northeast of the central plaza. Look for the sign that says "Ferrocarriles Unidos del Sureste." An information booth at the station is open from 0700-2200 daily; bus tickets are also on sale. Trains departing from Merida have no dining cars; bring a lunch or plan on buying from the food vendors at each stop. For

AIRPORT LOUNGE

Visitors traveling with **Mayaland Resorts** and **Mayaland Tours** now have a passenger facility at Merida International Airport. The lounge is located directly across from the baggage claim area where Mayaland clients are offered refreshments and a representative to help them with their itineraries.

the best information on train schedules, go directly to the train station. To walk downtown from the train station, turn west (right) from the main entrance along Calle 55 for five blocks to Calle 60; turn south (left) and three blocks will bring you to the plaza.

Warning!

Reports of train robberies have been repeatedly given to authorities on the second-class train bound from Mexico City to Merida. The first leg, Mexico to Palenque, appears to be trouble free, but travelers haved reported that shortly past Palenque and around the Tenosique area, thefts have occurred while they were sleeping.

By Bus

The main bus station is on Calle 69 between 68 and 70, tel. 21-91-50 (other stations noted below). The station houses both 1st- and 2nd-class companies. As you enter the station, 1st-class is on the left and 2nd-class on the right, both with baggage checking services. Ask at the information counter for the latest schedules. Bus transport on the Peninsula is excellent with routes going to all parts of Mexico. The following list will get you going to many places—for further information check at the bus terminal.

By Car

Good highways approach Merida from all directions. Be prepared for one-way streets and avoid arriving on Sunday—a large area in the center of town is closed to vehicles. If you don't know the city, it can be a real headache to drive to your hotel, since most are located downtown. If you should land in town on Sunday, flag down a cabbie and pay him to lead you to your hotel. He'll know how to get around the detours—worth the few pesos.

MERIDA BUS SCHEDULES

First-class buses from Merida to:

DESTINATION	FARE	TIMES
Mexico DF	US$25	1000, 1200, 1630, 1800, 2000, 2230
Villahermosa	US$10	1000, 1030, 1200, 1300, 1630, 1730, 2000, 2015, 2045, 2100, 2145, 2215, 2230, 2330
Campeche	US$3	0600, 1100, 1230, 1400, 1830, 2330
Cancun or Puerto Juarez	US$5	0630, 0700, 0800, 0900, 1000, 1200, 1300, 1400, 1500, 1600, 1700, 1800, 1900, 2000, 2200, 2300
Tizimin	US$3	0615, 1215, 1815
Valladolid	US$3	0615, 1630
Chichen Itza	US$2	0615, 0830, 1630
Chichen Itza roundtrip	US$4	departure 0830 and returns to Merida from Chichen at 1500
Playa del Carmen	US$6	0600, 0745, 1100, 2330, 2400

Second-class buses from Merida to:

Tulum	US$6.50	0600, 0745, 1100, 2330, 2400
Akumal	US$6	0500, 1100, 2400
Mexcanu	US$8	0530, 0730, 0930, 1100, 1300, 1400, 1600, 1700, 1900, 2030
Palenque	US$8.50	2330

AUTOTRANSPORTES DEL SUR

(Second-class) calle 50 and 67 from Merida to:

Hunucma	every two hours from 0500 to 1900
Celestun	every two hours from 0600 to 2000
Sisal	every hour from 0500 to 1900
Uxmal	0630, 0900, 1200, 1500, 1700
Ticul and Oxkutzcab	
	every hour from 0500 to 1900
Izamal	1000

AUTOBUSES DE PROGRESO

Calle 62 between 65 and 67 from Merida to:

Dzibilchaltun	0715, 1215, 1615
Dzitya	1115, 1515
Progreso	every 20 minutes from 0500 to 1900
	every 10 minutes in summer months

Car Rentals

Cars are available from several agencies in the airport terminal building, downtown Merida, and in most of the larger hotels. Advance reservations are advised during the busy winter months. One of the most economical agencies in the city is **Mexico Rent A Car** located on Calle 62 #483 E, between 57 and 59, tel. 23-36-37, 27-49-16. They rent (not new) VW bugs for about US$44 per day including full insurance, unlimited mileage, and taxes.

TAXI STANDS IN MERIDA

Mejorada	Calle 57	21-34-84
Near Itzaes Blvd.	Calle 57-A and 60	25-00-31
Plaza Hidalgo	Calle 59 and 60	21-25-00
Plaza Santa Lucia	Calle 55 and 60	21-23-65
Santa Ana	Calle 60 and 47	21-23-00
Santiago Plaza	Santiago	21-27-44

GETTING AROUND

Merida is laid out in a neat grid pattern of one-way numbered streets. The even-numbered streets run north and south, the odd east and west. The central plaza is the center of town and you can easily walk to most downtown attractions, shops, and marketplaces. Buses provide frequent service in and around the city and outlying areas. Bus stops are located at almost every corner along the main streets and buses go to any destination in the city. During the day, it's never more than 20 minutes between buses; they run less frequently at night. Average fare around town is less than a U.S. dime.

At one time, *calesas* were the only means of getting around the city; today they're a pleasant alternative. From near the plaza, *calesas* are a relaxing slow way to see aristocratic old houses with carved facades, marble entries, stone gargoyles, etched glass, and wrought-iron fences, some with their elegance slipping, others well maintained over several generations in this European-flavored residential district. In all honesty, however, the main streets are so busy and noisy it's best to get off them whenever possible.

Taxi Service

The gasoline taxi is fastest, although you can't always find one when you're in a hurry. Taxis are generally found at taxi stands in most neighborhoods and there's almost always a queue at any one of the parks. However, if it's late, any hotel, cafe, or disco will call one for you. They are not metered, so establish your fare in advance. The average fare around town is about US$2-3.

MERIDA CAR RENTALS

NAME	ADDRESS	TELEPHONE
Easy Way	Calle 59 #501	28-15-60
Panam	Calle 41 #483-A	23-07-30
	Montejo Palace Hotel	23-40-97
	Av. Itzaes	23-14-50
Budget	Paseo Montejo	27-27-08
	Holiday Inn	25-54-53
	Airport	24-97-91
	Next to Casa Balam	28-17-50
	Hotel Calinda	23-91-11
	In Progreso	5-03-00
	Hotel Fiesta Inn	5-00-34
Avis	Airport	23-78-56
National	Calle 62 #483	24-17-64
	Airport	24-51-96
Hertz	Calle 55 #479	23-89-75
Dollar	Airport	24-02-80
Colonial	Calle 57 #500	23-29-86

VICINITY OF MERIDA

Along the Merida-Progreso Hwy. wanderers will find two reasons to turn off the road. One is the small wood-carving community of Dzitya, and the other is the archaeological site of Dzibilchaltun.

DZITYA

Here artisans make tourist-oriented gifts out of sections of logs from the *huayacan* tree—such items as mortar and pestles, bowls, and animals, all left in their natural colors. Visitors are welcome to observe the locals at work on modern lathes in the small factories. An enthusiastic visitor that shows a genuine curiosity might be treated to a demonstration of an antiquated foot-pedaled lathe ingeniously operated with a piece of henequen twine.

DZIBILCHALTUN

Located 21 km from Merida along the Merida-Progreso Hwy., Dzibilchaltun is open daily from 0800-1700; admission is free. To the archaeologist, Dzibilchaltun (dseeb-eel-chawl-TOON) represents a valuable 19 square km of land. This is the oldest continuously used Maya ceremonial and administrative center on the Peninsula: from 2000 B.C. until the conquest. The map of the site shows close to 8,400 fallen structures. To the layman it does not offer the visual displays of the more fully reconstructed sites. For the amateur archaeologist, however, Dzibilchaltun is fascinating.

Dzibilchaltun's Temple of the Dolls

Sights Of Dzibilchaltun

Dzibilchaltun was unknown to the world at large until 1941 when archaeologists George W. Brainerd and E. Wyllys Andrews began their explorations. By 1965 several important buildings had been uncovered and repaired. Probably the most remarkable structure is the **Temple of the Seven Dolls,** where seven primitive clay dolls were found buried under the floor of the temple. These crude figurines depicted various deformities, such as a hunchback and a distended stomach. Possibly they were part of a ritual for protection against illnesses and deformities.

Anyone who has read E. Wyllys Andrews and Luis Marden articles in the Jan. 1959 issue of *National Geographic* (especially) will enjoy visiting the **Xlacah** (shla-KAH) *cenote* where the dive that was described took place. This natural pool is 44 meters deep and clear (not all *cenotes* have such clarity), and though work continues on and off, swimming here is great. Thousands of artifacts from ancient ceremonial rites were reclaimed from this sacred well, but only a few are on display at the small museum on the grounds.

Ecological Park

Dzibilchaltun is known not only for its archaeological wonders but is also heralded as a natural reserve where nature trails meander through typical forest which shows another face of Yucatan flora. Here visitors will see the low scrubby deciduous forest, endemic cactus, and palms. Many trees are labeled and birds abound, especially near the *cenote* where they feed and nest. A small snack bar and souvenir stand where you can purchase books and postcards is next to the museum.

Getting There

Direct buses depart from the second-class bus station in Merida on Calle 62 #524 (tel. 21-23-44) four times a day: 0500, 0715, 1215, 1615. The 30-minute ride is a good way to get to the site. The return trip isn't so dependable—it's best to go on one of the early buses if you want to return to Merida in the afternoon. Remember: there isn't another bus back to Merida after the 1615 bus arrives at the archaeological zone. Another alternative is to travel from Merida on the Progreso bus which leaves from the same second-class station every 15 minutes 0500-2100, and will drop you off at the crossroads on Hwy. 273 to the Dzibilchaltun archaeological zone (when you board the bus be sure to tell the driver where you wish to get off). This alternative leaves you with a four-km walk to the ruins. A return bus can be caught at the same spot. If driving, go from Merida on Hwy. 273 and look for the Club de Golf La Ceiba, then continue one km beyond and turn right (east) on the side road for four km to the entrance of Dzibilchaltun.

YUCALPETEN

On the Progreso Hwy. south of the city, turn right (west) at the junction. This road, which parallels the coast, goes to Yucalpeten, an active shipping and fishing port, and a popular vacation spot for Mexican families and students on *temporada* (summer break). The government runs a simple large hotel on the beach called **ISSTEY**, a two-story, modern cement building with two adult swimming pools and a shallow one for kids. It's moderately priced, clean, and each room has a bathroom with a shower. The rooms vary in size from doubles to family units with cooking facilities. The larger units provide hammock hooks to sleep extra people. In July and Aug. it's crowded and noisy with fun-seekers of all ages. In the middle of the week during winter months the place is seldom filled and makes a good stopover along the coast; about US$9 d. On the beach alongside the hotel is a *balneario,* which has a large pavilion cafe, dressing rooms, showers, *palapa* sun shelters, and easy access to the ocean (small fee).

The new modern **Fiesta Inn Hotel** has opened in Yucalpeten, the first of what is expected to be a large tourism development on the Gulf coast of the State of Yucatan. The luxury hotel offers all the amenities including two dining rooms, swimming pool, nicely decorated common areas, bar, friendly staff; rates are about US$62 d, plus tax. It's near a new marina that is expected to attract boaters from the southern coastal regions of the U.S.

Close by the Fiesta Inn Hotel is another upscale hotel, much smaller, but impressive, called **Hotel Sian-Ka'an.** Private terrace, kitchenette, ocean view, swimming pool, bar, restaurant, all just 30 minutes from Merida. For reservations call 23-12-67 in Merida, 395-5888 in Mexico City, telex. 1763128.

A few kilometers beyond Yucalpeten, the road continues through **Chelem** and **Chuburna.** Both small towns cater to summer tourists with simple *balnearios* and open-air cafes serving fresh fish. During the yearly migration season, when hundreds of birds pass by, most of these cafes serve a local delicacy, *pato* (duck), cooked in several different spicy sauces.

SISAL

Sisal is another port town that's lost most of its zing since henequen production fell off, slipping from a bustling, prosperous seaport to a small sleepy Gulf village. However, not for long. Plans for a large resort are in the works. For now walk through the old customs house for a taste of colonial days. A short pier off the main road makes a good spot to photograph the beached fishing boats. The beach east or west of town is clean, though the water can be silty in the afternoon when the breeze picks up. There are several lighthouses along this coast, and often with just a smile and your best Spanish (even if your best is not too good), you'll be permitted to climb the old stairway and take a look around. The lighthouse in Sisal, however, is a private home, and you must ask permission to visit their tower, a solid red-and-white structure located on the main road a block from shore. The view is worth the climb! A P1000 tip to the child who leads you up the stairway would be appreciated. If you have the urge to fish, you can easily make a deal with a resident fisherman to take you along for a reasonable fee. Sisal is a good place to catch red snapper and sea bass.

Accommodations And Food

There's little choice of accommodations in Sisal. The **Club Felicidades** east of the pier (a five-minute walk on the beach) offers 13 rooms (some a bit stuffy because of poor ventilation) with bathrooms that wouldn't receive a gold star for cleanliness. A double bed in each room takes care of one or two people for the same price; about US$5. **Balneario Felicidades** offers thatched-roof *palapas* on the beach where you dine; use of dressing rooms and showers (free). Located 600 meters from the main pier in Sisal. The food is good. **Club de Patos** is now operated strictly as a hunting club. If interested in hunting call Mayatours in Merida, tel. 23-02-02. Find good fried fish at a small cafe with six tables and no name on the main road one block away from the dock.

Getting There
Buses to Sisal are available at the Merida bus station at Calles 67 and 50 every 30 minutes, 0500-1900, a two-hour ride. Return to Merida from the Sisal bus station in town, two blocks from shore. Buses to Merida leave frequently from 0515-2020. Drivers note: some maps show a coastal road from Chuburna to Sisal; it does not exist! Mexican maps often show roads that are in the *planning* stage. To drive to Sisal from Merida, leave the city on Calle 60 going west, follow the signs that say Sisal-Hunucma. At Hunucma take Hwy. 25 to Sisal.

CELESTUN

A narrow finger of land separates the estuaries of Rio Esperanza from the Gulf of Mexico. On the tip of the one-km strip is a small fishing village, Celestun, which attracts Mexican visitors to its fine swimming beach on the north edge of town. Tourists wishing a luxury seaside resort should look elsewhere, but anyone who takes pleasure in studying birds will want to stop and stay a few days. During winter months, when birds are migrating from the cold climates of the north, many stop over at Celestun for a pause on their way to South America. Others make their home here until nature directs them back north. One of the most startling in hue of the many winged inhabitants is the flamingo, with an "S"-shaped neck and long spindly legs with webbed feet that enable it to walk through shallow water. Its color ranges from pale coral to flame red with black wing tips; and when a group of flamingos is seen standing on a beach, the vibrant colors melting together is a wonderful stroke to the senses. It's not unusual to see a blue heron or an *anhinga* perched on a tree stump jutting out of the water drying its wings.

Sights
The best time for birdwatching is in the morning before the day warms up. Protect yourself from the sun—wear a hat and use sunscreen if you plan on spending a few hours in an open boat on the estuary. Fishing boats along the Rio Esperanza can be hired to go into estuaries to see the birds. One kilometer before you reach town, open launches (available for hire) dock under the bridge that spans the river. These vessels are a little rickety, and some make so much noise they scare off the birds. Talk with your boatman and make sure he's willing to stop frequently for pictures (if that's your wish). The gracious Ositas family (on shore under the bridge) regularly takes people to see the flamingos. The captain will turn off the motor and quietly pole the boat as close as possible without scaring off the flock. Expect to pay approximately US$30-40 per boatload of about four persons.

Other than birds, Celestun offers little entertainment. The plain central plaza is a gathering place for townspeople, but everything moves in slow

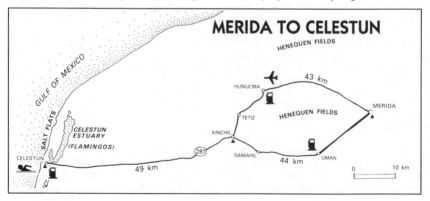

MERIDA TO CELESTUN

HENEQUEN FIELDS

GULF OF MEXICO

HUNUCMA

43 km

MERIDA

TETIZ

HENEQUEN FIELDS

SALT FLATS

CELESTUN ESTUARY

KINCHIL

(FLAMINGOS)

281

SAMAHIL

44 km

UMAN

CELESTUN

49 km

0   10 km

Yucatan flamingos

gear. Across the plaza is a simple pink stucco church, and on the opposite side is the market. The beach on the north edge of town is white and clean, but the choppy water gets silty in the afternoon with the rising wind. In the morning, it's a beautiful walk along the beach which meanders for miles. Many small cafes spill out onto the sand; parents sit at white tin tables, enjoy fried fish and beer, and watch their children play in the surf close by. Except for July and Aug., you and the fishermen have the beach to yourselves. For the artist and photographer, the harbor, with its hundreds of boats, fishermen, curious traps, and mended nets stretched out to dry, provides endless and colorful subjects. **Note:** Photographers, protect your lenses from blowing sand on this coast.

Accommodations

Living is simple and the jet set has yet to discover Celestun, keeping Celestun's few hotels in the budget category. The nicest location is on the sea front. **Hotel San Julio,** constantly blown by the wind, maintains clean simple accommodations with private bathrooms. Though downtown, there's easy access through the patio to the beach. Located on Calle 12 #92 (tel. 1-85-89 for reservations), modest rates. Another smaller hotel right on the beach is **Hotel Gutierrez.** Though Spartan, it has 10 comfortable rooms, each with two double beds and private bathroom. The three-storied stucco hotel is cooled with ceiling fans and sea breezes, especially the front rooms. The tile-floored rooms are clean (if you don't count the

constant, inevitable, blowing sand), with purified water and cold soda for sale in the lobby; about US$10, Calle 12 #22. Also on the same street (which faces the beach) is **Posada Martin,** simple and reasonable, on Calle 12 #76. The local police do not object to people sleeping on the beach, but a combination of wind and sand causes gritty discomfort. Those driving vans and campers are welcome to park on the beach, but pick a spot close to the road where the sand isn't so soft that you get stuck.

Food

A few small seafood cafes edge the beach. **Playarita** and **Restaurant Celestun** are the cleanest and both serve good food. Try a generous fresh shrimp cocktail for about US$3 or a succulent ceviche that ranks with any restaurant in Yucatan.

Celestun beach cafe

This is fish country and the closer you get to Campeche, the bigger the shrimp! Meet the incoming fishermen if you want to buy the freshest. The market is active with a good supply of fresh fruit and vegetables; it opens early and closes at 1300. The *panaderia* makes good bread, and the *tortilleria* opens by seven in the morning.

Services

The **bank** cashes travelers cheques Mon. to Fri. 0900-1330, located on Calle 12 #103. The **long-distance telephone** office (really a private home without a sign) is located on the corner of Calles 9 and 12 across from the plaza, open 1600-1800. Hotel Gutierrez has a phone; sometimes you can make a deal with them. The **post office** is just as difficult to find as the telephone office, but if you must mail a letter or buy stamps, walk toward the

sea to a home at Calle 7, open Mon. to Fri. 0800-1200. You'll find a **gas station** in town, and if you need a policeman, your best chance is to try the Palacio Municipal on Calle 7.

Getting There

From Merida, buses go out from the Autotransportes del Sur station, Calle 50 #531 at Calle 67, leaving hourly 0500-1400 and every two hours 1400-2000. Return trips begin at 0430 and follow the same hourly schedule until 1430; and then every two hours with the last bus leaving at 2030. The trip (OW) takes about one hour. From Merida by car follow the signs out of town marked Sisal-Hunucma. At Hunucma go to Kinchil and pick up Hwy. 281 to Celestun. There isn't a coastal road from Sisal to Celestun.

PROGRESO

Located on the Gulf of Mexico, Progreso is Merida's closest access to the sea, where Meridanos flock to escape the intense heat and sticky humidity of summer. On a good wide highway, it's an easy 33-km drive between the state capital and its once-bustling seaport. During the halcyon days of the henequen industry, ships were a regular part of the scene along the calm Progreso waterfront and its then-amazing two-km-long wharf. Expansive mansions built by henequen entrepreneurs still line the water's edge just east of town; however, they are vacation homes of Merida's well-to-do and some are used for rentals— adapting to the town's burgeoning new economy: tourism.

SIGHTS

Progreso, founded in 1856, is small (pop. 30,000), and with Yucalpeten taking over as the more important fishing port, the town leads a subdued existence most of the year. During the two weeks of Easter holiday, and in July and Aug., however, most of Merida arrives at this beach. The whole town comes to life; all the restaurants are open, usually quiet shops hustle, the beaches are filled with families enjoying the sun and the surf, and Progreso is transformed for the summer. The gra-

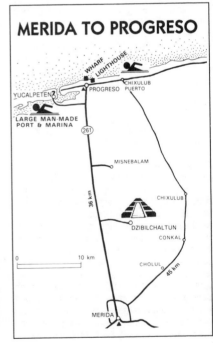

MERIDA TO PROGRESO

PROGRESO

1. Merida-Progreso Bus Station
2. I.S.S.S.T.E. (Hospital)
3. emergency service
4. long-distance telephone office
5. City Hall and Eligio Ancono Library
6. Chazaro Peres Sport Center
7. Church of Purisima Concepcion
8. post office
9. telegraph office

cious walkway along the shore, called the Malecon, is taking on a new look with a tourist center in the middle of town. This is to accommodate the many more visitors anticipated when cruise ships are able to dock offshore.

El Faro Lighthouse

Built (on the site of an earlier lighthouse) from 1885-1891, 40 meters high, it was originally lit with kerosene. Next it was lit with acetylene gas, and finally in 1923 it was electrified. A 1,000-watt lightbulb and a series of amazing reflectors create all the light seen far out to sea. A back-up generator ensures that there's always light to lead the *marineros* through the shallow Gulf waters and into Progreso. Open to the public 0800-1600. **Visitors:** a tip is certainly in order for the keeper after a visit.

Wharf

Progreso's claim that its original two-km-long wharf was the longest stone wharf in the world was true at the turn of the century when it was built. Again it may be the longest wharf in the

world with the new addition that was just completed. This extension and small island (seven km total), was created to enable luxury cruise ships to pull into Progreso for short visits. So far this has not come to pass! The bay is shallow at Progreso because it sits (as does most of the Yucatan Peninsula) on a limestone shelf that gradually drops off into the Gulf. (Geographers conjecture that at one time Yucatan, Cuba, and Florida were all one long extension of land.) The end of the original wharf sat in only 20 feet of water. Hence the extension was needed to accommodate large ships.

For 100 years Progreso's wharf was the scene of heavy international shipping—the days when the henequen industry was in its prime. Today, only a small percentage of henequen products are shipped. In addition, the wharf has lost some of its impact since the protected newer (1968) Yucalpeten harbor, six km west of Progreso, stole most of its thunder. However, some ships still tie up at the Progreso wharf to pick up honey, cement, sisal products, fish, salt, and steel—Mexican products going to foreign ports. The wharf is open to the public, either on foot or in a vehicle as long as you don't try to park. Pier fishermen will find lots of company with abundant local advice and fish stories—in Spanish. They say early in the morning or late in the afternoon you have only to throw out your hook to catch a string of fish in no time!

Beaches

Travelers just returning from the Caribbean side of the Peninsula will find the Gulf coast different. The water doesn't have the crystalline clarity and flamboyant shades of blue that make the Quintana Roo coast famous. But the beach at Progreso is nothing to apologize for; it's open and broad with clean sand. Except for the stormy season (June through Oct.), the warm water is calm. It's possible to walk a kilometer from shore into the sea and still have dry ears. A paved road and inviting palm-lined promenade wind along the breezy Malecon waterfront. The beach is dotted with *palapa* sun-shelters and a few cafes. For the energetic it's an invigorating walk east along the shoreline from the wharf seven km to Chixulub. Don't expect fascinating flotsam and jetsam, but you'll see shells aplenty—plus gangs of people in the middle of summer. During the winter, the beach is practically deserted except on weekends.

ACCOMMODATIONS

Progreso has a limited selection of accommodations. However, the choice for travelers is growing daily. Economy-minded travelers can usually find rooms to fit any budget if they're not too fussy; it's a little harder in July or August. On Calle 79 are several budget hostelries. Also try the **Hostel Malecon,** a big family-style house with a community bathroom for about US$5 s. Or **Hotel Real del Mar,** on the Malecon for about US$10 d. For those looking for cooking facilities, **Tropical Suites** provides stove and frig for about US$17.50, or a regular room for about US$10, just across from the beach. At the west end of town is the small, clean **Playa Linda** with private bath for about US$12 d. **Yaxac-**

tun Hotel is another clean simple hotel with a bathroom, fan, and friendly staff. They offer a Ping-Pong table and a cafe. On the corner of Calle 66 and 25; the rates are about US$9 d. Some backpackers claim to use the beach for overnight sleeping, but if you ask the town authorities for permission, they make it clear that camping is not allowed and that they'll check you into their "free" hotel involuntarily if you're caught. Beaches east and west of town are more likely places to camp than in the center of the promenade, which the town is trying to dress up to attract more tourists.

FOOD AND ENTERTAINMENT

Progreso's cafes are typical of Mexican seaside resorts: if you like sweet, fresh-caught fish you're in luck—but it's hard to find much else. Walk along Calle 79 for several budget cafes. Try **Soberani's** (of chain fame) located at Calle 30 #138; **El Cordobes,** an unpretentious restaurant in front of the plaza, serves economical dishes. Though pricey by Progreso standards, **Capitan Mariscos** is preferred by some, serving excellent seafood in an airy open-porched atmosphere. Despite tales of watered sangria, it was found to be "pure" and tasty. The "Capitan" provides dressing rooms and showers for guests who wish to swim. New small cafes are springing up every day as Progreso begins to be discovered by the world at large; keep looking, you'll find one that suits you.

If you're looking for breakfast on the waterfront in the off-season, when most cafes are closed

PROGRESO HOTELS

NAME	ADDRESS	TEL.
Tropical Suites	Calle 23, Av. Malecon	5-01-17
Playa Linda	Calle 23, Av. Malecon	
Yaxactun	Calle 66 #129	5-03-92
San Miguel	Calle 78 #148	5-13-57
Real Del Mar	Calle 23, Av. Malecon	
Rio Blanco	Calle 23, Av. Malecon	5-00-66
Malecon	Calle 23, Av. Malecon	5-03-85

DRIVING DISTANCES FROM PROGRESO
(DISTANCES IN KM)

From Progreso to:

Chabihau (village)	58
Chelem (village)	14
Chixulub (village)	5
Chuburna (village)	20
Club de Golf Yucatan (golf, hotel)	18
Dzibilchaltun (arch. zone)	16
Dzilam de Bravo (village)	84
Merida (city)	36
San Benito (coconut grove)	23
San Bruno (coconut grove)	30
San Cristanto (village)	52
Santa Clara (village)	72
Telchac Puerto (village)	43
Uaymitun (coconut grove)	17
Yucalpeten (marinas and hotel)	4

until later in the day, don't hesitate to walk into one of them. The cook/owner/family is usually there early. With a friendly request they'll fix you something—usually *huevos motulenos* (Yucatecan egg dish). More than likely you'll have a porch/dining room all to yourself while you watch birds diving for their breakfast in a deserted sea. During the summer, cafes come to life along the promenade in pleasant outdoor surroundings overlooking the beach and waterfront. There's a great bakery on the corner of Calles 27 and 60; for those not watching their cholesterol, they use real butter!

Many of the small restaurants feature live loud music during the holiday periods on the beach. A cinema shows mostly Mexican films. Sailing on the Gulf is available from the port of Progreso: day sailing, sunset trips, fishing, including sailing instructions; tel. 27-85-31. Snorkeling is not a big activity on this coast; visibility is poor much of the year.

SERVICES

On the main street you'll find the **post office** and the **telephone/telegraph office**. Three **banks** are open 0900-1330 Mon. to Fri.; Bancomer accepts Canadian dollars. For **taxi service** call 5-01-71/5-01-85. A **laundromat** is located on Calle 36 #58. In the event of a medical problem there are several **doctors**, all Spanish speaking. A Pemex **gas station** is on the main street one block south of the plaza; closed between 1300-1600. Visit the public market, busy for such a small city. This is a good place to mingle with the locals and experience a small slice of Progreso life.

PROGRESO PUBLIC SERVICES

NAME	TEL.	ADDRESS	HOURS
tourist department	5-01-04	Calle 30 #176	Mon.-Sat. 0900-1300, 1500-1900 Sun. 1000-1300
police	5-00-26		
medical service	5-00-45	IMSS 77 No. 129	(24 hours)
post office	5-05-65	Calle 31 #150 by plaza	Mon.-Fri. 0900-1800 Sat. 0900-1300
telegraph office	5-01-28	Calle 28 and 31	same as post office schedule above
taxi stands	5-01-55 5-01-71 5-01-98		
health center	5-00-53	Calle 74	

GETTING THERE

By Bus
From Merida, buses leave the depot (on Calle 62 between Calles 65 and 67) every 30 minutes daily 0500-2100; allow one hour for the trip. You'll be dropped off at the bus station in Progreso, located a few blocks from the center of town and a short walk from the Malecon.

By Car
Driving from Merida take Calle 60 at the central plaza, go north following the Progreso signs out of the city. Do not try to reach Progreso from Sisal or Celestun on a coastal road; you must return almost all the way to Merida.

For hitchhikers, Hwy. 261 is a good road for finding a ride because of busy traffic between Merida and Progreso; expect lighter weekend traffic.

Tour Groups
It's possible to travel to the Gulf coast with a tour group from any of the many travel agencies in Merida. Some provide lunch, some are longer, some are cheaper—it's easy to shop around since travel agencies are scattered all over Merida.

Independent Tours
Another possibility is to locate an independent cabbie/guide that takes pleasure in showing off the best in his country. Ask a Meridano cabbie to recommend someone. Don't hesitate to haggle over the rate which, depending on time of year and number of tourists, is negotiable. Regular travel guides are unionized and not willing to bargain. For a full day ending back in Merida, the fee will probably be the same for one to four passengers—ask. This can be a good deal if you're traveling with others; if traveling alone pass the word around your hotel. Tell the driver where you wish to go and what you want to see, how long you expect to be gone, your budget limitations for cafes and drinks, and then rely on his judgment.

PROGRESO BUS SCHEDULES

The Progreso Bus Station is located at Calle 29 #151 between 30 and 32.

Progreso - Merida (non-stop)
US$.45 one-way
US$.75 round trip
0500 (1st bus), 0520, 0540, 0600
After the 0600 bus there is one every 15 minutes until 2100.
The trip is about 45 minutes long.

Progreso - Merida (with stops)
US#.35 one-way
0500 (1st bus), 2100 (last bus). Bus leaves every 30 minutes.
The trip is 50-55 minutes long.

Progreso-Yucalpeten
US$.05 one-way
Local Bus System: 0600 (1st bus), 2100 (last bus)
mornings: bus leaves every 20 minutes.
afternoon: every 35 minutes.
Look for sign on the bus: "Puerto de Abrigo"

Progreso-Chixulub
US$.10 one-way
0600 (1st bus), 2100 (last bus)
Bus leaves every 20-30 minutes.

Progreso-Dzilam de Bravo
There are two buses daily: 0700 and 1400.

CHIXULUB

The coastal road from Progreso (east of the wharf) wanders behind a long string of summer houses for seven km to Chixulub Puerto. Many of these houses are available as rentals. Summer is high season, with prices in the same stratosphere. In the winter months the rental fees are quite reasonable, anywhere from US$150-300 monthly, depending on the size of the house. Real estate offices in Merida can help you out, or just ask around town at the beach. Several American and Canadian families regularly spend their winters in Chixulub Puerto.

Chixulub Puerto is a small fishing village with a dilapidated, half-missing wooden pier that no longer accommodates vehicles. However, the nimble-footed local pier fishermen hop across its missing planks and always come in with a good catch. This is a picturesque beach: broad, white, with a collection of worn fishing boats often beached on their sides. If you decide to stay a day or two for some quiet time, there's a motel available. Strolling around the small fishing village, you'll run into a *panadería* (bakery) where you can buy a tasty small loaf of French bread for about US$.50 and *pan dulce* for less. You'll also find a small Conasuper market, and seasonal fruit and vegetable stands by the side of the road.

ACCOMMODATIONS

So far accommodations are limited in Chixulub. You have two choices, the **Vistalmar** is on the beach; rooms have kitchenettes and balconies to enjoy the sunset on the sea. A good seafood restaurant is on the premises with showers and dressing rooms available; tel. 5-00-88. A reader just told us about another called **Chu-Juc Maria**, tel. 5-11-95.

FOOD AND ENTERTAINMENT

La Parilla Mexicana is located on the Progreso/Chixulub road. Good charbroiled meats, pizza, pasta, and salads; Calle 27 near 50. **Las Palmas** advertises itself as the first restaurant in Chixulub to change from sand floors to tile floors, and besides, the food is good. Just order a beer or drink and they'll bring you enough snacky things to make a meal; good seafood. Right next door at **Dino's Disco.** On Friday nights a video-bar comes to life; Saturday night is dance night. **Moctezuma/Chixulub** is a local hangout painted with fluorescent colors so it's easy to see in the dark; good seafood, and liberal snacks served with drinks.

DZILAM DE BRAVO AND VICINITY

Continuing along the coast east from Chixulub, the road parallels the sea for 75 km to Dzilam de Bravo. Along the way are several small villages, all tuned in to life on the sea. Forty km past Progreso is **Telchac Puerto,** the largest of these villages. On the road going into town a large coconut grove shelters **Los Cocos,** a *balneario* (day-use swim resort) with dressing rooms, *palapa* sun shelters, and a restaurant that serves fried fish, beer, and soda pop—prices reasonable and surroundings tropical. Investigate the lighthouse and the small flotilla of fishing boats—great picture possibilities.

Between Telchac Puerto and Dzilam de Bravo the road passes three small villages. On this section of the coastal road you'il see copra drying in the sun and a salt works. Just beyond the small village of **Chabihau** is a narrow strip of sandy beach good for camping. About 10 km farther is **Santa Clara,** located on the inland side of a small lagoon and crossed by many causeways. Strolling around these areas you'll discover several good beaches.

PARAISO MAYA

Located on the Progreso-Telchac road, 16 miles from Progreso and 47 miles from Merida's International Airport, this large new complex is a five-star resort with 163 a/c rooms. The view from the front is the white sand and blue-green water of the Gulf of Mexico and in the rear the scene is a pink lagoon and dozens of species of birds. The hotel offers luxury amenities including a fine restaurant, snack bar, cafeteria, swimming pool, disco, lobby bar, fishing, wind-surf and jet-ski equipment available, beach and poolside games, travel agency, car rental, and a 24-hour ambulance service. Paraiso Maya is a favorite with Canadian snow birds. Rates approximately US$70 s or d. For more information contact: ITI **Amigoteles,** in U.S. and Canada (800) 458-6888, in California (800) 227-0212, fax (714) 494-5088, in Merida Calle 62 #515, tel. 28-13-51, 21-36-09, fax (99) 23-27-00.

DZILAM DE BRAVO

The coastal road from Progreso ends at Dzilam de Bravo. In order to go farther around the Peninsula to San Felipe or Rio Lagartos, you must first return south on any one of the paved roads from the small towns, then catch another northbound road. All the paved roads return to Merida. About 13 km before Dzilam de Bravo, there's a small village cemetery where a wooden grave marker was found with the name Jean Lafitte. Historians question the validity of his burial here, since after his

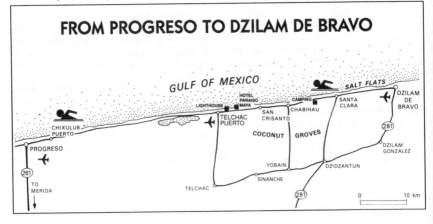

FROM PROGRESO TO DZILAM DE BRAVO

GULF OF MEXICO

SALT FLATS

HOTEL PARAISO MAYA

LIGHTHOUSE

CAMPING

SANTA CLARA

DZILAM DE BRAVO

CHIXULUB PUERTO

TELCHAC PUERTO

SAN CRISANTO

CHABIHAU

281

PROGRESO

COCONUT GROVES

DZILAM GONZALEZ

261

YOBAIN

DZIDZANTUN

TO MERIDA

SINANCHE

TELCHAC

281

0   10 km

Hotel Paraiso Maya

departure in 1826 there's no record of his return. But Pierre Lafitte, his brother, is known to be buried in the cemetery. The Yucatecan fishermen held both brothers in great esteem because of the brothers' good treatment of local sailors. Jean's marker, authentic or not, was moved to the museum at Puerto Aventuras on the Caribbean coast of Quintana Roo. If you decide to spend the night in Dzilam de Bravo, check out the simple **Hotel Dzilam,** about US$10 d.

IZAMAL

Izamal is a fine old colonial town (pop. 25,000) with Maya origins. Arriving Spaniards were determined to alter the importance of Izamal as a pilgrimage destination. Led by Friar Diego de Landa they lost no time tearing down most of the religious Maya ceremonial centers; to add insult to injury, they used the same stones to construct their own city buildings and churches. The original Maya city that the Spaniards destroyed was called Itzamna (variously translated as "City of Hills" or "Dew from Heaven"). The present-day colonial town is mostly ignored by tourists because it's off the tourist track and lacks such amenities as modern hotels. However, the town is well worth a detour.

SIGHTS

The most imposing structure in the small town is the yellow **Convent of Saint Anthony de Padua,** a church-convent complex built on what looks like a broad hill. Actually, the hill is the base of what was once a Maya temple, Popul-Chac, destroyed in the 1600s. The immense base measures 180 meters long and stands 12 meters high. The current church was designed by Fray Juan de Merida; construction began in 1533. Wander through the church grounds, and in one of the stark stone cells you'll see a huge caldron, metal tools, and a hanging rack still used to make candles for church use. The buildings surround a grassy courtyard (8,000 square meters, the largest in Mexico) with 75 arches—once a glorious yellow, now faded and splotched with age. The town plaza is surrounded by buildings all the same color, condition, and arched design with massive porticoed stone pillars and sheltered walkways. They all get a coat of paint periodically, unlike the ancient churches in most of the old out-of-the-way cities. During the colonial period the city must have been a shiny jewel in New Spain's showcase. Because most of the structures in Izamal are the same color, it's often referred to as Ciudad Amarilla ("Yellow City").

Archaeological Zone

Itzamna was already an ancient city when the Spaniards arrived. Although the archaeologists date it from the Early Classic Period (A.D. 300-

600), pottery carbon-dated to 1000 B.C. has been found. When standing on one of the stone stairways on the grounds near the church, you have a good view of a Maya temple called **Kinich Kakmo,** dedicated to the sun god. When you try to track it down from street level the structure mysteriously eludes you, even though the site is only two blocks northeast of the main plaza! One of the tallest pyramids in the Western Hemisphere, it has been only partially restored. If you decide to climb to the top, be aware that the upper stairway is not completely reconstructed. Once on the peak you'll have a striking view of the surrounding brush-covered landscape. Looking east, you can see for 50 km to Chichen Itza. As is the case with hundreds of ruins on the Peninsula, one day it will be excavated and scientists hope ancient rumors will become fact by finding the burial chamber of an honored ruler.

ACCOMMODATIONS AND FOOD

Most travelers to Izamal just pass through, stopping long enough to take a look around, which even with a climb to the top of local pyramid Kinich Kakmo should take no more than a couple of hours. However, if you decide to spend the night, there are few accommodations to look for, all very primitive and close to the main plaza. Ask for: **Hotel Kabul, Hotel Toto,** or **Hotel Canto,** whose rates average US$5-8. Remember, these provide little more than a roof overhead. One reader described the hotel rooms in Izamal as dark dungeons; many visitors opt to visit Izamal for the day only. You'll see several cafes, one under the arches of a yellow building near the plaza across from the bank. A few small stores sell minimal basics. The bank doesn't cash travelers cheques.

TRANSPORTATION

Driving on Hwy. 180 from Merida, turn left (north) at Hoctun; after traveling 24 km you'll reach Izamal. Highway 180 is a well-used road and hitching is comparatively simple during daylight hours. Along the road from Hoctun any second-class bus will stop for you with a wave of your arm.

At any hour of the day, you'll find a queue of *calesas* which serve as taxis parked in front of a broad stairway leading to the church and courtyard. These tiny horse-pulled buggies do an active business carrying locals (often whole families) around town. The *calesas* are not impractical bits of nostalgia for the tourists to admire (though you will), they're the only transportation some families have.

Izamal taxi stand

CHICHEN ITZA

Chichen Itza is one of the finest Maya archaeological sites in the northern part of the Yucatan Peninsula. Largely restored, Chichen Itza is about a three-hour drive from Cancun and about 2½ hours from Merida—a favored destination of those fascinated with Maya culture. Chichen Itza is a mingling of two distant cultures: ancient Maya and later-arriving Toltecs. Though there appears to be differences of opinions rising about the role of the Toltecs, for years scientists have theorized that the oldest buildings at Chichen Itza are good examples of Late Classic Maya construction from the 5th century to the 1100s when the Toltecs invaded and then ruled Chichen Itza for 200 years. The Toltecs built new structures and added to many already in place—all bear a remarkable similarity to those in the ancient Toltec capital of Tollan (today called Tula) 1200 km away in the state of Hidalgo.

Two centuries of mingling cultures added a new dimension to 800 years of Maya history. The carvings found on buildings of different eras vary between the rain god Chac (early Maya) to the cult of the feathered serpent (late Mexicanized Maya). Though Chichen Itza was most likely abandoned toward the end of the 13th century, Maya were still making pilgrimages to the sacred site when Montejo the Younger, the Spaniard who played a role in ultimately subjugating the Maya, settled his troops among the ruins of Chichen Itza in 1533. Although they placed a cannon on top of the pyramid of Kukulcan, they were unable at that time to conquer the elusive Indians, and after a year left Chichen Itza for the coast. The pilgrimages continued.

Today, a different breed of pilgrim comes to Chichen Itza from all over the world to walk in the footsteps of great rulers, courageous ball players, mysterious priests, and simple peasants. Chichen Itza is considered the best-restored archaeological site on the Peninsula. Restoration, begun in 1923, continued steadily for 20 years. Work is still done intermittently, and there are enough unexcavated mounds to support continued exploration for many years into the future.

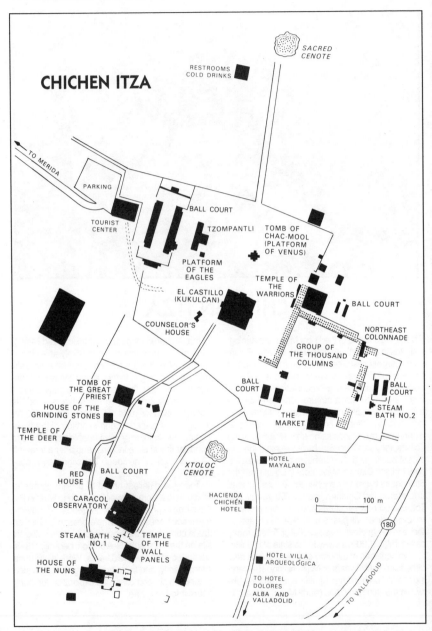

CHICHEN ITZA

Travel Tips

You can easily walk the 10-square-km grounds; two days is a relaxing way to do it, but for those with less time it can be done in a day—not as thoroughly, perhaps, but you will come away with a good idea of what Chichen Itza is about. Wear walking shoes for this entire expedition: climbing around in sandals can be uncomfortable and unsafe. For some, a short walk around the grounds will satisfy their curiosity, and they can say they've "been there." For a ruins-nut, however, the best advice is to spend the night either at a hotel adjacent to the ruins where you can be up and on the grounds as soon as the ticket taker is there (usually 0800), or at the nearby town of Piste with a good shot at getting to the site as early as possible. Two good reasons for arriving early are the weather (it's much cooler in the early hours) and the absence of the crowds that arrive later in tour buses. With two days you can study these archaeological masterpieces at your leisure, have a chance to climb at your own pace, and be there at the odd hours when the inner chambers open (only for short periods each day). This also allows time to return to your hotel for a leisurely lunch (maybe a swim), a short siesta, and an afternoon return visit (free with your ticket). The ruins are open daily from 0800-1700, although some of the structures have special hours (posted on the buildings or ask at the entrance). Admission is under US$1.50 pp, plus a small fee to use the parking lot. The lovely new visitors center offers clean restrooms, cafe, small museum, auditorium where short informative films are shown, bookstore, gift shop, and information center.

CHICHEN ITZA VISITORS CENTER SERVICES AND HOURS	
entrance	0800-1700, under US$2
museum	0800-1700
auditorium	0800-2100
information & Telephone	0800-2200
infirmary	0900-1700
money exchange	0900-1300
restaurant	0800-1700
handcraft booths	0800-2000
light & sound Spanish	1900-1935 US$1
light & sound English	2100-2135, under US$2
parking	0800-2200 US$.50

Children under 12 enter free; free entrance to everyone on Sundays and holidays.

SIGHTS

This large park-like area is easy to stroll through. Eighteen structures have been excavated, many of those restored. The uses for these buildings are not truly understood. Archaeologists can only study and guess from the few "real" facts that have been found. Near the Sacred Cenote a snack bar sells cold drinks, light snacks, postcards, and a few curios. A clean restroom is available at the back of the *palapa* building.

Temple Of The Warriors

On a three-tiered platform, the Temple of the Warriors stands next to the impressive **Group of a Thousand Columns**—reminiscent of Egypt's Karnak. Many of the square, stone columns have carvings still in excellent condition. In 1926 during restoration, a subtemple found underneath was named **Chacmool Temple.** The former color on the columns of the inner structure is still slightly visible. Close to the Thousand Columns on the east side of the plaza is a simple sweat house cleverly constructed with an oven and a channel under the floor to carry off the water thrown against the hot stones to create steam. Indian sweat houses are a combination religious and health-giving experience still used today on American Indian reservations.

The Platforms

Strolling the grounds you'll find the **Platform of Venus** and another called **Platform of Tigers and Eagles.** The flat square structures with a low stairway on each of four sides were used for ritual music and dancing and, according to Diego de Landa (infamous 16th-century Franciscan bishop), farce and comedy were presented for the pleasure of the public.

Temple Of The Bearded Man

At the north end of the ballpark sits the handsome **Temple of the Bearded Man.** Two graceful columns frame the entrance to a small temple with the remains of decorations depicting birds, trees, flowers, and the earth monster. It's doubtful whether anyone will ever know if the unusual acoustics here were used specifically for some unknown display of histrionics, or if it's accidental that standing in the temple one can speak in a low voice and be heard a good distance down the playing field, well beyond what is normal (much like in the dome of St. Peter's Cathedral in Rome). Was this the "dugout" from which the coach whispered signals to his players downfield? Some believe that only the upper class actually watched the game, and that the masses remained outside the walls and listened.

Great Ball Court

Of several ball courts at Chichen Itza (some archaeologists say nine), the most impressive is the **Great Ball Court,** the largest found yet in Meso-

carved serpents on top of the Temple of Warriors

america. On this field, life and death games were played with a 12-pound hard rubber ball in the tradition of the Roman Colosseum. The playing field is 135 meters by 65 meters, with two eight-meter-high walls running parallel to each other on either side of the playing field. The players were obliged to hit the ball into carved stone circles embedded in the vertical walls seven meters above the ground using only their elbows, wrists, or hips. The heavy padding they wore indicates the game was dangerous; it was also difficult and often lasted for hours. (In Diego de Landa's book written in the late 1600s, he mentions in two different places, "The Indians wore padding made of cotton with salt padding.") The winners were awarded jewelry and clothing from the audience. The losers lost more than jewelry and valuables, according to the carved panels on the site—they lost their *heads* to the winning captain! There is a theory circulating that says the *winners* of the game were granted the "privilege" of losing their heads.

Temple Of The Jaguar

On the southeast corner of the ballpark, the upper temple was constructed between A.D. 800-1050. To get there you must climb a steep stairway at the south end of the platform. Two large serpent columns, with their rattlers high in the air, frame the opening to the temple. The inside of the room is decorated with a variety of carvings and (almost visible) remnants of what must have been colorful murals.

Sacred Cenote

Today's adventurer can sit in the shade of a *palapa* terrace and enjoy a cold drink near the sacred *cenote* (say-NO-tay). This natural well is 300 meters north of Kukulcan. The roadway to the sacred well, an ancient *sacbe,* was constructed during the Classic Period. The large well, about 20 meters in diameter, with walls 20 meters above the surface of the water (34 meters deep), is where the raingod Chac supposedly lived; and to con him into producing rain, sacrifices of children and young adults were made here. Human bones have been found here. On the edge of the *cenote* is a ruined sweat bath probably used for purification rituals before sacrificial ceremonies.

In 1885, Edward Thompson was appointed United States Consul in nearby Merida. A young writer greatly interested in the archaeological

the observatory

zones surrounding Merida, he eventually settled in Chichen Itza and acquired the entire area, including an old hacienda (for only US$75). For many years he had studied Diego de Landa's account of human sacrifice still going on at the time of the Spanish conquest. Stories of young virgins and valuable belongings thrown into the well at times of drought over hundreds of years convinced him there was treasure buried in the muddy *cenote* bottom. From 1903-07, with the help of Harvard's Peabody Museum, he supervised the first organized dive into the well. Fewer than 50 skeletons were found, mostly those of children, male and female, smashing the virgin myth. Precious objects of jade, gold, copper, plus stone items with tremendous archaeological value were also dredged from the muddy water.

Thompson set off an international scandal when he shipped most of these important finds to the Peabody Museum by way of diplomatic pouch. He was asked to leave Yucatan and for years (1926-1944) a lawsuit continued over the booty. Ironically, the Mexican court ruled in favor of Peabody Museum, claiming that the Mexican laws concerning archaeological material were inadequate. After the laws were toughened up, the Peabody Museum, in a gesture of friendliness, returned many (but not all) of the artifacts from Chichen Itza's well of sacrifice.

The next large-scale exploration of the well was conducted in the 1960s, sponsored by the National Geographic Society with help from CEDAM (a Mexican organization of explorers and divers

noted for having salvaged the Spanish ship *Mantanceros* in the Caribbean). As Thompson suspected before his untimely departure, there was much more treasure in the *cenote* to be salvaged. Hundreds of pieces (including gold, silver, obsidian, copper bells, carved bone, and other artifacts, plus a few more skeletons) were brought to the surface. In order to see in this well, thousands of gallons of chemicals (an unusual experiment by the Purex Co.) were successfully used to temporarily clarify the water. The chemicals however destroyed many of the blindfish and shrimp in the *cenote*.

Observatory
One of the most graceful structures at Chichen Itza is the **Caracol,** a two-tiered observatory shaped like a snail, where advanced theories of the sun and moon were calculated by Maya astronomers. Part of the spiral stairway into the tower/observatory is closed to tourists in an effort to preserve the decaying building. The circular room is laid out with narrow window slits facing south, west, the summer solstice, and the equinoxes. The priests used these celestial sightings to keep (accurate) track of time in their elaborate calendrical system.

Kukulcan
The most breathtaking place to view all of Chichen Itza is from the top of Kukulcan, also called El Castillo. At 24 meters it's the tallest and most dramatic structure on the site. This imposing pyramid,

built by the Maya on top of another smaller pyramid, was probably constructed at the end of a 52-year cycle in thanksgiving for allowing the world to survive the elements—maybe even Halley's comet! Halley's swept by this part of the earth in A.D. 837 (and most recently in 1986); the construction of the second temple was approximately A.D. 850.

Kukulcan was built according to strict astronomical guidelines. Giant serpent heads repose at the base of the stairs. There are four sides of 91 steps with the platform on the top for a total of 365—one step for each day of the year. On 21/22 March and September (21/22 days of equinox) between 1200 and 1700, the sun casts an eerie shadow darkening all but one bright zigzag strip on the outside wall of the north staircase. This gives the appearance of a serpent slithering down the steep north-facing steps of the pyramid, giving life to the giant heads at the base. It seems to begin at the bottom in the spring and at the top in the fall. This was first noticed only 20 years ago. In the days when there were only a few people on the grounds watching, you could observe not only the serpent slithering down the steps, but also watch the shadow on the ground move toward the road to the sacred well—maybe looking for a sacrifice? Today the ground is covered with people. A visit including the dates of the equinox is a good time to observe the astronomical talents of the Maya, but be prepared for literally thousands of fellow watchers.

Be sure to make the climb into the inner structure of Kukulcan where you'll see a red-painted jade-studded sculpture of a jaguar, just as it was left by the Maya builders over a thousand years ago. Check the visiting hours since the inner chamber is not always open.

Others

The largest building on the grounds is the **Nunnery,** named by the Spaniards. From the looks of it and its many rooms, it was a palace of some sort built during the Classical Period. **Tzompantli,** meaning "Wall of Skulls," is a platform decorated on all sides with carvings of skulls, anatomically correct but with eyes staring out of large sockets. This rather ghoulish structure also depicts an eagle eating a human heart. It is presumed that ritualistic music and dancing on this platform culminated in a sacrificial death for the victim, the head

then left on display, perhaps with others already in place in a gory lineup. It's estimated that the platform was built between A.D. 1050-1200 after the intrusion of the Toltecs.

A much-damaged pyramid, **Tomb of the High Priest** is intriguing because of its burial chamber found within. Sometimes referred to as Osario (Spanish for "ossuary," a depository for bones of the dead), the pyramid at one time had four stairways on each side (like El Castillo) and a temple at the crest. From the top platform, a vertical passageway lined with rock leads to the base of this decayed mound. There, from a small opening, some stone steps lead into a cave about three meters deep. Seven tombs were discovered containing skeletons and the usual funeral trappings of important people, including copper and jade artifacts.

ACCOMMODATIONS

Only a few hotels are within walking distance of the ruins, all in the moderate price range; remember, most of the hotels listed add 15% government tax to the prices listed. **Hotel Mayaland** is a lovely colonial with 64 rooms, private baths, three dining rooms, swimming pool, and tropical gardens. This old hotel has been around since the early 1930s and provides visitors with the ambience of beauty and tranquility. A long winding staircase from the lobby, ornate leaded glass windows in the original dining room, tile floors, tall ceilings, and overhead fans lend an exotic ambience to the lovely hotel.

In 1988, UNESCO declared Chichen Itza the **Heritage of Humanity.** The Mayaland is located in the heart of this archaeological zone with over 100 acres of tropical-fruit and flowering trees filled with unique species of birds. This unique resort is in the process of being renovated (should be finished by the time you are reading this) and is scheduled for a large addition (sometime in 1991) which when complete will offer 164 rooms and Maya-type villas. Rates: about US$80 s or d, villas vary in price, two-bedroom Chac Mool Suite for up to four persons is about US$140, reservations suggested. These prices drop slightly in the summer. From the U.S. call Mayaland Resorts, tel. (800) 235-4079, 311 University Dr., Suite 403, Coral Springs, FL 33065; ask about their package deals including a family plan.

Hotel Hacienda Chichen Itza contains original bungalows of the early archaeologists. The narrow-gauge railroad tracks used in the 1920s for transportation and hauling still go through the outlying hotel grounds. The old mule train is also still in its place, but not used today. This hotel has lots of history, plus private bathrooms, a pool, dining room, and part of the rustic original hacienda. The hotel isn't used in the summer unless the traffic through Chichen is heavy. Rates about US$60 d, reservations suggested; from the U.S. call (800) 223-4084. **Villa Arqueológica,** owned by Club Med, at Chichen Itza is a pleasant hotel. "Almost" deluxe small rooms have private bath; plus *shallow* swimming pool, bar, covered patio, dining room, and a unique library filled with books concerning the Maya are also on the grounds. One of the biggest complaints from readers is that the hotel has no double beds, so as one reader put it, "it makes it difficult for *large* travelers to have romantic nights." The rooms are small though functional and some air-conditioners are noisy (listen to the air-conditioner in your room before you sign the register). But this hotel has a lighthearted ambience with a delightful garden and pool area. Don't forget to bring along your receipt, voucher, or any other communication that says you have reservations and have paid, because without it you could have a problem. This hotel has been known for overbooking. Rates are about US$48 s, $54 d; these prices drop slightly in the summer. Reservations are suggested; from U.S. call (800) 528-3100.

Hotel Dolores Alba, 2.2 km east of the ruins, is rustic, small, clean, with swimming pool, dining room, and private baths; US$20 d. Free transport to the ruins available. Mailing address: Calle 63 #464, Merida 97000, Mexico, tel. 21-37-45. Be sure to designate that you want a room in the Chichen Dolores Alba, since this address also takes reservations for its sister hotel, the Merida Hotel Dolores Alba.

Piste

Piste, 2.5 km west of Chichen Itza, has a unique tradition of providing the work force for the archaeological digs at Chichen Itza. Originally the men were chosen because they were the closest; now it's a proud tradition of the people. Piste is growing up. The once-quiet village is becoming a viable addendum to Chichen's services. More hotels and restaurants are available each month as the number of tourists interested in Chichen Itza grows. Be sure to look around at the many cafes and gift shops as well.

Piste Accommodations

The **Hotel Mision Chichen,** just a few kilometers west of the ruins on Hwy. 180 and just outside Piste is rustic, has a pool, a/c, and dining room, credit cards accepted. Rates are US$65 including breakfast and dinner, rates drop slightly in the summer. Reservations suggested; from the U.S. tel. (800) 223-4084. Nearby, you'll find the **Piramide Inn Hotel and Trailer Park.** With cement pads, electrical and water hookups, the hotel area

Mayaland dining room designed in the early 1920s

is peaceful, grassy, tree shaded, and has a swimming pool. Dining room is open to both hotel guests and trailer guests. Rates are moderate.

FOOD AND ENTERTAINMENT

The only restaurants within walking distance of the site are at the hotels. Check the hours since they're usually open for lunch only between 1230-1500. Bring your swimsuit—lunch guests are welcome to use the pool, a refreshing break in a day of climbing and exploring the ruins. Every evening a **sound and light show** is presented in both English and Spanish at the ruins. The English version is usually the second one of the evening and the fee is under US$2. Other than that there's no organized entertainment in Chichen Itza. However, the guests of the nearby hotels are generally well-traveled people, many with exciting tales to tell. Sitting under the stars on a warm night with a cold *cerveza* swapping adventure yarns is a delightful way to spend an evening.

TRANSPORTATION

From Cancun, Cozumel, Playa del Carmen, Akumal, and Puerto Aventuras many travel agencies and hotels offer day trips to outstanding pre-Columbian Maya sites nearby and some *not* so nearby. Look into the different options. Though some travelers may think a day trip just isn't enough time to really absorb the sights, it may be just what *you* are looking for. For those who wish to explore further, a few options to do it on your own would be renting a car (see "Car Rentals," p. 54), taking a local bus (check with the hotel concierge), or hiring a car and driver for two or three days (local travel agencies can recommend someone).

Chichen Itza lies adjacent to Hwy. 180, 121 km east of Merida, 213 km west of Cancun, and 43 km west of Valladolid. If traveling by car you have many options. The roads to Chichen Itza are in good condition, as long as you slow down for the *topes* (traffic bumps) found before and after every village and school. Hitchhiking at the right time of day will put you in view of many autos on Hwy. 180, but be at your destination before dark or you may spend the night on the roadside; there's little traffic on this road after sunset.

By Public Bus
Local buses leave from Cancun and Puerto Juarez (three-hour trip) to Piste; ask about the return schedule.

By Plane
Small planes offer commuter service to Piste from Cancun, Cozumel, and Chetumal. Check with Aerocaribe, tel. 4-12-31 in Cancun, tel. 2-08-77 in Cozumel, for information and reservations. A sample price is around US$60 OW to Cancun.

Packaged Trips
For some, being independent and free to turn down any unexpected road is the only way to travel. However, for others (maybe those who have never been to a foreign country) who don't wish to

---

BUS SCHEDULE TO CHICHEN ITZA

Local buses available from Merida to Chichen Itza as follows:
Autobuses de Oriente Ado, Calle 69 near 68 and 70, tel. 24-90-55

First-class: Merida-Chichen Itza	Departure Time: 0630
Second-class: Merida-Chichen Itza	Departs every hour from 0500 to 2100
First-class: Chichen Itza-Merida	Departure time: ask at the Chichen Itza tourist center information desk
First-class: Merida-Chichen Itza-Merida	Departs Merida: 0830 Departs Chichen Itza: 1400

drive or take local buses, or just don't know how to go about investigating these off-the-beaten-path destinations should look into packaged trips. Check with your local travel agent, or Sunday travel section of your local newspaper. Several companies in the U.S. specialize in Mexico. For the Yucatan area check with **Mayaland Resorts,** 3111 University Dr., Suite 403, Coral Springs, FL 33065, tel. (800) 235-4079 or (305) 341-9173, fax (305) 344-6547.

Escorted Tours

Escorted tours on modern a/c buses leave daily from Merida. Check with your hotel, or one of the many travel agencies in the city. They offer a variety of tours and prices; check around before you make a decision. The following tour is arranged by Yucatan Trails in downtown Merida (Calle 62 #482, tel. 21-55-52), where you can get price and time schedules. This is a creative way for a traveler to make a short trip to Chichen Itza on the way to Cancun. A scheduled 0900 bus stops at Chichen Itza for a couple of hours, and again in Valladolid for lunch, then drops you off in Cancun, arriving approximately 1800. Your luggage is safe in the same bus for the entire trip. So, although you don't spend a great deal of time at the ruins, you have the opportunity to make a brief visit enroute while transferring from Merida to Cancun. Fare is about US$40 pp including lunch.

Check with your travel agent either in the States or in Cancun or Cozumel; some agencies in Mexico provide a pickup service for those travelers who wish to spend the night at the archaeological zones. There are many other tours available, including custom tours.

VICINITY OF CHICHEN ITZA

THE BALANKANCHE CAVES

Only six km east of Chichen Itza, take a side trip to the Balankanche Caves. Here you'll travel down under the earth and see many Maya ceremonial objects that appear to have just been left behind one day, 800 years ago. Discovered in 1959 by a tour guide named Gomez, it was studied by prominent archaeologist Dr. E. Wyllys Andrews, commissioned by the National Geographic Society. What he saw, and what you can see today, is stirring: numerous stalactites, and a giant stalagmite resembling the sacred "Ceiba Tree" surrounded by ceramic and carved ceremonial artifacts. This was obviously a sacred site for the Maya—a site that perpetuates the mystery of the ancient people: Why did they leave? Where did they go? Who were they? Where did they come from in the very beginning? And what is the secret of their complex hieroglyphics?

At the entrance you'll find a parking lot, a cool spot to relax, small cafe, museum, interesting photos of Maya rituals, and guides; a light and sound show is offered nightly. The entrance fee is under US$1, light and sound show is under US$2; open 0800-1700. Surrounding the site you'll find a botanical garden with a variety of (identified) plants native to the areas around the Yucatan Peninsula.

Travelers Note: Remember that all museums and archaeological sites in Mexico are free on Sundays and holidays, children under 12 always free.

DZITNUP

After leaving the archaeological zone of Chichen Itza continue on the road toward Valladolid. A few kilometers before you reach Valladolid you'll see a small handmade sign that says Dzitnup. At the sign follow the road (about two km off the main road) and you'll find a delightful underground *cenote.* Wear your tennis or comfortable walking shoes and your swimsuit in case you decide to take a swim. After a reasonably easy descent (in

BALANKANCHE CAVES HOURS AND SERVICES	
Museum	0900-1700
Guided tour in Spanish US$1.25	0900, 1000, 1200, 1400, 1600
Guided tour in English US$2	1100, 1300, 1500

Cenote
Dzitnup

a few places you must bend over because of a low ceiling) underground you'll come to a beautiful circular pond of crystal-clear water. It's really a breathtaking place, with a high dome ceiling that has one small opening at the top letting in a ray of sun and dangling green vines. You'll see dramatic stalactites and a large stalagmite; catfish and blindfish swim in the placid water. It's typical of the many underground caverns and grottos that are common around the Peninsula, and well worth the small admission. When returning to the main road at the intersection of the Dzitnup/Hwy. 180, check out the southeast corner where you'll find another *cenote* on private property. For a few pesos they will take you down some steps to an open-air area with a scum covered *cenote*. Seeing the roots from trees at the surface reaching down into the *cenote* far below is an unusual sight.

VALLADOLID AND VICINITY

Take time to visit Valladolid, a short distance from Chichen Itza, and the second-largest city on the Yucatan Peninsula. Very colonial, the city's social life still centers around the downtown *zocalo*. Young couples sit in the park and hold hands, parents with small children enjoy the cool shade on a Sunday afternoon while the kids play hide and seek amidst the trees; this is a great place to meet the friendly Valladolidans. During fiestas, such as Candelaria Day, the park comes alive with music and the cool walkways are lined with stalls selling balloons, pottery, leather goods, and all manner of prepared goodies straight from *mamasita's* kitchen.

HISTORY

The valiant townspeople fought off Francisco de Montejo and his nephew when they attempted to capture the city in 1544. However, Francisco "El Mozo" (the son) was tougher. After finally conquering the city in the 16th century, he built large churches in Valladolid as a reminder to the indigenous people that the Spanish Christians were now in control and would not let up until they totally crushed the people's ancient beliefs—just as they had already crushed many of their temples. Perhaps to the outsider it may look as though this was accomplished, but anyone who has the opportunity to witness a religious event will recognize that the Maya didn't give up their beliefs—they just blended them neatly with the new Christianity forced upon them.

ECONOMY

Valladolid is the center of an agricultural district. Cattle-raising is becoming more popular as well as profitable. Note all the leather-goods shops in the city—great places to pick up belts, sandals, even a saddle! The people of the city, though not rich, appear to enjoy a good life.

SIGHTS

Churches
Valladolid has many churches. Some are no longer used for services, but instead offer exhibits of the city's history (San Roque for instance, Calles 41 and 38). Most of the ornate decorations that once lined the altars were removed either during the Caste War or the revolution. The architecture of these structures is graceful, powerful, and quite remarkable. The most well-known are the **Church of San Bernardino de Sienna** and the **Ex-Convent of Sisal,** built in 1552. The oldest churches in the Yucatan, they're located on Calle 41A, three blocks southwest of the *zocalo*. Also check out the following churches if you're into old architecture: **Santa Ana,** on Calles 41 and 34; **La Candelaria,** Calles 35 and 44; **Santa Lucia,** Calles 27 and 40.

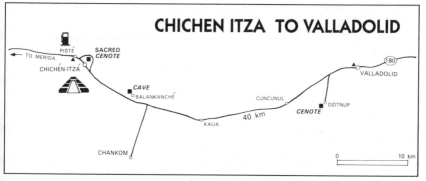

CHICHEN ITZA TO VALLADOLID

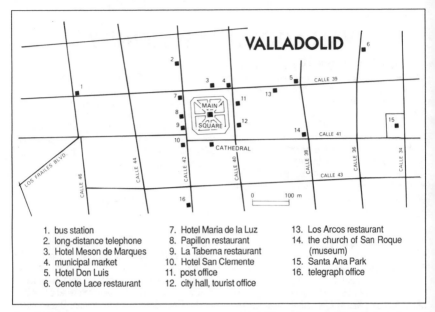

VALLADOLID

1. bus station
2. long-distance telephone
3. Hotel Meson de Marques
4. municipal market
5. Hotel Don Luis
6. Cenote Lace restaurant
7. Hotel Maria de la Luz
8. Papillon restaurant
9. La Taberna restaurant
10. Hotel San Clemente
11. post office
12. city hall, tourist office
13. Los Arcos restaurant
14. the church of San Roque (museum)
15. Santa Ana Park
16. telegraph office

Cenote Zaci

On Calle 36, between Calles 37 and 39, Cenote Zaci still attracts tourists, local and national. This particular lake always has a green scum on the surface which the Mexicans call lake lettuce (supposedly excellent feed for ducks and chickens). You see few gringos swimming in this water, but for about US$1, a young local teacher will make a beautiful dive from the top of a tall tree into the murky water. The cave itself is dark, very large, and littered—a sign of tourism.

When you climb back up the often-slippery stairs, stop at the museum (small thatched huts which house interesting exhibits of the area). You'll find a cafe and bar on the grounds. Open from 0800 till dark; a small admission is charged.

ACCOMMODATIONS

Valladolid offers a good choice of middle-class hotels. If you're looking for real luxury you won't find it; but with a little searching you can discover satisfactory lodging. Being close to the *zocalo* is convenient, since that's where most of the action takes place. However, here's one that's not on the *zocalo* but is really a good bargain for value received; **Hotel San Clemente** is a pleasant small hotel, with a/c, private bathrooms, good food, pool, located on Calle 42 #206, tel. 6-20-08; rates with fan about US$14, a/c US$17. The most expensive is probably the **Hotel El Meson del Marques,** across from the plaza, with a/c, pool, outdoor and indoor eating, often there's no hot water in the evening, gift shop; the building is said to have been the home of an old prominent family. Located on Calle 39 #203, tel. 6-20-73, rates start at about US$28 d. The **Hotel Maria de La Luz** gives a good first impression, with a swimming

VALLADOLID HOTELS

NAME	TEL.
El Meson de Marques	6-20-73
Hotel Maria de la Luz	6-20-71
San Clemente	6-22-08
Hotel Zaci	6-21-67
Don Luis	6-20-08
Ek-Balam	6-23-43

pool and curved sweeping stairway to the second floor—but it appears they spent their entire budget on the outside, since the rooms are quite basic. They include private bathrooms and are fan cooled; located on Calle 42, tel. 6-20-71. Rates about US$14 d. **Hotel Zaci** is fairly nice with plants and trees in the courtyard, a little more expensive, and located on Calle 44 #101, tel. 6-21-67.

A few cheapies include **Hotel Maria de Guadalupe,** which is reasonably clean, within walking distance to the *zocalo,* and close to the bus station. Located on Calle 44 #198, between Calles 39 and 41. Rates about US$11 d. Several others are available, but the only reason to recommend them is the price; so look them over carefully before paying your rent: **Hotel Osorno,** Calle 44 #188, **Hotel Maya,** Calle 41, and **Hotel Lilly,** Calle 44 #192.

SERVICES

You'll find most businesses and shops located on the streets that surround the *zocalo.* **Banks** are open Mon.-Fri. 0900-1330. The **police station** is on Calles 40 and 41, tel. 6-21-34. **Red Cross** is on Calle 40 #212, tel. 6-24-13, open daily 0800-1300, 1600-2000. The **pharmacy** is on Calles 39 and 42, open Mon.-Sat. 0630-2200, Sun. 0630-1300. The **laundromat** is on Calle 41, open Mon.-Fri. 1000-1800, Sat. 1000-1400. The **post office** is on Calle 40 #195A. The **telegraph office** is on Calle 42 #193B, open for money orders Mon.-Fri. 0900-1730.

TRANSPORTATION

The city is located on Hwy. 180, easily reached by bus from Merida, Cancun, Tizimin, and other connecting points. Many people choose to stay over in Valladolid while touring Chichen Itza (40 km distant) because hotels are much more economical.

The city is easy to get around. It's laid out in a grid pattern with even-numbered streets running north to south, odd-numbered streets running east to west. The *zocalo,* at the dead center of the city, is bordered by Calles 39, 40, 41, and 42. Seeing the city on foot is simple; maps of the area are available at the tourist office in the Palacio Munic-

ipal or at most of the hotels that surround the plaza.

TIZIMIN

At Valladolid, Hwy. 180 junctions with Hwy. 295. If traveling to Rio Lagartos follow Hwy. 295 north for about 52 km into Tizimin, center of Yucatan's cattle country. The small town has few tourists, though it has two attractions a visitor might contemplate. One, is a world-class disco called **Stravaganza** (which is rated one of the finest in all of Mexico), and second, flamingo watchers might prefer the two simple hotels in Tizimin over the low rated Hotel Nefertiti in Rio Lagartos. Take a look at **Hotel San Carlos,** Calle 54 #407, tel. 3-20-94, and Hotel San Jorge, Calle 53 #411, tel. 3-20-37. If you decide to stay in Tizimin, get to Rio Lagartos by 0700 and go directly to the Hotel Nefertiti and ask about a guide to the flamingos.

TIZIMIN
TO
RIO
LAGARTOS

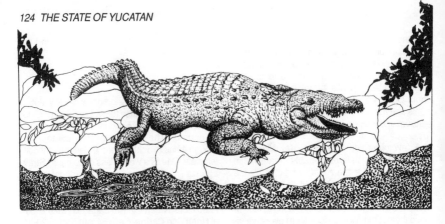

RIO LAGARTOS

A little more than 100 km from Valladolid on the northernmost point of the Yucatan Peninsula is a picturesque small fishing village called Rio Lagartos. A pleasant promenade meanders along the waterfront from where you can watch the fishing boats and the activities of the men who have been making their living plying the seas for generations. The isolated town is gradually catching up with the rest of Yucatan state. Rows of wooden clapboard houses line narrow streets where there are few autos. TV has come to town, cable and all.

However, Rio Lagartos is best known for its colonies of flamingos that return each year to nest. In April, May, and June, literally thousands of pink and cerise *Phoenicopterus ruber* flamingos throng in the shallow estuaries everywhere you look. The locals are very protective of their flamingos; during the brooding season, visitors are not allowed to approach the nesting area for fear they will disturb the birds while they guard their strange-looking mud nests which protrude above the surface of the shoreline. The sounds of outsiders cause them to rise in flight, often knocking fragile eggs from the nests. The rest of the year, it's an easy matter to rent a boat and guide; from Nov. to March there aren't as many birds, but the young are just beginning to color. At hatching, flamingos are mostly white, and at three months the black feathers along their wings begin to grow.

The town of Rio Lagartos is an amazing small community. Like the birds, people build their homes in swampy water that seems to flood a good bit of the land. While visiting you might see a cement foundation being poured right into the water. Besides the growing number of birdwatchers—which is still infinitesimal compared to the visitors to most other cities on the Peninsula—the main industry is fishing; many folks also work 16 km east at the Las Coloradas salt factory (in operation since Maya days). Even today, most of the employees of the factory are Maya.

SIGHTS AND ACTIVITIES

Beach Hiking
Rio Lagartos ("Lizard River") at one time was home to numerous crocodilians but before anyone realized what was happening, the animal was hunted out. Today, unless you set up camp in a mangrove-lined swamp, the only crocs you're likely to see are two kept in a fenced mud wallow on the beach near the hotel.

The small spit of land called Rio Lagartos Peninsula that separates the lagoon from the sea is nine km long from the head of the lagoon to **Punta Holohit.** This is a good walk for beach hikers. Chances are you won't see another soul; the utter isolation encourages the wildlife you *will* encounter. Wear some type of protective covering for your feet since some parts of this peninsula are covered with brush including cactus; other parts of it are quite narrow and you'll have to wade in the water. In certain sections, the beach is covered with shells, bits of coral, and driftwood; in other spots, you'll be accompanied by hundreds of water birds.

As you get closer to Punta Holohit, the land becomes marshy and finally gives way to a lagoon (three are nearby). The end of the marsh is about one km from Punta Holohit. Make arrangements to be dropped off or picked up at either end by the Nefertiti Hotel van.

Birdwatching

The shallow lagoons and canals wind for many kilometers in and around small islets and sandbars—an ideal place for birdwatching. Look for plover, white egret, heron, cormorant, pelican, and especially that star of Lagartos—the flamingo. As you meander through the water, you'll see flocks of these startling-pink birds covering the white beach or standing one-legged in the shallow water. The combination of colors—blue sky, white sand, green water, pink birds—is a breathtaking effect you'll not want to rush. The sandy beach is often tinted a soft coral, covered with the silky feathers of flamingos. Bring your binoculars and camera.

Tours To The Flamingos

Through Hotel Nefertiti you can arrange an early morning boat tour to the flamingos. Nicasio Kumul Medina is really a great captain/guide. He has an open launch and for about US$40 he will take one to four people on a three-hour trip from the boat dock near the hotel through the estuaries to find the birds (if you're going to see crocs, it's in these estuaries that you'll find them). Nico motors you out quickly but when the birds are spotted he knows all the right methods to get as close as possible without scaring them into the air and onto another (farther) sandbar. He cuts the motor at just the right moment, pulls out his long pole, lets the current help, and if you have a camera, he tries to keep the sun at your back. Be sure you settle your price early on. Even for just one person, Nico still charges US$40 for the boat trip.

The busiest times are in July (especially the feast day of Santiago on the 20th) and Easter week. Starting in May and through June and July, the flamingos fly to a distant cove and build their mud nests. They are kept under close scrutiny by the Ministry of Ecology and Urban Development. No one is permitted to get close to the nesting birds since the slightest disturbance sets them off, knocking the fragile eggs into the water with their long skinny legs. More and more people wish to see the flamingos. Hopefully these numbers will

Flamingos lay one egg in a cone-shaped mud nest.

be kept under control, adhering to the **Pronatura** guidelines of low-impact eco-tourism, which makes tourists happy as well as happy reproducing flamingos.

Bring protection from the sun (it's an open boat), water, and a snack if you can start out before breakfast—the best time to begin the day when flamingo hunting. Nico is well versed in the habits of flamingos, willing to tell you how they build nests, how, if a storm hits at nesting time, the usually calm water sweeps away their one egg, and how some shady characters (not locals) steal eggs and young birds to sell on the black market —illegal since this is a national park.

It's best to make arrangements the day before. Try to be on the water by 0700. Get all particulars straight before you begin your trip: how long it will last and where you will be going. During the heavy tourist season (Dec., March, April, July, and Aug.), expect the price to be higher. Don't forget your Spanish dictionary, for Nico, along with most of the local guides, speaks little English. Serious photographers: bring your long lens (a tripod helps, too) since many of your pictures will be taken with the birds in flight, seldom closer than 300 meters (unless you get lucky).

Swimming

For swimming, go to the north side of the Rio Lagartos Peninsula, a narrow strip of land that separates Gulf water from shallow estuaries. The only way there is by boat, and the easiest and most economical is a small shuttle run by the Nefertiti Hotel, usually less than US$2 pp RT (with a minimum of five people—find other travelers at the hotel or on the beach). The driver will drop you off at the beach and return at an agreed time. This beach is very isolated, and although there's usually a breeze, it's hot with no shade. Bring protection from the sun's intense glare, plus food and water—there are no facilities of any kind and very likely you will be the only visitors. Beware of the sudden drop-off when you go into the surf; within a meter of shore the water is waist deep. The sea here has a slight current and is not clear, so snorkeling isn't worth the effort of carrying equipment. As for fishing, don't bother in the estuaries: they're so shallow that you'll foul your line. On the seaward side, it's possible to find a sandbar where you'll probably have luck. If your Spanish is good, you might be able to arrange (for a fee) a trip with a fisherman in his boat. Bring your own equipment.

ACCOMMODATIONS

Hotel Nefertiti is the only hotel in Rio Lagartos. Located on the waterfront, you can't miss it—it's the only multi-storied building in town. The rooms are Spartan, and not noted for cleanliness, but have bathrooms and (usually) hot water. The first-floor rooms seem to have constantly wet floors from moisture oozing through the cement floor; ask for a second-floor room and inspect it carefully. Rates are about US$12.50 d. They have an open-air *palapa* dining room which seconds as a disco some nights. An alternative is to inquire at the cafe on the plaza; there may be a place where

you can hang your hammock for a reasonable fee. Another alternative if you have flexible transportation is to spend the night in Tizimin and rise very early and take a chance on catching Nico or another guide free that morning.

Camping

Along the shore about one km east of the Nefertiti Hotel, you'll come across a lovely *cenote*. Circling the *cenote* is a parking lot. There's little else in the area, but it's a beautiful, clean, and pleasant stopover for picnicking and swimming. It makes a quiet, deserted campground at night, but expect lots of company during the day when families and kids come to swim and have a good time, especially on weekends. Another alternative for camping is the **Rio Lagartos Peninsula** (see p. 124). About five km from Punta Holohit is a large flat area where the peninsula is so wide that you needn't worry about surf hitting your campsite. Don't forget your toothbrush, for there's no corner drugstore close by—nor even a corner.

FOOD AND ENTERTAINMENT

Again you have a limited choice in Rio Lagartos. The **Hotel Nefertiti Restaurant** is about as good as it gets. The seafood is always fresh; and though the decor is garish, the prices are moderate and you'll come away satisfied. For something cheaper, try the **Restaurant Negritos,** on the plaza; it serves mostly seafood. The small market has a limited selection but will keep body and soul together nicely. If you have transportation, a pleasant surprise is the food at the **Restaurant El Payaso** in San Felipe, 12 km west of Rio Lagartos. At night, music from the Hotel Nefertiti disco, **Los Flamingos,** filters across the water and can engulf the hotel (including almost every room). If you happen to have quarters overlooking the disco, you might as well use the free ticket they present you with when you check in because you'll "enjoy" the music one way or another.

SERVICES

Few services exist in this small town. Bring plenty of film for your camera, and don't bother even to look for a long-distance phone. The basketball court you may have noticed in the center of town is really the central plaza. On one side, you'll find the Catholic church, on the other, city hall. This little town really loves basketball, and if you happen to be there at the right time of the year, you'll see the whole town turn out for a game. The local authorities are helpful and willing to answer questions—when their office is open.

GETTING THERE

By Bus

From Valladolid, it's a two-hour bus trip to Rio Lagartos—which does not include the layover in Tizimin, where you have time to look the town over as you wait for your transfer. There are no direct buses to Rio Lagartos. The bus drops you off in front of the Restaurant Negritos, which also sells bus tickets.

By Car

At Valladolid, Hwy. 180 (heading north) junctions with 295 through Tizimin, ending in Rio Lagartos 103 km later. Beware of the *topes* (traffic bumps)! You'll find these all over Mexican highways to slow the traffic down as it approaches a village or a school. However, the *topes* (sometimes called *puntas* or "bridges") in this northern section of the Peninsula are higher and more deadly than most. If you hit these at any speed over 20 km an hour, the underside of your car will be destroyed—quickly! The highway in this north country has little

traffic and it's easy to find yourself speeding right along the two-lane road—and a *tope* sign gives short warning. Gasoline is available along this route; you'll find **Pemex** stations at Valladolid, Tizimin, and Rio Lagartos. On the Yucatan, one should never let fuel get low: although stations may be closely spaced, they suffer occasional non-delivery—leaving them empty for as much as a day or two. Top off your tank frequently. Driving along this part of the Peninsula, you'll find the landscape arid, mostly inhabited by range cattle. As is recommended in all of Yucatan, don't drive at night. It's very dark; animals often lie in the middle of the road; or worse, pedestrians walk in the road, invisible until hit.

Cycles

The roads on most of the Peninsula are flat. Highway 295 between Valladolid and Rio Lagartos is especially inviting to bikers. Though it's 103 km, the road has comparatively little traffic. Don't count on any commerce once past Tizimin until you reach Rio Lagartos, and as described, that's minimal.

Tours

If you're in Merida and would like to see Rio Lagartos and the birds with an escorted group, contact the **Yucatan Trails Travel Agency** (Calle 62 #482, tel. 21-55-52), which offers a two-day bird-watching excursion. This includes an overnight stop at the Hotel Nefertiti.

VICINITY OF RIO LAGARTOS

LAS COLORADAS

This small settlement is named for the color (mineral-laden reds and purples) of marshy swamps that surround the village. These ponds have been producing salt for centuries; Maya history indicates that they used the valuable mineral as an important trade item throughout Mesoamerica. Deposits in the water also inadvertently produce the brilliant colors of flamingos that nest in estuaries nearby! If you're interested in seeing what salt is like before it comes out of your shaker, check at the factory office. People will either refer you to the hotel

tours in Rio Lagartos or may offer you a personal tour of the premises. To get to Las Coloradas, go east on the crossroads one km south of Rio Lagartos. Travel about 14 km, till you cross the only high bridge across the river; continue another two km and you'll be in the small village.

You can travel by bus from Rio Lagartos but the only real reason to come to Las Coloradas is to see the flamingos—and the bus schedule pretty well rules that out. From Rio Lagartos buses leave daily at 1100 and 2000, returning at 1300 and 0500, double check the schedules, they change frequently. The road has a reasonable amount of traffic, so hitching is possible from the crossroad near Rio Lagartos. If while trekking you should see a boat close by going out to watch flamingos, you can usually join them en route if there's room (for a fee). There's little to see at Las Coloradas except maybe a hot little-league baseball game played near the road leading to the canals. There's a refreshment stand, but few other facilities.

SAN FELIPE

If you like small villages on the sea visit San Felipe, a fishing town 12 km west of Rio Lagartos. The small settlement offers few amenities but provides a relaxed and friendly atmosphere especially in the off-season. During spring and summer, the town fills up with campers; but during the rest of the year not many out-of-towners can be seen. Make sure you have pesos with you because you won't find a bank or post office (closest are at Panaba where there's a Bancomer).

San Felipe doesn't have a hotel, but if you find yourself unable to leave and are without camping equipment, ask at **La Herradura** grocery store (one block from the pier) about house or room rentals around town for very little money. These are not really designed for tourists, contain limited furnishings, and may be in need of a broom. There's a **cinema** (Cinema Morufo), a city hall (across from the cinema), and a good little restaurant called the **Restaurant El Payaso,** Calle 8 #55, open almost daily 0730-1830. Serving mostly seafood (great *ceviche),* prices are moderate and there's a bathroom for customers.

Camping

Most visitors who plan to stay over bring camping equipment and cross the estuary to Rio Lagartos Peninsula to set up their tents. In busy times, this wide flat area with tall shade trees near the tip of Point Holohit becomes a regular tent city. For a ride across the estuary, ask around at the stone wharf in San Felipe; a fisherman is always willing to haul you and your gear for a small fee. Tell him when you want to be picked up. If you're visiting for the day without any gear, you can swim out from the pier to a close islet for a lazy afternoon. Most of these mangrove islets and sandbars in the estuary are wonderful for birdwatching and a little isolated contemplation surrounded by the soothing sea.

Getting There

San Felipe can be reached by bus from Tizimin. If you're driving, fill up your gas tank before you leave Rio Lagartos or Tizimin since there's no gas station in between. Highway 295 meets an intersection one km south of Rio Lagartos; turn left (west) onto a single-lane paved road. When you come to a well-marked fork, take the road on the right, go past the cemetery on the edge of town and into San Felipe. Here, the road dead-ends on the main street which parallels the waterfront. This last section of road is one lane with turn-outs every kilometer in case you meet traffic coming in the opposite direction. The rule of thumb seems to be that outgoing vehicles closest to a turn-out pull over to allow incoming vehicles to pass.

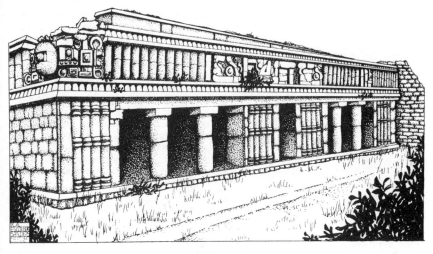

UXMAL

Located 80 km south of Merida (one-hour drive) in a range of low hills covered with brush, Uxmal is believed to have been the hub of a district of about 160 square km, encompassing many sites, including Kabah, Sayil, Labna, and Xlapak. The Maya word Uxmal (oosh-MAHL) means "Thrice Built," referring to the number of times this ceremonial center was rebuilt—in fact, it's believed that Uxmal was built five times. In many instances structures were superimposed over existing buildings, built almost entirely in the "Puuc" style of pure Maya design (without outside influences such as the Toltecs at Chichen Itza). Puuc indicates the "hill" style of construction (because of the location). The work at Uxmal was begun in the 6th and 7th centuries, the Classic Period. It is characterized by delicately carved pieces of stone which were worked mosaic style into delicate designs and rich facades. After surviving a thousand years, some of the sapodilla-tree lintels—the cross pieces over doorways and windows—were removed by John L. Stephens, taken to the U.S., and were (tragically) destroyed in a fire along with many other priceless pieces. Many consider Uxmal to be the most ornate and complete complex yet found on the Peninsula.

HISTORY

Varied historical claims have been made about this Classic site. Some believe that it was founded by Maya from Guatemala's Peten in the 6th century. Others contend that it dates back even further, perhaps to the Pre-Classic Period. By the time the Spaniards arrived it had been abandoned. An account of an early visit was given by Father Lopez de Cogulludo who explored the ruins in the 16th century, long after the Indians had abandoned the site. Without any facts to go on, he referred to the Quadrangle of the Nuns (Las Monjas) as the dwelling of the Maya "Vestal Virgins," who kept the "Sacred Fire." This comment demonstrates the beliefs the first Spaniards held about the evil of the Maya cult, based on some of the sacrificial rites they observed, no doubt. Cogulludo was followed by Jean-Fredric de Waldeck in 1836 who published a handsomely illustrated folio showing the structures of Uxmal peeking over thick brush. He compared them with the ruins of Pompeii. Only a few years later, the famous adventure duo, John L. Stephens and Frederick Catherwood, began their well-documented journey through the Peninsula in 1841. In the interim,

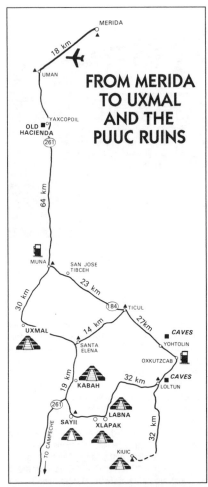

FROM MERIDA
TO UXMAL
AND THE
PUUC RUINS

the Indians must have cleared plots of land around Uxmal to plant corn, since Stephens comments that ". . . emerging from the woods we came unexpectedly on a large open field strewn with mounds of ruins and vast buildings on terraces and pyramidal structures grand and in good preservation"—shown beautifully by Catherwood's sketches.

Frans Blom

The first real excavations began in 1929 led by the noted Danish archaeologist Frans Blom. Blom was involved in many archaeological digs in the Maya hinterland, and his wife still lives among the Chiapas Indians today (see p. 176) carrying on her own work with the Indians she has come to love and crusade for—trying to save their Chiapas rainforest as well as their culture. Since Frans Blom, many other archaeologists have worked with the Mexican government at Uxmal; the result is a fine reconstructed site open for the enjoyment of the public. Much more will one day be excavated, and who knows what exciting finds will be discovered! But for now the small area (700 by 800 meters) of Uxmal presents some of the finest examples of pure Maya design, without Toltec influence.

Precious Water

Unlike most Maya centers in Yucatan, Uxmal was not built around a *cenote,* since there are none in this arid part of the Peninsula. Rainwater was collected by manmade installations of *chaltunes* (cisterns) built into the ground, sometimes right inside a house or under a patio. Another method for saving water was the use of *aguadas* (natural holes in the ground) that in time had silted solid. Because of the almost total absence of surface lakes or rivers in Yucatan, the collection of water was of prime importance for the survival of the Maya. Most of their religious ceremonies and idols were devoted to the worship of Chac, the rain god. The constant threat of drought inspired the people to build great centers of worship, with hundreds of carvings and mosaics representing him and his prominent, long, hooked nose.

THE TEMPLES OF UXMAL

House Of The Magician

This "pyramid" is the tallest on the grounds, rising 38 meters—shaped in a distinctive elliptical form rather than a true pyramid. The west staircase, facing the nunnery and quad, is extremely steep (60° angle). Before you begin your climb do some leg stretches to loosen your muscles! Under this west stairway you can see parts of the first temple built on the site; a date on a door lintel is A.D. 569. On the east facade, the stairway has a broader slant, and though it's still a steep incline, it isn't nearly so hard on the legs. In the upper part of the east staircase you can enter an inner chamber which is **Temple 2. Temple 3** consists of nothing

Uxmal

more than a small shrine at the rear of Temple 2. Climbing the west stairway brings you to **Temple 4** and an elaborate Chac mask with an open mouth large enough for a man to pass through. **Temple 5** dates back to the 9th century and is reached by climbing the east stairway. From this viewpoint you'll be able to see the entire site of Uxmal and the surrounding brush-covered Puuc hills.

Nunnery

The Nunnery, northwest of the House of the Magician, is a courtyard covering an area of 60 by 45 meters, bound on each side by a series of buildings constructed on platforms of varying heights during different periods of time. The buildings, which contain numerous small rooms, inspired the Spaniards to name it after the nunneries in Spain.

House Of The Turtles

A path leads south from the Nunnery to the House of the Turtles. This simple structure is six by 30 meters. The lower half is very plain, but the upper part is decorated with a frieze of columns; a cornice above that has a series of turtles along its facade. The turtle played an important part in Maya mythology.

Governor's Palace

Just south of the House of the Turtles is the Governor's Palace, considered by some to be the finest example of pre-Hispanic architecture in Mesoamerica. It sits on a large platform and measures almost 100 meters long, 12 meters across, and eight meters high. With 11 entrances, the lower facade is plain, but the upper section is a continuous series of ornate carvings and mosaics of geometrical shapes and Chac masks. Two arrow-shaped corbel arches add to the delicate design of this extraordinary building. A double-headed jaguar in front of the palace (presumed to be a throne) was first found by John Stephens in 1841.

UXMAL VISITOR CENTER SERVICES AND HOURS

entrance	0800-1700, under US$2
museum	0800-1700
auditorium	0800-1700
information booth	0800-1000
infirmary	0900-1700
restaurant	1200-2200
handcraft booths	0900-2000
light & sound, Spanish	1900-1945, US$1
light & sound, English	2100-2145, under US$2
parking	0800-2200 $1000 pesos

Note: Children under 12 enter free; free entrance to everyone on Sundays.

The Great Pyramid
Another large structure is the Great Pyramid (30 meters high), originally terraced with nine levels and a temple on the top. According to early explorers, at one time four small structures sat on each of the four sides of the top platform described as "palace-like." The top story is decorated in typical Puuc fashion with ornate carvings and stonework depicting flowers, masks, and geometric patterns.

Others
Walking through the grounds you'll find many other structures and a ball park. Visit the **Dovecote, Temple of the Old Woman** and **Phallic Collection, Temple of the Phallus,** other small structures, and as yet unexcavated mounds. You can pick up a guide (or he'll try to pick you up) at the entrance of the ruins. If you feel a need for this service, be sure you agree on the fee before you begin your tour. Also something to remember: every guide will give you his own version of the history of the ruins, part family legend (if you're lucky) and part fairy tale. And let's face it, no one

Hacienda Uxmal Hotel

really knows the history of this obscure culture shrouded by the centuries. Many good books are available on the archaeological ruins of the larger sites (see "Booklist"). Grounds are open from 0800-1700, admission charge is under US$1. A light and sound show is presented each evening in Spanish (1900) and English (2100); admission under US$2.

ACCOMMODATIONS

Uxmal is not a city; don't expect services of any kind. There are a few hotels with restaurants, and nothing else close by. To do justice to this fascinating antiquity, plan at least a full day to explore thoroughly. Because Merida is only an hour away, it's easy to make this a day trip by bus or car. Or continue on and spend the night in Ticul, 65 km (one hour) farther.

In Uxmal you have your choice of three excellent hotels within walking distance of the ruins. All are in the same price category—US$40-50 d. For budget accommodations a little farther out take a look at **Rancho Uxmal,** humble but clean and with a great restaurant. Other alternatives for budget accommodations are in Merida or in Ticul (see pp. 78-84 and p. 142).

Hotel Hacienda Uxmal
This older colonial-style favorite is in the process of being renovated and added to. For years it's been a favorite of visitors, with beautiful tile walkways and floors, large old-fashioned rooms with heavy carved furniture, tropical garden around the swimming pool, gift shop, and bar. A spacious dining room serves typical Yucatecan food as well as a broad selection of Continental meals. A new restaurant is being added and probably the most unusual addition is an arts and crafts *palapa* where guests can try their hand at making their own pottery and learning how to weave under the auspices of a local artisan. A kiln on-site will finish the work in time to take home. Rates: about US$70 d. Reservation information address: Royal American Marketing, 3411 University Dr., Suite 403, Coral Springs, FL 33065-5059, tel. in the states and Canada (800) 235-0479, in Florida (305) 753-8105, fax (99) 25-23-97.

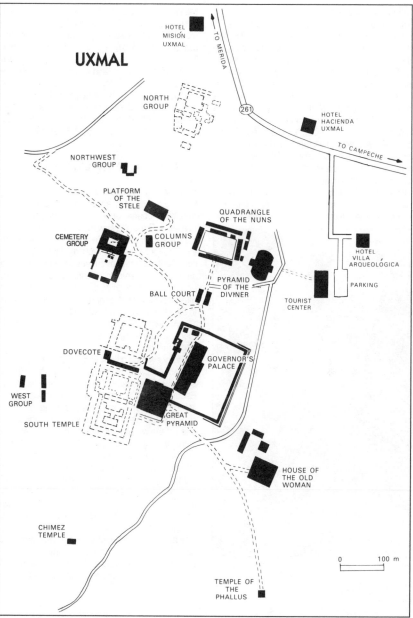

UXMAL

HOTEL MISIÓN UXMAL

TO MERIDA

261

HOTEL HACIENDA UXMAL

TO CAMPECHE

NORTH GROUP

NORTHWEST GROUP

PLATFORM OF THE STELE

CEMETERY GROUP

COLUMNS GROUP

QUADRANGLE OF THE NUNS

HOTEL VILLA ARQUEOLÓGICA

PARKING

PYRAMID OF THE DIVINER

BALL COURT

TOURIST CENTER

DOVECOTE

GOVERNOR'S PALACE

WEST GROUP

SOUTH TEMPLE

GREAT PYRAMID

HOUSE OF THE OLD WOMAN

CHIMEZ TEMPLE

0   100 m

TEMPLE OF THE PHALLUS

Villa Arqueológica
This hotel, newest of Uxmal's three hotels, is owned by a branch of Club Med. A clone of its sister hotels in Coba and Chichen Itza, the rooms are small, attractive, and functional, with twin beds on built-in cement platforms (no double beds available), a/c (a few readers have complained that the air-conditioners can be noisy), and private bathrooms with shower. Both floors look out onto a tropical courtyard. The flower-covered patio has a sparkling (shallow) pool, outside bar and table service, covered cabaña area, and a complete library on the history and culture of the Maya. You'll find some French dishes along with local specialties in the large dining room. The rates are about US$44 d and $38 s. Lunches and dinners average about US$11 pp—à la carte menu only. For more information and reservations, write to Club

learning to embroider

Med Inc., P.O. Box 29805, Phoenix, AZ 85038, tel. in U.S. (800) 528-3100. A little farther down the road (1 km) but still walking distance is **Hotel Misión Uxmal.** Transport to the ruins is available. This has all the modern amenities including a pool, bar, dining room, and nice rooms with private bath and a/c. Credit cards accepted, rates about US$65 d, including breakfast and dinner; if you only want a sandwich or soup or snack, just ask, it's available. Mailing address: 14 W 95th St., New York, NY 10025, tel. in U.S. (800) 223-4084.

FOOD AND ENTERTAINMENT

All three hotel dining rooms welcome visitors for lunch. Expect to pay about US$10.50 for a complete three-course lunch; ask what light meals are available. Bring your swimsuit for an after-lunch dip—great for cooling down before you return to the ruins for the next go-around. At the Uxmal Visitors Center located at the entrance to the ruins a small cantina serves cold drinks and light meals, and a kiosk just outside the entrance to the ruins offers cold drinks. If driving, another alternative is to take the road back toward Merida (Hwy. 261), 18 km north to Muna, or 11 km south to Santa Elena, where there are small cafes in the villages and a few on the road.

Every evening a **light and sound show** is presented in Spanish (1900) and English (2100) at the ruins overlooking the Quad of the Nunnery. Escorted tours to the shows are available from Merida. If you've never seen one of these shows, check it out. It's mood-altering to sit under the stars in the warm darkness surrounded by stark stone remnants and listen to Latin-accented voices and a symphony orchestra echo in stereo from temple to temple, narrating the (so-called) history of the Maya while colored lights flash dramatically on first one and then another of these stark structures. Sometimes Mother Nature adds her own drama: the rumble of thunder from a distant storm, or jagged streaks of luminous light in a black sky. The already eerie temples reflect a supernatural glow evoking the memory of the Maya, their mysterious beginnings and still unsolved disappearance. Admission is under US$2; reserve and buy tickets either at hotels in Uxmal, or at government tourist offices and travel agencies in Merida.

SHOPPING

The new visitors center at the entrance to the Uxmal site is modern and beautiful. With the visitor in mind, the center offers clean restrooms, gift shops, a small museum, an auditorium where a short film promoting the Yucatan Peninsula is shown, a bookstore with a good supply of English-language books about the various ruins on the Peninsula, an ice cream shop, and a small cafeteria and cantina.

Outside the entrance are kiosks where local women sell the *huipil* (Yucatecan dress). Their prices can be much better than in gift shops; frequently they're made by the saleswoman or someone in her family. Some dresses are machine-embroidered or made of polyester, though many are still handmade on white cotton with bright embroidery thread. Be sure you get what you want. The *huipiles* worn by Maya women always look snow white with brilliant colors. Don't forget to bargain.

The only other shopping at Uxmal is at the small gift shops adjoining the hotels near the ruins. Most of them sell the usual curios, clothing, tobacco, postage stamps, and postcards. The exception is the **Villa Arqueológico** where high-quality Maya reproductions depicting ancient idols are displayed. You can find reproductions in many places, but unlike these, most are not of the best quality and have very little detail. Here, the prices reflect the excellent workmanship.

GETTING THERE

Local buses leave Merida's main bus station (Calle 69 #544) daily starting at 0800 and continuing frequently throughout the day. Check at the bus station in advance since schedules are apt to change. Allow at least one hour for the trip (79 km)—be sure to check the return time to Merida. Buses to Uxmal leave Campeche from the ADO station (Gobernadores 289).

If driving, the highway (261) from Merida to Campeche City passes close to the Uxmal ruins, and is a good road. From Merida the drive takes about one hour, from Campeche allow two hours (175 km southwest). Travel agencies in Merida have tours available to visit the ruins at Uxmal. (See "Travel Agencies" in "Merida," p. 93.) Check with the government tourist office at Teatro Peones Contreras on Calle 61 in downtown Merida for more information.

BUS SCHEDULES TO UXMAL FROM MERIDA

AUTOTRANSPORTES DEL SUR
Calle 69

DEPARTING MERIDA	0600, 0700, 0900, 1200, 1500, 1700
DEPARTING UXMAL	0830, 1130, 1430, 1730, 1930

VICINITY OF UXMAL

MUNA

From Uxmal traveling north, Hwy. 261 passes through the rustic city of Muna. Lovers of 17-century architecture might enjoy a look at the large Franciscan church. In the late afternoon sun, the facade with its lacy belfries glows a mellow gold, almost hiding the decay that adds to its appeal. Early in the morning on the edge of the plaza, women sell small quantities of fresh fruits and vegetables. Opposite the plaza, a series of open stalls offers cold drinks and Yucatecan snacks including good *panuchos* (mini-burrito types); for the big appetite, go for the *tortas* or tamales. Try **Katty's** for a good breakfast; clean bathroom available. **Kristie's Curios,** a handicraft store next to Muna's gas station, has good bargains for curios and clothes, but buy soda pop anywhere else—it's cheaper. The boss, former manager at Loltun Caves for INAH, speaks English.

Close-by, **Yaxcopoil** (yawsh-koe-poe-EEL), a turn-of-the-century hacienda, is right off Hwy. 261 between Merida and Uxmal and is clearly marked. A half-hour visit (about US$.45) gives a great insight into what life must have been like in the days when Mexican haciendas operated like small fiefdoms. Hundreds of Indians provided the labor necessary to grow and harvest the thorny henequen plant which, until after WW II, made the owners of these small kingdoms millionaires. At Yaxcopoil there are remnants of the 1890s and 1900s furniture used in the drawing rooms and dining rooms giving a hint of the gracious life the *patrones* enjoyed. Take a look into the kitchen with its unique wood stove made from white tile, pictures of the family, framed documents showing dates of events, even the old safe. This is a stroll into the past. With luck you may have Ernesto Cuitam Yam as your guide . A Maya, he was born in Yaxcopoil. His parents are both still alive, 87 and 90, and tell of life on the hacienda when they worked—under much different conditions than now.

PUUC RUINS

An entire day could be spent making a loop from Uxmal to the Maya ruins of Kabah, Sayil, Xlapak, Labna, through the village of Oxkutzcab to see the caves of Loltun (see "Oxkutzcab," p. 140), and Mani. For the most part these are small sites and easy to see or photograph quickly, and the ornate Puuc design is well worth the time and effort.

Kabah

Kabah was constructed in A.D. 850-900. On Hwy. 261, 19 km south of Uxmal, structures are found on both sides of the highway. The most ornate building is the **Codz-Pop,** dedicated to the rain god, Chac. This temple is 45 meters long and six meters high. Part of the original rooftop comb (at one time three meters high), with its uneven rectangular openings, can still be seen. The entire west facade is a series of 250 masks with the typical elongated, curved nose, some almost a complete circle. This is Puuc architecture with a busy Chenes influence. The Chenes design, a name given by archaeologists to the heavy and ornate style, was added onto the existing structures. The beige, rust, brown, and gray colors come from the oxides in the earth that engulfed the building for so many years. Small pits on each mask are said to have been used to burn incense or oil; Codz-Pop must have shone like a Chinese lantern from great distances throughout the rolling countryside. Inside the building are two parallel series of five rooms each.

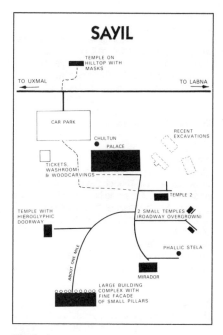

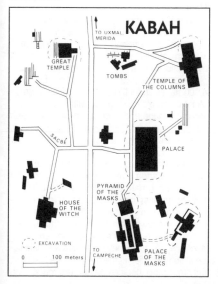

The Arch

West of the road is the impressive **Arch of Kabah.** It is presumed that this arch marks the end of a ceremonial *sacbe* built by the Maya from Uxmal to Kabah. A few more structures have been partially restored—look for the **Great Temple, Western Quadrangle,** and the **Temple of the Columns.**

Sayil

A short distance brings you to a side road and to Oxkutzcab (Hwy. 184); follow this road to Sayil (in Maya this word means "anthill." This is probably the most imposing site of the Loop. Several hundred known structures at Sayil illustrate a technical progression from the earliest, unornamented building to the more recent ornate **Palace** constructed in A.D. 730. The Palace is a large impressive building, over 60 meters long, with three levels creating two terraces, again showing the outstanding architectural talents of the Classic Period. The second level is decorated with Greek-style columns and a multitude of rich carvings including the everpresent rain god and one distinctive portrayal of a descending god (an upside-down figure also referred to as the bee god). By A.D. 800 this site was abandoned.

Because of the lack of rainfall in this area, *chaltunes* are found everywhere, including the sites of the ceremonial centers. One example of a *chaltune* that holds up to 7,000 gallons of water can be seen at the northwest corner of the Palace. Other structures to visit at this site include the fast-decaying **Temple Mirador** (on a path going south from the Palace) and the monument of a human phallic figure beyond.

Xlapak

Six km farther on the same road (east of Sayil) is the Xlapak turnoff. Though this Puuc site is small, do stop to see the restored building with its curious carvings: tiers of masks, curled Chac noses, collonettes, and geometric stepped frets. It's easy to pick out the light-colored areas of restoration compared to the darker weathered stones that were covered with bushes and soil oxides for so many years. The word Xlapak in Maya means "Old Walls."

Labna

Another Maya arch of great beauty is at Labna, located three km beyond Xlapak. More correctly the arch should be referred to as a portal vault. Be

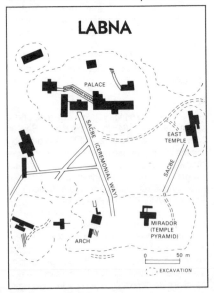

LABNA

PALACE

SACBE (CEREMONIAL WAY)

EAST TEMPLE

SACBE

MIRADOR (TEMPLE PYRAMID)

ARCH

0   50 m

⌐ ̄ ̄¬ EXCAVATION

sure to examine the northeast side of this structure to see two outstanding representations of thatched Maya huts, one on each side of the portal. This arch is one of the largest and most ornate built by the Maya; the passageway measures three by six meters.

The Palace

This Puuc-style structure was built at the end of the Classic Period, about A.D. 850. The elaborate multi-room pyramid sits on an immense platform 165 meters long, and the structure is 135 meters long by 20 meters high. A *chaltune* is built into the second story of the Palace and, according to archaeologist George Andrews, at least 60 *chaltunes* have been located in the Labna area, indicating a population of about 3,000 residents within the city.

El Mirador

This stark square building stands on a tall mound with a roof comb gracing the top. The comb on the small temple was originally decorated with a carved seated figure and a series of death heads. The carvings were still in place in the 1840s when John Stephens traveled through the Peninsula. The elements and time continue to wreak their destruction on the ancient structures of the Maya.

Mani

This small town, north of Ticul, was the scene of early surrender by the Xius (prominent Maya rulers with descendants still living in the state of Yucatan). Montejo the Elder quickly took over and by the mid-1500s a huge church/monastery complex was completed in only seven months by 6,000 slaves under the direction of Fray Juan de Merida. This old building, still with a priest in residence, is huge and in its day must have been beautiful with graceful lines and pocket patios. Fray de Merida also designed and built similar buildings at Izamal and Valladolid.

Historians believe it was in Mani that Friar Diego de Landa confiscated and burned the books held in reverence by the Maya. These codices, the first books produced in North America, were hand-lettered on fig bark carefully worked until it was thin and pliable, then coated with a thin white plaster sizing and screen folded. According to Landa they were filled with "vile superstitions and lies of the devil." Since that time, only four more codices have been found. The most recent (1977), though doubted to be genuine at first, is gaining more and more credibility among archaeologists. The remaining three books are in museums in Dresden, Paris, and Madrid. Replicas can be seen at the Anthropological Museum in Mexico City. The destruction of the codices was a monumental tragedy not only for the Maya—the loss to the world is incalculable. Only a little progress toward learning the mysterious glyphs has been made; who knows, the destroyed books may have been the lost key to their language, their history, and their mystery. It is hoped that other codices exist and will someday turn up—perhaps in an unexcavated tomb still buried in the jungle. Many villages still practice the ancient rituals of their ancestors and appoint keepers of the sacred records. However, these people have learned from the experiences of their ancestors and tell no outsiders of their task.

OXKUTZCAB AND VICINITY

This small village is known by outsiders because of its proximity to the caves of Loltun. The town itself is ordinary, but the people are friendly and appear semi-prosperous. Land in the area is fertile, and most mornings farmers and their families from outlying areas come to the produce market to sell large quantities of fruits and vegetables by the crate—unusual for most small-town markets. Approaching Oxkutzcab you travel through acres of healthy tall corn fields, giving you the same feeling you would have in a farm town near Kansas City, Missouri. Suddenly you're surrounded by citrus groves, banana trees, and coconut palms. Then you remember—you're in the tropics!

Triciclos
A large Franciscan church faces a barren plaza with ugly cement benches and a strange gazebo in the center. A graceful arched building along one side of the plaza is the government center. While looking around you find more examples of stark 16th-century Spanish-influenced architecture. Be careful crossing the streets—you might get run down in the bicycle traffic or overtaken by its three-wheeled cousin *(triciclo)* seen in many small towns all over the Peninsula. Similar to an Indonesian *becak,* it has a more utilitarian look and no overhead protection. But the result is the same: providing cheap transportation for the family, with dad (or paid "cabbie") pedaling in the back, mom and the kids sitting up front. When not filled with people it's used for hauling anything from a crate of live chickens to a modern TV set. Oxkutzcab's morning streets bustle with people coming to market, big and little trucks parked hither and yon unloading crates of healthy fresh produce. At 1300 all of this activity quiets down and with commerce completed, folks pack up and go home.

Triciclos *are fuel-efficient taxis seen all over the Peninsula.*

LOLTUN CAVES

Seven km southeast of Oxkutzcab, Loltun's underground caverns are the largest known caves in Yucatan. In addition to being a fabulous natural phenomenon, Loltun is an important archaeological find. Loltun means "Rock Flower" in Maya and in the caves are carvings of small flowers. Hieroglyphic inscriptions on the walls are "guestimated" by the guides to be more than a thousand years old. Throughout, *chaltunes* are placed strategically under the dripping roof to catch water. This saved water was called "virgin water," important in ceremonies that Maya priests directed to the rain god.

A Guided Walk

No one is allowed to visit the caverns without a guide—and for good reason. Loltun is immense, and it would be very easy to get lost in the meanderings from grotto to grotto, up and down, in total

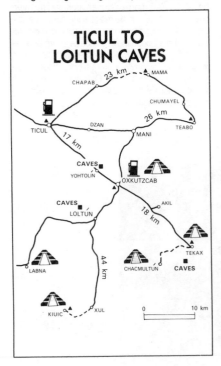

TICUL TO LOLTUN CAVES

LOLTUN CAVES ARCHAEOLOGICAL ZONE HOURS	
Guided tours about US$1	0930, 1100, 1230

darkness. (Select caverns have been wired for light and are turned on and off by the guide as the group moves through.) If you understand Spanish you'll enjoy a few giggles from the stories and anecdotes the guide weaves into his commentary as you stroll through chambers once lived in by thousands of Maya Indians.

Along the way the guide points out common artifacts used by the Indians such as stone *metates* (corn grinders) in the "kitchen." Numerous natural formations bear a startling resemblance to certain persons (like the Virgin of Guadaloupe) and animals (such as the distinct head of an open-mouthed tiger). Giant columns stand from floor to ceiling and when tapped give out a resonant hum that echoes through the darkened passageway. You'll see the stone-carved head now referred to as the Head of Loltun found by two Americans, Jack Grant and Bill Dailey, during an archaeological dig in the caves in 1959-60.

Toward the end of the two-hour tour you come to an opening in the roof of an enormous two-story-high cavern. The sun pours into the blackened room creating dust-flecked shafts of golden light. The gnarled trunk of a towering tree grows from the floor of the cave hundreds of feet up through the sunny opening, and flocks of birds twitter and flit in and around the green leafy vines that dangle freely into the immense chamber from above—breathless sights and sounds of nature not soon to be forgotten. Don't miss Loltun Caves.

Practicalities

Wear walking shoes in the caves. For the most part it's an easy two-km walk; however, it's dark, damp, and in a few places the paths between chambers are steep, rocky, and slippery. Buy your tickets (about US$1) at the office next to clean restrooms (no restrooms in the caves). Tours begin daily at 0900, 1130, and 1330. Have five or six thousand pesos for the guide at the end of the trip (he'll ask for it). Lectures are *usually* given in

Spanish only, but ask for an English-speaking guide when you buy your ticket; you might get lucky.

If you arrive early or need lunch or a cold drink after walking through the caves, stop at **Restaurant Guerrero,** a small cafe next to the cave exit.

The owner is friendly, the beer is cold, the food is good and moderately priced: *poc chuc* (barbecued pork fillet) with bean soup and handmade tortillas hit the spot. Escorted tours are available from Merida; contact Yucatan Trails Travel Agency located at Calle 62 #482, tel. 21-55-52.

TICUL

A busy small city, Ticul has a population of 20,000. Almost everyone is on a bicycle, motorcycle, or a *triciclo,* a three-wheeled bike with a small "seat" in front that serves as the local taxi service. For about US$.30 most townspeople can get a ride home from downtown, shopping bags and livestock included. For about US$1.20 the *triciclo* and driver can be hired for an hour.

It's a toss-up whether to designate Ticul a pottery town or a shoemaking center—it's really both. Shoes are offered for sale in many small shops lining the streets, and according to some Meridanos the prices are a bit cheaper here for good leather *zapatos* than in Merida. Signs extolling *fabricas* (factories) tell of the good value of visiting and buying pottery direct from the potter—complete with location directions. It's well worth a visit to one of these small *fabricas* to watch the artist at work, and probably the most famous is Arte Maya on Calle 23 #301 as you approach town on Hwy. 184 from Muna.

The raw clay used to manufacture urns, platters, bowls, and teapots is found at the hacienda Yo'k'at. The small factory/instruction center on the west side of town specializes in unglazed terracotta reproductions of classic Maya art. From the highway it's easy to spot, with very large (about two-meter-tall) miniatures of pyramids and idols as well as an awe-inspiring wall covered with masks of the Maya era. Operated by artist Wilbert Gonzalez, the gallery provides a selection of work: from that of his beginning students that's just "so-so," to outstanding, one-of-a-kind pieces done by Gonzalez himself. These pieces are crafted in terra-cotta as well as jade. They aren't cheap, but are museum-quality art. Gonzalez's work bears a special mark identifiable by him and Mexico's Anthropological and Historical Art experts so that there will never be a repeat of his incarceration for three months in the Mexico City jail for stealing original Maya art, when in fact the works were original Wilbert Gonzalez art.

SIGHTS

An elaborate high-domed 18th-century cathedral faces the plaza; next to it is a Franciscan monastery built 200 years earlier. Visit the popular marketplace in Ticul—the earlier in the morning the better—which has a good choice of fresh produce with some unusual fruits. In July and Aug. try the *guaya,* a cousin of the litchi nut. This fruit grows on trees in clusters, and from a distance resembles green grapes, but on closer examination they're much larger, with the same texture, size,

Maya art by artist Wilbert Gonzalez

and color of the outer green skin of a walnut. Crack the skin and eat the refreshing sweet jelly around the seed—tasty! Ticul, an agricultural center, is a pleasant small city and a good place to get an idea of Mexican life in the slow lane. You'll find few tourists.

ACCOMMODATIONS

Budget travelers find Ticul a good spot to overnight while visiting the Maya ruins on the "loop." These are simple hotels, check them out closely before signing the register. The **Hotel San Miguel** is clean and cheap, with rooms for about US$7 d, on Calle 28 near 23. Probably the nicest hotel is the **Hotel Sierra Sousa,** about US$8 d, clean, with fan and bathroom, located on Calle 26 near 23, opposite the market. **Motel Cerro Inn** (on the outskirts west of town) is a rustic motel with private bathrooms, lots of cooling shade trees, ceiling fans, and a large outdoor restaurant. Rooms are about US$7 d. For reservations write to Motel Cerro Inn, Ticul, Yucatan, Mexico. There's room for a few self-contained RVs on the motel premises (no hookups available). The owner is friendly and will make arrangements to accommodate RV caravans downtown, providing water and a small generator for about US$5 per day per RV. Another small hotel, **Conchita,** is located on Calle 21 #199.

FOOD

The open-air restaurant at the **Cerro Inn** serves good, simple food at reasonable prices. The cafe is open for breakfast, lunch, and dinner; good *huevos rancheros.* **Los Delfines** is a fine, clean restaurant serving better-than-ordinary food, located on Calle 23 #218-C, tel. 2-00-70. On the menu you'll find great seafood as well as a delicious beef *torta.* Try the chile relleno stuffed with shrimp—excellent! Another nice *tipico* eating spot is the **Restaurant Los Almendros,** north of the highway on Ticul's main street. Only Maya specialties are served and this is reputedly the originator of *poc chuc,* a very popular meat dish served all over the Yucatan Peninsula. A branch of this cafe (same name) is in Merida.

SHOPPING

Ticul is a center for leather and pottery, with ceramic and shoe shops on all the streets. In front of the cathedral, **Centro Artesano** carries locally handcrafted items. Though prices here are often the best, the shops have a better selection. If the local townspeople shout "heepie, heepie" at you, don't be alarmed. They're not expressing an opinion, they're inviting you to see their *jipi* hats, more commonly known as Panama hats. All through this area and near the Campeche border, folks have small underground rooms (caves) in their backyards where they weave the hats and store them during the dry season so the fiber of the *jijipa* (hee-HEE-pah) plant stays soft and supple while being woven. A few local merchants carry the fiber hats, but most are sold in the larger cities of Merida, Cancun, Cozumel, and Campeche.

GETTING THERE

Ticul is on the loop from Uxmal that takes in the important Maya sights of Kabah, Sayil, and Labna. Located 14 km west of Mani and 86 km southeast of Merida, odd truck-buses (passengers stand in the back of a truck) travel frequently between Muna, Ticul, and Oxkutzcab. Fare is about US$.20.

THE STATE OF CAMPECHE

THE LAND

Occupying the southwest section of the Yucatan Peninsula, the state of Campeche is bordered on the north and east by the state of Yucatan, on the northwest by the Gulf of Mexico, on the southeast by the state of Quintana Roo, on the southwest by the state of Tabasco, and on the south by Guatemala. Campeche covers 50,952 square km, with a population of over 600,000. In the north, the land is dry; however, just a few km south of the Campeche/Yucatan border, rivers begin to run, and the land becomes green and tropical. Several fine harbors are nestled along the Gulf coast and just a few km inland, rolling hills rise to low, jagged mountains.

CLIMATE

Though only a few hundred kilometers apart, the northern and southern parts of the state exhibit vastly different climates. The arid north stands in stark contrast to the thick lush rainforest of the southern and eastern parts of the state, which receive as much as 1,500 mm (60 inches) of rain each year. While the north has little visual water, in the south abundant lakes and rivers flow into the Laguna de Terminos. The farther south the more humid the weather. Even here some areas become parched after a long dry period.

FAUNA

Campeche harbors a variety of animals including peccaries, jaguars, tapirs, armadillos, ocelots, and deer; all can be seen (often close up) with a hike into the bush and a lot of patience. Bird hunting is a popular sport supported by quantities of wild duck, wild turkey, and pheasant. Other more beautiful birds (for watching only) include flamingos, parrots, and herons. The coastal waters along the Gulf are thick with barracuda, swordfish, dolphin, tuna, snapper, as well as lobster and shrimp from the tiniest to the largest.

HISTORY

Several Maya towns in various pockets of the state are believed to have been trade centers between central and southern Mexico, as well as important crossroads between the north and east part of the Peninsula. Twenty years after the first Spaniards arrived in Campeche, it was finally conquered by Francisco de Montejo. The state's capital, also called Campeche, was founded on 4 Oct. 1540, and soon developed into the major port of the state. During the 16th and 17th centuries the city was attacked repeatedly by vicious European pirates—it was destroyed and rebuilt several times over a period of many years. The Spanish crown finally approved the expenditure of funds to build a magnificent wall with protective bastions. This mighty rampart of immense proportions had gates that heaved open to give sanctuary to vessels fleeing from ships flying the "skull and crossbones." Portions of the wall are still standing. For years a part of the state of Yucatan, in 1863 Campeche became an independent state.

STATE OF CAMPECHE

ECONOMY

Lack of roads and communication systems isolated Campeche (along with the rest of the Peninsula) from the development of the rest of Mexico. Only since the beginning of the 1950s has Campeche really begun to enter the 20th century and join the outside world. Good highways have been built; logging the precious woods of the rainforest remains high in economic contributions; agriculture is starting to thrive; fishing has grown from a family industry to big business; and the greatest boon of all has been the discovery of offshore oil. With some fine archaeological sites attaining fame, tourism is also developing within the state.

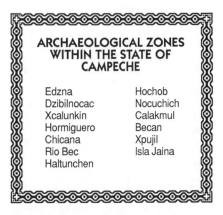

ARCHAEOLOGICAL ZONES WITHIN THE STATE OF CAMPECHE

Edzna	Hochob
Dzibilnocac	Nocuchich
Xcalunkin	Calakmul
Hormiguero	Becan
Chicana	Xpujil
Rio Bec	Isla Jaina
Haltunchen	

CAMPECHE CITY

Campeche, capital of the state of the same name, is a growing city with a population of 250,000. The city lies along the Gulf coast and is approximately five meters above sea level. Campeche is a latecomer in the growth of tourism compared to Quintana Roo and Yucatan. However, in recent years the city has realized the potential of its old wall, *baluartes,* and Maya ruins. These attractions, along with the feeling of old Spain, are drawing more tourists than ever. It has a long way to go before it's considered a tourist destination, however, and as a result today's travelers benefit from low prices. For example, Campeche's Ramada Inn is one of the most moderately priced of the entire chain.

HISTORY

Campeche's Pre-Columbian past is rich in Maya legend and its colonial past is steeped in pirates' lore. During pre-Hispanic times the Campechean coast bore the title of *La Ruta Maya* ("Route of the Maya"), a main artery for Maya traders traveling by land and sea. Ah Kim Pech was a medium-sized village on the shore of a small bay surrounded by hills. Until 22 March 1517, when the first Spaniards arrived in their village, the Maya people had never seen a white man. After 25 years—25 years of bloodshed for both the Spaniards and Indians— Maya power in Ah Kim Pech had been destroyed.

Despite the difference in arms (the Spanish musket against the Indian lance), innate intelligence and a deadly determination to repel the intruders gave the Maya a cunning that persisted an entire generation.

Pirates
In 1542 the present city of Campeche was established by Montejo the Younger, whose family conquered the Indians in Merida. After the Spaniards gained control of Campeche harbor, the financial attention of Francisco Hernandez de Cordoba (appointed viceroy to Mexico by the king of Spain) and Juan de Grijalva (Spanish explorer) enabled the city to blossom. Campeche City was destined to become a jewel of Spanish colonial development. The riches of the Peninsula were regularly channeled to Spain from here in ships belonging to the Spanish king. Tales of this great treasure drew the attention of those who resented Spain's hold on the fabled riches of the New World; seagoing highwaymen were determined to get their share—and more. A crafty breed of pirates began regular attacks on ships carrying the king's gold and silver. From 1558 for almost two centuries, the city of Campeche was harassed, burned, and sacked by buccaneers who'd taken up permanent residence—208 km away—on the Island of Tris (today called Ciudad del Carmen).

Accounts of Campeche's wealth eventually traveled through every major port in Europe; pirates (such as Laurent Graff "Lorencillo," Brasiliano, John Hawkins, William Parck, Diego el Mulato, Barbillas, James Jackson, and Pie de Palo "Pegleg") came all the way from England, France, Portugal, and Holland. In the 17th century the pillaging and killing increased. On 9 Feb. 1663 the buccaneers joined forces, gathered their ships on the horizon, and launched a furious attack. They completely wiped out the city, killing men, women, children—the worst massacre in the city's history!

Walled City

Finally, after so much misery and so many deaths, the Spanish crown agreed that the city needed

detail of beautiful tilework of the former Church of San Jose

protection. A plan was formulated and quietly the work began. On 3 Jan. 1668 the cornerstone of the new walled city was laid. The "wall" that surrounded Campeche was stout stone construction, from three meters thick to ship's height. Four gates in the wall were placed strategically around the city. Indeed, in an effort to make this bastion impregnable, the wall extended right into the water, with huge gates that allowed ships to pass through into the fort! Though finishing touches weren't made until 36 years later, the completion of a sturdy bastion (its counterpart unknown in the Americas) finally gave Campecheans a security against their invaders that would ultimately end the era of invasion. Still, isolated attacks upon the coastal cities south of Campeche continued from the pirates' notorious base island. In 1717, determined to wipe the bandits out, Captain Don Alonso Felipe de Aranda led a sneak attack which routed or killed all the pirates and burned their ships. Once and for all peace reigned over the Gulf coast.

After The Pirates

The next 200 years were spent developing a peaceful society, including the growth of an economy not dependent on the shipment of silver and gold. The initial rumblings of Mexican independence began during the second decade of the 1800s. By 1832 Mexico was free from Spanish colonial rule, many years and many presidents passed before peace settled over the country. Campeche, though isolated from much of greater Mexico's turmoil, suffered from its own problems of development. For years Campeche was part of an alliance with Merida, but in 1863, several years after the Caste War, it seceded and became part of the Federal Republic of Mexico as an independent state.

The People

Before the Mexican revolution, Campeche City was inhabited almost exclusively by descendants of colonial Spaniards. During the early glory days after the wall was built and the pirates were destroyed, life was good for the landowners. The Indians were slaves and suffered the same indignities as their fellows in the rest of the land. In 1813 the first moves were made to abolish slavery. Campeche settled into an era of humble existence that saw few economic changes for many years.

Campeche central plaza

The main industries were fishing and logging. The fishing trade helped the economy, but it was a local business until it began exporting fish to the U.S. and other countries in the 20th century. Even after tourists began visiting Mexico in the 1950s and '60s, the Peninsula was still not commonly considered a destination on visitors' itineraries.

Oil
Only after oil production began in earnest in the 1970s did the average Campecheans start living above the poverty level. All along the Gulf coast the oil industry is growing. And if the value of a barrel of crude quits its volatile swings, Mexico should benefit by its enormous quantities of "black gold" still untouched.

SIGHTS

Central Plaza
Located near the sea, the central plaza is bordered by Calles 8, 10, 55, and 57. This charming spot provides a resting place between walking tours around the city. Renovated in 1985, contemporary wrought-iron fences and benches have been installed. Though Campeche is endowed with the charm of 1700s architecture, the city fathers seem determined to add the cold glitz of spaceshapes, plastic, and glass. But even with its modern gazebo in the middle, the square's feeling of antiquity is overwhelming. The central plaza is bordered on one side by **Cathedral Concepcion,** the oldest Christian church on the Yucatan, constructed from 1540-1705. On Calle 10, the plaza faces **Los Portales,** another aging building with a graceful facade and arcaded passageways.

Old-time Sunday concerts are held in the plaza and the band could have stepped out of a Norman Rockwell painting, black shiny-brimmed hats and all. And don't be surprised when you don't hear Latin rhythms: some nights it's a great oompah band—with French horns, flutes, violins, and bassoons—blaring forth the excitement of a great orchestra. The plaza is the heart of the city: families gather, friends meet, and children run and play. The scene is reminiscent of evening time in small Spanish cities. The square glass building near the waterfront with the colorful mosaic is the **Palacio de Gobierno.** The concrete building next to it that somewhat resembles a flying saucer is **Congressional Hall.**

Regional Museum Of Campeche
This museum, located on Calle 59 between 14 and 16, is housed in a lovely old building with a colorful history, **The Casa del Teniente del Rey.** Its exhibits are a combination of colonial and archaeological/anthropological artifacts. Among other things, you'll see the famous jade mask from Calakmul. When Mexican archaeologists found the mask six years ago it was in many pieces; it has since been put together. Don't miss the exhibit of the wooden contraption used to deform the heads of newborn infants, giving them the deep

lofty guardhouse of old Spanish fort

sloping forehead considered beautiful by the ancient Maya. On display upstairs are many of the arms used in the days of the marauding pirates. **Note:** All museums in the state are open 0800-2000, Sun. 0800-1400, and are closed on Mondays. Small admission fee is charged every day except Sunday.

Forts

Many remnants of the city's fortifications remain more or less intact. Though neglected for years, even partially destroyed to make way for trolley tracks, the remaining ramparts have managed to survive modern architects and violent storms, and lend a wonderful old-world ambience to Campeche. What was formerly the sea wall and shipyard within the gate was filled in some years back to make way for a wide avenue and new buildings on the modern waterfront. You can visit seven of the eight original forts—**San Francisco, Soledad, Santiago, Santa Rosa, San Pedro, San Juan,** and **San Carlos**—now used as public buildings. Beneath some of them remains a labyrinth of passageways that at one time connected with various houses in the city and were used by women and children to elude kidnappers during attacks by ferocious buccaneers. If you have a guide, ask about the tunnels; some will take you to the few that are open, though most have been sealed for years.

Fort San Miguel

Fort San Miguel, 2 1/2 km west of town, has 18th-century construction including moat and drawbridge. One can feel the terror that motivated inhabitants to build such sturdy protection—so sturdy that it has survived 200 years. To get to the fort, follow the coastal road south until you come to the large statue of a man with a raised arm, a work entitled "The Resurgence of Campeche," then follow the signs.

Fort Soledad

Fort Soledad is the site of many stelae found in Campeche in a hall called **Dr. Roman Pina Chan.** Many of these carved stones are said to be 1,000 years old. This is the largest fort on the city's seaward side. See the Maya fountain close by. Easy to find near the waterfront on Calle 8 across from the central plaza; small entry fee.

Fort Santiago

Here you'll find the **Jardin Botanico Xmuch Haltum,** a small garden with many species of plants native to the arid plains in the north and the green jungle of the wet southern region. This walled garden is a short but worthwhile trip. Fort Santiago is located on Av. 16 de Septiembre near the waterfront. As well as enjoying the garden, each of these ancient gates is a wonder of architecture which shouldn't be missed.

Baluarte San Carlos

On the southwest corner of Circuito Baluartes is the former *baluarte* called San Carlos. It was one of the first fortresses built, today flanked by the Governor's Palace and the state Congress building. Between Calle 8, the Progress Fountain, and Av. 16 de Septiembre.

Larrainzur Indians (Oz Mallan)

1. Chiapas woman (Ministry of Mexico Tourism); **2.** weaving *henequen* (Oz Mallan);
3. cacao plantation (Oz Mallan); **4.** working the back strap weaver in San Cristobal (Oz Mallan)

1. jungle wildflowers; **2.** fruit, Cozumel; **3.** Yucatan orchid; **4.** water lilies; **5.** red ginger, Belize; **6.** *flamboyane* tree, Cozumel (all photos by Oz Mallan)

1. manatee mom and baby (Jess White); 2. pelican, Campeche (Oz Mallan);
3. parrots, Chiapas (Oz Mallan); 4. underwater sights, Cozumel (Oz Mallan);
5.Cozumel iguana (Oz Mallan)

1. Maya artifact (Museum of Anthropology, Mexico); 2. Mansion Carvajal, Campeche (Oz Mallan);
3. Maya mask (Museum of Anthropology, Mexico); 4. colonial architecture, Merida (Oz Mallan);
5. statue dedicated to motherhood, Merida (Oz Mallan);
6. first mestizo family in Mexico, Akumal (Oz Mallan)

1. Palenque; 2. Dzibilchaltun (photos by Oz Mallan)

1. Chichen Itza; **2.** Tulum; **3.** Cancun; **4.** Palenque; **5.** El Mirador (all photos by Oz Mallan)

1. flamingos, Celestun; **2.** Agua Azul, Chiapas; **3.** Isla Mujeres sunset (all photos by Oz Mallan)

1. Temple of Kukulcan, Chichen Itza; **2.** Uxmal (all photos by Oz Mallan)

1. market day in neighboring Guatemala; **2.** San Cristobal salesman; **3.** Tulum neighborhood
(all photos by Oz Mallan)

1. Stouffer Presidente, Cancun; 2. reclaiming sand from the ocean; 3. on Nichupte Lagoon, Cancun; 4. Camino Real ; 5. Fiesta Americana, Cancun (all photos by Oz Mallan)

1. typical Maya art; **2.** Maya sculpture; **3.** Franciscan church (all photos by Oz Mallan)

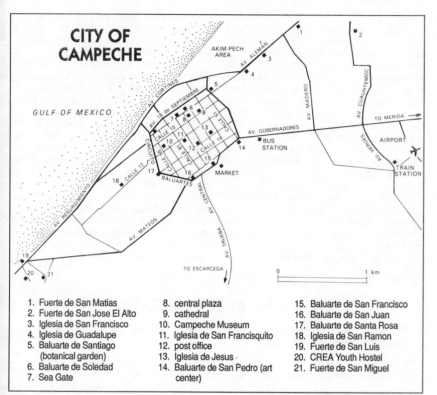

CITY OF CAMPECHE

GULF OF MEXICO

AKIM-PECH AREA

TO MERIDA

AIRPORT

TRAIN STATION

BUS STATION

MARKET

TO ESCARCEGA

0   1 km

1. Fuerte de San Matias
2. Fuerte de San Jose El Alto
3. Iglesia de San Francisco
4. Iglesia de Guadalupe
5. Baluarte de Santiago (botanical garden)
6. Baluarte de Soledad
7. Sea Gate
8. central plaza
9. cathedral
10. Campeche Museum
11. Iglesia de San Francisquito
12. post office
13. Iglesia de Jesus
14. Baluarte de San Pedro (art center)
15. Baluarte de San Francisco
16. Baluarte de San Juan
17. Baluarte de Santa Rosa
18. Iglesia de San Ramon
19. Fuerte de San Luis
20. CREA Youth Hostel
21. Fuerte de San Miguel

Ex-convent Of San Jose

The first lighthouse in Campeche was raised in 1864 and is located on the front of this former church. The original part of the structure, the Ex-convent of San Jose, was built by Jesuits in 1700; the adjacent building, a Jesuit college, was constructed in 1756. The baroque church, impressive with its quixotic talavera tile facade, provides an artesans' exhibit and shop.

History of the building is as varied as the city of Campeche: it's gone from church to army post to warehouse to gift shop/museum. The paintings on display represent a striking contrast: two giant religious murals are placed next to a modern artist's violent portrayal of what was wreaked upon the Maya Indians in the name of God.

Mansion Carvajal

Another interesting old building was a former mansion that has been restored to its original beauty,

and is maybe more beautiful! The building has a checkered history: formerly owned by a rich family named Carvajal, used as a hotel (Hotel Senorial) until the mid-1970s, and today it houses a small balcony cafe and handcrafted items donated by the DIF lady volunteers who raise money for cultural activities and promote Campeche under the auspices of the first lady (the state governor's wife). It's worth a visit just to see the Moorish-style architecture; the building also houses the offices of the first lady and her staff.

ACCOMMODATIONS

In a city the size of Campeche, one might expect a larger number of hostelries. Though not as many as expected, there's still a good selection in each of the three price categories, with a YH and trailer facilities to boot.

Budget

The **CREA Youth Hostel** (IYHF) is very clean and offers segregated dorms with bunk beds, about US$3 pp. There's a US$5 deposit for blankets, pillowslips, and towels. These articles are changed every three days, and the deposit is refunded when you leave. The well laid-out grounds are neatly kept and roomy, with a swimming pool, ball park, and cafeteria. Meals run from US$2-3. Breakfast is served 0730-0930, lunch 1400-1530, dinner 1930-2130. To get to the YH from the center of town, take the bus marked "Campeche Lerma" going south along the coastal highway to the corner of Agustin Melgar. If you're so inclined, it's about a 20-minute walk from the central plaza.

Another good value for your peso is **Hotel Castelmar,** located in an old colonial building three blocks south of the plaza. A relaxing patio with ornate tile provides a quiet place to visit or read. The large rooms each have ceiling fan, private bathroom, and hammock hooks; if you're lucky and have a choice, ask for a front room with a balcony. The management is friendly and willing to answer all questions. Rates are about US$7 d, located on Calle 61 #2, tel. 6-51-86.

Hotel Roma is very Spartan and unexciting and not always the cleanest (maybe rates half a star or less), but is only about US$6, on Calle 10 #254, tel. 6-38-97. **Hotel Reforma** is centrally located, very humble, fairly clean (but check). Rates are around US$8 d, located on Calle 8 #185, tel. 6-44-64. The best bargain of all is the **Hotel Colonial.** From the outside it looks new, painted a soft beige and white. Inside you'll find everything spotlessly clean, tile everywhere (although none of it matches), 1920s simple painted wooden furniture, sheets that might glow in the dark they're so white, hot water, bathroom, ceiling fans, a few a/c rooms (extra), purified water available downstairs, central area for reading or relaxing. Rates about US$9.50 d, cash only, pay daily, and the landlady means business. Located on Calle 14 #122, tel. 6-22-22.

CAMPECHE ACCOMMODATIONS

The state of Campeche has established a price structure on the star rating. Use the following as a *guideline* for a standard double, maximum rates:

★ = US$15, ★★ = US$21, ★★★ = US$35, ★★★★ = US$68, ★★★★★ = US$?—A five-star hotel can charge whatever they wish. Remember, a 15% tax is added to these rates.

NAME	ADDRESS	TELEPHONE	FAX
CREA Youth Hostel	Av. Agustin Melgar	6-18-02	—
Castelmar ★	Calle 61 #2	6-51-86	—
Reforma ★	Calle 8 #185	6-44-64	—
Central ★	Av. Gobernadores #462	6-32-87	—
Rona ★	Calle 10 #254	6-38-97	—
Colonial ★★	Calle 14 #122	6-22-22	—
El Viajero ★★	Av. Lopez Mateos #177	6-51-33	—
America ★★	Calle 10 #252	6-45-88	—
Campeche ★★	Calle 59 #2	6-51-83	—
Lopez ★★	Calle 12 #189	6-33-44	—
Alhambra ★★★★	Av. Resurgimiento #85	6-69-88	—
Baluartes ★★★★	Av. Ruiz Cortines	6-39-11	—
Ramada Inn ★★★★	Av. Ruiz Cortines #51	6-22-33	—

Moderate

Posada del Angel offers 15 rooms with a/c, hot water, and private bathroom, is clean, and there's a refrigerator for guest use. About US$10 s, US$12 d, located next to the cathedral on Calle 10 #309 between 53 and 55, tel. 6-77-18. In the colonial setting of an old three-story mansion, the **Hotel America** offers clean rooms with hot water, private bathroom, ceiling fans, marble floors, and colonial touches. It has 52 rooms, 38 have telephones. Rates are around US$12 d, located on Calle 10 #252, tel. 6-45-88. In a modern setting, friendly, family-run **Hotel Lopez** has (usually) clean rooms simply furnished with ceiling fans (a/c extra), hot water, bathrooms, and upstairs restaurant with TV. The colorful old hotel is beginning to show its age, but for the price it's worth it, US$10 s, US$15 d, US$17 t. Located on Calle 12 #189, tel. 6-33-44.

Almost Luxury

The **Ramada Inn** (formerly El Presidente) overlooks the sea, and has 118 nicely appointed rooms, a/c, coffee shop (open all day), dining room, bar, disco, and swimming pool. Non-guests can swim in the pool without charge. Chocoholics note: the dining room serves a good Bavarian chocolate cake. Reservations are needed for December. Rates are US$45 s or d, for a junior suite add US$2-4 more. Located on Av. Ruiz Cortines #51, tel. (981) 6-22-33/6-46-11, telex 75519, Apto. Postal 251. In the States, tel. (800) 228-2828. Credit cards accepted. **Hotel Baluartes** fronts the promenade that runs along the water across the street from the Ramada Inn. It's clean, has 104 well-furnished rooms, swimming pool (non-guests can swim for a small charge), sidewalk cafe, bar, dining room, and banquet facilities. Rates are about US$38 s, $45 d, plus tax. Located on Av. Ruiz Cortines, tel. 6-39-11.

Toward the south end of town across the street from the waterfront, the Moorish-style **Hotel Alhambra** is the newest (opened 1985) of the three nicer hotels. It offers 100 clean rooms (none have ocean views), private bathrooms, a bar, and a restaurant. This hotel is very popular with Mexican families during summer vacation. Rates begin at US$30 s, up to US$60 d. Located on Av. Resurgimiento # 85, tel. 6-69-88.

Trailers And Campsites

With complete hookups for trailers and RVs, the **Campeche Trailer Park** is a countrified spot eight km southwest of the central plaza near the small community of Samula. The bathrooms are clean with hot showers, the manager speaks some English, and soft drinks and cold beer are on sale. Turn from the ocean road onto Melgar and follow the signs. Several readers have had a hard time finding this place; if you're at your wits end, hail a cabbie and pay him to lead you into the trailer park. Address is Apto. Postal 241, Campeche, Campeche, Mexico. Trailers are also welcome to park beside the tourism office for US$2, no hookups; Av. Ruiz Cortines, Plaza Moch-Couoh.

FOOD AND ENTERTAINMENT

Budget

A number of fast-food-type cafes sell *tortas,* or if you yearn for a hamburger try the **Pinkus** cafes (Parke Pinkus on Campeche-Hampolol, or Pinkus Burger on Av. Francisco I. Madero). For real budget food, the food stands in the marketplace serve *tipico tortas,* beans, tortillas, *panuchos,* and tamales. Fruit lovers—try the unusual fruits you'll see at the markets or the buys of the season. Avocados, for instance, sell for about a nickel each. The **Nueva España Panaderia** makes great egg breads and sweet breads. Be there between 1230 and 1300 to get them hot and fresh! Located at Calle 10 between 59 and 61.

Moderate Cafes

Remember that this is seafood country, so take advantage of it. Try the excellent shrimp or stone crabs, or the fish specialty of the day which is usually sweet and fresh. Not to say that you shouldn't try other regional specialties. Though the **Miramar** restaurant (Calle 8 and 61) has been operating for many years, it has the flavor of today's Campeche, and is always busy with visitors and residents alike putting away excellent seafood. The **Balneario Popular** on the beach serves good seafood at reasonable prices. For great *tortas* and luscious desserts try **Maxim's** on Av. Lopez Mateos. **Video Taco** serves the best tacos in town with reasonable prices, a youthful atmosphere, and videos thrown in. Open from 1830 on, located on Av. Francisco I. Madero, two blocks south of

the marketplace

Av. Gobernadores. **Restaurant La Parroquia** is open 24 hours, serves *típico* food, sandwiches, and a wide variety of other dishes. Located on Calle 55 between 10 and 12. Another good eating place is the **Cafeteria Continental** on Calle 8 and 61.

Special Dining
The **303 Club** serves a good midday meal. What makes this restaurant special is the authenticity of its surroundings. Located in an old colonial building, it's obvious that it wasn't created (a la Disneyland) and decorated to look like old Spain; what you see is the real thing cared for and maintained over a very long period of time. The dining area is a series of 14 cozy rooms, each accommodating 8-16 people, many on the second floor. The menu is very "old continental," with unexpected extras such as pâté before dinner and a fresh basket of rolls and croissants brought with each course. Naturally, seafood is highlighted, but you can find

other tasty offerings, even a spaghetti dinner (a bargain at US$2), steaks, veal cutlets, rich desserts, and wonderful sangria, served in white linen elegance. Both the coffee shop and the grill at the **Ramada Inn** serve good food as well.

Discos
For night music the hotel discos are the best bet for adults—**Atlantis** at the Ramada Inn is considered the city's best. The **El Olones** at Hotel Baluartes and **Linderaja** at the Alhambra Hotel both have lively music, dramatic lights, and a bar. **Las Barajas** is another small disco-bar worth looking into.

Cinema
Five theaters offer Mexican films in Spanish: **De la Cruz,** Calle 8 between 51 and 53; **Jardin,** Calle 12 and Bravo; **Selem,** Calle 12 and 57; **Alhambra,** next to the Alhambra Hotel; **Estelar,** Av. Universidad between Ruiz Cortines and Lopez Mateos. For live theater, **Teatro Toro** is available. Check with the tourist office for monthly schedule of events.

SERVICES

Tourist Office
Located at the Plaza Moch-Couoh on Av. Ruiz Cortines near Calle 63 is a helpful tourist information center. You'll find at least one English-speaking staff member at all times. They hand out good street maps and hotel and restaurant information. They'll make local calls for reservations if you have trouble speaking Spanish. Open Mon.-Fri. 0900-1300, 1500-1800; open Sat. and Sun. 0900-1300; tel. 6-60-68/6-67-67.

Banks
Though Campeche appears to have banks everywhere, not all of them cash travelers cheques or exchange foreign currency. The two mentioned

---

State Department Of Tourism

Av. Ruiz Cortines
Plaza Moch-Couoh
Campeche, Campeche, Mexico
tel. 6-67-67/6-60-68

Campeche rainwater salesman making deliveries

below give good service: **Banamex** located on Calle 10 #15 is open Mon.-Fri. and will change money 1000-1200, tel. 6-52-52; **Bancomer** on Calle 59 #2A (across from Baluarte de Soledad on Av. 16 de Septiembre) is open Mon.-Fri., and will also change money 1000-1200, tel. 6-21-44.

Postal Service
Edificio Federal at Av. 16 de Septiembre and Av. Ruiz Cortines is open for both telegraph and postal business, selling stamps, accepting outgoing mail including registered mail, 0800-1900 Mon.-Fri.; Sun. for stamps only 0800-1400; tel. 6-43-90. Telegraph service is in the same building as the post office; go to the right as you enter the building. Open to send telegrams Mon.-Sat. 0800-2000, Sun. 0900-1300; for money orders Mon.-Fri., 0900-1730, Sat. and Sun. 0900-1200.

Medical
For medical emergencies ask the hotel to refer you to an English-speaking doctor, or call **Seguro Social,** tel. 6-18-55, located on Lopez Mateos on the south side of the city. Another choice is the Clinica Campeche, Av. Central #65, tel. 6-56-12.

Laundry
There's a laundromat on the south end of the Malecon called **Lavamatic.**

Emergency Numbers
Fire Dept., tel. 6-23-09. Policia, tel. 6-23-29. Red Cross, tel. 6-06-66/6-52-02.

GETTING THERE

Campeche is on the Gulf coast, 190 km southwest of Merida and 444 km northeast of Villahermosa (across the Tabasco state border). On the main highway, Campeche is a natural stopover for the trip between these two capitals.

By Plane
Campeche is serviced by small commuter airlines which offer frequent flights from Mexico City. Ask about shuttle flights from Merida. Though small, the airport is modern, two km northeast of the city, and taxis meet most flights. Check with your Mexican travel agent for flights within Mexico.

By Train
The train station is two km northeast of town center on Av. Heroes de Nacozari; taxi fare is about US$4 from downtown. The bus marked "China" passes in front of the station and can be caught at the market or Av. 16 de Septiembre downtown. The state tourist office has the most recent schedules, prices, and information. Trains to central Mexico or Merida run daily. Get to the station at least an hour early to buy tickets and re-check departure time; no sleeping cars are available at this time.

By Bus
Four blocks northeast of the city on Gobernadores

#289 between Calle 47 and Calle Chile, the bus station houses both first- and second-class buses. The **ADO** (first-class) terminal has a restaurant, waiting room, and baggage check-in facing Gobernadores; the second-class terminal is on the opposite side (enter through first-class or Calle Chile). ADO offers more frequent service to Ciudad del Carmen, Villahermosa, and Merida. Check the schedule at the terminal for departure times to the Caribbean coast, Chetumal, Mexico City, and all other destinations throughout Mexico. The second-class bus makes frequent trips to nearby archaeological zones, to Edzna daily at 0800 and 1430 (this bus drops you off and picks you up one km away from the ruins), and to Dzibalchen, near the sites of Dzbilnocac and Hochob; figure two hours OW at 0800, 1600, and 1900. You'll see countryside, with frequent stops made in small towns along the way. Archaeology buffs—talk to the tourist office to help arrange a trip to Calakmul, the site where the jade mask was found. It's difficult to reach, but worth it to see the important structures if you're a fanatic. At your hotel or travel agency ask about tours to the ruins.

By Car

Two good highways link Merida and Campeche: Hwy. 180 *via corta* (the short route), and Hwy. 260 *via larga* (the long route). If you're traveling roundtrip by car to or from Merida, try both roads to see more of the countryside (traveling time is almost the same both ways: two to three hours). Highway 180 runs south parallel to the coast, and crosses a bridge which brings you to Isla del Carmen; to continue south you must travel on a series of ferries from Isla del Carmen to the mainland. Staying on Hwy. 180 brings you to the state of Tabasco. To Chetumal (Caribbean coast) it's 421 km from Campeche; north to Cancun (Caribbean coast) it's 514 km.

GETTING AROUND

The old city within the ramparts of the ancient wall is well laid out, and once you figure out the numbering system for the 40 square blocks, walking is a piece of cake! The streets that run east to west, perpendicular to the sea, are odd-numbered from 51 on the north to 65 on the south. Streets running north to south are even-numbered, beginning with Calle 8 on the west through Calle 18 on the east (see city map). Most of the more popular sights and services are located within these ancient boundaries, set off by the seven remaining forts built by Spanish settlers. This old part of the city is surrounded by Circuito Baluartes on three sides, and by Av. 16 de Septiembre on the seaward side. The city outside the wall is creeping ever-outward toward the mountains, north and south, up and down the coast. Campeche has a good bus system covering the entire city, in and out of the wall, and the price is right for everybody—cheap. Bus stops are located on most corners or, as is so convenient in Mexico, they'll stop most anyplace. Remember that in Campeche west is always toward the water and east is inland.

Car Rentals

Getting around within the city is quite simple either on foot or by bus. But if you wish to visit the outlying areas at your leisure, car rental is recommended. Prices fluctuate daily with the season and the peso, so shop around for your best buy (see "Car Rental Info," in "Introduction"). Try **Hertz**, Prolongacion Calle 59, Edificio Belmar, tel. 6-48-55; **Autos y Camionetas de Renta**, Calle 57 #1, tel. 6-27-14/6-34-67; or **Easy Rent Car**, Hotel Baluartes, tel. 6-39-11.

TAXI STANDS

Taxi stands are located at the intersections of:

Calle 55 and Circuito, close to market
Calles 8 and 55, left of cathedral
Gobernadores and Chile, close to bus terminal
Costa Rica and Circuitos Baluartes
Central and Circuito Baluartes
or order up a cab by calling tel. 6-23-66/6-52-30

VICINITY OF CAMPECHE

ISLA JAINA

Burial Grounds Of The Elite

North of Campeche City, near the coast, lies the Island of Jaina, which has the largest known Maya burial ground on the Yucatan Peninsula. According to archaeologist Sylvanus Morley, who discovered the impressive site in 1943, Jaina was used for burial ceremonies for the Maya elite since A.D. 652. The most important and powerful dead were carried in long, colorful processions great distances from all over Central America to this small island. Bodies were interred in burial jars in a crouching position, with a statue resting on the folded arms. Some were found with a jade stone in the mouth; the skin was often stained red and then wrapped in either a straw mat or white cloth. Plates with food, jewelry, weapons, tools, and other precious items to accompany them to the other world were placed on their heads.

In 1950, more than 150 skeletal remains were discovered along the banks of Jaina rivers. The clay burial offerings (beautifully crafted figurines, some with moveable arms and legs) found on the island have given us detailed information about the customs of dress, religion, and working and living habits of the Maya. The clay figures have been compared to statues found in other ancient civilizations such as China, Greece, and Persia.

Climbing The Pyramids

The ancient Maya outdid themselves again in developing this offshore island. Jaina's low elevation was raised by building platforms made of *sascab* (limestone material) brought from the mainland in canoes. This material covered the brittle coral of the island and allowed the Jaina Indians to build two imposing pyramids, **Zacpool** and **Sayasol,** as well as altars and other ceremonial structures on the island.

If you decide to climb to the top of these structures for the magnificent view, use caution; the steps are narrow and steep. **Note:** Some sites have such a steep slant that a chain or rope has been attached from top to bottom to hang onto as

you climb the steps in an upright position—good idea, use it! However, many pyramids don't offer this thoughtful assistance, such as those on Jaina. Since the structures are so steep, try walking a zig-zag pattern, putting each foot sideways on each step and walking diagonally across the staircase, then making a "switchback" in the opposite direction till you reach the top. Or—some experienced climbers suggest—an easy (and very acceptable) way is to use both hands and feet in a crawling position straight up—don't look down!

Statues found on Isla Jaina at burial sites show anatomical realism and minute details indicative of everyday living. This man is wearing a false nose piece, which was considered a sign of class.

Jaina Development

Till now, the only visitors to Jaina were die-hard archaeology or Maya buffs willing to make a rough and tough trip to visit the island. Little resconstruction had been done on the pyramids, and for the average tourist there just wasn't a whole lot to see. Restoration is now being done in the archaeological zone and a study of the area's wildlife has shown that this would be an interesting stopover for tourists. A bridge has been put in place between the island and the mainland (a very short distance), and it looks as though there will soon be a Villa Arqueológica Hotel on the grounds of an old mainland hacienda to house tourists interested in this important archaeological zone. For now, anyone wanting to visit the island must go to the tourist office on Plaza Couoh in Campeche City and apply for a permit. The road to the bridge is bad (a low car might have problems), but should be paved by 1991. For those who like the pristine look of the Maya cities as Stephens and Catherwood saw them in the 1840s—better hurry! It will soon be another park with the distinct touches of the 20th century, bathrooms and all.

HECELCHAKAN

Around 75 km north of Campeche on Hwy. 180 going toward Merida, make a stop at Hecelchakan's **Museo Arqueologico del Camino Real.** Some fine examples of Jaina burial art are displayed here. Hecelchakan is a small city; the museum is easy to find near the center of town north of the church. Also, the next time you visit Mexico City, go to the Anthropological Museum at Chapultepec Park to see a superb exhibit of Maya art, including the best of the Jaina graves—or at least what's not in private collections.

Services

There's a large modern **Pemex** gas station as you approach Hecelchakan. This station is one of many that Pemex has and will be installing all over Mexico. Best of all, each station is scheduled to have a clean modern restroom. Information about the area is readily available from the Dept. of Tourism (brochures and maps in several languages, and Green Angel information).

EDZNA

As you approach Edzna on the road from Cayal (about 60 km southeast of Campeche), a tall pyramid rising from thick vegetation on the valley floor is visible from quite a distance. The site covers an area of six square km in the midst of a wide valley of cultivated land side by side with scrub forest bordered on two sides by a low range of mountains. This Maya city is off the beaten track, but easy to get to from Campeche.

The Temple Of Five Stories

People lived at this site as early as 600 B.C., and the existing structures are dated from around 300 B.C. to A.D. 200. The city grew and prospered until A.D. 900 when it (along with many other Classic centers) was suddenly deserted for reasons yet undiscovered. The largest structure is on the east side of a large open area called **Plaza Central.** This five-story pyramid has an open comb on top (seen only on some Maya structures) to add the image of more height and bring the temple closer to the sun. At one time this comb was covered with ornate stucco carvings and the rest of the building's stones were coated with smooth stucco and painted brilliant colors. Over the centuries the elements have worn away the stucco coating, exposing the rough stones beneath.

Edzna in Maya means "House of Grimaces"; the name comes from the masks that decorated the comb of The Temple of Five Stories. This structure sits on a base that measures 60 by 58 meters and is 31 meters tall. There are four levels of living quarters (used by Maya priests) with a shrine and altar on the highest level and the roof comb on top of that. Under the first-floor stairway is a corbel-vaulted tunnel that leads to an inner chamber. The architecture is simple compared to the ornate facades of the Puucs only a couple hundred kilometers down the road.

Surrounding Temples

At Edzna you can't help but be impressed with the elegant planning of each center. The buildings are gracefully placed around open plazas and platforms, blending nicely with nature. It must have been the Beverly Hills of its day. On the west side of the plaza is the restored **Temple of the Moon**

Unimaginatively named Temple of Five Stories sits on Plaza Central.

("Paal u'na"). On the two corners of the plaza stand the **Southwestern Temple** and the **Northwestern Temple,** with the sweat bath next door. Another plaza surrounded by structures not yet excavated (or previously excavated and overgrown again) is called **Grupo del Central Ceremonial.** Here beneath the vegetation you'll see the **Great Acropolis, Great House, Platform of the Knives,** and **Southern Temple.** Part of Edzna is below sea level but the Maya, with their incredible engineering skills, solved the drainage problem by building a complex system of underground canals and holding basins.

In the 1920s the American archaeologist Sylvanus Morley and Mexican archaeologist Enrique Juan Palacios studied the glyphs; those on the stairs of the Temple of Five Stories are still in remarkably good condition. More work was done in the 1940s by the Palenque specialists Alberto Ruz l'Huillier and Raul Abreu. In the 1980s a new ball court was uncovered. Eventually the remainder of this lost city will be excavated and studied. Edzna is open 0800-1700, small admission.

Getting There
If you're driving from Campeche, take Hwy. 180 east to Chencoyil, then go north on Hwy. 261 to Cayal where you turn right and continue to the Edzna site. The 60-km drive takes about one hour. From the bus station in Campeche a second-class bus leaves twice daily at 0800 and 1430. **Note:** the bus drops you off and picks you up about one kilometer from the site. Unless you have great faith in your hitchhiking skills, forget the 1430 trip since the only return bus passes the ruins between 1130 and 1200. Allow one hour for the trip. Campeche hotels will line you up with an escorted tour to the ruins, or check with any one of the travel agencies in the city.

LERMA

Seven km south of Campeche on Hwy. 180, just before reaching Lerma, a sign points to a dirt road that's marked Playa Bonita. You'll find a *balneario* that is advertised as "the nicest" beach in or around Campeche. Though it doesn't have the white sand and gorgeous blue sea of the Caribbean, the sandy beach has showers, lockers, dressing rooms, *palapa* sun shelters, and a large pavilion for food, drink, and music. This is a popular spot for Mexican vacationers during the summer *temporada*. Lovely homes line the shore.

Just past Playa Bonita is Lerma. This small in-dustrial city is really a suburb of Campeche, a fishing town that grew up along with now-large shipyards, fish-processing plants, and harbors filled with numerous commercial boats. Lerma is one of the main centers for exporting fish, a large part of the Campechean economy.

SEYBAPLAYA

Thirty-three km south of Campeche (on Hwy. 180), the small town of Seybaplaya has occupied this choice spot on the Gulf coast long enough to have been victimized by pirates—since it had no protective rampart. This small fishing village is an ideal place for artists and photographers. The waterfront is lined with posts where fishermen tie up their boats; at midday every post has a resident pelican that poses statue-like with wings extended, drying in the sun. You'll also see fishermen mending nets, drying them in neat rows along the beach, or unloading fish from open *lanchas*. Each of these broad boats has at least a 40-hp outboard motor and holds four working men and their equipment. If you'd like to buy fresh fish, halfway down the coastal road across from the waterfront is a public market (large green building). The shore along the center of town is definitely not for swimming, with remnants of dead fish and the workings of a fleet of boats. However, at the extreme north end of the bay is a dirt road to a bit of isolated beach called **Balneario Payucan** that's good for a cooling swim. At the junction of Seybaplaya and Hwy. 180 to Campeche, an open-air restaurant called **Veracruz** sits on the water's edge; the cafe serves great red snapper. Other than a couple more eating spots there's little else to see. Take the second-class bus from Campeche to Seybaplaya, RT twice daily; check at the Campeche bus station for current schedules.

SIHO PLAYA

If driving from Campeche south on Hwy. 180 toward Isla del Carmen, a few kilometers before you reach Champoton is **Hotel Siho Playa,** a relaxing spot on the water to spend a lazy afternoon and an overnight—or more. The original structure was an old hacienda, part of a large sugar plantation. Remodeled and added to some years back, it's a favorite with Mexican families. The rooms are

Fuerte de San Miguel is located high on a hill overlooking the bay, ready to blast pirates out of the water.

clean, with two double beds, a/c, and private bathroom with shower. A dining room overlooks the sea, and the garden is bordered with grass. The grounds are beginning to look overgrown and the common rooms have been allowed to get rather shabby, but there's a large swimming pool, and a sandy beach area for sunbathing or watching a continuous show of gliding man-o-wars and pelicans diving for their dinner. A stone quay jutting into the water is commonly covered with sunbathing iguanas. For the more energetic there's a tennis court and arrangements can be made for hunting and fishing. In summer months it's comparatively quiet with few guests and limited staff. The disco/bar closes down, with no outside service by the pool, and it isn't unusual for a lightning storm to knock out the electricity (even without power the cooks manage to prepare an outstanding fresh-fish dinner). Don't rule it out until you take a look—this is low-key tourism and might be just what you're looking for. Room rates are about US$30 d.

CHAMPOTON

Dating from pre-Hispanic days, this waterfront town is spread out on the banks of the Rio Champoton with a small lagoon at the river mouth. Because of its proximity to Guatemala it played an important role in the cultural exchange between Guatemala, Yucatan, and central Mexico. Earliest history places the Toltecs and then the Maya in Champoton, followed by the Spaniards in 1517. On the south side of the city you can still see the remnants of a fort built in 1719 to defend against violent pirate attacks. Today the small town is home to an ever-growing fishing fleet and a certain amount of fallout from the oil industry. In fact, all along the coast between Siho and Isla del Carmen, you'll see much more evidence of successful oil business than you're looking for.

WILDLIFE

This area has for years been the state's center for hunting. Mexico is beginning to realize that its wildlife will soon be gone if they don't take a stand on the destruction of these animals. As a result, more and more reserves are being created in Mexico. So here in the middle of thick jungle is an ideal spot to find exotic animals such as peccary, brocket and white-tailed deer, ocelot, jaguarundi, and puma. Bring your binoculars and camera and lots of film. Birdwatchers will enjoy seeing ocellated turkey, royal pheasant, crested guan, scaled pigeon, mourning and white-wing dove, and *chachalaca*.

CHAMPOTON ACCOMMODATIONS

The state of Campeche has established a price structure on the star rating. Use the following as a *guideline* for a standard double, maximum rates:

★ = US$15, ★★ = US$21, ★★★ = US$35, ★★★★ = US$68, ★★★★★ = US$?—A five-star hotel can charge whatever they wish. Remember, a 15% tax is added to these rates.

NAME	ADDRESS	TELEPHONE	FAX
Hotel Imperial ★	Calle 30 #12	8-00-10	—
Hotel Gemenes ★★	Calle 30 #10	8-00-08	—
Hotel D'Venecia ★★	Calle 38	8-01-45	—
Hotel Snook Inn ★★★	Calle 30 #1	8-00-18	—
Si-Ho Playa ★★★★	Campeche-Champoton Rd. km 40	6-29-89	—

The smartest way to conduct a wildlife safari in this jungle area is with a guide who knows the ropes; several are available. Check with the tourist office in Campeche for information. Ask about the Sansore family; they were formerly hunting guides with camps in the jungle and might be available as guides. The camps are primitive but the staff makes you very comfortable; the food is good (and plenty) with purified water and ice. For further information and brochures write to Jose Sansore, Hotel Castelmar, Campeche, Campeche, Mexico. Or telephone in Mexico, 6-55-38/6-23-56. Start writing at least two months in advance to allow time for an exchange of mail.

TRANSPORTATION

Both the coastal road (Hwy. 261) and Hwy. 180 go right through Champoton. First- and second-class buses pass through Champoton on their way to Ciudad del Carmen (check at the Campeche bus station on Gobernadores #289). The highway is usually busy with all kinds of traffic, which makes hitching relatively easy.

FOOD AND SERVICES

The restaurants are simple and—you guessed it—fish is usually the star on the menu. However, during certain times of the year you'll find wild game specialties such as *pato* (duck). Another favorite along the Gulf coast is *pan de cazon* (hammerhead shark). Though there are several banks, to exchange currency go to the **Banco del Atlantico,** open Mon. to Fri. 0900-1230, or **Banpais.**

ISLA DEL CARMEN

This sandbar/island has been occupied since the earliest Maya fishermen discovered it. In 1558 it was taken over by a band of pirates who chose this spot as their lair. Within striking distance of the port at Campeche City, the pirates attacked the ships time after time, killing the sailors and stealing the cargo of silver and gold on its way to the Spanish king. Called the Island of Tris at that time, the pirates maintained their stronghold until 1717 when they were finally killed or driven out by the army. Today the 38-mile-long island is inhabited by 80,000 people, mostly at Ciudad del Carmen (at the southwest end), the only city on the island. Formerly most of the townspeople were fishermen and coconut farmers; today new dimensions have been added—the oil industry, a thriving shipbuilding community, fish-processing plants, and a prosperous shrimp fleet that grows yearly.

SIGHTS

Ciudad del Carmen is not considered a tourist town, but for people curious about the oil and fishing industry and how it is developing in Mexico, this is a good spot to explore. Wander around the dock east of the ferry landing and you'll see shrimp-processing plants and one of the major fleets of shrimp boats on the Mexican Gulf—another place for picture taking. At the **Liceo Carmelita** there's a small archaeological museum with some locally found artifacts on display. The central plaza hosts free band concerts on Thurs. and Sun. evenings.

WATER SPORTS

Although other water sports are advertised (water-skiing, sailing, and swimming), by far the biggest attraction is fishing. Carmen is a crescent-shaped island creating a large lagoon (Laguna de Terminos) between it and the mainland. The lagoon's combination of fresh- and saltwater makes for delectable fish! Fishing charters are available for deep-sea sport, and just 15 minutes from the city are island streams where you can find snook, *corbina,* and *mojarra.* Swimming is best at either **El Playon** or **Playa Benjamin.** The resorts advertise snorkeling; however, if you've sampled the clear Caribbean water, Carmen's water will never satisfy you.

FIESTAS

The people of Ciudad del Carmen take part in a yearly festival on 15-31 July, paying homage to their patron saint, the Virgen del Carmen, with a great celebration. Everyone on the island participates in this lively event. If you like dancing, fireworks, and partying people, try to get there early for a room, or make reservations for this busy time.

FOOD AND ENTERTAINMENT

It's not difficult to find a cafe to fit your budget. The nicer hotels have the better dining rooms with more varied menus. Of course, shrimp and prawns are featured and are very sweet! The public market on Calles 39 and 20 is the usual source of quick and inexpensive tacos, tamales, *tortas*, and fried fish. Supermarkets have a fair selection of basics most of the time, and there are bakeries and *tortillerias*. Most of the nicer bars are in the hotels; however, you'll find a couple of active discos along the avenues.

SERVICES

Travel agencies include Ixtoc on Calles 35 and 30 and **Turismo Bahamita** on Calle 28 #150, tel. 2-15-00. Car rentals are available at **Auto Rentas del Carmen,** Calle 33 #21, tel. 2-23-76, and **Auto Panamericana,** Calle 22, tel. 2-23-26. The municipal **police** can be reached at tel. 2-02-05, the regional **hospital** at tel. 2-03-06. You'll see many banks; go to **Banpais** or **Banco del Atlantico** for currency exchange. The **ADO** bus station is located on Calle 24 #48; a taxi stand is located at the bus station, tel. 2-03-01.

GETTING THERE AND AROUND

With the active oil and fish industry at Ciudad del Carmen, the airport becomes more efficient each day. Several airlines now service the island. Reaching Isla del Carmen on Hwy. 180 from Campeche takes about three hours. From Champoton the road is narrow and a little hilly, often with lots of truck traffic. The new bridge, Puente de la Unidad ("Bridge of Unity"), longest in Mexico (3.25 km), connects the mainland with Isla del Carmen.

CIUDAD DEL CARMEN ACCOMMODATIONS

The state of Campeche has established a price structure on the star rating. Use the following as a *guideline* for a standard double, maximum rates:

★ = US$15, ★★ = US$21, ★★★ = US$35, ★★★★ = US$68, ★★★★★ = US$?—A five-star hotel can charge whatever they wish. Remember, a 15% tax is added to these rates.

NAME	ADDRESS	TELEPHONE	FAX
Hotel Villa Del Mar ★	Calle 20 #45	2-04-12	—
Roma ★	Calle 22 #117	2-05-10	—
Eli-Gar ★	Calle 35 #6	2-06-02	—
Costa Maria ★	Calle 26 #208	2-14-36	—
Col. Los Arcos ★	Calle 50 and 33	2-12-72	—
Acuario ★	Calle 51 #60	2-25-47	—
Hotel Zacarias ★★	Calle 24 #58	2-01-21	—
Hotel Linas ★★★	Calle 31 #132	2-05-66	—
Hotel Lli-Re ★★★	Calle 32 #25	2-05-88	—
Isla del Carmen ★★★	Calle 20-A #9	2-16-66	—
Hotel del Parque ★★★	Calle 33 #1	2-30-66	—
Los Andes ★★★★	Av. Periferico	2-23-88	—

Buses run frequently from Campeche to del Carmen; check schedules at the bus station in Campeche on Gobernadores #289. For ongoing trips south, north, or east, check in Ciudad del Carmen at the ADO first-class bus station (on Calle 24 #48). The second-class station is within walking distance of the central plaza.

To Tabasco
Anyone continuing to Villahermosa should be prepared for a long day—start early. From Ciudad del Carmen a series of ferry crossings ultimately brings you to the town of Frontera, the border town between the states of Campeche and Tabasco. Be prepared for a wait at each dock, and try to arrange to complete the entire trip in daylight. For a faster route to Tabasco, drive from Champoton south on Hwy. 287 which joins 186 at Francisco Escarcega, where you have the choice of traveling east to Chetumal in the state of Quintana Roo, or southwest toward Villahermosa in the state of Tabasco. This route takes you inland, eliminating Ciudad del Carmen and the ferry crossings through the estuaries.

ESCARCEGA

Escarcega is growing from a grubby little railroad stop (where you formerly thought twice before stepping off the train) to a fairly respectable village of 15,000. While far from being a tourist town, many adventurers pass through each year on their way to explore the surrounding jungle. It's also becoming an important crossroad connecting the Yucatan with the rest of the world, especially since the oil boom hit this part of the Peninsula. As outsiders come, services increase. Note: I'd still lock my car before leaving it parked on the street.

ACCOMMODATIONS

Escarcega lies 149 km south of Campeche, and is most often used as a gas stop on the way to Chetumal (270 km) and the east coast of the Peninsula. Merida is 355 km north, and Villahermosa is 297 km southwest. If you find it necessary to overnight, expect very Spartan hotels in the budget class (see chart, opposite page).

FOOD AND SERVICES

The cafe at the **Hotel Maria Isabel,** though simple, serves acceptable meals. Several other small cafes around are adequate. The **market** (beginning on Calle 31 on the corner of the plaza) has ample food supplies. There's a **Bancomer** on Calle 31 #26 for currency exchange. The **long-distance telephone** is found at Perez Martinez #30, open 0800-1300 and 1600-2000 daily. The **post office** is on Calle 28-A. The **Social Security**

Hospital can be reached at tel. 4-01-92. The **police** can be reached at tel. 4-00-39.

TRANSPORTATION

Escarcega is located at the junction of Hwys. 186 and 261. The town is 1½ km west of the highway. If driving follow the signs into town. Most of the services are downtown and accessible on foot, though it's easy to flag down a taxi. The **ADO Bus Station** is at the intersection of Hwy. 261 and Justo Sierra. The **second-class bus station** is on Justo Sierra and Calle 31. The **Caribe bus station** (for buses east to the Caribbean coast) is on Hector Perez Martinez three blocks west of the plaza. The **train station** is a half km up the tracks, north of Mendez. Two trains pass through daily headed for Campeche and Merida and two run in the opposite direction toward Coatzacoalcos and Mexico City. There are no first-class trains on this run.

ARCHAEOLOGICAL SITES NEAR ESCARCEGA

Chicana
Roughly 145 km east of Escarcega is Chicana. The turnoff is a half km from the ruins. An elaborate serpent mask frames the entry of the main palace, **House of the Serpent Mouth**—it's in comparatively good repair. Several hundred meters into the bush is another structure built at the same time, though not as well preserved. Throughout the area are small and large ruins,

ESCARCEGA ACCOMMODATIONS

The state of Campeche has established a price structure on the star rating. Use the following as a *guideline* for a standard double:

★ = US$15, ★★ = US$21, ★★★ = US$35, ★★★★ = US$68, ★★★★★ = US$?—A five-star hotel can charge whatever they wish. Remember, a 15% tax is added to these rates.

NAME	ADDRESS	TELEPHONE	FAX
Akim Pech ★	Escarcega-Villahermosa Rd.	—	—
Bertha Leticia ★	Calle 29 #28	4-00-11	—
El Yucateco ★	Hector Perez Martinez #102	—	—
Posada Escarcega ★	Calle 25 #15	4-00-79	—
Escarcega ★	Calle 32 #86	4-01-87	—

none of which have been restored. But if you're curious to compare the subtle differences of design and architecture of the ancient Maya throughout the Peninsula, it's worth a day's visit to this group.

Becan
On the main highway another two km is the turnoff to Becan. You'll see an unusual waterless moat, 15 meters wide and four meters deep, that surrounds the entire site. It's believed this protective-style construction indicates that warring factions occupied this part of the Peninsula during the second century. Historians claim that they were constantly at war with Mayapan, in what is now the state of Yucatan.

Xpujil
Six km east of Becan are three towers. Pass through the small village of Xpujil, then continue to this classic example of Rio Bec architecture: the remains of three false towers overlooking miles of jungle. On the back side of the central tower check out what's left of two huge inlaid masks. If you're in a vehicle that can handle a primitive jeep road, you can reach Rio Bec by taking the road south of the gas station near Xpujil.

This is also an ideal place for birdwatching in thick jungle with little or no tourist traffic. Don't forget your binoculars and bug repellent! If you're traveling by bus to Chetumal, check with the tourist office or a travel agency for bus trips to these sites. Though not restored, these ruins will give you an indication of what the archaeologists find when they first stumble upon an isolated site. You will have renewed wonder at how they manage to clear away hundreds of years of jungle growth, figure out a puzzle of thousands of stones, and end up with such impressive structures.

Calakmul Reserve
Located in the Peten region in the north of Campeche, 35 km from the border with Guatemala, Calakmul has given its name to one of the newest, largest Biosphere Reserves in Mexico. This site was once home to over 60,000 Maya. What may turn out to be the largest of all the structures built by the Maya, a massive pyramid looms 175 feet over a base that covers five acres.

For the past seven years an archaeological team from the Universidad Autonoma del Sudeste in Campeche has mapped 6,750 structures, uncovered two tombs holding magnificent jade masks, beads, and two flower-like earcaps, excavated parts of three ceremonial sites, and found more stelae than at any other Maya site. From the top of Pyramid 2, it's possible to see the Danta pyramid at Calakmul's sister site, El Mirador, also part of the Calakmul reserve on the Guatemala side of the border. Both of these sites predate Christ by 100 years.

Heading up the archaeological team at Calakmul, William Folan has made startling discoveries, but even more important he has been instrumental in pushing through the concept of the Biosphere Reserve. Today it has become a reality. Though it's not on the usual itinerary because of the difficulty reaching it, if you'd like more information contact the Campeche Tourist Office in Campeche City. See the October, 1989, issue of *National Geographic Magazine* for color photos of the Calakmul archaeological site.

THE STATE OF CHIAPAS

The Land
The southernmost state of Mexico, Chiapas is bordered on the west by Oaxaca and Veracruz, on the north by Tabasco and Campeche, and on the east by Guatemala. Covering 74,415 square km, it has a population of 2,000,000. While the low-lying coast and jungle areas are typically tropical, a large part of Chiapas is in the "highlands," thick rainforest with innumerable lakes, rivers, and waterfalls. The rugged mountains of the Sierra Madre del Sur, often crowned with thick clouds, average 1,500 meters in elevation and some peaks are as high as 3,000 meters. One of the few volcanos of this region is the 3,000-meter peak of Tacana, overlooking Mexico's southern Pacific coast and the city of Tapachula. This bustling German-influenced business center is a popular stopover to or from Guatemala—complete with smog. The state boasts one of the most magnificent of all Maya ruins, Palenque.

Climate
The tropical Chiapas lowlands are continuously hot and humid, especially during the rainy season,

May to October. Although rainfall can be as high as 4,000 mm (160 inches) in the mountains, it's somewhat less in the lowlands. But be prepared for cold weather in the highlands, especially in Dec. and January. Occasional hurricanes from the Gulf and the Caribbean pass over southern Mexico.

History
The earliest inhabitants of the Chiapas area are presumed to be the Olmecs. The Maya settled in

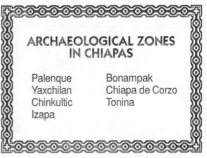

ARCHAEOLOGICAL ZONES IN CHIAPAS

Palenque	Bonampak
Yaxchilan	Chiapa de Corzo
Chinkultic	Tonina
Izapa	

during the Pre-Classic Period, and during the Classic Age created their most outstanding structures. After years of fighting, the Spaniards assumed control of the area in 1530 and, as in all of their conquests, subjugated the Indians. When made bishop in 1544, Bartolome de las Casas began to implement changes for the better. He tried to abolish slavery and managed to convince the Spanish crown to provide legal protection for Indians throughout the New World. Although marginally successful, it was a first step. Bishop de las Casas is held in great respect by the Indi-

ans of the area. On and off between the 16th century and Mexico's independence in 1823, Chiapas was under the legal jurisdiction of the Spanish in Guatemala. Repeated Indian uprisings against the Spanish colonialists and the Republic continued until 1911; the last was a gallant though futile effort by the Tzotzil and Tzeltal groups.

Economy
Chiapas has plodded along, mostly isolated from the world, but that's beginning to change. Along with increased tourism, the mining of oil, silver,

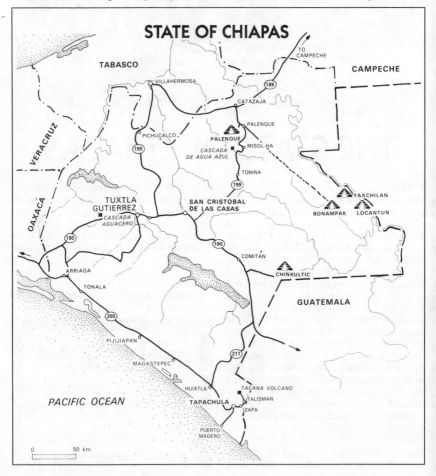

STATE OF CHIAPAS

HETZMEK

The Maya woman took the infant, about six months old, and spoke slowly and reverently to him in a Maya dialect as she placed a gold bracelet on each tiny wrist. The young mother and father watched the "godmother" intently as she introduced the infant to his future. On a table between them lay a book, a coin, a weeding blade, a gun, and a pair of scissors. "*Koten, Antonio Cuitok, ten kin mentik hetzmek tech*—Come, Antonio Cuitok, I make the *hetzmek* for you." She went on, "I give you all these things to hold; so that you learn them when you grow up." She picked up the book from the table, a Catholic Missal, and read several prayers from it, then placed it in the baby's tiny hands. "I give you this book so that you will learn to read." Then the blade—". . .that you will learn to farm"—the gun, etc., until all the items were given and explained.

Then the godmother placed the baby astride her left hip, a signal that he'd passed from infancy to babyhood. She then circled the table counter-clockwise nine times. Though the godmother was dressed in a beautiful white *huipil*, embroidered with bright flowers, the baby was dressed 20th-century style: a blue nylon romper suit.

The ceremony was complete, the baby's future now assured. The "nine lords of the night" would protect him—with some help from the Christian Church; the bracelets pledged good health during his first two years.

In each community, *hetzmek* is carried out in a slightly different manner. Some must call in a friend from another village because no one at home remembers all of it. Though the ceremony might differ from village to village, the child is always shown his potential future and placed astride the hip for the first time on this day. Who knows how many hundreds or thousands of years the ceremony has been repeated or when the Christian components became part of it. But its powerful roots signify the continuation of the Maya people.

---

gold, and copper is bringing new money into state coffers, providing a base to build more roads, extend advertising, and improve facilities for tourists. All of this means more money for Chiapecanos, even though the overall economic condition in Mexico makes it slow going. For many years the chief industry was timber harvesting and exportation, leading to the decimation of essential rainforest. (Many would like to see the timber industry stop altogether to preserve the rainforest; isolated Indian cultures, such as that of the Lacandones, depend on the forest for their unique way of life.) Today, Chiapas's economy includes cocoa beans, coffee, and most important, oil. Tourism is also making strides in the state, especially since Chiapas offers some of the finest ancient Maya stone cities on the Peninsula.

People
It should be pointed out that the "improving" economy is that of the mestizos and *ladinos* in Chiapas, *not* of the Indians. For them, life is very hard—their "economy" is almost nonexistent. In Chiapas, 80% of the population is of indigenous Maya origin and their average income is about US$5 per month. Many Indians live in villages in the outlying areas of the Chiapas Highlands—the fringe of civilization. Chiapas produces immense quantities of electricity, at Chicoasan Dam, though most indigens do not have that luxury, or paved roads, running water, or indoor plumbing. They die young, have a high infant mortality rate, are illiterate, suffer from poor hygiene, and many are alcoholics. They are in a hole from which they have been unable to extract themselves since the coming of Cortes in 1528. Problems are rife and the Indians can do little about it. More and more of their land is confiscated by rich and powerful landowners. The communities of the Chamula, Zinacanteco, Larrainzar, Zoque, Chol, and Lacandone, among others, still speak their own language, mostly Tzotzil and Tzeltal (some speak Spanish as a second language), and practice the traditions of the ancient past.

The Municipality Of San Andres Larrainzar
The Larrainzar group is an example of a people who are trying to improve their lifestyle with dra-

matic changes. The municipality consists of about 54 villages with 17,000 inhabitants scattered across the hilltops of the Chiapas Highlands. There are about 32 primary schools, many of which go only to the fourth grade instead of the usual sixth grade. The quality of education is inferior, and many children do not attend because they are needed at home to work. Most of the Larrainza do not speak Spanish, especially the women. These people are very poor. Their one-room homes with dirt floors are made of adobe (mud slapped onto stick frames) with either thatch or corrugated metal roofs; a few have tile shingles. Cooking is done over an open fire in the room and the smoke *eventually* escapes through the roof. (Often when you buy a piece of cloth that has been woven by these women, it smells of smoke.) Within their culture, women have always been considered inferior and have no voice in the community, though this is gradually changing.

Changes

Cantinas are not allowed within the villages (by a vote of the city fathers). Some of the men are involved in a training program to learn to become tailors. Making their own trousers cuts the price by about 50%. This program was in part sponsored by a Swiss benefactor who donated a heavy-duty commercial treadle sewing machine to each of several villages of the Larrainzar. He also provided a couple of bolts of fabric to each village to "seed" the operation.

It's a step. In the meantime, the people of the village continue to eke a living from poor soil in a cold climate on the top of tall mountains. Farming is their only way of surviving and corn is their main crop. Traveling through the highlands you see *milpas* (corn fields) planted up and down the vertical mountainsides; in many cases water must be hand-delivered to the crop. Corn tortillas and beans are the staples of their diet. Ofte i the only means of bringing cash into the house is by selling what other few vegetables they grow, as well as chickens, eggs, and sometimes a pig.

Women And Weaving

Another source of cash is derived from the women's weaving abilities. It doesn't bring in much, however, since competition to sell these beautiful pieces of cloth to the tourists is fierce. All the women from the outlying villages weave and

there are over 200,000 Indians living in the "neighborhood." Another problem is bringing their crafts to market since most Indians do not have transportation, especially those people living in isolated mountainous areas. Often "buyers," representing shops from other parts of Mexico, make trips into these villages and offer prices that are simply not just, then sell them in their trendy shops (far from Chiapas) at inflated prices. We all like a bargain, but it's high-handed robbery to pay US$.50 for a weaving that took five days to produce.

Village Stores

The villages are beginning to learn to work together. It is probably their only chance of survival. Fourteen villages have community stores (families within the community who donate become members). Each village specializes in one "product": four villages produce trousers and shirts, two more raise bees, four—rabbits, five—chickens, two—bread, and one village is organizing to weave the cloth for the women's skirts. Can you imagine getting everything done in a day if it was necessary to "make" each daily need from scratch, including the cloth? No wonder the people seldom have more than two changes of clothing—if that.

The author had the opportunity of visiting one of these hilltop villages when a group of Swiss visitors who donated a commercial sewing machine to the village some months before returned to see how the sewing program was progressing. It's a tough trip. The good paved road ends just after the turnoff to Chamula and Zinacantan (tour buses don't go past this point). Beyond the pavement it's best to have a 4WD vehicle. The road becomes potholed, ridged, and rough although it meanders through beautiful green mountains and along a lively river. Occasionally heavy rains flood the road turning it into a river of mud. Eventually this dirt track stops at the foot of a mountain. From here it's a hike on a narrow path to the top. When we began our trek, the air was clear and crisp, the sky blue, and the green trees all incredibly beautiful. As we approached the crest of the hill we could see the village, just a small group of houses constructed of adobe and red tile roofs. As is usual, all the women and little girls of the village were barefoot, each dressed in a dark wool skirt, a crisp white cotton blouse with colorful red woven designs trimming the neck and cuffs, and a white wool shawl worn in a variety of ways, but mostly bulging with a baby held inside. The men wore western trousers and shirts, machine-made straw hats, and generally cowboy boots; little boys were dressed just like their dads.

At the edge of the village, a brown-faced woman with dazzling white teeth under a shy smile offered three red plastic buckets. One was water to wash away the dust from our trek, the other contained a weak aromatic tea and tasted like the leaves of orange or lemon trees, and the third was filled with plastic glasses. The villagers did not hide their joy at greeting their Swiss benefactors. They spoke only Tzotzil so everything had to be translated by a young Mexican man into Spanish for the rest of us. The entire village took part in this meeting. Well-behaved children and women with quiet babies sat on planks of wood set on tree trunks and men in turn gave prepared reports on the progress of their sewing project

which would eventually enable several village men to become tailors. The men proudly reported that they were able to make pants for the village. It was then time for the women to speak, and they have a curious custom (perhaps because they're not used to being acknowledged?): when invited to speak they all begin speaking at the same time, in a whining, sing song, guttural tone—in the Maya dialect. Even with a translation it was hard to keep up with this part of the meeting.

The meeting lasted several hours until the Swiss guest of honor was fully apprised of how his project was taking form, and several requests were presented to him. At the end, the women streamed from the small meeting hut to their homes and rushed back with lunch that had been prepared early in the morning—an enormous pot of rice and another of beans along with more tortillas than I have ever seen at one time. They

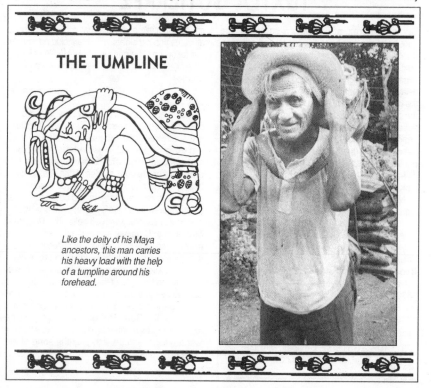

THE TUMPLINE

Like the deity of his Maya ancestors, this man carries his heavy load with the help of a tumpline around his forehead.

heaped rice and beans on each plate and topped them with a generous stack of tortillas. The tortilla served as a fork—once we got the hang of it. This was a very unselfish gesture since these people hardly have enough food to get by. Outsiders rarely get the opportunity to see the inner workings of a village in this part of Mexico. The people are suspicious, with good reason. Most of their day is spent doing simple things that we take for granted. Washing their hair at the community faucet; searching the surrounding hills for firewood for the cookfire (a continuous job); washing their laundry (and themselves) by hand in cold water. Medical care is nonexistent and a small group of Catholic nuns have brought in indigens from other villages to teach them about their illnesses and cures with herbal medicines, *curandero* style. This is a lost art to many of the Indians, and since there are no doctors among them, they are relearning how to prepare salves, tinctures, syrups, capsules, and soaps from the herbs and roots available to them in their environment.

Just as we were preparing to photograph (with permission) some of the women working on their backstrap looms, the clouds dropped onto the hilltop; it seemed wise to head down the trail while we could still see it. The day had been enlightening and I felt closer to my Indian friends with the hope that somehow I could help. **Note:** Anyone interested in helping these people with a donation, please drop me a note c/o Moon Publications, 722 Wall St., Chico, CA 95928, and I will send you an address where contributions can be made; the donations are tax deductible.

TUXTLA GUTIERREZ

Tuxtla Gutierrez, at one time a center for the Zoque Indians, has been the capital and commercial center of the state of Chiapas since 1892. The Tuxtla airport makes it a gateway to the rest of the state (even though flights in and out are frequently delayed by fog and rain due to the poor location of the city's airport). Tuxtla is a busy hub that reflects the growth of the state. The center of a thriving coffee-growing zone, its population numbers approximately 220,000. Although Chiapas is one of the most picturesque states in the Mexican Republic, its capital is a large busy city that could be located anywhere. But don't let that stop you from looking around. The city is definitely worth a one- or two-day stopover to see a few outstanding sights.

SIGHTS

Tours
If you have little time and want to see the most in the shortest, contact the tourism office (tel. 3-3478). Ask about their (economical and extensive)

city tour that takes you on a day-long excursion to all of the popular sights in Tuxtla including most of the following. The price is about US$7 including pickup at most hotels and lasts approximately six hours.

City Sights
The central plaza area is a fairly new "make-over" done by a recent governor of Chiapas. The plaza is a shady tree-lined square surrounded by modern government buildings and the rebuilt **San Marcos Cathedral.** The cathedral, all white with unusual (for Mexico) modern lines, has a stark beauty. Its German glockenspiel-type mechanism sends 12 carved apostles in and out of the tower every hour while a medley of international music is chimed beautifully with 48 bells. The **Regional Museum of Chiapas** has two halls with permanent exhibits: the archaeological collection on the first floor and the colonial exhibit on the second floor. The **Xiloteca** offers an exhibit of the types of wood found throughout the forests of Chiapas. It's easy to see why this part of the world has attracted lumber interests from all over the world for four centuries. The **Botanical Garden** is a cool place to wander if you're interested in the state's flora or just a quiet afternoon with only the song of the birds to accompany you.

State Tourist Office Of Chiapas
1a Av. Pte 1482
Tuxtla Gutierrez, Chiapas, Mexico
tel. (9-16-61) 2-07-32

AMBER

Amber comes from the resin of different kinds of pine trees which covered various regions of the earth 40 or 50 million years ago. Due to modifications caused by natural catastrophes the earth's crust suffered substantial alterations, and forests of now-extinct varieties of conifers were entombed within it. Among those classes of trees buried was the *succinifer* pine which, judging by the size of some pieces found, had the capacity to secret great quantities of resin, which were transformed into amber through an extremely long process of petrification.

Amber is hard and brittle, and emits a special aroma when it is burned. It is generally yellowish, although it can have many different tones such as white, pink, red, wine, brown, or black, among others. It can be either opaque or transparent, and, on occasion, marbled, all depending on its degree of purity.

Amber was attributed with magical properties by primitive civilizations, and there have been numerous references made about its importance since time immemorial. For this reason, it has become associated in Mexico with theories determining the commercial routes of Maya traders across Central America in ancient times.

There is evidence of amber's existence in the state of Chiapas as far back as 250 B.C. Until the arrival of the Spaniards, amber was principally used to make adornments such as nose- and lip-rings, earrings, and beads for necklaces. Subsequently it was distributed throughout the Yucatan Peninsula, Oaxaca, and what is now central Mexico by two Maya tribes of southern Mexico (Zoques and Zinacantecos). In the Mendocino Codex, amber is mentioned among the tributes paid to the Aztecs by the inhabitants of the Soconusco, the southwest coastal region of the state of Chiapas.

The first amber mines to be exploited were found in regions near **Simojovel**, a small town in the north of Chiapas. Throughout the years new veins have been discovered. Unfortunately for the amber miners, however, they have always been located in hard-to-reach places where there's constant danger of landslides.

To find amber deposits, miners begin by searching for layers of coal, a highly risky job because of the condition of the loose, shaky terrain. Once coal is located, a tunnel is drilled and large blocks of coal are cut away until the "hearth of amber" is found.

Generally raw amber is sold to the artisans of Simojovel, who, with the help of sandpaper and files, polish the pieces, giving them a beautiful finish. Once the amber has been polished, the artisans take advantage of the luminosity of its shine and create a great variety of pieces in imaginative forms. Some of these are vine leaves, which were made even before the Spanish conquest, as well as feet, hands, hearts, crosses, and other amulet designs clearly influenced by silver medals. Other shapes are red currant berries, feathers, raindrops, fangs, triangles, leaves, flowers, and tears. Amber is also found in earrings, rings, bracelets, and necklaces, multi-faceted pieces of amber which look like geometrically carved gems.

Sometimes trapped insects are found in amber, which considerably raises its value. Samples found have enabled entomologists to classify almost 75 species of insects which, according to investigators, belong to the Tertiary or Cretaceous periods.

The advantage of studying the insect specimens which have been preserved in amber is that the molecular structure on the insect remains intact without a mineral substitution of their organic tissues. These specimens offer excellent study conditions to biologists and archaeologists.

In Chiapas, tradition has endowed amber with magical properties. Certain Maya groups put bracelets hung with small pieces of amber on their children to protect them from the *evil eye*. With the passage of time, the mestizo population adopted this custom and added more modern attributes of *good luck* to the use of the amber.

Amber has had many names. The Greeks called it *electron* due to its capacity to accumulate electricity. Because of its resinous origins the Romans called it *succo* or juice and, due to its similarity to water bubbles with the reflection of sunrays within them, the Aztecs called it *apozonalli,* or water foam.

Shopping

Shops in Tuxtla are generally open daily from 0900 to 1400 and 1700 to 2100 except Sunday. The city is filled with modern shops including glitzy department stores, trendy dress shops, and beauty shops. Shoppers have access to all hi-tech appliances and equipment. For native crafts take a look around the public market. A visit to the city *mercado* is always fun and filled with bright colors. *Tipico* crafts as well as mounds of exotic fruits and vegetables and cold glasses of *tazcalate,* a tasty sweet drink made from local chocolate, cinnamon, and *pinole* (roasted corn), are sold here. The market is three blocks south of the main plaza.

Indian weavers from outlying areas are often seen selling their wares in the shade across from the plaza next to the "white" cathedral. A stop at **Bazar Ishcanal** will give you an overview of crafts from the entire state of Chiapas. Located on the ground floor of the **Plaza de Instituciones,** the same building that houses the government tourism office, this shop is also operated by the government. You'll discover fine embroidery, wooden carvings, pottery, leather products, jewelry, and weaving. These products are a good representation of both the indigenous as well as the Hispanic people of the state. The room is set up almost like a museum except that everything's for sale. Check out the amber jewelry. Vendors offering amber wrapped in plain brown paper can be found on most street corners. But it takes a trained eye to tell the difference between the real McCoy and the imitation. The government shop might be the place to buy it to be sure it's authentic.

Tuxtla Gutierrez Zoo

On the southeast side of the city in a forest called El Zapotal is the **Miguel Alvarez del Toro Zoo.** Built in 1980, this is probably the finest zoo in Central America, filled with animals and birds that are found in the wilds of Chiapas. A one-km-long trail meanders up and down the side of a hill under tall trees with hanging vines. The animals are housed in as natural surroundings as possible. You'll see the unusual *aarpia* (harpy eagle)—a very large bird (about one meter tall) with deep thick feathers around its eyes and feet—and other unusual birds including the brilliant South American macaw or the *guacamaya roja* and the *pavon,* the Chiapas state bird. A large puma named Mustafa responds to his name. Sleek healthy jaguars pace within their enclosure, the variety including the black jaguar—the delicate jaguar pattern shows through the ebony-shaded fur. Look for ocelots, javelina, coatimundi, and raccoons. There are families of spider monkeys swinging high up in the trees to the roar of their neighboring howler monkeys. The active, spinning, swimming nutria puts on a great show; and it's easy to watch with a great underwater viewing window. The zoo is a definite "must-see" when in Tuxtla Gutierrez.

ACCOMMODATIONS

Tuxtla has a good selection of hotels to choose from. Be sure to check out the rooms before you pay; some in the budget class are not always in tip-top condition.

pozole *vendor in Chiapa de Corzo*

Budget

The **CREA Youth Hostel (IYHF)** is located on 16 de Septiembre, tel. 1-12-01. The entrance is on the left of the youth center and cafe. Spotlessly clean dormitories (single sex) are furnished with bunk beds and the price includes a towel, pillowcase, and sheets. Curfew is 2100 and the doors are locked between 2100 and 0600. About US$6.
Hotel La Posada is simple, has a pleasant enough courtyard, bathrooms, friendly staff, and is close to the 2nd-class bus station on 2 Sur. If you're not in your room by 2200 you get locked out until 0600. Rates about US$6 s and US$7 d.
Hotel Santo Domingo is just a simple hotel; ask to see the room they assign you *before* you pay. It's conveniently located across from ADO, at 2 Norte Poniente #259A, tel. 3-48-39, and the price is moderate, about US$8.50 s, and US$10.50 d.

Moderate To Expensive

Hotel Bonampak, on Blvd. Dr. Belisario Dominguez #180, is a bit deceptive. The front building is box-like 1960s architecture, with clean rooms, nicely furnished, tile bathrooms, TV, telephones, and cushy beds. But look further: in the back section around the garden you'll find a different look—early 1900s bungalows built about 40 years ago, not fancy, but comfortable, pool close by. In the front building is a good coffee shop for breakfast, and in the back, the dining room (again, at least 40 years old) is a gracious old room with elegant architecture and sculptured, plastered domed ceilings. Formal ambience, wine list, and a great filet mignon for US$5. Rates about US$28.50 d. For something fancier, the bright pink **Hotel Flamboyant** is lovely with restaurants, cafes, bars, and all services. It's located farther out of town on Blvd. Dr. Belisario Dominguez km 1081. For reservations write to Apto. Postal 640, Tuxtla Gutierrez, Chiapas 29000, Mexico. Rates are about US$35 s and US$49 d.

OUTLYING AREAS

Chiapa De Corzo

Chiapa de Corzo (10 km from Tuxtla) and San Cristobal de las Casas are the only two cities in Chiapas that still have Spanish colonial architecture from the early 16th century. Chiapa de Corzo, the first city settled by the Spaniards, was once called Chiapa Español and San Cristobal de las Casas was the center of the Indian population. Chiapa de Corzo is a small laid-back city with mostly Indian inhabitants. It boasts the largest colonial fountain in the state, set regally under an elegant Moorish-style structure. Another 16th-century building is **Santo Domingo Cathedral,** a huge, though simple, white building that today stands next to the local soccer field. They say that its huge bell was cast in gold, silver, and copper in 1576, and that when it tolls it's heard for miles around the countryside. Vendors set up shop near the church and among other things sell "black" *pozole* in large (maybe a liter) round-bottomed tin cups. This thick drink is made from corn, chocolate, and cinnamon. It serves as a "fast-food" lunch for workers on the go in Chiapas. Eat your heart out, McDonald's.

Chiapa de Corzo houses the **lacquer ware museum** (alongside the *zocalo*) which exhibits wonderful examples of this colorful craft—from tiny delicate jewelry boxes to enormous wooden chests, each covered with an explosion of bright color and intricate designs. Also displayed are the wooden masks depicting the Spanish conquistadores (painted with vivid blue eyes) worn during the many celebrations in which the Spaniards are portrayed conquering the Indians. You can buy lacquer ware here, and you can even watch the craftsmen demonstrating their talents. Gift shops sell typical arts, crafts, and clothing from a few arcaded shops next to the *zocalo*.

It's a short walk from the town center to the *embarcadero* (city dock), where you can usually find a boat to take passengers on the Grijalva/Sumidero trip. The docks offer a relaxing respite; try one of the outdoor *palapa* cafes for a cold beer or light lunch with a good view of peaceful life on the river. Buses travel regularly from Tuxtla to Chiapa de Corzo.

Take a launch to get a look at the steep canyon walls from the level of the river. This awesome waterway was formerly a roaring series of mighty rapids that literally cut its way through the massive towering stone. In 1960 it took a team of surveyors nine days to travel through the hazardous white rushing water of the canyon. In 1981 the water was harnessed by the **Chicoasen Dam,** one of Mexico's largest. As a result, the tranquil riverway serves as a favorite recreational area for locals and visitors alike—a trip in a small boat to the dam and back takes about three hours. Along the water's edge the cliffs present interesting rock formations, caves (some large enough for the boat to pull into), waterfalls (during the rainy season), and an ever-changing vista of plants and trees.

Transportation is available to either the town of Chiapa de Corzo on the river or to the docks on Cahuare Beach where boats are available for trips through the canyon. Most of these small launches are open (bring a hat and sunscreen). Price of the trip varies depending on the number of passengers. Figure about US$60-80 per boat RT, and most boats hold 6-10 people. Check with the Tuxtla Gutierrez Tourism Office.

Sumidero Canyon

Another worthwhile trek is a drive into the mountains 22 km northeast of Tuxtla for a different view of the dramatic Sumidero Canyon. This spectacular perspective of the canyon is of the 14.3-km-long gorge with sheer cliffs that drop 1,800 meters into the Grijalva River. As you ascend into the mountains you'll find five lookout points with a diverse vista from each: La Ceiba, La Coyota, Las Tepehuajes, El Roblar, and at the end of the road Los Chiapas. At Los Chiapas you have a breathtaking look at the canyon, and the river zig-zagging far below. Here you'll find a small cafe, La Atalaya, selling regional tamales and the favored local drinks—*pozole, tazcalate,* or a steaming cup of excellent Chiapas-grown coffee. No instant coffee here!

A persisting "Tepechia" legend tells that the Chiapas Indians refused to be taken prisoners when it was apparent they would suffer defeat at the hands of the Spanish invaders. Men, women, and children chose instead to jump to their deaths from the top of the Sumidero cliffs. *Combis* leave Madero Park daily (as they fill up), taking passengers to the Sumidero Canyon. Ask at your hotel or at the tourism office at Edificio Plaza de las Insti-

Sumidero Canyon

tuciones, 2nd Floor, Blvd. Dr. Belisario Dominguez #950, Tuxtla Gutierrez, tel. 3-48-37.

Accommodations

Chiapa de Corzo's hotel is simple, usually clean, but not much more. Check it out. **Hotel Los Angeles** has a certain old charm, large rooms, tiled bathrooms, and windows that look out onto the street. On Julian Grajales #2, tel. 6-00-48, rates about US$6 s, US$7 d. Ask around town for another small hostelry called **Hotel Marisa** available for a little less money.

SAN CRISTOBAL DE LAS CASAS

A trip to Chiapas would not be complete without a visit to this lovely colonial city. One-story pastel-colored buildings with wrought-iron-covered windows and tile roofs line the streets, adding a special charm. But even more important is San Cristobal's Indian culture. This is the Indian center of the Mexican Highlands—a place to watch the people. Here you will see a diverse collection of native clothes that date back hundreds of years. Those in the know can identify villagers by the clothes they wear since each village uses its own central color and particular style when weaving the textiles to make their garments.

HISTORY

San Cristobal was founded in 1528 by the Spaniard Diego de Mazariegos after a brutal conflict with the Chiapan warriors described by Spanish historian Bernal Diaz as "the best warriors he had seen" while traveling with Cortes during the conquest of "New Spain." Originally named **Ciudad Real** ("Royal City") as so many were, it remains one of the charming colonial jewels of Mexico.

Most of San Cristobal's beautiful churches were built in the early years after the Spanish conquest.

The Indians provided the labor to build these structures and the rest of the city. They were little more than slaves and rose up frequently against their conquerors; each time they were crushed. The Catholic Church was supervised by the Dominican order during those years and not until the time of Bishop Bartolome de las Casas did their condition improve, and then only slightly. The city eventually honored de las Casas by changing its name from Ciudad Real to San Cristobal de las Casas.

SIGHTS

Churches

Churches abound! Even if you're not a "church" person, take a stroll just to investigate the beautiful architecture of these structures, and remember, some are over 450 years old! **Santo Domingo's** baroque facade glows a delicate rose color, and the intricate carvings, columns, statue niches, and statues are beautiful. The interior houses a sensational pulpit, one of Mexico's finest works of art. You'll see many nostalgic *retablos* (religious paintings frequently offered in place of money donations, or in thanks for favors. Remember, the painters were not professionals). It's not unusual to find an Indian healer (often a female *curandera*)

San Cristobal Catholic Church Archival Office is a treasure of history of the area.

performing rituals touching the stricken pilgrim with flowers and passing burning candles before the church altars. These are not Catholic ceremonies. But this is Indian country and religion is a very personal mix of the Maya past and the Catholic present. Other churches well worth seeing are the **cathedral** on the main square and the simple **Carmen Church.** Up many steps, high on a hill just west of downtown you'll find the **church of San Cristobal,** open just once a year during the fiesta on the feast of St. Christopher. There's a wonderful view of the town and the entire valley from this hill. Another building to check out is the **Hotel Santa Clara,** originally built for 16th-century conqueror, Diego de Mazariegos.

MUSEUMS

Na Balom Museum

An old-time resident in San Cristobal is Swiss-born Gertrude Duby Blom, known to everyone as Trudy. She and her late husband, Danish archaeologist Frans Blom, arrived in San Cristobal more than 40 years ago (when there weren't many gringos around) to excavate Muxquivil, Maya ruins outside of town. Frans had been involved with the archaeology of the Maya in several locations on the Yucatan Peninsula over the years and around the Bonampak area (Lacandone land). Both Frans and Trudy became very interested in the Indian lifestyle as they penetrated the highlands.

When the Bloms first made contact with the Lacandones, there were less than 250 of these people; today thanks to help from Trudy Blom and her efforts to preserve their forest habitat, there are more than 400. Many of the Lacandone men still wear the traditional white dress and long black hair. (Amazingly some of these very old Indians have not a sign of gray in their black tresses.)

Though the Lacandone are usually associated with the Bloms, they were first heard of after a visit in 1933 by French anthropologist Jacques Soustelle and his wife Georgette. Soustelle told the world of their hunting techniques that involved bows and poison-dipped arrows. They generally hunted monkeys, wild pigs, and wild turkeys. More intense contact with the outside world began during the last half of the 20th century when loggers began to harvest mahogany trees, which they dragged to the river and then floated to Tenosique.

The Lacandones worked for these loggers and earned money for the first time; logging is still going on in the area.

Frans Blom died in 1963 at the age of 70. Over the years, these indigenous people have become Trudy's cause. Even now, though into her late 80s, it's not unusual to see her going off into the forest on horseback—jewelry dangling, issuing orders to her companions like the best of generals. She has championed a mighty effort to preserve the rainforest that houses these Indians, and over the years has become their guardian angel. Trudy maintains a guesthouse on her property for the exclusive use of the Indians when they come to San Cristobal; they reciprocate in Lacandone country. The lovely home (cum museum/research center/library/guesthouse) is named Na Balom ("House of the Jaguar") from the Lacandone language.

Na Balom is open for guided tours Tues.-Sun. at 1630, admission fee is less than a dollar. The entire house (and garden) is a museum with interesting artifacts everyplace you look. There's an old chapel, and several rooms with extraordinary exhibits showing life in the jungle. The gardens cover a large area, and include developing vegetables, trees, flowers, and plants of the area. At one time, thousands of sapling trees were grown here from seed and given to the Indians to encourage them to replant the areas of their rainforest that have been destroyed over the years by logging and slash-and-burn farming.

In one of the patios is a small stage, painted in vivid colors and designs, where household celebrations are held. Although the Lacandones will not allow anyone else to photograph them, they've posed for thousands of pictures for Trudy, and she has marvelous portraits of these people throughout the house. The extensive library has books and articles covering all of Central America and is used by social scientists and students that come every year to intern under Trudy's stern guidance; and of course guests are welcome to browse.

About a dozen rooms are available for guests, though it's rare to get a room without a reservation. The rooms are colorful and earthy (about US$60 d), each furnished with the crafts of a different village, and most have fireplaces that you find burning brightly when the night is chilly. Dinner (included) can be a stimulating event. Guests (seated together around an immense table that

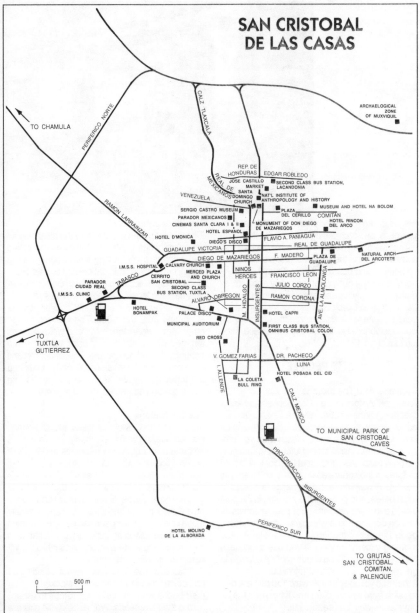

SAN CRISTOBAL DE LAS CASAS

TO CHAMULA

ARCHAELOGICAL ZONE OF MUXVIQUIL

PERIFERICO NORTE

CALZ TLAXCALA

RAMON LARRAINZAR

REAL DE MEXICANOS

REP. DE HONDURAS
EDGAR ROBLEDO

VENEZUELA

JOSE CASTILLO MARKET
SECOND CLASS BUS STATION, LACANDONIA

SANTA DOMINGO CHURCH
NAT'L INSTITUTE OF ANTHROPOLOGY AND HISTORY
MUSEUM AND HOTEL NA BOLOM

SERGIO CASTRO MUSEUM
PARADOR MEXICANOS
CINEMAS SANTA CLARA I & II

PLAZA DEL CERILLO
COMITÁN
HOTEL RINCON DEL ARCO

HOTEL ESPANOL

MONUMENT OF DON DIEGO DE MAZARIEGOS

HOTEL D'MONICA

DIEGO'S DISCO

FLAVIO A. PANIAGUA

GUADALUPE VICTORIA

REAL DE GUADALUPE

NATURAL ARCH DEL ARCOTETE

I.M.S.S. HOSPITAL
CALVARY CHURCH

DIEGO DE MAZARIEGOS
F. MADERO
PLAZA DE GUADALUPE

TABASCO

CERRITO SAN CRISTOBAL
MERCED PLAZA AND CHURCH

NINOS HEROES

FRANCISCO LEON

AVE. LA ALMOLONGA

PARADOR CIUDAD REAL

I.M.S.S. CLINIC

SECOND CLASS BUS STATION, TUXTLA

ALVARO OBREGON

JULIO CORZO

M. HIDALGO

INSURGENTES

RAMON CORONA

HOTEL BONAMPAK

PALACE DISCO

HOTEL CAPRI

MUNICIPAL AUDITORIUM

FIRST CLASS BUS STATION, OMNIBUS CRISTOBAL COLON

RED CROSS

V. GOMEZ FARIAS
DR. PACHECO

I. ALLENDE

LUNA

HOTEL POSADA DEL CID

LA COLETA BULL RING

CALZ MEXICO

TO TUXTLA GUTIERREZ

TO MUNICIPAL PARK OF SAN CRISTOBAL CAVES

PROLONGACION

INSURGENTES

HOTEL MOLINO DE LA ALBORADA

PERIFERICO SUR

TO GRUTAS SAN CRISTOBAL, COMITAN, & PALENQUE

0   500 m

San Cristobal street

fills the dining room) are often journalists, anthropologists, and archaeologists from far-flung corners of the globe, or adventurers like yourself with a keen interest in the Maya culture, along with the volunteers and possibly Trudy. Trudy has many opinions and is outspoken on many subjects, all making for lively conversation. For information on becoming a research volunteer, or for room reservations, write to Na Balom, Vicente Guerrero 33, San Cristobal de las Casas, Chiapas 29300, Mexico , tel. 8-14-18.

THE PEOPLE

Cameras And The Indians

First-time visitors to San Cristobal should know that the Indians—especially the Chamulans, Zinacantecans, and Lacandones—do *not* like to be filmed, and they like it *even less* when you produce a camera inside their churches. In Chamula you can purchase a permit at the city hall to take pictures in the square as long as it isn't a special holiday. A warning about cameras is posted in most hotels, and heeding the warning is the best way to avoid any problems. For photographers intent on coming home with pictures of the locals, go to the public market in San Cristobal (any morning except Sunday). If you use a long lens and stand in an inconspicuous spot it's possible to get pix of the people while they're busy shopping. If they see you they'll turn away. You can ask permission from your subject and if he/she asks for payment—well, that seems fair.

The Zinacantecans

Zinacantecan men are probably the most colorful with short white pants and tunics woven of red and white threads making them appear from a distance as pink, with bright-colored flowers or designs embroidered atop the woven cloth, pink tassels hanging loose, and hand-woven straw hats with semi-flat crowns and bright-colored ribbons streaming from the sides. The women, on the other hand, wear dark skirts and white blouses trimmed with a minimum of color, topped with a beautiful blue *rebozo* (shawl). The Zinacantecans have been merchants since the early 1600s and still today they travel around the region selling home-grown vegetables, fruit, and flowers.

The Chamulans

Visitors to San Cristobal will also see Chamulan women wearing white *huipils* with simple flowers embroidered around the necklines and black or brown wool skirts with red belts and sky-blue wool *rebozos* wrapped around their shoulders; there's almost always a baby tucked into the folds of the shawl. These garments are not only hand woven on a waist loom (or backstrap), but are generally made of wool that has been carded by the women from animals raised on the family plot. Chamulan men wear long white woolen tunics while the village leaders wear black tunics.

Visitors will see Chamulan women plodding up and down the hills with firewood stacked high on their backs with the help of a tumpline (strap) across their foreheads. Women and little girls are generally barefooted, men and little boys wear shoes. Here in the highlands most of the women from the outlying villages speak no Spanish, only an ancient dialect of Maya such as Tzotzil.

A Few Cultural Changes

Despite the influx of more and more tourists (mostly European), little change has taken place here. Still no high-rise hotels (thank heavens!), no Denny's, and always thousands of Indians dressed in their traditional clothing, bustling to the rhythm of San Cristobal's public market. Sadly the outside world has introduced a few variations in the lifestyle of the *i*ndigens. More and more men wear factory-made straw cowboy hats, and

among city-dwelling ladinos polyester clothing is raising its shiny head. Fortunately, the outlying villages such as San Juan Chamula and Zinacantan are still making their own flat-crowned hats and women still use the backstrap loom to weave the colorful fabric for their blouses and *huipils*.

PRACTICALITIES

Getting There

The city of San Cristobal, with its unique Indian population, attracts people (including many social scientists) from all over the world—fortunately in small numbers! Without a jet-class airport, it still

DOWNTOWN SAN CRISTOBAL DE LAS CASAS

NOT TO SCALE

takes time to get to 1,500-meter-high San Cristobal de las Casas. Thankfully, the roads are continuously being improved. Only 45 years ago you could figure a trip from Tuxtla Gutierrez to San Cristobal de las Casas was 12 hours by mule. Today it's a one-and-a-half-hour drive on a good road. However, if you plan on driving be prepared for steep, winding, hairpin curves with many

A CEREMONY FOR CHAC

Maya rituals are still practiced for many occasions, but usually within the confines of the village or the home—seldom when outsiders are around. These rituals are a fascinating marriage of Catholic and Maya mysticism. At a *Chachaac* rite, a Maya priest and the people beseech the rain god Chac for help. The altar (often set up in a clearing in a jungle) is made of poles and branches that would be at home in a Catholic church. With four distinct corners (with a tall candle at each), the altar has been dedicated to the four cardinal points—sacred in the Maya cult. In the center is a crucifix with a figure of Christ dressed, not in a loincloth, but in a white skirt embroidered with bright red flowers like a *huipil*.

The priest is a reverred village elder and is brought offerings of cigarettes, soda pop, sometimes food, maybe a raw chicken. Onlookers (usually only men) find stones and sit down in front of the priest for the ceremony.

The cigarette offerings are placed on one end of the altar next to small gourd-bowls. On the ground nearby lays a plastic-covered trough made from a hollowed log. At the beginning of the ceremony (dusk), the priest lifts the plastic sheet and drops something into the log. Kneeling on an old burlap sack with a young helper beside him he pours water into a bucket, adds ground corn and mixes it with a small bundle of leaves. The two of them pray quietly in Maya dialect to Chac for quite awhile. At some unseen signal, one of the men in the group throws incense on a shovel of hot coals. As the exotic aroma spreads, the priest begins praying in Spanish. Everyone stands up and chants Hail Marys and Our Fathers. The priest dips his sheaf of leaves in a gourd and scatters consecrated water in all directions—now the ceremony begins in earnest.

Young boys sit under the altar and make repetitive frog sounds (a sign of coming rain) while gourds of the sacred corn drink *zaca* are passed to each person. Christian prayers continue, and more *zaca* is passed around. The ceremony continues for many hours with occasional rests in between. Bubbling liquid sounds come from the log trough. It's a mixture of honey, water, and bark from a *balche* tree.

As the evening passes the priest takes intermittent naps between rounds of prayers. The men occasionally stop and drink beer, or smoke cigarettes from the altar. The young acolyte gently nudges the napping priest and the praying starts again. Each round of prayers lasts about 45 minutes, and nine rounds continue throughout the night. No one leaves, and the fervor of the prayers never diminishes.

At dawn, after a lengthier than usual round of prayers, the priest spreads out polished sacred divination stones on a burlap sack and studies them for some time. Everyone watches him intently and after a long silence, he shakes his head. The verdict is in: Chac has communicated and there will be no rain for the village this planting season.

The sun comes up and the men prepare a feast. Chac must not be insulted despite the bad news. Thick corn dough cakes, layered with ground squash seeds and marked with a cross are placed in a large pit lined with hot stones. The cakes are covered with palm leaves and then buried with dirt. While the bread bakes and the gift-chicken stews in broth, blood, and spices, gourds of *balche,* coca cola, or a mixture of both are passed around to all— for as long as they can handle it. The mixture is not fermented enough to be as hallucinogenic as it is proclaimed, but enough to make a strong man ill. The rest of the morning is spent feasting and drinking. Chac has spoken, so be it.

The priest accurately forecast the weather. No rain fell the rest of that spring or summer, and the villagers didn't raise corn in their *milpas* that year.

switchbacks and dramatic canyon drops. The incessant rain plays continual havoc with the roads, so what may be a smooth highway one month can be potholed and cracked the next.

Accommodations
Accommodations in San Cristobal range from very nice with fireplaces and private bathrooms to simple *posadas* with Spartan rooms and shared baths. It can get very cool at night in these mountains so be sure you have enough blankets before the desk clerk goes to bed. If there's a fireplace in your room, make sure you have enough firewood to keep you going. The nicer hotels fix a fire for you at the first chill. In some of the less expensive places you must pay for the firewood. If you plan on staying at one of the more upscale hotels, reservations are a good idea since many tour groups use these facilities, especially during the high season from 15 Dec. through 15 April. Check with your travel agent, though many of the budget hotels aren't available through an agency. **Note:** If you decide to write directly to Mexico, address your letter to the hotel, either street or box number, San Cristobal de las Casas, Chiapas 29300, Mexico. Don't forget, look at your room before you pay your money, especially the budget hotels, and ask if hot water is a given.

Hotels
The traveler on a budget should have no trouble finding good budget rooms. Here's a few to start with: **Casa de Huespedes Margarita,** is located on Calle Real de Guadalupe #34, tel. 8-0957. Dorm rooms and private rooms are available, all with shared baths. A *tipico* courtyard and small cafeteria make for good sociable evenings. Rate for a single room is about US$6, US$8 d. Ask about (cheap) laundry service. Check the bulletin board by the reception area, good information. For a little more charm check out one of the 33 rooms at **Hotel Palacio de Moctezuma** on Av. Juarez #16, tel. 8-0352. A cozy place with mini-courtyards, greenery, and intimate salons. This modern, clean hotel offers a dining room with fireplace as well as good food. Rooms are small but carpeted; US$17 s, US$21 d.

For a step up in price you get a little more atmosphere and sometimes a little more space and usually a private bathroom. The **Molina de la Alborada** is located south of town about five kilometers, at Periferico Sur, km 4, tel. 8-0935. Write to

Apto. 50. Fifteen rooms, each with a fireplace, are located on the outskirts of the woods. This is a laid-back rancho sort of a place to relax and enjoy the sounds of the woods in rustic surroundings; horses for hire. Having a car is convenient, though the owners run a bus to and from downtown San Cristobal. Nine-hole golf course, restaurant, and trailer park are also available for guests; about US$20 d, includes bathroom.

The **Hotel Santa Clara** is well worth checking out, even if you decide you don't wish to stay—it is the former home of Conqueror Diego de Mazariegos. Located at Insurgentes #1 Plaza Central (tel. 8-1140; fax 8-1041), near the center of town. It's quite simple but has lovely 16th-century touches such as wooden beams and carvings. Rates are about US$18 s and US$21 d. There's a restaurant and bar on the premises.

Hotel Posada Diego de Mazariegos
Some consider this the finest hotel in San Cristobal. It's situated in two buildings across the street from each other at 5 de Febrero #1, tel. 8-0833, 8-0621, or 8-0513. Many of the rooms have a fireplace; specify that you want one when you make reservations and again when you check in. The rooms have nice wood touches and the bathrooms are quaint with hand-painted tiles and bathroom sinks. The courtyards are filled with plants, and the large central court is covered with plastic so it can be used year-round, rain or shine; it can get stuffy. A few suites are available, but the fireplaces in these are in the living room and some nights it gets chilly enough to want the fire as near the bed as possible! There's a good restaurant with a warming fire going when needed, coffee shop, bar, laundry service, car rental, and travel agency, and often "imported" Indian women weaving and selling their textiles on the spot. This hotel is a popular destination for tour groups, many from Europe, so it is often very busy and mealtime gets hectic.

Another upscale hotel is **Hotel Bonampak** located at Calzada Mexico #5, tel. 8-1621, five minutes from downtown. Fifty rooms with private bathrooms, clean, good service, and the rates are reasonable at about US$35 d. Another favorite if you can get in is **Na Balom Musem.** About a dozen rooms are available for guests, though it's rare to get a room without a reservation. For information on this delightful house see "Na Balom Museum," p. 176.

SAN CRISTOBAL ACCOMMODATIONS

The state of Chiapas has established a price structure on the star rating. Use the following as a *guideline* for a standard double:

★ = US$15, ★★ = US$21, ★★★ = US$35, ★★★★ = US$68, ★★★★★ = US$?—A five-star hotel can charge whatever they wish. Remember, a 15% tax is added to these rates.

NAME	ADDRESS	TELEPHONE	FAX
Santa Lucia	Dr. Clemente Robles #21	8-03-15	—
Rancho San Nicolas	end of Calle Francisco Leon	8-00-57	—
Posada Lucella	Calle Insurgentes #55	8-09-56	—
Posada Tepeyac	Calle Real de Guadalupe #40	8-01-18	—
Casa de Huespedes Margarita	Calle Real de Guadalupe #34	8-09-57	—
Posada Vallarta ★	Calle Hermanos Pineda #10	8-04-65	—
Hotel Real Del Valle ★	Calle Real de Guadalupe #14	8-06-80	—
Hotel San Martin ★	Calle Real de Guadalupe #16	8-05-33	—
Hotel Villa Real ★★	Calle Benito Juarez #9	8-29-30	—
Hotel Capri ★★	Calle Insurgentes #54	8-00-15/ 8-13-18	—
Hotel Fray Bartolome de las Casas ★★	Ninos Heros and Insurgentes #2	8-09-32	967-8-35-10
Hotel Parador Mexicanos ★★	Av. 5 de Mayo #38	8-15-15/ 8-00-55	—
Hotel Dimonica II ★★	5 de Febrero #18	8-13-63	—
Molina de la Alborada ★★ (send mail to Apto. Postal 50)	Periferico Sur km 4	8-09-35	—
Hotel Maya Quetzal ★★	Carreta Internacional #71	8-11-81	8-09-84
Hotel Palacio de Montezuma ★★★	Av. Juarez #16	8-11-42/ 8-03-52	—
Hotel Dimonica I ★★★	Calle Insurgentes #33	8-29-40	8-07-32
Hotel Español ★★★	I de Marzo #1	8-00-45	—
Hotel Mansion del Valle ★★★	Diego de Mazariegos #39	8-25-82/ 8-25-33	—
Hotel Santa Clara ★★★	Plaza Central Insurgentes #1	8-11-40/ 8-08-71	8-10-41/ (telex) 78151
Hotel Ciudad Real ★★★	Plaza 31 de Marzo #10	8-01-87	—
Hotel Posada Diego de Mazariego ★★★	5 de Febrero #1	8-08-33/ 8-06-21	—
Hotel Bonampak ★★★	Calzada Mexico #5	8-16-22/ 8-16-21	—
Hotel Balom ★★★★	Vincente Guerrero #33	8-14-18	—

Camping And Trailer Sites

East of town, **Rancho San Nicolas** offers services for tenting or trailering as well as cabins, all with hot showers, cooking facilities, electricity, and dumping. Rates for campers US$2 pp, for rooms US$6 d. For more information write to Calle Francisco Leon, tel. 8-0057.

There are many hotels, *posadas, and huespedes* in San Cristobal; most are very close to the town center. All you have to do is walk the streets and look or go to a local coffee shop, strike up a conversation with some of the other visitors that usually hang out and you'll get plenty of suggestions. The prices for hotels in San Cristobal are among the best in Mexico.

Food

Normita serves good local specialties in a tiny cafe, with fireplace and unique wooden tables. This isn't fancy, but good and reasonable; Av. Benito Juarez and Calle Jose Flores, no credit cards. Take a look at the semi-trendy **Fogon de Jovel,** something different for unpretentious San Cristobal. Designed for the tourist (expect busloads), the selection of dishes is large, the waiters are costumed, and you might catch a marimba band/folkloric show. On Av. 16 de Septiembre #11, tel. 8-1153, accepts credit cards. **Unicornio** is a great gathering place for expats. If you need a hamburger, this is an acceptable place to have one; they even have whole-wheat bread. Sunday is *paella* day (be prepared to peel multitudes of the tiniest shrimp you've ever seen). On Insurgentes #35, a few blocks south of the *zocalo*.

The dining room at the **Posada Diego de Mazariegos** serves good meals, is open only during meal hours, and has a nice atmosphere including a fireplace for those chilly days. Wandering through the city you'll find a number of small cafes and coffeehouses. Remember, this is coffee country and it usually plays host to many student travelers from around the world who often like San Cristobal so much that they stay for a month or a year. The coffeehouses become pleasant, vibrant gathering places for these adopted citizens. Most of the cafes in San Cristobal are tiny and serve regional food, though more are changing their menus to include continental style, with the increase in tourists. But until there's a jet-sized airport, San Cristobal should maintain its unique ambience.

Shopping

Shops can be found on every corner of San Cristobal; most carry the hand-woven textiles and *tipico* clothing of Chiapas (as well as Guatemala), hand-woven straw hats festooned with ribbons, bows and arrows made by the Lacandone Indians (without the poison), as well as leather goods and other souvenirs of the state. Bargain—the people expect it. For more fine regional crafts visit the **San Jolobil** co-op at the ex-Convento de Santo Domingo at 20 de Noviembre. This is a true co-op run by the Tzeltal and Tzotzil craftsmen. Here you'll find outstanding textiles with set prices, most of which are quite moderate. Open daily from 0900 till 1400. The public market on Av. Utrilla is large but mostly devoted to the needs of the locals. This is a pulsing gathering spot for the *indigens* every morning except Sunday, which is the day that most of the outlying villages have their own market. It's at these Sunday markets that you will see outstanding woven textiles and leather goods. Market days are perfect people watching days. **Note:** Be careful with your camera if in one of the villages where people object to having their photos taken.

Getting Around

The best way to see the city is on foot. For the outlying areas a car is a big advantage, although driving around the narrow streets of San Cristobal as well as outlying villages can be nerve racking. **Collectivos** (small buses) travel on Utrilla between the *zocalo* and the market. **Taxis** can be found on the *zocalo* and will take visitors to outlying villages as well as to Tuxtla Gutierrez. Tour buses make a variety of excursions; check with local travel agencies or the **tourist office** in the municipal palace on the *zocalo*, open Mon. through Fri. 0800 to 2000, Sat. 0800 to 1300 and 1500 to 2000, Sun. 0900 to 1400.

Car Rental

A **Budget Rent-A-Car** office is located in the Hotel Posada Diego de Mazariegos, tel. 8-1871, or if flying into Tuxtla Gutierrez, rent a car at the airport.

Travel Agencies

Jovel, Calle Real de Guadalupe #26-G, tel. 8-2727; **A.T.C.** on Av. 5 de Febrero #1A, tel. 8-25-50; **Lacantun,** Calle Madero #19-2, tel. 8-25-87,

8-25-88. Check for city tours as well as excursions to the outlying sights including the **Caves of San Cristobal** and horseback outings.

Horseback Riding

Horseback riding is popular throughout the hills surrounding San Cristobal. Check with your hotel; several have horses available or can tell you where to go. Ask about horses *and* guides at the **El Molino de la Alborada** hotel, the **El Rocoveco Bookstore,** or the tourist office. Having a guide is really a good idea if you plan to ride through the villages in the countryside. Make arrangements and/or reservations a day in advance.

Services

A laundromat, **Lavanderia Patty,** is located at 16 de Septiembre and 1 de Mayo. The **post office** is located at Cuauhtemoc and Crescencio Rosas. **Bookstores** selling English-language books are located at **El Recoveco** on the *zocalo,* **Cafeteria El Mural** on Av. Crescencio Rosas, **El Sol y La Luna** at Calle Real de Guadalupe #24-D, and **La Galeria** at Av. Hidalgo #3.

OUTLYING VILLAGES

San Juan Chamula

Visitors are welcome in the village of Chamula. One of the favorite attractions is the village church. To visit get the necessary permit at the government building on the main square of the village (small charge per person)—hang on to it because you *will* be asked to produce it at the church. Remember, no cameras here—you use it, you lose it!

This is a very personal place for these people; you will witness people prostrated before their "favorite statue." Groups of two or three musicians scattered about the church add a low-pitched tintinnabulation of ancient instruments, hundreds of tapers placed reverently on the floor in front of each penitent glow in the dim light, families kneeling together reverently pray—pausing now and then for a glass of *pash* (a potent sugarcane liquor). The church is no longer officially Catholic; there are no clergy and haven't been for some seven or eight years since the Chamulans kicked all mestizos and ladinos out of their village. The rituals are now the interpretation of the Indians—who were baptized Catholic. At first glance the church looks Catholic, but soon you'll notice a few differences.

The floor is usually covered with pine needles. The statues of the saints are dressed in many layers of brilliantly flowered cloth with mirrors hung around their necks. It's said that the innermost layer of clothing is woven with the sacred symbols of the ancient Maya. These clothes are changed once a year on the feast of the saint. At that time the statue is carefully undressed, washed scrupulously clean, and new garments for the year are reverently placed on the statue. An exotic aroma greets you as you walk in the door of the church: a mixture of fresh pine, flowers, incense, and candles.

Larrainzar Indian family

Chamulan Holidays

A visit to the Chamula church is a scene to be experienced. The days before Ash Wednesday are especially colorful, with interesting ceremonies around the central square that include all of the Chamulan barrios (small hamlets) scattered around the countryside. The men gather into three groups, much like army platoons preparing to attack. They dress in special costumes including high-heeled huaraches, tall cone-shaped hats covered with monkey fur and topped with colorful ribbons, knee-length pants, a red-tassled white scarf, and brilliantly striped cummerbunds. Some carry a cane made from the penis of a bull, others wave flowered cloth banners on tall poles. Tooting horns and clouds of incense signal the time to run. Little boys join into the festivities running behind the men—learning their future. At an unseen signal they stop, slowly wave the banners over the incense and then begin running again. The *casiques* (head men) of the different villages crowd together on a second-floor balcony of the government building wearing their ribboned hats, each holding under his arm a silver-headed rod (sign of his authority). What a colorful scene, and you can't take even one picture! Another time of great ceremony is Good Friday.

Comitan

It's a long drive to Comitan, but some consider the town—along with the Montebello Lakes beyond —well worth the trip. If driving, you'll travel south on highway 190 (Pan American Highway) which takes you very close to the Guatemalan border. It's not unusual to see jeeps or trucks filled with Guatemalan soldiers and their guns. This road takes you past **Amentenango del Valle,** a pottery-making village where you will find Tzeltal craftsmanship, where bowls and other items are made without a wheel. Natural-colored pottery is sun-dried then fired in a traditional pit with an open fire, rather than in a kiln of very high temperatures. Don't expect the pottery to be as durable as most, but it is a *tipico* souvenir. Children will try to sell you their own handmade crafts—small primitive animals that more than likely have not been fired. The price is right (bargain) and they are cute remembrances to take home to a child.

Continuing down the highway brings you to **Comitan,** a town built on a roller-coaster site with steep hills. This is a good overnight stop if you plan on a full day of exploring the lakes beyond. The small town has limited accommodations; take a look at **Lagos de Montebello** (on the highway) if you're traveling on a budget. Comitan makes a dynamite local liquor called *comitecho* from sugarcane and yes it is really fiery! **La Casa de la Cultura** is a small museum (next to the church on the *zocalo*) with curious regional Maya artifacts from close by including the archaeological site of **Chinkultic.** The Comitan *zocalo* is pleasant with a historical monument and colonial ambience. Take the opportunity to fill your gas tank before you leave town.

Lagunas De Montebello National Park

The lakes are about a 60-minute drive from Comitan (51 km).

Located in the **Lacandone Forest,** this setting was made for photos. The lakes reflect a myriad of colors from pale blue, to lavender, deep purple, and reddish black, covering an area of 13,000 square miles (the official slick printed brochure from the Mexico City Tourism Office tells us there are 16 lakes in all. In Chiapas, the local tourist office says there are 59, with access to 50 by way of a paved road).

A few kilometers off the main highway a dirt road leads to Lake Tziscao where you'll find single-sex dormitories, 33 bunks in all as well as a small cafeteria and a camping area. These are very Spartan accommodations—not everyone will be happy to spend the night here. Also off the paved road you'll find the turnoff to the Maya site of **Chinkultic,** with a pyramid standing guard over the Guatemala/Mexico border. You may even see the Guatemalan army.

PALENQUE

Palenque is a *do-not-miss* attraction on any itinerary of Maya ruins. The setting, on a lush green shelf at the edge of the Sierra de Chiapas rainforest, adds to the serenity of this noble compound of ornate carvings and graceful design. Located in the west part of the Peninsula about 150 km southeast of Villahermosa and 10 km from Santo Domingo (also called Palenque Town), the site is open from 0800 to 1700; there's a small admission fee as well as a fee for parking. The museum on the grounds is open 1000-1700, and the tomb in the Temple of the Inscriptions is supposed to be open (which means the light is on) from 1000 till 1600. Ask about this one when you buy your ticket. There's a cold-drink stand and souvenir stall at the entrance, but no bathroom.

The structures are continually being excavated and restored. It may be several lifetimes before all of the still-buried ruins are revealed. But those structures that have been freed from the jungle offer a mysterious, awe-inspiring vision of great pomp and opulence. Experts say some 8-11 km of unexcavated buildings surround the present site.

In a recent breakthrough, scholars have been able to decipher enough of the many glyphs to construct a reasonable genealogy of the Palenque kings, from the rule of Chaacal I (A.D. 501) to

the demise of Kuk (A.D. 783). But it was during the reign of Lord Shield Pacal and his son, Chan-Bahlum (A.D. 615-701), that Palenque grew from a minor site to an important ceremonial center. Again we see the brilliance of the Classic Period, with beautiful sculpture, unusual life-size carvings, and innovative architectural design. These buildings are outstanding even as compared with other sites of the same period constructed throughout the Peninsula, Guatemala, and Honduras.

Passed By
Somehow the conquistadores missed Palenque completely, although Cortes passed within 35-45 km of the site. By that time, however, Palenque had been long abandoned. The earliest recorded comments on Palenque were made by a Spanish army captain, Antonio del Rio, who passed through in March 1785. He drew maps and plans and excavated by royal order for one year. The Spaniard was highly criticized by archaeologist J. Eric Thompson for "bulldozing" the ruins. Captain del Rio broadcast wild and fantasy-like assumptions about the beginnings of the Maya. After visits by a few other laymen who took home strange drawings, it wasn't long before the people in Europe envisioned Palenque as the lost city of Atlantis or part of Egyptian dynasties. When Amer-

Palenque Palace

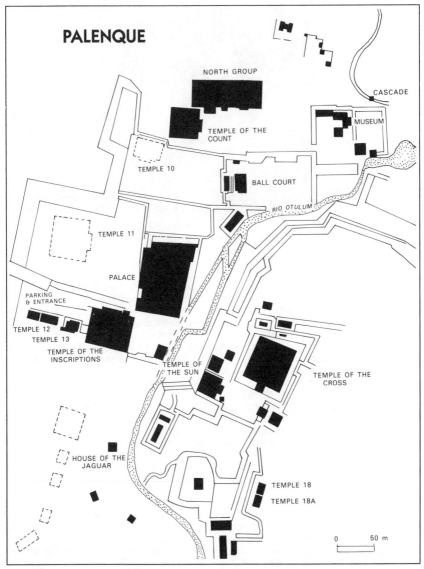

PALENQUE

NORTH GROUP

CASCADE

MUSEUM

TEMPLE OF THE COUNT

TEMPLE 10

BALL COURT

RIO OTULUM

TEMPLE 11

PALACE

PARKING & ENTRANCE

TEMPLE 12

TEMPLE 13

TEMPLE OF THE INSCRIPTIONS

TEMPLE OF THE SUN

TEMPLE OF THE CROSS

HOUSE OF THE JAGUAR

TEMPLE 18

TEMPLE 18A

0   50 m

icans John L. Stephens and Frederick Catherwood wrote about the site and drew outstanding realistic reproductions in the mid-1800s, a true picture of Palenque began to emerge.

Everywhere on the grounds you'll see reminders of the great leader Lord Shield Pacal. Carvings of him and his family, as well as some of the finest examples of Maya funerary art, are

Temple of the
Inscriptions

found in many of the structures. Palenque is renowned for its extraordinary stucco bas-relief sculpture. Rather than work in smaller figures, typical of much Maya art, the Palencanos often created figures as tall as three meters.

TEMPLE OF THE INSCRIPTIONS

After walking through the entrance and past Temple XII (also known as Temple of the Skull—look for the carved skull on the lower right corner) and XIII on the right side of the road, you'll come to Temple of the Inscriptions. This 24-meter-high pyramid kept a secret hidden within its depths for over a thousand years, until 1952. At the top of the eight-stepped pyramid is the Temple, where magnificent tablets of glyphs tell the ancestral history of the Palenque rulers. The rear gallery is divided into three chambers. Here, Mexican archaeologist Alberto Ruz L'Huillier (in 1949) first uncovered a stairway filled with rubble cleverly hidden under a stone slab floor of the center chamber.

Untouched Crypt
At the foot of the stairs another sealed passage was found, in front of which were clay dishes filled with red pigment, jade earplugs, beads, a large oblong pearl, and the skeletons of six sacrificial victims. When the final large stone door was removed, Ruz experienced the lifetime dream of every archaeologist: before him was an untouched crypt dating back hundreds of years. He had found the burial site of Lord Shield Pacal. On

15 June 1952, after three years of excavating the steep passageway, Ruz entered the small room for the first time. The centerpiece of the chamber is the sarcophagus topped by a flat, four-meter-long, five-ton slab of stone. The magnificent slab is beautifully carved with the figure of Pacal in death, surrounded by monsters, serpents, sun and shell signs, and many more glyphs that recount death and its passage. The walls of the chamber are decorated with various gods, from which scientists have deduced a tremendous amount about the Palencanos's theology.

Further Discovery
Working slowly to preserve everything in its pristine state, Ruz didn't open the lid of the sarcophagus for six months. It took a week of difficult work in the stifling, dust-choked room to finally lift the five-ton slab. On 28 Nov. 1952, the scientists had their first peek into the sepulcher. In the large rectangular cement sarcophagus they found another body-shaped sarcophagus (a first in Maya history), within which was Pacal's skeleton, with precious jewelry and special accoutrements to accompany him on his journey into the next world. A jade mosaic mask covered the face, under which his own teeth had been painted red. (The mask was exhibited at the Anthropological Museum in Mexico City until 24 Dec. 1985, when it was stolen along with several other precious historical artifacts. The mask was recovered in 1989.) It is estimated that Pacal was taller than the average Maya of the time. A disagreement between scientists stemming from different methods of decipher-

ing the number-glyphs has given various ages at death. Some say he was 80-100 years old, while others say he was 60 at the most. We may never know for sure.

This excavation began a new concept in Maya archaeology. It was formerly believed that the pyramids had served a single function, as a base for temples brought closer to the heavens. But now it's possible that other pyramids were used as crypts for revered leaders as well. All of this bears a resemblance to the culture and beliefs of the Egyptians, and imaginative students of history have tried to link the two cultures—so far unsuccessfully.

The Climb

The Temple of the Inscriptions is probably the most difficult climb at Palenque, but don't let that stop you. To reach the Temple as the Maya did, you walk up the front of the structure, 69 very steep steps. Take it slowly! At the top, while catching your breath, study the fine panels and carvings in the Temple, then begin your trip down the stairs into the depths of the pyramid. Occasionally the lights of the abrupt stairway leading down into the crypt are off; check with the ticket-taker before you make the climb. The steps can be slippery, and without light it's pitch black! An iron gate allows you to view the burial chamber without entering the room (a flashlight helps). The magnificent carved slab is suspended several centimeters above the sarcophagus.

Note: An easier climb to and from the Temple from ground level can be made on the back side of the structure.

Around the back side of the Temple, you'll find a path through the forest and up a hill to the small moss-covered **Temple of the Foliated Cross**, which seems to be in imminent danger of takeover by the thick jungle once again.

OTHER SIGHTS

The Palace

Palenque's Palace is one of the unique structures on the Yucatan Peninsula. Located to the right and across from the Temple of the Inscriptions, the Palace occupies the unusually large space of a city block. The four-story tower, another rarity of the Classic Maya, will immediately catch your eye. It's believed that the tower was constructed to give a good view of the winter solstice (22 Dec.) when the sun appears to drop directly into the Temple of the Inscriptions. It was also used to make astronomical calculations—an important part of their daily lives. A dominating structure, larger-than-life panels are still clearly recognizable throughout the site; various glyphs which line steps and walls give an insight into the life of the Maya during the reign of Pacal. The Palace sits on a platform 10 meters high, and labyrinth underground passageways and tunnels can be explored.

Palenque

More Temples

While wandering the grounds of Palenque you'll discover more than 10 buildings and several courtyards on different levels; discoveries continue to be made today. The restored buildings cover a fairly small area, making it easy to investigate each structure. Other buildings to look for are the **Temple of the Cross, Temple of the Sun, Temple of the Count, Temple XIV,** and the **North Group.** Many still have distinct carved tablets within. Visit the **ballpark,** where today you're apt to

see a vigorous baseball game going on, with the steps of a once-sacred temple serving as bleachers! Near the north group of buildings (turn left as you enter the grounds), a small **museum** displays a selection of artifacts found on the Palenque site; small admission fee. Near here a stream feeds a small pool ideal for a refreshing dip. The small structure sitting kitty corner from the Temple of the Inscriptions entrance is a memorial to Alberto Ruz L'Huillier.

SANTO DOMINGO

The community of Santo Domingo, more and more referred to as Palenque Village, is eight km from the archaeological site. The small town

bulges at its seams with the influx of tourists interested in the Palenque ruins. Hotels, cafes, curio shops, a large shady plaza, and a tourist informa-

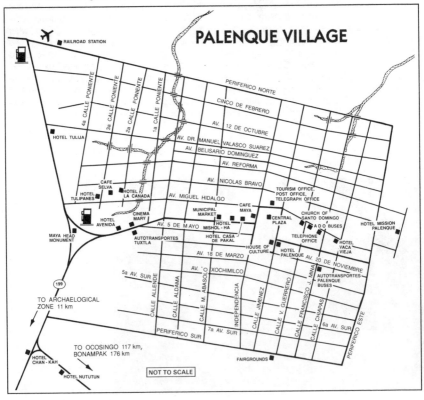

PALENQUE VILLAGE

NOT TO SCALE

tion office help make the traveler feel welcome. Again, ask before you take pictures of the people anywhere in Chiapas.

Economy

The town itself has matured over the past 10 years from a dirt-road village to an amiable small town. Much of the surrounding area has been cleared of trees and jungle (to the consternation of ecologists) and converted to cattle-grazing land. Some of the small farms are growing into large agricultural complexes. Fine mahogany forests have been destroyed by outside lumber companies who have bought the timber rights from local Indians. Many say this will ultimately destroy the lush rainforest and the culture of the Indians that has survived in this isolated world for centuries.

Tourism is beginning to take hold as the biggest moneymaker for the city. The largest numbers of visitors come in tour buses and pass through quickly. However, for years Palenque has been a gathering place for backpackers from all over the world—and psilocybin seekers. The wise pilgrim will ask fellow travelers rather than locals about the mushroom trade, since the government has offered good rewards to be informed of 'shroom activity.

ACCOMMODATIONS

For such a small town it's amazing how many hotels are scattered about. Most are simple inns in the budget category, but upgraded hostelries are springing up each year. Look at your room before moving in (or paying) and make sure you have ample blankets (this can be cold country in the winter). For reservations check with your travel agent, or contact the hotel (write to the street address or Apto. Postal number, Palenque, Chiapas 29960, Mexico. Allow about six weeks for return mail.

Budget

If money is the main concern, the **Hotel Regional** offers small rooms with overhead fans. It's reasonably clean with tile floors and private toilets. Rates about US$9 s, US$11 d. Located on Av. Juarez #79, tel. 5-01-83. Another, **Posada Charito,** offers fans, bathroom with cold-water shower, reasonably clean. Rates about US$7 s. Located on Av. 20 de Noviembre #15.

The old **Hotel Palenque** is near the Plaza. The rooms are simple and almost clean (unless there's been a change, it was going downhill), there's a courtyard that is often cluttered with hotel paraphernalia, choice of fan or a/c. Rates about US$12 s and US$23 d. Located at Av. Cinco de Mayo and Jimenez; tel. 5-01-03/5-01-88. Several other budget hotels in town include the **Hotel Avenida,** Av. 20 de Noviembre, tel. 5-01-16; **Casa de Huespedes Leon,** Av. Hidalgo; and the **Hotel Misol-Ha,** Av. Juarez #12, tel. 5-00-92. Take a look at the rooms—the only consistent fact is that they are cheap!

A step up but with budget prices is **Hotel Vaca Vieja** at Av. Cinco de Mayo #42, a side street that parallels Av. Hidalgo. This is still a little gem for the money. Clean, each of the 12 rooms has a private bathroom with tile shower, overhead fan, and tile floors. The only problem is the hot water disappears frequently, without warning—sometimes the water goes completely! An open skylight down the middle of the upper corridor lets in light and moisture, nurturing the lovely plants which add a nice touch to the simple hotel. On the main floor the small dining room serves excellent food and is very reasonable. The cook is willing to adapt dishes on the menu for vegetarians, ask. Rates about US$12 s, US$15 d; tel. 5-03-77.

Moderate

Hotel Chan Kah Centro is a new hotel downtown, clean, modern, and reasonable. (Same owners as the Chan Kah Cottages on the road to the ruins.) It offers bathrooms, fans, restaurant on the first floor, and a terrace on the second floor. For reservations write to Apto. Postal 26. Be sure to indicate "Hotel Chan Kah Centro." Rates are about US$25-30 d, tel. 5-03-18. On the main highway coming into town from Villahermosa (about one km north of the plaza), you'll see the newish **Hotel Tulija.** The rooms are simple, a/c, private bath, swimming pool, and a/c dining room that serves a big lunch for around US$2.50. Rates about US$20 s, US$25 d. Another moderate hotel in Santo Domingo is the **Hotel Casa de Pakal.** It's located in the central part of town at Av. Juarez #12 and offers 16 clean (though small) rooms (often closed during off-season). Rates about US$14 s and US$20 d. The **Hotel La Canada** is one km from the central plaza; cottages and rooms are secluded by tall shade trees. Register at the thatched-roof restaurant, La Chanampa, before you get to the hotel; be sure to specify if you want air-conditioning since only some of the rooms are equipped. Rates are about US$28 d. This is a peaceful tropical spot but also has a lively disco close by. Often filled with groups, reservations are suggested, Apto. Postal 91, Calle Canada #14, tel. 5-00-20.

Nicer Hotels

A few hotels have rooms a cut above average, or are sensationally located. The following fall into that group. If you're a birdwatcher (or not), you'll enjoy **Suites Chan Kah. Note:** A car is really helpful here. Roomy cabañas with large open porches are perched on the edge of an arm of a river in the midst of thick jungle. (Ask not to be put in one on the entry road.) The rooms are well kept, fan cooled, with decorative bathrooms and lots of privacy. Shallow, stone-lined pools in a large garden offer cooling relaxation and reading areas. An attractive *palapa*-roofed building houses the reception desk, lounge area, and dining room, with jungle vines dangling exotically down the open sides. The food is good and they serve cocktails. From your front porch, you can see many exotic creatures of this jungle. Guests have claimed to spot the elusive quetzal bird with its rich blue-green plumage, once common in the area and used by Maya royalty for headpieces and religious ritual. The owner, Roberto Romano, speaks English, is a font of information about Palenque, and

can sometimes be found at mealtimes in the dining room, except during the off-season (check the rooms out first at that time!). In answer to the oft-asked question about drinking the water (which comes from a spring behind the Temple of the Inscriptions at the ruins), Señor Romano passes out a little card that explains it this way: "This water endowed the men who lived thousands of years ago on this site with the capability of a superior mind and who by drinking it brought to light the zero and discovered the infinite." However, if you still have doubts, ask for bottled water. Rates about US$46 d. The hotel is located about three km east of the ruins; transportation provided. For reservations write to Suites Chan Kah: Apto. Postal 26.

A little more about Chan Kah; a reader related an experience that makes all travelers feel good. The young traveler decided to go out on the town and have a few drinks. To protect himself (from himself), he decided to take only the money he could afford to spend that evening. The rest of the pesos he slipped under his mattress. The evening was fun, he spent his allotment, came back to Chan Kah and after a good night's sleep left bright and early the next morning. Fifty miles later, on his way to San Cristobal, he remembered he hadn't retrieved his money from under the mattress. When he and the manager returned to the room, he found the maid had already cleaned and changed the sheets. Expecting the worst, he slipped his hand under the mattress and—did you guess?—there was the roll of pesos, all of them,

airy open-sided dining room at Hotel Chan Kah Centro, Palenque

PALENQUE ACCOMMODATIONS

The state of Chiapas has established a price structure on the star rating. Use the following as a *guideline* for a standard double:

★ = US$15, ★★ = US$21, ★★★ = US$35, ★★★★ = US$68, ★★★★★ = US$?—A five-star hotel can charge whatever they wish. Remember, a 15% tax is added to these rates.

NAME	ADDRESS	TELEPHONE	FAX
El Kichen	Col. Pakalna	5-04-29	—
Posada Santa Ursula	Col. Pakalna	5-04-29	—
Posada Charito	Av. 20 de Noviembre	5-01-21	—
Posada Santo Domingo	Av. 20 de Noviembre	5-01-46	—
Posada Alicia	Av. Valazco Suarez	5-03-22	—
Santa Elena ★	De La Vega	—	—
Lacroix ★	Hidalgo #30	5-00-14	—
Vaca Vieja ★	Cinco de Mayo	5-03-88	—
Regional ★	Av. Juarez #79	5-01-83	—
Avenida ★	Av. 20 de Noviembre #216	5-01-16	—
Misolha ★★	Av. Juarez #12	5-00-92	—
Palenque ★★	Av. Cinco de Mayo	5-01-88	—
Suites Bonampak Chan Kah Centro ★★	Av. 20 de Noviembre	5-02-05	—
Nututun ★★★	Palenque-Ocosingo Rd., km 3	5-01-00	—
Tulija ★★★	Catazaja-Palenque Rd.	5-01-04	—
Casa de Pakal ★★★	Av. Juarez #8	—	—
Canada ★★★	Calle Canada #14	5-01-02	—
Tulipanes ★★★	Calle Canada #6	5-02-30	—
Chan Kah ★★★	on the road to the Palenque ruins	5-03-18	—
Mision Palenque ★★★★	Rancho San Martin	5-02-41	—

neatly returned after the bed had been made.

Approximately 2.2 km southwest of town on the road to Agua Azul is the **Hotel Nututum** in a lush green setting on the Rio Chacamax River. Most of the rooms are modern, with bathroom, TV, fan, a/c, and a few have kitchen facilities; several of the rooms are of the older variety used when the newer ones are filled—ask for a newer room. There's swimming in the river, and an outdoor dining room that overlooks the water and jungle. A small gift shop sells cards, T-shirts, suntan lotion, and a few sundries. Nighttime entertainment is presented during the high-season. Rates about US$35 d, suites higher; popular with groups. Expect cheaper rates without advance reservations especially in the off-season. A car is a necessity. For reservations write to Apto. Postal 74, tel. 5-01-00.

Almost Luxury
The **Hotel Mision Palenque** is one of the newest and most modern hotels in the area. Complete with 160 rooms and suites, terraces, a/c, telephones, large swimming pool, green garden

areas, bar, live music, travel agency, parking, and indoor/outdoor restaurant, the hotel also provides transportation to and from Villahermosa airport and the Palenque archaeological zone. While staying at the Mision Palenque, try something a little different: follow the path into the jungle to the natural mud baths, an earthy soak complete with (free) beer and soft drinks. Room rates about US$55. For reservations write to Hotel Mision Palenque, Rancho San Martin, tel. 5-02-41.

RVs And Camping
Maria del Sol is a new campground with good facilities. All hookups for trailers, including hot and cold showers, are provided and there's a clean pool and a good restaurant called **Maria del Mar.** Rates about US$6. Located on the road to the Palenque archaeological site just before you come to the Hotel Chan Kah. Frequent minibuses travel back and forth from downtown Santo Domingo to the ruins right past this trailer park (about US$.30). Another local campground is the **Mayabel,** located about 2.2 km east of the ruins. It's a grassy area with trees and space for either tents or camping vehicles; hammock huts and hammocks are available but it's suggested you travel with your own hammock and mosquito netting (found easily at any marketplace); bring bug repellent and spray your netting as well as yourself. Toilet and shower facilities are fairly clean. The *señora* in the office will keep valuables while you're out sightseeing. Mailing address: Apto. Postal 20.

FOOD AND SERVICES

Palenque has many small cafes with reasonable prices and over the last couple of years a few new, almost trendy cafes have sprung up. The marketplace is an inexpensive place to pick up picnic fixings or to eat a reasonably priced *comida corrida.* The **Mayan Restaurant** on the plaza serves good regional food. **La Francesa** is clean, pleasant, and the food is good. The hotel dining room at the **Hotel Vaca Vieja** serves top-quality budget food in clean surroundings for few pesos. **El Paraiso** is located 2½ km beyond the Ocosingo turnoff on the way to the ruins. Here diners find a reasonably priced *palapa* atmosphere; reasonably priced it's a good place to try the *tipico* and delicious *huevos*

motulenos as well as an inexpensive *comida corrida.* For a special evening and a little more money try **Restaurant Bar Hardy's La Selva.** The food is good, great drinks, and the tropical *palapa* atmosphere is pleasing. You'll find indigenous artisans at the site along with *tipico* music. La Chanampa (at La Canada Cottages) also offers a tropical ambience and a (smaller) good menu, with occasional marimba music and moderate prices. The dining rooms at the **Nututum** and the **Chan Kah,** both out of town, serve meals in a lovely atmosphere. At least two bakeries make delicious breads and pastries. Keep looking, the town is growing small eateries like weeds.

Services
The **bank** cashes travelers cheques 0900-1200. The **post office** is a block off the *zocalo* on Av. Independencia (about US$.33 to mail postcards internationally). The **long-distance telephone office** is located in the ADO bus station (24 Av. Hidalgo), open Mon. to Sat. 0800-1400 and 1630-2000. When calling collect (always cheaper) have your name, the city, state, and number you want written down and be prepared for a long wait: there's only one operator and one line out of the village! The rumor is that this might be changing—believe it when you see it. Close to the ADO station (28 Av. Hidalgo) is a 24-hour **medical clinic;** they speak Spanish only.

TRANSPORT

By Train
Getting to Palenque is a matter of choosing among a variety of transportation modes. The train, at one time the only way to go, is a marvelous sightseeing expedition and very economical. From Merida it's an overnight trip (sleeping cars are not available). From Mexico City, pullman service is available and the route takes you through beautiful jungle with rushing rivers and waterfalls. This train travels between Merida and Mexico City; check at departure points for current prices and schedules. (A taxi from the train station to town is about US$.55.)

By Bus
Buses to Palenque arrive frequently from a number of cities: from Mexico City (14 hours); twice

daily from Merida (eight hours); from Villahermosa (two hours); twice daily on ADO; and on the 2nd-class bus more frequently. In Palenque the 2nd-class bus station is on Calle 20 de Noviembre, and the ADO 1st-class station is on Av. Hidalgo, three blocks north of the central plaza.

By Car

Car rentals are available both at the airport and the large hotels from Villahermosa, and it's a pleasant drive. The road is in good condition most of the year, and it takes about two hours to cover the 150 km. Drive 114 km on Hwy. 186 to the Cataja junction, then take the road to the right another 27 km to the village of Palenque. From there it's nine km to the ruins site. The road from San Cristobal de las Casas to Palenque (Hwy. 199) is a fair road. Upkeep is an ongoing problem and you may encounter rough spots and occasional potholes due to the excessive rain. Figure about five to six hours because of the twists and curves and steep switchbacks through the mountains. **Note:** It's strongly suggested that this drive be made during daylight hours, and never pass a gas station without topping off your tank; the next station down the road may be out of gas.

By Air

When flying to Mexico, it's convenient to fly into Villahermosa, pick up a reserved rental car at the airport, and continue on to Palenque. A small landing strip is serviced by air-taxi from Villahermosa, Tenosique, San Cristobal, and Tuxtla Gutierrez. Check with the tourism office; the strip is closed "temporarily" on and off throughout the year.

Getting Around

The town of Palenque is small and can easily be covered on foot. If you're staying at one of the hotels out of town, it's a different matter: you can either rent a car, call and wait for a taxi, or hitch. Taxis are reasonable and easy to flag down in the village. Even better, daily bus service *(collectivo)* runs frequently to and from the village to the ruins (about US$.35).

VICINITY OF PALENQUE

Misol-Ha

The lush rainforest around Palenque has an unbeatable combination of tall trees, thick tropical plantlife, beautiful waterfalls, and rushing streams. Don't leave Palenque without first exploring the surrounding areas! Taking the Ocosingo road for 20 km, a side road goes off to the left leading to Misol-Ha, a breathtaking waterfall (Misol-Ha means "Waterfall" in Maya). The falls plunge from a height of 30 meters into a large shimmering pool, perfect for a cool swim.

AGUA AZUL

When returning to the main Ocosingo road, continue another 50 km to a side road that turns off to the right for four km to Agua Azul—in Maya Yax-Ha ("Blue Water"). As you climb up into the mountains you'll see the locals (including youngsters) making their way to small villages carrying large loads of wood, sweet potatoes, full hands of bananas, all carried on their backs with tumplines around their heads. *Milpas* are cut out of the thick forest; small huts, mostly with tin roofs, are grouped here and there. As you climb higher, the view below is dazzling with brooks and rivers cutting across the green valley floor.

Agua Azul has more than 500 cascades crashing onto a limestone bed. The water boils and whirls, flows and ebbs, all a luxuriant blue. Calm pools provide good swimming and the large grassy area (that fills with people when tour buses arrive) is great for flaking out and picnicking.

OTHER SITES NEAR PALENQUE

Ocosingo, 118 km from Palenque. See ruins of Tonina. Try the good cheese manufactured here; adequate overnight facilities.

Grutas de San Cristobal, a large cavern 10 km southeast of Cristobal.

just a few of dozens of cascades at Agua Azul

Camping is permitted for a small fee at the site; in fact, campers will meet many fellow backpackers from all over the world, especially Europeans. You might see kayakers taking a turbulent ride down the cascades after toting their kayaks up into rampant wild jungle! The hardy might enjoy a hike upstream, following the cascades over rickety bridges (or just a log flopped across a rushing waterway!) and into the small village above the falls. It takes plenty of time; start out early.

Back at Agua Azul there's a small cafe, bathrooms (for a fee), plus the Lacandone Indians selling handmade arrows that not too many years ago were dipped in poison before being used. Truckloads of kids (mostly girls) dressed in dirty flowered dresses sell fruit carried in washtubs on their heads. **Note:** These girls really *don't* accept "no" very graciously. These Indians present a very intimidating attitude, totally unlike those found in the northern Yucatan Peninsula. Most speak no Spanish, only their own dialect which can be Tzeltal, Tzotzil, or one of many others. Ask before you take their pictures.

Getting There

The most convenient way to see the mountains around Palenque is with a car. From Palenque a local bus brings you within a 1½-hour walk to Agua Azul. From the drop-off point it's a steep treacherous four-km climb the rest of the way to the cascades. A backpack gets very heavy on this road. You may get lucky and hitch a ride, but don't count on it. Another alternative is a minibus tour offered by the tourism office in Santo Domingo. If day tripping, allow enough time to arrive at your final destination before dark. There's a fee for camping.

BONAMPAK

One of the important discoveries of a ceremonial center was Bonampak, about 160 km southeast of Palenque very near the Guatemalan border. Unfortunately, since its discovery by the outside world, it's fascinating murals have lost some of their luster and are not considered by the ordinary tourist as a "must-see" site. However, Bonampak reinforces the hope that uncountable archaeological treasures still wait to be uncovered in the dense jungles and rainforests of Mesoamerica.

THE DISCOVERY OF BONAMPAK

The story goes that in 1946 a young American conscientious objector, Charles "Carlos" Frey, took refuge in the jungles of east Chiapas in a small village called El Cedro. He soon became a familiar figure wandering the paths around the village and eventually met Kayon, one of 250 remaining Indians from the Lacandone *caribal* (village) located between the Lacanha and Usumacinta rivers. A warm friendship grew between the two men, and Frey began to learn the language of the Indian. The American was accepted so completely by the tribe that Kayon offered him one of his five wives. This small group of Indians lived isolated in the rainforest, still practicing polygamy and worshiping the ancient gods. Eventually, Kayon led Frey deep into the thick forest and shared the knowledge of a secret ceremonial center of his ancestors. Frey found nine structures and stelae scattered around the overgrown site. But the greatest discovery was the brilliantly colored frescoes in Building 1.

Breaking The News

Apparently this discovery was too much for Frey to keep to himself, and he told Mexican federal authorities of the magnificent find. At first his news was not met with too much enthusiasm, probably because getting there was a treacherous trip through some of nature's worst hazards, including trespassing on the land of aggressive, xenophobic Lacandone Indians. But, with the help of another American, John Bourne, Frey managed to pique the interest of several Mexican archaeologists; over the next few years several scientific expeditions were made to Bonampak. In 1949, Frey personally organized an expedition of Mexican artists, archaeologists, architects, photographers, and chemists, sponsored by the Mexican National Institute of Fine Arts. This trip would pave the way for future scientific research, but it ended in tragedy. Carlos Frey lost his life attempting to rescue an engraver, Franco Lazaro Gomez, when their canoe overturned in the rampaging water of the Lacanha River. Perhaps the initial tragedy was the breach of trust between two friends, Frey and Kayon. None of this stopped other scientists from studying the site. Once a trip for adventurers *only*, roads—though still not the best—are being built and improved each year.

Murals

The most exciting finds at Bonampak were the murals found in the **Temple of the Frescoes.** After removing hundreds of years of thick brush and grasping vines that had engulfed the building, three rooms were found to contain brilliantly colored murals depicting a broad view of life during the era. The paintings covered all four walls in

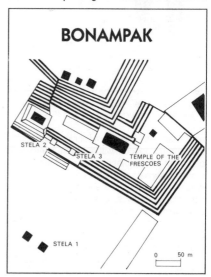

A variety of monkeys, including the spider monkey, live in the rainforest.

Restorations

To see the paintings it was necessary to scrape off the accumulation of centuries of limestone. The walls were then washed with kerosene, which temporarily brought out the brilliant colors; sadly, however, this was a mistake. The kerosene weakened the adhesion and contributed to the murals' deterioration. Today, there is very little color left on the walls. Fortunately, these fine paintings were duplicated in precise color and content by the early artists. You can see replicas in several places. At Tuxtla Gutierrez's Hotel Bonampak there's a large-scale reproduction from the central chamber; others are found in Villahermosa at the state museum; and farther away, Mexico City's Anthropological Museum has a full set of reproductions from each chamber. The murals are considered the finest example of fresco art thus found in the Maya world.

GETTING THERE

A trip to Bonampak is an adventure; it may be only for the dedicated archaeology buff. Be prepared to rough it in the jungle if you intend to spend the night. Unless you fly, you must travel over rough gravel roads in a 4WD-vehicle or minivan; during the rainy season the road becomes impassable. When you arrive there are no facilities. Although most of the Indians in the area are aloof and keep their distance, there have been reports of robberies, even from locked cars. Women backpackers traveling alone should be wary of offers of hospitality, which have been used as a ruse for theft. Obviously, not all offers of kindness are would-be threats. Just use common sense when dealing with these Indians.

By Plane

Flying to Bonampak is expensive. However, if you're a dyed-in-the-wool Mayaphile, this is another means of getting to see the ruins (which doesn't take very long) and it's possible to combine the trip with a stop at Yaxchilan, a larger, more architecturally important site. Trips can be arranged in small air-taxis from Villahermosa, Tenosique, Palenque, and San Cristobal de las Casas. When making arrangements make sure you have at least an hour at Bonampak and two hours at Yaxchilan, which seems to be the norm. The flight av-

each chamber. Almost from floor level and continuing around the room without interruption was a parade of people that caused great excitement among scientists and artists alike. The panels brought into view a cross section of the past with servants, rulers, musicians, soldiers at war, children, women, victims of sacrifice—two dimensional and all life size. The colors used were deep siennas, Venetian reds, and brilliant emerald greens, while unpainted lime was left white and outlined in black giving added brilliance to the scenes.

erages US$400-600 for a four-passenger plane, so traveling in a group saves a few pesos. Make all financial arrangements in advance, you know, like the taxi ride. For information, check at the tourist office in Palenque, travel agencies, or in San Cristobal at the Na Balom Museum.

By Car

The State Tourist Office across from the main plaza in Palenque offers an on-again off-again jeep trip that takes around six to seven hours each way. Ask about stopping at the Lacandone village of **Lacanja.** Check with **Anfitriones Turisticos de Chiapas,** located on Allende and Juarez; tel. 5-0210. Check also with the travel agency at the **Hotel Mision Palenque.** All of these trips require some trekking and climbing. For the hardy adventurer, river-boat trips are available through the **Foundation for Latin American Research,** #635 S. Green Valley Circle 213, Culver City, CA 90230.

If driving your own car, continue on the road from the Palenque ruins. Be prepared for a rough road the last half of the trip; if it's raining, expect an impassable muddy mire. Four-wheel drive vehicles are available for rent in Palenque and San Cristobal de las Casas. Chains should be carried at all times; and bring an extra tank of gas. The only other way to get there is the way of the Indians: walking and boating down the river. From Palenque it's 160 km through thick rainforest.

Safety Tips

When traveling through the rainforest (especially if you're on your own) it's wise to dress for the occasion and carry a few extra necessities: a flashlight, a sharp knife (preferably a machete that will handle sturdy vines), extra batteries, and a strong bug repellent (Muskol is good). Wearing long, lightweight cotton pants (jeans get hot) helps to ward off insects and scratches from jungle growth. Make sure you have good water-repellent shoes (boots are best), and a waterproof coverup wouldn't hurt. If you're sleeping in a hammock, bring good mosquito netting (some dangerous flying critters out there thrive on fresh blood and can cause severe problems). Before you leave home ask your doctor about malaria pills (some malaria

Chiapas fruit vendors at Agua Azul. Some of these young women speak no Spanish, only Tzeltzal. Photographers take note— they have strong religious beliefs; please don't take photos without permission.

medication must be taken in advance of exposure), and check with the State Department for a list of any other tropical diseases that might be ravaging the locals (hepatitis, etc.). Remember the other usuals if you're on your own; bring water and your own victuals. If this seems a little drastic, remember what Mom used to say—a stitch in time saves you know what!

YAXCHILAN

Larger, and also deep within the rainforest, Yaxchilan's curious carved structures are set on hills and valleys overlooking the imposing Usumacinta River. Although many of these ancient temples have been restored, you know as you stroll through the once-elegant site that Yaxchilan belongs to the jungle and its occupants. At dawn you hear the poetry of birds and at dusk the roar of the howler monkeys. While examining the carved artistry of the Maya dating back to the 7th and 8th centuries you can almost feel the eyes of four-footed jungle residents patiently hiding until intruders leave.

In Yaxchilan with a good guide you will trace the life of such Maya luminaries as Shield Jaguar I and II along with Bird Jaguar and his wife, Zero Skull. Some of the carvings are almost beyond recognition, but several carved lintels are still amazing in Temple 33. You'll see stone altars and under a protective roof some extraordinary panels depicting life as it was hundreds of years ago. The usual tour lasts two hours—not long enough to climb to each of the temples, two of which are at least a kilometer above the plaza. Some of the paths are steep. The site offers a ballpark, stelae, roof combs, carved lintels, carved thrones, and scenes including bloodletting rituals that were apparently required of royalty before major ceremonies. Many of these are fragmented and scattered, most from the passage of time and the elements, but some from deliberate acts of man. This is a magnificent site, but go with someone who knows the archaeological history—it makes it far more interesting to have an idea of what transpired here, even if it's mostly guesswork.

THE STATE OF TABASCO

Technically, only three Mexican states make up the Yucatan Peninsula: Campeche, Yucatan, and Quintana Roo. However, to provide continuity for anyone studying the Maya culture it would be a mistake not to include the classic past of the Olmec culture, which flourished in the nearby jungles and hills of what is today the Mexican state of Tabasco.

The Land
Geographically, there's a vast difference between Tabasco and its northern neighbors. In Tabasco the land is flat near the sea, and only swells into gentle hills as it nears the border of Chiapas. Water is everywhere: swampy marshland, lakes, small brooks, spectacular waterfalls, and two large navigable rivers (Usumacinta and Grijalva) as well as smaller ones (including the San Pedro and the Chacamax, which begins in Chiapas). The soil is rich and fertile, with so few rocks that the Olmecs had to travel many miles to find the material to carve their colossal heads. Much of the land is covered with thick rainforest, rich stands of co-conut, healthy banana groves, and cacao planta-

tions. The state occupies 25,337 square km. Most of the 1,065,000 inhabitants are mestizo and Chontal Indians, with the greatest density of people in and around the capital, Villahermosa.

Climate
Tabasco is tropical—hot, humid, more sticky than its neighbors in the north. Most of the approximately 1500 mm (60 inches) of yearly rainfall occurs between May and October. The driest season, when most visitors come, is between 15 Dec. and 15 April. But don't be surprised by showers at any time of the year in the tropics.

ARCHAEOLOGICAL ZONES WITHIN TABASCO

La Venta	San Miguel
Comalcalco	Jonuta

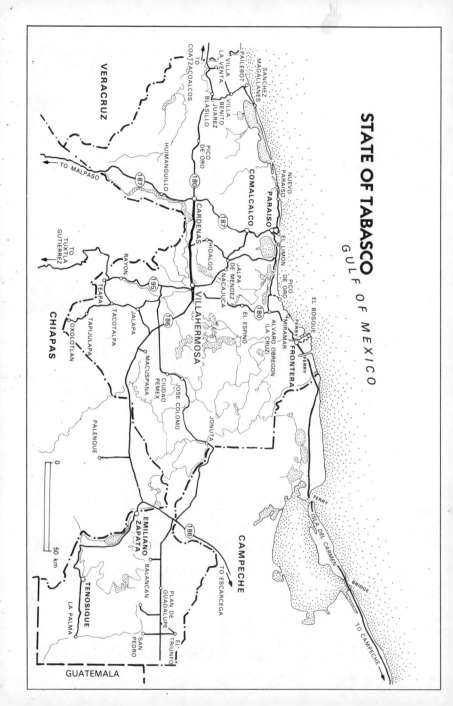

History

This was the first land of the Olmecs, predecessors of the Chontal Maya that followed. It has been determined that the Olmecs preceded all others; their society is considered the mother of Mesoamerica. The Olmecs flourished from about 1200-400 B.C., the first progressive society in the Americas. More than likely they were the first to begin carving in stone and building ceremonial centers.

For the most part, their centers had been long deserted by the time the Spanish first stepped on Maya land. Arriving on the coast of Tabasco in 1519, Cortes faced his first battle with the Maya on the Gulf coast and established a city called Santa Maria de la Victoria in honor of his initial victory. But his success was short-lived, as the Indians fought it out for 20 years more before Francisco de Montejo really gained control of the land. As the Peninsula developed and the riches of the New World began flowing from the Gulf ports to Spain, pirates attacked often enough to make living on the coast a day-to-day gamble. In 1596 the city was moved inland and renamed Villahermosa de San Juan Bautista.

Life went on with little agitation. An oblivion settled over the colony until the 1821 break from Spain, which was followed by chaos in the rush for positions of leadership. Internal conflict continued until 1863's invasion by the French. This act was the catalyst that finally brought Tabascans together, and the French were ungraciously ousted from their lands.

The age of President Porfirio Diaz (1876-1911) was the longest period of peace in Mexico during its first 100 years of independence. But though modernization and economic advances began throughout most of the country, Tabasco and the other southern states barely felt this wave of progress. Foreign capital was welcome; British and U.S. oil industries saw the potential and the seed of Tabasco's future growth was planted. The country mopped up after the bloody revolution (1910-20) and began putting its economic life together. Nationalization of foreign industry slowed things down, but ultimately the government-sponsored Pemex oil company brought Tabasco into the 20th century.

Economy

If you haven't been to Tabasco in the last 10 years, you'll be surprised at the changes that have taken place since the introduction of oil into the state's economy. A side effect is the upsurge of agriculture with the introduction of modern machinery and improved methods, enabling the state to become a viable world-class producer of the excellent Tabasco banana and cocoa bean products.

The state is growing into a center for culture as well as for big business. The people are swept up in this pattern and though the present economic conditions in the country have slowed the progress that was marching across Tabasco, many of the state's inhabitants have benefited from the oil boom—with better paying jobs, improved housing, upgraded roads, and a higher standard of living. The cities have discovered the "new" industry: tourism. Now a lot of effort is spent trying to attract tourists with modern hotels, restaurants, and an advertising campaign extolling the natural beauty of this green state along with the archaeological attractions available in Tabasco,

VILLAHERMOSA

The Olmecs, Mexico's oldest culture, left a rich history; travelers interested in the ancient past should not leave the Yucatan Peninsula without a visit to Tabasco's capital, Villahermosa. Two archaeological sites are Comalcalco, the largest and most important Maya site in Tabasco, and La Venta Park.

Today, Villahermosa combines the sophisticated look of a big city with the friendly atmosphere of a small town (pop. over 500,000). You can't help but notice a happy independent feeling among the Villahermosans. The cafes, parks, and shops are alive with chattering bustling people who seem content with their present lifestyle and proud of their ancient heritage. Walking the streets of Villahermosa you notice an abundance of museums, public buildings, schools, and more recently, union buildings with long lines of men waiting for jobs. Doctors' offices are everywhere. Perhaps due to their growing sophistication, Villaher-

mosans have switched from the ancient *curanderas* (healers), *brujas* (witches), and *espiritualistas* (spiritualists) to more modern medicine.

SIGHTS

La Venta Park

The original site of the Olmecs's art was in **La Venta** ("The Marketplace"), just off the Gulf coast 127 km west of Villahermosa near the border of Veracruz. Although the ruins were known and first investigated by Frans Blom in 1925, if it weren't for the intrusion of the Pemex oil drills, an entire Olmec ceremonial center might still be an obscure footnote in ancient history. With oil development in the region threatening to destroy the site, the entire complex was moved to the outskirts of Villahermosa and today occupies a park laid out in the precise configuration in which the site was

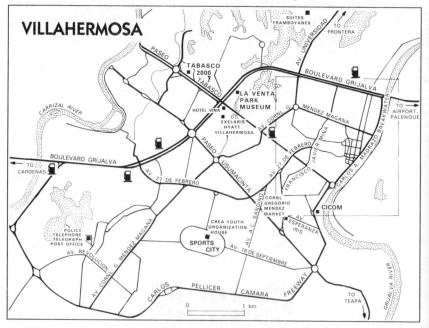

found by petroleum engineers. Called **La Venta Park Museum** (a must-see!), you'll find colossal heads and unusual sculptures not found anyplace else on the Peninsula. However, the true-blue archaeological buff should take a trip to the original site. As wonderful as La Venta Park is, the wonder of the Maya really comes through when visiting the "real McCoy." Nearby, archaeologists have discovered a series of large heads made from wood, a first! They are terribly decayed and filled with fungus, but scientists are trying different methods of treating the wood. This will take many months, hopefully the heads will then be on display to the public.

La Venta Park Museum

The park is a combination outdoor museum and wildlife preserve, with small animals running freely and others in cages or, as in the case of the crocodiles, within their own muddy moat. (Next door pay a visit to the children's zoo and park. A large greenery-filled walk-through aviary contains a marvelous array of tropical birds including colorful toucans.) The complex was conceived by Carlos Pellicer Camara, poet and much-revered Tabasco statesman. A self-guided tour (brochures with explanations are available at the entrance for a small fee) leads you by way of concrete footprints through the trees and tropical foliage past five giant heads more than two meters tall and weighing over 15 tons each. No one has yet figured out how the Olmecs (without the wheel) managed to move these giant basalt heads and altars weighing up to 30 tons, since the raw material comes from an area almost 100 km distant.

The park, three km from the center of Villahermosa, is located on the lovely **Laguna de las Ilusiones.** (The lagoon is a relaxing resting place with a high-flying jet of water that shoots rainbow crystals toward the hot midday sun.) The Olmec culture left a diverse collection of carvings at La Venta. Along with the giant carved heads wearing war helmets and having facial features displaying thick down-turned lips (which are supposed to typify the jaguar), other more delicate carvings are scattered here and there. Dwarfs coming out of doorways, or framed within structures, along with a mammoth altar and an arrangement of stone pillars called the **Jaguar's Cage,** are part of this outstanding collection. You'll see stone carvings of animals, including the unusual manatee, along

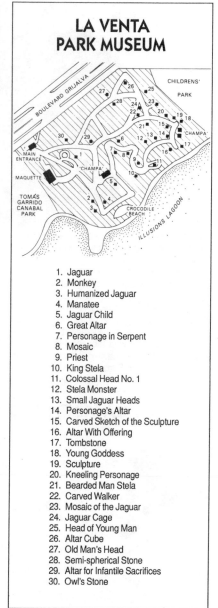

LA VENTA PARK MUSEUM

1. Jaguar
2. Monkey
3. Humanized Jaguar
4. Manatee
5. Jaguar Child
6. Great Altar
7. Personage in Serpent
8. Mosaic
9. Priest
10. King Stela
11. Colossal Head No. 1
12. Stela Monster
13. Small Jaguar Heads
14. Personage's Altar
15. Carved Sketch of the Sculpture
16. Altar With Offering
17. Tombstone
18. Young Goddess
19. Sculpture
20. Kneeling Personage
21. Bearded Man Stela
22. Carved Walker
23. Mosaic of the Jaguar
24. Jaguar Cage
25. Head of Young Man
26. Altar Cube
27. Old Man's Head
28. Semi-spherical Stone
29. Altar for Infantile Sacrifices
30. Owl's Stone

*La Venta Park
sculpture*

with stelae depicting various unique scenes such as the bearded man, all placed in appropriate settings.

The park also houses a cafe and bookstore. Every evening except Wed., a good **sound and light show** is presented at 1900, 2010, and 2115 for a small fee. The park is open daily except Wed. from 0830-1700, small admission fee. La Venta Park is located at the intersection of Boulevard Grijalva and Paseo Tabasco. From Madero near the center, buses marked Tabasco 2000, Circuito 1, Foviste, and Parque Linda Vista go to La Venta (ask the driver when you board). Taxis are reasonable and easy to flag down. After visiting the park, if you're still in the mood to explore, from La Venta it's an enjoyable walk along a busy boulevard (Paseo Tabasco) to two more parks, Tabasco 2000 and Parque La Choco.

Tabasco 2000

This series of new buildings is developing into an impressive cultural center. It includes a modern **Palacio Municipal,** a convention center with facilities for large groups, often presenting plays and other entertainment, and a planetarium that offers permanent exhibits and occasional special shows.

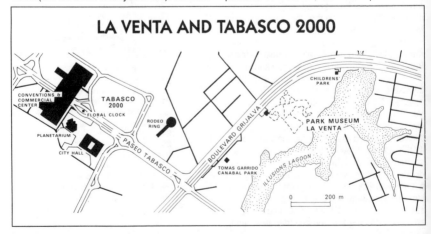

LA VENTA AND TABASCO 2000

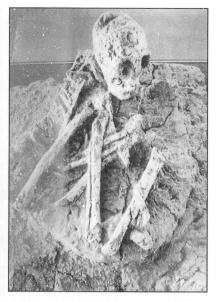

CICOM museum has artifacts such as this exhibit, which shows bodies buried in large clay pots in a fetal position.

If you haven't time to see a scheduled evening show (Tues., Fri., Sat., and Sun.), stop by for a tour of the building. The planetarium exhibits (in Spanish) depict the environment and energy of Tabasco—it's worth a visit. Lovely fountains and walkways make a pleasant stroll. Whether you want to shop or not, stop in and take a look at Tabasco's most modern shopping mall, the Tabasco 2000 commercial center. This mall is unusual for this part of Mexico with its polished marble floors and glass-enclosed shops that carry everything from well-stocked camera equipment to the latest in fashions and the newest in electrical appliances that are becoming a way of life in the growing metropolis.

CICOM

Another well-laid-out complex of interest to the visitor along the Grijalva River is CICOM *(Centro de Investigaciones de las Culturas Olmeca y Maya),* an investigation center for the Olmec and Maya cultures. One of the main attractions is the **Museo Regional de Antropologia Carlos Pellicer Camara,** a well-designed museum dedicated to Carlos Pellicer Camara. Documentation of the history of Tabasco and the Olmec, Toltec, and Maya cultures is beautifully presented throughout four floors. You'll see Olmec and Maya pottery, clay figurines, stone carvings, and delicate pieces of carved jade, along with explanatory photos showing the sites where they were discovered. One exhibit is devoted to Carlos Pellicer Camara and his life. This poet, also an anthropologist, is much re-

The man is six feet tall.

spected by Villahermosans and is remembered and honored in many ways throughout the city.

On the grounds of the CICOM complex is a complete and efficient installation dedicated to the study of the ancient cultures including offices, laboratory, workshops, auditorium, classrooms, and lecture halls for special seminars. This is also the location of a growing business center with a cafe, Ministry of Education, office handcrafts center, and the very impressive **Teatro Esperanza Iris.** This beautiful theater presents entertainment Wed. to Sat. at 1900 and 2130. However, people are graciously welcome to look into the building most times during the day. Designed as an opera house, it seats 1300 people. The **Casa de Artes,**

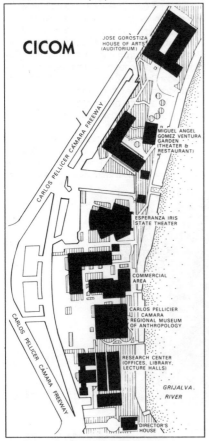

CICOM

JOSE GOROSTIZA
HOUSE OF ARTS
(AUDITORIUM)

CARLOS PELLICER CAMARA FREEWAY

MIGUEL ANGEL
GOMEZ VENTURA
GARDEN
(THEATER &
RESTAURANT)

ESPERANZA IRIS
STATE THEATER

COMMERCIAL
AREA

CARLOS PELLICER
CAMARA
REGIONAL MUSEUM
OF ANTHROPOLOGY

RESEARCH CENTER
(OFFICES, LIBRARY,
LECTURE HALLS)

GRIJALVA
RIVER

CARLOS PELLICER CAMARA FREEWAY

DIRECTOR'S
HOUSE

part of the complex, offers classes in art, handcrafts, music, drama, classical and folkloric dancing—everyone is welcome. Performances and exhibits are presented regularly by students.

Parque La Choco

A little beyond Tabasco 2000 is La Choco Park. During Villahermosa's artisan festival in May, this park comes to life, with hundreds of booths presenting a wide variety of crafts and cuisine from regions throughout the state. If you feel the need for a refreshing swim, La Choco has a large clean swimming pool open Mon. to Sat. 0700-2100. There's a fee and you must pass inspection by the pool doctor. Check with the Tourist Office for particulars.

Zona Remodelada

The old narrow streets of the original central areas, nicely tiled and closed off to traffic, are referred to as **Zona Remodelada.** The tree-lined streets bring you past small shops and tiny cafes bustling with people. Every place you go in Villahermosa is busy, but with a friendly laid-back atmosphere.

Deportivo Recreativo

This is really an impressive layout! Blocks and blocks devoted to sports of all kinds are located south of the main part of Villahermosa. Here Tabascans take part in baseball, basketball, aerobics, football, tennis, volleyball, soccer, and swimming. There's a huge playground and even (what looks like) a resident circus for the children. The grounds are well landscaped with monuments, fountains, and wide walkways. There's a large CREA building (youth organization house, day use only) where many activities are planned for Villahermosa's young people. The city fathers are to be commended for creating such a fine sports complex open to everyone for a token fee. No doubt oil money had something to do with this.

Museum Of Popular Art

This small museum displays the culture of the people of more recent history, between the time of the Spanish occupation and the discovery of oil. In the former home of noted sculptor Angel Enrique Gil Hermida is the room of Indian Music and Dances. Here you can see the dresses and masks and musical instruments used since the time of the Spanish conquest. A changing exhibit introduces you to whatever custom is taking place at the time of year you happen to visit. For example, between 31 Oct. and 15 Nov., you'll see typical displays as they appear in homes to commemorate *El Dia de Muerte* ("Day of the Dead," in the U.S. known as All Souls' Day, the day after Halloween). Skeletons are dressed with an article of the deceased's clothing and set on a shrine in a prominent place in the home. Also at the shrine, favorite foods are arranged along with candles and a religious picture or symbol. According to belief, eternity opens its doors during this time and the deceased are allowed a visit to enjoy some earthly pleasures. Cemeteries overflow with visitors, and cart vendors do a thriving business selling skeleton and skull candies, flowers, and soft drinks. It's not a gloomy time, just a melancholy holiday celebrated graveside all over Mexico, which the people take very seriously. After the cataclysmic earthquake hit Mexico City in 1985 Sept., the cemeteries were more crowded the following Nov. than they had ever been.

A Spanish-speaking guide takes you through the very small museum. Thatched huts of the rural areas have been recreated. In detail you'll see how the cooking is done, how food in baskets is hung from the ceiling in the huts made of tall smooth saplings placed close together with a *palapa* roof. There's little furniture in these humble homes, but they accommodate many hammocks. A movable bathtub has its place in the corner of the room. Waist-high slanted washtubs on stands (still commonly seen outdoors on wash day in rural areas all over the Peninsula) show the fine art of scrubbing clothes by hand without breaking the back. On the museum premises is a library, a bookstore, and a small shop selling typical handcrafts.

Marketplace

Visit the marketplace in Villahermosa for an introduction to some exotic foodstuffs. Besides small stalls displaying mounds of herbs and spices with piquant aromas and colors of ochre, sienna, saffron, and rust, there are rows of dewy fresh vegetables and fruits, and game animals not usually seen in the grocery store back home. Right out of the jungle, hanging up in front waiting to be bought, some already skinned, are iguanas, peccary, pheasant, and *paskenkly;* there's also ordinary chicken, beef, pork, and fresh fish.

Wash tubs like the one pictured have been in use for hundreds of years.

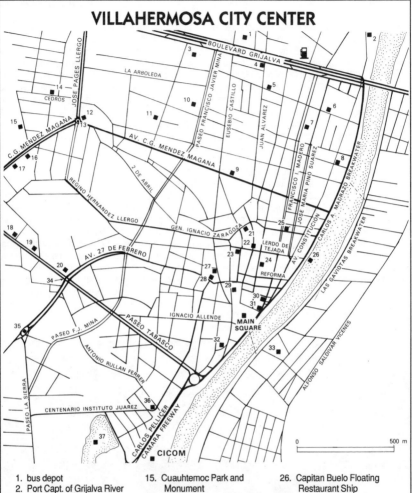

VILLAHERMOSA CITY CENTER

1. bus depot
2. Port Capt. of Grijalva River
3. Maya Tabasco
4. Kansas Steak House
5. Tabasco I and II Cinema
6. Jose Maria Pino Suarez Market
7. Galan Cinema
8. Choco's Hotel
9. Di Bari Pizzeria
10. ADO Buses
11. Pemex Hospital
12. Suites San Angel
13. Young Men Heroes Monument and Plaza
14. Country Steak House
15. Cuauhtemoc Park and Monument
16. Sahara Compound (Disco, Restaurant Alhambra, Snack Bar Mezquita and Oasis Bar)
17. Chez Monette Restaurant
18. Lion's Club
19. Manuele Mestre Ghigliazza Park and Monument
20. cathedral
21. Hotel San Francisco
22. tourist information booth
23. post and telegraph central offices
24. telephone central office
25. Manuel R. Mora Library
26. Capitan Buelo Floating Restaurant Ship
27. Jose Marti Library
28. House of Culture
29. Government Palace
30. Mexicana Airlines
31. Superior Cinema
32. Hotel Plaza Independencia, Restaurant, Bar, Car Rental
33. Flag Monument
34. Mendez Magana Monument & Plaza
35. City Clock Fountain and plaza
36. Suarez Cinema
37. Recreation Park "Laguna de la Polvora"

VILLAHERMOSA ACCOMMODATIONS

The state of Tabasco has established a price structure on the star rating. Use the following as a *guideline* for a standard double:

★ = US$15, ★★ = US$21, ★★★ = US$35, ★★★★ = US$68, ★★★★★ = US$?—A five-star hotel can charge whatever they wish. Remember, a 15% tax is added to these rates.

NAME	ADDRESS	TELEPHONE	FAX
BUDGET			
Hotel Balboa	Hermanos Bastar Zozaya #505	2-45-50	—
Hotel La Paz	Av. Madero #923	2-33-62	—
Posada Bariloche	Pino Suarez #3311	—	—
Hotel Frisa	Constitucion #1025	2-29-59	—
Hotel San Rafael	Constitucion #232	2-01-66	—
MODERATE			
Hotel Choco	Constitucion and Lino Merino	2-94-44	—
Hotel Miraflores	Reforma #304	2-00-22	—
Plaza Independencia	Independencia #123	2-12-99	—
Hotel Ritz	Av. Madero #1009	2-16-11	—
Hotel Madan	Av. Madero #408	2-16-50	—
DELUXE			
Exelaris Hyatt Villahermosa	Av. Juarez #1601 Colonia Linda Vista	3-44-33 (800)-228-9001	—
Hotel Holiday Inn Tabasco Plaza	Prolongation Paseo Tabasco #1407 and #2000	3-44-80	—
Hotel Cencali	Av. Juarez and Paseo Tabasco	2-60-00	—
Villahermosa Vina	Paseo Tabasco and Ruiz Cortines	5-00-00	—

ACCOMMODATIONS

Budget
The best selection of budget hotels is on Madero or in the Zona Remodelada. Inconveniently, it's about a 20- to 30-minute walk to these areas from the ADO 1st-class and 2nd-class bus stations. Luckily taxis are easy to find and economical. Overnight camping and trailer parking are allowed at the Sports City complex, also a considerable distance from the bus depots. Keep in mind that Villahermosa is a busy city and the best-value rooms are taken quickly, which makes room-hunt-ing a first priority upon arrival. To all hotel prices add 15% tax.

A few humble hotels are mentioned only be-cause of their budget value. **Hotel Malecon** offers ceiling fans, private bathrooms, and no hot water, and it's not too clean. Its only saving grace is its price, about US$4.50 d. Located on Calle Lerdo #106 and Malecon. The **Hotel Providencia** is Spartan, noisy, not always clean (look first), with small rooms. On Constantinople #216, it's be-tween Reforma and Lerdo, six blocks south of Fuentes; rates US$7 s or d; tel. 2-82-62. **Hotel San Rafael** is another simple hostelry that offers a living room with a TV, hot water, private bathrooms, ceiling fans, and there's a restaurant and bar next door. Located on Constitucion #240, rate is about US$6 d.

Moderate
These hotels are all near the city center. The **Hotel Don Carlos** is comfortable with clean rooms, bathrooms, a/c, TV, telephones, dining room, cocktail lounge, travel agency, and car rental.

Luxury
Since Villahermosa is growing fast, more and better hotels are being added all the time. The best one, **Exelaris Hyatt Villahermosa,** is nicely fur-

VILLAHERMOSA BANKS		
NAME	ADDRESS	TEL.
Banamex	Av. Madero #201	3-81-20
Bancomer	Av. Zaragoza and Juarez	4-07-26
Banco Serfin	Av. Madero	2-17-35
Banco del Atlantico	Av. Mendez	2-88-88

nished, with room service, a/c, restaurant, coffee shop, disco, large swimming pool and patio area, sauna, laundry, tennis court, and car rental. Located at Av. Juarez #106, Colonia Linda Vista room rates about US$64.50 d, and for US$2 more you can stay on the Regency floors which include complimentary continental breakfast and afternoon drinks along with a private lounge; tel. 3-44-44, in the U.S. tel. (800) 228-9001. **Hotel Holiday Inn Tabasco Plaza** is one of the newest and offers modern accommodations in the city. The rooms are spacious, and well furnished, with deluxe bathrooms, room service, beautiful dining room, bar, disco, swimming pool, every service you need. About US$60 d. Find it at Prolongacion Paseo Tabasco #1407, Tabasco 2000, tel. 3-44-00. Two other luxury hotels nearby are the **Hotel Cencali,** on Juarez and Paseo Tabasco, tel. 2-60-00, and **Hotel Villahermosa Viva,** Paseo Tabasco and Blvd. Ruiz Cortines #1281, tel. 5-00-00.

FOOD

You can get as exotic with your food as you wish in Villahermosa. A few cafes specialize in pre-Columbian recipes. For instance, how about cooked turtle in green sauce, or *tamales de chipilin, pejelagarto* (lizard meat), or *chirmol de congrejo* (a spicy rabbit stew), *mondongo en ajiaco* (tripe and vegetables), or just plain iguana stew? For a drink that's native to the area, try *pozole* (made of corn and raw cacao beans); *cacawada* is another tasty drink (sweetened cacao beans mixed with water though it doesn't taste anything like chocolate). Before roasting, the flesh around the beans has a tart fruity flavor—very refreshing.

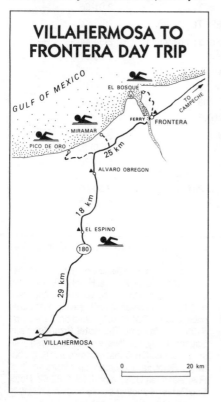

VILLAHERMOSA TO FRONTERA DAY TRIP

GULF OF MEXICO

EL BOSQUE

TO CAMPECHE

FERRY FRONTERA

MIRAMAR

PICO DE ORO

25 km

ALVARO OBREGON

18 km

EL ESPINO

180

29 km

VILLAHERMOSA

0   20 km

VILLAHERMOSA NIGHTLIFE

Show Bar El Candil	Hotel Choco's	Constitucion and Lino Merino
Bar Safra	Hotel Exelaris Hyatt	Av. Juarez #106
Lobby Bar Plataforma	Hotel Exelaris Hyatt	Av. Juarez #106
Bar El Fandango	Hotel Villahermosa Viva	Paseo Tabasco
Bar La Selva	Maya Tabasco	Blvd. Cortines #907
Bar Las Garzas	Hotel Plaza Independencia	Independencia #123
Bar Miraflores	Hotel Miraflores	Reforma #304
Bar Miragua	Hotel Manzur	Madero #422
Lobby Bar El Jaguar	Holiday Inn Hotel	Paseo Tabasco, Tabasco #2000

DISCOS

Estudio "8" Discotheque	Hotel Maya Tabasco	Mendez #505
Discotheque La Troje	Hotel Villahermosa Viva	Paseo Tabasco
Disco Snob	Hotel Exelaris Hyatt	Av. Juarez #6

Restaurants

Choosing a restaurant can be tough since there's a large selection. For the budget traveler the food around the bus station is nothing to write home about. As usual the cheapest meals are available at the market, off Pino Suarez near Zozaya. Lots of Conasupo supermarkets are scattered throughout the city. Here are a few good, economical restaurants: **Tacos El Rodeo,** Calle Hidalgo; **Rico Mae Tacos,** Madero between Zaragoza and Mendez; **Restaurant Gemenis II** (good wild game, seasonal wild pig, pheasant, mountain lion), across from Rico Mae Tacos; **Cafe Su Casa,** look for the Cabal sign at the intersection of Suarez, Madero, and Reforma; and **DiBari Pizzeria,** Av. Mendez #712.

Though more costly, if you have the yen for a good steak try either the **Kansas Grill,** Alvarez #803, or **Country Steak House,** Cedro #209. **Old Canyon** at Tabasco 2000 is worth a trip to take a look; it's like stepping into an old Hollywood western, cowboys and all. If you're looking for an outstanding (pricey) continental meal, have dinner at Hyatt's **Bogambilia**. The food is exquisite, the ambience is romantic, and the night we were there the entertainment was a very mellow jazz band from Mexico City. It's well worth the splurge,

about US$50 for a complete meal for two including wine.

For a change of pace from Latin food try **La Pagoda,** Ninos Heroes 167, or **McTavish Pub** (at Garcia and Madrazo). And if you like window-shopping, you'll find many more cafes all over the city serving *tipico* cuisine and the exotic, along with black beans and spicy *mole* sauces.

Sea Fare

For something a little special, take a lunch or dinner cruise along the Grijalva River on board the small restaurant-ship *Capitan Buelo*. The lunch trip is a breezy tour with a peek into life on the busy river. The food is nicely served, fresh fish the specialty. If you order the shrimp cocktail, don't be surprised when it's served to you "naked"—they bring many bottles of interesting condiments and fresh lime, all meant to be added by the diner. The shrimp is so fresh and sweet it's delicious *au naturel.*

At night, the small ship takes on a sparkling dimension. For the most part you sail along black banks, so your attention turns to the linen decor, the food, or perhaps a special companion to share the stars reflecting on the quiet river. This is not a cheap dinner, but with the boat excursion included

---

State Dept. of Tourism
Retorno Via 5 #104, 2nd floor
Edificio SEFCOT
Villahermosa, Tabasco, Mexico
tel. 3-80-00/3-57-62

---

it's good value, about US$17 (get current price at your hotel or Dept. of Tourism). The trip is made daily (except Mon.) at 1330, 1530, and 2100; catch the floating restaurant at the pier on the Madrazo Breakwater at the foot of Lerdo de Tejada. During winter's high season reservations are suggested, tel. 2-31-71/2-49-97.

ENTERTAINMENT

Villahermosa sports a variety of nightspots, mostly in the hotels scattered around town. Some are small and cozy, others are wild and vibrate with music into the wee hours. Some are just for dancing, others also have floorshows. Look them over, try them *all* for fun!

Tabasco 2000
The Tabasco 2000 **planetarium** puts on impressive Omnimax 70 documentaries. Shows are presented Tues.-Fri. 1800 and 2000; Sat. and Sun. at 1700, 1830, and 2000. The planetarium is next to the Palacio Municipal in the Tabasco 2000 Complex. Also check for events that might be taking place in the **Teatro Esperanza Iris;** call the tourist office, tel. 2-31-71.

SPECIAL EVENTS

EXPOTAB Annual Fair
During the second half of April, this fun event brings the town to life. Decorated folkloric floats, art exhibits, food booths, livestock judging, dances, cockfights, and the election of the Flower Queen make April a good time to visit if you like lots of activity.

Nautical Marathon
Something different in May is an internationally acclaimed marathon on the Usumacinta River. Four categories of boats cover a distance of 600 km from Tenosique to Villahermosa over four days.

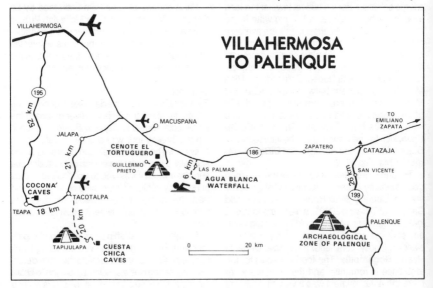

VILLAHERMOSA TO PALENQUE

VILLAHERMOSA

195

52 km

JALAPA

21 km

MACUSPANA

CENOTE EL TORTUGUERO

GUILLERMO PRIETO

LAS PALMAS

6 km

AGUA BLANCA WATERFALL

186

ZAPATERO

TO EMILIANO ZAPATA

CATAZAJA

ZAPATA

199

SAN VICENTE

26 km

COCONA' CAVES

TACOTALPA

20 km

TEAPA   18 km

TAPIJULAPA

CUESTA CHICA CAVES

PALENQUE

ARCHAEOLOGICAL ZONE OF PALENQUE

0   20 km

Villahermosa Emergency Telephone Numbers

Fire Department	3-91-41
Highway Patrol	3-22-14
Red Cross	3-35-93
State Tourism Office	3-80-00
Social Security Hospital	3-00-31

Participants come from all over Mexico and bordering countries to this big event. Cash prizes are awarded and everyone has a good time. For more information call the State Tourism Office at 2-31-71, or write to Carlos Izundegui Rullan, Director of Tourism, #101-A Zaragoza, Villahermosa, Tabasco, Mexico.

GETTING THERE

Considered a gateway to central Mexico, Villahermosa is easily reached by many means. A fine transportation network connects with Mexico City, Chiapas, Guatemala, the Quintana Roo coast, and the rest of the Yucatan Peninsula, although to link up with the national train service you must travel 58 km to Teapa.

By Plane

Villahermosa has a busy airport. Flights arrive daily from many cities in Mexico as well as connecting international flights from Madrid, Paris, London, Rome, the U.S., and several points in the Orient. You can make direct flights to Mexico City, Oaxaca, Merida, Tuxtla Gutierrez, and other large cities, as well as to special destinations in small air-taxis: Bonampak, Ciudad del Carmen, Emil-iano Zapata, and Palenque. **Mexicana Airlines** (Madero 109, tel. 2-27-15/2-11-69) flies in and out of Villahermosa.

When you arrive at the airport (tel. 2-43-86), you have the choice of a taxi or *combi* service to your hotel or the center of town. It's at least a 45-minute walk to town center. There are numerous auto rentals within the a/c air terminal plus a coffee shop, restaurant, and several gift shops. The staff at the state tourist information booth located in the terminal is very helpful, provides detailed city maps, and there's almost always someone who speaks English along with several other languages.

By Bus

Buses from all over Mexico arrive frequently. The **ADO** 1st-class bus station is located at Mino and Merino, in the northeast section of the city; tel. 2-14-46. The 2nd-class bus station, called **Central de Autobuses de Tabasco,** is on Grijalva. Both stations are very busy; you can find transportation to anyplace in Mexico from these two spots.

By Car

Highways into Villahermosa are easy driving from both north and south. From Campeche and points east take Hwy. 186. From Campeche along the coastal route take Hwy. 180. From Veracruz along the coast take Hwy. 180 east. From San Cristobal de las Casas and points south take Hwy. 190. These all converge in Villahermosa. If driving from the airport into downtown Villahermosa, have a few 1000-peso notes ready for the toll. Local taxis take a roundabout detour to eliminate paying, but make sure you know where you're going before trying it.

VICINITY OF VILLAHERMOSA

COMALCALCO

Ruins

A beautiful pastoral site of green rolling hills and plains, Comalcalco is a 55-km drive northwest of Villahermosa. Built in the Classic Period between A.D. 200-700, its distinct architectural design is different from the sites in the north part of the Peninsula. Because of a lack of stone, the building method was to compact earth and clay creating high platforms. Next, kilned bricks for the structures, walkways, and domes were held together with mortar made from ground oyster shells. The entire facade was then faced with stucco, which was often molded into beautiful ornamentation: glyphs, masks, human and animal figures, religious symbols, and high polychromatic reliefs. Most of the artwork is barely visible now after centuries of exposure to the elements. The stucco surface is almost totally gone, exposing the bricks that so closely resemble those made today. **Note:** The bricks are fragile and you are not permitted to climb on the pyramids—wherever the signs read *No Subir!*

Several mounds are now bare of any structure; the original structures were built of wood and have long since deteriorated. **Temple #1,** the immense structure on the left as you walk from the entrance, has the best remaining example of the stucco high relief that once covered most of the structures. Today these valuable remnants of history are covered with glass and have been roofed over to deter any further deterioration. The facial features of these figures are unique, with thick strangely shaped lips, somewhat resembling the colossal heads in La Venta, yet vastly different in style. The Palenque site in Chiapas flourished at the same time as the Chontal Maya here in Comalcalco, and artifacts indicate there was communication and trading between the two sites. At the entrance to the ruins is a small museum, a gift/book shop (that doesn't have much to sell), and a snack stand; a small admission to the site is collected and it's open 0800-1700.

The walk up a hill to the **Palace** reveals a lovely view of the green countryside below and mounds scattered here and there but not yet excavated. From the top of the hill you'll see healthy cattle, unknown to the Maya Indian, living in the shadows of the ancient structures. While wandering you'll discover a sunken courtyard, many halves of the traditional corbel arch, and the remains of small display niches all through the structures. The Chontal Maya were as talented and creative as the rest of the Maya throughout Mesoamerica.

The entomologist might enjoy observing giant beetles often seen in the trees near the buildings at the entrance. The insect is the size of a man's hand and about three inches thick, shiny black in color, and apparently common in this rural part of the state.

Getting There

You can reach Comalcalco from the Villahermosa ADO 1st-class bus station on Mina and Merino.

Comalcalco's kilned-brick construction is evident here.

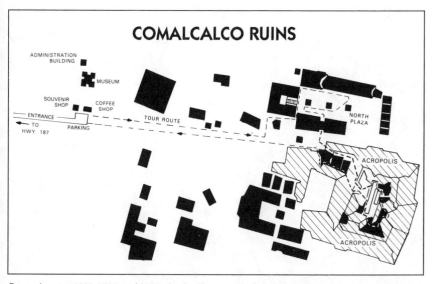

COMALCALCO RUINS

ADMINISTRATION
BUILDING

MUSEUM

SOUVENIR
SHOP   COFFEE
SHOP

ENTRANCE
TO   PARKING   TOUR ROUTE
HWY. 187

NORTH
PLAZA

ACROPOLIS

ACROPOLIS

Buses depart at 1230, 1730, and 2030; check with the driver for return-trip information. If driving take Hwy. 180 west from Villahermosa to the city of Cardenas, and when you come to the junction with Hwy. 187, continue on 187 to Comalcalco. Just beyond the ruins is cacao bean country. A chocolate factory (ask at the Comalcalco gift shop) gives a tour if it's the right time of year (harvest season usually begins around 15 Oct., but the weather determines the exact date and when the factory begins operating).

DAY TRIPS

Comalcalco Loop

A good day trip is the visit to Comalcalco, then continuing through the small city of Paraiso, with a stop at Puerto Ceiba on the coast of the river, perfect for marvelous scenery and a lunch stop of fresh fish and shrimp in an outdoor cafe on the edge of the river. Making a loop on your return trip to Villahermosa by way of one of several different highways (watch for signs marked Villahermosa) gives a pleasant change of landscape.

Allow a full day with an early start for this trip. You'll travel through small towns with colorful churches painted in bright blues and yellows, very

atypical. Dense groves of trees—coconut, banana, and cacao—are thick along the highway. Tabasco is the largest producer of bananas in Mexico, especially in this area. With lots of banana stands along the way you can pick up either a large hand or just a few for an energy snack—very cheaply. You'll see coconut being worked all along here in preparation for copra. And if you have never seen the cacao bean grow, make a point of looking for a cacao plantation. This area is loaded with them, small family affairs that welcome visitors. The bean looks much like a pale greenish-yellow ridged squash about the size of an elongated cantaloupe. It grows not only on the branches of the tree, but strangely, from the trunk also.

Agua Blanca Falls

This trip is best done by car. Agua Blanca or Iztac-Ha is the name of the Maya princess who, according to legend, shed the tears that created these magnificent waterfalls. The **Mampulli River** emerges at the highest point of Cerro de las Perdices, a green tropical forest where walkways and steps have been provided for the trek. It's a lovely walk, often with few tourists. The walkways take you through deep shadowed paths with the sounds of water and unseen creatures every-

Comalcalco stucco carving shows unusual style of the Chontal Maya.

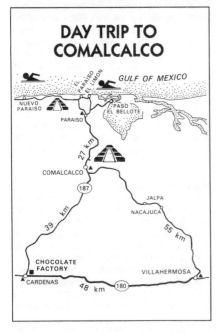

DAY TRIP TO COMALCALCO

where. The falls foam and bubble over large boulders and small rocks falling into whirling pools, finally resting in calm blue ponds. This is a perfect place for a refreshing dip.

This is a popular destination for Tabascans, and on holidays it is often filled with family groups enjoying picnics. Barbecue grills are provided, as well as restrooms, shops, and a small restaurant selling refreshments. To get to Agua Blanca Falls from Villahermosa, head southeast toward Marcuspana on Hwy. 186 for 71 km where you'll see a sign for the Agua Blanca turnoff directing you another 11 km.

If on your way back to Villahermosa and there's still plenty of daylight, you may want to take the three-km road off to the right to take a quick look around Marcuspana, location of the first city built by the Pemex oil company.

SOUTH OF VILLAHERMOSA

Teapa And The Puyacatengo River
Another trip for those traveling by car is a 62-km drive from Villahermosa heading south on Hwy.

Much of the Olmec sculpture portrays people in or climbing out of various altars or windows.

195 to **Puyacatengo,** another fabulous river that crisscrosses the state. After 58 km you pass Teapa, one of the old cities of Tabasco. It's worth a walk-through for a brief glimpse of the town. There are plenty of places to explore in this area, and if you decide to continue on to Tacotalpa, Tapijulapa, and Oxolotan (depending on how much time is spent at each stop), stay at **Parador Puyacatengo,** a beautiful location where you can swim in the river and enjoy nature. This is a very simple hostelry, with food available.

Tacotalpa

A sign at Teapa will direct you to the road to Tacotalpa, another thriving farming community with an interesting history. In pre-Columbian days, before there were state borders breaking up the area, this was one of the centers of the Zoque Indian Empire. The nearby Indian capital city was named Tuchtli, now called Tuxtla Gutierrez, in present-day Chiapas. In 1598, after the intrusion of the conquistadores, the leaders of the Spanish government and their families moved from the pirate-plagued coastal region to the safety of Tacotalpa. In 1795 the capital moved back to the coast and the city has grown as an agricultural center since. Its economic activity involves cattle, corn, beans, bananas, cacao, and sugarcane.

Tapijulapa

Continuing south you'll come to Tapijulapa (over 90 km from Villahermosa), a charming town on the banks of the Oxolotan and Amatan rivers. You'll enjoy a stroll through the cobblestone streets lined with white houses with red-tile roofs and colonial facades. For the ambitious, a trek to the highest hill in town brings you to an old church and offers a spectacular view of the entire area. Bring your camera. Just south of the city are the **Poana** and **De Cuesta caverns** for spelunkers.

CAVES FOR EXPLORERS

Most of these caves are within reasonable distance of downtown Villahermosa. Ask your hotel clerk for easy directions. Some offer sound and light shows, and all should be explored by experienced spelunkers.

Grutas de Poana	Carretera Tacotalpa Xicotencatl km 12
Grutas de Tulija	Carretera Tenosique Guatemala km 5
Grutas de Cacona	Ejido Eureka Belen Teapa km 15
Grutas de Agua Blanca	Carretera Villahermosa-Macuspana km 69

Another possible adventure in Tapijulapa is a trip in a dugout canoe from the Tapijulapa Wharf to **Villa Luz.** Meandering down the river you'll pass lovely landscapes, multiple waterfalls, brooks of sulphurous water, and beautiful birdlife along the shoreline. Villa Luz was the home of one of the political heroes of Tabasco, Tomas Garrido Canabal. His home is open to visitors.

Oxolotan

Farther south on the highway leaving Tapijulapa is Oxolotan. Here the biggest attraction is the **Country and Indian Theater.** Performances are usually during the day, presented against a backdrop of majestic hills and river banks. Check at the Tourist Office in Villahermosa for schedule information.

THE STATE OF QUINTANA ROO

THE LAND AND SEA

The state of Quintana Roo (say kin-taw-nuh-ROW) is located on the east coast of Mexico's Yucatan Peninsula, bordered by the state of Yucatan to the northwest, Campeche to the west, and the country of Belize to the south. Quintana Roo occupies 50,350 square km and has a population of 200,000. Mostly flat, this long isolated state is covered with tropical forest and boasts the most beautiful white-sand beaches on the Peninsula. Several islands lie offshore, and the magnificent 250-km-long Belize Reef runs parallel to the Quintana Roo coast from the tip of Isla Mujeres to the Bay of Honduras, whose undersea life provides world-class diving. Chetumal, capital of the state, borders Belize, formerly known as British Honduras.

HISTORY

This stretched-out coastal region was ignored by Mexico longer than the rest of the Peninsula because of its dense jungle and notorious Chan

Santa Cruz Indians. When defeated by the Spanish, many Maya took refuge in this coastal territory, keeping would-be intruders easily at bay with their xenophobic reputation until the beginning of the 20th century. The only real Spanish settlement, Bacalar, on the southern end of the state, was destroyed twice, once by pirates and again during the Caste War by rioting Maya. Quintana Roo was held as a territory of the Republic for 73 years, then admitted as the 30th state to the United Mexican States in 1974. Not until the 1970s were highways built, when Mexico finally realized that Quintana Roo possesses all the elements of one of the most beautiful resort areas in the world.

Naming A Territory

If you're wondering how Quintana Roo got its name, it's rather a disappointing story. For many years the east coast of the Yucatan Peninsula remained a desolate no-man's land; it had no name because few if any people ever spoke about it. But, when it became a territory it needed a name. As is often the custom in Mexico, the territory was named for an army general, undoubtedly a sterling soldier who deserved the honor. But sadly the

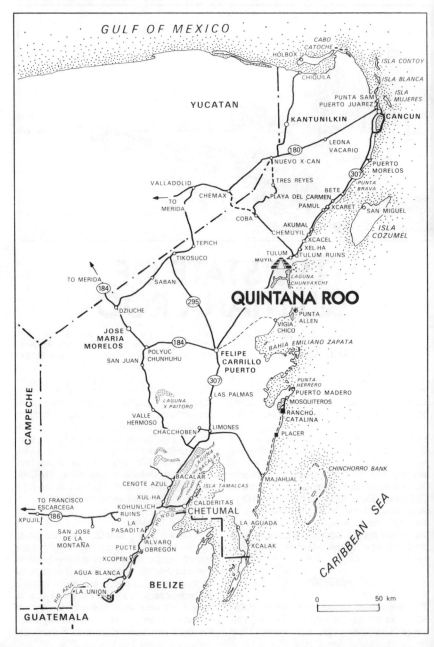

man had not fought a battle in, nor had he ever traveled to, the territory of this Caribbean paradise. His name was Andres Quintana Roo.

ECONOMY

Until recently the economy of this lost territory amounted to very little. For a few years the chicle boom brought a flurry of activity centered around the harbor of Isla Cozumel. Native hardwood trees have always been in demand; coconuts and fish-

ing were the only other natural resources that added to the economy—but none on a large scale. Today the face of Quintana Roo is changing rapidly. Tourism is its number-one attraction thanks to the development of Cancun into a multimillion-dollar resort. Building and construction continues south down the peninsula bringing new roads which give access to until-now unknown beaches and unseen Maya structures. By 1995 Cancun will have 25,000 rooms available to visitors from around the world.

ISLA DE COZUMEL

INTRODUCTION

Cozumel ("Land of the Swallow") is a Caribbean island surrounded by water the color of imperial jade. Edged with stretches of white sand and craggy castles of black limestone and coral, its shoreline is continuously washed by an inquisitive, restless sea. The island rose from the sea in the Pliocene or Pleistocene epoch to its maximum height of 45 feet above sea level. At 47 km long and 15 km wide it's the largest of the three islands off the east coast of Quintana Roo—and the largest island in the Republic of Mexico. The other islands lying off the Quintana Roo coast are Isla Mujeres and Contoy. Cuba is 95 miles north and

Cancun is 30 miles northwest. Across a 3,000-foot-deep channel that's 19 km offshore, Cozumel was a sacred mecca for Maya noblewomen who traveled in large dugout canoes to worship Ixchel, the goddess of fertility.

A calm sea on the lee (west) side of the island makes it ideal for swimming, diving, water-skiing, windsurfing, beachcombing, or relaxing in the sun. It's also the developed side, where clusters of buildings in the (only) town of San Miguel de Cozumel house 50,000 residents and visitors. Offices, shops, banks, markets, hotels, restaurants, and two docks are all concentrated in this small seaside town. The east coast is another world, with few people and little activity but dotted with isolated coves and bays, some with placid water, others

Cozumel coastline

with spectacular surf crashing on the beach and spraying mist on passing windshields. Clear water and the proximity of at least 20 live reefs make snorkeling a must, even for the neophyte. Exploring the Maya ruins in the overgrown interior of the island is an adventure by motorcycle, bike, car, or foot. The people of Cozumel, in their quiet way, are accepting and friendly to the growing number of visitors who come each year. Although Cozumel, with its lively discos and steady influx of divers and cruise ships, is more upbeat than Isla Mujeres, it still lacks the jet-set feeling of Cancun

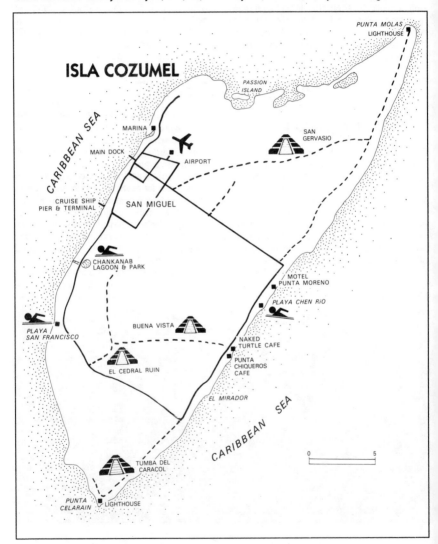

—perhaps because it's a real town where fishing and diving flourished long before outsiders arrived.

Climate

The climate is warm year-round (average 80° F). The heaviest rains begin in June and last through October. It's possible for rain to fall almost every day during that time, but the usual afternoon shower is brief and the ground absorbs moisture quickly. In most cases any travel interruption is minimal, though there are the exceptions. The rainy season occasionally opens up and lets loose torrents. During wet months, expect high humidity. November through May is generally balmy, with lower humidity and an occasional cool evening (average 78° F). But remember, tropical climes can change from mellow to miserable very quickly—and then to mellow again.

FLORA AND FAUNA

Birds

In 1925, Ludlow Griscom from the American Museum of Natural History was one of the first ornithologists to discover Cozumel's varied and concentrated birdlife. Since then, Cozumel has been

ARCHAEOLOGICAL ZONES IN QUINTANA ROO

Tulum	Xelha
Coba	Kohunlich

considered a prime birding site; outside of town, civilization has not intruded into natural habitat. Except for the network of above-ground plastic water lines paralleling graded roads, the tangled brush, tall trees, and an occasional abandoned hut all ensure protected nesting grounds for these exotic winged creatures. If you enjoy watching birds, then getting up very early and trekking into one of several swampy areas on the island is worth the effort. One such place is located close to town behind the Sol Caribe Hotel. Here, at dawn, you're likely to see flocks of small multi-hued parrots, blue warblers, macaws, and spindly legged white egrets, while listening to a glee club of sounds echoing through the trees and across the murky water. Another marshy area that attracts fowl is just south of the junction where the cross-island

Hummingbirds are seen everywhere in the Yucatan bush. The tiny bird was an important part of Maya art and religion.

road meets the east shore. A large swamp, accessible by car, parallels the coast behind the Punta Celerain Lighthouse.

Other Animals

Iguana and other lizards skitter through the jungles; armadillos, deer, small foxes, and coati also call the Cozumel jungle their home. The iguana, more visible than the others because of its size and large population, is often seen sunning atop rocks along the east shore or even in the middle of the warm paved road that parallels the beach. Though the iguana is described as timid and said to move slowly, the traveler with a camera has to be lightning-fast to capture it on film. Once an outsider is spotted, it slips quickly into its underground burrow or up the nearest tree. The secret is not to be seen by the wary creature. (Photographers—keep trying, it can be done!) The iguana found in Cozumel is commonly shades of dark green, can grow up to two meters long, including its black-banded tail, and has a comb-like crest of scales down the middle of its back. Varicolored species are found on the Yucatan mainland.

Plantlife

Cozumel has never been known for its agriculture, partly because of the shortage of water. However, during the early 1900s chicle sap was gathered from numerous *zapote* trees, which grow wild in the interior. Evidence of abandoned huts can be seen now and then where farmers once tried to eke a living from the thin, rocky soil. Coconut palms grew thick near the sea (before the devastating "yellowing" disease destroyed many trees) and it's still not unusual to see a sprouted coconut bobbing up and down in the surf. Many coconut trees take root that way, but if grown too close to the sea, they produce poor-tasting fruit. Take a stroll through the cool botanical garden at **Chankanab National Park,** where hundreds of tropical plants found on the island have been planted and labeled. A small entry fee (US$2) gives access for the day to the lagoon and beach.

Marinelife

Brilliantly colored fish, from tiny two-inch silver bait fish traveling in cloud-like schools to the grim thick-lipped grouper, lurk in and around graceful, asymmetrical formations of coral reminiscent of their names: cabbage, fan, and elk. You'll see rainbow-

hued parrotfish, yellow- and black-striped sergeant majors, French angelfish, yellow-tailed damselfish, and shy silver-pink squirrel fish with their big sensitive-looking eyes. In shallow coves, daring Bermuda grubs come up out of the water to eat from your hand; watch the teeth!

HISTORY

Earliest Maya And Spanish

Cozumel's history alternates with bursts of unique activity and years of obscurity. During the post-Classic Period, Cozumel was not only a sacred island but an important trading center. Artifacts, especially pottery remnants of the female figure made in distant parts of Mesoamerica, were left by women who traveled from all over Quintana Roo to worship Ixchel at shrines scattered throughout the jungle. At one time during the Caste War, the talking cross cult was active on the island. After that era the island existed undisturbed until 1517, when it was briefly visited by Juan de Grijalva, who traveled from Cuba on a slave-hunting expedition.

He was soon followed by Spaniard Hernan Cortes, who embarked on his history-changing course in 1518. Cortes used Cozumel as a staging area for his ships when he launched his successful assault on mainland Indians. It was here that Cortes first heard of Geronimo de Aguilar, a Spanish shipwreck survivor of several years before. Aguilar had been living as a slave with his Indian captors. One story claims that when he heard of Cortes's arrival, he swam 19 km from the mainland to meet him. Because of Aguilar's fluency in the Maya tongue, he became a valuable accomplice in Cortes's takeover of the Indians. Francisco de Montejo also used Cozumel as a base in his war on the mainland. With the influx of Spaniards and accompanying diseases the Maya all but disappeared. By 1570 the population had dropped to less than 300.

Pirates And Chicle

The sparsely inhabited island led a placid existence until the late 1600s when it became a refuge for bandits of the sea. Pirates such as Jean Lafitte and Henry Morgan favored the safe harbors of Cozumel, especially during violent storms. The buccaneers frequently filled their water casks at

Chankanab Lagoon and created general havoc with their heavy drinking and violent fights, disrupting life within the small population of Indians and Spanish. By 1843 the island of Cozumel had been totally abandoned. Then refugees from the Caste War began to resettle it.

Cozumel again became a center of activity when the chewing gum industry began to grow in the U.S. For centuries, the Maya had been satisfying their thirst by chewing raw sap from the *zapote* tree which grows on Cozumel and throughout most of Central America. In the early 1900s, the developed world was introduced to this new sweet, bringing an economic boom to the Quintana Roo coast. New shipping routes included Cozumel, one of the best harbors along the coast suitable for large ships. Several big companies made fortunes on the nickel-pack of chewing gum, while the Indians who cut their way through the rugged jungle to tap the trees managed only subsistence. Because of these gum companies, however, obscure but magnificent jungle-covered ruins hidden deep in the forests were discovered, fascinating the urban explorers. This was the beginning of a large-scale interest in the Maya ruins by outsiders that continues into the present. At one time the only route to Cozumel was by ship from the Gulf of Mexico port of Progreso. Cozumel's shipping income dwindled gradually as airstrips and air freight became common on the Peninsula. In addition, synthetics replaced hard-to-get chicle and are now used almost exclusively in the manufacture of chewing gum.

WW II And Cousteau

In 1942, as part of their defense network guarding the American continent, the U.S. government made an agreement to protect the coastline of Mexico. The American Army Corps of Engineers built an airstrip on Cozumel where the Allies also maintained a submarine base. After the war, the island returned to relative obscurity until 1961, when a TV documentary produced by oceanographer Jacques Cousteau introduced the magnificent underwater world that exists in and around its live reefs. Since 1974 statehood, Quintana Roo (including Cozumel) has enjoyed (or suffered) a rebirth into the world of tourism.

The Mexican government is making progress developing its beautiful Caribbean coast. For years it was believed that Cozumel itself would always maintain its pleasant small-town ambience, with just a smattering of tourism to add spice to the small island, and would never grow into a high-rise city; the water supply cannot support an enormous increase of people, plus everything needs to be shipped across the 19-km stretch that separates it from the mainland. But now the word is out, and the historical "Land of the Swallow" is about to see a new desalinization plant and the development of hotels on San Francisco Beach due to be open in 1991-92.

SAN MIGUEL DE COZUMEL

Cozumel has only one city: San Miguel. Though it's no longer a sleepy fishing village, it still has a relaxed, unhurried atmosphere, a good selection of restaurants from budget to gourmet, and hotels in every price range. Grocery stores, curio shops, banks, a post office, telegraph office, dive shops, and anything else you might need are available. The main street, known either as Malecon ("Seawall") or Av. Melgar, depending on which map you're studying, extends 14 blocks along the waterfront. The main dock is at the foot of Av. Juarez, in the center of town. Plaza del Sol, the large central plaza, boasts modern civic buildings and an imposing statue of the late Mexican president Benito Juarez. The surrounding streets are closed to vehicular traffic making it a pleasant place to stroll, shop, and enjoy the tranquility of Cozumel. In spring, masses of orange *flamboyane* (poinciana) flowers bloom on the surrounding shade trees under which local townspeople gather for festivals, religious celebrations, or friendly chats. Cafes and gift shops line the north side of the plaza.

ACCOMMODATIONS

Deluxe

The newer, more modern hotels located on or across the street from the waterfront are north and south of town. Most of these fit the deluxe category. Sand hauled from the east side of the island covers razor-sharp coral and limestone, creating beautiful white beaches for their patrons (and the public). The hotels offer a variety of lures to get you out of town: spacious palm-shaded grounds, beach activities, diving equipment, charming outdoor patios and thatch-roofed bars, swimming pools, tennis courts, lively entertainment, and modern restaurants, with tour services and car rentals right on the premises. Taxis charge about US$3 from town to the hotel zones (one to four passengers). One of the newer hotels, Plaza Las Glorias is an exotic experience—pretty and pink, it's right on the beach and features in-house diving and services. Walking distance to downtown, the five-star hotel offers 163 a/c rooms, outdoor pool, restaurant, swim-up bar, music, Mexican fiesta night, dancing, and all with spectacular ocean views. Junior suites offer roomy sitting areas and balconies. For more information and reservations call (800) 342-2644 in the U.S.; in Cozumel, Av.

Rafael Melgar, km 15, tel. (987) 2-19-37, fax (817) 685-9443.

Hotel Sol Caribe offers 350 a/c rooms and those on the upper floors have lovely views of the bay. Everyone should take a look at its extraordinary Maya-style entry. The hotel imparts a comfortable upscale atmosphere with a pool area that meanders through the garden and includes a well patronized swim-up bar, a large *palapa* outdoor cafe, outdoor music, and intimate dining room with piano melodies in the evening. The beach club across the road offers diving services as well as a small beach. Ask about the Fiesta Mexicana where great entertainment is served up with an immense Mexican buffet. For more information contact **Fiesta Americana,** tel. (800) 223-2332.

Another good old standby is the newly refurbished **Stouffer Presidente Hotel,** which has one of the best beaches on the San Miguel side of the island. Visitors find a friendly atmosphere, 260 a/c rooms (ask if you want a sea view!), some on the lower floors open directly onto the beach, others have balconies. The sport buff has multiple choices including tennis, diving, snorkeling along the hotel's shore, and a pool. Car rental is on the premises (it's four miles to town), bars, discos, indoor and outdoor cafes, daytime marimba music, boutique, sports equipment rental, travel agency,

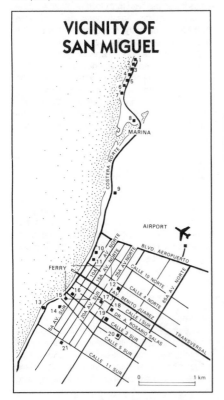

VICINITY OF SAN MIGUEL

1. Mayan Plaza Hotel
2. El Cozumeleno Hotel
3. Cabanas del Caribe Hotel
4. Playa Azul Hotel
5. Cozumel Caribe Hotel
6. Cantarell Hotel
7. Mara Hotel
8. Club Nautico de Cozumel
9. Condumel Condos
10. Los Portales Restaurant
11. Pizza Rolandi
12. Gonzalo de J. Rosado Library
13. El Hippopotamo Disco
14. post and telegraph office
15. Aqua Safari Diving
16. Maya Cozumel Hotel
17. Benito Juarez Municipal Market
18. Lion's Club
19. Javier Rojo Gomez Baseball Park
20. Children's Park
21. Health Center (S.S.A.)

Plaza Las Glorias

and the Presidente's giant bath towels; reservations suggested, tel. (800) 472-2427.

Moderate

You can still stay on the waterfront (across the road) for a good price. **Hotel Club del Sol** is a simple hotel with a great ambience. Enjoy a swimming pool, a/c, dive shop, open-air cafe with good food, and rooms that are simply furnished, and across the road there's a small snorkeling area. Rates US$55 d, for more information call **Cancun Yucatan Adventures,** tel. (800) 6CANCUN in the U.S., (707) 765-1000 in California. Senior citizens, check with Cancun Yucatan Adventures for a discount!

Another old standby is the **Hotel Baracuda,** only rated one star, but it is on the beach with 23 very simple rooms with balconies, restaurant, dive shop, and only a half mile from town. Rates about US$60 d, tel. 2-00-02, Apto. Postal 163, Cozumel, Quintana Roo 77600, Mexico.

Condominiums

Condos have not taken over the Cozumel shoreline—yet! A few are popping up here and there and one of the older but finest to rent is the small, intimate, well-laid-out **Condumel,** a 20-minute walk or a five-minute cab ride north of town. Condumel has its own beach and swimming dock where iguana sunbathe with the visitors. The condos each have one bedroom with a king-size bed, living room with sleeper sofa, roomy modern marble bathroom with tub and shower, and well-

equipped kitchen ready for the cook. A few basic food items, including beer and purified water, are chilling in the fridge in case you don't want to go shopping right away. Fans and the offshore breezes usually keep your rooms cool, but there's also a/c if you want it cooler. Maid service is included in the price, and laundry service is available. Just ask, and you can borrow fins, mask, and snorkel to use while there. Rates for up to five people are US$88 per night 16 Dec. to 31 May; US$65 per night 1 June to 15 December. The fifth person sleeps in a hammock. For reservations write to Condumel, attn. Ruth, P.O. Box 142, Cozumel, Quintana Roo 77600, Mexico; or call in Mexico (987) 2-08-92. Owner Bill Horn also manages Aqua Safari dive shop.and will arrange diving trips and equipment. Anyone that doesn't need to be on the waterfront will find a cluster of new townhouses about 10 blocks from the *zocalo*. White stucco, red-tile roofs, tile floors, three bedrooms, a/c, swimming pool, daily maid service, good storage area for scuba equipment—total cost per night is US$125. For more information contact **Cancun Yucatan Adventures, tel.** (800) 6CANCUN, (707) 765-1000 in California.

Hotels For Divers

Some hotels go out of their way to accommodate divers. One such hotel is the 12-room **Safari Inn** located above Aqua Safari Dive Shop downtown on Av. Melgar across from the Safari boat dock. The hotel is modern but simple, clean, a/c, and very convenient for diving expeditions. The rates are US$30 d, $35 t, $40 quad, and $45 for five. Write to Safari Inn, Box 142, Cozumel, Quintana Roo 77600, Mexico for package information; tel. 2-01-01/2-06-61. Other hotels also offer dive packages; write for prices: **Casa Del Mar,** and **La Ceiba Hotel,** 8117 Preston Rd., Suite 170, Lockbox No. 4, Dallas, Texas 75225.

Budget

Hotels in the center of San Miguel are often less expensive and within walking distance of cafes, discos, shops, and the seafront promenade. A wide variety of rooms is available: some small and sparsely furnished, others expansive with heavy colonial decor, central courtyards, restaurants, and

COZUMEL ACCOMMODATIONS

NAME	ADDRESS	TELEPHONE	FAX
Cabanas Del Caribe ★★★★	—	2-00-17	75-23-74
Cantarell ★★★★	—	2-01-44	—
Caribbean Suites ★★★	—	2-01-44	—
Casa Del Mar ★★★	—	2-16-65	75-32-65
Casitas La Plaza ★★	—	2-08-78	—
Cozumel Caribe ★★★★★	—	2-01-00	—
El Barracuda ★★★	—	2-00-02	—
El Cozumeleno ★★★★	—	2-00-50	75-32-69
Fiesta Americana Sol Caribe ★★★★★	—	2-07-00	—
Galapagos Inn ★★★	—	2-06-63	—
La Ceiba Beach ★★★★★	—	2-08-12	75-32-65
La Perla ★★★	—	2-01-88	—
Hotel Bahia ★★★	Av. Rafael Melgar #25	2-02-09	—
Hotel Mara ★★★★	—	2-03-00	75-38-43
Mary Carmen ★★★	Av. 5 Sur #4	2-05-81	—
Maya Cozumel ★★	Av. 5 Sur	2-00-11	—
Mayan Plaza ★★★★★	—	2-02-72	73-32-74
Mesan San Miguel ★★★	north side of plaza	2-02-33	—
Paraiso Caribe ★★★	15A Av. Norte #599	2-07-40	—
Playa Azul ★★★★	—	2-00-33	75-32-66
Plaza Las Glorias Cozumel ★★★★★	—	2-20-00	68-27-69
Suites Turquesa ★★	—	2-15-54	—
Villa Blanca ★★★	—	2-07-30	—
Villa Del Rey ★★★	—	2-16-00	—
Vista Del Mar ★★★	Av. Rafael Melgar #45	2-05-45	—
Presidente Cozumel ★★★★★	—	2-03-62	75-32-63

comfortable gathering places to meet fellow travelers. Some hotels offer an economical junior suite with cooking facilities and private bath, a great bargain for families or small groups. Most have ceiling fans; some have a/c. With few exceptions, higher winter rates prevail from the middle of December through Easter week, and reservations are recommended. Rates quoted in the hotel chart are for a double room during high season and can fluctuate; add 15% tax. Since the economy of Mexico changes almost daily, double-check prices upon arrival if reservations aren't made in advance. There are no youth hostels on the island.

Take a look at the **Hotel Mary Carmen;** this small pleasant though simple hotel is just a stone's throw from the *zocalo,* discos, restaurants, shops, and all other downtown activities. The 28 rooms are clean and surround a nicely cared for garden. Rates are about US$25 d; tel. 2-05-81, 5 Av. Sur #4.

Out-of-town Hotels

The only motel on the windward (east) shore is budget-class **Punta Morena,** set on a low rise overlooking the sea with (very) Spartan accommodations: cooking facilities, electricity that goes off when the generator quits at 2300 (public power is on its way), an open-air restaurant, bar (pricey

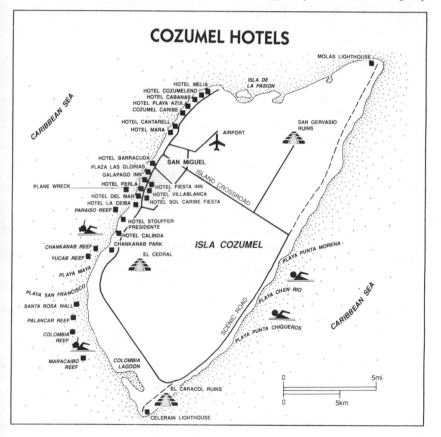

COZUMEL HOTELS

MOLAS LIGHTHOUSE

ISLA DE LA PASION

CARIBBEAN SEA

HOTEL MELIA
HOTEL COZUMELENO
HOTEL CABANAS
HOTEL PLAYA AZUL
COZUMEL CARIBE
HOTEL CANTARELL
HOTEL MARA

AIRPORT

SAN GERVASIO RUINS

HOTEL BARRACUDA
PLAZA LAS GLORIAS
GALAPAGO INN
HOTEL PERLA

SAN MIGUEL

PLANE WRECK

HOTEL DEL MAR
HOTEL LA CEIBA
PARAISO REEF

HOTEL FIESTA INN
HOTEL VILLABLANCA
HOTEL SOL CARIBE FIESTA

ISLAND CROSSROAD

HOTEL STOUFFER PRESIDENTE
HOTEL CALINDA
CHANKANAB PARK

ISLA COZUMEL

CHANKANAB REEF
YUCAB REEF

EL CEDRAL

PLAYA PUNTA MORENA

PLAYA MAYA

PLAYA SAN FRANCISCO
SANTA ROSA WALL

PALANCAR REEF

PLAYA CHEN RIO

COLOMBIA REEF

SCENIC ROAD

CARIBBEAN SEA

PLAYA PUNTA CHIQUEROS

MARACAIBO REEF

COLOMBIA LAGOON

EL CARACOL RUINS

0   5mi
0   5km

CELERAIN LIGHTHOUSE

even for soda), and a beguiling view of the rough coast. A few sleepy monkeys tethered to the trees constitute an advertised "zoo" on the path to a beach with miles of shore to explore; rates are about US$17 d. This hotel was heavily damaged during Hurricane Gilbert, but rumor has it that it will be back to normal by the time you have this book in hand.

Camping

Cozumel has no campgrounds with facilities. However, hidden coves and isolated beaches on the east side of the island let the outdoorsperson enjoy roughing it. Bring everything needed to camp, including water. Don't expect even a tiny *tienda* to buy forgotten items. If you ask the tourism office about beach camping, they'll tell you to get permission from the navy, which occupies the large building south of town, on the ocean side across from the Costa Brava cafe and hotel.

FOOD

San Miguel has a variety of ways to spotlight mealtime. Fast-food stands and restaurants abound and fit all budgets. Seafood is exquisite and fresh. Yucatecan specialties simply must be tasted! *Camarrones con ajo* (shrimp with garlic), *caracol* (conch), and tangy *ceviche* (fish or conch marinated in lime, vinegar, chopped onions, tomatoes, and cilantro) are all tasty treats. *Huachinango Veracruz* (red snapper cooked with tomatoes, green pepper, onions, and spices) is popular, and snapper is caught off the reef year-round; eating it a few hours after it's caught makes a good fish dinner perfect. Fresh seafood at its best is sold in most cafes.

Moderate Cafes

Budget-class **La Economica,** two blocks from the plaza heading inland, gives ample servings of *pescado frito* (fried fish) and *carne asada* (grilled meat) for about US$2.50. Another budget-class cafe is **Los Morroes**—great Mexican hamburgers. Both of these cafes are off the main drag behind the plaza. Prowl around on these back streets—more and more small cafes are opening up, and prices are usually cheaper than those near the ocean. **Las Tortugas,** Av. 10 between

Av. Juarez and Calle 2 Norte, serves good tacos.

Pepe's, one-half block south of the plaza on Av. 5 Sur, noted for its relaxed atmosphere and reasonable prices, has been popular for 20 years. **El Portal,** an open cafe facing the waterfront, serves tasty family-style food. A sturdy breakfast of bacon, eggs, beans, and toast costs about US$2.50. Open for breakfast, lunch, and dinner.

Las Palmeras at the foot of the pier in the center of town has been serving good food for many years and is always busy. Have dinner and a drink at **Costa Brava,** on Av. Melgar across from the navy buildings on the waterfront. The food and prices are very good. A simple breakfast begins at about US$2, set lunch starts at US$2.50, and you can indulge in usually high-priced shrimp, crab, or lobster dinners at reasonable prices. If the chef has had a good night, he treats his customers to an after-dinner glass of Xtabentum, spicy liqueur made in Yucatan.

Italian

If you're ready for something different, try the Swiss-Italian specialties at **Pizza Rolandi** on Av. Melgar #22. Good pizza, lasagna, calzone, and salads, plus beer and great sangria. The outdoor patio/dining room is a pleasant place to be on a balmy Caribbean evening; indoor dining available in case of rain. **Karen's Pizza** is another place for fun and good food. Try the *taaaaalll* glass of beer, served in a wooden holder, in their large outdoor patio located on the closed-to-vehicles section of downtown.

Mexican Entrees

For the zany crowd, **Carlos and Charlie and Jimmy's Kitchen,** north of the plaza on Av. Melgar, tel. 2-01-91, is a lively restaurant that specializes in fun. Any respectable beer drinker owes it to himself to witness the beer-drinking contests held nightly. Sound like a place to drink and not eat? Surprisingly, the food is terrific and includes good Mexican entrees. Open nightly. For a leisurely lunch in a tropical atmosphere, **Las Gaviotas,** out of town past the Hotel Playa Azul, sits right over a blue silk sea. A thatch roof over the patio protects diners from the hot sun. *Mole* lovers, try the enchiladas. Excellent Mexican club sandwiches with fresh-roasted turkey (no plastic-flavored pressed stuff—yet!). The view of clear water

Cozumel's new museum is conveniently located on the oceanfront.

Scaramouche (Av. Melgar), **Grips** ... Norte), and **Neptuno** (Av. Melgar ... **idente**, **Sol Caribe**, **Plaza** ... **Ceiba**, and the **Mara** have ... and often during dinner ... maraderie and exerc... **cuentro**, a resta... and domino e... open daily ...

Spe...

Hot...
On V... , the **Pres-idente** and **Sol Caribe** hotels present a Mexican buffet and folkloric entertainment (about US$25), offering literally dozens of tasty dishes, fun, and good music and dancing. Reservations can be made through most hotels.

Street Vendors And Markets

During spring and summer, street vendors offer mangos on a stick, peeled and artistically carved to resemble flowers, about US$.50 each with your choice of lime or chili powder garnish, or both! A good selection of grocery stores, fruit vendors, and two bakeries make it easy to eat on the run. Nothing tastes better than a crusty hot *bolillo* (hard roll) fresh from the oven, a bargain at US$.25 each. The bakeries (one is a block north of the main

... **Comercial** on Av. Juarez facing the plaza, and **Comercial Caribe** on Av. Juarez closer to the waterfront, are grocery stores stocking a wide variety of canned goods, fresh produce, notions, and alcoholic drinks. Expect American-made products to cost more. Looking for plain Mexican ground coffee in Cozumel markets is frustrating; instant coffee and coffee grounds with sugar added are often all you can find. If you're desperate, American brands are available (at inflated prices) at **Pama** on Av. Melgar.

ENTERTAINMENT

Discos are popular in Cozumel. At night the town jumps with lively music, as energetic people meet and mingle. Dancing continues till morning at

(Seafront/10 ...Calle 11). **Pres-** ...**Las Glorias, La** ...music at cocktail hour ...For a quiet evening of ca- ...se for the brain, go to **El En-** ...rant where San Miguel's chess ...thusiasts enjoy challenging visitors, ...rom 0800; Calle 1 Sur and Av. 10 Sur.

reefs, and corals surrounding the island, and artifacts of historic Cozumel. This small nonprofit museum is definitely worth seeing (small admission) and offers a bookstore, library, and meeting room; on the second floor there's a pleasant outdoor cafe overlooking the sea. Anyone interested in joining the **Group of Friends of the Museum,** write to Av. Melgar and Calle 6 Norte, Cozumel, Quintana Roo 77600, Mexico; tel. 2-08-41/2-15-57.

cial Events
...e **Billfish Tournament** is held every year in May, bringing fishing enthusiasts from all over, especially boaters from the U.S. who cross the Gulf of Mexico to take part in the popular event. **Carnaval,** a movable fiesta usually held in February, is a great party with street parades, dancing, and costumes—all with a tropical flavor. Another popular event is the celebration of the patron saint of San Miguel, held the last week of September.

Cinemas
Cinema Cozumel is on Av. Melgar at Calle 4 Norte; **Cine Cecilio Borgues** is on Av. Juarez and Av. 35; showtime 2115 at both. Sometimes U.S. films are shown with original soundtrack and Spanish subtitles, but most are Spanish-language films.

The Museum
The **Museo de la Isla de Cozumel** is located on the waterfront north of the plaza in an old building that once housed a turn-of-the-century hotel. There are lovely informative exhibits of the wildlife,

Bullfights
For those into the traditional attractions of Mexico, a bullfight is scheduled on Wednesday mornings at 0930 during the high season. Check with your hotel for price and reservations.

The Plaza
On Sunday evenings local citizens and tourists meet in the central plaza. Only a few women still wear the lovely white *huipils.* Men in their best white hats look crisp and cool in the typical *guayabera* with its open collar and tailored pleats. Families (sometimes three generations) gather in the plaza to hear Latin rhythms and the tunes of the day presented by local musicians. The charming white gazebo takes on a modern look with the addition of powerful speakers placed around the park. Children, dressed as miniatures of their parents, run, play, and chatter in front of the live band. It's hard to say who does the best business—the balloon man or the cotton-candy vendor. This is a nice place to spend an evening under the stars, meeting the friendly folk of Cozumel.

SHOPPING

You can buy almost anything you want in Cozumel. Gift shops are scattered all over town. You'll see black coral jewelry, pottery of all kinds, and typical Mexican clothing and shoes. A few trendy fashion houses carry the latest sportswear, T-shirts, and elegant jewelry. One of the nicer gift shops, **La Concha,** displays traditional folk art from all over Mesoamerica including beautiful Guatemalan weavings in flamboyant colors; Av. 5 Sur #141 near the plaza, tel. 2-12-70. A small shop that sells a conglomeration of unique souvenirs and artwork is **The Flea Market** (formerly Antiques and Artifacts) on Av. 5A Norte between

Calle 2 Norte and Calle 4 Norte on the west side of the street: you'll find Cuban cigars, old coins, weird sculpture, Xtabentum (in fact they give you a taste of this Yucatecan liqueur to introduce you to it before you decide whether to buy it or not), artwork from strange to talented, and good English-language books. While you're there, pop into the **Na Balom** crafts shop next door, a little different, but what the heck, you're already there! The gift shops of some hotels also carry a limited selection of English-language reading material. **La Belle Ondine,** on Melgar at Calle 4 Norte, has an unpredictable selection and also sells maps of the coastal area.

SERVICES

The four banks in town—**Bancomer, Banpais, Banco del Atlantico,** and **Banco Serfin** are all on the main plaza: exchange dollars or travelers cheques 1000-1230. Since the advent of the cruise ships, almost everyone in town will accept dollars, but be sure you know the daily rate. There have been complaints that cruise-ship passengers often are taken advantage of with the exchange; know your rates and count your money. The **long-distance phone office** is on Calle 1 on the south side of the plaza, open 0800-1300 and 1600-2100. Long-distance calls can be made from many hotels as well. Calling collect will save a good part of the added tax. The **post office** is on Melgar close to Calle 7, open 0900-1300 and 1500-1800 Mon. to Fri.; the **telegraph office** in the same building is open Mon. to Fri. 0900-2030, Sat. and Sun. 0900-1300, tel. 2-01-06/2-00-56. **Office of Tourism** (booth in plaza) is a font of information, usually manned by someone who speaks English. A complete list of hotels in every

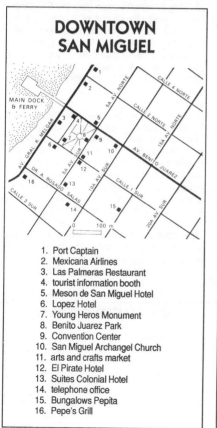

DOWNTOWN SAN MIGUEL

1. Port Captain
2. Mexicana Airlines
3. Las Palmeras Restaurant
4. tourist information booth
5. Meson de San Miguel Hotel
6. Lopez Hotel
7. Young Heros Monument
8. Benito Juarez Park
9. Convention Center
10. San Miguel Archangel Church
11. arts and crafts market
12. El Pirate Hotel
13. Suites Colonial Hotel
14. telephone office
15. Bungalows Pepita
16. Pepe's Grill

EMERGENCY PHONE NUMBERS

Police	2-00-92
Fire Department	2-08-00
Hospital	2-01-40
Red Cross	2-10-58
Ambulance	2-06-39
Clinic (24 hours)	2-10-81

price bracket is available along with maps of the island and any general info you might need; tel. 2-14-98.

For **taxi** service it's usually a matter of standing on the sidewalk and waving your arm, or waiting on Av. Melgar at the foot of the downtown dock—taxis queue along the sidewalk on the waterfront. The taxi office is on Calle 2 Norte, tel. 2-02-36/2-00-41, and any hotel will call a taxi. The closest **U.S. Consular Office** is in Cancun, tel. 3-10-15. Cozumel has one **gas station,** five blocks from downtown at Av. Juarez and Av. 30, open 0700-midnight daily. Cozumel has government-sponsored **Green Angel** motorist assistance. If your car should break down on the coastal highway, stay with it until they come by to give you gas, parts, or whatever help you need to get you on your way. The Green Angels cruise only on paved roads during daylight hours.

Laundry can be left at **Lavanderia Mañana,** Av. Circumvalacion #101. Charge is by the kilo, open 0700-2000, Mon. to Sat., usually one-day service. Pickup service on request, tel. 2-06-30.

Camera Shops

Several camera stores in town sell film, rent underwater cameras, and have one-hour color-print processing service. **Aquascene,** tel. 2-03-79, ext. 102, is next to La Ceiba Hotel. **The Flash Camera Shop** is in Discover Cozumel Dive Shop (weather reports available here), tel. 2-02-80/2-03-97.

Medical Services And Pharmacies

In the event of a medical emergency, contact your hotel receptionist for an English-speaking doctor. **Hospital y Centro de Salud,** a small clinic with a doctor on duty, is open 24 hours a day, Av. Circumvalacion, tel. 2-10-81. One pharmacy, **Los Portales,** is located on Calle 11 Sur, tel. 2-07-41. Another is in Centro Comercial on the north side of the plaza. **Farmacia Joaquin** is on the plaza in front of the clock tower; open 0900-1300 and

1700-2100, tel. 2-01-25. If still in need of help, call the American Consular Office in Cancun, tel. 3-10-15. Dr. Manuel Marin-Foucher Lewis is located on Adolfo Rosado Salas #260, tel. 2-09-12/2-09-49. Three dentists are listed in Cozumel's Blue Guide: Z. Mariles, tel. 2-05-07, T. Hernandez, tel. 2-06-56, and Escartin, tel. 2-03-85.

GETTING THERE

By Boat

Passenger ferries come and go to Playa del Carmen from the downtown dock in San Miguel; car ferries use the **International Pier** (in the process of being repaired) across from the Sol Caribe Hotel where cruise ships dock. If crossing with a car, arrive 1½ hours early and be prepared with exact change and your car license number when you approach the ticket window—or you may lose your place in line and possibly on the often-crowded ferry that docks in Puerto Morelos.

By Air

Air travel from various points on the Yucatan Peninsula is becoming more common. There are flights from Merida to Cozumel (Aero Caribe), and from Playa del Carmen to Cozumel (Aero Caribe, runs hourly during most of the year, about US$10 pp OW); schedules change with the season. The airport is approximately three km from downtown San Miguel. Taxis and minibuses meet incoming planes. Taxi fare to town is about US$2 pp in a collective taxi (a van) that will take you to your hotel; it's more for the return trip in a private taxi. When departing, an airport-use tax (about US$10) is collected. This tax applies to all international Mexican airports, so hang on to US$10 or $12 (price varies) for each international airport city

AIRLINES SERVING COZUMEL	
United	2-04-68
Mexicana	2-02-63
Continental	2-05-76
Aero Cozumel	2-09-28
American	2-09-88

BY BOAT TO AND FROM COZUMEL

The new modern "waterjet" boat, the MV *Mexico* is quite comfortable and conveniently holds many passengers in airline-type seats, refreshments served. On the long ride to and from Cancun and Cozumel, a movie is shown (Mexican usually). Price around US$2.50 pp.

SCHEDULES TO AND FROM COZUMEL

From Playa del Carmen	0515	0645	1300	1500	1700
From Cozumel to Playa del Carmen	0430	0600	1200	1400	1600
From Cancun	0930	2030			
From Cozumel to Cancun	0715	1800			

The regular boats are still running; the price is about US$.50. Schedules are subject to change, so check it out.

From Playa del Carmen to Cozumel	0700	1100	1930		
Sundays only	0600	0900	1200	1600	1930
From Cozumel to Playa del Carmen	0500	0900	1800		
Sundays only	0400	0700	0900	1400	1800

AUTO FERRY SCHEDULES FROM PUERTO MORELOS

To Cozumel Sun., Mon., Tues.	0600	1200
To Puerto Morelos Sun., Mon., Tues.	1000	1600
To Cozumel Wed. and Fri.	0600	1500
To Puerto Morelos Wed. and Fri.	1100	
To Cozumel Thurs. and Sat.	1000	
To Puerto Morelos Thurs. and Sat.	0600	1400

where you plan to stay 24 hours or more. Change your money in town, as banks and some shops (when purchasing) give the best exchange rates, with hotels notoriously giving the worst. Cozumel has many small duty-free shops with a good selection of gifts. Reading materials, especially English-language pictorial books about the area are found here and there. The airport has a dining room upstairs, and on the ground level a coffee bar opens for snacks, but usually not before the earliest flights.

GETTING AROUND

Getting around on the island is easy; it's flat and the roads are maintained. It's easiest in the city of San Miguel. The roads are laid out in a grid pattern with the even-numbered *calles* to the north of the town plaza, odd-numbered *calles* to the south; numbered *avenidas* run parallel to the coast. Travelers, especially backpackers, should be aware that only escorted tourist buses make trips outside the immediate area of San Miguel. To go to hotels north or south of town, either take a taxi or go by car. Escorted tours around the island are available through any travel agency or your hotel.

Several transport options exist for exploring the outlying areas of the island on your own—which everyone should do! Avenida Juarez begins in downtown San Miguel at the dock and cuts across the middle of the island (16 km), then circles the south end. The road around the north end of the island isn't paved. Walking the flat terrain is easy, but distances are long. All of downtown San Miguel is easily reached on foot. The 70 km of paved island roads are flat and easily explored by bike (rented at **Ruben's,** south side of the plaza,

BIKE RENTALS ON COZUMEL

Hotel Aguilar, 5 Av. Sur #22, tel.2-0307
Hotel Lopez, south side of plaza, tel. 2-0108
JB Motoscooter, 2 Calle Norte
Rentadora Caribe, 3 Calle Sur, tel. 2-0961
Ruben's, south side of plaza and at the cruise
     ship terminal. tel. 2-0144, hotel delivery

CAR RENTALS ON COZUMEL

Hotel Aguilar, 5 Av. Sur #22, tel. 2-0307
Avis, Hotel El Presidente, tel. 2-0389, and
     airport, tel. 2-0099
Budget, 5 Av. Norte, tel. 2-0009, and airport,
     tel. 2-0903
Cozumel Maya Rent, tel. 2-0655
Hotel Cozumeleno, tel. 2-0344
Hertz, Hotel Cozumel Caribe, tel. 2-0100
Rent un Carro, Adolfo Salas 2, tel. 2-0111

tel. 2-01-44, for about US$28 per day) and 125cc motorcycles (available to rent at several other shops in town; motorbikes and 125cc motorcycles rent for about US$30 daily). Remember to bargain, at certain times of the year you'll get a discount—supply and demand.

Taxis will take you anywhere on the island and are available by the day; agree on price before your tour begins. Traveling with a local cabbie is often a real bonus since drivers know the island and its hidden corners better than most guidebooks (other than this one of course!). Remember, when the cruise ships arrive, all the taxis are at the International Pier, leaving the rest of the visitors high and dry. Ask at your hotel for ship times if possible and plan your movements around it. The same goes for the larger shopping centers: they are jammed when the ships are in port. Another option for seeing Cozumel is renting a car, which means total freedom to explore. Car rentals run approximately US$54 daily.

ARCHAEOLOGICAL SITES

Nine Maya sites are scattered across the island. A few are difficult to reach, and only the hardy

hiker will want to make the attempt. Most ruins on the island are of the "oratorio" type: small square buildings, low to the ground, with short doors that led early Spaniards to believe the places were once inhabited by dwarfs (a myth no longer believed). **El Cedral** is the exception; though the temple is small, major ceremonies were probably held on this site. The story goes that a Maya site was destroyed when the U.S. Army Corps of Engineers built an airstrip in dense jungle (now the location of the new Cozumel airport).

El Cedral

Several of the ruins are easily reached by car or motorbike. Just beyond San Francisco Beach on the main highway leaving town, a paved road takes off to the left and ends in 3.5 km at **El Cedral.** Small and not enormously impressive, this is the oldest Maya structure on the island. Amazingly, it still bears a few traces of the paint and stucco of the original Maya artist. But the deterioration indicates that hundreds of years have passed it by. A tree grows from the roof, with thick, exposed roots interminably tangled in and around stones of the ancient structure. Fat iguana with bold black stripes tracing their mid-sections guard the deserted, mold-covered rock structure; sounds of cows blend with the songs of countless birds and the resonant buzz of unseen insects. Located in what is now a small farm settlement, El Cedral was once used as a jail in the 1800s. Right next to it is a rustic, modern-era stucco church painted vivid green. Go inside and take a look at two crosses draped with finely embroidered lace mantles—a typical mixture of Christianity and ancient cult, which some believe is associated with the "talking cross cult."

Aguada Grande

Aguada Grande is more difficult to reach. After crossing the island (via Av. Juarez) to the beach, turn left on the dirt road and travel 21 km to another dirt road going inland; it's about a 1.5 km hike to the site. This is .75 km from the northern tip of the island, the **Punta Molas** lighthouse, and **El Real** (30.5 km from San Miguel). The beach along here is difficult because of a rocky shoreline—you make better time on the dirt road. At about km 12, prepare for one of the most beautiful beaches on the island.

San Gervasio

San Gervasio is a well-preserved and recently reconstructed group of structures. Travel east on Av. Juarez, then left (north) on a dirt road (look for the San Gervasio sign) for approximately 10 km until it dead-ends at the entrance to the site. The silence of these antiquities looming in the midst of dense brush, with only birds singing in the tall trees, overwhelms the visitor with an image of what it must have been like centuries ago when only the Maya visited. San Gervasio has a snack bar for cold drinks and is open from 0800-1700, small entry fee. Be prepared, guides will offer their services for about US$10 for two people, a bit pricey when you can do just as well in this small area by getting solid information at Cozumel's museum (downtown) first and then buying the green map, usually available at La Concha.

WEST SHORE BEACHES

Chankanab Lagoon

Chankanab, nine km south of San Miguel, is a national park. A small crystal-clear natural aquarium is surrounded by a botanical garden of 352 species of tropical and subtropical plants from 22 countries, as well as those endemic to Cozumel. The lagoon contains more than 60 species of fish, crustaceans, turtles, and intricately designed coral formations. This is a wonderful shady park to spend hours watching underwater activity. The lagoon is shallow, and until recently swimmers could go from the lagoon to Chankanab Bay (on the sea) through underwater tunnels; the tunnels have collapsed and no longer assure safe passage. Now there's *no swimming.* Don't bring your crumbs and stale tortillas: caretakers frown on anyone feeding fish in Chankanab Lagoon. Without the tunnels opening to the sea, scientists must work at protecting life in the small area. Save food offerings for your short walk from the lagoon to the bay, where hundreds of fish will churn water along the shore to get a scrap of anything.

Chankanab Bay

This is a popular beach for sunbathers, swimmers, divers, and snorkelers to explore limestone shoreline caves. Showy sea creatures have no fear of humans invading their domain. For adventurous scuba divers, the coral reef which is close offshore is two- to 16-meters deep. A sunken

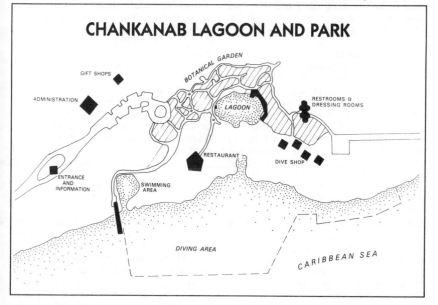

CHANKANAB LAGOON AND PARK

Chankanab Lagoon

boat, rusty anchors, coral-crusted cannons, and an antiquated religious statue all make for eerie sightseeing among the fish. A well-equipped dive shop is located here for rentals, air, sales, and certification instruction. Several gift shops, a snack stand, and a restaurant are all conveniently located near the beach where shade *palapas,* freshwater showers, dressing rooms, and lockers are all included in the small entrance fee of US$2.50. This is a national park open from 0900-1700 daily.

San Francisco Beach
Following the main road past Chankanab (14 km from town), you'll come to **Playa San Francisco** on the right. This 3.5 km of busy beach has two open-air restaurants, dressing rooms, bar, gift shops, volleyball net, wooden chaise lounges, and snorkeling equipment rental (US$5 per day). During the week, it's relatively quiet, but during busy seasons and on weekends it's inundated with tourists, many brought by bus from cruise ships that anchor in the downtown harbor. San Francisco is also a popular Sunday destination for local citizens. Fresh fish and Mexican specialties are served to the accompaniment of loud, live music, romping kids, and chattering adults. The bay is usually filled with dive boats attracted to nearby San Francisco Reef (see p. 244). Rumor has it that hotel construction here is planned for the future. No one knows exactly how the new hotel construction will affect Sunday-afternoon fun at San Francisco Beach.

Beach Clubs
On the main road from town going south toward San Francisco Beach, a small *balneario* called **Paloma Beach Club** is a pleasant place to spend an afternoon: good fresh fish and cold *cerveza* served at the outdoor cafe, white-sand beach, and good swimming and snorkeling. More and more of these little beach clubs are popping up along this area. Another one, **Playa Maya,** four km south of Chankanab, offers a small, calm swimming area on a narrow strip of sand. A snack stand is open daily, and you'll find beach facilities, dressing rooms, and a bar.

Isla De Passion
This tiny island in **Abrigo Bay** has secluded beaches and a rocky shoreline good for underwater exploring (no cafes, restrooms, or any other facilities). Often the destination of Robinson Crusoe picnic trips, it is now a state reserve.

WINDWARD BEACHES

South To North
From **San Francisco Beach** around the southern end of the island are many beaches. Some are good for swimming; some are dangerous for swimming but great for beachcombing. Add sunning, camping, and birdwatching to provide more than enough reason to visit this shoreline which stretches from **Punta Molas** at the north tip to **Punta Sur** at the south. To visit beaches on the

east shore north of the island-crossing highway, take either a motorcycle or 4WD for the unpaved sandy road. If you rent a jeep for this trip, make sure that the 4WD hasn't been disengaged by the rental agency. Because of its condition, the 24.5-km road is seldom used, and few people see these beautiful beaches. If you decide to hike along this coast, you'll make better time in many areas on the road than on the rocky portions in between sandy beaches.

The first two beaches, **Santa Cecilia** and **Playa Bonita,** are good beachcombing spots, and Playa Bonita is a good camping beach (no facilities). For the real adventurer, the *Brown Map of Cozumel* shows trails from this dirt road to various little-known Maya ruins, abandoned *cenotes,* and caves. This kind of jungle trek requires carrying all essentials. From the Maya site at **Castillo Real** to the north, no more sandy beaches come before the lighthouse on Punta Molas. Many ships have sunk along this violent shore: cannons and anchors are occasionally found to prove the legends.

Chen Rio
At the end of the cross-island highway is tiny **Mescalitos Cafe.** Turn right (south) and the first beach is Chen Rio (km 42). Space for tent campers and a few camping vehicles is on a broad flat area next to the beach. Chen Rio is also the site of the only motel on the east side of Cozumel, **Punta Morena.** From here the beach becomes **Playa de San Martin** and after that, **Punta Chiquiero,** with a protected cove for swimming in crystalline water. A small restaurant, the **Naked Turtle,** sits on the edge of a lovely crescent bay with white sand. A bar serves *ceviche,* snacks, hard and soft drinks; next door is the dining room. You can camp on the beach—with a tent or a vehicle—but there are no facilities. If driving an RV, check with the restaurant owners before you park.

Isolated Beaches
Along the highway from here to Punta Celerain is access to many beaches and the remains of a few small ruins. A dirt road meandering parallel to the coast behind sand dunes leads to **Punta Celerain Lighthouse.** All along this road you'll find paths turning out to the left, all leading to beautiful isolated beaches. Along the dirt road a small conch-shaped structure was restored (and is now being restored once again because of hurricane damage). One of the docents at the museum in town explains how the small openings at the top were used as a warning—the wind blowing through creates a fog-horn effect. According to archaeologists

Cozumel's reefs make it a favorite divers' destination.

it was built between A.D. 1200-1400 as a ceremonial center and navigational guide using smoke and flames tended by the Maya keeper. Behind this small building, a dirt path over a sand dune goes to another great beach for swimming, sunbathing, and beachcombing.

Punta Celerain

This lighthouse is four km from the main road. From a distance it appears white, tall, and regal; up close it needs a paint job. Next to the lighthouse is a small army base with soldiers on guard. An exciting spot, it's well worth the detour to wander around the point where a strong surf crashes over the irregular black limestone shore in great clouds of misty surf, spraying tall geysers through jagged blowholes. The family at the lighthouse is friendly, and usually you'll run into them on the grounds either doing their laundry or cooking. Ask to climb to the top for a spectacular 360-degree view of the island (a tip wouldn't hurt); don't forget your camera and wear comfortable walking shoes. The view one way is a long strip of white sand with a lacy scalloped edge of turquoise waves; in the opposite direction you'll see red marshy swamps in the middle of green scrub jungle; beyond it all—unending sea. On Sundays the lighthouse keeper sells cold drinks and fried fish. The soldiers nearby often hike back to the barracks carrying several iguana ready to be prepared for lunch, much like their ancient ancestors did.

Back on the paved road just as it rounds the curve and turns north, a large sign warns of the consequences of taking turtle eggs. There's a stiff fine for this since the turtle is a protected species; they come to shore here in large numbers during the summer to lay their eggs. You'll often find a soldier (with tent) standing guard over the sign. This coastal watch keeps tabs on the boating activity between Cozumel and the Yucatan coast; boatloads of illegal drugs are frequently picked up along here. A return to the paved highway takes you through the hotel zone and on into downtown San Miguel.

WATER SPORTS

Snorkeling

Snorkeling and diving are the most popular outdoor activities on Cozumel. If you can swim but haven't tried snorkeling, Cozumel is the finest place to begin. For those who don't know, snorkeling is floating along the surface of the water with your face (in a mask) underwater while you breathe through a plastic tube called a snorkel. The little glass window on your mask gives you heady visions of the colorful underwater world found nowhere else. For beginners, it's easy to find a fascinating marine environment close to shore without swimming or boating; in many cases you need only step from your hotel. Along the lee side of the island almost all beaches are ideal sites. If it's your first time, practice with a snorkel and mask while sitting in shallow, calm surf with your face underwater and breathe through the snorkel that protrudes above the surface. (Or use your bathtub to learn before leaving home.) Once accustomed to breathing with the tube, the rest is simple. Wear fins which make it easier to maneuver in the water. A few easy-to-reach snorkeling sites include: Chankanab Bay and San Francisco Beach, Presidente Hotel beach, Hotel Cozumel Caribe beach, and La Ceiba Beach (where there's an underwater plane wreck). Rental equipment is available at hotels and dive shops. For the pros, check with a dive shop and you'll find many trips that motor groups to a suitable reef daily.

Scuba Diving

If you've always wanted to learn to scuba dive, here's the place to do it. A multitude of dive shops and instructors offer certification, or instruction sufficient for one dive, so use a lot of common sense finding a *qualified* instructor. Look at his qualifications, ask if he's ever had an accident while in charge, ask about him around town (try the harbor master). It's your life you're placing in his hands. Thousands of people come to Cozumel because of the surrounding reefs, and there are occasional accidents! Fairly simple dives for the neophyte are on offshore fringing reefs. Caves and crevices line the shore, and coral heads rise to within

Aqua Safari boats wait for passengers for an all-day dive trip.

three meters of the surface. Some experienced divers prefer wall diving, while others find night diving more exciting. Certain reefs are for only the most expert diver. Boat reservations must be made in advance. Diving is an exciting sport, and the clear waters around Cozumel allow outstanding photographs; underwater camera rentals are available at some dive shops. **Note:** All divers should be aware that even touching the delicate coral reef kills it. Take care not to scrape your equipment or push off from the coral with your feet. These delicate creations of nature take millions of years to build.

DIVE SPOTS

Plane Wreck
The average non-diver wouldn't think of a wrecked plane as a reef. However, if it sits on the bottom of the sea it serves as a reef by affording schools of fish shady hiding places on the white sandy bottom. A 40-passenger Convair airliner (engines removed) reposes upside down after being purposely sunk in 1977 for the Mexican movie production of *Survive II*. The water's clarity allows a clear view of the submerged wreck, located 100 meters off the La Ceiba Hotel pier. Beyond the wreck are huge coral heads in 14 meters of water. At the plane wreck, a 120-meter trail has been marked with underwater signs which point out the various types of marinelife on La Ceiba reef. The visibility is up to 30 meters, and the average depth is 9-17 meters. A pillar of coral is an impressive sight and multicolored sponges are outstanding here.

Paraiso Reef
About 200 meters off the beach just south of the International Dock (between the Presidente and the dock), **North Paraiso Reef** can be reached either by boat or from the beach. It averages 9-17 meters deep and is a site of impressive star and brain coral, and sea fans. The south end of the reef, farther offshore and located south of the International Dock, is alive with churning reef life. This is a good spot for night diving.

Chankanab Caves And Reef
For easy-access diving, go to **Chankanab Lagoon.** A series of three caves on the shoreline provides a unique experience. Along the shore, steps are carved from coral for easy entry into water that surges into large underground caverns. Within seconds, you're in the first cave filled with hundreds of fish of all varieties. Striped grunt, snapper, sergeant majors, and butterfly fish are found in all three caves. Dives average 5-12 meters.

A boat is needed to dive Chankanab Reef, several hundred meters offshore south of Chankanab Lagoon (sometimes referred to as Outer Chankanab Reef). There's good night diving here in depths of 8-15 meters where basket starfish hang out with octopi and jail-striped morays. At the drop-off, stunning coral heads are at a maximum depth of 10 meters; in some spots coral is within three meters of the surface. Coral heads are covered with gorgonians and sea fans; striped grunt and mahogany snapper slowly cruise around the base. This is a good location for snorkelers and beginning divers.

Tormentos Reef
This is a medium-depth reef with innumerable coral heads in 8-12 meters of water above a sandy bottom. The heads are decorated with fans, gorgonians, and sponges. With little current, you can get excellent photos. Along the sandy bottom are great numbers of invertebrates: flamingo tongue shell, arrow crab, black crinoid, coral shrimp, and sea cucumber. When the current is going north, the farthest section of the reef drops to 21.5 meters, where you'll see deep-sea fans, lobsters, and immense groupers.

Yocab Reef
One km south of Punta Tormentos, Yocab Reef is fairly close to shore, shallow (good for beginners), and alive with such beauties as queen angelfish, star and brain coral, sponge, and sea whip. The coral reef is about 120 meters long, with an average depth of nine meters, and coral heads from the floor about three meters. When there's a current it can be two or

three knots. (The local bus makes daily runs to this beach for about US$.25.)

Tunich Reef

A half-km south of Yocab—directly out from Punta Tunich—this deeper reef (15-24 meters) has about a 1½-knot current or more, and when it's stronger you could be swept right along to Cuba! It's loaded with intricately textured corals, and the water activity attracts manta rays, jewfish, and barracuda; a good reef to spot shy moray eels.

San Francisco Reef

Another popular reef is located one km off San Francisco Beach. The abbreviated (one-half km) coral runs parallel to shore; this is a boat dive into a site teeming with reef fish of many varieties and brilliant colors. Depths average 17-19 meters.

Santa Rosa Wall

This sensational drop-off, which begins at 22 meters and just keeps going to the black bottom of the Caribbean, really gives you a feeling for the ocean's depth. Strong currents make this a drift-dive, a site for experienced divers only (watch your depth gauge). You'll discover tunnels and caves, translucent sponge, stony overhangs, queen, French, and gray angelfish, white trigger fish, and many big groupers.

Paso Del Cedral

This flat reef with 22-meter garden-like valleys is a good wall dive. In some places the top of the reef begins 15.5 meters from the surface. Sealife includes angelfish, lobster, and the thick-lipped grouper.

Palancar Reef

The reef most associated with Cozumel Island is actually a five-km series of varying coral formations about 1.5 km offshore. Each of these formations offers a different thrill. Some slope, and some drop off dramatically into winding ravines, deep canyons, passageways, or archways and tunnels with formations 15 meters tall—all teeming with reef life. Startling coral pinnacles rise to 25 meters from the sloping wall. Much deeper at the south end, the top of the reef begins at 27 meters. **Horseshoe**, considered by some to be the best diving in the Caribbean, is a series of coral heads which forms a horseshoe curve at the top of the drop-off. The visibility of 66-86 meters plus a solid bronze, four-meter-tall, submerged modernistic sculpture of Christ, make this a dramatic photo area. The statue, created especially for the sea, was sunk on 3 May 1985, with great pomp and ceremony and the presence of Ramon Bravo, well-known TV reporter and Mexican diver. The much-discussed reef lives up to its good press.

Colombia Reef

Several kilometers south of Palancar, Colombia Reef is a deep-dive area, with the top of the reef climbing from 25-30 meters. This is the same environment as Palancar, with canyons and ravines; here the diver may encounter giant turtles and huge groupers hiding beneath deep overhangs of coral. Seasonally, when the water cools down, you'll see spotted eagle rays (water temperature averages 74° in winter and 82° in summer). This reef is best for experienced divers, as there's usually a current; visibility is 50-66 meters.

Maracaibo Reef

At the southern tip of the island, this reef is an exhilarating experience. For the experienced only, Maracaibo is considered by most to be the ultimate challenge of all the reefs mentioned. At the deepest section, the top of the wall begins at 37 meters; at the shallow area, 23 meters. Unlike many other reefs, coral formations here are immense. Be prepared for strong currents and for who-knows-what pelagic species, including shark. Dive boats do not stop here on their regular trips and advance reservations are required for this dive.

Other Good Diving Areas

Not shown on most maps are **Cardona Reef, La Francesa Reef, Barracuda Reef,** and parallel to Barracuda, **San Juan,** for *experienced divers only*—currents can be as much as six knots. In that kind of current a face mask could be ripped off with the wrong move. The faster the current, the clearer the water and the more oxygen, definitely a specialty dive (somewhat like a roller-coaster!). Check with Aqua Safari for more information, including length of time to reach these reefs; three hours in a slow boat, an hour in Aqua Safari's fast boats. Reservations necessary. A handy scaled map-guide with water depths around the island (and other reef information), *Chart of the Reefs of Cozumel Mexico,* is put out by Ric Hajovsky; it's available at most dive shops.

DIVE TRIPS

Note: Many package dive trips originate in the U.S., with airfare, hotel, and diving included. Unless you have your own boat, many of the reef dives mentioned may be arranged through one of the many dive shops in town, the boatmen's co-op, or by some of the hotels that have their own equipment and divemaster. All equipment is provided and sometimes lunch and drinks. Prices vary, so shop around. For beginners, scuba lessons for certification or a resort course for one-day dives are available at most of the same shops. Be sure to check the qualifications and track record of the dive shop and divemaster you choose. A few are outstanding, most are good.

Also, shop around for your needs and level of diving. **Aqua Safari** has an excellent reputation for safety, experience, good equipment, and happy divers who return year after year. Aqua owns two large fiberglass boats geared for 16-18 divers each, with platforms for easy entry and exit. The boats leave from in front of the dive shop at 0930 returning at 1600, and operate daily except Sun., Christmas, and New Year's Day. A typical dive day consists of two dives on different reefs with a stop at the beach for a seafood lunch. The first dive is usually about 19-25 meters, the second dive about 13 meters. The exact location is determined by the divemaster on each boat according to the weather conditions, currents, and divers' requests and experience. The fee is about US$40 plus 20% tax (check; these prices change often). This includes two tanks, weights and belt, backpack, dive guide, lunch, and refreshments. Additional gear may be rented: regulator with pressure gauge, horsecollar B.C., tanks for beach diving (includes weights, belt, and backpack), mask, snorkel, and fins. They have a few lights available for night diving but suggest that you bring your own. During the winter months water temperature drops slightly and it's suggested you bring a wetsuit top. Aqua Safari Dive Shop hours are 0800-1300 and 1600-1830.

For a quickie morning dive **Blue Angel**

Aqua Safari Dive Shop

Divers, with a six-diver capacity, is back by 1330. The boat is fast and comfortable, with easy entrance and exit. Ricardo Madrigal, a divemaster who caters only to advanced divers, can be reached at tel. 2-16-31; he supplies tanks, weights, and belts—*only.* All other scuba equipment must be supplied by the diver. Ricardo first checks your ability, and when satisfied that you're in the expert class makes specialty trips to the mainland for diving and camping or trips to the Barracuda and San Juan reefs in his Bertrim twin-engine boat. All scuba divers must show a certification card before going on boats or renting tanks.

Notice To Divers
Since 1980, a refuge has protected marine flora and fauna on the west coast of Cozumel from the shore up to and including the Drop-Off (El Cantil). It is illegal to fish or to remove any marine artifacts, including coral, from the area. So, scuba divers and snorkelers, take only pictures. No one wants this product of millions of years to be damaged; on the contrary it must be protected and saved for future generations of divers to enjoy.

DIVE SAFETY

Because of the growing influx of divers to Cozumel from all over the world, the small island continues to increase safety services. The newest is the **SSS** (Servicios de Seguridad Sub-Acuatica) available for US$1 per dive day (at participating dive shops). This entitles

AFFILIATED DIVE SHOPS

Adriana Boat	Dive Cozumel
Aqua Safari	Dive Paradise
Anita Boat	Dives Unlimited
Blue Angel	Diving World
Careyitos	Fantasia Divers
Clear Water Divers	Kaapalua
Cruisers Divers	Neptuno Divers
Del Mar Acuaticos	Palancar Divers
Deportes Acuaticos	Pro Dive
Discover Cozumel	Yucab Reef

COZUMEL DIVE SHOPS

Aqua Safari, south of the plaza, on Malecon at 5 Calle Sur, tel. 2-01-01/2-06-61. For more info (including hotel reservations): Box 41, Cozumel, Quintana Roo 77600, Mexico

Aventuras Tropicales, on Malecon north of the plaza, tel. 2-03-93

Blue Angel Scuba School, Villablanca Hotel, tel. 2-07-30

Bonanza Boat Trips, north of the plaza on 2 Calle Norte, tel. 2-05-63

Caribbean Divers, Hotel Cantarell, Mayan Plaza, and Cabana del Caribe

Deportes Acuaticos, four blocks north of the plaza on Calle 8, a short distance from the Malecon, tel. 2-06-40. Underwater cameras available

Discover Cozumel, south of the plaza on the Malecon; also at Chankanab Lagoon, tel. 2-02-80

Fantasia Marina, south of town, in front of Hotel Sol Caribe, tel. 2-07-25

La Ceiba, south of town, at Hotel La Ceiba, tel. 2-03-79

SCUBA Cozumel, south of the plaza on Malecon, tel. 2-06-27; also at the Galapagos Inn, two km south of town, tel. 2-08-53

Sociedad Cooperativa, tel. 2-00-80

Viajes y Deportes del Caribe, south of town, at the Hotel El Presidente, tel. 2-03-22

the distressed diver to the use of Cozumel's hyperbaric chamber, marine ambulance, and fully trained round-the-clock personnel (each facility offers 24-hour service). All divers are welcome to use these services; however, non-participants pay regular commercial rates, so check with the dive shop before you choose.

OTHER WATER ACTIVITIES

Boat Tours
For the non-diver, glass-bottom boats provide a close-up view of Cozumel's flamboyant underwater society. Small boats cruise along the lee side of the coast, and bigger motorized launch-

es travel farther out to the larger reefs. Prices vary accordingly. Ask at your hotel or one of the dive shops. From US$2-6 pp. Another popular cruise is the "Robinson Crusoe," which also varies in size and type. One boat is even designed to look like a pirate ship out of the 1600s. Destinations vary, though they're usually along the lee side, which guarantees a white beach for good swimming. The crew dives for and cooks lobster or fish over an open fire for your lunch. Depending on how extensive the lunch, prices start at about US$15.

Charter Boats
Customized boat trips can be arranged through Bill Horn at **Aqua Safari,** tel. 2-01-01, for crossing the channel to Tulum for a day of sightseeing at the Maya ruins; return trip at your leisure. Trips to Cancun and Isla Mujeres or some other mainland destinations can also be arranged.

Off-island Excursions
Trips to Cancun, Isla Mujeres, Playa del Carmen, or a number of other mainland destinations can be arranged. Boat/plane/bus excursions to the Maya ceremonial centers are offered through your hotel or travel agency. Tulum is close by boat or plane and too good to miss. Xelha, a natural aquarium harboring thousands of tropical fish is also a pleasant stopover when going to the ruins at Coba or Tulum.

Fishing
Cozumel boasts good deep-sea fishing year-round. Red snapper, tuna, barracuda, dolphin, wahoo, bonito, king mackerel, and tarpon are especially plentiful March through July, also the high season for marlin and sailfish. Hire a boat and guide for the day at the downtown dock or at Club Nautico de Cozumel. Small to large boats, including tackle, bait, and guide, cost from US$125 to US$825, half and full day, depending on size of boat, number of people, and season. Arrangements can be made at the boatmen's co-op, tel. 2-00-80, Pancho's, tel. 2-02-04, or by contacting Club Nautico de Cozumel at Marina Puerto de Abrigo Banco Playa, Box 341, Cozumel, Quintana Roo 77600, Mexico; tel. 2-01-18.

Miscellaneous
Instruction and rental equipment for windsurfing and water-skiing can be found at **Pancho's,** two blocks northeast of the plaza, corner of 2 Calle and 10 Av. Norte, tel. 2-02-04. At the Hotel Presidente south of town, **Viajes y Deportes del Caribe** offers boat rentals (small and large fishing boats, ski boats, sailboats, and motorboats). Windsurfing instruction and sail boards are also available. Hobie Cats, jet skis, windsurfers, and sailboats can be rented at the Mayan Plaza Hotel beach.

Other Activities
Several hotels north and south of town have tennis courts and for a small fee non-guests can use them. **Sea Horse Ranch** offers horseback expeditions into the Cozumel bush, where you will see off-the-track Maya ruins and even the **Red Cenote.** English-speaking guides explain the flora and fauna of the island. Regular tours leave daily Mon. through Sat., reservations needed, tel. 2-19-58.

CANCUN

It's a well-known story: a wise Mexican computer in 1967 chose a small, swampy finger of land in an isolated part of the Mexican Caribbean, and pixels flashed, "Let There Be Tourists." And so it happened—Cancun resort was born. Designing Cancun, an island shaped like a seven with a bridge at both ends connecting it with the mainland, began from the ground up in 1968: new infrastructure, modern electrical plants, purified tap water, paved tree-lined avenues, and buildings which fit into the landscape (reincarnated Mayas could almost mistake some of them for new pyramids). When the first hotels opened their doors in 1972, visitors began coming and haven't stopped since.

For some, the name Cancun conjures immediate images of sugar-fine sand, a palette-blue sea, and flashing dollar signs. Think again! The beaches *are* stunning, the water *is* enticing, and it *does* take lots of money to enjoy Cancun if you just "drop in" at one of the fabulous resorts in the hotel zone. However, with careful shopping for package deals from your travel agent or in the travel pages

of your local newspaper you'll find something to fit every pocketbook. It's the best of both worlds—you just have to look a little harder for the less-expensive world.

At one end of the bridge is the "island," the hotel zone where the most elegant hotels are located; on the other end is Cancun city, where new moderately priced hotels and condos continue to be built. Hotels in the city serve up the flavor of Yucatan in the moderate US$30- to $100-a-night category and offer easy access to crowded sidewalk cafes (good for meeting people), romantic dinners, hot discos, intimate bistros, cinemas, buses, and a multitude of shops to explore—all within a few kilometers of the beach and lagoon. But if you need a shot of luxury, Hotel Row is the place to get it. Here, the most modern hostelries on Mexico's Caribbean coast provide a first-rate vacation in a sunny tropical setting. There's glamour, excitement, excellent service, great entertainment, lavish rooms, and epicurean delights—to say nothing of the surroundings, which bombard the senses with nature's simple beauty.

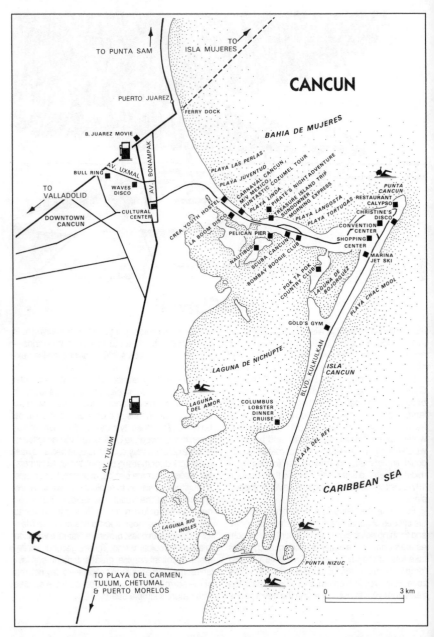

TO PUNTA SAM

TO ISLA MUJERES

CANCUN

PUERTO JUAREZ

FERRY DOCK

BAHIA DE MUJERES

B. JUAREZ MOVIE

AV. UXMAL

AV. BONAMPAK

BULL RING

TO VALLADOLID

WAVES DISCO

DOWNTOWN CANCUN

CULTURAL CENTER

Playa Las Perlas

Playa Juventud

Playa Linda

CREA YOUTH HOSTEL

LA BOOM DISCO

NAUTIBUS

PELICAN PIER

SCUBA CANCUN

BOMBAY BOOGIE CLUB

CARNAVAL CANCUN, MI MEXICO CANCUN, FUNTASTIC COZUMEL TOUR

PIRATE'S NIGHT ADVENTURE

TREASURE ISLAND TRIP

SUNDOWNER

MORNING EXPRESS

Playa Langosta

Playa Tortugas

PUNTA CANCUN

RESTAURANT CALYPSO

CHRISTINE'S DISCO

CONVENTION CENTER

SHOPPING CENTER

MARINA JET SKI

POK TA POK COUNTRY CLUB

Laguna de Bojorquez

Playa Chac Mool

GOLD'S GYM

LAGUNA DE NICHUPTE

BLVD KUKULKAN

ISLA CANCUN

LAGUNA DEL AMOR

COLUMBUS LOBSTER DINNER CRUISE

Playa del Rey

CARIBBEAN SEA

AV. TULUM

LAGUNA RIO INGLES

PUNTA NIZUC

TO PLAYA DEL CARMEN, TULUM, CHETUMAL & PUERTO MORELOS

0   3 km

SIGHTS

Archaeological Zones

Cancun has little to offer the archaeology buff compared to the larger sites at Chichen Itza, Uxmal, and Palenque. But surprisingly, structures built on this narrow strip of land have contributed important information to our knowledge about the people that lived here hundreds of years ago. Remnants of two sites, **Del Rey** on the south end of the island (close to Club Med) and **Yamil Lu'um** next to the Sheraton Hotel, are both worth a look; Yamil Lu'um is also on the highest point of mostly flat Cancun. The two small temples (15 meters high) were probably used as watchtowers and lighthouses along this navigational route. Between 400-700 years old, they were first noted by two intrepid American explorers John L. Stephens and Frederick Catherwood in 1841.

Scenic Spots

All of Cancun is scenic. But the most scenic beaches are on the seaward side of the island, extending 21 km and parallel to Paseo Kukulcan. If

Modern hotels line the shore, with an ancient Maya structure in the foreground.

you haven't been to Cancun since before Hurricane Gilbert, you will see some rearrangements of the beaches. In some areas sand was whisked out to sea, in others the beach was widened with sand deposits. Walking along the coast is rated a five-star activity, and it's free (all beaches in Mexico are public). The panorama is capricious—the color of the sea changes subtly throughout the day from pale aqua at dawn to deep turquoise at noon to cerulean blue under the blazing afternoon sun to pink-splashed purple during the silent sunset.

Nichupte Lagoon

This large lagoon which parallels Paseo Kukulcan is a combination of sweet water fed by underground springs and saltwater that enters from two openings to the sea. In certain areas where the water is still and swampy, mangroves provide hiding places for the cayman, little brother of large crocodilians found on other parts of the Peninsula. Birdlife is plentiful, with a treasure trove of over 200 cataloged species including herons, egrets,

DRIVING DISTANCES FROM CANCUN

Airport	20 km
Akumal	104 km
Aventuras (playa)	107 km
Bacalar	320 km
Chemuyil	109 km
Chetumal	382 km
Chichen Itza	192 km
Club Med	25 km
Coba	167 km
Kohunlich	449 km
Merida	312 km
Pamul	92 km
Playa del Carmen	65 km
Puerto Juarez	2 km
Puerto Morelos	32 km
Punta Sam	7 km
Tulum	130 km
Valladolid	152 km
Xcaret	72 km
Xelha	123 km

ospreys, screaming parrots, and parakeets; the sooty tern returns here to nest each year. The best way to see the lagoon and its wildlife is by boat. One of the many travel agents or your hotel can arrange a boat and a guide who knows his way around. Along the north end of the lagoon the marinas bustle with activity, and the trim greens of the Pok Ta Pok golf course extend out over the water. Nichupte is a favorite for water-skiing, sailing (Sunfish and Hobie Cat rentals), and sailboarding. Restaurants from exotic to generic are open all day, with a variety of shopping centers offering something for everybody. The arts and crafts center offers those who find bargaining stim-

ulating a chance to practice the art. For the more timid who may be used to paying the marked price, there are also shops which have become very Americanized. *Almost* all businesses in Cancun accept plastic money.

BEACHES

Note!
The water on the ocean side of Cancun can be hazardous. Pay particular attention to warning signs, and if in doubt, don't swim. Each year a few people drown off the beaches of Cancun because of a lack of respect for the power of this beautiful sea.

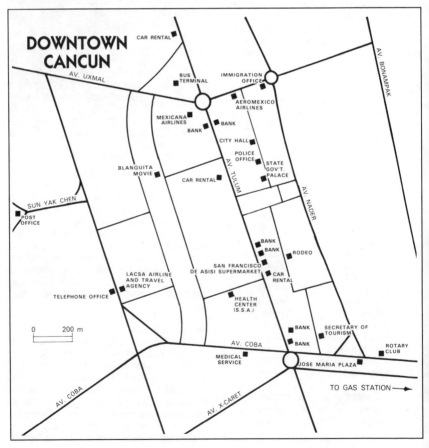

DOWNTOWN CANCUN

AV. UXMAL
CAR RENTAL
BUS TERMINAL
IMMIGRATION OFFICE
AV. BONAMPAK
AEROMEXICO AIRLINES
MEXICANA AIRLINES
BANK
BANK
CITY HALL
POLICE OFFICE
STATE GOV'T. PALACE
BLANQUITA MOVIE
CAR RENTAL
AV. TULUM
AV. NADER
SUN YAK CHEN
POST OFFICE
BANK
BANK
RODEO
SAN FRANCISCO DE ASISI SUPERMARKET
CAR RENTAL
LACSA AIRLINE AND TRAVEL AGENCY
TELEPHONE OFFICE
HEALTH CENTER (S.S.A.)
0   200 m
BANK
SECRETARY OF TOURISM
ROTARY CLUB
AV. COBA
BANK
MEDICAL SERVICE
JOSE MARIA PLAZA
AV. COBA
AV. X-CARET
TO GAS STATION →

Bus To The Beach

Cancun is one big beach, or more accurately, a series of breathtaking beaches laid end to end and around corners and curves. It's simple to reach any beach by bus; the route begins in downtown Cancun, making a circuit along Paseo Kukulcan, through the hotel zone, past the Convention Center, and on to the last hotel, whichever that happens to be at the time you're visiting. Bus stops are frequent and marked with blue signs that say Parada. However, most drivers will stop for a waving arm almost anywhere (if there's room). Bus fare is about US$.50 to anyplace.

Beginning Snorkelers

Cancun's beaches are for relaxing and soaking up the sun. The sandy sea-floor along here doesn't provide hiding places for the kind of sealife that prefers cool caves and rocky crevices. (Don't despair; there are a number of reefs in the area with rich marinelife to explore.) But for beginners (including children), this is a great place to learn to snorkel—and sun-loving fish such as tanned beauties and burnt-back beach nappers will provide the thrill of accomplishment when viewed for the first time through the glass. Guests at the Camino Real Hotel have a lovely, calm manmade lagoon ideal for learning, with tropical fish and sea turtles from small to very large to swim with.

Lifeguards

The hotels on the island all have beaches with various activities; some provide *palapa* sun shelters, volleyball courts, aerobic classes, bars, restaurants, showers, restrooms, and towels for their guests, and most importantly, lifeguards. Everyone is free to use the 60-foot strip of sand along the sea on any part of Cancun; signs indicating this are prominently posted everywhere by Sectur, the Ministry of Tourism. Visitors staying in the city have been known to spend their entire vacations (on their own towels) under the eye of a hotel lifeguard.

Public Beaches

Don't expect lifeguards or showers; some have snack stands and good parking areas. **Playa Linda** is close to the city (10 minutes by bus) located on Paseo Kukulcan near the Nichupte bridge. Two km past Playa Linda on Paseo Kukulcan is **Playa Tortuga,** easily spotted by a sign that

reads Playa Recreativa. The water is crystal clear, calm, and deep; on the beach is a *palapa*-covered snack bar. RV travelers often park here.

Around the point beyond the Convention Center is **Playa Chacmool.** This stunning beach displays the vibrant colors that make the Caribbean famous. You can walk out to sea 14 meters in shallow water before it begins to drop off. Check the tide conditions on the sign just south of the beach cafe—the water at times gets rough.

The Surf

There isn't a beach suitable for surfing anywhere on Cancun. Where protected by the reef, the Peninsula is a placid sea ideal for swimming. After leaving the city, the first stretch of beach from the youth hostel to Hotel Cancun Viva provides calm water and is also protected from strong currents and dangerous surf. The water at the lagoon is usually calm, but not as clear as the sea. Along the lagoonside you'll find many marinas and headquarters for water activities. On the east (the Caribbean or windward) side from Punta Cancun to Punta Nizuc the surf can be as high as three feet, and at certain times you'll encounter an un-

---

WATER SAFETY

The usual precautions apply. Don't swim alone in isolated places; take small children to calm surf areas, especially if there isn't a lifeguard. Common sense protection with sun-screen lotions, broad-brimmed hats, and dark glasses are suggested for anyone still walking around in winter-whites (skin). Familiar brands of American sun-screen lotions are available at all pharmacies and many hotel gift shops—but will cost much less in the States.

Familiarize yourself with the beach before splashing into the surf. Most of the beaches are posted with surf-condition signs (in Spanish) which specify the condition each day with a colored flag. Red is high surf or undertow—dangerous; yellow is medium high surf—use with caution; green is calm. While swimming, if you feel yourself being pulled out to sea, don't panic, and don't wear yourself out trying to swim to shore. Instead, swim parallel to the beach in either direction, and usually after swimming three or four meters you'll be out of the undertow—then swim to shore.

dertow. If you don't see a water-condition sign, ask at the concession stand—or *don't* swim. The calmest and most protected beaches on the windward side face Bahia Mujeres on the north end of the island.

WATER SPORTS

The Reefs

One of the most popular reefs despite its shallow depths is **Chital,** a short distance north of Hotel Stouffer Presidente on the island. The reef is made up of two sections, both about 20 meters wide. Expect a one-knot current and clear visibility up to 33 meters. **Cuevones Reef,** about three km north of Punta Cancun, is just what its name tells us in Spanish, "small caves." Here the body of the reef is comprised of elkhorn, rock, and brain coral. The series of caves varies in size from a five-meter cavern to a two-meter hole, all at a depth of about 10 meters. With an amazing 45-meter visibility, divers find themselves surrounded by large schools of reef fish, groupers, amberjack, and the ever-lurking predators, barracudas. **Manchones Reef** is a shallow reef closer to Isla Mujeres (three km south) than to Cancun (eight km northeast). Its 10-meter depth, 60-meter visibility, lack of current, and abundant sealife make it an ideal learning reef for beginning scuba divers.

Snorkeling

The experienced snorkeler will want to observe the beauty of the reefs, which are mainly made up of a variety of uniquely shaped and textured coral. In the immediate vicinity the most popular snorkeling areas are Chital, Cuevones, and Manchones reefs. They are home to large populations of reef fish, including blue chromis and barracuda. Chital, two km north of the island, has good snorkeling with depths between two and five meters. Cuevones and Manchones reefs are between Cancun and Isla Mujeres, with depths of 10-15 meters. Usually dive boats will take snorkelers along (room permitting) on scuba trips. Tour boats leaving daily for Garrafon Beach on Isla Mujeres carry snorkeling equipment. Garrafon is a logical spot for beginners and intermediates. Non-divers, bring dry bread to feed the little critters. They'll jump from the water and eat out of your hand—watch the fingers! Snorkeling equipment is available for rent at all the marinas and some of the hotels.

Dive Certification

Cancun has a good selection of dive shops; check with the marinas for recommendations. Before a diver can rent equipment, it's necessary to show a certified diver's card. If not certified, resort courses (for one dive accompanied by the divemaster) and certification classes (around 40 hours) are offered. For class info call **Mundo Marina,** PADI, tel. 3-05-54; **Neptune,** NAUI, tel. 3-07-22; **Aqua Tours,** tel. 3-02-07.

Scuba Diving

For the experienced scuba diver, Cancun would be second choice; Cozumel is unquestionably *numero uno!* For dive spots, however, none of the Caribbean is dull. An abundance of rich sealife surrounds each of the reefs; though around Cancun they're somewhat shallow, the beauty and excitement of the scenery are still dramatic. At **Punta Nizuc** (next to Club Med), experienced divers can explore the starting point of the Belize Barrier Reef that runs parallel to the Quintana Roo coast south 250 km to the Gulf of Honduras. This reef is the fifth-longest reef in the world after the Great Barrier Reef, Australia (1,600 km); Southwest Barrier Reef, New Caledonia (600 km); Northeast Barrier Reef, New Caledonia (540 km); Great Sea Reef, Fiji Islands (260 km); Belize Reef (250 km).

Windsurfing

For anyone who doesn't know, a windsurfer (also known as a sailboard) is comprised of a surfboard with a sail on a mast attached to the board by a swivel joint. This is controlled by a standing passenger who manipulates the sail with a wishbone tiller. It's a great wind-powered sport; in a brisk breeze the sail billows and this surfboard-cum-sailboat takes its sailor on an exhilarating ride skimming across the waves at mind-boggling speeds. Lessons are available at most of the marinas or the International Windsurfer Sailing School at Playa Tortuga, tel. 4-20-23. Usually six hours of lessons give you a good start. Sailboards are available to rent at many of the hotels and at the marinas.

Sailboats

If your idea of a ride in the wind includes a deck under foot and a tiller in hand, Hobie Cat and Sunfish rentals are available at a few hotels and most of the marinas. These small boats will give you a good fast ride if the wind is up. Negotiate for the fee you prefer to pay (remember, you're in Mexico)—sometimes you can get a good daily rate, better than the hourly rate posted.

Water-skiing
Most water-skiers prefer Nichupte Lagoon, although skiers are seen on calm days in Bahia de Mujeres north of the island. Equipment and instruction information are available from the marinas.

Jet-skiing And Parasailing
One of the new speed thrills on the lagoon is jet-skiing, obtained by means of a small motorized sled that will slowly circle around the driver should he or she fall off (rentals available at most marinas). Parasailing is popular at the busy beaches. The sailor, strapped into a colorful parachute and safety vest, is pulled high over the sand and surf by a speedboat; after about 10 minutes of "flying" he is gently deposited back on land with the help of two catchers. Once in awhile the rider is inadvertently dropped in the bay—usually to the guffaws of the beach crowd.

Marinas
Cancun offers many marinas with a variety of services. Some provide diving equipment and boats to the best scuba grounds; others have docks for a variety of sports equipment, including a flight on an ultralight, and still other docks are pickup points for organized boat tours. (See chart on following pages.)

FISHING

Deep-sea Fishing
Fishermen come to Cancun for what is considered some of the finest game fishing in the world. Charters are available and easily arranged with a day or two advance reservation. For information on half- and whole-day trips, call the marinas or check with your hotel. On full-day trips you can cap off the afternoon with a fish barbecue on the beach (ask the captain in advance). One of the most exciting game fish, the sailfish, runs from March to mid-July, bonito and dolphin from May to early July, wahoo and kingfish from May to Sept., and barracuda, red snapper, bluefin, grouper, and mackerel are plentiful all year.

Shore Fishing
Once you find a place to fish from shore, you'll catch plenty. Try fishing in the lagoon off the Nichupte bridge. Perhaps now you're spoiled, used to seeing the crystal-clear water of the Caribbean; well, the water is not as clear, but the fish are down there. Expect needlefish or possibly barracuda, and rumor has it that an occasional shark takes a wrong turn at the bridge and finds itself in the lagoon. Contrary to universal belief, this type of shark is good eating.

ESCORTED TOURS

Organized Boat Trips
Many tour boats are available for a variety of trips, most going to nearby Isla Mujeres: glass-bottom boats slowly drift above flamboyant undersea gardens, or on a musical cruise you can dance your way over to the small island. These tours often include snorkeling, and the necessary equipment is furnished. The *Aqua-Quin* is a motorized trimaran going twice daily to Isla Mujeres for snorkeling at Garrafon Beach, a buffet lunch, open bar, music, and fun. Reservations required; check at Hotel Camino Real or Hotel Fiesta Americana marina—fare is about US$40 pp.

The B/M *Carnaval Cancun,* a large triple decker that cruises to Isla Mujeres, serves a buffet lunch on board with an open bar, stops for snorkeling, and allows time for shopping in downtown Isla Mujeres. Called the Skin Tour, the boat leaves the Playa Linda pier daily; fare is about US$32.

Another popular cruise is the *Carnaval's* "party animal's cruise," which includes a calypso cookout on the beach, with an open bar, music, limbo contest, and other games (with prizes) that can last the whole night through. Fare is about US$42. For reservations check with your hotel or travel agency. To get information on trips that explore the lagoon, visit the Del Rey ruins, or take sightseers to nearby reefs, ask at your hotel or call one of the marinas.

The *Nautibus* (referred to as a floating submarine) is a double-keeled boat with transparent panels and individual stools in two air-conditioned compartments. In the submerged keels passengers feel as if they're of swimming among the schools of fish that live in Chital reef. Hundreds of sergeant majors rush alongside the windows, and

CANCUN MARINAS

NAME:	**Aqua-Quin**
ADDRESS:	marina at hotels Camino Real and Fiesta Americana
PHONE:	3-01-00
HOURS:	0830-1800
SERVICES:	diving, snorkeling, windsurfing, fishing; catamaran tours to Isla Mujeres
NAME:	**Aquatours**
ADDRESS:	km 6.25 Av. Kukulcan
PHONE:	—
HOURS:	0830-2000
SERVICES:	boat slips, diving, fishing, water-skiing, yacht tours, market (all credit cards accepted)
NAME:	**Carlos N' Charlies**
ADDRESS:	km 5.5 Av. Kukulcan
PHONE:	3-08-46
HOURS:	0730-2300
SERVICES:	boat tours and sportfishing
NAME:	**Carnaval Cancun**
ADDRESS:	Playa Linda Pier
PHONE:	—
HOURS:	1000-1600
SERVICES:	*Carnaval* cruiser to Isla Mujeres, includes open bar, continental breakfast, buffet, lunch, live music
NAME:	**Fiesta Maya**
ADDRESS:	km 8 Av. Kukulcan
PHONE:	3-03-08/3-04-18
HOURS:	1000-1600
SERVICES:	trips to Isla Mujeres via glass-bottomed *Fiesta Maya* (no credit cards accepted)
NAME:	**Krystal Divers**
ADDRESS:	Hotel Krystal
PHONE:	—
HOURS:	0800-1900
SERVICES:	dive trips—US$50 (two tanks), plus lessons—US$15; snorkel equipment rental—US$9 per day; boogie board rental—US$5 per hour
NAME:	**Lucky Hooker**
ADDRESS:	Playa Linda Pier
PHONE:	4-21-01/4-29-76
HOURS:	0900-1700
SERVICES:	Contoy Island tour, Tues.-Sat.—US$46; Lucky II fishing tour—US$40
NAME:	**Mauna Loa**
ADDRESS:	km 9 Av. Kukulcan
PHONE:	4-17-16
HOURS:	0900-1700
SERVICES:	jet-skiing, water-skiing, speedboats, kayaks, windsurfing, diving, fishing, snorkeling trips, charters available

CANCUN MARINAS

NAME: **Mundo Marina, S.A.**
ADDRESS: km 5.5 Av. Kukulcan
PHONE: 3-05-54
HOURS: 0800-2100
SERVICES: big and small game fishing, dive and snorkel trips, boat tours, charters

NAME: **Neptuno**
ADDRESS: Hotel Verano Beat
PHONE: —
HOURS: 0800-1600
SERVICES: dive tours and lessons, underwater videos, snorkeling and fishing tours, tour to Isla Mujeres via trimaran

NAME: **Pelican Pier Avioturismo**
ADDRESS: km 5.5 Av. Kukulcan
PHONE: —
HOURS: 0730-2000
SERVICES: Cessna air taxi; fishing—US$66 pp, or four hours for US$240, six hours US$336, eight hours US$384; rides in ultralight plane—US$40 (Visa and MasterCard accepted)

NAME: **Royal Marina**
ADDRESS: Omni and Oasis hotels
PHONE: 5-03-91/5-06-41
HOURS: —
SERVICES: diving, snorkeling trips, jet-skiing, water-skiing, windsurfing/sailing school, *Columbus* lobster-dinner cruise, Captain's Cove Restaurant, 7-11 market, and more

NAME: **Scuba Cancun**
ADDRESS: km 5 Av. Kukulcan
PHONE: 3-10-11/4-23-36
HOURS: 0900-1800
SERVICES: dive trips, night dives, certification courses, Cancun's only decompression chamber, PADI and NAUI training facility, Tropical Cruiser Tours, Playa Langosta dock. For tours, to Isla Mujeres: Morning Express 1000-1700; Treasure Island, closed Sundays. For reservations and details call 3-14-88.

NAME: **Uno Mas/Roman Lopez**
ADDRESS: Mundo Marina
PHONE: 3-05-54
HOURS: —
SERVICES: light-tackle fishing tours, reservations required

NAME: **Wild Goat**
ADDRESS: km 5 Av. Kukulcan
PHONE: —
HOURS: 0800-2000
SERVICES: fishing—US$34 pp (shared boat); Contoy Island trip—US$40 pp; or charter the "Goat Boat" (maximum six persons)—four hours US$240; six hours US$350; eight hours US$385; full day US$450 (Visa and MasterCard accepted)

Nautibus

the boat travels directly over unique coral formations.

Traveling to the reef on *Nautibus*'s top deck, you get a good view of one of the channels along the mangrove-lined Nichupte Lagoon under the Playa Linda bridge, and a look at the beaches in front of many upscale hotels on the way to the reef. The entire trip takes just under two hours, with three daily departures (1000, 1200, and 1400) from San Marino Pier in the hotel zone. Fare is about US$20 and includes all the beer and sodas you can drink.

Self-guided Tours

If you prefer to investigate Garrafon Beach on your own, it's easy and cheap. On Av. Tulum catch the city bus marked Ruta 1-A to Puerto Juarez (runs every 15 minutes). Take the passenger boat to Isla Mujeres (about US$.50), and from here if you want to spend your day diving, take a taxi to Garrafon Beach (about US$2, one to four passengers), or walk the five km to the beach (its a long sweaty walk). Garrafon admission is about US$1, snorkeling equipment rents for about US$5 (per day). A snack stand serves light lunch and cold drinks. If there's time before the last ferry back to Cancun, take a look at the town of Isla Mujeres.

OTHER SPORTS

The **Pok Ta Pok Club de Golf** has tennis courts and a well-kept 18-hole golf course designed by Robert Trent Jones. The golf club is a great sports center, with a pro shop, swimming pool, marina, restaurant, bar, and even its own small restored Maya ruin. Temporary club membership allows you to play golf or tennis at the club; arrangements can be made through your hotel. Greens fees about US$30. Many of the hotels on the island also have tennis courts, some with night lighting for a fee.

ACCOMMODATIONS

Deluxe
Every hotel on the "island" or hotel zone fits into the deluxe category. All offer at least one swimming pool (sometimes more) and good beaches; an assortment of restaurants, bars, and nightlife; beach activities and gardens; travel, tour, and car agencies; laundry and room service. In fact, a few tourists find everything for a complete vacation under one roof and stay pretty close to the hotel. Rates on the island begin at about US$80 and can get as expensive as you wish.

The hotels themselves showcase brilliant architecture, using the lines that would best fit into nature's environment, with a suggestion of the ancient Maya thrown in; add extraordinary comfort and total luxury for an overall description of the majority of the hotels in Cancun's hotel zone. If a rainy afternoon discourages beaching, take a tour of the hotels. It would take a whole book just to describe all the hotels in Cancun, so we have chosen a few that are beautiful, comfortable, and offer the ultimate in luxury. See a complete list of Cancun hotels beginning on p. 261.

Hyatt Regency And The Hyatt Cancun Caribe: Both are sensational hotels. The Regency's breathtaking 18-floor-high central atrium takes in the entire lobby, where afternoon drinks are accompanied by piano music. A bubbling waterfall separates the two swimming pools, where daily games of volleyball keep the actives busy. The views are breathtaking and the services perfect. The rooms are beautifully appointed with mini-bars and cable TV, and babysitting is available. Each hotel offers their "special hotels within the hotels," like the Regency Club in the Hyatt Cancun Caribe, where services include complimentary continental breakfast and afternoon cocktails and snacks, along with luxury amenities in the rooms.

The **Hyatt Cancun Caribe** has recently been remodeled and for a little more money the Regency Club villas offer lovely sitting areas and share a private pool, jacuzzi, and comfortable clubhouse near the pool for complimentary breakfast and afternoon cocktails. For reservations and information about both hotels call Hyatt's toll-free number in the States, (800) 228-9000. And if you want to have a really scrumptious dinner New Orleans style, go to the **Blue Bayou** at the Hyatt Cancun Caribe. Fourth- and fifth-time returnees continue to rave about the exquisite food at the Blue Bayou. Not only will you hear great jazz, but authentic Cajun and Creole cuisine are served amid a lush setting of waterfalls and bayou swamp—Louisiana swamps never looked like this!

Camino Real: One of the all-time favorites is the durable **Camino Real Cancun.** Spread out on lovely grounds on the tip of the island; you never feel crowded. The new **Tower** on the premises offers complimentary continental breakfast, afternoon tea, and snacks; morning wake-up service means a hot cup of coffee served by the Tower butler at your requested time. The rooms have beautiful views with private balconies, and color cable TV. In the main building live music is played at cocktail hour and in the evening. Take your choice of several restaurants including bars, and coffee shops. Gourmands, do try dinner at the Calypso. A few menu favorites are: chilled lobster gazpacho, *camarones empanizados con coco fresco* (jumbo shrimp breaded with fresh coconut), and apple tort aruba, a flaky crust with juicy apples surrounded by flowers sculpted from peaches, plums, grapes, and kiwis. The Camino Real has its own small lagoon inhabited by colorful fish and turtles. Be sure to watch the turtles being fed, scrubbed, and cared for. This is also a calm body of water great for learning windsurfing and snorkeling.

Crowne Plaza Holiday Inn: When walking from the lobby to the pool area, you see an optical illusion that makes the far end of the pool fade into the horizon of the sea behind, giving the impression that the pool continues into the Caribbean and the horizon. Crowne Plaza Holiday Inn hotel is decorated in bright Mexican purples and blues against elegant marble in an immense airy lobby surrounded by public rooms. All 380 rooms are very comfortable, have an ocean view, security box, and balcony; guests will find several great

Camino Real Hotel offers its own small lagoon with an opening to the sea. There you can see turtles and many colored tropical fish.

A bird's-eye view of the Elexaris Hyatt Regency Hotel's pool

restaurants and bars. **Alghero** specializes in Italian and Mediterranean/Arabic food; **Los Gallos** offers Mexican specialties. The sports nut has four swimming pools and a well-equipped health club.

Hotel Krystal Cancun: This is one of the all-time greats in Cancun, and it just continues to get better. Comfort and service are the bywords. Each of the 330 rooms looks as though it has been decorated individually, with luxury in mind. Rooms offer servibars, satellite TV, and room service; the health club offers tennis and racquetball courts, private clubroom pool and hydromassage pool.

TIPPING

Tipping is of course up to the individual, but for a guideline on the Peninsula the following seems to be average.

Porters: About US$.50 per bag. If you're staying at a hotel with no elevator and three flights of stairs and lots of luggage, you may wish to be more generous.

Hotel Maids: If staying more than one night, US$1-2 per day left at the end of your stay.

Waitresses: 10-15% is average.

Tour Guides: For an all-day trip, US$5 is appropriate, and the driver US$1.

When visiting a ruin, cave, or lighthouse you will usually be accompanied by a young boy to show you the way—US$.50 is customary.

Tipping taxi drivers is not customary.

The Krystal Club is a private club on the top floors of the building that offers complete access to all services in the entire hotel, along with private clubroom pool, and exclusive lounge with magnificent food and beverage service. Every guest in the hotel needs to know there are two restaurants at the Krystal that should be shared with that very special person. The **El Mortero** is a duplication of a 17th-century hacienda located in Durango in the north part of Mexico. When you step through the door into the outdoor patio, you leave the 20th century behind. The ambience is colonial Mexican with old-time charm, and guests have a choice of haute Mexican cuisine or continental food. If you're lucky, a very old, leathery-faced cook will come out into the candlelit patio and sing a romantic Latin love song accompanied by Mexican musicians and the bubbling water of the plant-lined fountain. The second choice takes you to distant Casablanca at **Bogart's**. Slow ceiling fans, high-backed wicker chairs, low light, and small intimate dining rooms with moorish architecture present the perfect background for a romantic dinner. For reservations and more Krystal information, contact Hotel Krystal Cancun, 12625 High Bluff Dr., Suite 205, San Diego, CA 92130, tel. (800) 231-9860, fax (619) 792-1872.

Hotel Cancun Palace: When you walk into the spacious lobby of the Hotel Cancun Palace a tranquil elegance predominates: rich woods, marble floors, skylights, greenery, and marvelously textured fabrics in pale grays and beige. Each room is spacious and includes full bar, king-size

CANCUN ACCOMMODATIONS

NAME	RATING	TELEPHONE	FAX	NO. OF ROOMS
Antillano	★★★	—	—	48
Aquamarina Beach	★★★★★	4-4205	—	—
Aristos	★★★★	3-0011	3-0078	222
Bahia de Mujeres	★★★★	3-0415	—	—
Beach Club Cancun	★★★★★	3-1597	3-1177	78
Calinda Quality Inn	★★★★	3-1600	3-1857	280
Camino Real Cancun	GT	3-0100	3-1739	205
Cancun Clipper Club	—	3-1130	—	—
Cancun Playa	—	5-1111	5-1151	266
Cancun Plaza	★★★★★	5-0072	5-0236	190
Cancun Viva	★★★★★	—	—	210
Caribbean Club	—	4-4340	—	90
Caribbean Suites	—	3-2300	5-1593	—
Caribe Mar	★★★★	3-0811	—	—
Carisa y Palma	★★★	3-0211	—	122
Carrousel	★★★★	3-0513	—	149
Casa Maya	★★★★★	3-0555	3-0881	237
Castel Flamingo	GT	3-1544	—	—
Castel Sol y Mar	★★★★★	3-1832	4-4521	—
Club Caribe Cancun	★★★★	3-0811	3-0384	113
Club Internacional	★★★★	3-0855	—	200
Club Lagoon	★★★★	3-1111	3-1326	70
Club Las Perlas	★★★	3-0869	3-1471	81
Club Mediterranee	GT	4-2900	4-2090	410
Club Privado	★★★★★	—	—	420
Club Verano Beat	★★★★	3-0772	3-0772	77
Coconut Inn	★★★	—	—	—
Condessa Cancun	GT	5-1000	5-1800	474
Crowne Plaza Holiday Inn	GT	5-1050	5-1050	380
Dos Playas	★★★★	3-0500	—	29
El Pueblito	★★★★	5-0849	4-0422	239
Fiesta Americana Condessa	GT	5-1000	5-1800	474
Fiesta Americana Playa Cancun	GT	3-1400	3-2502	636
Fiesta Inn	★★★★	3-2200	3-2532	84
Flamingo	★★★★★	3-1544	3-1029	69
Fontain Marina Club	★★★★	—	—	94
Galerias Plaza	★★★	—	—	58
Girasol	★★★	3-0624	3-2246	110
Green 16	★★★	3-1415	—	288
Hotel Beach Cancun Club	★★★★★	3-1177	5-0439	157
Hotel Cancun Handall	★★	—	—	58
Hotel Cancun Palace	GT	5-0533	5-1593	388
Hotel Colonial	★★★	4-1535	—	—
Hotel Hacienda	—	4-1208	—	—

GT= *Gran Turismo*—better than the best

continued

CANCUN ACCOMMODATIONS (CONT.)

NAME	RATING	TELEPHONE	FAX	NO. OF ROOMS
Hotel Plaza Del Sol	—	4-3888	—	—
Hyatt Cancun Caribe	★★★★	3-0044	3-1514	162
Hyatt Regency Cancun	GT	3-0966	3-1349	291
Imperial Las Perlas	★★★	3-0193	3-0106	53
Intercontinental Cancun	GT	5-0755	5-0021	239
Kokai	★★★	—	—	62
Krystal Cancun	GT	3-1133	3-1790	330
Laguna Cancun Resort	—	3-0070	—	48
Las Velas	★★★★★	3-2150	3-2118	226
Mary Tere	—	4-2473	—	42
Mauna Loa	—	3-0693	—	—
Maya Caribe	★★★★	3-2000	3-0650	40
Miramar Mision	★★★★★	3-1755	3-1136	179
Novatel	★★	429-99	—	40
Oasis Cancun	GT	5-0877	5-0131	1200
Omni Cancun	GT	5-0741	4-0689	281
Palace Hotel	GT	5-0533	—	—
Parador Hotel	—	4-1922	—	—
Paraiso Radisson	★★★★★	5-0112	5-0999	283
Park Inn Sol y Mar	—	5-0500	5-0934	257
Piramides del Rey	GT	3-1988	—	42
Playa Blanca	★★★★★	3-0028	3-0904	150
Plaza Caribe	—	4-1377	—	—
Plaza Kokai	★★★★	4-3666	—	48
Plaza Las Glorias	★★★★	3-0811	3-0901	112
Ramada Renaissance	★★★★	5-0100	5-0354	239
Royal Caribbean	★★★★★	—	—	92
Royal Mayan	—	5-0144	5-0032	200
Salvia Condominiums	★★★	3-2286	3-2568	80
San Marino	★★★	3-0815	—	42
Sheraton Resort	GT	3-1988	3-1450	745
Sierra Intercontinental	GT	—	—	261
Sina Suites	★★★	3-1017	—	—
Soberanis	★★★	4-1858	—	20
Solynar	★★★★★	—	—	156
Stouffer Presidente	★★★★	3-0200	3-2515	—
Suites Atlantis	—	4-1622	7-3362	—
Suites Brisas	★★★★★	4-1643	5-0060	25
Suites Caribbean	—	3-2300	3-2072	—
Suites Dos Playas	—	3-0500	7-3374	—
Suites Kin-Ha	—	3-2152	3-2147	85
Suites Las Gaviotas	—	3-1499	—	—
Suites Marbella	—	3-0572	—	—
Terramar Plaza Suites	★★★★	3-1588	3-1479	72
Tropical Oasis	★★★★★	5-1364	5-1363	154

CANCUN ACCOMMODATIONS (CONT.)

NAME	RATING	TELEPHONE	FAX	NO. OF ROOMS
Tucan Cun Beach	★★★★★	5-0058	—	39
Vacation Clubs International	★★★★★	3-0855	3-0206	200
Valma Kan	★★★★★	5-0107	5-0168	40
Villas Cerdena	★★★★	3-2055	—	26
Villas Kin-Ha	★★★★	—	—	193
Villas Marlin	★★★★	5-0532	5-0411	60
Villas Maya Cancun	—	4-1762	—	—
Villas Plaza	—	3-1022	3-2270	40
Villas Presidente	★★★★	3-0022	—	—
Villas Tacul	★★★★★	3-0000	—	23
Viva	★★★★★	3-0800	3-2087	210

beds, art and ornaments, splendid views, balconies or terraces, a/c, suites with outdoor hot tubs—all of this on a 492-foot-oceanfront beach with the turquoise sea and sand just a few feet from your hotel. For the ambitious, add tennis and a health spa to the list of swimming, jet-skiing, fishing, sailing, snorkeling, and scuba diving. For the less ambitious, the pools are lined with chaise lounges near waterfalls, snack bar, pool bar, sunken bar, lobby bar, and gourmet restaurants that offer seafood and international cuisine. Excellent Mexican food is served at **Las Golandrinas,** or have breakfast and lunch with gentle breezes from the sea at the enchanting outdoor **Palapas Cafe Las Redes.** For more information and reservations contact Hotel Cancun Palace, Blvd. Kukulcan km 14.5, Box 1730, Cancun, Quintana Roo 77500, Mexico; tel. (800) 346-8225, fax (305) 375-9508.

Cancun Sheraton Resort: The Sheraton hotel, as one of the "experienced" hotels around, is kept in marvelous condition with frequent remodeling and additions. The 745 rooms and 211 suites are modern and comfortable, with satellite TV, minibars, and individually controlled air. The grounds are beautifully kept and include two swimming pools, ample chaise lounges for sun worshipers, and a great shopping arcade; beach lovers have half a mile of white-powder sand and blue sea to frolic in. Archaeology buffs will even find on the grounds a small remnant of the Maya past, **Yamil Lu'um,** one of the few remaining Maya structures

in Cancun. Visitors play tennis on one of six lighted courts, visit the fitness center with sauna, steam bath, and whirlpool, or play golf on the minicourse; children enjoy the playground.

The newest addition is the seven-story Sheraton Towers, a separate new building with 167 rooms, each with a balcony and a spectacular view of the turquoise sea, some suites with terraces and jacuzzis. The Towers offers private Towers Lounge, special concierge, coffee or tea with your morning wake-up call, continental breakfast in the Towers Lounge, daily newspaper, clothes pressing, hors d'oeuvre service each evening, and luxurious amenities in the rooms like hair dryers, safety boxes, alarm clocks, and a special treat from the pastry chef upon retiring.

The Sheraton offers a variety of restaurants and bars to all of its guests: **La Gaviota, La Duna,** and the **Yalma Caan Lobby Bar** has a lively happy hour with the sea in the background; and **Daphny's Video Bar** continues late into the night with snappy entertainment in colorful surroundings. For more information and reservations in Canada and the U. S., call (800) 325-3535 or call your travel agent.

Fiesta Americana Plaza Cancun And Villas: Located between Nichupte Lagoon and the Caribbean Sea, the **Fiesta Americana Plaza Cancun And Villas** is a unique mix of Colonial, Moorish, and Caribbean architecture. A cloud of pink from a distance, the complex includes 636 rooms and suites scattered about in 26 villas and

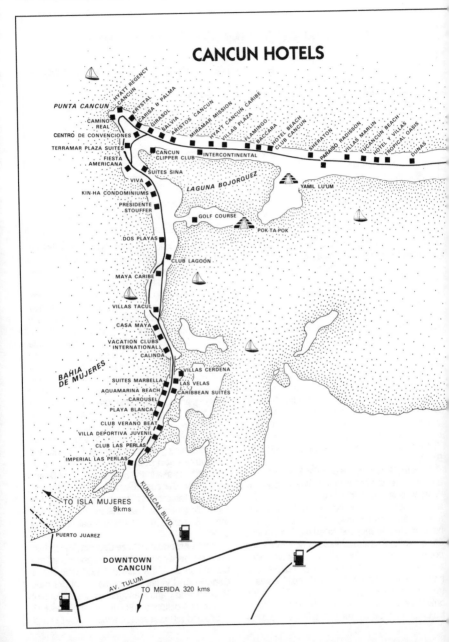

CANCUN HOTELS

PUNTA CANCUN

HYATT REGENCY CANCUN
KRYSTAL
CARISA B PALMA
GIRASOL
SALVIA
ARISTOS CANCUN
MIRAMAR MISSION
HYATT CANCUN CARIBE
VILLAS PLAZA
FLAMINGO
BACCARA
HOTEL BEACH
CLUB CANCUN
SHERATON
PARAISO RADISSON
VILLAS MARLIN
TUCANCUN BEACH
HOTEL V VILLAS
TROPICAL OASIS
DUNAS

CAMINO REAL
CENTRO DE CONVENCIONES
TERRAMAR PLAZA SUITES
FIESTA AMERICANA

CANCUN CLIPPER CLUB
INTERCONTINENTAL

SUITES SINA

VIVA
KIN-HA CONDOMINIUMS
PRESIDENTE STOUFFER

LAGUNA BOJORQUEZ

YAMIL LU'UM

GOLF COURSE

POK-TA-POK

DOS PLAYAS

CLUB LAGOON

MAYA CARIBE

VILLAS TACUL

CASA MAYA

VACATION CLUBS INTERNATIONAL
CALINDA

BAHIA DE MUJERES

VILLAS CERDENA
LAS VELAS

SUITES MARBELLA
AQUAMARINA BEACH
CAROUSEL
PLAYA BLANCA
CLUB VERANO BEAT
VILLA DEPORTIVA JUVENIL
CLUB LAS PERLAS
IMPERIAL LAS PERLAS

CARIBBEAN SUITES

TO ISLA MUJERES 9kms

PUERTO JUAREZ

KUKULCAN BLVD.

DOWNTOWN CANCUN

AV. TULUM

TO MERIDA 320 kms

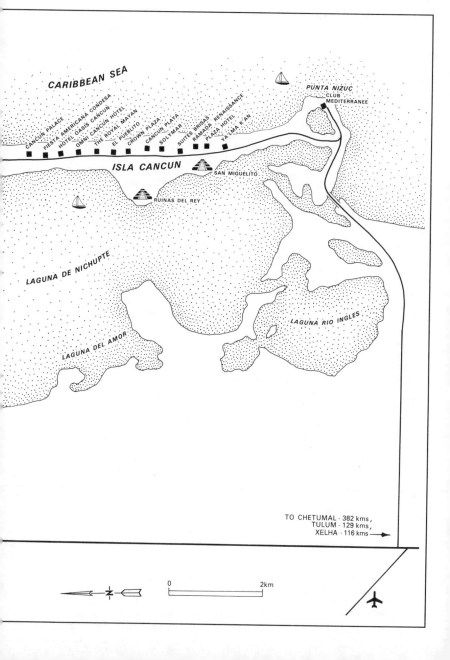

CARIBBEAN SEA

PUNTA NIZUC
CLUB MEDITERRANEE

CANCUN PALACE
FIESTA AMERICANA CONDESA
HOTEL OASIS CANCUN
OMNI CANCUN HOTEL
THE ROYAL MAYAN
EL PUEBLITO
CROWN PLAZA
CANCUN PLAYA
SOLYMAR
SUITES BRISAS
RAMADA RENAISSANCE
PLAZA HOTEL
YA LMA K'AN

ISLA CANCUN

SAN MIGUELITO

RUINAS DEL REY

LAGUNA DE NICHUPTE

LAGUNA RIO INGLES

LAGUNA DEL AMOR

TO CHETUMAL - 382 kms,
TULUM - 129 kms,
XELHA - 116 kms

0   2km

one tower. Rooms decorated in pastel colors are cozy and comfortable, a/c, with views of either the sea or the lagoon. Four pools and 500 yards of white-sand beach encourage guests to hang around. Tennis, squash, and racquetball courts are on the premises along with instructors for all manner of water sports. Five restaurants and three bars cater to every taste. Try **Las Cupulas** with its special Italian cuisine. For more information and reservations call (800) 223-2332.

Fiesta Americana Condessa: Scene of the Miss Universe contest in 1989, the **Fiesta Americana Condessa** is a smashing hotel. Guests enter through a 117-foot-tall *palapa* at the entrance (with escalator, thank you), the highest *palapa* roof in Mexico. The Disney people helped with the design of the hotel—and it shows. The magnificent lobby is decorated with stylized marble floors, jewel-toned fabrics, upholstered smart wicker furniture, and brilliant stained-glass awnings, which extend over the bars and here and there. The hotel is reminiscent of a small (upscale) Mexican village with greenery everywhere. Rooms are comfortable, many with spectacular views. Swimming pools are joined with arched bridges, and excellent restaurants scattered about offer a variety of ethnic foods to choose from. If you just can't drag yourself out of the pool try a game of backgammon on a floating table available for the asking. For the health buff, there are three a/c indoor tennis courts and a complete spa and gym. For more information and reservations call (800) 223-2332.

CAFE DE OLLA

Served at the
Sheraton Towers Breakfast Buffet

Recipe: 1 small earthen pot
3 tbs. of dark roasted
  coarse ground coffee
1 cinnamon stick
3 cloves
dark brown sugar to taste
1 liter of water

Bring water to boiling in pot, add coffee, cinnamon, and sugar. Bring to boil again, strain and serve. Optional: Add tequila to taste. Especially good brewed over an open fire!

Hotels—A Little Less Glitzy

Of course there are many more luxury hotels to choose from in Cancun, but your choices aren't limited to expensive resorts. Many smaller inns offer an entirely different ambience with charm and grace. **Sina Suites** is a lovely small complex that is a real buy. You have a choice of either one or two beautifully furnished bedrooms, plus two bathrooms, kitchen with all facilities for cooking, and living room. The hotel has two swimming pools, beach towels, maid service, and a terrific little cafe with reasonably priced meals near one of the pools. Both suites have a couch in the living room that makes into a bed. Price in high season is about US$151 per night, but negotiable. For more information contact Carlos Sandoval, Apto. Postal 919, Cancun, Quintana Roo 77500, Mexico, tel. 3-10-17/3-10-18, telex Siname 73433. A **Club Med** is located very close to Punta Nizuc in the hotel zone. Make reservations in advance.

Condominiums

Cancun is sprouting condos everywhere you look. While one wonders when the building will end, they provide some of the best bargains in town for families or small groups. For as low as US$130 a night, a family of five can stay in lovely surroundings near the beach with a pool, cooking facilities, often two bathrooms, and daily maid service included in the price.

Rates can soar much higher or at certain times of the year can even be less. Travel agents can help you find them or you can write directly to the managers. For the daring, good buys come if you just arrive on the scene without reservations, go from condo to condo, and negotiate the price of one that isn't reserved. However, you run a certain risk of not finding what you want, especially during the winter months. The following company rents condos from the U.S.: Luxury Villas of Cancun, Box 18225, San Antonio, TX 78218, tel. (800) 531-7211.

Moderate

Moderate accommodations are found in bustling downtown Cancun. The biggest drawback to this location is the absence of beach, but blue sea and white sand are accessible in short order by bus every 15 minutes. Some hotels provide free transportation for their guests. Sometimes crowded, these hotels are good bargains. The Yucatecan ambience pervades, and each has a helpful staff

CAN FOREIGNERS OWN LAND IN MEXICO?

As a result of legislation in 1971, it is possible for a foreigner to own land within the coastal zone of Mexico. The ownership is through a *fideicomiso* (trust). This process requires the foreigner who is purchasing to mandatorily place the title to the property in trust with a Mexican financial institution empowered to act as a trustee. The foreign owner is then conveyed a beneficial interest in the trust, which means the foreigner may live on the property, rent it, or in general treat the property as if it were owned with a fee simple title.

Should the foreigner wish to sell, the transaction occurring is the assigning of rights acquired through the *fideicomiso*. The maximum duration of such a trust is 30 years. After the 30-year period, the trust must be either renewed or the property sold at fair market value. As in any real estate transaction, it is recommended that you consult a lawyer first.

Beautiful new condos are springing up all over the Caribbean coast—some are good buys —but they were terrific buys five years ago. Who knows what will happen in another five years.

willing to answer questions about the city. The hotels have private baths, a/c, hot water, phone in room, swimming pool, bar, and restaurant. The rates run from about US$40 d to about US$100. **Hotel Hacienda,** Av. Sunyaxchen #39, tel. 28-13-51 is a low-key pleasant hotel with 40 a/c rooms, swimming pool, pool bar, beach club service and transportation, cafe, parking, and a travel agency on the premises. Rates in summer are US$28 s or d, in winter US$35 s or d. For information in the U.S. call ITI, (714) 494-8129, (800) 227-0212. Other choices are **Hotel Plaza Caribe,** corner of Av. Uxmal, tel. 4-13-77; **Hotel Cancun Handall,** Av. Tulum, tel. 4-19-47; **Hotel America Cancun,** Av. Tulum and Calle Brisa, tel. (800) 262-2656, 4-15-00; **Hotel Plaza del Sol,** Av. Yaxchilan, tel. 4-38-88; or **Novatel,** Av. Tulum and Uxmal, tel. 4-29-99.

Youth Hostel
The best bargain in Cancun is the **CREA Youth Hostel** on Paseo Kukulcan next to Club Verano Beat. Located in the hotel zone, the YH has a beach (not always in the best condition), swimming pool, bar, inexpensive dining room, and 650 bunk beds in women's and men's dorms. Rates are about US$10 pp, bedding included, plus a US$7 deposit.

Budget
These hotels, though simple, are *usually* clean and offer a/c and hot water. Some rates begin as low as US$20. *Please understand that these rates change with supply and demand.* Try negotiating in May, June, and September. Choices include

Hotel Rivemar, about US$45 d, Av. Tulum, tel. 4-17-08, and **Hotel Tulum,** about US$35, Av. Tulum, tel. 4-13-55. **Hotel Coral** advertises its price as about US$11, but take a look (we haven't seen it), Av. Sunyaxchen 50, tel. 4-05-86. **Hotel Cotty** costs about US$20, Av. Uxmal 44, tel. 4-13-19.

Hotel El Rey Caribe is a small family-run motel-like inn set in a well-kept simple garden with pool and hot spa. Rooms are old but presentable and include kitchenettes, a/c or ceiling fan; rates from US$37 to $70. Near the corner of Uxmal and Nader, Apto. Postal 417, tel. 4-20-28. **Hotel Kokai** is downtown, a simple small hotel with 48 rooms, a/c, lobby bar, swimming pool, jacuzzi, a small roof garden, and 12 suites with kitchens. Prices start at around US$50, and a continental breakfast is about US$3 at the small dining room in the lobby. For more information and reservations write to: Uxmal 26, Cancun, Mexico, or call 4-36-66, telex Ikeame 73341.

FOOD

Restaurants
If you stayed for three or four months, it might be possible to sample each of the fine restaurants in Cancun city and the island—maybe. Most budget cafes are found on Av. Tulum and Av. Yaxchilan. For more *tipico* food and ambience, walk along Av. Yaxchilan until you find a place that appeals to you. On the two main streets, Av. Tulum and Uxmal, many resort-like touristy sidewalk cafes are busy, noisy, Americanish, and fun! For the epi-

curean explorer, there's Swiss, French, Chinese, Italian, Mexican, Arabic, Polynesian, Texan, Yucatecan, and continental; there's fast food, simple-food, fancy food, seafood, homemade, rushed, and romantic, hamburgers, hot dogs, tacos, and *tortas,* and don't forget the great Creole food at the Hyatt's Blue Bayou. This is gourmet headquarters for the state of Quintana Roo, and all you have to do is look! Most restaurants accept credit cards.

A curious food fact: Mexico is one of the leading coffee producers of the world, but in spite of this most restaurants in Mexico serve instant coffee. Cancun, however, is the exception. Almost all of its cafes serve good brewed coffee—brewed decaf is available in only a few. On some Cancun menus you can find an old traditional favorite, *cafe de olla* (coffee cooked and served in a small earthen mug). Remember, in Mexico it's considered an insult for a waiter to submit a bill before it's requested; when you're ready to pay, say, *"La cuenta, por favor"* ("The bill please").

The following restaurants represent a few of Cancun's ethnic assortment. Cajun: **Blue Bayou,** very elegant, Hyatt Cancun Caribe Villas and Resort, tel. 3-00-44, reservations recommended. Chinese: **Mauna Loa,** Polynesian atmosphere, nice, shows 1900-2100 nightly, Mauna Loa Shopping Center, tel. 3-06-93, reservations required. French: **Du Mexique,** a tastefully chic restaurant, casual, Av. Coba downtown, tel. 4-10-77, reservations required. All major credit cards accepted except Diners; **L'Alternative,** casual- elegant, Av. Kukulcan and Bonampak downtown; **Maxime,** sophisticated-elegance, casual, Av. Kukulcan, Pez Volador #8, oceanfront (next to the Casa Maya Hotel), tel. 307-04/304-38. German: **Karl's Keller,** German beer-garden atmosphere, casual, Plaza Caracol.

International: **El Mural,** quietly elegant, Carrousel Hotel, tel. 3-03-88; **El Pirata,** lively, casual, 19 Azucenas St. downtown, tel. 4-13-38; **La Ola,** Caribbean view, casual, Hotel Suites Brisas; **Peacock Grill,** garden dining, casual, Hotel Plaza Caribe downtown, tel. 4-13-77; **Plaza Girasoles,** open-air patio, casual, Hotel Plaza del Sol, 31 Yaxchilan downtown, tel. 4-38-88. Reservations required; **Seagull,** ocean view, casual, Calinda Hotel, tel. 3-16-00; **Tunkul,** elegant, Hotel Oasis, tel. 5-08-67. Italian: **Don Giovanni,** traditional Italian, casual, Av. Kukulcan, near Mexicana, down-

town, tel. 4-50-63; **Savio's,** elegant bistro, casual-chic, Plaza Caracol II, accepts all major credit cards except Diners; **Scampi,** elegant, quiet, dressy, Hyatt Regency Hotel, tel. 3-09-66, reservations required. Japanese: **Tokyo Surf Club,** light, fun, casual, 3 Calle Azucenas downtown. Mediterranean: **Alghero,** intimate, Mediterranean style, dressy, Crowne Plaza Cancun, tel. 5-10-50.

Mexican: **Careyes Restaurant,** elegant, dressy, Hotel and Villas Tropical Oasis; **El Campanario de los Armandos,** wild Mexican party, casual, 12 Av. Coba downtown, tel. 4-41-80; **El Cortijo,** Mexican party atmosphere, casual, Plaza Flamingos; **Fonda del Angel,** very "old Mexico," casual-nice, 85 Av. Coba downtown, tel. 4-33-93; **Pericos,** lively, casual, 71 Av. Yaxchilan, tel. 4-31-52; **Restaurant Mexicano,** very elegant, dressy, La Mansion-Costa Blanca Shopping Center, hotel zone, tel. 3-22-20; **The Mine Co.,** a Mexican fiesta atmosphere, casual-nice, Av. Kukulcan next to Verano Beat, tel. 3-07-72/3-06-70; **Xenia,** high-style Mexican, nice, Cancun Plaza Hotel, hotel zone, tel. 5-00-72.

Seafood: **Captain's Cove,** elegant, tropical dining, casual, Av. Kukulcan across from the Royal Mayan, Omni, and Oasis hotels; **El Pescador,** a homey restaurant, casual, Tulipanes #28 downtown, tel. 4-26-73; **La Bamba,** lively Caribbean/Mexican atmosphere, ocean view, casual, Playa Langosta, hotel zone; **Mi Casa,** high-style, casual, on the beach at km 4 of the Puerto Juarez-Punta Sam Hwy.; **Soberanis,** lively, singles bar, Av. Coba and Tulum, downtown, tel. 4-11-25/ 4-18-58.

Spanish: **Olé y Olé,** traditional Spanish style, nice, Plaza Terramar, tel. 4-13-38, reservations recommended. Swiss-Italian: **Casa Rolandi,** Mediterranean atmosphere, casual, Plaza Caracol, tel. 3-18-17.

For a great roast beef sandwich (under US$4) on crisp French bread, good bagels, excellent breakfast, a brownie sundae, tabouleh, or a choice selection of imported beer, try lunch at **Cafe Amsterdam** downtown, run by a Dutch woman. The food is great, the prices reasonable. **100% Natural** on Sunyaxchen serves good vegetarian, makes great shakes. **Pollo Goyo** offers a big menu with satisfying salads, good chicken, and a "bucket of soup."

Groceries
Mercado Municipal, six blocks north of the bus station on Av. Tulum, is well supplied; come early for the best selection of fresh produce and meat. **Javier Rojo Gomez** behind the post office on Sunyaxchen is a smaller version of Mercado Municipal. **Super Carniceria Cancun,** Av. Sunyax- chen 52, sells familiar American-style cuts of meat. **San Francisco de Assisi Super Market** on Tulum is a modern well-stocked market designed for one-stop shopping (somewhat novel to much of Yucatan): butcher case, bakery counter, row upon row of groceries, liquor, electric appliances, even clothes. Another smaller supermar-

MEXICAN WINE

It would seem the most natural thing in the world for Mexico to produce good wines, considering the Spanish conquistadors came from a land with a long history of growing rich flavorful grapes and were experts in the field of fermentation. Pre-Hispanics didn't have wine as the Spanish knew it, but did make fermented beverages from such things as corn. It was not long before vine cuttings were brought to the New World and colonists were tending vineyards. By 1524 wine was so successful that Mexican wines were soon competing with Spanish wines. Pressure from vintners at home forced King Felipe II to outlaw its production in Mexico. However, over the years church-use continued and no doubt many gallons of the forbidden drink found its way to private cellars. But for all practical purposes and development, the industry was stopped before it had the opportunity to make itself known around the world.

Not until 1939 under then-president Lazaro Cardenas did Mexican wine-making begin to make a name for itself. Experts from around the world are beginning to recognize the industry in general and several of the wines are considered world-class. Over 125,000 acres of vineyards are under cultivation in the states of Baja California Norte, Aguascalientes, Queretaro, and Zacatecas. It's the vineyards of Baja that produce almost 80% of the country's wines located within the so-called "international wine belt" (between latitudes 30 and 50). Some of the well-known wineries (and their wines) from this area are: **Domecq** (Padre Kino, Calafia, Los Reyes, and Fray Junipero); **L.A. Cetto** (Don Angel); and **Santo Tomas.**

The wineries, **Cavas de San Juan** (Hidalgo, Edelmann, Carte Blanche, etc.) and **Casa Martell** are found in Queretaro, some 2,000 miles south of Baja. This was due to the suggestion of a University of California professor of enology who came to the conclusion that the area's 6100-foot elevation compensated for its being outside the celebrated "wine belt." Zacatecas is the location of the relatively new and promising **Union Vinicola Zacateca** (Los Pioneros), and Aguascalientes of **La Esplendida** (Armilita) and **Valle Redondo.**

According to Walter Stender of ACA Imports, some Mexican wines are even being imported to the U.S. Please note: Mexican wines don't age well and need not be impressed by dates. In other words, the whites are ready when released, the reds need "age" no more than 18 months.

If you want champagne, remember to ask for *vino espumoso* or "bubbly wine." A label that reads *methode champenoise* means the French system for producing sparkling wine was used. Mexico signed an agreement with the French government not to label its sparkling wines *champagne*—along with all other major wine-producing nations of the world except the U.S. Of course there are many imported wines from all over the world available in the fine restaurants of Cancun—many from California— but while in Mexico be adventurous and try the Mexican wine. A personal favorite is L.A. Cetto's white.

ket, **Glorietta Supermarket** is on Av. Tulum just past the *glorieta* (traffic circle).

Bakeries

Indulge yourself in fine Mexican pastries and crusty *bolillos* at the **Panificadora Covadonga** on Av. Tulum, a few hundred meters north of Av. Uxmal. Another smaller bakery is **Los Globos** on Tulipanes just west of Av. Tulum. The **Glorietta Market** and **Don Giovanni Bakery** have delicious baked goodies.

ENTERTAINMENT

Nightlife

Cancun has a marvelous choice of nighttime entertainment. It's easy to dance the night away at any one of a number of inviting places. Most of the hotels on the island have discos in motion until the early hours of morning. Some *cantinas* offer live bands ranging from jazz to popular marimba to reggae and several hotels offer Mexican "fiestas"

Fiesta night at the Hyatt Regency Hotel offers excellent tipico *food and dancers.*

weekly, including *tipico* dinners, traditional dances, and colorful costumes. The **Lone Star Bar** in downtown's Hotel Maria de Lourdes advertises that they "speak Texan," has great down-home country-western music, and is busy at happy hour when they serve each patron a free margarita (2000-2200 Sun., Tues., and Thurs.). **The Mine Co.** disco next to the YH on Paseo Kukulcan charges a small cover. The **Mauna Loa** at the Convention Center presents two Polynesian floor shows nightly, but after 2300 the place transforms into a hot disco.

For zany fun with wild and comedic waiters as well as exceptionally good food (try the Mexican combination plate with *carne asada*), you can't beat **Carlos N' Charlie's,** on Paseo Kukulcan. For more romantic live music try **La Cantina** in Cancun at 1900 at the Convention Center. And for a serene romantic spot to begin or end an evening, watch Cancun's sensational sunset or glittering stars in **La Palapa,** a mellow bar in a thatch-roof pavilion on the end of its own pier over the lagoon at Hotel Club Lagoon Caribe, Paseo Kukulcan. La Palapa serves snacks, exotic drinks, and has live music and dancing from 2100-1330.

Bars And Nightclubs

Cancun has some of the most upscale, modern discos in Mexico with all the newest effects to make for the best entertainment. Check out: **Aquarius Disco,** high-tech disco, dressy, Hotel Camino Real, tel. 3-01-00; **Bombay Boogie Club,** very splendid, dressy, Av. Kukulcan next to the Bombay Bicycle Club; **Casis Lobby Bar,** contemporary elegance, nice, Hyatt Cancun Caribe Villas and Resort, tel. 3-00-44; **Christine's Disco,** superb sound and light show, dressy, next to Hotel Krystal, tel. 3-11-33; **Daphny's Video Bar,** casual and fun, Sheraton Hotel, tel. 3-19-88; **Extasis Disco,** high-tech, sophisticated, nice, km 3.5 Av. Kukulcan; **Gifry's Piano Bar,** elegant, chic bar, stylish, same entrance as L'Alternative Restaurant, Av. Coba downtown, tel. 4-12-29; **La Boom Disco,** high-tech disco, nice, km 3.5 Av. Kukulcan; **Lobby Bar,** elegant, classy, casual-nice, Hotel Hyatt Regency, tel. 3-09-66; **Tropical Oasis Piano Bar,** casual, Hotel and Villas Tropical Oasis; **Mexican Fiesta** at Hyatt Regency, a full-on party, casual, tel. 3-09-66, ext. 2; **Reflejos Video Bar,** upbeat and lively, casual-nice, Hyatt Regency, tel. 3-09-66.

Cancun Evening And Dining Cruises

Two favorite dinner cruises are the **Columbus "Lobster Dinner Cruise,"** featuring a superb charcoal-grilled lobster, spectacular sunsets, and casual atmosphere, Royal Marina, tel. 3-13-57 or 3-18-53, reservations required; and **Pirate's Night,** casual, tel. 3-14-88, reservations required.

Cinema

Unlike most Peninsula cities, the majority of films shown in Cancun are usually American made with Spanish subtitles. Expect the bill to change every three or four days. However, **Cines Cancun,** Av. Xcaret #112, tel. 4-16-46, and **Cine Royal,** Av. Tulum, offer Mexican films that provide a cultural experience. Some of the larger hotels have their own movie theater and large-screen TV.

Shopping Centers

La Mansion-Costa Blanca, a small, exclusive, and painted hot-pink mall, features unique boutiques, several of the city's top restaurants, a money exchange, and a bank. **El Parian** shops are constructed around a lovely garden off to one side of the Convention Center. A lot of variety here in terms of shops, plus a money exchange and several good restaurants. **Las Velas,** though small, includes a pizza parlor, liquor store, exotic leather shop, art gallery, fancy-dress boutique and more. **Mauna Loa,** a diminutive cluster of shops that faces the lagoon just opposite the Convention Center, encompasses a bookstore/pharmacy, real estate office, convenience store, a few interesting boutiques, a marina, a pizza parlor, and two of Cancun's top restaurants. **Mayfair Gallery,** one of Cancun's newer malls, is located opposite the Fiesta Americana Hotel and contains a wide variety of boutiques and restaurants in a lovely atrium-roofed, two-story building. **Plaza Caracol,** one of Cancun's biggest and most contemporary shopping centers, is conveniently located in the hub of the hotel zone, fully air-conditioned, and elaborately finished with marble floors and lots of windows. This two-story mall consists of over 200 shops and boutiques, including signature stores of the world's most famous labels: Gucci, Fiorucci, Christian Dior, Benetton, and more.

Plaza Flamingo is the newest addition to Cancun's plethora of modern malls. This one-story center with Maya-inspired architecture, beautiful marble floors, and high-tech lighting features over 100 shops plus several restaurants, including a

Denny's that serves good enchiladas (true, true!), and **Golds,** a fully equipped gym. **Plaza La Fiesta** is actually a huge one-floor department store featuring all the fabulous crafts of Mexico; they offer a particularly fine selection in gold and silver jewelry.

Plaza Lagunas, at the center of the hotel zone, features all manner of sportswear, including those of famous designers. Various small restaurants, a snack bar, and an ice cream parlor are set among the shops. **Plaza Nautilus,** a modern, two-story plaza with over 70 businesses, is a potpourri of shops and art galleries, including a bookstore, video games arcade, and two fine restaurants. **Terramar,** located opposite the Fiesta Americana Hotel, is a city block of shops, eateries, real estate offices, a pharmacy, and a small hotel.

Downtown, **Plaza America** is located on Av. Kukulcan just as you leave town going south. This large mall houses over 40 shops, a money-exchange house, snack bar, and a fine French restaurant among other upmarket boutiques and craft shops. **Plaza Bonita** is housed in a large hacienda-style structure replete with hand-painted Mexican tiles and a collection of many fine shops, boutiques, eateries, and imported goods.

TO GET MARRIED IN CANCUN

Call 4-13-11, ext. 129 to make an appointment with Sr. Pedro Solis Rodriguez, official of the Civil Registry. When you go to the Civil Registry Office at the city hall located downtown on Av. Tulum have available from bride and groom:

✔ Tourist cards

✔ Birth certificates

✔ Blood tests

✔ Passports or driver's licenses

✔ Final divorce decrees if applicable

✔ The names, addresses, ages, nationalities, and tourist card numbers of four witnesses

✔ Pay fee to the cashier at the city hall, about US$35.

✔ Fill out application which you will be given by the judge.

✔ Very important: these things must be done at *least* two days before the wedding.

Plaza Mexico on Av. Tulum is an air-conditioned mall which specializes in Mexican crafts, among them Maya textiles, leather goods, wood carvings, stoneware, and sportswear. **Plaza Safa,** a lovely arcade which fronts Av. Tulum, houses a snack bar, a series of shops, a money exchange, and a very popular cantina on the second floor. **Tropical Plaza,** an interesting new mall, has shops selling everything from jewelry to designer clothing; there's also a bank, travel agency, real estate office, and a great restaurant for beef eaters. It's next door to Plaza Mexico. **Via Benetto** is a colorful arcade lined with a wide range of shops featuring everything from silver jewelry to textiles. Access from Av. Tulum.

Craft Markets
In the hotel zone, **Coral Negro** is located next to the Convention Center. This market is a collection of approximately 50 stalls selling handicrafts from all parts of Mexico. Located downtown on Av. Tulum, **Ki Huic** is Cancun's main crafts market. Over 100 different vendors feature just about every kind of craft and souvenir you can imagine. **Plaza Garibaldi,** also downtown at the center of Av. Tulum and Uxmal South, contains 90 stalls of serapes, tablecloths, traditional clothing, onyx, and other handcrafted items.

Miscellaneous
Alberto's Jewelers, 21 Av. Tulum, Plaza Mexico and Plaza Tropical, downtown. **Foto Omega— Prints and Supplies,** 103 Av. Tulum and 45 Av. Uxmal, tel. 4-38-60/4-16-79. **Pama** is a modern department store featuring imported cosmetics, perfumes, and food stuffs as well as sportswear, designer clothing, and more.

SERVICES

Laundromat
A large pleasant laundromat is located downtown at 5 Av. Nader. Either you can do it yourself or pay extra to have it done for you—laundry and dry cleaning are tremendously cheaper here than at the hotels. A shady patio offers chairs for waiting.

Medical Information
Most hotels in Cancun can provide the name of a doctor who speaks English. For medical assistance or an emergency, call 3-01-63 or the American Consular Office, tel. 4-16-38.

Post Office And Telegrams
The post office is west of Av. Tulum on Av. Sunyaxchen; open 0900-1200 and 1500-1700, Mon. to Sat., tel. 4-14-18. Telegraph office, tel. 4-15-29.

Consulate
To reach the American consular agent, call 4-16-38.

Tourist Information
One info center is downtown on Av. Tulum next to the Ki Huic shopping mall; another is at the El Parian Convention Center in the hotel zone, tel. 4-33-40. The informed staffs are bilingual, cheery, and genuinely helpful. Ask for maps, brochures, prices, schedules, or directions. The chamber of commerce is also a good source of information, tel. 4-12-01.

Travel Agencies
With the advent of the tour guide's union, tours to Tulum and Chichen Itza are the same price at every agency, US$21 and $29 respectively. **Best Day** in the Kin-Ha Condominiums lobby, tel. 3-21-55/3-20-19, offers scheduled tours to Chichen Itza, Tulum, and Xel-Ha; private tours to Cozumel, Isla Mujeres, etc. can be arranged. **Buen Viaje** at Hotel America, downtown, tel. 4-54-41, open 0800-1500, offers scheduled tours to Chichen Itza, Tulum, Cozumel, Isla Mujeres, and Contoy Island. **Contours Operadora** is at Av. Tulum and Claveles St. downtown, tel. 4-25-74/4-61-95, open 0830-1330 and 1630-2000, closed Sundays. Services include: all local and Yucatan tours, all travel arrangements. **Ceiba Tours,** 146 Av. Nader, S.M. 3, downtown, tel. 4-20-62/4-19-62, open 0700-2200, offers scheduled tours to Chichen Itza, Tulum, Merida, Isla Mujeres, Cozumel, and Con-

EMERGENCY NUMBERS

Police	4-19-13
Fire	4-12-02
Air-Vac Medical Life Service, Houston, Texas	(713) 961-4050

toy; ask about private tours. Additional services: national and international airline tickets. **Incentives and Vacations Inc.** at Suites Lomas, S.M. 4, downtown, tel. 4-61-33, open 0800-2000, can provide tours to Chichen Itza, Tulum, and Isla Mujeres.

Intermar Caribe, Plaza Quetzal, hotel zone, tel. 3-02-44, open 0700-2000. Scheduled tours: Tulum, Chichen Itza, Coba, Isla Mujeres, Cozumel; private and charter groups. **Mayaventuras,** 11 and 12 Av. Coba, tel. 4-22-44, open 0800-1300 and 1600-2000. Scheduled tours: Chichen Itza, Tulum, Cozumel, Isla Mujeres, and Contoy Island, plus airline ticketing. **Mexicanos Profesionales de Viajes,** Hotel Fiesta Americana (lobby), tel. 3-14-00/3-14-26, open Mon.-Sat. 0800-2000, Sun. 0800-1800. Tours: Chichen Itza, Tulum, Cozumel, Isla Mujeres; horse riding at Rancho Victoria. **Turismo Aviomar,** 30 Venado, S.M. 20, downtown, tel. 4-67-42, 4-66-56, or 4-64-33, fax 4-64-35, open 0800-2000. Tours and services: Chichen Itza, Tulum-Xel-Ha, Cozumel, Isla Mujeres, Uxmal, and Merida; airline ticketing. **Turismo Caleta,** Plaza Quetzal Ste. 11, hotel zone, tel. 3-16-59, 3-05-91, or 3-25-38, open 0800-2000. Tours: all local services and tours.

Viajes Cancun Holiday, S.A., Plaza Bombay, tel. 3-01-61/3-00-05; open 0800-2000. Tours: Chichen Itza, Tulum and Coba, city tours to Isla Mujeres, Cozumel, Chichen Itza, Uxmal (nightly light and sound show), and Merida; flights using the Helicar service can be arranged. Visa and MasterCard accepted. **Viajes Inolvidables,** Plaza Quetzal, tel. 3-17-82/3-10-41, open 0730-2000. Tours: Chichen Itza, Tulum, Cozumel, Isla Mujeres, etc. Additional services: national and international packets. **Viajes Thomas Moore, S.A.,** km 16 Av. Kukulcan across from the Royal Mayan, tel. 5-01-44, ext. 164, or 5-02-66, open 0800-1900. Tours: Chichen Itza, Tulum, Isla Mujeres, Merida, Uxmal, Cozumel, Contoy, plus windsurfing lessons, jet-ski and water-ski bookings. Banamex and MasterCard accepted. **Viajes Turquesa,** Suites Lomas, S.M. 4, downtown, tel. 4-20-75/4-35-95, open 0700-1400 and1600-1900. **Visusa,** 64 Av. Bonampak, downtown, tel. 4-30-95/4-28-82, open 0800-2000 daily. Tours: Chichen Itza, Tulum, Isla Mujeres, Cozumel, and Uxmal. Visa is accepted. **Wagons Lits,** Calinda Hotel, Camino Real Hotel, tel. 3-08-47/3-08-24, open 0800-2000. Tours and services: Tulum, Chichen Itza, and more; airline ticketing.

Immigration

Remember that you must turn in your Mexican visitor's card when you leave the country. If you should lose it, need an extension, or have any questions, call Mexican Immigration, tel. 4-28-92 and at the airport, tel. 4-29-92.

Bookstores

Don Quixote Bookstore in downtown Cancun on Tulum (one block south of Tulipanes) carries a limited supply of English-language books, both fiction and nonfiction. Most of the island's hotel gift shops sell American magazines as well as a supply of paperback novels, Spanish-English dictionaries, and several English-language newspapers: *The News* (published in Mexico City), *Miami Herald, New York Times Weekly Review,* and *USA Today.*

GETTING THERE

Airport

Quintana Roo's busiest airport is Cancun's International Airport, 20 km south of Cancun. Along with everything else around this infant city, the airport is new and shiny and continues to grow and add to its facilities each season. By the time you are reading this book a new runway should be in operation; that makes two. Visitors from many cities in the U.S. arrive daily on **Mexicana, Aeromexico, United, Continental, Lacsa,** and **Eastern** airlines. **Aerocaribe** and **Aerocozumel** bring passengers on daily flights from Isla Cozumel. Car rentals, taxis, and yellow-and-white *combis* are available at the airport to bring you to town or the island (hotel zone). Remember to reconfirm your flight 24 hours in advance and be at the airport one hour before local flights or two hours before international flights; an airport tax of about US$10 is collected upon departure.

By Bus

From Merida and Chetumal, buses make frequent trips daily, linking smaller villages to Cancun en route. The bus terminal is located in downtown Cancun on Av. Tulum. Call or go to the terminal for complete schedules—they change frequently.

Car Rentals

Car rentals are available from Mexican and American agencies at Cancun airport and many hotels. Remember there is a hefty drop-off fee in a city other than the origination point. The 320-km, four-hour drive from Merida to Cancun is on a good highway (Hwy. 180) through henequen-dotted countryside, historic villages, and archaeological ruins. From Chetumal (Hwy. 307) It's 343 km (four hours) along a well-maintained highway through thick tropical brush parallel to the Caribbean coast. Car rentals in Cancun can be found at: **Avis,** Viva Hotel, tel. 3-08-28, open 0800-1400 and 1600-1900; **Budget,** 15 Av. Tulum downtown, tel. 4-02-04/4-21-26, open 0730-1330 and 1600-1900, all major credit cards accepted; **Cuzamil Car Rental,** Av. Kukulcan km 9.5, hotel zone, tel. 3-00-43, open 0800-1300 and 1600-2000.

Dollar Rent-A-Car, 235 Av. Tulum downtown, tel. 4-22-29, open 0800-1300 and 1600-1900, all major credit cards except American Express accepted; **Economovil Rent,** Cancun Airport, tel. 4-84-82, all major cards accepted; **Hertz,** 35 Reno, S.M. 20 downtown, tel. 4-13-26/4-46-92, open 0700-2200, all major credit cards accepted; **Rentautos Kankun,** Plaza Caribe Hotel downtown, tel. 4-11-75, open 0800-1300 and 1700-2000, Mon.-Sat., all major credit cards accepted; **Xel-Ha Car Rental,** 13 Av. Tulum downtown and at the airport, tel. 4-13-38/4-41-38, open 0800-1600 daily.

AIRLINE DIRECTORY

Airline	Office	Telephone	Arrivals	Departures
American	Airport	4-29-47 4-26-51	Dallas	Dallas
Aerocaribe	Av. Tulum at Uxmal	4-12-31 4-13-64	Cozumel Isla Mujeres Chichen Itza	Cozumel Isla Mujeres Chichen Itza
Aeromexico	—	4-56-40	Mexico City	Los Angeles
Continental	Airport	4-25-40	Los Angeles Houston	Los Angeles Houston Denver
Eastern	Airport	4-28-70	New Orleans	New Orleans
Lacsa	Av. Taxchilan 5	4-12-76	Guatemala New Orleans	New Orleans San Jose
Mexicana	Av. Coba	4-12-65 4-11-54	Mexico Miami Dallas Philadelphia	Mexico Miami Dallas Philadelphia
United	Airport	4-28-58 4-25-28	Chicago	Chicago

ISLA MUJERES

Isla Mujeres is just 13 km across the bay from Cancun via several transportation options. Many visitors return year after year, hop the ferry, and spend a few hedonistic days relaxing or diving on the outlying reefs of Isla Mujeres. This finger-shaped island lying off the east coast of the Yucatan Peninsula is eight km long and 400 meters at its widest point. While exploring the small island, take a walk through Fortress Mundaca, snorkel along the coast, visit the lighthouse, and see the marine biology station—devoted to the study of the large turtle. Visitors are not encouraged, but if you're a science buff and can speak the language, give it a try.

Though the overflow of tourists from Cancun and Cozumel is very noticeable, the island is relatively quiet, especially if you choose to visit during the off-season—June and Sept. are great! For some adventurers, Isla Mujeres is a favorite even though it's "growing up" with more visitors than ever. Everyone should snorkel at least once at teeming Garrafon Beach (it's teeming with fish *and* tourists!). The easy-going populace is getting used to all the people; the small town still smiles at backpackers. Travelers from budget to (almost) deluxe can easily find suitable lodging, though in the budget category it's getting harder.

Isla Mujeres has a large naval base, with many ships in its harbor. By the way—the Mexican Navy doesn't like people photographing the base, ships, or crewmen on duty. If you're struck with the urge to photograph *everything,* ask someone in charge first. Before tourism, fishing was the prime industry on the island, with turtle, lobster, and shark the local specialties. Today the turtle is protected; they may *not* be hunted during any time of the year. The eggs are *never* to be taken and stiff fines are given to those who break this law.

History
One legend tells us that the name Isla Mujeres ("Island of Women") comes from the buccaneers who stowed their female captives here while conducting their nefarious business on the high seas. Another more prosaic (and probably correct) version refers to the large number of female-shaped clay idols found on the island when the Spaniards arrived. Archaeologists presume the island was a stopover for the Maya Indians on their pilgrimages to Cozumel to worship Ixchel, female goddess of fertility and an important deity to Maya women.

The city is 10 blocks long and five blocks wide. Avenida Hidalgo, the main street, is where the central plaza, city hall, police station, cinema,

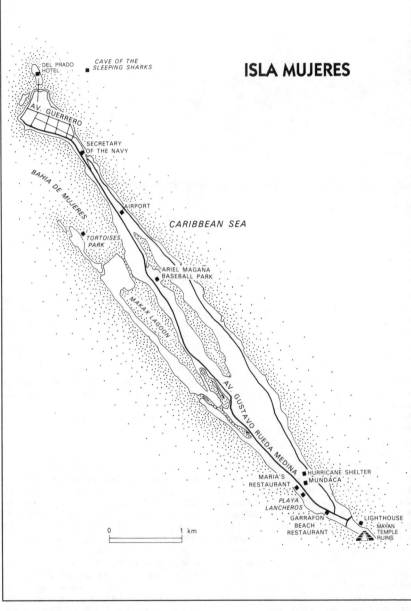

ISLA MUJERES

DEL PRADO HOTEL

CAVE OF THE SLEEPING SHARKS

AV. GUERRERO

SECRETARY OF THE NAVY

BAHIA DE MUJERES

AIRPORT

CARIBBEAN SEA

TORTOISES PARK

ARIEL MAGAÑA BASEBALL PARK

MAKAX LAGOON

AV. GUSTAVO RUEDA MEDINA

HURRICANE SHELTER

MARIA'S RESTAURANT

MUNDACA

PLAYA LANCHEROS

GARRAFON BEACH RESTAURANT

LIGHTHOUSE

MAYAN TEMPLE RUINS

0   1 km

farmacia, and large supermarket are located. Most streets are really only walkways, with no vehicles allowed (although they frequently squeeze by anyway). The ferry terminal is three blocks from the plaza; if you're traveling light, you can walk to most of the hotels when you get off the ferry. Otherwise, taxis queue up along Av. Hidalgo close to the ferry dock.

SIGHTS

Garrafon National Park

Snorkeling at Garrafon Beach has been heralded for years. However, so many day trippers come each day from Cancun that the beach is not only terribly crowded from 1000-1400, but many of the fish seem to be hanging out someplace else. Get there early in the morning for the best snorkeling! Garrafon Beach is five km out of town with a close-in coral reef that's a great spot for beginners. It has little swell and is only a meter deep for about five meters offshore, after which the bottom drops off abruptly to six meters. This is a good place to introduce children to the beauties of the ocean through a glass. The brazen fish—which aptly describes Bermuda grubs—gaze at you eye to eye through your mask; if you have food they'll follow you almost onto shore. Feeding the fish stale bread or tortillas makes for good pictures—the fish literally jump out of the water to grab the treat, so watch your fingers!

Swim past the reef and you'll see beautiful angelfish that seem to enjoy hanging around a coral-encrusted anchor and a couple of antiquated ship's cannons. For the non-snorkeler, there are *palapa* sun shelters and beach chairs on the sand—that is until the tourist boats from Cancun arrive. After that the beach gets crowded and loses its tranquility. Garrafon is a national park, open from 0800-1700; about US$1 pp admission. The ticket taker doesn't arrive until 0800, but even earlier someone will usually let you in.

Built into the steep cliff which backs the beach are a dive shop (snorkel, mask, and fins for about US$6 a day), a seafood cafe, lockers, showers, and changing rooms. Taxi fare (up to four passengers) from town to Garrafon is about US$3, from Hotel Del Prado at the northern tip of the island, US$3.50. Coral outcroppings along this beach add much to the beauty of Garrafon, but can be razor sharp and dangerous. Even the coral that isn't dangerous should be avoided—don't walk on it or scratch your initials into it. It took millions of years to establish and it's ridiculous to kill it in one thoughtless moment.

Maya Ruins

A short distance past Garrafon, at the southern tip of the island on a cliff overlooking the sea, is what's left of an ancient Maya temple used as a coastal observation post. It's little more than a pile of stones now after Hurricane Gilbert's devastation. It's still a beautiful lookout point if you happen to be in the "neighborhood." To get there, continue on the main road from Garrafon until you can see the lighthouse road going off to the right, then take a well-traveled dirt path to your left. These ruins were first seen and described by Francisco Hernandez de Cordoba in 1517. In addition to being a temple of worship to Ixchel, goddess of fertility, there were narrow slits in the walls of the temple facing the four cardinal points which were used for sophisticated astronomical observations—part of Maya daily life. Today, the lighthouse keeper looks after what's left, sells fresh fish *ceviche,* and makes colorful hammocks and black coral jewelry. A friendly guy, he's more than happy to let you try out the hammocks, will answer all questions (if asked in Spanish), and loves to pose for the camera (especially for a tip). This is a magnificent spot to see both the open sea on the windward side of the island and peaceful Mujeres Bay on the protected side. If traveling by taxi, ask the driver to wait while you look around. Or let him go—you can walk back to Garrafon Beach and catch a taxi to town (till 1700). The walk to town is long and sweaty—figure about two hours.

Fort Mundaca

To make a visit to Fort Mundaca meaningful, dwell on a touching local legend from the mid-1800s. It tells of a swashbuckling slave-trading pirate, Fermin Mundaca de Marehaja, who fell in love with a young woman on Isla Mujeres, Prisca Gomez, also called *Triguena* ("Brunette"). In some versions she was a visitor from Spain, in others she was from the island. After 10 years of plying the seas and buying and selling slaves, he retired to the land to court her, unsuccessfully. Coincidentally, pirates were slowly being put out of business by the British Navy right about then. Mundaca built a lavish estate to woo her further, but to no avail. She married another Mujeres man and ultimately moved to Merida and the high life, leaving the heartsick slave-trader behind to live alone in the big house with only his memories of the past. If you're a romantic, you'll feel a haunting melancholy while strolling in the once-gracious gardens of this deserted, almost destroyed estate. Mundaca lived the remainder of his lonely life on the island and left behind this inscription on his tombstone—*"como ere yo fui; como soy tu seras"* ("like you are I was; like I am you will be"). Fate can be fickle—and perhaps just.

Rumor has it that the government is going to restore Mundaca and make it into a park, which would be nice since it is literally rotting away now. To get to Fort Mundaca from downtown, follow the signs that say Hurricane Shelter, then take the dirt path going to the left 4.5 km from town.

Just before the Mundaca turnoff, there's a dirt road to the right (at four km) that takes you to the small center for marine biology studies. Again, this is not officially open to the public; however, visitors have been known to gain entrance simply by knocking on the door and asking.

Beaches
The closest beach to downtown is **Playa Norte,** also called Coco Beach and Nautibeach (perhaps because of the topless girls?), on the north edge of town, the lee side of the island. Here you can relax in the sun and swim in a blue sea that's as calm as a lake. In this shallow water you can wade for 35 meters and still be only waist deep. At the west end of the beach are *palapa* cafes, with both soft and hard beverages.

Four km south toward Garrafon on the main road out of town is **Playa Lancheros.** Several giant turtles swim around, caged in a large sea pen, and submit to being ridden by small children—as long as they can stay seated on the slippery-backed animal. At one time the beaches attracted sun-worshipers, and a large *palapa* cafe sold good fried fish, snacks, drinks, and fresh fruit. Now it seems more a place for the fishermen who still bring in a good catch to this shore, and it's not unusual to see them cleaning nurse and tiger sharks caught close by. A bus from town travels as far as Playa Lancheros about every half-hour; fare is about US$.30. Very close by is a much nicer beach called **Hacienda Gomar.** Here the beach is clean, and in outdoor *palapas* you can get good food; the cost is very little more than Playa Lancheros.

WATER SPORTS

Snorkeling And Scuba Diving
The snorkeler has many choice locations to choose from, and the common-sense approach is to snorkel with a companion. **Garrafon** is good, and the east end of **Playa Norte** has visibility up to 33 meters near the wooden pier, though on occasion the sea gets choppy here, clouding the

Isla Mujeres waterfront

water. The windward side of the island is good for snorkeling if the sea is calm; don't snorkel or even swim on the windward side on a rough day and risk being hurled against the sharp rocks. Besides being cut, an open wound caused by coral laceration often becomes infected in this humid climate.

The dive shops on the island sponsor trips to nearby reefs for snorkeling and scuba diving. A lot of press has been devoted to Isla Mujeres's **Sleeping Shark Caves.** Ask at the dive shop for detailed information. Although some divemasters will take you in among the sluggish though dangerous fish, others feel that it isn't a smart dive. Bill Horn, experienced diver/owner of Aqua Safari Dive Shop on Isla Cozumel, warns that there's always danger when you put yourself into a small area with a wild creature. In a cave, even if a large fish isn't trying to attack, the swish of a powerful tail could easily send you crashing against the wall. Reasons given for the shark's somnambulant state vary with the teller: salinity content of the water, or low carbon dioxide. Between Cancun and Isla Mujeres, experienced divers will find excitement diving **Chital, Cuevones, La Bandera,** and **Manchones** reefs. Diving equipment can be rented from **Mexico Divers** at two locations—Av. Rueda Medina and Garrafon Park, or at **El Canon,** Av. Rueda Medina, tel. 2-00-60.

Fishing

Deep-sea fishing trips can be arranged through any of the marinas. Spring is the best time to catch the big ones: marlin and sailfish. The rest of the year you can bring in good strings of grouper, barracuda, tuna, and red snapper. **Mexico Divers** (Av. Rueda Medina) just left of the boat dock offers a day-long deep-sea fishing trip which includes bait, tackle, and lunch. The **Boatmen's Cooperative** is helpful with questions about destinations, fishing trips, and boat rentals, tel. 2-00-86.

Robinson Crusoe Trip

If you enjoy group trips, take the Robinson Crusoe boat trip which includes snorkeling for a few hours at Garrafon Beach, a visit to the turtle pens, a cruise to Manchones Reef, and a *tikin chik* feed of fresh fish, caught by the crew and cooked over an open fire on a hidden beach somewhere along Isla Mujeres's coast. For more information ask at the Boatmen's Cooperative or your hotel.

The Yucatecan boatmen keep a sharp watch for the reef between Isla Mujeres and Isla Contoy. Hundreds of ships over the past 400 years have been wrecked on the reef that runs parallel to the coast from Quintana Roo to the Bay of Honduras.

Boat Regattas

Sailors from the southern U.S. have the opportunity to take part in sailing regattas each year. Organized by the Club de Yates of Isla Mujeres and started in 1968 from St. Petersburg, many participants come for this event scheduled for either the last week in April or the first week in May. Every two years in the spring groups sail to the island from Galveston, Texas, and from New Orleans. This is a challenging trip for the adventurous navigator.

This is also a great time for a party. The town opens its homes and hearts to people that have in many cases been returning for years and have become friends. The boaters reciprocate and open their vessels to the islanders. The kids of Isla Mujeres work all year long learning dances, and the women make the costumes for cultural entertainment. An annual basketball game takes place between the "Bad Boys" of the island and the boaters that visit, and no matter how they try, the boaters always lose. The name "Bad Boys" indicates these are the worst players on Isla Mujeres! During Regatta Amigos, everyone has a good time. In 1989, almost the entire population of 182 local children were onboard one boat, attacking adults with water balloons on another—boats head to head. The town provides food, tequila, and bands; with music everywhere, there's dancing in the streets and a queen is chosen by the Commodore of the Regatta. This is good fun and it happens several times a year. During religious holidays visitors will find the same kind of good times. For more info and dates contact Club de Yates de Isla Mujeres, Av. Rueda Medina, tel. 2-02-11/2-00-86.

Dock Facilities

The marinas in Isla Mujeres are getting more sophisticated with many services available. **Pemex Marina** in the bay offers electricity, water, diesel, and gasoline, tel. 2-00-86. At the navy base dock you'll find a mechanic, tel. 2-01-96. **Laguna Makax** offers only docking facilities. For boating emergencies call either by radio, using the word "Neptuno" for the Coast Guard, or on VHF channel 16 or band 2182. Use channel 88 to get clearance to enter the country. Gasoline for cars and boats is at Av. Rueda Medina, tel. 2-02-11.

ACCOMMODATIONS

You'll find a surprising number of hotels on this miniscule island. Most of them are small, simple, family-run inns downtown near the oceanfront. None can really be considered luxury class, but some offer more services than others. Since most are clustered downtown, it's simple to shop (on foot) until you find the one that suits you.

First-class

Posada del Mar is an older multi-storied a/c hotel. Rooms overlook the waterfront with swimming either in the sea or the hotel's own lovely pool. A *palapa* dining room, bar, and snack pavilion adjoin the pool. From the boat dock turn left and walk four blocks. Rates about US$40 d; Av. Rueda Medina #15-A, tel. 2-02-12.

Facing the windward side of the island, a fairly new hostelry called **Hotel Perla del Caribe** offers pleasant rooms with private bathrooms, a/c or fan (ask for your choice), snack bar, and pool; rooms have terraces and balconies—be sure to *ask* for one facing the sea (great view of the coast). The hotel's (rough-water) beach is good for sunbathing and walking; swimming only when the sea is calm. The staff is very friendly; we looked at four rooms before we found the one we wanted, and they were still smiling in the end when they brought our luggage. Credit cards okay, rates are about US$56 d during high season, but prices drop as much as 40% during the summer; three suites with kitchens are available. For reservations write to Av. Madero and Guerrero, North Point, Isla Mujeres, Quintana Roo, Mexico, tel. 2-04-44.

On the northernmost tip of the island, the modern **Hotel Del Prado** (formerly the El Presidente) lies on a shallow lagoon. A lovely white beach blooms with colorful *palapas* adjacent to a swimming pool with swim-up bar, outdoor dining, a/c, coffee shop, clean (almost Spartan) rooms, tile bathrooms (with giant bath towels, typical of the hotel chain), a friendly helpful staff, gift shop, tobacco shop, and snorkeling equipment for rent. Credit cards accepted, about US$75 d; tel. 2-01-22/2-00-29.

Another pleasant small hotel is the **Na Balam** on Los Cocos beach just a short walk to the sea. All junior suites with cooking facilities, also patios and balconies; a *palapa* is open all day for drinks and food. Rates are about US$54 d. Located on Calle Zazil-Ha (the road to Hotel Del Prado), tel. 2-02-79. For something small and intimate and away from town, check out **Maria's Kan Kin Restaurant Francaise** near Garrafon Beach. Just a few rooms available. For the visitor who plans on a longer stay, two-bedroom apartments are available on the beach at Chez Megaly (this is special!), located at Av. Rueda Medina Playa Norte, tel. 2-02-59.

A Little Better Than Moderate

These hotels are clean, with pleasant staffs and charming surroundings that make them stand out from the others in this category. From the boat dock turn left for two blocks, then right for a half block to **Hotel Berney.** This three-story 40-room hotel is built around a patio and small pool, with restaurant and bar, about 200 meters from the

ISLA MUJERES ACCOMMODATIONS

NAME	ADDRESS	TELEPHONE
Belmar	Av. Hidalgo	2-04-30
Caribe Maya	Av. Madero	2-01-90
Carmelina	Av. Guerrero #9	2-00-66
Cielito Lindo	Av. Rueda Medina #78	—
El Caracol	Av. Matamoros #5	2-01-50
El Marcianito	Av. Abasolo #10	2-01-11
El Zorro	Av. Guerrero #7	2-01-49
Hotel Berney	Calle Abasolo	2-00-25
Hotel Cabanas	Av. Carlas Lazo #1	2-01-79/2-02-13
Hotel Del Prado	Puerto Norte	2-01-22/2-00-29
Isla Mujeres	Av. Miguel Hidalgo #3	2-02-67
Isleno	Av. Guerrero and Madero	2-03-02
Las Palmas	Av. Guerrero #20	—
Margarita	Av. Rueda Medina N. #9	2-01-46
Maria Jose	Av. Madero #27	2-01-30
Maria de los Angeles	Juarez #35	—
Na Balam Jr. Suites	Calle Zazil Ha #18	2-04-46
Osorio	Av. Madero and Juarez	2-00-18
Perla Del Caribe	Av. Madero and Guerrero	2-04-44/2-02-36
Poc Na Youth Hostel	Matamaros #15	2-00-90/2-00-53
Posada Del Mar	Av. Rueda Medina #15	2-00-44/2-03-00
Posada San Jorge	Juarez #29–AN	2-01-54
Roca Mar	Av. Guerrero & Bravo	2-01-01
Rocas del Caribe	Av. Madero #2	2-00-11
Su Casa Sur	Ocean Front Houses	2-02-65
Vistalmar	Av. Rueda Medina	2-00-96

beach. The rooms are simple (though colorful), clean, and have purified tap water. About US$22 s or d, summer, US$25 s or d, winter; all rooms with fans. Located on Av. Abasolo #3, tel. 2-00-26; in the States call ITI (714) 494-8129, (800) 227-0212.

Close to the central plaza on the windward shore is **Hotel Rocamar,** a three-story hotel with balconies overlooking the often wild sea. From the boat dock it's one block to the right and two blocks to the backside of the island. The hotel provides lounge chairs for sunning on the beach; remember, swimming can be treacherous here. Clean rooms, hot and cold water, ceiling fans, bar, restaurant serving good food, and a friendly staff. Rates about US$26 d; Av. Nicolas Bravo, tel. 2-01-01.

Cabañas Maria del Mar blends the old and the new. Located on Nautibeach and one of the nicest on the island, the newer rooms offer a/c in a two-story building, about US$45 d. The old cabañas are thatched, comfortable in a laid-back tropical way, about US$35. **Bucanero** is a new hotel located above the Bucanero restaurant. Just a few rooms on the second and third floors, ask in the restaurant for prices of hotel rooms. Right across the street is **Pizza Rolandi;** they also have rooms over the restaurant—ask in the restaurant.

Moderate
Actually, as a reader told us, the **Hotel Gomar** is "better than moderate." Opened in early 1990, the hotel is conveniently located across from the ferry,

has good-sized rooms (with Simmons mattresses), private bathrooms, and fans, is clean, and has a friendly staff. Rates are around US$30 d.

Budget
As you will soon discover, budget-priced hotels are no longer as easy to find as they once were. Please look at budget hotel rooms carefully before paying your money; they change from day to day. What can be clean and friendly one day, can be dirty the next. Hot water can be an elusive, unreliable item. If these things are more important than your pocketbook, don't look at budget hotels.

The youth hostel **Poc Na** has reopened for business. For the backpacker this is really a terrific bargain. The hostel offers clean, dormitory-style rooms, communal baths and toilets, and rates less than US$5 per day (including a locker) plus a few returnable deposits, and extra charges if you choose to use the hostel's linens. The cafeteria is simple with few choices but its food is adequate and inexpensive. Poc Na is located at 15 Matamoros Ave., tel. 2-00-90.

Try the **Las Palmas Hotel** on Playa Norte; it's clean and was renovated in 1989, rates are US$12 d. For another wallet-saver, take a look at the **Caribe Maya;** it's old but clean and has 20 rooms which rent for about US$13 d. The **Hotel Lopez** offers pleasant, *usually* clean, simple rooms for about US$15 d, located on Av. Juarez #29-A North.

FOOD AND ENTERTAINMENT

As always, seafood is the highlight of most restaurant menus on Isla Mujeres; the fish is caught right in the front yard. Around town are dozens of indoor and outdoor cafes, simple and informal, plus a number of small fast-food places selling *tortas,* tacos, and fried fish.

Bucanero
On Hidalgo, this large outdoor cafe serves good seafood and Yucatecan specialties for breakfast, lunch, and dinner. Prices are reasonable—a breakfast of bacon, eggs, beans, and toast runs about US$3. Good fried fish and *chiliquiles*.

Miramar Restaurant
It's always nice to discover a cafe with good food, good service, and a nice ambience, and what makes it even nicer is to get letters from readers who tell me it's still great! That's the Miramar. Not to be considered a fancy cafe, but open-sided, it's located on the seaside of the *malecon* where you have a great view of the harbor. You can see the ferries come and go and watch the fishermen

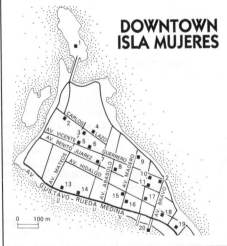

DOWNTOWN ISLA MUJERES

1. Hotel Del Prado
2. El Cabanas Hotel
3. Poc Na Hostel
4. Social Security Clinic (I.M.S.S.)
5. post and telegraph office
6. Javier Rojo Gomez Market
7. Ciro's Restaurant
8. Office of Tourism
9. Hotel Rocas del Caribe and Restaurant
10. Magana Movie
11. city hall, police, and traffic office
12. Immaculada Concepcion Church
13. Posada del Mar restaurant and bar
14. lighthouse
15. Osorio Hotel
16. Martinez Hotel
17. public library
18. telephone office
19. port captain
20. ferry terminal

ISLA MUJERES EATERIES

NAME	ADDRESS	TELEPHONE
Abarrotes	Av. Hidalgo	2-01-75
Bad Bones	next to the north lighthouse	—
Brisas Del Caribe	Av. Rueda Medina	2-03-72
Bucanero	Juarez #13 and Hildago #11	2-02-36
Buho's Restaurant, Bar, & Disco	Carlos Lazo #1	2-02-11
Carnitas	Av. Hidalgo #4	—
Ciro's Lobster House	Av. Matamoros #11	2-01-02
El Garrafon Restaurant	Garrafon Park km 7	—
El Limbo Restaurant & Bar	Hotel Roca Mar	2-01-01
El Patio	Av. Guerrero #4	—
El Peregrino	Madero #8	2-01-90
Gomar	Av. Hilgado and Madero	2-01-42
Guillermos	Calle Benito Juarez	—
Hacienda Gomar	beach road to Garrafon	2-01-42
La Estrellita Marinera	Av. Hidalgo	—
La Melosita	Av. Hidalgo #17 and Abasolo	2-04-45
La Pena	Av. Guerrero South	—
Las Palapas	Playa Cocos north beach	—
Los Jardines	Calle Morelos	2-03-59
Malos Huesos Cafe	Rueda Medina and Lopez Mateos	—
Miramar	Av. Rueda Medina	2-03-63
Mirtita	Av. Rueda Medina	—
Pizza Rolandi	Hidalgo between Madero and Abasolo	2-04-30
Roberts	Calle Morelos	2-04-51
San Martin	mercado municipal	—
Sergio's Restaurant Gallery	Av. Guerrero 3-A Sur	2-03-52
Taqueria Alex	Av. Hidalgo	—
Tequila Video Bar	Matamoros and Hidalgo	2-00-19
Tropicana	Nicolas Bravo and Rueda Medina	—
Villa Del Mar	Rueda Medina #1 Sur	2-00-31

cleaning their catch and tossing scraps to the waiting pelicans, and on top of that find good food and friendly waiters. Whole fried fish is good and the price is about US$4; *ceviche* is the same price.

Sergios

On Guerrero, this is a combination cafe, bar, and art gallery with an open-air second-story dining room. The food is tasty (though the servings are rather small); try the chicken tacos. The lobster is good—and no longer a bargain anywhere! At cocktail hour, 1800-2000, drinks are two for one.

The owner/artist Sergio is friendly and willing to answer questions about the island.

Pizza Rolandi

This small cafe has good food and usually efficient staff. In March of 1988, Isla Mujeres was caught in a tremendous tropical storm. It wasn't raining buckets—it was raining truckfuls. The early lunch crowd would ordinarily be emptying out and a new crowd coming in, but no one was moving. The water had risen knee deep in front of the cafe and no one was too anxious to get out into it except the kids paddleboarding up the street. Rolandis played host to the entire crowd for hours, making space under the dry-roofed part of the patio for everyone. The coffee kept coming all afternoon. There was lots of laughing, visitors got acquainted with each other as well as with the waiters and management. Hurray for Pizza Rolandi—and be sure to try their garlic bread; it's great with beer. A pizza for two averages US$6. Ask about the few hotel rooms on the upper floors of Pizza Rolandi. On Av. Hidalgo between Madero and Abasolo, tel. 2-04-30.

Ciro's

On Matamoros and Guerrero, this is a fancier restaurant with glass-topped tables; in the evening light reflects from old-fashioned glass lamps mounted on the walls. The clean, modern, fan-cooled, open-sided dining room serves all day. Good food, moderate prices, well-stocked bar, and choice seafood, including excellent shrimp-in-garlic as well as lobster. Good bargain breakfast: bacon and eggs with toast and black beans about US$2.50. Special omelettes with ham, bacon, and cheese are just a little more.

Maria's Kan Kin Restaurant Francaise

If your palate yearns for something continental, get a taxi and have an elegant lunch at **Maria's** (close to Garrafon Beach). She serves in a *palapa* dining room overlooking the Caribbean. A small seawater tank holds live lobsters from which you can take your pick. The sophisticated menu offers curries, snails, and rabbit, and her prices are accordingly more expensive. Closed Sunday. A good meal for two with a cocktail can average US$15 to $30.

Chez Megaly

Head for the pink buildings on Nautibeach. Sit by the sea and enjoy Caribbean food with a European flavor. Good food with a great view. Located at Av. Rueda Medina Playa Norte, tel. 2-02-59; closed Monday.

Other Cafes

Other food places offer poolside barbecues, including **Del Prado** and **Gomar's** colorful Mexican patio; food is good though pricey. Be sure you try the *licuados* (liquefied fruit in sweetened water and ice) at a small open stand across from the play-

ground. The **Cafe Mirtita** on the main road across from the sea serves great (brewed) coffee and all-around simple good food. It's very clean and reasonable. A newish addition is a wild and crazy place called **Bad Bones,** serving *good* American specialties. From the dock turn left and head north, it's next to the north lighthouse and doesn't look like any other cafe on the island. Twice we went there for lunch and it was closed, but they seem to be open for dinner consistently.

Markets

If you prefer to cook your own there are several places to buy groceries. The *mercado municipal* opens every morning till around noon; it has a fair selection, considering everything must come from the mainland. There are two well-stocked supermarkets that have liquor and toiletries. **Mirtita** (Juarez #14, tel. 2-01-27) is open 0600-1200 and 1600-1800. Larger **Super Bertino** (Morelos #5, tel. 2-01-57) is on the plaza, open 0700-2100. **La Melosita** is a mini-super open from 1000 till 2400, with candies, piñatas, film, sundries, cigarettes, gifts, and snacks. Located on Av. Hidalgo #17 and Abasolo, tel. 2-04-45. **Panaderia La Reina** makes great *pan blanco* and *pan dulce,* open 0600-1200 and 1700-2000.

Entertainment

Isla Mujeres has a few good nightspots. A new glitzy disco is the **Casa Blanca.** Lots of locals as well as tourists report a good time; Av. Hidalgo #1, tel. 2-02-67. The **Calypso** (Rueda Medina Playa Norte, 2-01-57), the **Tequila Video Bar,** and **Broncos Video Bar** are all good, noisy fun for an evening.

Other evening activities: Spanish-language movies (theater on Morelos near the plaza), ball games in the plaza, an occasional boxing match, dancing in the plaza during special fiestas, listening to the military band that comes to the navy base, or (the most common) visiting in the plaza or sitting by the sea and watching the stars reflect off the water.

Special Event

The **Isla Mujeres International Music Festival** takes place the second weekend in October and lasts for 12 days. The island rocks with bands and dancers from everywhere. Reservations are a must, and if anyone is interested in playing, a spe-

ISLA MUJERES SHOPPING HINTS

NAME	ADDRESS	COMMENTS
Artesanias Prisma	Garrafon Park	souvenirs and crafts
Bazar Pepe's	Av. Hidalgo #4	clothing and souvenirs
Caribbean Queen Handicrafts	Madero Norte #25	wool rugs, Mexican curios, gifts
Caribbean Tropic Boutique	Av. Juarez #3	souvenirs and crafts
El Nopal	Guerrero and Av. Matamoros	authentic clothing and crafts
Gomer Restaurant and Boutique	Hidalgo and Av. Madero	clothing
Isleno T-shirt & Shell Shop	Av. Guerrero 3-A Norte	—
La Loma	Av. Guerrero #6	arts, crafts, collectors masks
La Melosita	Av. Hidalgo #17	piñatas, mini-super
Mariola Boutique	Garrafon Park	souvenirs
Mari-Tona	Garrafon Park	clothing and souvenirs
Paulita	Morelos and Av. Hidalgo	imports
Rachat & Rome	in front of main pier	fine jewelry
Vamily	Av. Hidalgo and Parque	clothing and souvenirs

cial permit is needed. For more reservations call Armadillo Tours in Austin, Texas; for information about playing, contact Rod Kennedy Productions, Box 1466, Kernville, TX 78629, tel. (512) 257-3600.

SERVICES

A well-stocked **drugstore** is at Av. Juarez #2. **Farmacia Lily** is on Av. Francisco Madero and Hidalgo. A limited selection of **newspapers** and **magazines** can be found on the corner of Juarez and Bravo. Check at the **photo studio** for film. Two banks in town will change money Mon.-Fri. 1000-1200: **Bank Atlantico** (Av. Juarez #5) and **Banco Serfin** (Av. Juarez #3). The **post office** (Av. Guerrero #15) is open 0800-2000 Mon. through Fri., half-day Sat., and is closed Sun. and holidays. General delivery will accept your mail and hold it for 10 days before returning it. Addresses should read: your name, Lista de Correos, Isla Mujeres, Quintana Roo, Mexico. The **telegraph office** next to the post office (Av. Guerrero #13) is open 0900-2100 weekdays and on Sat., Sun., and holidays from 0900-1200. Money orders and telegrams will be held for 10 days only. Address to your name, Lista de Telegrafos, Isla Mujeres, Quintana Roo, Mexico. A **long-distance telephone** is in the lobby of the Hotel Maria Jose at Av. Francisco Madero. Also, Club de Yates offers long-distance telephone service for a small service charge (on Av. Rueda Medina in front of the gas station). Some hotels offer long-distance phone service, but be sure to ask about the service charge on collect calls.

Travel Agencies
For all of your travel needs contact **Club de Yates de Isla Mujeres.** They can fix you up with side trips to the mainland or fishing trips from Isla Mujeres. Even if you don't want a ticket but have a problem while you're on the island, stop in and ask for help—they'll do their best to help you out. To get to Club de Yates coming off the dock, turn left and walk about 150 meters; their office is on the left.

IMPORTANT TELEPHONE NUMBERS

city hall	2-00-98
police station	2-00-82
customs office	2-01-89
chamber of commerce Av. Juarez	2-01-32
Office of Tourism Av. Guerrero	2-01-88

Medical

In the event of a medical emergency there are several options on Isla Mujeres. Ask your hotel manager to recommend a doctor. If that's not possible the following medical contacts might be helpful. **Centro de Salud** (health center) is located at Av. Guerrero on the plaza. Emergency service 24 hours daily, open for regular visits 0800-2000; tel. 2-01-17. Doctor Antonio Torres Garcia is also available 24 hours, tel. 2-03-83. An English-speaking doctor, Dr. Antonio Salas, is open daily, 1100-1400 and 1700-2100; tel. 2-01-95/2-04-77.

GETTING THERE

Many hotels and travel agencies arrange escorted day tours to Isla Mujeres. But for the independent traveler who wishes to do it on his own it's quite easy. It can be confusing not knowing that there is more than one boat going to the island from different departure points. One is a car ferry (also takes walk-on passengers) and the others are passenger boats.

For those traveling the Peninsula by bus, it's easier to make ongoing connections in Puerto Juarez than in Punta Sam. A passenger boat from the Puerto Juarez dock is located a few kilometers north of Cancun and makes trips almost hourly throughout the day from 0500-1800; it takes just under an hour, and costs about US$.50. Check the schedule since it changes often. At the foot of the dock in Puerto Juarez you'll find a Tourist Information Center sponsored by the municipal government, with bilingual employees and a restroom (small fee); ask for a map of Isla Mujeres.

A car ferry leaves Punta Sam (five km south of Puerto Juarez) daily and carries passengers and cars. You really need a good reason to bring a car to this short island with narrow, one-way streets. RVs can travel on the ferry, but there are very few places to park and no hookups. The trip on the ferry from Punta Sam is slightly longer than from Punta Juarez. If driving, arrive at the ferry dock an hour before departure time to secure a place in line; tickets go on sale 30 minutes in advance.

Aerocaribe flies from Cancun and Cozumel to Isla Mujeres three times a week. Fare is about US$35 OW, and the schedule changes constantly; be sure to check this out well in advance. For airport info on Isla Mujeres, call 2-01-96. In Cancun and Cozumel check with your hotel or travel agency.

Note: Be aware of the time that the last passenger boat leaves Isla Mujeres. If you haven't a hotel reservation you might have to sleep on the beach, and it can rain anytime of the year in the tropics.

passenger ferry from Cancun to Isla Mujeres

BOAT SCHEDULES TO AND FROM ISLA MUJERES

Please keep in mind that transportation on the water to and from Isla Mujeres is referred to either as a boat or a ferry. There is a difference. The ferry carries cars and passengers, the boat carries only passengers. The biggest difference, however, is that the ferry leaves from Punta Sam (much less frequently) and the boats leave from Puerto Juarez often, all day long. Know the schedule to save valuable vacation time, it can change anytime. If you're going to the island without reservations hoping to get a room (and yes it can be done—*usually*), be sure to know when the last boat or ferry leaves the island—just in case. A recent traveler was having such a good time snorkeling that he neglected to look for a room till too late, slept on the beach—and it rained. Price for passengers is about US$.50 pp, and for cars about US$1.50. **Delicate stomachs note:** on a rough day, take the car ferry for a smoother ride.

BY BOAT FROM PUERTO JUAREZ		FROM ISLA MUJERES TO PUERTO JUAREZ		BY CAR FERRY FROM PUNTA SAM TO ISLA MUJERES		FROM ISLA MUJERES TO PUNTA SAM	
0530	1330	0430	1330	0715	1200	0600	1315
0830	1530	0630	1530	0945	1430	0830	1600
1030	1630	0730	1730	1000	1715	1100	1830
1130	1730	0830			1945		2100
	1915	0930					
		1130					

GETTING AROUND

Mujeres is a small and mostly flat island, and in town you can walk everywhere. The eight-km length is a fairly easy trek for the experienced hiker. Other options include taxi, bicycle, motorcycle, or the municipal bus. A tour around the island in a taxi (three passengers) and back to your hotel should cost about US$8-9 and takes about an hour, including stops to watch the lighthouse keeper making hammocks, see what's left of the Maya temple on the south tip, and observe turtles at Playa Lancheros.

By Bicycle
Bicycle rentals are available at **Arrendadora Maria Jose** on Madero #16, tel. 2-01-30; **Arrendadora Carmelina** on Av. Guerrero #6; and **Arrendadora de Bicicletas Ernesto** on Av. Juarez #25. Rental fee is around US$10 per day.

By Motorcycle
Most of the motorcycles on the island are newish and come with standard or automatic shift for the same rate. Be sure to check the bike for damage before you take responsibility. Beware of narrow one-way streets and numerous children darting back and forth. Rates are fairly standardized in most of the *rentadoras*. **Pepe's Moto Rental** (Av. Hidalgo and Matamoros) charges about US$60 per day or US$10 hourly for a Honda 250. This is the best size for two people. The smaller bikes rent for US$20 daily, US$3.50 hourly—all require a deposit. It's quite simple to rent, no minimum age and no driver's license required at either of the following: **Gomez Castillo** (Av. Bravo and Hidalgo, tel. 2-01-42) and **Moto Servicio Joaquin** (Av. Juarez #7B, tel. 2-00-68).

By Taxi
Taxis are many, easy to get, and have reasonable fares. To go anyplace downtown the fare is about

US$1. At the taxi stand on Av. Rueda Medina all fares are posted; open 0600-2300, tel. 2-00-66.

By Bus

The municipal bus operates 0600-2100 daily; about US$.25. It runs from Posada del Mar on Av. Rueda Medina to Colonia Salinas (a small suburb of homes facing the windward side of the island), departures every half-hour.

CONTOY

From Isla Mujeres, take a one- or two-day trip to Contoy, an island 24 km north of Mujeres. The small bit of land (2.5 by .5 km) is a national bird sanctuary. Outside of wayward flamingos, heron, brown pelicans, the magnificent frigatebird, oliva-ceous cormorants, and a couple of humans at the biology station, you'll find only a lush isolated is-land—the kind of place around which fantasies are spun. From a tall viewing tower (about three stories of steps) open to the public, you can see most of the island. Under a shady arcade there's an information display with lighted photos of nu-merous birds, including full details of each spec-imen. A white beach close by provides a refresh-ing swim with delicate tropical fish. Often you'll swim amid large schools of young trumpetfish, al-most transparent as they glide through the water sucking up small fish and shrimp. Tiny flying fish in groups of 10-30 or more skim the surface as they flee large predators. A day at Contoy is well worth the money. Check around for the best rate; about US$25 pp, depending on the type of boat.

Getting To Contoy

Among others, trips are provided by Richard Gai-tan aboard his 10-meter sailboat, the *Providencia*. The two-day trip is well worth the time, which in-cludes all meals (mostly fresh-caught fish, liquor extra), snorkeling equipment, a cruise around the island, and time for hiking and exploring. Bring your own sleeping bag for the beach, and don't forget sunscreen, bug repellent, and mosquito net-ting. The boat anchors close to shore near some excellent birdwatching sites (bring your camera and Fielding's *Mexico Bird Guide*). Rick can be contacted at the Boatmen's Cooperative in town.

Other boatmen offer one-day trips departing 0800 and returning 1930. These cruises typically include a stop at the reef to snorkel (equipment provided), fishing off the end of the boat en route (if you wish), a light breakfast snack of *pan dulce* and fresh fruit, and a delicious lunch of *tikin chik* (fresh fish caught along the way and barbecued at Contoy) along with Spanish rice and green salad. Soda and beer are extra. The captain often treats his passengers to a lime/salt/tequila drink on the return trip. Most of the boats are motor/sailers, usually motoring north to Contoy and raising the sail for the trip back to Isla Mujeres. Many of the boats are neither luxurious nor too comfortable (wooden benches), but look forward to meeting about 15 people from various parts of the world. Check at the marinas or at Dive Mexico for Con-toy trips. Signs giving full information are seen lit-erally all over town, or contact the Cooperativa, tel. 2-00-86.

PUERTO MORELOS AND VICINITY

Anyone looking for isolation can find it on Quintana Roo's Caribbean coast from just below Cancun to Boca Paila. Along this 153-km stretch are dozens of fine beaches, some with camping facilities, several with modest cabañas, and a few with more deluxe accommodations. Others offer nothing but nature's gifts: the sun, white sand, and blue sea—free! Often the only way to spot the entrance to these beaches is by noting the kilometer count on small highway signs that begin at Chetumal and end at Cancun (360 km). To get to some of them you must leave Hwy. 307 at the Tulum turnoff and continue on the uneven, potholed road that parallels the sea. This road ends at Punta Allen, an isolated bit of paradise with little more than a lobstering village, but what a place to forget about civilization for awhile!

Hurricane Gilbert hit this Quintana Roo coastal area in Sept. 1988. This was one of the most devastated areas. The small town of Puerto Morelos suffered tremendous damage and is taking much longer than other towns to put back together, mainly because of money. However, these people are survivors, and slowly docks, homes, hotels, and other structures are being rebuilt. We have attempted to mention those places (which may have been your favorites) and the status of their reconstruction.

Puerto Morelos

Puerto Morelos, on the northern Caribbean coast, is 17 km south of Cancun. It has limited accommodations and few attractions to detain ordinary tourists. At one time its only claim to fame was the vehicle ferry to Cozumel. But more and more people are beginning to notice Puerto Morelos's peaceful mood, lack of tourists, and easy access to the sea. As with some of the other towns on the Caribbean coast, divers are bringing low-key attention to this small town, using it as a base to explore the rich coastline. Until Hurricane Gilbert, Puerto Morelos had been the coastal headquarters of CIQRO (Centro de Investigaciones de Quintana Roo), an ecological-study organization sponsored by the Mexican government, the UN, and other environmental groups dedicated to maintaining the ecosystem of the Quintana Roo

coast. The building was thrashed and there was little sign of activity when last seen, but ask one of the locals for the most current information and CIQRO's present location.

Canoe Harbor

In pre-Hispanic times this was a departure point for Maya women making pilgrimages in large dugout canoes to the sacred island of Cozumel to worship Ixchel, goddess of fertility. Remnants of

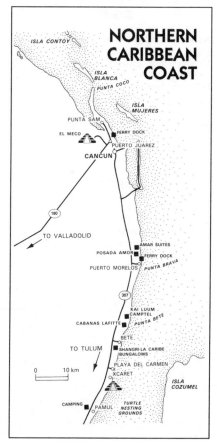

Maya structures are located near the coast and throughout the jungle. Though small, the ruins are not considered insignificant, but as usual there's a shortage of money to investigate and restore them. The descendants of Indians in these parts occasionally find artifacts dating to pre-Columbian times, which sadly are often sold to private collectors, and their archaeological value is never measured. If caught with the genuine article, whether a pottery shard you may have picked up at one of the ruins or a piece bought from a local, you will be fined and your treasure taken from you. Remember that old Latin saying, *Caveat emptor!*

SIGHTS

A short walk through town reveals a central plaza, shops, a cantina, and nearby military base. Puerto Morelos's most spectacular attraction is its reef which begins 20 km north of town. Directly in front of Puerto Morelos, 550 meters offshore, the reef takes on gargantuan dimensions—between 20 and 30 meters wide. For the scuba diver and snorkeler this reef is a dream come true, with dozens of caverns alive with coral and fish of every description.

ACTIVITIES

Snorkeling
Snorkeling is best done on the inland side of the reef where the depth is about three meters. Snorkelers can expect water clarity up to 25 meters along the reef.

Scuba Diving
The reef has been a menace to ships for centuries. Early records date losses from the 16th century. Many wrecks have become curiosities for today's divers, who come from great distances to explore the Quintana Roo coast. Puerto Morelos can provide the most experienced diver with exciting destinations, including a wrecked Spanish galleon with coral-crusted cannons—clearly visible from the surface five meters above. Looking for another kind of excitement? **Sleeping Sharks Caves** are eight km east of Puerto Morelos. Intriguing, yes, but the sharks still claim proprietorship.

Fishing
A never-ending variety of fish provides good hunting for sportsmen. Onshore fishing is only fair off the pier, but if you're interested in deep-sea fishing, ask around the plaza or make arrangements at the hotel **Posada Amor.**

ACCOMMODATIONS

Budget
No one minds if campers spread their sleeping bags north and south of the lighthouse away from town, houses, and hotels. Choose a high spot (so you'll stay dry). It can get gritty if the wind freshens, and if it's very still be prepared for mosquitoes. Remember, the beach is free and this is a safe, peaceful town.

The **Posada Amor** is a simple, 19-room, friendly, family-run hotel with ceiling fans, shared baths (some private), and hot water; rates about US$20. They offer a good restaurant with a continental breakfast for about US$3, a fresh salmon plate US$5.50, and fried chicken US$4.50. If you're adventurous ask about a tour that's a little out of the ordinary, offered by a veterinarian involved in the Sian Ka'an Reserve. Manuel picks up passengers around 1400, then takes them to a boat where they become part of the work crew. Dinner is served onboard while traveling. Ultimately the boat arrives at Manuel's work area and passengers will see crocodiles, turtles, and birds. The crocodiles are dealt with at night, counted, tagged, and cared for. This is a night trip since the crocs are out and easily spotted with a light that catches the red glow of their eyes. Anyone expecting a luxury boat shouldn't even consider this trip. It's only for those interested in the fauna of the Sian Ka'an and curious about crocs and turtles. It's a great photo safari and the cost is about US$45 pp. Ask at the Posada Amor for reservations.

Apartment Living
Going south on the same street as the Posada Amor, across the street from the school and the beach look for the **Reef Inn,** four comfortable, clean, efficiency apartments that have cooking facilities, washer, hot water, and small living room. The manager speaks English; rates are about US$20 d, US$25 for three or four persons, add US$5 if you plan to use the kitchen. At Av. Rafael

and Melgar #4, Puerto Morelos, Quintana Roo 77580, Mexico. If you arrive when no one is home you'll see a perfect example of the casual environment in this little town. You will find a note that says:

1. Put your luggage inside.
2. Lock door and take key.
   (It's in the doorknob.)
3. See room rates on envelope.
4. Deposit money in envelope.
5. Turn this sign around.
   (On the back it says occupied.)
6. Put envelope in slot in Apt. 4
   (manager).

I'll make change later if needed. Be back soon, thanks, manager.

Almost Deluxe
Since Hurricane Gilbert, **Hotel Playa Ojo de Agua** has been rebuilt with 12 modern rooms including a kitchen, ceiling fans, dive shop, and pool. This beautiful beach just north of town center is as lovely as ever. Write for information: Ernesto Munoz, Calle 12 #96, Colonia Yucatan, Merida, Yucatan 97000, Mexico.

Bed And Breakfast
Before Gilbert, **Amar Suites** was a large stucco

house on the beach. It was knocked down, but the owners have already constructed five small cabañas that sleep two to four people. Each has a loft bedroom, simple cooking facilities, toilet and shower, fan, TV (!), and a small sitting area. These are very Spartan accommodations close to the sea. Summer (low) rates are US$20, and winter (high) rates are US$40. For more information write to Apto. Postal 136 A, Cancun, Quintana Roo 77500, Mexico.

FOOD AND SERVICES

Restaurants
Several small budget cafes serving typical Mexican food and good seafood circle the main plaza. The **Posada Amor Restaurant** can usually be depended on for outstanding *mole poblano* and other regional dishes at moderate prices. The **Maison del Tiburon** is a good vegetarian restaurant; **Dona Zenaidas Restaurant** offers a good selection of local fare. The **Pelican** and the **Palmeras** both serve fair pizza and hamburgers. On the way out of town south of the turnoff on Hwy. 307, check out the *palapa*-roofed **Oasis Carib,** a vegetarian cafe.

Markets
Local markets carry fresh fruit and vegetables plus

This tranquil dock offers good fishing.

QUEEN CONCH

A popular easy-to-catch food beautifully pack-aged—that's the *problem* with the queen conch (conk). For generations inhabitants of the Carib-bean nations have been capturing the conch for their sustenance. The land available for farming on some islands is scant, and the people (who are poor) have depended on the sea—especially the conch—to feed their families. Even Columbus was impressed with the beauty of the peach-col-ored shell, taking one back to Europe with him on his return voyage.

The locals discovered a new means of making cash in the 1970s—exporting conch meat to the U.S. The shell is also a cash byproduct sold to throngs of tourists looking for local souvenirs. An easy way to make money—except for one thing: soon there will be no more conch! In recent years the first signs of overfishing have become evident: smaller-sized conch are being taken, and fisher-men are finding it necessary to go farther afield to get a profitable catch.

It takes three to five years for this sea snail to grow from larvae stage to market size. It also takes about that long for planktonic conch larvae carried into fished-out areas by the currents to replenish themselves. What's worse, the conch is easy to catch; large (shell lengths get up to 390 cm) and heavy (about three kg), the mollusk moves slowly and lives in shallow crystalline water where it's easy to spot. All of these attributes are contributing to its demise.

Biologists working with various governments are trying to impose new restrictions that include closed seasons, minimum size of capture, a limit on total numbers taken by the entire fishing industry each year, limited numbers per fisherman, restrictions on the types of gear that can be used, and most impor-tant—the cessation of exportation. Along with these legal limitations, technology is lending a hand. Re-search has begun, and several mariculture centers are now experimenting with the queen conch, raising

1. These tanks hold juvenile queen conch.
2. conch larvae stage
3. From these tiny shells…
4. …grow these beautiful large mollusks.

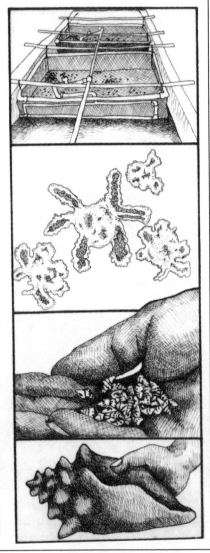

animals in a protected environment until they're large enough for market or grown to juvenile size to be released into the wild.

A new research center at Puerto Morelos is in operation and recently released its first group of juvenile conchs to supplement wild stock. This is not always successful. Sometimes one group of larvae will survive, and the next 10 will not—for no clear-cut reason. In the wild, not only does the conch have man to contend with, it also has underwater predators: lobsters, crabs, sharks, turtles, and the ray.

The conch is not an endangered species yet—but it must be protected for the people that depend on it for life.

---

a limited selection of sundries. Supplies of basic food items can be sketchy and intermittent. If camping or backpacking, it's advisable to stock up in Cancun. Two pharmacies in town appear well stocked with the usual.

Services

Puerto Morelos has one of the few **gas stations** along this route (also at Tulum, Playa del Carmen, and Puerto Felipe Carrillo). If driving, be advised to top off your tank whenever you find a gas station. Besides being few and far between, it's not unusual for a station to run out of gas, so get it wherever and whenever possible. If you run out near the coast and can find a dive shop, they're usually willing to help out with a couple of gallons of outboard motor gasoline. Though laced with oil, it might get you to a gas station without doing irreversible damage to your car. Also, many rural towns have a supply of gas in five-gallon drums even though you don't see a sign or a gas pump. Ask at the local store. *Larga-distancia* telephone service is found just south of the military camp, open 0800-1300 and 1600-1930 daily. The **bank** is open to cash travelers cheques from 0930-1300, Mon. to Friday.

TRANSPORT

Getting There

Buses from north and south stop at Puerto Morelos frequently. From Cancun it's about a 40-minute drive, from Chetumal about five hours. Hitching is reasonably easy from the larger towns (Chetumal, Cancun, Puerto Felipe Carrillo, Playa del Carmen); try Hwy. 307 where the service roads enter the towns.

Vehicle Ferry

The vehicle ferry to Cozumel departs Puerto Morelos daily beginning at 0600 (see "By Boat To And From Cozumel" p. 237). Check the schedule the night before, in case it changes. Be at the dock two or three hours early to get in the passenger-car line. It also expedites things to have correct change and the car's license number. The ticket office is open 1700-1800. The trip takes two hours and can be a rough crossing so put on your elastic cuffs if you tend to get seasick (see "Health" p. 41). For those with sea legs (and stomachs), light snacks are sold on the passenger deck.

PUNTA BETE

Punta Bete, a four-km stretch of beach, is a complete tropical fantasy—swaying palms hover along the edge of pure white sand, with gentle blue crystal waves running across the shore. Swimming is perfect in the calm sea, and 10-20 meters offshore the rocky bottom makes a perfect snorkeling area. As recently as 1965 there were no tourists along this part of the coast. At that time Quintana Roo was only a federal territory. There wasn't even a road to this fine white-powdered beach. Family groups, mostly descendants of the Chan Santa Cruz Indians, tended their small, self-sufficient *cocales* (miniature coconut plantations). Together a family harvested enough coconuts each year to earn spending money from the resulting copra. The custom continues today (although a coconut blight begun in Miami in 1980 has spread south to the Quintana Roo coast, in some areas decimating the coconut palms). We saw one man wrestle two 70-kilogram bags of fresh coconuts (a harvest representing several months' labor) onto a bus to Merida (three hours each way), sell them in the public market, and come home with about US$50!

pure water supply comes from nearby wells (boil it anyway); fires are not allowed, so if you want to cook, bring a backpacking stove. To camp on the beach the rate is about US$4 pp; a few cabañas rent for about US$10 d: individual bathrooms, no electricity, fairly clean. A small cafe/bar is open part of the day. For reservations write to: Familia Novelo Cardenas, Attn. Sr. Miguel, Av. Sur #548, Cozumel, Quintana Roo, Mexico; tel. 2-18-36.

El Marlin Azul Bungalows
Hurricane Gilbert destroyed this once-charming small resort. The word is they will start rebuilding soon. For information write to: El Marlin Azul, Calle 61 #477, Merida, Yucatan, Mexico.

Note!
Before shedding your shoes to stroll along the southern part of Punta Bete beach, look it over. Often-sharp little bits of coral hide in the sand. When swimming beware of the sharp limestone in the shallow places; if you have diving booties they are ideal around here.

ACCOMMODATIONS AND FOOD

Along the four-km stretch are several resorts in a variety of price ranges. Each of them (depending on your travel style) is ideal.

Budget
You have a choice of two campgrounds right next to each other—one also offers small cabañas. **Xcalacoco** (shkah-lah-CO-co) **Beach** is a trailer park next to the sea for campers and self-contained recreational vehicles, moderately priced, with showers and toilets. Next door, **Xcalacoco Campground** can be a social experience if you wish. However, it's still large enough to lose yourself in your own little coconut grove, hammock slung between palms (close enough to the sea that breezes blow the mosquitos away, but be prepared with bug repellent and mosquito netting anyway). On the grounds are clean bathrooms and showers, separate *palapas* for socializing—or for cover in case of an unexpected shower. The

TURQUOISE REEF RESORTS

Luxury Campout Kai Luum Camptel
For the traveler who wants to avoid the glitz of the high-rise but doesn't want the work of setting up a campsite, Kai Luum is the lazy man's campout. In the tradition of the British safari, it's camping with a touch of class. Though there's no electricity, Kai Luum offers modern tents on the beach with large comfortable beds, communal hot and cold showers, clean toilets very close by, and daily maid service. Each tent is shaded by a shaggy *palapa* roof and strung with two hammocks facing the sea for lazy afternoons.

The restaurant is one of the great attractions at Kai Luum—the food is outstanding. Prepared by Maya cooks, the menu is overseen by owner Arnold Bilgore, who happens to have a gourmet touch and plans something new and unusual (often continental) every day. The dining room is a large *palapa* structure on the sand, where a sumptuous buffet breakfast always includes trop-

*Shangri-La cabañas,
Punta Bete*

ical fruits, fresh juice, sweet rolls, hot coffee, tea, chocolate, and a different hot dish each day. Dinner is served under the sparkling light of hundreds of candles. Arnold jokes that next to the church, Kai Luum is the biggest buyer of candles in Mexico. The bar is at one end of the dining room: each person makes and keeps track of his own drinks with a numbered pegboard. The whole feeling of the resort is much like the honor system at the bar —relaxed, intimate, friendly. If you have a problem, see Mino, Arnold's son who grew up on the beach and is now the manager of the operation. The restaurant attracts travelers from other resorts in the area as well. There are no telephones, so if you aren't staying at Kai Luum and would like to eat at the restaurant you must drop by and make arrangements in advance.

Everyone enjoys browsing in Kai Luum's boutique where the discerning shopper can purchase unique treasures from throughout Latin America, including hand-woven fabrics and colorful clothing from Guatemala. If you find something too big to carry home, the management will pack and ship it for you. You have a choice of water sports at the new activity center near the Capitan Lafitte swimming pool next door (walking distance). Called **Buccaneer's Landing,** the activity center serves all three Turquoise Reef Resorts, **Kai Luum, Cabañas Capitan Lafitte,** and **Shangri-La.** They've got a personable, highly skilled and trained staff, including a registered PADI dive instructor; boats and state-of-the-art equipment are available for rent. Other activities including snorke-

ling trips, beach picnics, and fishing trips are offered as well as scuba instruction, PADI certification, check-out dives, and a short "resort course" which entitles you to dive for the length of your holiday.

Buccaneer's Landing offers **Vagabonder** daytrip suggestions to various sights close by, including appropriate travel tips and maps. If you've always wanted to see Belize, ask about extended Vagabond trips that include both the Punta Bete coast and Belize. Rates at Kai Luum are US$40 pp, double occupancy (surcharge for holiday periods), and include breakfast, dinner, and 15% government tax. Three persons maximum in each tent, no children under 16. Economical three-day rates available during the summer. No credit cards, travelers cheques okay. For accommodation reservations write to Turquoise Reef Group, Box 2664, Evergreen, CO 80439, in Colorado tel. (303) 674-9615, from anywhere else tel. (800) 538-6802, fax (303) 674-8735.

Deluxe

Cabañas Capitan Lafitte has been around for many years, and it is as well known for its charming managers, Jorge Fuentes and family, as it is for its fine service, wonderful beach location, good food, swimming pool, and pleasant game room. All provide a serene backdrop for welcome camaraderie among the people who return year after year from distant parts of the globe. The stucco oceanfront cabañas have double and king-size beds, hot water, ceiling fans, private bath, and

Kai Luum dive masters, Cassie and Richard

along with daily maid service each room is provided with a handmade reed broom to help keep the sand out. Buccaneer's Landing (see "Kai Luum" above), a full dive shop on the premises, has a good selection of rental equipment including sailboards. The management provides transport by skiff to nearby Lafitte Reef, an exciting snorkeling destination. Here, a lazy day of floating on the clear sea will bring you face to face with blue chromis, angelfish, rock beauties, and often the ugly grouper—a great place to use your underwater camera. Fishing is another satisfying sport—you'll always come away with a tasty treat that the restaurant chef will be happy to prepare for your dinner. Hands off the large handsome turtles you may see and don't expect to find turtle soup or conch *ceviche* on the menu. The management makes it clear that they support the preservation of these endangered species. And speaking of species, every afternoon between 1700 and 1800 a flock of small colorful parrots flies over the swimming pool; unmistakable with

their awkward wing movements and peculiar squawk.

Each week the hotel staff and guests get together and have a *fiesta*—not the impersonal version that you see at the big clubs, but the type of good time that a family has at a Mexican birthday party where everyone takes part. The waiters demonstrate rhythmic dance skills, balancing filled glasses on their heads, then teach anyone else that wants to give it a try—it's not easy! A zesty smorgasbord of *tipico* food is served. It's a down-home party, Maya style.

During high season it's best to have reservations. Rates include breakfast and dinner, US$57 pp double occupancy, children six and under no charge, 7-12 US$28.50 per night, 13 and over full rate. Ask about the economical summer-season three-day package and El Cofre, a large two-story beachfront duplex for large families. No credit cards, cash and travelers cheques only. Car rentals are now available at Lafitte. For more information and reservations write to: Turquoise Reef Group, Box 2664, Evergreen, CO 80439; from Colorado tel. (303) 674-9615, from anyplace else tel. (800) 538-6802, fax (303) 674-8735.

A delightful addition to the coastline just beyond Punta Bete is **Shangri-La Caribe.** Exotic bungalows with private baths, fan, tile floor, hot water, beach bar, swimming pool, and pool bar; car rentals available on-site. Rates include breakfast and dinner, about US$57 pp, oceanfront suites US$175 per day for one to four persons, children under six free in same room with parents, 7-12 US$28.50, 13 and over full charge. No credit cards.

TRANSPORT

Getting There
If arriving by plane in Cancun, taxis are available; arrange your price before you get in the cab. Figure approximately US$45 (up to four passengers). From Playa del Carmen (a ferry arrival point from Cozumel), taxi fare is less. Car rentals are available at Cancun Airport, which is a straight shot north on Hwy. 307; look for the large sign on the left side of the road that says Capitan Lafitte; here you'll find both Lafitte and Kai Luum. From Capitan Lafitte it is approximately eight km farther to Shangri-La.

PLAYA DEL CARMEN

For years there was but one reason to go to the small village of Playa del Carmen—the Cozumel Island ferry dock. And though thousands of people pass through here each year on their way to or from Cozumel (a popular island 19.2 km off the Quintana Roo coast), many come just to enjoy the laid-back pleasures of the small town. Playa offers the latest transportation to get to Cozumel—conventional boat, water jet, and flights from the airport near the center of town. But the town is taking on a personality of its own and adds to its modest beginnings each year. Nature did its part by endowing the small town with a broad beautiful beach, one of the finest in Quintana Roo. It's still uncluttered by high-rises—but maybe not for long! Condominiums have begun to spread along the beach south of the dock, with promises of more coming. A new multi-stoned hotel is in progress right on the beach at the foot of the dock (formerly the location of the Playacar Hotel), and several corporate hotel chains, including Hyatt, are negotiating for a piece of beach close by. Small simple hotels are popping up everywhere overnight. The same two funky campgrounds still hold their space near the beachfront, but who knows for how long!

Visitors have a vast selection of restaurants to choose from, several dive shops, and a busy efficient bus terminal. This once slow-moving fishing village is becoming a "destination" to consider while traveling along the Caribbean coast. Swimming is a pleasure and Playa's proximity to attractions such as Tulum, Xelha, Cancun, and coastal Hwy. 307 makes it a convenient stopover. For lovers of early morning walks along the water, the long beach is perfect to stroll for hours, sometimes without seeing another soul—almost a thing of the past. If you enjoy watching crabs scurry about, wading in the surf, or catching fluttering sea birds in the eye of a camera lens, then early morning on the beach at Playa del Carmen is just the place for you.

Traffic Note

The road going to the dock is now a one-way street; watch the signs and follow the traffic flow which turns left just before the dock and takes you in front of the military base, through the parking lot, and then left along the plaza. There's a white-suited man that gives out traffic tickets quite regularly, then asks for payment right then—US$5. He may indeed be a policeman, but it's doubtful. However, to avoid the hassle, watch the signs.

SIGHTS

By far the nicest thing to do in Playa del Carmen is to enjoy the people and the sparkling Caribbean. Take a walk through the village. Only two or three years ago you would've been escorted by children, dogs, little black pigs, and incredibly ugly turkeys. Nowadays mostly tourists crowd the streets—everywhere. Once off the main thoroughfare into town the streets are potholed and bumpy. Playa's lack of sophistication and topsy-like growth is appealing. The milkman no longer delivers milk from large cans strapped to his donkey's back; now he travels the streets in a dilapidated unmarked station wagon. At the familiar honk the village ladies bring their jars and pots to be filled. The number of small curio shops, cafes, and cantinas increases daily, and there's a movie theater. Yes, Playa del Carmen has become a "tourist resort," and the increase in prices reflects this metamorphosis. However, it's still a bargain compared to Cancun or Cozumel.

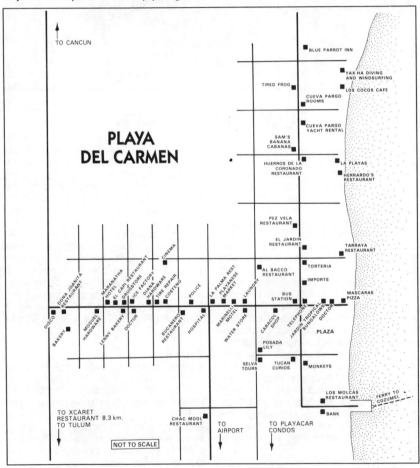

The cool early hours are best for walking along the beach. Warm afternoons are perfect for swimming and snorkeling, snoozing on the sand, or watching the magnificent man-o-war frigate bird make silent circles above you, hoping to rob another bird of its catch. Ferries from Cozumel come and go all day; in addition, luxury cruise ships anchor close by in the bay, and tenders bring tourists to shore who crowd into all the gift shops. The ships' passengers have a choice of lounging on the beach, hosted by Los Molcas Hotel (for now), or being escorted immediately to large modern buses and whisked off to the more famous sights of Xelha and Tulum. You can count on Playa del Carmen's beach being filled with jet-setters when ships are in port; the rest of the time it plays host to a mixed conglomeration of young and old, archaeology buffs, students of the Maya culture, backpackers, adventure seekers, sun-lovers who prefer the ambience of Playa del Carmen over Cancun, independent travelers from many parts of Europe, and just plain folks who enjoy the white sand and blue Caribbean wherever they find it.

Outdoor Activities

Windsurfers are available for rent or lessons at the **Cueva Pargo Hotel** dive shop (north of the dock on the beach). A little pricey, but talk to Huacho, the owner—he's negotiable. This part of the coast generally has an eight to 10-km breeze with a gentle swell, giving you a good sailboard ride. Though swimming is wonderful and the water clean, it's not crystalline directly in front of Playa del Carmen; a short distance north or south of the wharf are great reefs with clear water and active undersea life on view to snorkelers. The best fishing is offshore; ferry traffic discourages most fish around the wharf. The **Molcas Hotel** offers deepsea fishing, a five-hour trip with bait and tackle provided. **Cuevo Pargo Dive Shop** takes diving and fishing groups and provides equipment; fees are negotiable.

Dive Adventure

For an unusual dive adventure, ask Huacho at Cuevo Pargo (Box 838, Playa del Carmen, Quintana Roo 77710, Mexico.) about **Calypso Scuba Safari**. This involves a deluxe camp on wheels—a super-bus with toilets, showers, freezer, and kitchen, along with tents, good food (including fresh lobster and good tender steaks), beach equipment from windsurfers to parlor games, and stopovers in extraordinary camp- and dive sites along the Caribbean.

ACCOMMODATIONS

You can still see remnants of damage wrought by Hurricane Gilbert, but the village has picked itself up, rebuilt where necessary, and continued to improve. Many new small hotels are available and others are better than ever.

Luxury

Until the new hotel is completed, the closest to luxury lodging is the **Villas and Condominiums Playacar** located on the beach on the south side of the boat dock. These are privately owned and rented when not in use by their owners. They are beautifully designed in a convenient location either right on the beach or a short walk away. A five-minute stroll from town, each has one to three bedrooms, a fully equipped kitchen, washer and dryer, and living room. Some have balconies, and there's a swimming pool. These are great for families or small groups, or for those who prefer to do their own cooking. Prices begin at US$80 for a one bedroom, depending on time of year. For more information write to Box 396, Cancun, Quintana Roo 77500, Mexico.

Almost Luxury Class

Los Molcas Hotel is very close to the foot of the ferry dock and the beach. It has nicely decorated, air-conditioned, spacious rooms with private bath, plus swimming pool, dining room, terrace dining, and three bars. The hotel offers tours to Chichen Itza, Tulum, and Coba, diving equipment, and laundry service. Rates start at about US$80 double. For reservations write to Turismo Aviomar, SA, Calle 60 #469, Merida, Yucatan 97000, Mexico .

Suites Quintas is a lovely place to stay; if it were on the beach it would be rated "luxury," but it's located on the main street into town about halfway to the highway. The suites are about US$75 double. The complex is clean, modern, nicely furnished, air-conditioned, and beautifully decorated—except for one thing; no toilet seats! I have a feeling that will change if many Americans stay there.

Moderate Hotels

A modern pleasant motel-style hostel, **Maya Bric** offers a swimming pool, cafe, and 18 clean rooms with fans, bathroom, and hot water—all just a few minutes' walk from downtown cafes, the dock, and the beach; about US$28 d, less in the summer. The **Hotel Costa del Mar** complex sits on the beachfront next to the Blue Parrot. Spacious but rather sterile rooms, tile bathrooms, hot water, and a small pool, plus an indoor and beach restaurant (prime rib advertised for US$18!). The **Maranatha Hotel** is on the north side of the main street coming into town. They offer a swimming pool, dining room, bar, tile floors, fans, private bathrooms, some with kitchenette, double beds, and they take MasterCard and Visa. **Jardin Tropical** is an unexpected surprise. Located between a dentist's office and a gift shop across from the park two doors up from Mascaras restaurant and the beach, once through the gates you'll find yourself in a small tropical garden complete with Tony the Parrot and three small *palapa* bungalows. Some rooms have private bathrooms; others share. One bungalow is large enough for a family. Mosquito netting furnished. Prices start at US$30 d, discounts for extended stays. You can always just show up and take your chances, but for reservations send a two-day deposit c/o Christine, Box 1434, Cancun, Quintana Roo 77500, Mexico. Allow a couple of months for roundtrip/letters.

A Robinson Crusoe-type hotel is the **Blue Parrot Inn** on the beach north of town. It's a whimsical stucco tower structure with *palapa* roof, tile floors, spotlessly clean shared bathrooms, lots of hot water, one or two double beds in each room, and an ice chest with soda and beer (in the more expensive rooms) along with purified water. For a midnight swim you need only step out your front door. Each room has a view of the water, and just a short walk north on the white sand takes you to where you can watch fishermen throw their nets or return in their open launches with the morning catch.

The Blue Parrot offers a large selection of rooms from simple thatch-roof rooms on the sand to spacious two-story stucco cabañas with fantastic views. A beachside deli serves up cold drinks and light snacks.

Room rates begin at US$40-140 during the high season and US$25-65 during the low season. For more information and reservations write

to Box 652737, Miami, FL 33265, tel. (904) 775-6660, toll-free (800) 634-3547. Or directly to Mexico write to Box 64, Playa del Carmen, Quintana Roo 77710, Mexico, fax (52) 988-44564 (address to "Caja 20," Cancun, Quintana Roo 77500, Mexico).

Cabañas Nuevo Amancer offers private baths, double beds, and *palapa* roofs for US$20-25. Clean and pleasant. For reservations write to Arlene King, Apto. Postal 1056, Cancun, Quintana Roo 77500, Mexico.

Budget Hotels

Playa del Carmen has a CREA youth hostel. You can't miss the sign as you come into town. Good value—too bad it's not closer to the beach. Follow the signs from the main street into town about one km. Fairly new, clean, single-sex dorms, dining room with reasonably priced food, basketball court, and auditorium; it's well worth the effort.

Faces Hotel sits on the side of a small hill a few minutes from the beach. Some consider this the best buy in Playa del Carmen. The entrance is on Av. 5 Norte, and the hotel offers clean rooms with screens, hot water, shared and private bathrooms, and fans, plus a swimming pool in a small garden with lots of greenery. Managers Alba and Marcel take good care of their visitors. Depending on the season and which room, rates range from US$10 to $30. The owner of Faces also owns Hotel Trinidad and Hotel Galleria in Merida.

The **Tucan** is a good buy for a simple hotel. Follow the signs; it's about two blocks beyond the Blue Parrot turnoff. The rooms have overhead fans, hot water, group refrigerator, mosquito netting, peace and quiet (usually), and friendly staff. It's one of the best structures on Av. 5 Norte; rates are about US$20 s or d. Another whimsically named cabaña resort is the **Tired Frog**. Located five blocks north of the bus station; follow the signs (past Bananas Cabañas). This is a relaxed *palapa*-roofed setting with double beds, private bathrooms with hot water, and a laid-back patio. The transplanted American owners are great. Rates are around US$25 d, and prices drop drastically in the summer. For reservations write Apto. Postal 149. The old standby, **Posada Lily** has watched Carmen grow from a wide spot on the beach to a viable resort. One block west of the plaza, on the main road coming into town from Hwy. 307, it's the bright blue motel; clean, with a hot shower and good ceiling fans.

Another quaint place to stay is **Cuevo Pargo Hotel,** with nine rooms that share clean bathrooms and showers. Purified water, ceiling fans, simple, homey atmosphere. Before Gilbert there were a couple of houses with kitchenettes available that slept three to four. No information on these right now. Room rates start at US$20-30. Owner Huacho Corales takes groups on his sailboat for scuba day trips; for those interested in larger adventures, overnight trips are available to the cayes off Belize, Chinchorro Reef, or your choice. Write to Cuevo Pargo, Box 838, Cancun, Quintana Roo 77500, Mexico.

Camping

The two campgrounds in Playa del Carmen are dirty, noisy, and not recommendable, but if you're a masochist, check them out: **Las Ruinas** and **Brisa del Mar.**

FOOD

New restaurants are springing up even faster than hotels in Playa del Carmen. Around the central plaza several small cafes serve a variety of good inexpensive Mexican, Italian, and Chinese food. The **Molcas Hotel** serves good food, but it's hard to spend less than US$20 there for a meal. If you want to stick with the typical Yucatecan food at moderate prices or are looking for good fresh seafood, try **Dona Juanitas** on the main road close to Hwy. 307. Two fishermen's sons provide only the freshest catch, which is nicely prepared. **La Deseada,** three blocks north of the bus station on the second floor, formerly served only scrumptious bakery goodies. Now it serves great chicken and fish dishes along with such refreshers as fruit and yogurt shakes.

Chac Mool restaurant is clean and serves great Yucatecan food and a hearty breakfast, moderately priced. **El Jardin** is a small open cafe on the corner, one block inland from Las Ruinas campgrounds. The cafe serves good breakfasts and quick lunches, open from 0700 to 1200 only.

A good Italian restaurant, **Mascaras,** is on the first block off the beach across from the plaza. Their pizza and pasta are excellent. Try the spinach cannelloni—marvelous! Be sure to take

This relaxed family enjoys living out of their camper on the beach for several months each year.

a close look at the brick wood-burning oven where most everything is baked. Mascaras makes good fresh limeade, served in bulbous glasses with lots of purified ice. You can also get *big* margaritas and cold Yucatecan Leon Negra *cerveza.* Adding to the international variety of foods available, there is a Chinese restaurant called **Yut Kun** north of the square on the same street as Mascaras. For variety try the nachos at **La Caballa,** or lunch at **Ixchell. Flippers Cafe** is clean, and has good food and a lively clientele. Another do not miss is **Limones** at **Bananas Cabañas.** It's a bit more expensive than the average cafe in Playa, but you can't argue with success; it's worth it. Remember, you do not go to Limones to eat, you go to *dine.*

Groceries

Several small grocery stores around the plaza and on the main street coming into town have an ample supply of fruit, vegetables, and basics. A good variety of meat is available at the butcher shop, and there's a **rosticeria** that sells fresh roasted chicken. Nearby is the purified ice shop, a drugstore, and bakery. Liquor is sold across from the Molcas Hotel and several other locations in town.

ENTERTAINMENT AND SERVICES

The cinema is usually open on weekends with Spanish-language films. Dona Juanitas cafe becomes a disco with videos later on in the evening. As usual, people gather at the plaza and poke around the gift shops. Sitting on the end of the pier and watching the stars is *muy bueno* on the Caribbean; when you tire of that, a before-dinner drink on the patio of one of the many outdoor cafes generally comes with lots of fellow travelers to swap travel stories with.

Services

If taking the ferry to Isla Cozumel for the day, park your car at the public parking lot just beyond the **military camp** right on the waterfront, a half block from the dock; fees are posted. Somehow, one feels secure leaving the car next to the army camp, but do lock up regardless. (Rumors are wonderful in the small villages of the Caribbean coast. The newest is that the car ferry will soon be moving from its home port at Puerto Morelos to a new dock just south of Playa del Carmen.) **Banco del Atlantico,** located up the street from the ferry dock cashes travelers cheques (fee charged) between 1000 and 1230 Mon. to Friday. *Larga-distancia* phone service is located across from the plaza next to the vegetable stand, open daily from 0800-1300 and 1500-2000. There are now three phone lines into Playa del Carmen, easing the waiting time. Maybe by the time the new hotel is completed, Playa will have complete telephone service. Two **hardware stores** will help you out with twine, a gas can, or a knife blade, and there's a **doctor** *and* a **dentist** in town (ask at your hotel). Playa del Carmen has postal service now, a small building between the police station and the mayor's office.

GETTING THERE

By Air

Playa del Carmen's small airstrip is five blocks south of the main plaza and is open from 0700 to 1700 daily. Most of the flights go to and from Isla Cozumel (about US$10 OW). Reservations are not necessary, but if it's convenient, drop by the airport and make them in advance to ensure a

seat. Otherwise, arrive at the airport an hour before you wish to fly. The first flight leaves Playa del Carmen at 0720, then every hour thereafter during the busy season. Check the schedule; it's always subject to change.

By Taxi

Taxis at Cancun International Airport will bring you to Playa del Carmen. If there are several passengers, you can make a good deal—bargain with the driver before you start your journey. Expect the trip from Cancun to Playa to cost about US$40-50. Nonmetered taxis meet the incoming ferry at Playa del Carmen and are available for long or short hauls; again, make your deal in advance. A trip from Carmen to Tulum (with three passengers) can be about US$25-30 roundtrip, depending on supply and demand, and the time of year. If you're interested in a good diving spot, tell the cabbie. He may share with you his favorite cove that you'd never find on your own, and in fact he might join you for a swim.

By Ferry

Five round-trips leave each day from Playa del Carmen to Cozumel, with a choice of the old ferry or the new modern jetboat. The ferry crossing is usually a breeze. However, the calm sea does flex its muscles once in awhile making it difficult to berth the boat snugly against the dock. When this happens, hefty crewmen literally swing each passenger over the side into the capable hands of two other strong-armed receivers on the dock—quickly followed by the individual's luggage. This adds a bit of adventure to the voyage. But if it isn't your forte, delay your departure till the next day—the sea seldom stays angry for long. Young boys with imaginative homemade pushcarts or three-wheel *triciclos* meet incoming ferries at the dock to carry luggage for a small fee. (See "By Boat To And From Cozumel," p. 237.)

By Bus

Three bus lines provide this small town with the best bus transportation on the coast. From Merida via Cancun (a five-hour trip), three 1st-class buses and seven 2nd-class buses arrive daily. Buses arrive frequently from Chetumal and other points south as well. Playa del Carmen is an ideal base for many attractions along the Quintana Roo coast. Buses going north to Cancun's bright life travel the 65 km in 50 minutes. If sightseeing on the bus south to Chetumal, just a word to the driver and he'll drop you off at the turnoff to Tulum, to Xelha Lagoon National Park entry road, or one of the small beaches south along the coast. Ask what time his schedule brings him back, since you must be on the highway waiting to return to Carmen.

Hitching
Because of the ferry traffic, this is a good place to try for a hitch going north or south.

XCARET

About an hour's drive south of Cancun and a half km off the highway along a rocky bumpy road, **Xcaret** is hidden behind a couple of small *palapas.* Having lived here for years, the family collects a small entrance fee, less than US$.50, but mainly concentrates on their small ranchito and corral near the restored ruins of Xcaret. Not spectacular themselves, the ruins you see near the parking area are just the tip of the iceberg according to archaeologist Tony Andrews. He tells us that there are many, many more structures scattered throughout the bush in the area. This was another important location of the ancient Maya. It seems, whether by accident or just because their location near the Caribbean required navigational lookouts, the Maya often placed their ceremonial structures in magnificent locales.

A path from the small structures leads to a cave below a large rock that shows a hidden *cenote,* but looking down you'd never know water was there. If you need convincing, drop a rock; ripples expose crystal-clear water. Just beyond the ruins is a small *caleta* (cove) reminiscent of a serene watercolor painting. There's not a sandy beach here, just a dark limestone-edged lagoon filled with darting fish of brilliant colors. After you make your way across the rocks, the *caleta* eventually opens out to the sea. The whole bay is no bigger than a football field, but must be seen for its quiescent harmony.

Visitors will find a dive shop offering rental snorkeling gear; close by on the small cliff overlooking the bay, a low-key patio-cafe serves cold drinks and snacks (another cafe at the corner of the turnoff on Hwy. 307 called **Rancho Xcaret** serves excellent fresh fish). This is a lovely quiet vista.

Sacbes
Archaeologists will continue excavating this area which is rich with hidden history. They are convinced they'll eventually find traces of a *sacbe* beginning at Coba and ending at Xcaret. The scientists conjecture that this small cove was used as a protected harbor and debarkation point for Maya

Ruins attract visitors to Xcaret.

Xcaret cove

sailors traveling up and down the coast in dugout canoes. Hopefully they will eventually have the funds needed to excavate the hundreds of structures scattered throughout the area.

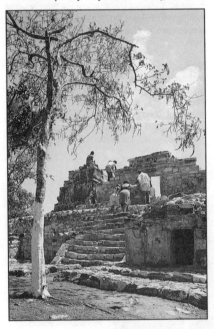

Xcaret ruins

Cave Diving
Along the limestone shore it's possible to enter a water-filled cave and swim (with scuba gear) inland a considerable distance underwater. At the mouth of the cave a layer of saltwater floats over fresh water from an underground river that flows from the cave opening into the sea. Swimming farther into the cave ultimately brings you to a shaft of light coming from an opening in the roof of the cavern; you can then climb out back into the jungle near the small ruined Maya structures. This area of the coast is dotted with similar caves and waterways.

Snorkeling
Xcaret is a marvelous spot for beginning snorkelers, especially children. The water is shallow and there's little current, though you must either climb over the rocks to enter the water, or jump off the small wooden platform. But it's not necessary to go much beyond the limestone shoreline to discover colorful denizens of the sea, such as resident schools of parrotfish and blue and French angelfish. One problem is fighting off the tourists that have discovered the lovely small *caleta*. Come early in the day and you might have the small bay almost to yourself. Although most folks make Xcaret a one-day trip, there are several simple rooms available for around US$25.

PAMUL

Another small beach that deserves exploring is Pamul. If you're a natural pack rat, you'll like the beachcombing here: shells, coral, and sometimes interesting jetsam from ships far from Yucatan shores. This is not one of the wide white beaches so common along the coast; in some places Pamul is steep and rocky, in others narrow and flat. The water is crystal clear, allowing you to examine the fascinating life within the shallow tidepools cradled by rocks and limestone. Snorkeling is better the closer you get to the reef 120 meters offshore. On the way the sea bottom drops off to about eight meters and its colorful underwater life can absorb you for hours.

Diving Near Pamul

If you are self-contained with your own compressor and equipment, the Quintana Roo coast offers miles and miles of pristine dive spots, and the waters near Pamul are especially ideal for scuba diving. The south end of Pamul's beach is sandy, but the shallow water along here harbors the prickly sea urchin—look before you step, or wear shoes while you're wading. Fishermen and divers along this coast are a jovial group always ready for a beach party, potluck style, when fishing is good—especially during lobster season (15 July through 15 March).

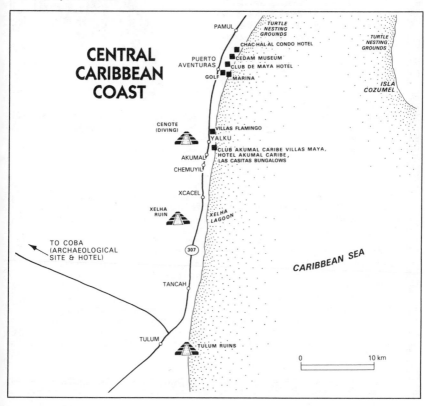

Turtles

If it's a bright moonlit night in July or August, you may be treated to the unique sight of large lumbering turtles coming ashore and laying thousands of eggs in the sand. If you're there a few weeks later it's even more exciting to watch the tiny (about eight cm in diameter) hatchlings make their way down the beach to begin life in the sea. Much has been written about protecting the turtles of the Caribbean from man, but nature in the form of egg-eating animals provides its own threat to this endangered species. On the beach of Pamul, more than half the eggs are scratched up from the sand and eaten by a variety of small animals that live in the adjacent jungle.

Practicalities

You have a choice of two lodgings in the area,

GIANT TURTLES AND THE INDIANS

At one time the giant turtle was plentiful and an important addition to the Indian diet. The turtle was captured by turning it over (no easy matter at 90-100 kilos) when it came on shore to lay its eggs. Any eggs already deposited in a sandy nest on the beach were gathered, and then the entire family took part in processing this nourishing game. First, the parchment-like bag of unlaid eggs was removed from the body, then the undeveloped eggs (looking like small hard-boiled egg yolks). After that, the meat of the turtle was cut into strips to be dried in the sun. The orange-colored fat was put in calabash containers and saved for soups and stews, adding rich nutrients and considered an important medicine. They wasted nothing.

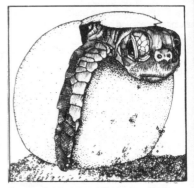

Today CIQR, a protective organization, along with the government keeps a sharp lookout along the coast for egg poachers during the laying season. Turtle-egg farms are being developed to ensure the survival of this ancient mariner. Sadly, the poacher of the '90s travels the entire coast, and each beach is hit night after night. The turtle can lay as many as 200 eggs in an individual nest or "clutch." One beach may be the instinctual home for hundreds of turtles (at one time thousands) that return to the site of their own hatching each year.

Turtles can live to be a hundred years old, which means they can lay a lot of eggs in their lifetime. But as the poachers steal the eggs on a wholesale basis, the species could eventually be wiped out entirely. If caught, poachers are fined, and can be jailed—though the damage has been done. When released they usually return to their lucrative habits. In most Mexican marketplaces a ready market for these eggs exists among superstitious men who believe the eggs are an aphrodisiac.

The survival of the giant sea turtle lies within the education of the people—locals and visitors alike. Shoppers will see many sea turtle products offered for sale: turtle oil, tortoise shell combs, bracelets, rings, buttons, carvings, and veneer inlaid on furniture and jewelry boxes, plus small stuffed, polished hatchling paper weights. **Note:** It is against the law to bring these products into the U.S. and other countries. If discovered they will be confiscated. Sadly, many travelers are not even aware of the law, and often the products get by the inspectors. If tourists refused to purchase these products, the market would dry up—a big step toward preserving these gentle lumbering beasts.

Cabañas Pamul, a small hotel on the beach, or the campground at the south end of the hotel. The hotel would be considered Spartan but it's usually clean and does have electricity between sunset and 2200, hot and cold water, and shared bathrooms, a little pricey for what you get—about US$34 d for a cabaña. The campground has room for 15 RVs. All spots have electricity and water, eight are large pads with sewerage hookups (US$8), seven will accommodate small trailers (US$5), and you can use the showers and toilets in the hotel. Camping fee is about US$1 pp, which includes bathroom privileges. The small cafe next to the hotel is run by the family that owns the hotel and usually offers fresh-caught seafood plus other typical dishes at reasonable prices, open 0800-2000. A small *cenote* nearby provides water for Pamul; do boil it for drinking. Otherwise, bottled water can be bought from the hotel manager. Mailing address is Apto. Postal 1681, Cancun, Quintana Roo 77500, Mexico.

PUERTO AVENTURAS

The corridor between Cancun and Chetumal is buzzing with the growth of new resorts, both large and small. One of the most ambitious developments is an enormous marina (advertised as the largest in the Caribbean) located just a few minutes south of Akumal. Some of these waterways are left from the days of the Maya, simply improved and opened to the sea. In other cases they are totally manmade and will soon be ready to moor almost 300 boats up to 120 feet in length with a draft of 10 feet.

The Marina
At the marina yachtsmen will find everything they need: gas and diesel, a spare-parts store, minor maintenance shop, purified water and ice, bait, 24-hour radio station and medical service, restrooms and showers, car rentals, travel agencies, shopping center, hotels, yacht club, and restaurants. Access into the marina is through a carefully planned channel, well marked for navigation and ready with an escort service through the reef 24 hours a day.

Golf, Tennis, And Diving
Construction has been in progress for almost two years, and while much has been completed, it will probably be another two years before the entire community will be finished. An 18-hole golf course is a big attraction at Puerto Aventuras and will be the scene of world-class golf tournaments. Nine holes were just about ready for playing when Hurricane Gilbert drove tons of salt water on the new grass. Nine holes should be ready for play by the time you're reading this book. Condos will be spaced around the golf course with an upscale hotel in the center of the fairways. Golf carts will be available for rent.

One tennis court is completed and work is in progress on several more. Eventually there will be an international tennis club with 25 courts. But the big attraction is expected to be the University of the Sea, a five-star PADI institution for diving instruction where divers will not only learn about div-

exercise time, Puerto Aventuras

ing but can take continuing courses on the preservation of the Belize Reef which runs from the tip of Isla Mujeres to the Bay of Honduras in Belize.

A nautical shopping village meanders on and around the marina with a boutique, supermarket, Carlos 'N' Charlie's restaurant, and other small shops getting ready to open.

CEDAM Museum

Artifacts brought from the sunken ship *Mantanceros* are seen at the CEDAM Museum located along the waterfront. There's a small collection of belt buckles, cannons, coins, guns, tableware, and various clay relics from Maya ruins along the Quintana Roo coast. The *Mantanceros* ("Our Lady of the Miracles"), a Spanish merchant ship that left Cadiz, Spain, in 1741 headed for the New World loaded with trade goods, foundered and sank on the reef two km north of Akumal. No one knows for certain why the *Mantanceros* sank since there were no survivors. However, the CEDAM organization spent several years salvaging it, beginning in 1958. Research suggests the ship probably engaged in a violent battle with a British vessel and then drifted onto the treacherous reef now known as Punta Mantanceros. For more detailed information on the finds of the *Mantanceros* read *The Treasure of the Great Reef* by Arthur C. Clark.

Hotels

In June 1989 Puerto Aventuras's first hotel, the **Club de Maya,** celebrated its grand opening with the Miss Universe entrants as the first visitors. The Club de Maya is a small, intimate hotel with 30 rooms. It faces the marina on one side and a shimmering white beach and the translucent water of the Caribbean on the other. The hotel has a swimming pool, pool bar, lobby bar, dining room with a Swiss-trained chef, health spa called Body And Sol, and a juice bar. All water-sports equipment is available. The rooms are spacious, with views of the marina or the ocean, tile floors, king-size beds, game room, and 1st-class room amenities.

Two condo-hotels are ready for occupancy, each with complete kitchen facilities, living room, balconies, and access to slips for the boaters. Hotel manager Rene Hersberger tells us that every effort will be made to keep prices at a reasonable level. Rates are about US$100 double, and the **Chac-Hal-Al** condos with kitchen average about US$139 per night. For reservations and more information, contact Royal American Marketing, tel.(800) 451-8891 or (305) 341-9173.

AKUMAL

About 100 km south of Cancun, Akumal Bay is a crescent of intensely white sand along the blue Caribbean. This quiet beach is home to an ever-growing resort that survives nicely without telephones, TVs (well, one or two have shown up—with satellite dishes!), or bustling activity. The traveler desiring the tropical essence of Yucatan *and* a dash of the good life will appreciate Akumal. Compared to Cancun it could not be described as luxury class but is more luxurious than many of the small resorts along the coast. It offers a good range of hotel rooms, dining, and activities.

The barrier reef that runs parallel to the Quintana Roo coast protects Akumal Bay from the open sea and makes for great swimming and snorkeling. Proximity to the reef and easy access to the unspoiled treasures of the Caribbean make it a gathering place for divers from all over the world. For the archaeology buff, Akumal is 10 km north of Tulum, one of the few walled Maya sites located on the edge of the sea. From Tulum, it's five km north to Xelha, a natural saltwater aquarium where divers (even amateurs) snorkel or scuba among surrealistic limestone formations

that give the eerie impression of an ancient sunken city. In Maya, Akumal means "Place of the Turtle," and from prehistoric times the giant green turtle has come ashore in summer to lay its eggs in the warm sands of the Caribbean.

Flora
Akumal is surrounded by jungle. In March, bright red bromeliads bloom high in the trees, reaching for a sun that's rapidly hidden by fast-growing vines and leaves. These "guest" plants that find homes in established trees are epiphytes rather than parasites: they don't drain the sap of the host tree but instead sustain themselves with rain, dew, and humidity; their leaves absorb moisture and organic requirements from airborne dust, insect matter, and visiting birds. The bromeliad family encompasses a wide variety of plants, including pineapple and Spanish moss. The genus seen close to Akumal is the tillandsia, and the flame-red flower that blooms on the tops of so many of the trees here is only one variety of this remarkable epiphyte. While searching out bromeliads, you undoubtedly will see another epiphyte, the orchid.

History

Akumal was a small part of a sprawling working coconut plantation until 1925, when a *New York Times*-sponsored expedition along the then-unknown Quintana Roo coast stumbled on this tranquil bay; it was another 33 years before the outside world intruded on its pristine beauty. In 1958, Pablo Bush formed the nucleus of CEDAM, a renowned diver's club, and introduced Akumal to world-class divers. Soon the word was out. The first visitors (divers) began making their way to the unknown wilderness. At that time, the only access to Akumal was by boat from Cozumel. A road was built in the 1960s. Since then, Akumal has continued to grow in fame and size each year, but it was Bush who introduced this part of Mexico as the "diving capital of the world." Though many people come here, it still remains beautiful, tranquil, a place to study the sea and stars.

The Beach

The porous sand of Quintana Roo never gets hot enough to burn. There are kilometers of white shore to beachcomb, with lots to investigate: conch shells, lacy red seaweed, an occasional coconut that has sprouted after soaking in the sea for months, and the ever-present crabs, all sizes and colors, popping in and out of their sandy holes. Take a walk at dawn. The sun bursts from the sea, spotlighting leaping fish as they jump at winged breakfast-bugs hovering just above the surface of the water. When the sun rises higher, late sleepers stake out spots on the beach and create a colorful patchwork of beach towels on the sand. Fortunately, the beach is so large that it never gets crowded—only coveted spots under shady palms become scarce. A *palapa* bar, open until 1800, serves beer, cocolocos, piña coladas, and more. This is a friendly place to meet other travelers and swap adventure stories.

WATER ACTIVITIES

Two dive shops on the beach rent equipment, including boats and motors, for scuba divers and snorkelers. The **Kapaalua Dive Shop** offers a three-day dive certification course. If you just want to make one dive on the reef, instructors give a four-hour "resort course," providing equipment, transportation, and one escorted dive. If you decide to take a resort course from any dive shop, check to make sure that you'll be making the dive one-on-one with a dive master. Kapaalua is fully PADI certified. Many divers come for the excitement of exploring the wreck *Mantanceros,* sunk in 1741. Although it was completely salvaged, a job that took CEDAM several years, the sea still yields an occasional coin or bead from this ancient Spanish merchant ship. A good collection of memorabilia from the *Mantanceros* is on display at the CEDAM Museum at Puerto Aventuras (just a few kilometers north) open 0800-1700 daily, with a small entry fee. A multitude of dive spots are hidden in the reefs about 130 meters offshore.

Caribbean Sea, Akumal Bay

Dive Shops

Akumal's dive shops have excellent equipment for rent, and they offer a good selection for sale. Rental fees vary slightly between both shops. Contact the **Kapaalua Dive Shop** for advance dive information: Akutrame Inc., P.O. Box 13326, El Paso, TX 79913, tel. in Texas (915) 584-3552, outside of Texas (800) 351-1622; from Canada call (800) 343-1440. Kapaalua is a PADI training facility. Rentals include kayaks and sailboards.

Snorkeling

Akumal Reef not only protects the bay from the open sea but also provides calm swimming areas ideal for snorkeling. A good spot within wading distance is the rocky area on the north end of the bay. Floating along the surface of the water and looking through your private window into the unique world below can be habit-forming along this coast. Take it slow and easy, and you won't miss anything. Search the rocks and crevices that you'll drift over, even the sandy bottom—what may look like a rocky bulge on the floor of the sea may eventually twitch an eye and turn out to be a stonefish hiding in the sand: hands off, it's deadly. You'll even see a new crop of sea urchins growing once again. Most of the urchins disappeared after the **El Niño** current passed through several years ago.

Fishing

World-class fishing is done farther out to sea, where piscatorial game, including marlin, sailfish, and bonito, grow to enormous size. The **Kapaalua Dive Shop** will arrange outings with all gear provided; make reservations in advance if possible.

Yalku Lagoon

Though within walking distance from Akumal, finding Yalku from the highway can be tricky—but not impossible. Driving south from Pamul, the unmarked entrance is a dirt road across from a ranch house with a broad stone wall and a tall windmill. This secluded tiny replica of Xelha Lagoon is worth a snorkel for the many fish you'll see in a quiet hideaway. Parrotfish gather here in numbers and make a multicolored glow just below the surface. A current of fresh water flows into this small lagoon which is at most three meters deep; the visibility is about five meters. This is just a stony little pond—no rooms, no cafes, no toilets,

no tourists, just fish and you. On the ocean side of the Yalku, lovely villas are springing up on private property. From Akumal it's about a half-mile stroll north on the road that runs past Half Moon Bay.

ACCOMMODATIONS

There are limited accommodations at Akumal. During the off-season you'll have little difficulty finding a room. However, if traveling between 1 Dec. and 15 April, make reservations. No camping is permitted at Akumal, but just a few kilometers south good beaches with camping facilities are available at Xcacel (sha-SELL) and Chemuyil (shem-oo-YEEL). The hotels at Akumal are all on the beach, close to the sea—perfect for a tropical vacation.

Hotels

While Akumal cannot be considered a budget resort area, the most economical choice is **Club Akumal Caribe Villas Maya,** the original cottages built for the CEDAM diving club. The owners replaced the elderly thatch roofs with Western-style coverings a few years ago. These roomy cabañas on the beach are clean, with private bath, tile floors, a/c, and cooking facilities in some; even the lighting has been improved for readers. There are plenty of water sports, but if you prefer land sports, check out their tennis and basketball courts. Bungalow rates start at about US$64 d, including tax; the oceanfront hotel is about US$92 d, including tax. **Villas Maya** also offers three lovely condos on a separate beach around the point north of Akumal Bay. Each has two bedrooms, two bathrooms, fully equipped kitchen, and living room with two sofa beds. These rent for US$115 per night for up to four adults; two children could also be squeezed in. For something special ask about the Cannon House Suite and Cannon House Studio.

One of the newest facilities on Akumal Bay is the beachfront hotel (still part of Villas Maya) offering 21 rooms on three floors, with lovely views of the Caribbean and the garden area, which includes a swimming pool and a pool bar. The rooms each have full bath, compact refrigerator, and a small porch or balcony. Winter rates are US$92 d, including tax. These rooms are just a few steps from the sea, Lol Ha restaurant, and all the other facilities of Akumal.

Club Akumal Caribe beachfront hotel

Villas Flamingo, four smashing new villas built on Half Moon Bay (the next bay north), is close enough to Akumal for guests to enjoy its restaurants and other facilities, as well as luxury living. Each villa has an enormous living room, an ocean view and tasteful furnishings, fully equipped kitchen, dining room, upstairs bedroom (or two), large terrace with barbecue grill, daily maid service, laundry facilities, a/c, and a swimming pool shared by the four individual villas. Prices range from around US$105 up to US$300, depending on size of villa, number of people, and season. For reservations and information on all of Club Akumal's facilities, including dive packages with a room and some meals, contact Akutrame Inc., P.O. Box 13326, El Paso, TX 79913, tel. in Texas (915) 584-3552, outside of Texas toll-free (800) 351-1622; from Canada call toll-free (800) 343-1440.

Las Casitas Akumal, at the north end of the beach with the bay at your front door, has airy, furnished condominiums with two bedrooms, two baths, living room, kitchen, and patio; daily maid service included. Walking distance to restaurants, grocery store, snack stand, dive shop, sandy beach, and beach bar. Up to five persons, US$115 plus tax; for reservations and information write: 6900 Skillman #201, Dallas, TX 75231, tel. in Texas (214) 553-1552, in Mexico tel. 4-10-45/4-16-89. **Hotel Akumal Caribe** (also known as **Ina Yana Kin),** on the south end of the beach, is a two-story hotel. All rooms are simple but delightful, with private bath and terrace, plus bar, restaurant,

swimming pool, fishing and diving arrangements, car rental office, disco, game room, and lounge with cable color TV. Rates are about US$80 d. Make reservations through your travel agent or write: Hotel Akumal Caribe, Av. Bonampak and Coba, suites Atlantis, local 10, Cancun, Quintana Roo 77500, Mexico.

Just around the bend from Half Moon Bay (going north) **Quinta del Mar,** another lovely villa, faces the sea and can accommodate over six people. Three bedrooms, 3½ baths, living room, dining room, fully equipped kitchen, red-tile floors, and lots of windows to bring in the luxuriant outdoors. Terraces on both floors have stunning views of the Caribbean. Though having transportation is much more convenient, Quinta del Mar is within walking distance (one km) from the dining rooms and activities of Akumal Beach. It's also a short walk to Yalku Lagoon and a swim in your own private aquarium. Weekly rates: summer US$900, winter US$1300, holidays US$1500. For more information contact Arlene Pargot, 850 Washington Ave., Martensville, NJ 08836, tel. (201) 469-6932. This area is a residential park with building lots for sale.

FOOD

Next door to the dive shop on the beach, **Lol Ha** serves the best food at Akumal. Open for breakfast and dinner, you can expect tasty food, especially wonderful fresh fish, and a friendly staff!

Prices are not cheap (though much cheaper than Cancun), but the food is worth it. When you sit down for breakfast a basket of homemade sweet rolls is brought to your table immediately, and if you should happen to be here on Thanksgiving, the cook prepares a turkey dinner American-style (almost), and all gringos in the area come and party well into the night, using the pilgrims as a good excuse. Adjacent to Lol Ha is a snack bar serving lunch from noon to 1730, and **Pizzas Lol Ha** serves from 1300-2100. The beach bar is open for drinks from 1100 to 2300; between 1600 and 1700, happy hour means half-price drinks. The largest of several restaurants in Akumal is **Zasil** open for breakfast, lunch, and dinner. On the north end of the beach next to Las Casitas, it's housed under an enormous traditional *palapa* roof with a garish obtrusive sign that for a minute makes you forget you're in paradise. Several times a week, a busload of tourists is brought in from cruise ships that anchor off Cozumel, Cancun, and Playa del Carmen—don't eat here then! A smaller open-air restaurant at the south end of the beach is part of the **Ina Yana Kin Hotel** complex. The food is generally good, specializing in Mexican rather than Yucatecan entrees. Their continental breakfast is served with a large platter of fresh tropical fruit.

Akumal is a family vacation spot, and to prove it kids can discover great ice cream cones at **El Bucanero Ice Cream Parlor.** Just before the main entrance/arch to Akumal resort, a small general/grocery store called **Super Chomak** sells a limited selection of groceries, cold drinks, liquor, beer, ice, sundries, fresh fruit, and vegetables. If you plan on staying at Akumal for any length of time and you're cooking, the store takes orders for chicken and meat. Attached to the store is a small fast-food window selling tacos and *tortas;* open from 0700-2100.

ENTERTAINMENT

Usually you can find a disco that's open. During high season or any time there's an appreciative audience, music continues into the wee hours. More and more nighttime entertainment is springing up along the coast between Chetumal and Cancun though as yet it's comparatively tame. Without the bright glare of city lights, however, Mother Nature provides her nightly spectacular of stars, moon, and rippling water—far better than any Hollywood screen.

SHOPPING

Two gift shops, one next to Zasil and a larger one called **Mariselva Boutique** farther down the beach, sell a little of everything: typical Maya clothing, leather sandals, shawls, postcards, pottery, original Maya art and reproductions, black coral and silver jewelry, and a good selection of informative books (in English, French, and German) about the Peninsula and the Maya. Stamps are sold at the Villas Maya lobby, and mail is taken from there to the post office every day except weekends and holidays.

CHEMUYIL

Chemuyil (shem-oo-YEEL) is a tranquil beach with natural attributes of powder-fine sand, a turquoise sea, and crowds of shady coconut palms. More crowded than three years ago, the water is calm, thanks to the reef, and snorkeling and fishing attract many day visitors for a fee of about US$1 pp. The Romano family who run this beach resort also make a home for various wildlife. Last noted was a friendly spider monkey (named Montezuma) who swings freely in the trees and rooftops, and thinking he's part of the human family greets visitors to Chemuyil. The other boarder, Daktari, is a young jaguar that enjoys bathing in the sea with the youngest member of the Romano family, Danny. This will have to stop soon, he's growing up!

The entrance fee (US$2) is paid at the front gate after you turn off Hwy. 307 at the sign direct-

This baby "tigre" from a neighboring jungle needed to be hand fed after its mother was killed.

ing you to Chemuyil. Feel free to park your camper here among the trees for about US$3 pp; public restrooms and showers available. Pay fees and get information at the circular *palapa* refreshment stand near the entrance of the parking lot.

The "Chemuyil Special," devised by an international clientele and Eduardo on a rainy day at the bar, is a refreshing drink served in a coconut-shell bowl with straws. It has strong overtones of Kahlua but slips down as easily as a chocolate ice cream soda. **Warning!** It tends to sneak up on the unwary. No wonder this bar becomes a fiesta every night, and you really can dance on the bar! If on the next day you suspect a hangover, Eduardo can fix you up with a "Mexican Alka Seltzer." First he brings out a "mystical" slice of the *zapote* tree and sets it on the counter. Then he puts a jigger on top of the wooden round. He pours tequila almost to the top, and finishes filling it with Squirt. Placing the wood round on top of the jigger he gives it three sound taps on the counter, upside down, then the bedeviled one gulps it quickly. Actually, the ceremony is worth the time, as long as it's *someone else* taking the cure!

ACCOMMODATIONS AND FOOD

The stand serves small packaged sweets, donuts, coffee, juice, and bananas plus beer, tequila, and fresh seafood, including lobster if the traps have lured any captives. They serve a large (very expensive) seafood platter which includes a healthy serving of all seafood delicacies in season like fish, shrimp, lobster, and crab, enough for five to eight people, for about US$87.

Although the barkeep does his best to control the cannibal flies that hover around the refreshment stand, if you're going to eat, sit at one of the colorful umbrella tables on the beach; the breeze helps a little.

Chemuyil can get crowded during the busy winter season. Day trippers from Cancun drive their rental cars to this beach, but only occasionally does it appear to be overcrowded with overnighters. Camp on the south end of the beach to avoid the day trippers. Trailers can park in the parking lot for about US$7 per night (plus the entry fee)—no hookups, but use of showers and bathrooms is included in parking fee.

Anyone can be a successful fisherman in this bay; it takes little more than throwing a baited hook into the surf five or six meters off the beach.

If you want to fish for something special, make arrangements with Eduardo or his son Danny to take you in a launch farther out to sea—the hunting grounds for great red snapper. Other trips can be arranged, including snorkeling or a short jungle trek to a nearby site of Maya ruins.

XCACEL

The beaches just keep coming, one right after the other—and all beautiful! Though this coast really hasn't been discovered by most of the world, some have found it and keep returning year after year. You can count on meeting some fascinating people: day trippers from Cancun, people in camper vans, on cycles, and some on foot. A few pack everything they can in campers and RVs and spend an entire exotic winter among Xcacel's (sha-SELL) palms for very little a month. For one night, a fee of about US$2 pp provides a clean shower and toilet but no hookups or electricity and often the space gets crowded fast (this price is bound to go up). For about US$.50, day trippers can use the beach, showers, and restrooms. The small restaurant here has gotten pricey, and is open only from noon-1600. A hamburger is about US$6; fish is less. On certain days groups from cruise ships anchored in Playa del Carmen or Cancun are bused to Xcacel for lunch at this little restaurant and the whole place gets a bit congested. If you're cooking your own meals, bring plenty of food and water; it's a long trek to the local Safeway.

Surf And Sand
The sea directly in front of the campgrounds can be rough, but only a few hundred meters north the reef shields large waves, producing calm water again—great swimming, fishing, snorkeling, and scuba diving on the reef. When beachcombing, wear shoes along this strip of beach to protect your feet from sharp little bits of coral crunched up in the sand. This is a good place to find shells, especially in front of the campgrounds after a storm. All manner of treasure can be found, from masses of dead coral (all white, now) to sea urchin shells, keyhole limpets, maybe even a hermit crab carrying an ungainly shell on his back.

Hiking
If you're a hiker or birdwatcher, take the old dirt road which runs parallel to the shoreline from Chemuyil to Xelha, about five km in all. The road edges an old coconut grove now thick with jungle vegetation. Just after dawn, early birds are out in force looking for the proverbial worm or anything else that looks tasty. If at first you don't see them, you'll surely hear them. Look for small colorful parrots or brilliant yellow orioles; you may even see a long-tailed motmot. If you decide to hike to the mouth of Xelha National Park, bring your snorkeling gear, especially if you get there before all the tour buses. Don't forget sunscreen and bug repellent.

XELHA

Xelha (shell-HAAH), a national park on Yucatan's east coast, is just five km south of Akumal. Xelha's lagoon consists of fresh and saltwater inhabited by rare and colorful tropical fish. Through small openings from the sea, a multi-fingered aquarium has developed through the centuries, providing a safe harbor for such exotic underwater life as the brightly hued parrotfish. As a national park, the lagoon is protected from fishing, thereby preserving these beautiful creatures for all to see. Xelha gets unbelievably crowded at certain hours when tour buses bring passengers from cruise ships docked at Cancun, Cozumel, and Playa del Carmen. Come early to avoid the crowds; Xelha is open from 0800-1700 and admission is about US$1. **Note:** Do not wear tanning lotions or oils before jumping into the lagoon. These potions are hard on fish and other marinelife.

SIGHTS

Ruinas De La Xelha

Across the highway and about 200 meters south of Xelha lies a small group of ruins. Be prepared for a bit of a stroll from the entrance. The structures are mostly unimpressive except for the **Templo de Pajaros** (Temple of the Birds). Protected under a *palapa* roof, one wall still shows remnants of paintings and it's possible to make out the tails and outlines of the original art depicting birds and Chac (the Maya rain god). To get up close you have to climb out onto a small bamboo platform, but from there you have an excellent view. Other buildings to see are the **Mercado** and **Temple of the Jaguar.** A young boy is always available to guide you around; certainly worth a dollar or so.

Along a dirt path farther into the jungle you'll find an enchanting *cenote* surrounded by trees covered with bromeliads, orchids, and ferns. Dozens of swallows put on a graceful ballet, swooping and gliding low over the water, stealing a small sip each time. Thick jungle and vines surround the crystal-clear water and it's a perfect place for a swim. Wear a swimsuit. It's offensive to the Mexicans to have you skinny-dipping in their country—in fact it's against the law; some Mexican po-

lice will throw you in the slammer if they catch you. And although nudity on the beach is more common now then ever before, you still run a risk of being penalized.

Museum

The small maritime museum formerly at Xelha has moved north to Puerto Aventuras and is open 0800-1700.

ACTIVITIES

Snorkeling

You can stroll around the lagoon and see the bottom through incredibly clear water. Snorkeling is allowed in marked areas, and equipment is available to rent for about US$5 per day (and a wait in a long line after the tour buses arrive). In one of many underwater caverns that punctuate the lagoon's coast, you'll see the remains of a decaying

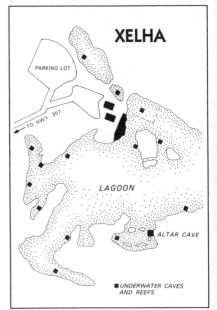

XELHA

PARKING LOT

TO HWY. 307

LAGOON

ALTAR CAVE

■ *UNDERWATER CAVES AND REEFS*

Xelha Lagoon

Maya temple altar. There's little to authenticate its origins, but it is believed to have been located on the now-submerged shoreline. Little islands, narrow waterways, and underwater passages are marvelous to snorkel in amid beautiful coral formations and a variety of warm-water fish.

Other Activities

The lagoon is surrounded by tropical vegetation and paths that wander around the 10 square acres of water. Small platforms over the rocky limestone shore provide a perfect place for the non-swimmer to study the fish and sea creatures below. There are no shallow wading areas along the lagoon edge, but you'll find frequent platforms with steps to climb in and out of the marked areas where swimming and snorkeling are permitted. **Note:** The steps get very slippery! It's tempting and fun to feed the fish, which is okay as long as you give them the nutritious prepared food sold in plastic bags at the entrance under the large arch. Please do not throw your lunch leftovers into the water! The well-fed fish often ignore them and since the incoming and outgoing water moves slowly from the sea, the lagoon quickly becomes polluted.

PRACTICALITIES

Xelha has a cafe open during the day for lunch, snacks, and drinks. Lovers of coconut milk can buy the whole nut from a straw-hatted vendor who deftly swings his machete, preparing the fruit to order (straws included) under the cooling shadows of a palm tree. Not too many years ago, coconut milk was the only refreshment available. Outside the entrance to Xelha, large shops offer a variety of Yucatecan crafts, clothing, leather goods, locally carved black coral, postcards, and other arts and crafts.

TULUM RUINS

Five km south of Akumal on Hwy. 307, a side road leads to Tulum, the largest fortified Maya site on the Quintana Roo coast. Tulum, meaning "Wall" in Maya, is quite small (the area enclosed by the wall measures 380 by 165 meters). It has 60 well-preserved structures that reveal the stylized Toltec influence and an impressive history. The sturdy stone wall was built three to five meters high, with an average thickness of seven meters. Originally this site was called Zama ("Sunrise"). Appropriately, the sun rises directly out of the ocean over Tulum, which is perched on a cliff 12 meters above the sea. The first view of this noble, then-brightly colored fortress impressed the Spaniards in Juan de Grijalva's expedition as they sailed past the Quintana Roo coast in 1518. This was their first encounter with the Indians on this new continent, and according to ships' logs, the image was awe-inspiring. One notable comment in the log of the Grijalva expedition mentions seeing "a village so large, that Seville would not have appeared larger or better."

HISTORY

Tulum was part of a series of coastal forts, towns, watchtowers, and shrines established along the coast as far south as Chetumal and north past Cancun. Archaeologists place the beginnings of Tulum in the Post-Classic Period after the Maya civilization had already passed its peak, somewhere between A.D. 700-1000. Although a stela dated A.D. 564 was found at Tulum, investigators are certain it was moved there from some other place long after it had been carved and date figures were cut into it after it was moved. The structures reveal a strong Toltec influence, such as flat roofs, plumed serpents, columns, and even pottery shapes that have definitely been established as Toltec.

Talking Cross
From 1850, Tulum was a part of the Chan Santa Cruz Indians' "Talking Cross Cult." The Spanish had taught the Indians Catholic rituals, many reminiscent of Maya ceremonies; even the cross reminded them of their tree of life. In fact for centuries the gods had been speaking to their priests through idols. In order to manipulate the Indians, a clever revolutionary half-caste, Jose Maria Barrera, used an Indian ventriloquist, Manuel Nahuat, to speak through the cross. They began three years after the Caste War ended at a cross in a forest shrine near what is now known as Felipe Carrillo Puerto but was then called Chan. A voice from the cross urged the Indians to take up arms

Tulum

against the Mexicans once again. Bewildered, impressed, and never doubting, they accepted the curious occurrence almost immediately. The original cross was replaced with three crosses that continued to "instruct" the simple Indians from the holy, highly guarded site. This political-religious cult grew quickly and ruled Quintana Roo efficiently. The well-armed, jungle-wise Chan Santa Cruz Indians (also called Cruzob) successfully kept the Mexican government out of the territory for 50 years. Even the British government in British Honduras (now known as Belize) treated this cult with respect, more out of fear of their power than out of diplomacy, and because they needed the timber trade. Around 1895 the Indians requested that the Territory of Quintana Roo be annexed by British Honduras, but the Mexican government flatly refused and sent in a new expeditionary force to try once again to reclaim Quintana Roo.

The Mexican army was doomed from the outset. They fought not only armed and elusive Indians but constant attacks of malaria and the jungle itself. The small army managed to fight its way into the capital of Chan Santa Cruz, where they were virtually trapped for a year. The standoff continued until the Mexican Revolution in 1911, when President Porfirio Diaz resigned.

Four years later the Mexican army gave up, the capital was returned to the Indians, and they continued to rule as an independent state, an embarrassment and ever-present thorn in the side of the broadening Mexican Republic. This small, determined group of Indians from another time zone managed to keep their independence and culture intact while the rest of the world proceeded into the 20th century. But life in the jungle is tough on everyone. With famine, measles epidemic, malaria, and 90 years of fighting (and beating) the Mexican army, the Chan Santa Cruz Indians' population was reduced to 10,000. Weary, in 1935 they decided to quit the fight and were accorded the recognition given to a respected adversary. When their elderly leaders signed a peace treaty, *most* of the Chan Santa Cruz Indians agreed to *allow* Mexico to rule them. This was probably the longest war in the Americas.

Into The Twentieth Century
One of the few pure Chan Indian villages left in 1935 was Tulum, and today many residents are descendants of these independent people. Even

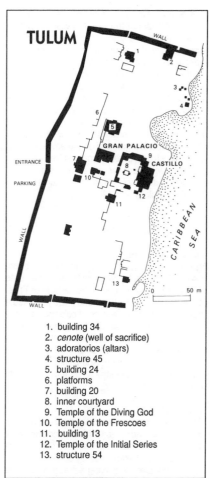

1. building 34
2. *cenote* (well of sacrifice)
3. adoratorios (altars)
4. structure 45
5. building 24
6. platforms
7. building 20
8. inner courtyard
9. Temple of the Diving God
10. Temple of the Frescoes
11. building 13
12. Temple of the Initial Series
13. structure 54

after signing the treaty, the Indians still maintained control of the area and outsiders were highly discouraged from traveling through. A skeleton imbedded in the cement at the base of one of the temples at Tulum is the remains of an uninvited archaeologist, as a warning to other would-be intruders.

All of this has changed. With foresight, the Mexican government in the '60s recognized the beautiful Quintana Roo coast as a potential tourist draw, and the new state entered the 20th century.

The advent of roads and airports has paved the way for the rest of the world to visit the unique ruins of Tulum. Workmen have been modernizing and enlarging the Tulum airstrip. The indigenous people welcome tourists and what they represent—money—at least for now.

The once-thick stands of coconut trees along this part of the coast were part of an immense coconut plantation that included Akumal and Xelha and was owned by a gentleman named Don Pablo Bush. Bush initiated the CEDAM organization made up of a group of daring archaeological divers. Bush and CEDAM donated Xelha Lagoon to the government for use as a national park. CEDAM stands for Conservation, Education, Diving, Archaeology, and Museums.

SIGHTS

Tulum Structures
Tulum is made up of mostly small ornate structures with stuccoed gargoyle faces carved onto the corners of buildings. In the **Temple of Frescoes,** looking through a metal grate you'll see a fresco that still bears a trace of color from the ancient artist. Archaeologically, this is the most interesting building on the site. The original parts of the building were constructed around 1450 during the late Post-Classic Period. And as is the case with so many of the Maya structures, it was added to over the years.

Diving God
Across the compound a small *palapa* roof protects a carved descending god. This winged creature is pictured upside down, and has been described as the God of the Setting Sun by some historians. Others interpret the carving as representing the bee; honey is a commodity almost as revered on the Peninsula as maize. Because so little is known about the glyphs of the Maya, it may be many years before this and other questions can be fully answered and understood, if ever.

El Castillo
The most impressive site is the large pyramid which stands on the edge of the cliff overlooking the sea. The building, in the center of the wall on the east side, was built in three different phases. A wide staircase leads to a two-chamber temple

Tulum

on the top. Two serpent columns divide the entrance and above the middle entrance is another carved figure of the Diving God. The climb to the top rewards you with a breathtaking bird's-eye view of the ocean, the surrounding jungle with an occasional stone ruin poking through the tight brush, and scattered clearings where small farms are beginning to grow. Until the 1920s the followers of the "Talking Cross Cult" kept three crosses in a shrine in this pyramid. It was only after the curious, as well as respectable archaeologists, showed an active interest in obtaining the crosses that the Maya priests moved the Tulum crosses to X-Cacal Guardia, where they supposedly remain today, still under the watchful protection of the Maya priesthood.

Tulum's archaeological zone is open daily from 0800-1700. At 0800 few tour buses have arrived yet, making the cooler early hours a desirable time to explore and climb the aged structures. Opposite the main entrance to the site are a number of open stalls with typical tourist curios along with a growing number of small cafes selling soda pop and snacks. A small fee is paid across the street from the entrance to the ruins. Parking is available directly outside the Tulum site (if not filled with tour buses). On a recent visit, 29 tour buses were counted in front of Tulum. The fumes alone will surely destroy this marvelous old site if this kind of abuse continues.

Village Of Tulum

A few kilometers past the road to the Tulum archaeological zone on Hwy. 307 is the pueblo of Tulum. This small village has had a delayed reaction to all the tourists that come to their famous ruins down the road. The town has little to offer except a few simple markets, fruit stands, a couple of *loncherias,* and maybe most importantly a couple of mechanics. You'll spot one on the highway on the left side of the street just as you drive into town. There's no sign, but the large number of cars on the property is a dead giveaway. The owner and his son are good, cheap, and willing to help if they can.

ACCOMMODATIONS AND FOOD

Only a few places to overnight are available in the immediate area of Tulum. Following the paved road from the parking lot south along the coast you'll come to a series of unspoiled beaches edged by what remains of once-thick stands of coconut trees. Between Tulum and Punta Allen there are only simple cabañas on the beach. Many don't have public power and depend on gas lanterns or small generators for part of the day; most have a good supply of cold water and some sell bottled water, but if not, boil your drinking supply. Expect Spartan accommodations all in the budget class. Remember that when you choose budget lodgings what was funky but clean one month may be a dirty dive the next month. Look at the rooms carefully—do you see fleas on the floor? If linens are furnished, check them out to make sure they're clean as well, the bathrooms and shower rooms ditto. Is there electricity? Gas lanterns? Candles? Make sure that you get what you expect or are led to expect. If you require deluxe rooms, your best bet is to headquarter at Akumal, 25 km north. The beach camps along the coast are open to RV parking, though most don't have hookups; ask the manager if in doubt.

Camping

Two combination cabaña/campgrounds side by side are on the beach immediately south of the Tulum ruins. Follow the paved road going from the parking lot (about a 12-minute walk). The cabins are tiny. Bring everything—hammock, drinking water, bug repellent, mosquito netting, food (Tulum village has a few markets and small cafes where you can find inexpensive meals). If you're camping it helps to have a tent; when the wind blows it gets mighty gritty on this beach. The fees are minimal, about US$2 pp.

Budget

El Crucero Motel is conveniently located at the crossroads of Hwy. 307 and the Tulum ruins entrance road. It's a 10-minute walk to the ruins, and several restaurants are close. The rooms are plain, *usually* clean, and rates are about US$10 d. A guest recently reported the rooms "dirty and with bugs," but one month before another reader reported the rooms *adequate. Caveat emptor!* A few kilometers south of the parking lot, **Cabanas Don Armandos** offers 30 very Spartan cabañas with one bed and room for a hammock (mosquito netting a must!), communal toilet and showers, cold water, candles, sheets, and bottled water supplied. A restaurant bar on the premises, Zasil Kin, serves good food, open from 0700 to 2130. This is a family-run operation; ask for the special of the day, it's usually delicious. Cabañas rent for about US$11 for two, camping available on the beach for US$3 pp. A little difficult to find, look for the sign Zasil Kin a few kilometers past the ruins on the bumpy road, officially called Boca Paila Road.

Another small group of 15 cabañas built in the spring of 1989 and called **Nohoch Tunich** is very primitive, but on a beautiful piece of the Caribbean coast. Expect tiny rooms, simple communal toilets, cold-water showers, and a small cantina serving cold drinks and simple meals. Very pleasant managers/owners. Rates for two are US$11 year-round.

Cabañas Chac Mool is at the end of the paved road leading south from the Tulum parking lot. You'll enjoy quaint *palapa* huts with hanging double beds and mosquito netting, screenless shutters that open up onto the outdoors, community bathrooms and hot-water showers, a dining room that serves excellent vegetarian dinners as well as chicken and fish, a bar, and a beautiful bay good for swimming and snorkeling. About US$30 double. Continue on the same road (seven km from Tulum) and on the left is a white wall (covered with colorful paintings and dominated by a bright yellow submarine) that surrounds small stucco cabañas. **Cabañas Arrecife** is reasonably modern, stucco built, very clean, with well-kept grounds and (usually) an abundant water supply (boil your drinking water or use bottled), about US$15. The owner's wife cooks meals for guests. Another camp, **Cabañas Tulum,** includes small cabañas with beds, bathrooms, ceiling fans, and cold water. In the summer of 1989 it was looking pretty run down and dirty. Rates US$22. Maybe the owner was on summer vacation—check it out carefully if that's all that's left! There's a restaurant on the premises and a white beach that now hosts topless visitors.

Ana y Jose is another beach resort built in the summer of 1989. It's developing into one of the nicest small cabaña groups along this Tulum road, all with private tile bathrooms, tile floors, cold water, and double beds. All-stone construction and red-tile roofs with pleasant little touches like hanging plants puts it a cut above many of the resorts along here. A colorful *palapa* restaurant overlooking the sea serves three meals a day. Rates during off-season are US$25 and US$30 to US$35 high season. Peppi, the owner/manager will show you around and speaks fairly good English. For more information contact: Ana y Jose Restaurant and Cabañas, in the States ask for Bill Kearns, tel. (702) 348-9368, fax (702) 348-0646; in Mexico write to Carr. Boca Paila, km 7, Tulum, Quintana Roo 77500, Mexico, tel. 4-11-17 in Cancun.

Cafes

Several readers have sent us troubling reports of Tulum's **Restaurant El Faisan y Venado** (overcharging and rudeness), so try it at your own risk. This is deer country, but don't be fooled by the name of the cafe: the government has cracked down on serving the over-hunted *venado* ("deer"). Across from the gas station is a restaurant called **Alexandros.** Formerly vegetarian, the food is okay and fairly reasonable, and the place is *usually* clean. The **Crucero Motel Cafe** serves reasonably priced simple food. A few fast-food stands at the **bazaar** across from the entrance to the ruins serve tacos, *tortas,* combination plates, and cold beer and soda. For more deluxe meals try the restaurants at Akumal (**Lol Ha** is good) or Puerto Aventuras about 20 and 25 km north of Tulum.

TRANSPORTATION

Getting There

The best way to get around on Hwy. 307 is by car. However, public buses going north and south stop at El Crucero Motel about every one to two hours from 0630-2030. From here you can also catch a bus to Valladolid which passes Coba at 0600 and noon; the return bus leaves Coba at 0600 and 1600. Both 1st- and 2nd-class buses are usually crowded by the time they reach Tulum; 1st-class allows no standing. Be there in plenty of time, the buses don't wait. It's always a good idea to check with the bus driver about destination, times, and return trips.

This is a busy place, so it's not difficult to hitch a ride.

COBA

This early Maya site covers an immense area (50 square km) and hundreds of mounds are yet to be uncovered. Archaeologists are convinced that in time Coba will prove to be one of the largest Maya excavations on the Yucatan Peninsula. Only in recent years has the importance of Coba come to light. First explored in 1891 by Austrian archaeologist Teobert Maler, it was another 35 years before Coba was investigated by S. Morley, J. Eric Thompson, H. Pollock, and J. Charlot under the auspices of the Carnegie Institute. In 1972-75 the National Geographic Society in conjunction with the Mexican National Institute of Anthropology and History mapped and surveyed the entire area. A program funded by the Mexican government continues to explore and study Coba, but it is time-consuming, costly work, and it will be many years before completed.

Coba seems to be the favorite Maya ceremonial site of many independent travelers. The fact that the jungle hasn't been cleared away or all the mounds uncovered adds a feeling of discovery to the visit. For the visitor interested in exploring, it's important to know that the distances between groupings of structures are long (in some cases one to two km), and they're not located in a neatly kept park such as Chichen Itza. Each group of ruins is buried in the middle of thick jungle, so come prepared with comfortable shoes, bug repellent, sunscreen, and a hat. A canteen of water never hurts.

Flora And Fauna

Coba in Maya means "Water Stirred by the Wind." Close to a group of shallow lakes (Coba, Macanxoc, Xkanha, and Zalcalpu), some very marshy areas attract a large variety of birds and butterflies. The jungle around Coba is perfect for viewing toucans, herons, egrets, and the motmot. Colorful butterflies are everywhere, including the large, deep-blue *morphidae* butterfly as well as the bright yellow-orange barred sulphur. If you look on the ground, you'll almost certainly see long lines of cutting ants. One double column carries freshly cut leaves to the burrow, and next to that another double column marches in the opposite direction, empty jawed, returning for more. The columns can be longer than a kilometer, and usually the work party will all carry the same species of leaf or blossom until the plant is completely stripped. It's amazing how far they travel for food! The vegetation decays in their nests, and the mushrooms which grow on the compost are an important staple of the ants' diet. The determined creatures grow up to three cm long.

People

Thousands of people are believed to have lived here during the Classic Period. Though the numbers are drastically reduced, today pockets of people still maintain their archaic beliefs side by side with their Christian faith. They plant their corn with ceremony, conduct their family affairs in the same manner as their ancestors, and many villages still appoint a calendar-keeper to keep track of the auspicious days to direct them in their daily lives. This is most common in the Coba area because of its (up till now) isolation from outsiders, and because these people have maintained a very low profile when it comes to their ancient heritage.

THE RUINS

White Roads

The most important reason to visit Coba is to view the archaeological remains of a city begun in A.D. 600. These structures built near the lakes were scattered along a refined system of *sacbe* (roads). The remains of 40 *sacbe* have been found crisscrossing the entire Peninsula, but there are more here than in any other location. They pass through what were once outlying villages and converge at Coba, an indication it was the largest city of its era. One such *sacbe* is 100 km long and travels in an almost straight line from the base of Nohoch Mul (the great pyramid) to the town of Yaxuna. Each *sacbe* was built to stringent specifications: a base of stones one to two meters high, about 4.5 meters wide, and covered with white mortar. However, in Coba some ancient roads as wide as 10 meters have been uncovered.

The Pyramids

While you wander through the grounds it helps to use the map. When you enter, follow the dirt road a few meters until you come to the sign that says Grupo Coba directing you to the right. A short distance on the path brings you to the second-high-

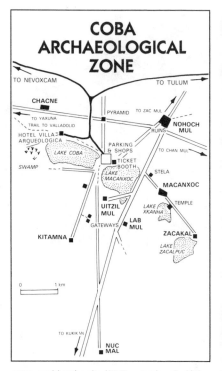

est pyramid at the site (22.5 meters), called **Iglesia.** After climbing many stone steps, from the top is a marvelous view of the surrounding jungle and Lake Macanxoc. Farther to the right (southeast on a jeep trail) is a smaller pyramid called **Conjunto Las Pinturas,** so named because of the stucco paintings that once lined the walls, minute traces of which can still be seen on the uppermost cornice of the temple. From the summit of this structure is a dizzying view of **Nohoch Mul,** tallest pyramid on the Peninsula (42 meters, a 12-story climb!). At the fork just beyond the Grupo Coba, a path to the left leads to that great temple. Watch for signs and stay on the trail.

Scientists conjecture there may be a connection between the Peten Maya (hundreds of miles south in the Guatemalan lowlands) and the Classic Maya that lived in Coba. Both groups built lofty pyramids, much taller than those found in Chichen Itza, Uxmal, or elsewhere in the northern part of the Peninsula.

Undiscovered

All along the paths are mounds overgrown with vines, trees, and flowers—many of these unexcavated ruins. More than 5,000 mounds wait for the money it takes to continue excavation. Thirty-two Classic-Period stelae (including 23 that are sculptured) have been found scattered throughout the Coba archaeological zone. For the most part they are displayed where they were discovered. One of the better preserved can be seen in front of the Nohoch Mul group. Still recognizable, it has a nobleman standing on the backs of two slaves and dated 780 in Maya glyphs.

ACCOMMODATIONS

There's one deluxe hotel in Coba, the **Villa Arqueológica,** part of a chain that has placed hotels at archaeological zones in several parts of Mexico, including Uxmal and Chichen Itza. Each hotel has a well-equipped library with many volumes containing histories of the area and the Maya people. Run by the owners of Club Med, it has *small* attractive rooms, a/c, shallow swimming pool, outdoor bar and dining, good *típico* and French food, and a gift shop which carries quality reproductions of Maya art. It's hard to predict seasonal highs since groups from Europe are bused in all year long; reservations could be important even though the hotel is often quiet. Rates are US$48, meals extra; in the U.S. for reservations call (800) 528-3100.

A couple of other modest inns are located on what could be called the main street of Coba. **Restaurant Isabel** is no longer a restaurant, but you'll find a few simple *cabanitas* for under US$8 d; *very* Spartan but clean, with electricity, two beds, and cold water only. **Bocadito's** cabins are a little more uptown—private bathroom, cold water, two beds, and a place for a hammock.

FOOD AND GIFT SHOPS

Food And Gift Shops

Where three years ago there was nothing, tiny shops and outdoor cafes are springing up near the entrance to the Coba ruins. You'll find cool drinks and good snacks at **Restaurant Cinco Lagos** and **Restaurant Coba.** These are close to small gift shops that carry the *usual* and include black coral factories on-site. One gift shop advertises their available bathroom (there's a public restroom across the street from the ruins site). In Coba you'll find the cafes at the inns clean and pleasant. The food, though limited in choice, is *típico* and can be quite good. **Bocadito** has pleasant surroundings and tasty, inexpensive food. Close by, a tiny bakery sells good *pan dulce,* and a small store sells cold soda pop. The food at **Villa Arqueológica** is fairly good though pricey, and if you bring your swimsuit you can take a dip after lunch and relax in their garden. The bar serves a terrific planter's punch, especially welcome when

A roof has been placed over this carved stela to help preserve it from nature's constant attack.

ruins at Coba

you come out of the jungle hot, sweaty, and tired from hiking and climbing the pyramids. Sandwiches cost about US$4.50, full meals average US$8-10.

Getting There

Getting to Coba is easiest by car. The roads are good, and from Coba you can continue on to Valladolid, Chichen Itza, and Merida, or the coast highway (307) that goes south to Chetumal and north to Cancun. If traveling by local bus your schedule is limited to two buses a day. Northbound buses depart Tulum at 0600 and noon, stopping at Coba town at 0730 and 1330 before continuing to Valladolid. Taxis at Coba are available to take you to Nuevo Xcan. From here you

can catch a bus to Merida. Southbound buses leave Valladolid at 0400 and 1400, stopping at Coba at 0600 and 1800 on the way to Tulum and points north on Hwy. 307. When you get on and off the bus, ask the driver about the return trip and times. These schedules change frequently! Bus travelers tell of waiting in Coba for a bus that just skips it entirely at certain times of the year. It's a three-km walk to the highway, where other buses pass. (If you're planning to spend the night, make sure you have reservations or get there very early in the day.) You'll often run into travelers on the trail at the Coba ruins who are willing to give you a ride. Organized bus tours are available from hotels and travel agencies in Cancun, Playa del Carmen, and Cozumel.

MUYIL: ANCIENT MAYA SEAPORT OF SIAN KA'AN

One of the larger Maya sites within the Sian Ka'an Reserve is Muyil, also known as Chunyaxche. Situated on the edge of the karstic limestone shelf about 25 km south of Tulum, it has been the recent subject of a study conducted by Tulane University and the Quintana Roo Regional Center of INAH. Along with mapping the site to determine its size and settlement pattern, graduate students from Tulane and men from the village of Chumpon have been excavating for ceramics in order to provide dates of occupation and are learning the use of the seaport at Muyil.

Architectural Discoveries

The potsherds dug up at the area indicate that Muyil was settled about 1 A.D. and occupied continuously until the Spanish conquest began. The author of the report, archaeologist Elia del Carmen Trejo, notes that since no Spanish ceramics have been identified and because there is no mention of a settlement at Muyil in books from the period, he suspects that the population of Muyil perished in the 40 years following the conquest. Many fascinating tidbits of information have been discovered. A large *sacbe* (roadway) at Muyil runs at least .5 km from the site center to near the edge of the Muyil Lagoon. The upper (western) half of the road runs through mangrove swamp. There are six structures spaced along the roadway approximately every 120 meters. They range in size from small two-meter-high platforms to the large *castillo,* one of the tallest structures on the east coast. All but the westernmost of the structures faces westward, away from the lagoon. They have center stairways facing westward to the roadway running to the west. The Maya always used directional precision that dealt with their beliefs involving the sun and Venus. The sections of roadway between each structure begin on center at the foot of each stairway, but when they arrive at the next structure to the west, they connect with it at the northeast corner, not on the centerline. It is as though one were always meant to pass these structures along their north side; as yet no one knows why.

The *castillo,* located in the midpoint of the *sacbe,* stands 21 meters above the water level of the lagoon. At the summit is a solid round masonry turret, which is (up till now) unique on ancient Maya structures. From the summit it's possible to see the Caribbean.

Locals report that Juan Vega (nicknamed "white king of the Maya") operated a chicle business at Muyil in the early 1900s. During the height of the post-Caste War conflict, Juan Vega was kidnapped by the Maya Indians as a young child. His entire family and young companions were put to death, but because he was carrying religious books and could read he was allowed to live. The Maya had a curious acceptance of the Christian religion. Because of certain similarities they managed to weave it into their own beliefs and would listen with conviction to the advice of Juan Vega given from his books.

Although Vega was a captive of these people, he was given tremendous respect and spent his entire life in the village, marrying a Maya and raising a family of mestizos in the village of Chumpon. Chumpon is referred to by knowledgeable outsiders as the "jungle vatican." Vega saved the lives of many Mexican soldiers that were captured and doomed by the Maya until he stepped in and read to them the laws of the Christian God from his worn books. In 1961, Quintana Roo was still a no-man's land without roads, and only through a fluke Vega was described to Paul Bush by a relative from the village of Chumpon who feared the man was dying of an illness.

Fortunately, Paul Bush, a compassionate man, acted quickly. With the help of the relative and the use of a small plane (to spot the hidden jungle village) and a helicopter to pick up the sick man (by foot it was a three-day expedition into the village), Juan Vega was rescued—but only after he asked the chief's permission to leave. The man was very ill, but after surgery and a long stay in a Mexico City hospital, he was once again fit. While in the hospital the newspapers gave an account of Vega and his past. This brought an old soldier to visit Juan Vega, one who lived only because of the in-

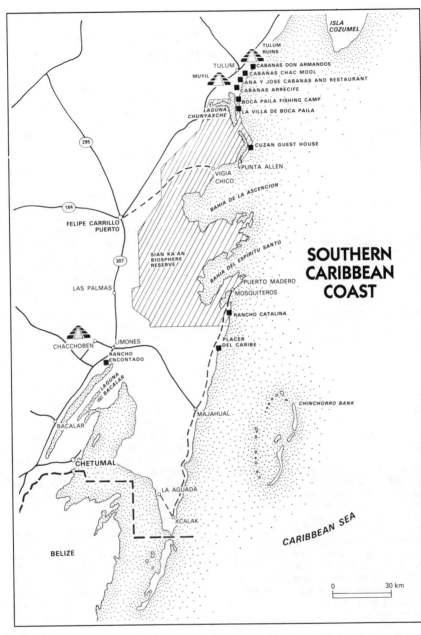

ISLA COZUMEL

TULUM RUINS
TULUM
CABANAS DON ARMANDOS
MUYIL
CABANAS CHAC MOOL
ANA Y JOSE CABANAS AND RESTAURANT
CABANAS ARRECIFE
BOCA PAILA FISHING CAMP
LAGUNA CHUNYAXCHE
LA VILLA DE BOCA PAILA

CUZAN GUEST HOUSE

PUNTA ALLEN
VIGIA CHICO

295

BAHIA DE LA ASCENCION

184

FELIPE CARRILLO PUERTO

307

SOUTHERN CARIBBEAN COAST

SIAN KA'AN BIOSPHERE RESERVE

BAHIA DEL ESPIRITU SANTO

LAS PALMAS

PUERTO MADERO
MOSQUITEROS

RANCHO CATALINA

CHACCHOBEN
LIMONES

RANCHO ENCONTADO

PLACER DEL CARIBE

CHINCHORRO BANK

LAGUNA BACALAR

BACALAR

MAJAHUAL

CHETUMAL

LA AGUADA

XCALAK

BELIZE

CARIBBEAN SEA

0   30 km

tervention of the "white Maya king." Vega had one request while in Mexico, to visit *Abuelitos* (the virgin of Guadaloupe). When able, he made his pilgrimage to the shrine and then happily returned to his isolated village and family in Chumpon. Juan Vega made a complete recovery and lived in Chumpon until his death a few years later.

ROAD TO PUNTA ALLEN

If you're driving south to Punta Allen on the Boca Paila Rd. (south from the Tulum parking lots and parallel to the coast), fill your gas tank at the Tulum crossroads gas station since there's not another on the coastal road to Punta Allen (57 km). (Traveling north on Hwy. 307, the next gas station is in Playa del Carmen, traveling south to Chetumal, there's one in Felipe Carrillo Puerto.) After leaving Hwy. 307 from Tulum on Boca Paila Rd., the road to Punta Allen appears to be paved and smooth—fooling the uninformed! The road is only smooth for about six km beyond the ruins, and then it becomes potholed, ridged, and rugged. Though it's slow going, bumpy, and uncomfortable, all vehicles can handle this all-weather road.

Boca Paila Fishing Lodge
This pricey small resort caters to fishermen looking for excellent saltwater fly-fishing for bonefish. It offers seven bungalows, food, and excellent service. In some cases clients are flown in from Cozumel or Cancun; weekly price includes round-trip land transfer from Cancun or Cozumel, six days of fishing, accommodations, food, boat, and shared guide. Prices begin at US$1725 double occupancy, less for non-fishing spouses. Daily price is about US$285 double occupancy. Call in the U.S. (800) 245-1950, in Pennsylvania tel. (412) 935-1577, or write Frontiers, Box 161, Pearce Mill Rd., Wexford, PA 15090.

Casa Blanca Lodge
Another great fishing lodge is located on Ascension Bay. Again this is a small resort for the fisherman (and a non-fishing spouse) with room for 14 guests. The attractive lodge is located on a palm-covered point just 100 feet from the edge of the blue Caribbean. The modern comfortable rooms are spacious and an open-air *palapa* is a bar/gathering spot where the evening is spent telling tall fishing stories. Weekly rates begin at US$2295 pp, double occupancy, including roundtrip air transport from Cancun, accommodation, food, boat, fuel, shared guide, fishing license, and 15% government tax. For further information contact Frontiers, Box 161, Pearce Mill Rd., Wexford, PA 15090, tel. (800) 245-1950, (412) 935-1577, fax (412) 935-5388.

Trekkers find many campsites along Quintana Roo's Caribbean coast.

Across The Bridge

Another 10 km beyond La Villa de Boca Paila is the Boca Paila Bridge. The new wooden bridge crosses the canal connecting the lagoons with the Caribbean. This exotic spot, crowded with tropical vegetation and coconut trees, offers stretches of lonely beach north and south of the mouth of the lagoon. The water, though warm and inviting, is not clear enough for snorkeling or diving. The beach is open to campers. Be sure to bring all necessities, including food and water.

Continuing on the road, south of the bridge is **El Rancho Retiro,** a wonderful beach located on a picturesque bay. It reminds one of a Tahitian island before the tourists discovered it. **Note:** Since the death of the owner, the cabañas have pretty well suspended operations. Behind the cabañas the

explorer will find a lagoon called **Laguna Chun-yaxe,** a stopover for migrant birds, including flamingos, herons, egrets, and many others. This area is all part of the **Sian Ka'an Reserve,** where there are over 300 species of birds living close by. **Bird Island,** a small island in the lagoon, hosts two species of crocodiles and is a great place to explore and observe all manner of wildlife.

Though this is wild country, some families have lived here for many years. Most are fishermen and some will provide boat outings upon request. The setting is lovely, right on the edge of the bay where dolphins come to frolick every autumn. Visitors tell of petting the lovely creatures in the shallow water. It's necessary to travel about a kilometer around the bay for the best swimming spot.

Exploring Ancient Caves

If you're traveling with a small boat (rubber raft is best), narrow canals said to be built by the Maya curve inland to remnants of isolated ceremonial centers—all small and none restored or even excavated. This is a trip for intrepid adventurers with sturdy muscles; in some spots the channel narrows, and you have to carry your boat overland or wade through muddy swamps. Caves are scattered about—some you can swim into, others are hidden in the countryside; Maya glyphs still intact on the inside walls suggest the Indians may have lived in them. Taking along a guide familiar with the area is suggested. Bring a flashlight, bug repellent, sunscreen, a hat, and walking shoes that will survive in the water.

For the hardy type with lots of time, walking the 347 km from Puerto Morelos to Chetumal or Punta Allen can be high adventure. Taking at least three or four weeks (or longer if you take time to smell the flowers), this trip is only for the fit. While the main highway (307) is the most direct route to Chetumal, it often veers away from the beach and is oftentimes boring and flat with little to see except cars. Trekking to Punta Allen, Boca Paila Rd. sometimes disappears behind sand dunes, but it's never that long a trudge to dozens of fine beaches where you might be seduced into staying a day or a month—or forever.

In most cases there's no place to stay except the beach, where there are lots of coconut trees on which to sling your hammock—a tropical paradise. The Maya believe the hammock is a gift from the gods, but be sure to have mosquito net-

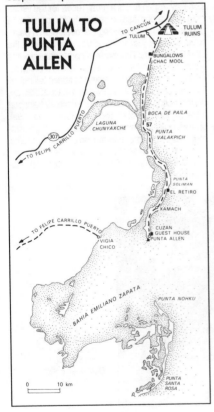

TULUM TO PUNTA ALLEN

TO CANCÚN
TULUM
TULUM RUINS
BUNGALOWS
CHAC MOOL
BOCA DE PAILA
LAGUNA CHUNYAXCHE
57
PUNTA VALAKPICH
307
TO FELIPE CARRILLO PUERTO
PUNTA SOLIMAN
EL RETIRO
XAMACH
TO FELIPE CARRILLO PUERTO
CUZAN GUEST HOUSE
PUNTA ALLEN
VIGIA CHICO
BAHIA EMILIANO ZAPATA
PUNTA NOHKU
PUNTA SANTA ROSA
0   10 km

ting with you for your nights under the stars. Simple cabaña resorts are springing up as Cancun continues to spread southward down the Quintana Roo coast, but be prepared for long stretches on this dirt road with nothing but vacant beach and small ranchitos.

Restaurants are also sparse on this stretch of road until you reach Punta Allen; come prepared with your own victuals and water. Once you reach Punta Allen you either have to hoof it back or make arrangements with a villager for a ride.

PUNTA ALLEN

Punta Allen, part of the Sian Ka'an Reserve, is a small fishing village on a finger of land that overlooks a large bay called Bahia de la Ascencion. In the last century, ships would occasionally drift off course onto the dangerous reef that stands just off the coast. Maya boatmen, however, expertly navigate in and out of the submerged reefs and shallow spots that lie hidden across the mouth of the bay.

Considered the hottest lobster grounds in Mexico, wildlife groups in association with the local lobster cooperative and the Mexican equivalent of the National Science Foundation are studying the way the Yucatecan fishermen handle the spiny crustaceans. The villagers don't use lobster traps as we know them but instead create artificial habitats. The lobsters grow sheltered in these habitats, and when they reach a predetermined size, the fishermen graff them by hand. For centuries the Maya built habitats from the spine of a particular palm tree which is becoming extinct from overuse. Fishermen within the Sian Ka'an reserve have been urged to use alternative materials.

Scientists (with manpower provided by organizations of volunteers such as Earth Watch) have been tagging and mapping the growth areas each summer since 1982 to decide if this concentration of lobsters leads to over-harvesting, or if protecting the habitat reduces the natural mortality rate of the open sea. Once they make their determinations perhaps they will be able to help prevent the lobster industry from being wiped out in Punta Allen as it has been in other once-rich lobster-growing areas. Over-harvesting the lobster has depleted the spiny delicacy in several areas in the Gulf of Mexico and in Baja's Todos Los Santos Bay.

SIGHTS

Along the way to Punta Allen you'll discover several beaches with white sand surrounded by thick jungle. The village itself is small and typical but not glamorous. Snorkeling, swimming, and fishing are good on some of the offshore islands. Walks will introduce you to unusual birds and maybe even a shy animal. Marshy areas close by are good for observing the nesting grounds and natural habitats of nearly 300 classes of birds identified by ornithologists.

ACCOMMODATIONS

All beaches are free to campers; certainly the polite way is to ask permission of the local villager whose house you'll be in front of before setting up camp. Dispose of your trash and leave the beach clean. RVs can park on the beach, but there are no facilities. Swimming here is not the best, but the fishing is great!

Few accommodations are available at Punta Allen. For a long time the only place was **Cuzan Guest House,** a group of basic *palapa* cabañas, some shaped like tepees. Earth Watch expeditions stay here. If you need all the modern conveniences of the States, *don't* come to Punta Allen. However, if you're interested in learning about the culture of a Maya fishing village, and your tastes run to low-key adventure, sleeping in primitive cabañas in hammocks (a few beds are available), community bathrooms (two only), simple food that is mostly from the sea—lobster is served frequently during the lobster season (15 July through 15 March)—then come along. Arrangements can be made with Armando, if he's not fishing, to take you motoring in his fishing launch to the reef, where snorkeling is outstanding. Another popular outing is a trip to **Cayo Colebre,** a small uninhabited island off the coast, where in spring you'll see hundreds of man-o-war frigates hanging like kites overhead, displaying the brilliant red mating pouches under their beaks to attract females. Fishing off Colebre, as well as several other uninhabited islands close by, is excellent. Ask about two-night Robinson Crusoe trips. Rooms at Cuzan Guest House begin at US$20. Breakfast and lunch are US$5 each, dinner US$12. Remember, this is a fisherman's house and not a resort! If you

have any questions write to Sonia Lilvik, Apto. Postal 703, Cancun, Quintana Roo 77500, Mexico. Allow a couple of months for return mail.

Note: When going to Punta Allen, start out early in the morning to allow yourself enough time to get back in case it's not for you.

FELIPE CARRILLO PUERTO

Anyone that has driven Hwy. 307 from Tulum to Felipe Carrillo Puerto in the past five years can't help but notice the varied changes taking place. Only a few years ago the main activity seen along this two-lane road was machete-swinging workmen battling to keep thick jungle vines and ferns from overtaking the roadway. Today, trees have been removed and jungle has been cleared away to make room for small ranchitos. The people keep a few cattle and pigs, and grow corn, squash, and tomatoes. Also large areas have been planted with citrus trees, a government-backed experiment to help the farmers.

From Tulum to Chetumal it's an easy drive that takes you through Felipe Carrillo Puerto. For anyone curious about the past of the Maya Chan Santa Cruz Indians (also called Cruzob) it's well worth a stopover to investigate this small colonial city with some of the richest history in Quintana Roo. It has yet to be discovered en masse by tourists and remains a simple quiet town.

Around an unexciting central plaza several small hotels offer moderately priced rooms, not fancy, but clean. The **Esquivel Hotel** is owned and operated by a family that can trace its beginnings back as far as the Caste War in the 1800s. **Faison y Venado** is a newer hotel on Hwy. 307 which also houses a good cafe. *Venado* (deer) meat is on the restricted list and *not* on the menu; however, the waiter will quietly offer it to those customers he feels comfortable with. For anyone interested in preserving what's left of the deer population along this coast, don't order *venado* if it's offered. Another long-time stopover, the **24 Hour Cafe,** still serves reasonably priced, tasty food. The bus station is close by in case you choose to continue your journey by bus.

Felipe Carrillo Puerto is an eclectic mix of modern young folks shopping for the latest hit at **Videolandia** and some of the oldest Maya (descen-

dants of the once-violent Cruzob) who are still hoping for British help to conquer the Mexicans and get them out of their homeland.

Chan Santa Cruz History
When the Caste War was going badly for the Maya, smart leaders reintroduced the "talking cross." This unearthly oracle encouraged the Indians, dictating tactical orders, and predicting victory in their fight against the outsiders. The talking cross gave them strength, and told them they were the chosen race, true Christians, and children of God.

In a way, they *were* the victors; they managed to resist and hold off intruders from the late 1840s to the early 1900s. A few old-timers still cling to the belief that one day the Maya will once again control the Quintana Roo coast. These aged traditionalists still sanctify the cult of the "talking cross" almost 90 years after being conquered by the Mexican federal army. Their fathers and grandfathers rejected the peace treaty negotiated between their leaders and the Mexicans, took their families into the jungle, and began new villages where they continued their secretive lifestyle, calling themselves *separados*.

The "talking cross" has a long history. Early Spaniards in the 1700s reported seeing one at Cozumel. The cross itself had been an important symbol in the ancient Maya cult, representing the four cardinal points. Studies indicate that the Maya knew full well that a human voice was responsible for the "talking," but they believed it was inspired by God. Who can prove otherwise?

Chan Santa Cruz Today
Chan Santa Cruz (meaning "Small Holy Cross"), is now called Felipe Carrillo Puerto. Today's city folk refer to old-timers as *antiguos,* and while the younger generation has too many modern things

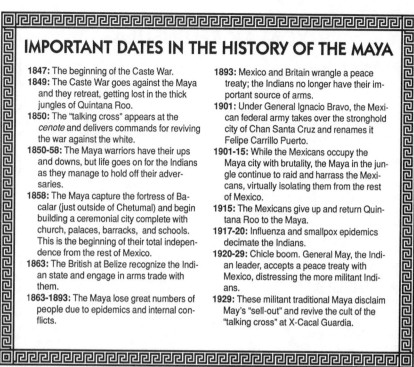

IMPORTANT DATES IN THE HISTORY OF THE MAYA

1847: The beginning of the Caste War.
1849: The Caste War goes against the Maya and they retreat, getting lost in the thick jungles of Quintana Roo.
1850: The "talking cross" appears at the *cenote* and delivers commands for reviving the war against the white.
1850-58: The Maya warriors have their ups and downs, but life goes on for the Indians as they manage to hold off their adversaries.
1858: The Maya capture the fortress of Bacalar (just outside of Chetumal) and begin building a ceremonial city complete with church, palaces, barracks, and schools. This is the beginning of their total independence from the rest of Mexico.
1863: The British at Belize recognize the Indian state and engage in arms trade with them.
1863-1893: The Maya lose great numbers of people due to epidemics and internal conflicts.

1893: Mexico and Britain wrangle a peace treaty; the Indians no longer have their important source of arms.
1901: Under General Ignacio Bravo, the Mexican federal army takes over the stronghold city of Chan Santa Cruz and renames it Felipe Carrillo Puerto.
1901-15: While the Mexicans occupy the Maya city with brutality, the Maya in the jungle continue to raid and harrass the Mexicans, virtually isolating them from the rest of Mexico.
1915: The Mexicans give up and return Quintana Roo to the Maya.
1917-20: Influenza and smallpox epidemics decimate the Indians.
1920-29: Chicle boom. General May, the Indian leader, accepts a peace treaty with Mexico, distressing the more militant Indians.
1929: These militant traditional Maya disclaim May's "sell-out" and revive the cult of the "talking cross" at X-Cacal Guardia.

to enjoy to actively take part in the ancient tradition, one gets the feeling that deep within themselves these youngsters admire the *antiguos's* tenacity and belief in the impossible dream.

TRANSPORTATION

Cycling
Since most of the Yucatan Peninsula is flat and the primary arteries are in good condition, the Caribbean coast sees a few cyclists. When exploring off the main roads, cyclists should be prepared for bumpy, irregular, and hard-packed dirt surfaces which become a muddy morass when it rains. Bring spare tires and a repair kit. Repairs are a big problem in most areas; few cycle shops exist. With a motorcycle you can travel almost any road on the Peninsula, but beware of the swampy shoulders near the sea.

Other Transport
You can expect frequent bus service between Chetumal and Cancun. Buses travel from all over the Yucatan Peninsula to Hwy. 307 and up and down the Caribbean coast.

XCALAK PENINSULA

Xcalak Peninsula History

This low-lying limestone shelf bounded by the Quintana Roo mainland on the west, Espiritu Santo Bay on the north, Chetumal Bay on the south, and the Caribbean sea on the east is a mosaic of savannah, marsh, streams, and lagoons, dotted by islands of higher ground with dark soil and high forest, a rich refuge for Quintana Roo wildlife. The jungle has kept hidden for centuries the remainder of Maya life that once thrived on this narrow peninsula.

From a report of a survey made in Feb. 1988 by archaeologists Anthony P. Andrews (University

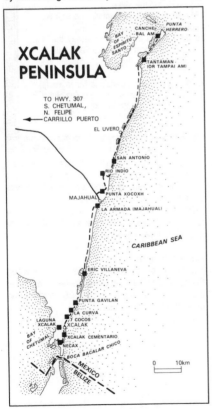

of South Florida), Tomas Gallareta Negron (Tulane University), and Rafael Coboa Palma (Tulane University), I learned of a reconnaissance of archaeological sites on the coast of the Xcalak Peninsula. This survey focused on the coastal strip between Punta Herrero on Espiritu Santo Bay and Boca Bacalar Chico, the canal that divides the Xcalak Peninsula from Ambergris Caye in Belize. Only sites on the shoreline and its immediate vicinity were visited; the interior areas were not surveyed. Money and time were devoted to the most threatened sites along the rapidly developing coast. Only in recent years a rough dirt road has opened this once isolated area to home builders and a few (so far) small resorts, but many new developments are on the drawing boards.

Early explorers Sylvanus Morley and Thomas Gann sailed up the coast from Belize in 1918 visiting a number of sites along the east coast. In 1926, Herbert Spinden and Gregory Mason passed by the area, and then in 1958 an amateur explorer, Michel Peissel, traveled down the coast, reporting Maya sites at San Lorenzo, San Antonio, Rio Indio, and Guadalupe. Other reports were made in 1973 and again in 1984. Although these were not in-depth studies, with each expedition more unknown archaeological structures were reported.

The coastline itself is a series of sandy beaches and dunes interrupted by rocky promontories that often connect with the offshore Belize Reef that runs along the entire coast. This shore is dominated by still-healthy coconut plantations planted in the early 20th century. Andrews suggests that prehistoric sites located on the high ground behind mangrove-fringed estuaries are likely to have been the parent communities of the fishing villages and camps whose remains have been found along the shoreline. Very little is known about the pre-conquest history of the Xcalak Peninsula because it was already abandoned by the time the Spaniards attemped (unsuccessfully) to establish a village at Espiritu Santo Bay in 1621. However, it became a sanctuary for Maya refugees fleeing Spanish control in the interior as well as a haven for pirates, British logwood cutters, and Belizean fishermen.

Maya construction using chit *palm*

Thick jungle hides many sites that will some day shed more light on the Maya past and their unique lifestyle. One local man tells of vine-shrouded structures where statues remain intact—the average person is not interested in fighting thick undergrowth with machete in hand and wading through muddy swamps to satisfy his or her curiosity. This is the realm of scientists—and (sadly) grave robbers. Hopefully the development and pillage of the Xcalak Peninsula will not move faster than scientific exploration.

PLACER

For the explorer looking for virgin territory, a drive along the Xcalak Peninsula is an adventure—though long! A paved road breaks off the highway (307) just south of the Limones road and meanders toward the sea for 57 km through varied scenery. Much of this land has been cleared of jungle, and small ranchitos are scattered about. In some areas mangrove swamps line the highway and are home to a large variety of birds, including hundreds of egrets and the graceful white heron. However, in August 1989, the "rainy" season, so little rain fell that many of the swamps were dry and the birds were elsewhere. Closer to Hwy. 307, the tall trees which have been left are covered with green and red bromeliads, orchids, and ferns. In spring colorful flowers brighten the landscape.

After about 55 km on this paved road, there's a turnoff to the left (north) going to Uvero and Placer. Many getaway houses are growing up along this part of the coast as well as the beginning of a few small diving destinations. You can count on this area being fairly deserted for a long time, at least until they pave the road! Right now, the road is potholed and extremely rough! It takes about an hour and 10 minutes of slow going to travel to a small resort called **Placer del Caribe** which caters especially to divers. This is a charming place, with four beautifully furnished spacious rooms, hot and cold water, tile bathrooms, comfortable beds, and a broad terrace with cushy chaise lounges to laze on while overlooking the beach and sea. A little farther down the beach Placer del Caribe has four *palapa* bungalows. This resort caters to divers interested in exploring **Chinchorro Bank** and fishermen looking for bonefish. Chinchorro Bank is a virgin wonderland of crystalline water where lobster, conch, and sunken ships are just waiting for

Modern history of the area began with the founding of the port of Xcalak in 1900 as a military base for a project to dredge a canal across the southern end of the peninsula. The project never got off the ground and instead a small rail line was laid between Xcalak and La Aguada on Chetumal Bay. In the following years, lighthouses were built at Xcalak and Punta Herrero. Large coconut plantations of several kilometers each were established at El Uvero and Xcalak. Smaller plantations and fishing camps were set up at Tantaman, Rio Indio, Benque Soya, Majahual, Rio Huach, and Punta Gavilan. In 1910 Xcalak's population numbered 544 with a few additional people scattered among the *cocales* (small coconut plantations) and ranchos along the coast. Many of the original colonizers were Yaqui Indians deported from their homeland in northwestern Mexico following their resistance to the Diaz regime. In the ensuing years, the population has fluctuated. The major industries—*cocales* and fishing—have been disrupted several times with the onslaught of major hurricanes.

divers. Pilots are welcome to land their small planes on a private strip close by (check, it's often closed). Non-divers are welcome, though there's little else to do except relax and enjoy the sun, sea, and stars. There's no electricity at Placer, but the managers run a generator a good part of the evening. Guests enjoy meals family style in the main house. For all information and reservations (recommended) concerning Placer del Caribe, call in the U.S. (800) 237-7552. Drop-in rates in August 1989 were US$75 per room (two persons), meals included. Dive packages for a five-night stay including lodging, meals, boat transportation to dive site, and guide run US$650 pp. These prices have fluctuated a lot over the past two years, call for current information. **Note:** This is a long way from Cancun, so start out early if you don't have reservations—just in case a return trip becomes necessary.

Rancho Catalina

If you continue on the road past Placer del Caribe to km 42, you'll find a simple lodge devoted to fishermen and divers. This small retreat run by an American couple, Kathy and Steve (no language problem here!), is on a white-sand beach dotted with coconut palms. A reef close by makes it perfect for snorkelers as well as fishermen. Away from the busy world, they offer two basic, comfortable rooms with private tiled bathrooms (with more on the drawing board), cold water (admittedly the water pressure is weak and the water merely dribbles out of the faucet), a simple wooden clubhouse, family-style dining, pleasant fellowship, and a boat to take you on fishing or diving expeditions. Prices are US$65 d, including room and all meals. Fishing and diving expeditions extra. For more information write: Kathy Lomax-Brisco, Apto. Postal 77, Chetumal, Quintana Roo 77500, Mexico. Allow plenty of time for your mail to get there and be returned.

MANATEE BREEDING PROGRAM

The state of Florida, under the auspices of the Miami Seaquarium and Dr. Jesse White, has begun a captive/breeding program hoping to learn more about the habits of the manatee and to try to increase the declining numbers. Several manatees have been born in captivity; they along with others that have recuperated from injury or illness will be or have been released into Florida's Crystal River where boat traffic is restricted. They are tagged and closely observed. Florida maintains a 24-hour hotline where people report manatees in need of help for any reason. Rescues can include removing an adult male from a cramped storm drain or rushing to the seaquarium newborns that somehow managed to get separated from their mothers and have washed ashore. These newborns are readily accepted by surrogate-mother manatees and are offered nourishment (by way of a thumb-sized teat under the front flipper) and lots of TLC. Medical aid is given to mammals that have been slashed by boat propellers as a result of cruising boats. The manatee has a playful curiosity and investigates anything found in its underwater environment, many times sustaining grave damage.

OVERLAND TO XCALAK

To go to Xcalak don't turn off to the left onto the unpaved road as you would to get to Placer; stay on the paved road until it dead ends at Majahual on the sea, a geographic point on the map but no town. A military camp guards the point, but they're just a bunch of friendly kids ready with smiles and information (unless, of course, you're a bad guy). Here turn right on the dirt road (south) to reach Xcalak, another 66 km. The jungle along this road hasn't been disturbed much and is teeming with animals and noisy birds. From Majahual, the road parallels the coast to Xcalak. This trip is especially conducive to travel in a small camper. Like an early explorer, you'll discover miles and miles of isolated beach—few facilities, just the turquoise sea, not a very pretty beach, transparent white crabs, a variety of fish waiting to be caught for your dinner, and curious birds checking out the newest visitor to their deserted paradise. It's all free—so far.

Bring plenty of food, water, and especially gasoline since you'll not see another gas station until you're back on the highway. This isolation won't last too much longer, however, as several attempts are being made to open businesses. You'll see a sign that says **Kates Restaurant** at km 8. Aha, you thought, a beachcombing American selling hamburgers and beer. Wrong! Don't say Kates à la Kate Jackson, say Kah-TAYS, as in the gnomes and little people of Maya legend. Very little more than a *palapa* hut, owner Arturo is happy to see visitors and serves fresh fish, strong coffee, beer, and not much more. You can camp on his beach for a small fee, water is available, and that's about it. The turtles still come to lay their eggs during the summer.

About three quarters of the way to Xcalak, you'll run into a surprise—a quaint group of 10 cabañas called **Hotel de Palapas** built of wood and *palapa*, with such niceties (in the middle of nowhere) as private tile bathrooms, hot meals, a bar, and a huge *palapa* roof. This is run by a Dutch woman whose interests include saving and raising baby turtles in a dish pan until she's certain they'll survive alone in the sea. A fascinating lady, she's always delighted to entertain visitors. Rates are about US$30 d. Since she's so far out and has no means of communication it is not really known if she is there from one month to the next. *If* you happen to be in the neighborhood, on your way to Xcalak, or just exploring, look around; if you find her let me know her status.

XCALAK

Xcalak (shka-LAK), a tiny fishing village located across the bay from Chetumal, is the southernmost tip of Quintana Roo. Trekking there is an extraordinary expedition for those with a wellspring of energy and plenty of time. If you plan to stay for a few days, bring your camping gear even though Xcalak does have a small simple hotel (and a large new one is on the drawing board). A couple of *tiendas* sell simple food and supplies. Local fishermen can be hired to take you across the reef to breathtaking **Chinchorro Bank,** 26 km off the coast, which covers a large area (43 km north to south, 17 km east to west). Scuba divers call this world-class diving, with crystal-clear water and a huge variety of colorful fish, delicate coral, and

Xcalak Peninsula

three sunken ships clearly visible from above. Xcalak is just a short distance from a channel that separates Mexico from Belize's Ambergris Caye. In days past, Mexican soldiers dug by hand the often-shallow channel to ensure border security between the two countries.

Back On The Road To Chetumal
On Hwy. 307 between Felipe Carrillo Puerto and Chetumal you'll see turnoff signs for several villages; some have small Maya sites, including **Chacchoben, Ichpaatun, Chichmoul, Tupak, Chacmool, Los Limones**—all minor archaeological sites off the main track but in the middle of the historical area where the Chan Santa Cruz Indians held court for so many years.

BACALAR

Thirty-eight km north of Chetumal (on Hwy. 307) lies a beautiful multihued lagoon called **Las Lagunas de Siete Colores** (The "Lagoon of Seven

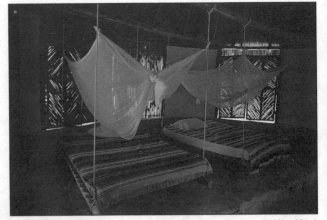

Hanging beds take the place of hammocks in many small resorts along this coast; this is Cabañas Osho.

Colors"). Bacalar, complete with 17th-century. Fort San Felipe, is a small town founded by the Spanish to protect themselves from the bands of pirates and Maya that regularly raided the area. Today, part of the fort has a diminutive museum housing metal arms used in the 17th and 18th centuries. A token assortment of memorabilia recalls history of the area. The stone construction has been restored, and cannons are still posted along the balustrades overlooking beautiful Bacalar Lagoon. The museum is open daily except holidays, small entry fee charged.

Near the town plaza and across from the old fort is a small budget *casa de huespedes*—not fancy, a youth hostel and a trailer park. Close by, built into the side of a hill overlooking the colorful Bacalar Lagoon, is **Hotel Las Lagunas,** moderately priced, with clean rooms and private baths. Special touches make it an out-of-the-ordinary stopover: local shells decorate walls and ceilings, and ornate fences are neatly painted in white and green. The friendly owners, Señor Carlos R. Gutierrez and his wife, can usually be found in the outdoor dining room. A small pool (filled only during high season) and outdoor bar look out across the unusually hued Lagunas de Siete Colores. A diving board and ladder make swimming convenient in the lagoon's sometimes blue, sometimes purple, sometimes red water; fishing is permitted and you can barbecue your catch on the grounds. Rates are about US$25-30 d. Ask about a bungalow including kitchen facilities. Reserve in advance during the tourist season and holidays; the rest of

the year there are few people around. Write: Hotel Laguna, Bacalar, Quintana Roo, Mexico. Send one night's fee and allow plenty of time for the mail to reach its destination.

Close by is the **Laguna Milagros Trailer Park** with tent camping also permitted, about US$2-3 pp. Restrooms, showers, sun shelters, narrow beach, small store, and open-air cafe combine to offer an exotic milieu on the edge of the lagoon.

Rancho Encantado

Thirty-five miles north of Chetumal (200 miles south of Cancun) an enchanting small resort lies on the edge of Bacalar Lagoon. Part of the **Turquoise Reef Group** that specializes in laid-back, relaxing resorts that excel in "doing nothing," this mini resort includes six *casitas* built with native hardwoods and Mexican tile and sits in a lush Eden of tropical shrubs, coco palms, and fruit trees—all just a few steps from the shore of Bacalar Lagoon. Each unit contains a small sitting room, convenience kitchen/dining room, bathroom, stove, refrigerator, and deck with a view of the garden or lagoon. A 40-foot *palapa*-roofed structure is the social center of the resort. Here visitors enjoy a tropical buffet breakfast and candlelit dinner (both included in the room rate; US$110 d including Mexico's 15% tax).

If you don't wish to "do nothing," you can be as vigorous as you desire with a variety of activities. The archaeology buff has the rarely visited **Kohunlich** Maya site with its giant masks close at hand, as well as several undeveloped sites across the border in northern Belize. Take an excursion through the Quintana Roo savannah to tour Mexico's southern Caribbean coastline, or plan a scuba trip to the Caribbean's **Chinchorro Banks.** Rancho Encantado offers boat rides through the mangroves, a picnic on a deserted island, bird-watching, snorkeling, or windsurfing. Ask about the private villa with three bedrooms, 2¹/₂ baths, and private dock located on the waterfront a short distance from Rancho Encantado; price given on request. For more information and reservations contact the Turquoise Reef Group, Box 2664, Evergreen, CO 80439; in Colorado tel. (303) 674-9615, the rest of the U.S. tel. (800) 538-6820, fax (303) 674-8735.

PLACES TO VISIT

Cenote Azul
Thirty-four km north of Chetumal (on Hwy. 307) is a circular *cenote* 61.5 meters deep and 185 meters across filled with brilliant blue water. This is a spectacular place to stop for a swim, lunch at the outdoor restaurant, or just a cold drink.

Kohunlich
Sixty-seven km west of Chetumal on Hwy. 186, turn right and drive eight km on a good side road to this unique Maya site. The construction continued from late Pre-Classic (about A.D. 100-200) through Classic (A.D. 600-900). Though not totally restored nor nearly as grand as Chichen Itza or Uxmal, Kohunlich is worth the trip if only to visit the exotic **Temple of the Masks** dedicated to the Maya sun god. The stone pyramid is under an unlikely thatch roof (to prevent further deterioration from the weather), and unique gigantic stucco masks stand two to three meters tall. The temple, though not extremely tall as pyramids go, still presents a moderate climb. Wander through the jungle site and you can find 200 structures or uncovered mounds from the same era as Palenque. Many carved stelae are scattered throughout the surrounding forest.

Walking through luxuriant foliage, you'll discover a green world. Note orchids in the tops of trees

giant masks of Kohunlich

plus small colorful wildflowers, lacy ferns, and lizards that share cracks and crevices in moldy stone walls covered with velvety moss. The relatively unknown site attracts few tourists. The absence of trinket sellers and soft-drink stands leaves a visitor feeling that he or she is the first to stumble on the haunting masks with their star-incised eyes, mustaches (or are they serpents?), and nose plugs—features extremely different from carvings found at other Maya sites. Even the birds hoot and squawk at your intrusion as if you were the first. Like most archaeological zones, Kohunlich is fenced and opens from 0800-1700; small fee. Camping is not allowed within the grounds, but you may see a tent or two outside the entrance.

CHETUMAL

Chetumal, a good base for the many sights in the southern section of Quintana Roo, is also the gateway to Belize. The capital of this young state, Chetumal is without the bikini-clad, touristy crowds of the north and presents the businesslike atmosphere of a growing metropolis. A 10-minute walk takes you to the waterfront from the marketplace and most of the hotels. Modern sculpted monuments stand along a breezy promenade that skirts the broad crescent of bay. Also explore the back streets, where worn wooden buildings still have a Central American/Caribbean look. The largest building in town—white, three stories, close to the waterfront—houses most of the government offices.

Wide tree-lined avenues and clean sidewalks front dozens of small variety shops. The city has been a free port for many years and as a result has attracted a plethora of tiny shops selling a strange conglomeration of plastic toys, small appliances, exotic perfumes (maybe authentic?), famous-label clothes (ditto), and imported foodstuffs. Because the tax in Chetumal is only six percent instead of the usual 15, it's a popular place for Belizeans and Mexicans to shop. The population is a handsome mixture of many races, including Caribe, Spanish, Maya, and English. Schools are prominently scattered around the town.

CLIMATE

Chetumal is hot and sticky. Though sea breezes help, humidity can make the air terribly uncomfortable. High temperatures in Aug. average 100° F, in Dec. 86° F. In the last 34 years, three destructive hurricanes have attacked the Mexican Caribbean coast, and Hurricane Janet all but destroyed Chetumal in 1955. Not something to be too concerned about though—these devastating blows are infrequent. The most comfortable time to visit is the dry season from Nov. to April.

FLORA AND FAUNA

Chetumal is noted for its hardwood trees, such as mahogany and rosewood. (Abundance of wood explains the difference in rural housing between the north and south ends of the Peninsula. Small houses in the south are built mostly of milled board, some with thatch roofs; structures with circular walls of slender saplings set close together are still common in the north.) Copious rainfall in the Chetumal area creates dense jungle with vine-covered trees, broad-leafed plants, ferns, and colorful blossoms. Orchids grow liberally on the tallest trees. Deer and javelina roam the forests.

SIGHTS

Calderitas Bay
On Av. Heroes eight km north of the city is **Calderitas Bay,** a breezy area for picnicking, camping, and RVing. The trailer park is one of the few in the state that provides complete hookups for RVs, including a dump station and clean showers, toilets, and washing facilities. Right on the water's edge, the spotless camp is in a park-like setting fringed with cooling palm trees. Even amateur divers will find exotic shells, and the fishing is great. Nearby public beaches have *palapa* shelters which are normally tranquil, but on holidays they're crowded with sun- and fun-seekers.

Isla Tamalcas
Tiny **Isla Tamalcas,** two km off the shore of Calderitas, is the home of the primitive *capybara.* This largest of all rodents can reach a length of over a meter and weigh up to 50 kilograms; it's found in few other places in the world. The animal is covered with reddish-yellowish-brown coarse hair, resembles a small pig or large guinea pig, has partially webbed toes, and loves to swim. It's referred to by the locals as a water pig, and is a favorite food of the jaguar. Isla Tamalcas is easily accessible from Calderitas Beach.

ACCOMMODATIONS

Although Chetumal is not considered a tourist resort, its low taxes and location on the Belize border make it a desirable marketplace and busy stopover for both Mexicans and Belizeans. If traveling without reservations, arrive as early in the day as possible to have your choice of hotel rooms. During the holiday season it's wise to reserve in advance. Most of the hotels listed are

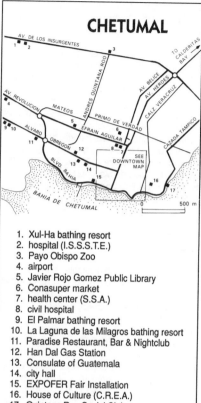

CHETUMAL

1. Xul-Ha bathing resort
2. hospital (I.S.S.S.T.E.)
3. Payo Obispo Zoo
4. airport
5. Javier Rojo Gomez Public Library
6. Conasuper market
7. health center (S.S.A.)
8. civil hospital
9. El Palmar bathing resort
10. La Laguna de las Milagros bathing resort
11. Paradise Restaurant, Bar & Nightclub
12. Han Dal Gas Station
13. Consulate of Guatemala
14. city hall
15. EXPOFER Fair Installation
16. House of Culture (C.R.E.A.)
17. Quintana Roo Social Club

within walking distance of the marketplace, downtown shops, and waterfront.

Higher Priced
Chetumal doesn't have a true luxury hotel. The **Del Prado** (formerly the El Presidente) comes closest with general cleanliness, a/c, pretty garden, and large clean swimming pool, a bar with evening disco music, and a quiet dining room with a friendly staff that serves a varied menu; about US$80 d, Av. Heroes con Chapultepec, tel. 2-05-44. The **Hotel Continental-Caribe** *advertises* itself as luxury, has a/c, restaurant, pool, bar with evening entertainment, and though the rooms are

clean the overall appearance is not. Prices range from about US$65, Av. Heroes 171, tel. 2-04-41.

Moderate

The moderately priced hotels for the most part are friendly (some clean, some not, look before you pay), usually fan-cooled, and have hot water. Prices range from US$12 to US$35 d at: **San Jorge,** Av. Juarez #87, tel. 2-10-65; **Maria Dolores,** Av. Alvaro Obregon #206, tel. 2-05-08; and **Tulum,** Av. Heroes #2, tel. 2-05-18. The following hotels are small, modern, friendly, have a/c, restaurant, bar, and evening entertainment: **Hotel Real Azteca,** Av. Belize #186, tel. 2-07-20; **El Dorado Hotel,** Av. 5 de Mayo #21, tel. 2-03-15; and **Hotel Caribe Princess,** Av. Alvaro Obregon #180, tel. 2-09-00. Prices begin at US$15.

Budget

The budget traveler has a choice of several hotels, a youth hostel at Bacalar, or camping at Calderitas Bay. Some of the *posadas* are Spartan without hot water; a few have food available. At the following hotels, prices range from about US$10: **Colonial,** Benjamin Hill #135, tel. 2-15-20; **Tabasco,** Av. Zaragoza #206, tel. 2-20-45; **America,** Othon P. Blanco #11.

FOOD

It's easy to find a cafe to fit every budget in Chetumal. Walk down the street to Av. Alvaro Obregon for several fast-food cafes. On the same street, for seafood try **El Pez Vela;** for chicken go to **Pollos Sinaloa.** On the corner of Av. Efrain Aguilar and Revolucion is **Los Pozos,** a regional cafe serving typical Yucatecan dishes. If your taste buds yearn for good American red meat, try **Buffalo Steak,** Av. Alvaro Obregon #208. For *helado* and *postres* try **Carlena,** Av. A. Lopez Mateos #407, or **Fonagora,** on the corner of Av. Heroes con Lazaro Cardenas. The **public market** has just about everything you could need; three **Conasuper** markets can provide the rest.

ENTERTAINMENT

For dancing, try one of these small discotheques: **El Elefante,** Blvd. Bahia; **Focus** at the Hotel Continental, Av. Heroes #171; **Huanos Astoria,** Av.

Reforma #27; **Sarawak** at Hotel Del Prado, Av. Heroes and Chapultepec. Cinemas and theaters include: **Campestre,** Av. A. Lopez Mateos con Milan; **Avila Camacho,** Calle 22 de Enero; **Leona Vicario,** Av. Alvaro Obregon and Independencia; **Cine Juventino Rosas,** Av. Hidalgo. The larger hotels usually have a TV in the lobby; the Del Prado Hotel provides one for each room. **Javier Rojo Gomez Public Library** is on Av. Efrain Aguilar.

SPORTS

A yearly event in Chetumal is the auto road race. Open to drivers from all over the globe, it's gaining prominence in the racing world. This event takes place in December and hotel reservations should be made well in advance.

A popular sport in both Chetumal Bay and Bacalar Lagoon is windsurfing. State competitions are held in both areas yearly. What a great place to fly across the sea! Make reservations early since many others will have the same idea. For

children's parade on the first day of spring, Chetumal

more information, write to the Secretaria de Turismo, Palacio de Gobierno #20. Piso, Chetumal, Quintana Roo 77500, Mexico.

SERVICES

The **post office** is on Calle 2 A. You can send a telegram from **Telegrafos Nacionales,** Av. 5 de Mayo. **Long-distance** phone calls can be made from Tico-Tico, Av. Alvaro Obregon #7, or Novedades Caribe, Av. Heroes. For any **medical** emergency, there are several hospitals and clinics. Ask at your hotel for a doctor who speaks English. One **pharmacy** is on Carmen Ochoa de Merino y Heroes, tel. 2-01-62. Four **gasoline stations** and at least seven mechanics are in town. Several **banks** will cash travelers cheques Mon. to Sat. 0900-1300. First- and 2nd-class buses use the new bus station on the outskirts of town. Ask about the Batty Bus to Belize that makes the trip daily. A visit to the **tourism office** is helpful; ask for their *Guia Turistica,* which lists cultural activities, monuments, and murals open to the public along with addresses of all banks and other solid information about Chetumal.

TRANSPORT

By Air
Chetumal's small modern airport still has only a few flights each day. An airport van provides transportation to hotels or downtown. Check with Aeromexico and Aerocaribe for possible flights in and out of Chetumal.

By Bus
Buses from points all over Mexico arrive throughout the day at the new modern Chetumal bus station located on the highway south of town. Taxis are available from the station into town. With the expanding road system, bus travel is becoming more versatile and is still the most inexpensive public transportation to the Quintana Roo coast. Buses to Chetumal arrive from Merida (5½ hours) and Mexico City (22 hours), plus frequent trips from Cancun and Campeche.

By Car
A good paved road connects Merida, Campeche, Villahermosa, and Francisco Escarcega to Chetu-

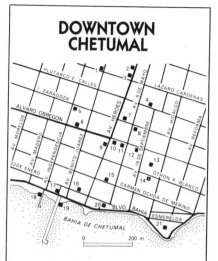

DOWNTOWN CHETUMAL

1. telephone office
2. El Presidente Restaurant
3. El Caracol Shopping Center and Fonagora (cultural center)
4. post and telegraph offices
5. Conasuper market
6. Leona Vicario Cinema
7. Arts and Crafts House
8. Superfama supermarket
9. Big Ben Hotel
10. Baroudi Hotel
11. Sergio's Pizza
12. Caribe Princess Hotel
13. Josefa Ortiz de Dominguez Gardens
14. Sagrado Corazon de Jesus Church
15. Aeromexico Airlines
16. state government office
17. Immigration Office
18. Fishing Club
19. El Mulle Amusement Park for Children
20. Sailor's Monument
21. state congress

mal; Hwy. 307 links all of the Quintana Roo coastal cities. There's little traffic, and gas stations are well spaced if you top off at each one. Car rentals are not yet available at the Chetumal airport; go to the Del Prado Hotel for Avis. Chetumal is an economical place to rent your car since there's only a six percent tax instead of the usual fifteen.

CROSSING INTO BELIZE

Chetumal, Mexico, is a bridge away from the country of Belize. For the explorer, the archaeology buff, the diver, or the curious, it's easy to take a side trip into what was formerly British Honduras. The Rio Hondo River forms a natural border between Quintana Roo and Belize. Chetumal is the only land link between the two countries, from which Belize is easily reached by Batty bus or taxi. There's rarely a problem crossing the border as long as you show a valid passport. If you look poor you'll be asked to show money or proof of onward travel. If driving you must buy insurance with Belizean dollars; money-changers are waiting for you as you cross the border. The rates seem comparable to bank rates; however, you always take a slight risk when you buy local money from a street vendor. U.S. citizens and *most* others don't need visas, but a few countries do; check with your embassy before leaving home. Other than U.S. citizens that plan to travel on to Guatemala from Belize, check with the Guatemalan Embassy in Chetumal; Guatemala is not represented in Belize.

Tour Group
If you have never visited Belize, you may find the first time easier with a tour guide who knows his way around the country. Many are available from the States and Canada. **International Expeditions,** a company out of Alabama offers several good trips with small groups and each expedition is designed for your particular interest. For the nature lover an 11-day **Naturalist Quest** expedition offers all transportation, lodging, and most important, is accompanied by a knowledgeable naturalist that takes the group into the beautiful forests and State Reserves created to save the treasures of Belize, including the **Jaguar Sanctuary** and the **Howler Monkey Sanctuary**. Another expedition visits most of the Maya archaeological sites in the country with a guide who knows how to bring to life the story of the Maya. Those interested in the offshore cayes will find a trip to Belize's islands a relaxing way to investigate the rich sealife of the Belize Reef. Ask about trips to nearby Costa Rica. For more information contact **International Expeditions,** 1776 Independence Court, Birmingham, AL 35216, tel. (800) 633-4734, (205) 870-5550. For details about traveling in Belize including accommodations, restaurants, attractions, diving, and everything else you ever wanted to know about the country, buy *Belize Handbook,* my newest book published by Moon Publications (see the ad in the back of this book).

ESCORTED TRIPS TO THE YUCATAN PENINSULA

A Potpourri Of Trips

A unique bus company, **Green Tortoise,** takes travelers of a special ilk all over the U.S. in buses that have rebuilt interiors to accommodate sleeping and seating. And though the Green Tortoise goes to many places, we'll give you the specifics for trips to the Yucatan Peninsula with other like-minded folks who enjoy "doing" things in Mexico during the day and traveling at night while one of two drivers (always two drivers on trips to Mexico) takes the wheel. Travelers bring sleeping bags and sleep on foam-covered platforms and bunks in the bus; meals are cook-out affairs where everyone helps. This is much like a camping trip and if you need a regular shower more than two-three times a week, better not come. There are no toilet facilities on the bus, but stops are planned to meet passengers' needs. The itineraries are decided beforehand and once in a region, a day is loosely planned with as much free time as desired by passengers. Food is not included in the fare; meals in a city are the responsibility of the passenger, for cook-outs everyone chips in US$3 per meal. Trips planned include the **Jungle-Yucatan-Highlands Loop,** 3¹/₂ weeks, US$699 plus food and one-way airfare from Mexico City to home; **Golden**

Coast-Jungle Loop, combining San Francisco and Mexico City-Yucatan, 5¹/₂ weeks, US$699 plus food plus one-way airfare from Mexico City to home; **Yucatan-Belize Loop,** RT from Mexico City, 3¹/₂ weeks, US$599 plus food plus roundtrip airfare to Mexico City. For more information contact Green Tortoise Adventure Travel, Box 24459, San Francisco, CA 94124, tel. (415) 821-0803.

Vagabonders is the travel division of the **Turquoise Reef Group.** The Vagabonders' **Dive Bundle** includes seven nights and eight days. A diver's surf-and-turf splurge on the Turquoise Reef includes lodging, meals, four two-tank dive days, and more. Another special trip is called the **Vagabonder's Whole Enchilada,** 14 nights and 15 days spent making a circle of three countries of the Maya world (Belize, Mexico, and Guatemala) with relaxing intervals on the beaches of the Caribbean. Includes lodging, meals, guides, transportation and more. Some of these trips are offered to guests already at a Turquoise Reef Resort in the state of Quintana Roo and originate from one of three locations along Mexico's Caribbean coast: Kai Luum, Capitan Lafitte, or Shangri-La Caribe. The **Vagabonder's Potpourri** is a five-night/six-day trip that gives the traveler an

a camping tour

intimate look at the Yucatan Peninsula, with its Maya treasures, and a taste of village and city life. This journey includes Merida, Uxmal, Labna, Sayil, Kabah, Chichen Itza, Valladolid, Coba, Tulum, and Xelha. For more information contact the Vagabonders, Box 2664, Evergreen, CO 80439, tel. (303) 674-9615 or (800) 538-6802.

Far Horizons: Cultural Discovery Trips originate in Miami, Dallas, or Los Angeles. First stop is the **Museum of Anthropology** in Mexico City where an overview of Maya prehistoric culture will be explained; from there a visit to Teotihuacan will illustrate how that ancient city heavily influenced Maya art and architecture. Other areas of Maya culture visited include Palenque, Tulum, Coba, Edzna, Labna, Sayil, Kabah, Uxmal, Rio Bec, and Chichen Itza. For more information write or call Far Horizons, Box 1529, San Anselmo, CA 94960, tel. (415) 457-4575.

Tropical Adventures offers a complete dive package in Isla Cozumel. The package includes seven nights at one of the top oceanfront resorts (choices include budget lodgings for less), boat diving, beach buffet lunches on all full-day dives, boats, guides, tanks, weights, belts, backpacks, and unlimited air for shore diving. Cozumel is considered a world-class dive site, plus offers the bonus of a multitude of archaeological sights to see on land. Low airfares available through Tropical Adventures. For more information call or write Tropical Adventures, 170 Denny Way, Seattle, WA 98109, tel. (800) 247-3483 or (206) 441-3483, fax (206) 441-5431.

For the explorer interested in seeing the colonial as well as the low-key part of Mexico's Caribbean, **Mex Treks** offers a 10-day adventure excursion which combines the vibrant and colorful city of Merida (and its many nearby Maya archaeological sites) with the private **Jungle Island Hideaway** on the Caribbean Sea. In Merida accommodations are at an intimate old colonial home with terraces, pool, art, and tropical foliage. At the **Habitat**, the primitive diving and fishing camp is on the wild south coast of Quintana Roo in the middle of a working coconut plantation within Sian Ka'an, the national ecological reserve comprising more than 1.3 million acres. The Habitat fronts the beach, where on one side guests will find sand dunes, sea, and the offshore barrier reef (fifth largest in the world) and on the other side a huge inland estuary bordered by mangrove swamps, coconut forests, and nesting islands for many varieties of tropical birds. The jungle stands on the opposite shore of the estuary. Time is spent snorkeling or scuba diving, fishing, exploring the jungle, or lying in the sun. For more information write to Mex Treks, Calle 68 #495, Merida, Yucatan 97000, Mexico, tel. 21-40-32/21-46-55. Allow plenty of time for roundtrip mail to Yucatan.

Honeymoon time is anytime and the **Honeymoon Of Your Dreams Plus** is waiting at the Cancun Sheraton Resort and Towers. This special package includes a luxury suite with terrace and private jacuzzi, daily breakfast in your room or in the restaurant, domestic champagne, welcome drink, free day or night tennis and free use of the fitness center. Three nights and four days, US$539 per couple. Or another choice at the same hotel is the **Honeymoon Down Mexico Way** in the new deluxe **Towers,** where guests will enjoy a Caribbean view, welcome drink, daily continental breakfast in the lounge, bottle of domestic champagne, free day and night tennis and complimentary use of the fitness center along with very special butler service; three nights, four days, US$369 per couple.

Underwater Adventure Tours offers seven-night trips to Cozumel. Accommodations are at **La Ceiba** beachfront hotel and include daily dive/boat trips to Palancar Reef and vicinity, unlimited air for offshore diving, tanks, backpacks, and weights. A five-night trip is also available which includes daily breakfast, standard accommodations, four boat trips to Palancar Reef and vicinity, air, equipment, and 15% tax. For more information call or write Underwater Adventure Tours, 732 W. Fullerton, Chicago, IL 60614, tel. (800) 621-1274.

Bargain Hunting?

For those travelers looking for bargains, **Cancun Yucatan Adventures,** a company located in Petaluma, California, deals exclusively with tour packages to Cancun and the Yucatan Peninsula. It advertises that it can beat any prices you can come up with. They handle 30 different properties and use Mexicana airlines. Clients stay not only in hotels, but also in condos and lovely villas along the Caribbean coast. For more information call (800) 6-Cancun.

BOOKLIST

The following titles provide insight into the Yucatan Peninsula and the Maya people. A few of these books are easier obtained in Mexico, but all of them will cost less in the U.S. Most are non-fiction, though several are fiction and great to pop into your carry-on for a good read on the plane, or for any time you want to get into the Yucatecan mood. Happy reading.

Coe, Michael D. *The Maya.* New York: Thames and Hudson, 1980. A well-illustrated, easy-to-read volume on the Maya people.

Cortes, Hernan. *Five Letters.* Gordon Press, 1977. Cortes wrote long letters to the king of Spain telling of his accomplishments and trying to justify his actions in the New World.

Davies, Nigel. *The Ancient Kingdoms of Mexico.* New York: Penguin Books. Excellent study of pre-conquest (1519) indigenous people of Mexico.

De Landa, Bishop Diego. *Yucatan Before and After the Conquest.* New York: Dover Publications, 1978. This book, translated by William Gates from the original 1566 volume, has served as the base for all research that has taken place since. De Landa (though the man destroyed countless books of the Maya people) has given the world insight into their culture before the conquest.

Diaz del Castillo, Bernal. *The Conquest of New Spain.* New York: Penguin Books, 1963. History straight from the adventurer's reminiscences, translated by J.M. Cohen.

Fehrenbach, T.R. *Fire and Blood: A History of Mexico.* New York: Collier Books, 1973. 3,500 years of Mexico's history told in a way to keep you reading.

Ferguson, William M. *Maya Ruins of Mexico in Color.* Norman: University of Oklahoma Press, 1977. Good reading before you go, but too bulky to carry along. Oversized with excellent drawings and illustrations of the archaeological structures of the Maya Indians.

Franz, Carl. *The People's Guide to Mexico.* New Mexico: John Muir Publications, 1972. A humorous guide filled with witty anecdotes and helpful general information for visitors to Mexico. Don't expect any specific city information, just nuts and bolts hints for traveling south of the border.

Greene, Graham. *The Power and the Glory.* New York: Penguin Books, 1977. A novel that takes place in the '20s about a priest and the anti-church movement that gripped the country.

Heffern, Richard. *Secrets of the Mind-Altering Plants of Mexico.* New York: Pyramid Books. A fascinating study of many subtances used from the ancients in ritual hallucinogens to today's medicines.

Laughlin, Robert M. *The People of the Bat.* Smithsonian Institution Press, 1988. Maya tales and dreams as told by the Zinacantan Indians in Chiapas.

Lewbel, George S. *Diving and Snorkeling Guide to Cozumel.* New York: Pisces Books, 1984. A well-illustrated volume for divers and snorkelers going to Cozumel. The small, easily carried volume is packed with hints about different dive sites, reefs, and marinelife of Cozumel.

Meyer, Michael, and William Sherman. *The Course of Mexican History.* Oxford University Press. A concise one-volume history of Mexico.

Nelson, Ralph. *Popul Vuh: The Great Mythological Book of the Ancient Maya.* Boston: Houghton Mifflin, 1974. An easy-to-read translation of myths handed down orally by the Quiche Maya, family to family, until written down after the Spanish conquest.

Riding, Alan. *Distant Neighbors*. Vintage Books. A modern look at today's Mexico.

Sodi, Demetrio M. (in collaboration with Adela Fernandez). *The Mayas*. Mexico: Panama Editorial S.A. This small pocketbook presents a fictionalized account of life among the Maya before the conquest. Easy reading for anyone who enjoys fantasizing about what life *might* have been like before recorded history in the Yucatan. This book is available in the Yucatecan states of Mexico.

Stephens, John L. *Incidents of Travel in Central America, Chiapas, and Yucatan*. 2 vols. New York: Dover Publications, 1969. Good companions to refer to when traveling in the area. Stephens and illustrator Catherwood rediscovered many of the Maya ruins on their treks that took place in the mid-1800s. Easy reading.

Thompson, J. Eric. *Maya Archaeologist*. Norman: University of Oklahoma, 1963. Thompson, a noted Maya scholar, traveled and worked at most of the Maya ruins in the 1930s.

Thompson, J. Eric. *The Rise and Fall of the Maya Civilization*. Norman: University of Oklahoma Press, 1954. One man's story of the Maya Indian. Excellent reading.

Werner, David. *Where There is No Doctor*. California: The Hesperian Foundation. This is an invaluable medical aid to anyone traveling not only to isolated parts of Mexico, but to anyplace in the world where there's not a doctor.

Wolf, Eric. *Sons of the Shaking Earth*. University of Chicago Press. An anthropological study of Indian and Mestizo people of Mexico and Guatemala.

Wright, Ronald. *Time Among the Maya*. New York: Weidenfeld & Nicolson, 1989. A narrative that takes the reader through Maya country of today with historical comments that help put the puzzle together.

MAYAN GLOSSARY

MAYA GODS AND CEREMONIES

Ahau Can — Serpent lord and highest priest

Ahau Chamehes — Deity of medicine

Acanum — Protective deity of hunters

Ah Cantzicnal — Aquatic deity

Ah Chhuy Kak — God of violent death and sacrifice

Ixchell — Goddess of birth, fertility, medicine and credited with inventing spinning.

Ahcit Dzamalcum — Protective god of fishermen

Ah Cup Cacap — God of the underworld who denies air

Ah Itzam — The water witch

Ah kines — Priests, lords who consult the oracles, who celebrate ceremonies and preside over sacrifices.

Ahpua — God of fishing

Ah Puch — God of death

Ak'Al — Sacred marsh where water abounds

Bacaboob — The *poureres,* supporters of the sky and guardians of the cardinal points, who form a single god, *Ah Cantzicnal Bacab.*

Bolontiku — The nine lords of the night

Cihuateteo — Women-goddesses who become divine through death in childbirth (Nahuatl word)

Chac — God of rain and agriculture

Chac Bolay Can — The butcher serpent living in the underworld

Chaces — Priest's assistants in agricultural and other ceremonies

Cit Chac Coh — God of war

Hetxmek — Ceremony when the child is first carried astride the hip

Hobnil Bacab — The bee god, protector of beekeepers

Holcanes — The brave warriors charged with obtaining slaves for sacrifice. (This word was unknown until the post-classic era.)

Itzamna — Lord of the skies, creator of the beginning, god of time

Hunab Ku — Giver of life, builder of the universe and father of Itzamna

Ik — God of the wind

Ixtab — Goddess of the cord and of suicide by hanging

Kinich — Face of the sun

Kukulcan — *Quetzal*-serpent, plumed serpent

Metnal — The underworld, place of the dead

Nacom — Warrior chief

Noh Ek — Venus

Pakat — God of violent death

Zec — Spirit lords of beehives

FOOD AND DRINK

alche — Inebriating drink, sweetened with honey and used for ceremonies and offerings.

Ic — chili

Itz — sweet potato

Kabaxbuul — The heaviest meal of the day, eaten at dusk and containing cooked black beans.

Kah — pinole flour

Kayem — ground maize

Macal — A type of root

Muxubbak—tamale

On—avocado

P'ac—tomatos

Op—plum

Uah—tortillas

Tzamna—black bean

Za—maize drink

Put—papaya

ANIMALS

Acehpek—dog used for deer hunting

Ah Maax Cal—the prattling monkey

Ah Maycuy—the chestnut deer

Ah xixteel Ul—the rugged land conch

Yac—mountain cat

Yaxum—mythical green bird

Bil—hairless dog reared for food

Ah Sac Dziu—the white thrush

Cutz—wild turkey

Cutzha—duck

Hoh—crow

Icim—owl

Keh—deer

Kitam—wild boar

Muan—evil bird related to death

Que—parrot

Thul—rabbit

Utiu—coyote

Tzo—domestic turkeys

Jaleb—hairless dog

MUSIC AND FESTIVALS

Zacatan—a drum made from a hollowed tree trunk, with one opening covered with hide.

Ah Paxboob—musicians

Bexelac—turtle shell used as percussion instrument

Chul—flute

Chohom—dance performed in ceremonies during the month of *Zip,* related to fishing.

Hom—trumpet

Tunkul—drum

Kayab—percussion instrument fashioned from turtle shell

Okot uil—dance performed during the *Pocan* ceremony

Oc na—festival of the month of *Yax.* Old idols of the temple are broken and replaced with new.

Pacum chac—festival in honor of the war gods

ELEMENTS OF TIME

Chumuc Kin—midday

Chunkin—midday

Chumuc akab—midnight

Haab—Solar calendar of 360 days which is made up with five extra days of misfortune which complete the final month.

Emelkin—sunset

Kin—the sun, the day, the unity of time

Kaz akab—dusk

Potakab—time before dawn

Yalhalcab—dawn

PLANTS AND TREES

Kan ak—plant that produces a yellow dye

Kikche—tree of which the trunk is used to make canoes

Kuche—red cedar tree

Ki—sisal

Kiixpaxhkum—chayote

K'uxub—annatto tree

Piim—fibre of the cotton tree

Taman—cotton plant

Tauch—black *zapote*

Tazon te—moss

Ha—cacao seed

MISCELLANEOUS WORDS

Yuntun—slings

Xul—stake with a pointed fire-hardened tip

Xanab—sandals

Xicul—sleeveless jacket decorated with feathers

Ah Kay Kin Bak—meat seller

Cha te—black vegetable dye

Chi te—eugenia, plant for dyeing

Ch'oh—indigo

Ek—dye

Chaltun—water cistern

Halach uinic—leader

Hadzab—wooden swords

Mayacimil—smallpox epidemic, "easy death"

Pic—underskirt

Ploms—rich people

Suyen—square blanket

NUMBERS

hun	one
ca	two
ox	three
can	four
ho	five
uac	six
uuc	seven
uacax	eight
bolon	nine
iahun	ten
buluc	eleven
iahca	twelve
oxlahum	thirteen
canlahum	fourteen
holahun	fifteen
uaclahun	sixteen
uuclahun	seventeen
uacaclahun	eighteen
bolontahun	nineteen
hunkal	twenty

SPANISH GLOSSARY

While on the Yucatan Peninsula you'll find many people in the larger cities who speak English. However, once you're in rural villages and isolated beaches, speaking Spanish becomes a necessity. Most Mexican people appreciate the effort you make, even if it's not perfect. On the peninsula don't be surprised to find some people who speak no English or Spanish, only a Mayan dialect. This group grows smaller every year.

The ideal way to prepare for your trip is to begin practicing Spanish before you leave. Most bookstores in the States sell simple Spanish-language tapes that are accompanied by a book. These tapes are great in the car on the way to work, while shaving, gardening, doing the dishes, etc. Repetition succeeds.

Berlitz's *Spanish For Travelers* is a great help used along with a pocket dictionary. It is quite common in Mexico's hotel gift shops, but small English-Spanish dictionaries are not as common. Buy them before you leave home. Mayan language dictionaries are not as easy to find, though limited grammar books are available on the peninsula.

Spanish is not difficult to speak if you learn a few simple grammatical rules:

Vowels:
a: pronounced as in father
e: as in ray
i: as in gasoline
o: as in stole
u: as in crude

Consonants are similar to those in English. A few exceptions:
g: before a, o, or u pronounced hard as in go; before e or i pronounced like an *h*.
h: silent
j: pronounced like an English *h* (with air)
ll: like *y* in you
n: pronounced ny as in Spanish senor

q: pronounced as *k*
r: rolled with the tongue (takes a little practice)
x: between vowels it's pronounced like a gutteral *h* as in Spanish Oaxaca
y: pronounced ee

GREETINGS

Hello, Hi.	*Hola!* or *Bueno!*
Good day.	*Buenas dias* (in the morning). *Buenas tardes* (in the afternoon).
Good night.	*Buenas noches.*
How are you?	*Como esta usted?*
Very well.	*Muy bien.*
How goes it?	*Que tal?*
Goodbye.	*Adios* or *Hasta la vista.*
So long.	*Hasta luego.*
Please.	*Por favor.*
Thank you.	*Muchas gracias.*
You're welcome.	*De nada.*

COMMON EXPRESSIONS

Just a moment, please.	*Un momento, por favor. Momentito*
Excuse me.	*Perdoneme. Disculpeme.*
I am sorry.	*Lo siento.*
Do you speak English?	*Habla ingles?*
Do you understand me?	*Me comprende? Me entiende?*
I don't understand.	*No entiendo.*
I don't know.	*No se.*
How do you say ... in Spanish?	*Come se dice ... en espanol?*
What?	*Como?*
Please repeat.	*Mande?*
Show me.	*Enseneme.*

This is good.	Esta bueno.
This is bad.	Esta malo.
Yes.	Si.
No.	No.
What time is it?	Que hora es?
What's going on?	Que pasa?
How much is it?	Cuanto cuesta?

GETTING AROUND

Take me to	Lleveme a ....
Where is ...?	Donde esta ...?
the road to ...	el camino a ...
Follow this street.	Siga esta calle.
Which way?	Por donde?
near	cerca
far	lejos
to the right, ...left	a la derecha, ...izquierda
straight ahead	derecho
open, closed	abierto, cerrado
How far?	Hasta donde?
entrance, exit	la entrada, la salida
airplane	avion
airport	el aeropuerto
airline office	la oficina de aviones
train station	la estacion de tren, ...del ferrocarril
taxi stand	el sitio
taxi	el taxi
Please call me a taxi.	Pidame un taxi, por favor.
How long does it take to go there?	Cuanto se tarda en llegar?
What will you charge me to take me to ...?	Cuanto me covra para llevarme a ...?
bus	autobus or camion
bus stop	la parada
How much is a ticket to ...?	Cuanto cuesta un boleto a ...?
When are there buses to ...?	A que hora hay camiones a ...?
I want a ticket to	Quiero un boleto a ....
Is there a toilet on the bus?	Hay bano en el camion?
Where does this bus go?	Donde va este autobus?

When does one (it) leave?	Cuando sale? (...llega?)
Down! (To tell the bus driver you want to get off the bus.)	Bajan!
I'm going to	Me voy a ....
reserved seat	asiento reservado
reservation	reservacion
first class	primera clase
second class	segunda clase

CAR AND MAINTENANCE

gas station	una gasolinera
gas	gasolina
regular (gas)	nova
Fill it up, please.	Lleno, por favor.
Please check the oil.	Vea el aceite, por favor.
brakes	los frenos
map	el mapa
air	aire
radiator	el radiador
battery	la bateria
repair garage	un taller mecanico
mechanic	un mecanico
jack	un gato
towtruck	un grua
tire	una llanta
hole	bache
speed	velocidad
stop	alto
traffic bumps	topes

SERVICES

telegraph office	la oficina de telegrafos
public telephone	el telefono publica
post office	el correo
How much is it?	Cuanto cuesta?
postage stamp	estampilla
post card	tarjeta ostal
bank	el banco
Where is the ladies' room? ...the men's room?	Donde esta el bano de damas? ...de senores?

ACCOMMODATIONS

hotel	*un hotel*
a room	*un cuarto*
single	*sencillo*
double	*doble*
triple	*para tres*
with a ceiling fan	*con ventilador*
with air conditioning	*con aire acondicionado*
without air conditioning	*sin aire acondicionado*
bed	*la cama*
hammock	*la hamaca*
pillow	*la almohada*
blanket	*la cobija*
towel	*la toalla*
bathroom	*el bano*
shower	*la regadera*
soap	*jabon*
toilet paper	*papel sanitario*
hot water	*agua caliente*
cold water	*agua fria*
quiet	*tranquilo*
bigger	*mas grande*
smaller	*mas pequeno*
with a view	*con vista*

DINING

restaurant	*un restaurante*
breakfast	*desayuno*
lunch	*almuerzo*
lunch special	*la comida corrida*
supper	*cena*
dinner	*comida*
menu	*la carta*
house specialty	*especialidad de la casa*
knife	*un cuchillo*
fork	*un tenedor*
spoon	*una cuchara*
napkin	*una servilleta*
plate	*platillo*
salt	*sal*
pepper	*pimienta*
butter	*mantequilla*
bread	*pan*
French (style) bread	*pan blanco*

sweet roll	*pan dulce*
pastries	*postres*
roll	*bolillo*
sandwich on a roll	*torta*
toast	*tostada*
coffee	*cafe*
cold water	*agua helada*
hot water	*agua caliente*
purified	*purificada*
soft drink	*un refresco*
beverages	*las bebidas*
liquified fruit drink	*liquado*
ice	*hielo*
the bill	*la cuenta*
tax	*impuesto*
tip	*propina*
waiter	*el mesero,* or more commonly: *joven*
to get a waiter's attention	*Oiga!*
Bring me	*Traigame ....*
beer	*cerveza*
a table	*una mesa*

calabash	small tree native to the Caribbean whose fruit, a gourd, is dried and used as a container on the peninsula
calesa	horse-drawn buggy seen in some cities on the peninsula
chiliquiles	Corn chips and bits of chicken
cochinita or *pollo pibil*	chicken baked with spices in banana leaves
conch	large edible mollusk common to the Caribbean; often eaten as *ceviche* or pounded and fried
escabeche	spicy Spanish style of cooking meat and game
naranja	a sour orange used extensively in cooking
panuchos	small fried tortillas topped with blackbeans, lettuce, meat or poultry, and spices
pok chuc	broiled meat, tomato, onion, and sour orange
sopa de lima	chicken broth, lime juice, tomato, onion

INDEX

Page numbers in *italics* indicate information in captions, callouts, charts, illustrations, or maps.

A

Abrigo Bay: 240
accommodations: 37-39; *see also* specific place
activities: 44-47; *see also* specific place
agriculture: 2-3, 40-41
Agua Azul: 195-196
Agua Blanca Falls: 217-218
Aguada Grande: 238
Aguilar, Geronimo de: in Quintana Roo 226
airlines: *see* transportation/specific place
Akumal: 309-313; accommodations 311-312; beach 310; entertainment 313; flora 309; food 312-313; history 310; shopping 313; water activities 310-311
Alecrane Reef: diving on 77
amber: 171
Amentenango del Valle: 185
anteaters: 10
antiques: in Merida 90
Arch of Kabah: 137
archaeological sites: Bonampak 197-200; Campeche state 145; vicinity of Campeche 155-159; in Cancun 251; in Chiapas 165; Chichen Itza 111-119; vicinity of Chichen Itza 119-120; Coba 323-326; in Comitan 185; vicinity of Escarcega 162-164; in Isla Mujeres 277; in Izamal 109-110; Kohunlich 339; Loltun Caves 140-141; vicinity of Merida 98-102; Palenque 186-190; vicinity of Palenque 195; in Quintana Roo 225; in San Miguel de Cozumel 238-239; in Tabasco 201; Tulum 318-322; in Uxmal 129-135; vicinity of Uxmal 136-139; Villahermosa 204; Yaxchilan 200; in Yucatan state *71*; on Xcalak Peninsula 337

armadillos: 9-10
art galleries: in Merida 90
art, Maya: 28-29

B

Bacalar: 221, 337-339
Balankanche Caves: 119
ballparks, Maya: 29
banks: *see* services/specific place
Barracuda Reef: scuba diving at 245
Bazar Ishcanal (Tuxtla Gutierrez): 172
beaches: 46; in Cancun 252-254; in Isla Mujeres 279; in Progreso 104; in Rio Lagartos 124-125, *126*; in San Miguel de Cozumel 239-242; *see also* specific place
Becan: 163
Belize: 344
Belize Reef: 2
Bird Island: 330
birds/birdwatching: 11-13, 47; in Cancun 251-252; in Celestun 100; in Contoy 288; in Rio Lagartos 125-126; on Xcalak Peninsula 339; *see also* fauna/specific place
Blom, Frans: 176; in Tabasco state 204; in Uxmal 130
Blom, Gertrude Duby: 176
Bonampak: 197-200, *197*
bullfighting: 33-34; in San Miguel de Cozumel 234
butterflies: 13, *13*

C

Calakmul Reserve: 163-164
calendar, Maya: 27
Caleritas Bay: 341
cameras: 63-64
Campeche City: 145-154, *149*; accommodations 149-151, *150*; entertainment 151-152; food 151-152; history 145-147;

services 152-153; sights 147-149; transportation 153-154; vicinity of 155-159
Campeche, state of: *3*, 143-164, *144*; climate 143; economy 145; fauna 143; history 144; land 143
camping: 37; *see also* accommodations/specific place
Cancun: 249-274, *250, 252*; accommodations 258-267, *261-263, 264-265*; beaches 252-254; economy 24; entertainment 270-272; food 267-270; services 272-273; sights 251-252; sports 258; transportation 273-274
capybara: 341
Cardona Reef: scuba diving at 245
car rental: 54-55
Casas, Bartolome de las: 166; in San Cristobal de las Casas 175
Caste War: 19-20, 69, 72
Castillo Real: 241
Catherwood, Frederick: 2; in Palenque 186; in Quintana Roo 251; in Uxmal 129
caymans: 8
Cayo Colebre: trips to 331
CEDAM: 320
CEDAM Museum (Puerto Aventuras): 308
Celestun: 100-102, *100*
Cenote Azul: 339
cenotes: 1-2
ceremonies: Maya 26-27
Cerro de las Perdices: 217
Chaacal I: 186
Chabihau: 108
Chacchoben: 337
Chachaool rite: 180
Chacmool: 337
Champoton: 159-160
Chamula Indians: 167, 178-179
Chan-Bahlum: 186

Chankanab Bay: 239-240
Chankanab Caves: scuba diving at 244
Chankanab Lagoon: 239, *239;* scuba diving at 244
Chankanab National Park: 226
Chankanab Reef: scuba diving at 244
Chan Santa Cruz Indians: 20, 318, 332
Chemuyil: 314-315
Chen Rio: 241
Chetumal: *3,* 340-343, *341, 343;* accommodations 341-342; climate 340; entertainment 342; fauna 340-341; flora 340-341; food 342; services 343; sights 341; sports 342; transportation 343
Chiapa de Corzo: 173-174
Chiapas, state of: *3,* 165-200; climate 165; economy 166-167; history 165-166; land 165; people 167
Chicana: 162-163
Chichen Itza: 111-119, *112, 121;* accommodations 116-117; entertainment 118; food 118; services *113;* sights 113-116; tours 346; transportation 118-119; vicinity of 119-120
Chichmoul: 337
chicle: in Quintana Roo 226-227
Chicoasan Dam: 167, 173-174
Chinchorro Bank: scuba diving at 335, 337, 339
Chinkultic: 185
Chital: 254
Chital Reef: scuba diving at 279
Chixulub: 107
Chol Indians: 167
Chontal Indians: at Comalcalco 216; in Tabasco state 201, 203
Chumpon: 327
Chunyaxche: *see* Muyil
churches: 68; in Merida 94; in San Cristobal de las Casas 175-176; in Valladolid 121
CICOM (Villahermosa): 207-208, *208*
Ciudad Real: *see* San Cristobal de las Casas
clothes, traditional: 179; *see also huipils; guayaberas*
clubs: 68
Coba: 323-326, *324;* accommo-

dations 325; fauna 323-324; flora 323-324; food 325-326; people 324; ruins 324; shopping 325-326; tours 346; transportation 326
Coco Beach: 278
Colombia Reef: scuba diving at 245
Comalcalco: 216-218, *217;* day trips 217-218, *218*
communications: 66-67
conch: 292
condominiums: 38; *see also* accommodations/specific place
conservation: of reefs 5
Contoy: 288
coral: 4, *5*
Cortes, Hernan: 18
Cozumel: *see* Isla de Cozumel
crafts, Maya: purchasing 171
crafts, Tzeltal: 185
cruises: to Contoy 288; *see also* transportation/specific place
Cruzob Indians: *see* Chan Santa Cruz Indians
Cuevones Reef: 254; scuba diving at 279
currency: 67
Customs, U.S.: 65

D
De Cuesta Cavern: 219
Del Rey: 251
Diaz, President Porfirio: 203
diving: *see* scuba diving
dress, traditional: *see* clothing, traditional
Dzibilchaltun: 98-99
Dzilam de Bravo: 108-109, *108*
Dzitnup: 119-120
Dzitya: 98

E
economy: 23-24; *see also* agriculture
education: 30; studying in Mexico 67-68
Edzna: 156-157; tours to 346
El Castillo: 320-321; *see also* Kukulcan
El Cedral: 238
El Cedro: 197
El Centenario Park Zoo (Merida): 92
electricity: 67

El Faro Lighthouse (Progreso): 103-104
El Mirador: 138, 164
embassies, U.S.: 68
emergencies: *66; see also* first aid; health care; services/specific place
entry and departure: 65-66
Escarcega: 162-164
estuaries: 12-13; *see* birds/birdwatching
events: *see* fiestas and celebrations
Ex-convent of San Jose: 148-149

F
fauna: 7-13
Felipe Carrillo Puerto: 318, 322-333
fiestas and celebrations: 31, *35-36*
first aid: 45, 59-63
fish/fishing: 5, *5,* 24, 46; in Akumal 311; in Cancun 255; in Chemuyil 315; in Isla Mujeres 279; in Playa del Carmen 299; in Puerto Morelos 290; in Punta Allen 331; in Punta Bete 296; lodges in Quintana Roo 329; in Xcacel 315; on Xcalak Peninsula 336; licenses 5; *see also* economy; specific place
flamingos: 12; in Las Coloradas 127-128; tours in Rio Lagartos 125-126; *see also* birds/birdwatching
flora: 14-16, 47; *see also* specific place
food: 40-43
fossil fuels: *see* economy
Frey, Charles "Carlos": 197
funerary art, Maya: 187-188

G
Garrafon National Park: 277
getting around: 48-53; *see also* specific place
getting there: 48-53; *see also* specific place
Gilbert, Hurricane: 5-6
golf courses: 47; *see also* specific place
Green Angels: 94
Grijalva River: 174
Grijalva, Juan de: 318; in Quintana Roo 226

guayabera: 234; purchasing in Merida 89; *see also* clothing, traditional

H
Hacienda Gomar: 278
hammocks: 90; purchasing in Merida 89-90
health care: 57-63
Hecelchakan: 156
henequen: *73; see also* economy
Hernandez de Cordoba, Francisco: 277
hieroglyphics: 29
history: 17-22
holidays: *see* fiestas and celebrations
horseback riding: at Isla de Cozumel 248; in San Cristobal de las Cosas 184
hostels: 39; *see also* accommodations/specific place
hotels: 38; *see also* accommodations/specific place
housing, Maya: 29, 30-31
huipils: 234; purchasing in Merida 88-89; *see also* clothing, traditional
hunting: 47
Hurricane Gilbert: 285

I
Ichpaatun: 337
iguana: 7-8, *7*
industries: 23; *see also* economy
insects: 13
insurance: 54
Isla de Cozumel: 223-227, *224;* climate 225; fauna 225-226; flora 226; history 226-227
Isla del Carmen: 160-162
Isla de Passion: 240
Isla Jaina: 155-156
Isla Mujeres: 275-288, *276, 282;* accommodations 280-282, *281;* beaches 278; entertainment 282-285; events 284-285; food 282-285, *283;* history 275-277; services 285-286; shopping *285;* sights 277-278; transportation 286-288, 293; water sports 278-280
Island of Tris: *see* Isla del Carmen
Isla Tamalcas: 341
Ixchel: 275, 277, 289

Izamal: 109-110

J
jaguar: 10-11, *10*
jet-skiing: in Cancun 255

K
Kabah: 137, *137;* tours to 346
Kayon: 197
Kohunlich: 338
Kukulcan: 115-116

L
La Bandera Reef: scuba diving at 279
Labna: 138, *138;* tours to 346
Lacandone Forest: 185
Lacandone Indians: 167, 176, 178
La Casa de la Cultura (Comitan): 185
La Ceiba's Park (Merida): 92
La Choco Park (Villahermosa): 208
Lafitte, Jean: in Quintana Roo 226
La Francesa Reef: scuba diving at 245
lagoons: formation of 6
Lagos de Montebello: 185
Laguna de las Illusiones: 205
Lagunas de Montebello National Park: 185
land: 1-3
Landa, Diego de: 2, 18; in Izamal 109; in Mani 138-139
language: 30
Larrainzar Indians: 167
Las Coloradas: 127-128
Las Lagunas de Siete Colores: 337-338
La Venta Park (Villahermosa): 204-205; museum 205-206, *205*
Lerma: 158
L'Huillier, Alberto Ruz: in Palenque 188
Loltun Caves: 140-141, *140*
Los Cocos: 108
Los Limones: 337

M
Mampulli River: 217
manatees: 11; breeding program 336

Manchones Reef: scuba diving at 279
Mani: 138-139
Mansion Carvajal (Campeche City): 149
maquiladora industry: 24; *see also* economy
Maracaibo Reef: scuba diving at 245
Marcuspana: 218
marinas: in Cancun 255, *256-257*
Maya Indians: 17, 25-29; art 91; culture 26-31; physical characteristics 25-26; religion 26
Mazariegos, Diego de: in San Cristobal de las Casas 175, 176
Merida: *3, 72-97, 75, 80, 100, 102, 130;* accommodations 78-84, *78-79;* cultural events 91-92; economy 72; entertainment 84-87; food 84-87, *85;* history 72; services 93-94; shopping 87-91; sights 73-77; tours to 346; transportation 95-97; vicinity of 98-102
Merida, Juan de: in Mani 138
Miguel Alvarez del Toro Zoo (Tuxtla Gutierrez): 172
mining: *see* economy
Misol-Ha: 195
money: 23, 67
Montejo, Francisco de: 121, 138; in Campeche 144; home of 76; in Tabasco state 203
Montejo the Younger: 121; in Campeche 145; in Chichen Itza 111
Morgan, Henry: in Quintana Roo 226
Mulsay's Park (Merida): 92
Muna: 136
Mundaca de Marehaja, Fermin: 277
Mundaca, Fort: 277-278
Municipality of San Andres Larrainzar: 167
Museo de la Isla de Cozumel (San Miguel de Cozumel): 234
Museo Regional de Antropologia Carlos Pellicer Camara (Villahermosa): 207
Museum of Anthropology (Mexico City): tours to 346
Museum of Popular Art: 208-209

museums: in Bacalar 338; in Chiapa de Corzo 173; in Merida 76-77; in Palenque 190; in San Cristobal de las Casas 176-178; vicinity of San Cristobal de las Cosas 185; in San Miguel de Cozumel 234; in Tuxtla Gutierrez 170; in Villahermosa 205-206, 207, 208-209; in Puerto Aventuras 308; in Xelha 316; *see also* sights/specific place
music: in Merida 91-92
Muyil: 327-329

N
Na Balom Museum (San Cristobal de las Casas): 176-178
natural gas: *see* economy
Nautibeach: 278
Nichupte Lagoon: 251-252
Nohoch Mul: 324

O
ocelot: 11
oil: *see* economy
Olmec Indians: 17, 139-141, 165-166; art 204; in Tabasco state 201, 203, 204
Oxolotan: 220

P
Pacal, Lord Shield: 186; burial site of 188
Palancar Reef: scuba diving at 245
Palenque: 186-190, *187, 214;* sights 188-190; temples 188-189; tours to 346
Palenque Village: *see* Santo Domingo
Pamul: 305-307
Panama hats: purchasing in Merida 89
Paraiso: 217
Paraiso Reef: scuba diving at 244
parasailing: 46; in Cancun 255; *see also* specific place
Parque La Choco (Villahermosa): 208
Paso del Cedral: scuba diving at 245
passports: 65
peccaries: 10
people: 25-26
photography: 47, 63-64

Pinacoteca Del Estado (Merida): 77
pirates: in Campeche 145-146; in Champoton 159; in Isla del Carmen 160; in Quintana Roo 221, 226-227; in Tabasco state 203
Piste: 117-118
Placer: 335-336
Playa Bonita: 241
Playa Chacmool: 253
Playa del Carmen: 297-303, *298;* accommodations 299-301; activities 299; entertainment 302; food 301; services 302; sights 298-299; transportation 302-303
Playa de San Martin: 241
Playa Lancheros: 278
Playa Linda: 253
Playa Norte: 278
Playa Tortuga: 253
Poana Cavern: 219
postal service: 66; *see also* services/specific place
Progreso: 102-106, *102, 108;* accommodations 104, *104;* entertainment 104-105; food 104-105; services 105, *105;* sights 102-104; transportation 106
Puerto Aventuras: 307-308
Puerto Ceiba: 217
Puerto Morelos: 289-293; accommodations 290-291; activities 290; food 291-293; services 293; sights 290
puma: 11
Punta Allen: *330,* 331-332
Punta Bete: 294-296
Punta Celerain Lighthouse: 241, 242
Punta Chiquiero: 241
Punta Molas: 240
Punta Nizuc: scuba diving at 254
Punta Sur: 240
Puuc Ruins: *130,* 136-139
Puyacatengo River: 218

Q
quetzals: 12-13; *see also* birds/birdwatching
Quintana Roo, state of: *3,* 221-343, *222;* economy 223; history 221; land and sea 221

R
radio: 67
Rancho Catalina: 336
Rancho Encantado: 338
reefs, coral: 4-6, *4*
regattas, boat: in Isla Mujeres 279-280
Regional Museum of Campeche (Campeche City): 147-148
Regional Museum of Chiapas (Tuxtla Gutierrez): 170
religion: Catholicism 19; Maya 26; Talking Cross Cult 20, 227, 318-319, 332
reptiles: 7-9
restaurants: *see* food
Rio, Antonio del: in Palenque 186
Rio Lagartos: *123,* 124-127; accommodations 126; activities 124-126; entertainment 126; services 126-127; sights 124-126; transportation 127; vicinity of 127-128
RV parks: *see* accommodations specific place

S
sailing: in Cancun 254-255
salt factory: in Las Coloradas 127
San Carlos, Baluarte: 148
San Cristobal de las Casas: 175-185, *177;* accommodations 181-183, *182;* activities 184; food 183; history 175; people 178; services 184; shopping 183; sights 175-178; transportation 179-180, 183; vicinity of 184
San Felipe: 128
San Felipe, Fort: 338
San Francisco Beach: 240
San Francisco Reef: scuba diving at 244-245
San Gervasio: 238-239
San Juan: scuba diving at 245
San Juan Chamula: 184-185
San Marcos Cathedral (Tuxtla Gutierrez): 170
San Miguel de Cozumel: 227-252, *228, 235;* accommodations 227-232, *230-231;* beaches 239-242; entertainment 233-234; food 232-233; services 235-236; shopping 235; sights 234; transportation 235-238; water sports 243-248

San Miguel, Fort: 148
Santa Cecilia: 241
Santa Clara: 108
Santa Rosa Wall: scuba diving at 245
Santiago, Fort: 148
Santo Domingo: 190-195, *190;* accommodations 191-194, *193;* economy 191; food 194; services 194; transportation 194-195
Santo Domingo Cathedral (Chiapa de Corzo): 173
Sayil: 137-138; tours to 346
scuba diving: 44-46; in Akumal 310-311; in Cancun 254; in Isla Mujeres 278-279; in Merida 77-78; in Pamul 305; in Puerto Aventuras 307-308; in Puerto Morelos 290; in Quintana Roo 243-247; tours 346; in Xcacel 315; on Xcalak Peninsula 335, 337, 339; in Xcaret 304
sealife: 4-5
sea turtles: 9, 278, 306, *306*
Seybaplaya: 158
Sian Ka'an Biosphere Reserve: 15-16, 320, 321; tours to 346
Sierra Madre del Sur: 165
Siho Playa: 158-159
Sisal: 99-100
Sleeping Shark Caves: snorkeling and scuba diving at 279, 290
snakes: 8
snorkeling: 44-46; in Akumal 310-311; in Cancun 253, 254; in Chemuyil 315; in Isla Mujeres 278-279;in Playa del Carmen 299; in Puerto Morelos 290; in Punta Allen 331; in Punta Bete 296; in Quintana Roo 243; tours in Merida 77; in Xcacel 315; on Xcalak Peninsula 336, 339; in Xcaret 304; in Xelha 316;
Soledad, Fort: 148
sooty terns: 12; *see also* birds/birdwatching
Stephens, John: 2; in Palenque 186; in Quintana Roo 251; in Uxmal 129
study: in Mexico 67-68
Sumidero Canyon: 174, *174*

T
Tabasco 2000 (Villahermosa): 206, *206*
Tabasco, state of: *3,* 201-220, *202;* climate 201; economy 203; history 203; land 201
Tacana: 165
Tacotalpa: 219
Talking Cross Cult: 20, 227, 318-319, 332
Tapijulapa: 219-220
tapirs: 10
Teapa: 219
Teatro Peon Contreras (Merida): 92
Telchac Puerto: 108
telegraph service: 66; *see also* services/specific place
telephone service: 66, *66; see also* services/specific place
telephone service: 66, *66*
television: 67
Temple of the Inscriptions (Palenque): 188-189; museum 190
tennis: 47; *see also* specific place
Teotihuacan: tours to 346
Thompson, J. Eric: in Palenque 186
Ticul: 141-142, *140*
timber industry: *see* economy
time: 67
Tizimin: 123, *123*
Toltec Indians: 17; in Champoton 159; in Chichen Itza 111
Tormentos Reef: scuba diving at 244
tourism: *see* economy
tourist information centers: *see* services/specific place
tours: to Yucatan Peninsula 345-346; *see* services/specific place; transportation/specific place

trailer parks: *see* accommodations specific place
transportation: 48-53; by air 50; by bus 51, 53; by car 48-50; driving distances *51;* by ship 53; tours 53; by train 50
travel agencies: *see* services/specific place; transportation/specific place

Tuchtli: *see* Tuxtla Gutierrez
Tulum: 318-322, *319, 330;* accommodations 321-322; food 321-322; history 318; sights 320; tours to 346; transportation 322
Tulum, village of: 321
Tunich Reef: scuba diving at 244
Tupak: 337
turtles: *see* sea turtles
Tuxtla Gutierrez: *3,* 170-174; accommodations 172-173; shopping 171-172; sights 170-172; vicinity of 173-174
Tziscao, Lake: 185

U
Usumacinta River: 200
Uxmal: 129-135, *130;* accommodations 132-134; entertainment 134; food 134; history 129-130; services *131;* shopping 135; temples of 130-132; tours to 346; transportation 135; vicinity of 136-139

V
Valladolid: 121-123, *121, 122;* vicinity of 123
vehicle permits: 65
Villahermosa: *3,* 204-215, *204, 210, 214;* accommodations 210-212, *211;* entertainment 213-214; events 214; food 212-213; sights 204-210; transportation 214-215; vicinity of 216-220
Villa Luz: 219

W
water sports: 44-47; in Cancun 254-255; in San Miguel de Cozumel 243-248
water-skiing: 46; in Cancun 255; *see also* specific place
what to take: 55-56
windsurfing: 46; in Cancun 254; in Chetumal 342; on Xcalak Peninsula 339; *see also* specific place
wine, Mexican: 269

X
Xcacel: 315

Xcalak: 336-337
Xcalak Peninsula: 324-339, *334*
Xcaret: 303-304
Xelha: 316-317, *316;* tours to 346
Xiloteca (Tuxtla Gutierrez): 170
Xlapak: 138
Xpujil: 163

Y
Yalku Lagoon: 311
Yamil Lu'um: 251
Yaqui Indians: 335
Yaxchilan: 200
Yocab Reef: scuba diving at 244
Yucalpeten: 99

Yucatan, state of: *3,* 69-142, *70;* economy 69-71; history 69

Z
Zinacantecan Indians: 167, 178
zoos: *see* sights/specific place
Zoque Indians: 167, 170; at Tacotalpa 219

ABOUT THE AUTHOR

As a child Chicki Mallan discovered the joy of traveling with her parents. The family would leave their Catalina Island home yearly, hit the road and explore the small towns and big cities of the U.S. This urge didn't go away, even later with a good-sized family to tote around. At various times Chicki and kids have lived in the Orient and in Europe. When not traveling, lecturing, or giving slide presentations, Chicki and husband Oz live in Paradise, a small community in the foothills of the Sierra Nevada. She does what she enjoys most, writing magazine and newspaper articles between travel books. She has been associated with Moon Publications since 1983, and is also the author of *Guide to Catalina Island, Belize Handbook,* and *Cancun Handbook.* In 1987, Chicki was presented the Pluma de Plata award from the Mexican Ministry of Tourism for an article she wrote about the Yucatan Caribbean published in the *Los Angeles Times.* In 1990 she and Oz received the Westin Hotels award for Media Coverage of Mexico. Chicki is a member of the Society of American Travel Writers.

ABOUT THE PHOTOGRAPHER

Oz Mallan has been a professional photographer for the past 40 years. Much of that time was spent as chief cameraman for the *Chico Enterprise-Record.* Oz graduated from the Brooks Institute of Photography, Santa Barbara, in 1950. His work has often appeared in newspapers across the country via UPI and AP. He travels the world with his wife Chicki, handling the photo end of their literary projects which include travel books, newspaper and magazine articles, as well as lectures and slide presentations. The photos in *Yucatan Handbook* were taken during many visits and years of travel on the Yucatan Peninsula.

ABOUT THE ILLUSTRATORS

The banner art in each chapter was done by Kathy Escovedo Sanders. She is an expert both in watercolor and this stipple style which lends itself to excellent black and white reproduction. Kathy is a 1982 California State Long Beach graduate with a BA in Art History. She exhibits drawings, etched intaglio prints, and woodcut prints, as well as her outstanding watercolor paintings. In the April 1982 issue of *Orange Coast* magazine, a complete photo essay illustrates Kathy's unique craft of dyeing, designing, and etching eggs. Her stipple art can also be seen in Chicki Mallan's *Guide To Catalina and California's Channel Islands* and *Belize Handbook.*

Diana Lasich Harper has illustrations in many Moon guides. She received her degree in Art from San Jose State University and continued studying as she traveled through Japan, where she learned wood-block printing, *sumie,* and kimono painting. Her wonderful animal drawings are also seen in *Guide To Catalina and California's Channel Islands.*

Louise Foote is a talented artist as well as a mapmaker. She is also an archaeologist and has spent some time on various digs around Northern California concerned with American Indians. Louise executed many of the maps, as well as the wild canary illustration and design sketches.

Bob Race, illustrator and cartographer, has always been interested in maps, especially the technique and material used in drawing them. After receiving a BA in Art in 1974, he earned an MA in Painting and Drawing one year later. For the following 14 years he taught fine art at the college level, and in 1989 he began working at Moon Publications. Evolved from his teaching and personal work is an interest in the primitive and fine arts of other cultures.

STATE CAPITALS: AVERAGE TEMPERATURE AND RAINFALL

CITY OF CAMPECHE
(CAMPECHE)

MONTH	AVERAGE TEMPREATURE (° Fahrenheit)	AVERAGE RAINFALL (Inches)
JAN	72	0.7
FEB	74	0.4
MAR	77	0.5
APR	79	0.2
MAY	81	1.7
JUNE	81	6.1
JULY	80	7.0
AUG	81	6.7
SEPT	81	5.7
OCT	80	3.4
NOV	76	1.2
DEC	74	1.2

CITY OF CHETUMAL
(QUINTANA ROO)

MONTH	AVERAGE TEMPREATURE (° Fahrenheit)	AVERAGE RAINFALL (Inches)
JAN	72	3.0
FEB	75	0.9
MAR	77	1.1
APR	80	1.2
MAY	81	5.5
JUNE	82	7.0
JULY	82	5.1
AUG	82	4.2
SEPT	81	5.5
OCT	79	8.4
NOV	75	3.4
DEC	75	3.7

CITY OF MERIDA
(YUCATAN)

MONTH	AVERAGE TEMPREATURE (° Fahrenheit)	AVERAGE RAINFALL (Inches)
JAN	73	1.2
FEB	74	0.6
MAR	78	0.8
APR	81	1.0
MAY	82	3.2
JUNE	81	5.9
JULY	81	5.5
AUG	81	5.1
SEPT	81	6.0
OCT	79	4.0
NOV	75	1.2
DEC	74	1.2

CITY OF GUTIERREZ
(CHIAPAS)

MONTH	AVERAGE TEMPREATURE (° Fahrenheit)	AVERAGE RAINFALL (Inches)
JAN	71	0.0
FEB	73	0.2
MAR	77	0.4
APR	80	2.2
MAY	81	3.0
JUNE	79	9.2
JULY	78	7.0
AUG	78	6.1
SEPT	77	8.0
OCT	76	3.2
NOV	73	0.2
DEC	70	2.5

CITY OF VILLAHERMOSA (TABASCO)

MONTH	AVERAGE TEMPREATURE (° Fahrenheit)	AVERAGE RAINFALL (Inches)
JAN	72	5.5
FEB	75	3.9
MAR	77	1.8
APR	80	1.8
MAY	83	3.5
JUNE	83	8.0
JULY	82	7.6
AUG	83	7.6
SEPT	82	10.0
OCT	80	11.0
NOV	76	5.6
DEC	73	7.1

METRIC CONVERSION

Mexico offically uses the metric system of weights and measures. The following tables will help you make quick conversion.

liquid measure: To roughly convert liters to quarts and gallons—one liter is approximately one quart; four liters about one gallon. To be more exact, multiply liters by 2.642 and divide by 10 to obtain gallons.

weight: To roughly convert kilos (kilograms, 1000 grams) to pounds—one kilo is about 2 lbs. More exactly, multiply kilos by 2.2046 to obtain lbs.

distance: In order to convert kilometers (1000 meters) to miles—multiply by 0.6

airpressure in automobile tires is expressed in *kilopascals*. Multiply pound-force per square inch (psi) by 6.89 to find *kilopascals* (kPa).

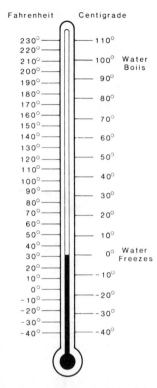

temperature conversions: To convert Fahrenheit to Celsius, subtract 32 from the Fahrenheit temperature, multiply by 5 and divide by 9. To convert Celsius to Fahrenheit, multiply by 9, divide by 5 and add 32.

It helps to carry a small pocket calculator with you to make these conversions quickly.

LIQUID MEASURE		WEIGHT		DISTANCE	
Liters	U.S. Gals.	Kilograms	Pounds	Kilometers	Miles
5	1.3	0.5	1.1	1	0.625
8	2.1	1.0	2.2	8	5.0
10	2.6	5.0	11.0	25	15.6
20	5.3	10	22.0	60	37.5
30	8.0	25	55.1	100	62.5
50	13.2	50	110.2	110	68.75

MOON HANDBOOKS
The Ideal Traveling Companions

Open a Moon Handbook and you're opening your eyes and heart to the world. Thoughtful, sensitive, provocative, and highly informative, Moon Handbooks encourage an intimate understanding of a region, from its culture and history to essential practicalities. Fun to read and packed with valuable information on accommodations, dining, recreation, plus indispensable travel tips, detailed maps, charts, illustrations, photos, glossaries, and indexes, Moon Handbooks are ideal traveling companions.

TO ORDER BY PHONE: (800) 345-5473 Monday-Friday 9 a.m.-5 p.m. PST

The Americas Series

NORTHERN CALIFORNIA HANDBOOK   by Kim Weir
An outstanding companion for imaginative travel in the territory north of the Tehachapis. Color and b/w photos, 69 maps, illustrations, booklist, index. 760 pages.   **$16.95**

NEVADA HANDBOOK   by Deke Castleman
Nevada Handbook puts the Silver State into perspective and makes it manageable and affordable. 34 b/w photos, 43 illustrations, 37 maps, 17 charts, booklist, index. 302 pages. **$12.95**

NEW MEXICO HANDBOOK   by Stephen Metzger
A close-up and complete look at every aspect of this wondrous state. 8 color pages, 85 b/w photos, 63 illustrations, 50 maps, 10 charts, booklist, index. 350 pages.   **$11.95**

TEXAS HANDBOOK   by Joe Cummings
Seasoned travel writer Joe Cummings brings an insider's perspective to his home state. 12 color pages, b/w photos, maps, illustrations, charts, booklist, index. 482 pages.   **$11.95**

ARIZONA TRAVELER'S HANDBOOK   by Bill Weir
This meticulously researched guide contains everything necessary to make Arizona accessible and enjoyable. 8 color pages, 194 b/w photos, 74 illustrations, 53 maps, 6 charts, booklist, index. 505 pages.   **$13.95**

UTAH HANDBOOK   by Bill Weir
Weir gives you all the carefully researched facts and background to make your visit a success. 8 color pages, 102 b/w photos, 61 illustrations, 30 maps, 9 charts, booklist, index. 452 pages.   **$12.95**

WYOMING HANDBOOK   by Don Pitcher
All you need to know to open the doors to this wide and wild state. Color and b/w photos, illustrations, 66 maps, charts, booklist, index. Approx 450 pages.   **$12.95**

ALASKA-YUKON HANDBOOK   by Deke Castleman, Don Pitcher, and David Stanley
Get the inside story, with plenty of well-seasoned advice to help you cover more miles on less money. 8 color pages, 26 b/w photos, 92 illustrations, 90 maps, 6 charts, booklist, glossary, index. 384 pages.   **$11.95**

WASHINGTON HANDBOOK   by Dianne J. Boulerice Lyons
Covers sights, shopping, services, transportation, and outdoor recreation, and has complete listings for restaurants and accommodations. 8 color pages, 92 b/w photos, 24 illustrations, 81 maps, 8 charts, booklist, index. 425 pages.   **$12.95**

OREGON HANDBOOK   by Ted Long Ishikawa and Stuart Warren
Brimming with travel practicalities and insider views on Oregon's history, culture, arts, and activities. Color and b/w photos, illustrations, 28 maps, charts, booklist, index. 422 pages.   **$12.95**

BRITISH COLUMBIA HANDBOOK   by Jane King
With an emphasis on outdoor adventures, this guide covers mainland British Columbia, Vancouver Island, the Queen Charlotte Islands, and the Canadian Rockies. 8 color pages, 56 b/w photos, 45 illustrations, 66 maps, 4 charts, booklist, index. 396 pages.   **$11.95**

GUIDE TO CATALINA AND CALIFORNIA'S CHANNEL ISLANDS   by Chicki Mallan
A complete guide to these remarkable islands, from the windy solitude of the Channel Islands National Marine Sanctuary to bustling Avalon. 8 color pages, 105 b/w photos, 65 illustrations, 40 maps, 32 charts, booklist, index. 262 pages.   **$9.95**

YUCATAN HANDBOOK   by Chicki Mallan
All the information you'll need to guide you into every corner of this exotic land. 8 color pages, 154 b/w photos, 55 illustrations, 57 maps, 70 charts, appendix, booklist, Mayan and Spanish glossaries, index. 391 pages.   **$12.95**

CANCUN HANDBOOK AND MEXICO'S CARIBBEAN COAST   by Chicki Mallan
Covers the city's luxury scene as well as more modest attractions, plus many side trips to unspoiled beaches and Mayan ruins. Color and b/w photos, illustrations, over 30 maps, Spanish glossary, booklist, index. 257 pages.   **$9.95**

BELIZE HANDBOOK   by Chicki Mallan
Complete with detailed maps, practical information, and an overview of the area's flamboyant history, culture, and geographical features. *Belize Handbook* is the only comprehensive guide of its kind to this spectacular region. Color and b/w photos, illustrations, maps, booklist, index. 201 pages.   **$11.95**

The Pacific/Asia Series

BALI HANDBOOK   by Bill Dalton
Detailed travel information on the most famous island in the world. 12 color pages, 29 b/w photos, 68 illustrations, 42 maps, 7 charts, glossary, booklist, index. 428 pages.   **$12.95**

INDONESIA HANDBOOK   by Bill Dalton
This one-volume encyclopedia explores island by island the many facets of this sprawling, kaleidoscopic island nation. 30 b/w photos, 143 illustrations, 250 maps, 17 charts, booklist, extensive Indonesian vocabulary, index. 1,050 pages.   **$17.95**

PHILIPPINES HANDBOOK   by Peter Harper and Evelyn Peplow
Crammed with detailed information, *Philippines Handbook* equips the escapist, hedonist, or business traveler with a thorough introduction to the Philippines's colorful history, landscapes, and culture. Color and b/w photos, illustrations, maps, charts, index.
550 pages.   **$12.95**

SOUTH KOREA HANDBOOK   by Robert Nilsen
Whether you're visiting on business or searching for adventure, *South Korea Handbook* is an invaluable companion. 8 color pages, 78 b/w photos, 93 illustrations, 109 maps, 10 charts, Korean glossary with useful notes on speaking and reading the language, booklist, index. 548 pages.   **$14.95**

SOUTHEAST ASIA HANDBOOK   by Carl Parkes
Helps the enlightened traveler to discover the real Southeast Asia. 16 Color pages, 75 b/w photos, 11 illustrations, 169 maps, 140 charts, vocabulary lists and suggested readings, index. 874 pages.   **$16.95**

HAWAII HANDBOOK   by J.D. Bisignani
Winner of the 1989 Hawaii Visitors Bureau's Best Guide Book Award and the Grand Award for Excellence in Travel Journalism, this guide takes you beyond the glitz and high-priced hype and leads you to a genuine Hawaiian experience. 12 color pages, 318 b/w photos, 132 illustrations, 74 maps, 43 graphs and charts, Hawaiian and pidgin glossaries, appendix, booklist, index. Approx. 870 pages.   **$15.95**

KAUAI HANDBOOK   by J.D. Bisignani
Kauai Handbook is the perfect antidote to the workaday world. 8 color pages, 36 b/w photos, 48 illustrations, 19 maps, 10 tables and charts, Hawaiian and pidgin glossaries, booklist, index. 236 pages.   **$9.95**

MAUI HANDBOOK: Including Molokai and Lanai   by J.D. Bisignani
"No fool-'round" advice on accommodations, eateries, and recreation, plus a comprehensive introduction to island ways, geography, and history. 4 color pages, 60 b/w photos, 72 illustrations, 34 maps, 19 charts, booklist, glossary, index. 350 pages.   **$10.95**

OAHU HANDBOOK   by J.D. Bisignani
A handy guide to Honolulu, renowned surfing beaches, and Oahu's countless other diversions. Color and b/w photos, illustrations, 18 maps, charts, booklist, glossary, index.
354 pages.   **$11.95**

BIG ISLAND OF HAWAII HANDBOOK   by J.D. Bisignani
An entertaining, yet informative text, packed with insider tips on accommodations, dining, sports and outdoor activities, natural attractions, and must-see sights. Color and b/w photos, illustrations, 20 maps, charts, booklist, glossary, index. 347 pages.   **$11.95**

SOUTH PACIFIC HANDBOOK   by David Stanley
The original comprehensive guide to the 16 territories in the South Pacific. 20 color pages, 195 b/w photos, 121 illustrations, 35 charts, 138 maps, booklist, glossary, index. 740 pages.   **$15.95**

MICRONESIA HANDBOOK:
Guide to the Caroline, Gilbert, Mariana, and Marshall Islands   by David Stanley
Micronesia Handbook guides you on a real Pacific adventure all your own. 8 color pages, 77 b/w photos, 68 illustrations, 69 maps, 18 tables and charts, index. 288 pages.   **$9.95**

FIJI ISLANDS HANDBOOK   by David Stanley
The first and still the best source of information on travel around this 322-island archipelago. 8 color pages, 35 b/w photos, 78 illustrations, 26 maps, 3 charts, Fijian glossary, booklist, index. 198 pages.   **$8.95**

TAHITI-POLYNESIA HANDBOOK   by David Stanley
All five French-Polynesian archipelagoes are covered in this comprehensive guide by Oceania's best-known travel writer. 12 color pages, 45 b/w photos, 64 illustrations, 33 maps, 7 charts, booklist, glossary, index. 225 pages.   **$9.95**

NEW ZEALAND HANDBOOK   by Jane King
Introduces you to the people, places, history, and culture of this extraordinary land. 8 color pages, 99 b/w photos, 146 illustrations, 82 maps, booklist, index. 546 pages.   **$14.95**

BLUEPRINT FOR PARADISE: How to Live on a Tropic Island   by Ross Norgrove
This one-of-a-kind guide has everything you need to know about moving to and living comfortably on a tropical island. 8 color pages, 40 b/w photos, 3 maps, 14 charts, appendices, index. 212 pages.   **$14.95**

The International Series

EGYPT HANDBOOK   by Kathy Hansen
An invaluable resource for intelligent travel in Egypt. 8 color pages, 20 b/w photos, 150 illustrations, 80 detailed maps and plans to museums and archaeological sites, Arabic glossary, booklist, index. 510 pages.   **$14.95**

PAKISTAN HANDBOOK   by Isobel Shaw
For armchair travelers and trekkers alike, the most detailed and authoritative guide to Pakistan ever published. 28 color pages, 86 maps, appendices, Urdu glossary, booklist, index. 478 pages.   **$15.95**

MOSCOW-LENINGRAD HANDBOOK   by Masha Nordbye
Provides the visitor with an extensive introduction to the history, culture, and people of these two great cities, as well as practical information on where to stay, eat, and shop. Color and b/w photos, illustrations, maps, charts, booklist, index. Approx 250 pages.
$15.95

IMPORTANT ORDERING INFORMATION

TO ORDER BY PHONE: (800) 345-5473 Monday-Friday 9 a.m.-5 p.m. PST

PRICES: All prices are subject to change. We always ship the most current edition. We will let you know if there is a price increase on the book you ordered.

SHIPPING & HANDLING OPTIONS:
   1) Domestic UPS or USPS 1st class (allow 10 working days for delivery):
      $3.50 for the 1st item, 50 cents for each additional item.

Exceptions:
   Moonbelt shipping is $1.50 for one, 50 cents for each additional belt.
   Add $2.00 for same-day handling.
   2) UPS 2nd Day Air or Printed Airmail requires a special quote.
   3) International Surface Bookrate (8-12 weeks delivery):
      $3.00 for the 1st item, $1.00 for each additional item.

FOREIGN ORDERS: All orders which originate outside the U.S.A. must be paid for with either an International Money Order or a check in U.S. currency drawn on a major U.S. bank based in the U.S.A.

TELEPHONE ORDERS: We accept Visa or MasterCard payments. Minimum order is US$15.00. Call in your order: (800) 345-5473. 9 a.m.-5 p.m. Pacific Standard Time.

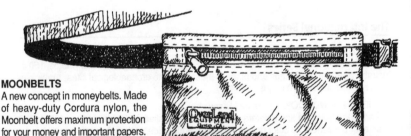

MOONBELTS
A new concept in moneybelts. Made of heavy-duty Cordura nylon, the Moonbelt offers maximum protection for your money and important papers. This pouch, designed for all-weather comfort, slips under your shirt or waistband, rendering it virtually undetectable and inaccessible to pickpockets. Many thoughtful features: one-inch-wide nylon webbing, heavy-duty zipper, and a one-inch high-test quick-release buckle. No more fumbling around for the strap or repeated adjustments, this handy plastic buckle opens and closes with a touch, but won't come undone until you want it to. Accommodates traveler's checks, passport, cash, photos. Size 5 x 9 inches. Available in black only.   **$8.95**

ORDER FORM

Name:_____Date:_____

Street:_____ _____

City:_____

State or Country:_____Zip Code:_____

Daytime Phone:_____

Quantity	Title	Price

Taxable Total _____

Sales Tax (6%) for California Residents _____

Shipping & Handling _____

TOTAL _____

Ship to: ☐ address above ☐ other (fill in below)

_____

_____

_____

Make checks payable to:
Moon Publications, Inc., 722 Wall Street, Chico, California, 95928, USA
We Accept Visa and MasterCard
To order: Call in your Visa or MasterCard number, or send a written order with your Visa or
MasterCard number and expiration date clearly written.

Card Number: ☐ Visa ☐ MasterCard

☐☐☐☐ ☐☐☐☐ ☐☐☐☐ ☐☐☐☐

expiration date:_____

Exact Name on Card: ☐ same as above ☐ other (fill in below)

_____

signature_____

WHERE TO BUY THIS BOOK

Bookstores and Libraries:
Moon Publications guides are sold worldwide.
Please write sales manager for a list of wholesalers
and distributors in your area that stock our travel
handbooks.

Travelers:
We would like to have Moon Publications guides
available throughout the world. Please ask your
bookstore to write or call us for ordering information.
If your bookstore will not order our guides for you,
please write or call for a free catalog.

MOON PUBLICATIONS, INC.
722 WALL STREET
CHICO, CA 95928 USA
tel: (800) 345-5473
fax: (916) 345-6751

Not since the days of Quetzalcoatl has the air borne such a legend.

The lore of our ancestors tells of a god who ruled the skies.

His name was Quetzalcoatl, the Plumed Serpent.

He is remembered for the gifts he brought to our people. A calendar, and corn to sustain them. And legend has it that his kind heart still shines as the planet Venus.

Today, another legend soars in the skies of our homeland. Mexicana. We'll help you discover the greatest gifts of Mexico.

With our first flight sixty-seven years ago, we began making history. We were the first international airline flying in North America. Now, we offer more non-stops to more destinations in Mexico than any other airline.

Come. Discover the wonders of Mexicana's Mexico. We'll show you the mysterious homeland of Quetzalcoatl like only a native can.

Call your travel agent, or Mexicana at 1-800-531-7921. No other airline can give you so much to worship.

mexicana
Discover Mexicana's Mexico.

2nd Class
  5:00 AM Tulum-Coba - Volladolid
10:00 AM   ⊥
17:00 PM

          one hour

10/8 DH910·682·770 thru 779 $200/C
        ⊥   ·759 $20/ D
   HH917·324·852 & 853 $100/B